||||| ||| || ||||||| |||| |||||
D1244553

THE GASTEROMYCETES
OF THE
EASTERN UNITED STATES
AND CANADA

WILLIAM CHAMBERS COKER

JOHN NATHANIEL COUCH

TOGETHER WITH
A SUPPLEMENTARY ARTICLE

THE GASTEROMYCETAE OF OHIO:
PUFFBALLS, BIRDS'-NEST FUNGI
AND STINKHORNS

BY

MINNIE MAY JOHNSON

DOVER PUBLICATIONS, INC.
NEW YORK

Published in Canada by General Publishing Company, Ltd., 30 Lesmill Road, Don Mills, Toronto Ontario.

Published in the United Kingdom by Constable and Company, Ltd., 10 Orange Street, London WC 2.

This Dover edition, first published in 1974, is an unabridged republication of the work originally published in 1928 by The University of North Carolina Press.

This Dover reprint also includes as an appendix an unabridged republication of "The Gasteromycetae of Ohio: Puffballs, Birds'-Nest Fungi and Stinkhorns" by Minnie May Johnson. This essay was originally published in the *Ohio Biological Survey Bulletin 22* (Vol. IV, No. 7, pp. 271-352).

International Standard Book Number: 0-486-23033-3
Library of Congress Catalog Card Number: 73-91490

Manufactured in the United States of America
Dover Publications, Inc.
180 Varick Street
New York, N.Y. 10014

CONTENTS

PREFACE.. ix
ARTIFICIAL KEY TO THE FAMILIES............................ 1
FAMILY PHALLACEAE.. 3
FAMILY HYSTERANGIACEAE.................................. 15
FAMILY HYMENOGASTRACEAE................................ 24
FAMILY SECOTIACEAE...................................... 53
FAMILY LYCOPERDACEAE.................................... 58
FAMILY ARACHNIACEAE.................................... 144
FAMILY SPHAEROBOLACEAE................................ 146
FAMILY TYLOSTOMATACEAE................................ 149
FAMILY SCLERODERMATACEAE.............................. 160
FAMILY NIDULARIACEAE.................................. 173
FAMILY CALOSTOMATACEAE................................ 185
LITERATURE.. 194
INDEX... 197

PREFACE

It seems to be generally felt that there is need for a handbook of Gasteromycetes. There has been in this country no comprehensive treatment of the species as a whole and in logical order with convenient keys, and as a result this highly interesting and varied group has been neglected by many who would otherwise enjoy their study. Lloyd, Morgan, and Peck have been the principal recent students of the Gasteromycetes and their publications are indispensable. Morgan included all the families except Hysterangiaceae and Hymenogastraceae, which were nearly unknown in America at that time, and established several new genera. Lloyd was occupied with these plants for years and has published a large number of good photographs, several monographs, and many notes. His collections, which are the largest in America, are available, and so are Peck's, but so far as this group is concerned Morgan's, unfortunately, have been almost destroyed.

In preparing this book we have studied all available species microscopically and have compared types and authentic specimens in many cases. To this end the senior author has visited the following herbaria: Persoon's at Leiden, Bresadola's at Stockholm, Kew Herbarium, New York Botanical Garden Herbarium, Curtis Herbarium, Schweinitz Herbarium, Lloyd Herbarium, and the Pathological and Mycological Herbarium at Washington. This last contains Michener's herbarium which includes many important plants from the Schweinitz Herbarium. To a number of correspondents we are indebted for generous gifts of material. Among these are Dr. W. A. Murrill, Mr. C. G. Lloyd, Miss Edith Cash, Mr. John Dearness, Dr. Homer D. House, Mr. H. C. Beardslee, Dr. Roland Thaxter, Mr. F. W. Pennell, Miss E. M. Wakefield (Kew), Professor N. Patouillard (Paris), Dr. G. F. Weber, Dr. C. L. Shear, Mr. Elam Bartholomew and Mr. G. H. Cunningham (New Zealand).

Other members of the botanical staff of this University have been of much assistance. Most of the microscopic work has been done by Dr. Couch and the drawings have been made by him and Miss Alma Holland, the latter having done all the ink work and drawn many of the spores. Nearly all the written matter and most of the photographs are by the senior author and the microscopical work and drawings have been carefully supervised.

The literature has been referred to throughout this work under families, genera and species, but for convenience we list on page 194 the more important general works dealing with the entire group or with several families.

W. C. C.

Chapel Hill, N. C.
June, 1927.

ARTIFICIAL KEY TO THE FAMILIES

Plants emerging at maturity from a soft volva or "egg;" the spores borne in a slimy, brown, bad-smelling liquid at the top of a stalk or net or several columns......................*Phallaceae* (p. 3)
Not as above
    Plants with a distinct firm or gelatinous stalk which carries the spore-bearing sac, the latter in our representatives having a distinct apical mouth through which the spores escape as a dry powder.
        Stalk firm and fibrous; mouth not red. ....*Tylostomataceae* (p. 149)
        Stalk gelatinous; mouth red......................................*Calostomataceae* (p. 185)
    Plants without a distinct, terete or gelatinous stalk; if a stalk is present it is thick and expands gradually into the swollen spore-bearing part above.
        Plants small, shaped like cups or tumblers or subspherical, at maturity opening in most of the species over the entire top by the collapse of a veil (or rarely by the crumbling of the peridium) to expose a number of small flattened peridioles with hard coats which contain the spores, the whole looking like a little nest containing eggs.
                        Nidulariaceae (p. 173)
        Plants growing on wood; very small, spherical, exploding at maturity and throwing out to some distance a single minute peridiole ....*Sphaerobolaceae* (p. 146)
        Not as above
            Peridium without a distinct outer layer that falls away or splits; at maturity opening at the top by irregular lobes, or by an irregular tear, or by crumbling or rotting away. Elongated threads (capillitium) not present among the spores.
                Gleba not formed of hollow chambers, but of sterile plates cutting out irregular blocks which are stuffed with the fertile tissue; at maturity crumbling into a dusty powder......................................*Sclerodermataceae* (p. 160)
            Gleba formed (at least when young) of hollow chambers which are lined with the hymenium.
                Peridium rotting away after maturity, the gleba (at least in species we are treating) turning into a slimy or gelatinous mass.
                    Tramal plates radiating from the base and not intimately onnected with the peridium..........................*Hysterangiaceae* (p. 15)
                    Tramal plates not radiating from the base and intimately connected with the peridium.......................*Hymenogastraceae* (p. 24)
                Peridium crumbling away after maturity, the glebal chambers remaining intact and falling apart as fine sand-like particles......*Arachniaceae* (p. 144)
            Peridium without a distinct outer layer; at maturity opening ventrally by separating around the stem and expanding more or less; capillitium not present.
                        Secotiaceae (p. 53)
            Peridium with a distinct outer coat (*Calvatia rubro-flava* is an exception) which falls away in flakes or wears away by degrees at maturity, or dehisces equatorially, or (in *Geaster*) splits into star-like rays to expose the thin, pliable or (in *Calvatia*) fragile and brittle inner peridium; gleba composed of small, hollow chambers lined with the hymenium (obscure in *Disciseda*); spores mixed with a true capillitium of long, slender, branched or unbranched threads (broken up into short sections at maturity in *Disciseda*) and escaping as dust through a definite (except in *Calvatia*) pore or slit. (In several small species of *Lycoperdon* the outer peridium is very thin, obscure and persistent, and in *Myriostoma* there are several pores)..................................*Lycoperdaceae* (p. 58)

1

PHALLACEAE*

Plants consisting at first of a white, elastic, oval or subspherical "egg," which consists of three coats, the central one soft and gelatinous, which break at maturity to allow the elongation and exposure of the curious, spongy, and in some species brightly colored receptaculum of various shapes which bears above either on itself or on a specialized appendage the slimy, deliquescing gleba which contains the spores, and which in nearly all cases has a very strong and offensive odor by which insects are attracted to scatter the spores. Basidia, so far as known, club-shaped (very peculiar in *Anthurus*), with several (4–8) sessile (no mucro), smooth, minute, apical spores.

The family is divided into two subfamilies or by some authors (as Corda and Fischer) into two distinct families which are separated by the position of the gleba and by other important microscopical characters. These subfamilies may be simply defined as follows:

Gleba (and spore slime) borne on the inner side of the receptaculum..............*Clathreae*
Gleba borne on the outer surface of the receptaculum..........................*Phalleae*

The unique genus *Phallogaster*, placed by Morgan, its author (l. c., **15**: 171, pl. 11. 1892), and by Thaxter (Bot. Gaz. **18**: 117, pl. 19. 1893) in the Phallaceae, but differing from them in the absence of a volva and in other ways, is treated by Fischer in the Hysterangiaceae (l. c., Pflanzenfamilien, p. 307), and we are following him in this. *Phallogaster*, *Protubera*, and *Protophallus* mark a distinct advance toward the Phalloids and indicate their descent from the Hysterangiaceae. The last mentioned genus is, in fact, so Phalloid-like that it is placed by its author among them. It is distinctly intermediate between the two families and if put in the Phalloids, their family characteristics would have to be modified.

As the number of our species of Phalloids is small, we key all of them under the family, and for the convenience of students we include all species described from the United States.

LITERATURE

Atkinson. Origin and Taxonomic Value of the Veil in *Dictyophora* and *Ithyphallus*. Bot. Gaz. **51**: 1, pls. 1–7 and one text figure. 1911.
Bambeke. La Relation du Mycélium avec le Carpophore chez *Ithyphallus impudicus* et *Mutinus caninus*. Mém. Acad. Roy. Belgique, 2nd ser., **2**: 1910.
Bambeke. Recherches sur certain éléments du mycélium d'*Ithyphallus impudicus*. Bull. Acad. Roy. Belgique, No. 6, p. 280. 1914.
Burt. A North American *Anthurus*. Mem. Boston Soc. Nat. Hist. **3**, No. 14: 1894.
Burt. The Phalloideae of the United States—I. Bot. Gaz. **22**: 273, pls. 11 and 12. 1896.
Burt. The Phalloideae of the United States—II. Bot. Gaz. **22**: 379. 1896.
Burt. The Phalloideae of the United States—III. Bot. Gaz. **24**: 73. 1897.

* A peculiar new plant, *Claustula Fischeri*, recently described from New Zealand (Curtis, l. c.) is obviously related to this family, but if included would necessitate modification of the family characters. The receptaculum is a complete hollow sac bearing the hymenium on the entire inner surface. The spores are larger than in typical Phalloids and have a very distinct mucro. There is also no obvious slime.

Conard. The Structure of *Simblum sphaerocephalum.* Mycologia 5: 264, pls. 96 and 97. 1913.

Corda. l.c., 5: 70, pl. 6, fig. 49, pl. 7 and pl. 8, fig. 51.

Cunningham. *Clathrus cibarius,* the "Bird-cage Fungus." New Zealand Journ. Sci. and Tech. 5: 247, figs. 1–4. 1922.

Cunningham. *Aseroe rubra,* an Interesting New Zealand Phalloid. New Zealand Journ. Sci. and Tech. 6: 154, figs. 1–4. 1923.

Curtis, K. M. The Morphology of *Claustula Fischeri,* gen. et sp. nov., a New Genus of Phalloid Affinity. Ann. Bot. 40: 471, pl. 15 and 6 text figs. 1926.

Fischer. Beiträge zur Morphologie und Systematik der Phalloideen. Ann. Myc. 8: 314, pl. 5. 1910.

Fischer. Unters. z. vergleichenden Entwicklungsgeschichte u. Systematik d. Phalloideen—I. Denkschriften d. Schweiz. Naturforschenden Gesellschaft 32: 1. 1890; II. Ibid 33: 1. 1893; III. Ibid 36: 2. 1900.

Gerard. Additions to the U. S. Phalloidei. Bull. Torr. Bot. Club 7: 29. 1880.

Gerard. Correlation between the Odor of Phalloids and their Relative Frequency. Bull. Torr. Bot. Club 7: 30. 1880.

Holttum. Observations on the expansion of *Dictyophora indusiata* Desv. Gard. Bull. Straits Settlements 3: 281. 1924.

Lloyd. The Phalloids of Australasia, figs. 1–25. Cincinnati, 1907.

Lloyd. Concerning the Phalloids. Myc. Notes No. 24: 293, figs. 131–135 and pls. 91–93. 1906; No. 26: 325, figs. 160–163 and pls. 112–121. 1907; Nos. 28–30: 349, figs. 167–223. 1907–08.

Lloyd. The Phalloids of Japan. Myc. Notes No. 31: 400, figs. 236–242. 1908.

Lloyd. Synopsis of the Known Phalloids, figs. 1–107. Cincinnati, 1909.

Lohwag. Der Übergang von *Clathrus* zu *Phallus.* Arch. f. Protistenkunde 49: 237, with 7 figs. 1924.

Long. The Phalloids of Texas. Journ. Myc. 13: 102, pls. 102–106. 1907.

Möller. Brasilische Pilzblumen. Jena, 1895.

Penzig. Ueber Javanische Phalloideen. Ann. Jardin Bot. de Buitenzorg, ser. 2, 16: 133, pls. 16–25. 1899.

Schroeter. In Cohn's Krypt.-Fl. Schlesien 3, pt. 1: 687. 1889.

For other literature see p. 194 and Fischer as cited there.

Key to the Phalloids of the United States*

Clathreae

Receptaculum composed of a stout, netted globe . . . .*Clathrus cancellatus* (p. 6)

Receptaculum composed of two to five stout columns fused only above . . . . . .*Clathrus columnatus* (p. 5)

Receptaculum composed of a relatively short stalk which divides above into three or more arms which are simple, widely separated and united at their tips, the gleba enclosed in the apical part of the arms . . . .*Colus Schellenbergiae* (p. 7)

Receptaculum composed of a single distinct, relatively long stalk bearing a subglobose, netted, sporebearing part on the end; red above . . . .*Simblum sphaerocephalum* (p. 7)

Receptaculum as above, but color yellow all over . . . .*Simblum texense*

Receptaculum stalked as in *Simblum,* but the apical spore-bearing part composed of several (usually six) short, hollow arms, incurved and meeting above at first and enclosing the gleba; stalk white . . . .*Anthurus borealis* (p. 8)

Phalleae

Gleba (and spore slime) borne on the upper part of the stalk itself

Stalk 10–17 cm. long, tapering gradually from the center upward to a rounded point; spores 4.7μ long . . . .*Mutinus Curtisii* (p. 10)

Stalk 6–8 cm. long, nearly cylindrical except for the tapering base (at times), the tip rather abruptly rounded and the spore-bearing part more or less sharply delimited from the sterile part; spores 3.7–4.8μ long . . . .*Mutinus Ravenelii* (and *M. caninus,* if that is different.) (p. 9)

* All except *Simblum texense* are found east of the Mississippi.

Gleba borne on a pendent cap hanging from the stem tip
  An obvious netted veil absent
      Outer surface of cap strongly pitted by reticulated plates......*Ithyphallus impudicus* (p. 12)
      Outer surface of cap not pitted but minutely granular; stalk white.......*I. Ravenelii* (p. 11)
      Outer surface not pitted but nearly smooth to longitudinally rugose; stalk red
                                                                        I. rubicundus (p. 13)
  An obvious netted veil-like indusium pendent from the stem apex and exposed for some distance
      below the cap...*Dictyophora duplicata* (p. 13)

CLATHRUS Mich.

Receptaculum without a single distinct stem, but composed of an inflated hollow network or of several curved columns meeting and fused above; in all cases having the spore-bearing gleba attached to the inner side above as a slimy mass.   Odor offensive. Only a few species are known and but two have been found in the eastern United States.

For other species see Lloyd, Syn. Known Phalloids, p. 54.   For literature see under the family.

There is evidence that both of the following species are poisonous.   Farlow reports the killing of hogs within twelve to fifteen hours by *C. columnatus* in North Carolina (Bot. Gaz. **15**: 45.   1890).

Clathrus columnatus Bosc
  Laternea columnata Nees

Plates 1 and 105

Eggs subspherical, about 2.5 cm. thick, bursting above into several flaps to allow the expansion of the receptacle which consists of 2–5 (in our plants 4–5) stout, spongy, curved and very delicate columns with separate, pointed, basal ends which remain in the volva, the distal ends incurved and completely fused into a flat roof from which hangs within the dark slimy mass of the spore-bearing gleba.   Color of the receptacle rosy red, the base pale to colorless; volva watery white, attached at base by a cord-like root.   Odor about that of a stink horn, strong and fetid.

Spores (of No. 4949) smooth, elliptic, minute, 1.8–2.4 x 3.7–4.8μ.

This plant seems to be entirely southern in its range (but see Saccardo's Sylloge **7**: 19) and confined to the sandy coastal plain of North Carolina southward.   It was originally described from South Carolina and is also known from the Gulf states (see Long, Mycologia **9**: 274.   1917).   An interesting anomaly is shown by one of our plants (pl. 1).   There is a natural perforation on one side at the top just about the center of one of the columns, exactly like the more numerous perforations in *C. cancellatus* and in *Simblum*.   For development and microscopic detail, see Burt, Bot. Gaz. **22**: 273, pls. 21 and 22.   1896.

Illustrations: Bosc.   Mag. der Gesell. naturforschender Freunde Berlin **5**: pl. 5, fig. 5.   1811.
  Burt.   As above.
  Fischer.   Pflanzenfamilien **1**, pt. 1: fig. 120 B.
  Lloyd.   Myc. Works, pl. 92.
  Lloyd.   Phalloids of Australia, fig. 20.
  Möller.   Brasilische Pilzblumen, pl. 2, figs. 3 and 4; pl. 7, fig. 17 (as *Laternea*).
  Nees von Esenbeck.   Syst. Pilze Schw., pl. 36b, fig. 262.   1817.

North Carolina. Smith's Island. In a sandy road, December 29, 1921. Couch and Grant, colls. (U. N. C. Herb., No. 4949).

Fayetteville. Lawrence, coll. Reported by Farlow (Bot. Gaz. 15: 45. 1890).

South Carolina. Georgetown. In sandy soil near Silver Hill Farm, Dec. 29, 1922. Coker, coll. (U. N. C. Herb., No. 6013).

Santee Canal. Ravenel, coll. (Curtis Herb.).

Also from South Carolina by Ravenel in Fungi Car. Exs. No. 70 (N. Y. B. G. Herb. and Phil. Acad. Herb.).

Florida. Eustis and Orange Bend. Underwood, coll. (N. Y. B. G. Herb.).

Mississippi. Trice, coll. (Curtis Herb.).

Louisiana. St. Martinsville. Langlois, coll. (N. Y. B. G. Herb.).

Porto Rico. Cook, coll. (U. S. Nat'l. Herb.).

Clathrus cancellatus Linn.

C. *ruber* Mich.

C. *albus* Mich.

C. *flavescens* Mich.

C. *volvaceus* Bull.

This beautiful species has been reported in the United States only from Georgia (Schweinitz; Syn. Fung. Car. Sup., No. 537, as *C. ruber*) and Florida (Lloyd; Myc. Notes, p. 296; Syn. Known Phalloids, p. 54) and New York (Peck; Bull. Torr. Bot. Club 7: 29. 1880). The last reference is in some doubt and may refer to *C. columnatus*, as suggested by Lloyd (Myc. Notes, p. 150). It differs from *C. columnatus* in the more globular receptaculum in the form of an open net-work. The color is red above, paler below; base surrounded by the conspicuous white volva with a central cord-like root. The dark, slimy, ill-smelling gleba containing the smooth, elongated spores is said to cover the entire inner surface of the thick, spongy elements of the net-work.

Illustrations: Barla. Champ. Nice, pl. 45, figs. 5–12.

Bulliard. Champ. Fr., pl. 441.

Fischer. Pflanzenfamilien 1¹: fig. 129 A. Copied by Lloyd on pl. 92, fig. 7.

Lloyd. Myc. Notes, p. 326, fig. 160; Syn. Known Phalloids, fig. 70; also pl. 92, fig. 7, and pl. 112.

Micheli. Nova Plant. Gen., pl. 93 (as *C. ruber*).

Nees von Esenbeck. Syst. Pilze Schw., pl. 36b, fig. 261 (as *C. ruber*). 1817.

Jamaica. Howe, coll. (N. Y. B. G. Herb.).

Bahamas. Acklin's Island. Brace, coll. (N. Y. B. G. Herb.).

Porto Rico. Britton and Wheeler, colls. (N. Y. B. G. Herb.).

COLUS Cav. & Séch.

Fruiting bodies with a distinct hollow stalk which is seated in a smooth volva, the wall with or without chambers, dividing above into several elongated arms which are united at their tips and simple, or capped by a group of meshes like those of *Simblum*. Gleba borne within the arms or meshes, deliquescing into a dark slime.

The original species (*C. hirudinosus*) and one other (*C. Mülleri*) are the only ones with a netted apex, the others have simple arms which taper up and are united at their tips only. Lloyd has separated the latter group as the genus *Pseudocolus* (Synopsis of the Known Phalloids, p. 51). Through *C. Mülleri* the genus approaches *Clathrella*. The species given below is the only one ever found in the northern hemisphere and is known only from the type locality.

For literature see Fischer, Lloyd and Penzig as cited under the family.

PLATE 1

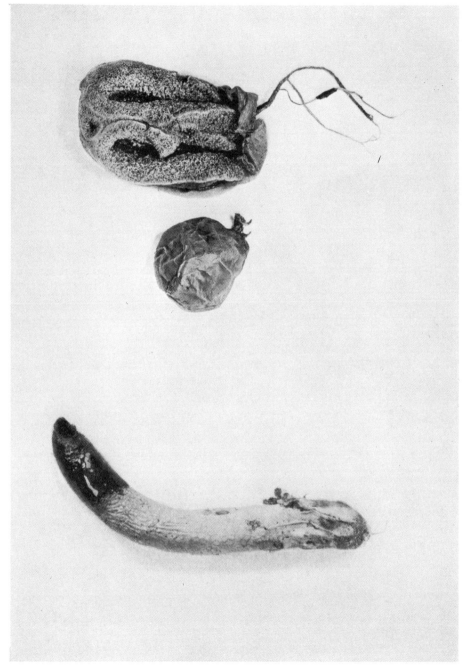

Mutinus Ravenelii. No. 741 [left]
Clathrus columnatus. No. 4949 [right]

Colus Schellenbergiae Sumstine

This species has been collected but once, and this is the only record of a *Colus* in the northern hemisphere. We copy below the original description (Mycologia **8**: 183. 1916):

"Volva dark-brown, smooth, globose, 2-3 cm. in diameter, breaking at maturity into several irregular segments; receptaculum stipitate, the stipitate portion cylindric, hollow, reticulate-pitted, white below, orange-colored above, slightly enlarged upward, dividing into three arms; arms arched outward, united at the apex, transversely wrinkled, cylindric or sometimes compressed so as to appear triquetrous, orange-colored, attenuate upward, 3-6 cm. long; gleba dark green, borne on the inner side of the arms, foetid; spores hyaline, ellipsoid-ovoid, 4.5-5.5 x 2-2.5μ."

The species is near *C. javanicus* (See Penzig, l. c., p. 160) and may be the same, as no important differences appear from the descriptions. *Colus Garciae* Müller from Brazil has much the same appearance, but differs principally in the absence of chambers in the wall of the stem, a remarkable peculiarity for a Phalloid.

Pennsylvania. Pittsburg. Sumstine, coll. (Carnegie Mus. and N. Y. B. G. Herb. and U. N. C. Herb.).

SIMBLUM Klotzsch

Receptaculum formed of a distinct, hollow, delicate stalk which is transformed above into a somewhat larger inflated network which bears the gleba slime on the inside. Volva watery white; receptaculum bright colored, red (in our species) or yellow, rarely whitish; odor offensive.

Only a few species are known and only two are North American. For literature see under the family.

Simblum sphærocephalum Schlecht
Simblum rubescens Gerard
S. rubescens var. *Kansensis* Cragin

Plates 2, 3 and 105

Stalk long, club-shaped, hollow, spongy, tapering downward to a narrow attachment in the bottom of the large, white, toughish, inflated volva; terminated above by the subglobose structure of thick, anastomosing strands that holds the dark slime containing the spores. Color bright red above, fading to pale below; odor strong and repulsive. The entire plant is about 7-9 cm. high and the stalk about 1-1.6 cm. thick above, its honeycombed wall 3-4 mm. thick near the top and only 1 mm. thick below. Spores (of No. 1427) elliptic, smooth, 1.4-2 x 3.7-4.4μ.

This is a rare plant in the United States and has not been reported before from North Carolina (for distribution see Lloyd's Myc. Notes, p. 220. 1905). It is said to be common in South America. The only other North American species is *S. texense* which differs from the present one in its yellow color and longer spores, which are 3 x 7μ (see Long, l. c., p. 112, pl. 106, fig. 11).

Our plate 3 shows an abnormal variation of two plants springing from one volva and fused at their tips. This is apparently of not rare occurrence as a similar example is shown in Lloyd's Myc. Notes No. 24, fig. 133, from a photograph of a Brazilian plant by Rick, and another such is illustrated by Gerard in his plate 2 (as cited below).

Illustrations: Gerard. Bull. Torr. Bot. Club 7: 8, pls. 1 and 2. 1880.
> Long. l. c., pl. 106, fig. 10.

1426.   In apple orchard, October 26, 1914.
1427.   In grass on campus, fall of 1902.   A large number of plants.
5910.   On ground in pasture, November 20, 1922.
5917.   On ground in pasture by branch, November 22, 1922.   Several plants.
7142.   On ground in pasture, September 25, 1923.

ANTHURUS Kalch.

Phalloids with a hollow, spongy, subcylindrical stem springing from a volva and bearing at the top several spongy arms which in youth embrace the dark gleba which covers their inner faces and sides; at maturity either remaining connivent at the tips or bending more or less strongly outward.

There is a difference of opinion as to the correct definition of the genera *Lysurus* and *Anthurus*. As originally described, in *Lysurus* the gleba is borne on the outside faces of the arms, while in *Anthurus* the gleba is described as enclosed within the arms in youth and covering their inner and side faces at full maturity, a dorsal zone remaining bare. We are following Burt and Fischer (Phalloideen, part 3, p. 41) in including our species in *Anthurus*. Lloyd (Syn. Known Phalloids, p. 35) and Rea (Trans. Brit. Myc. Soc. 2: 57. 1904) would put the species in *Lysurus*, modifying that genus to include certain species with the gleba on the inner surfaces of the arms.

The genus *Anthurus* is described by Kalchbrenner (Grevillea 9: 2. 1880) as having the stem conspicuously flaring at the top and passing into several broadly spreading arms which bear the spore slime on the inner surface. The description does not state that the arms pass directly into the stem without a groove or abrupt change of texture, but the original figure of the type species (*A. Mullerianus*) has this appearance, and Fischer's figures of the same species are in agreement. *Anthurus aseroeformis*, a better known plant, is said to have this structure. Lloyd thinks these two species may be the same (Myc. Notes, p. 408, fig. 244).

In the eastern United States there is but one representative, and that is found in the northern and central sections. There may be another American species, as a name (*Lysurus Texensis* Ellis) has been referred to without description (Bull. Torr. Bot. Club 7: 30. 1880), and Lloyd mentions a red *Lysurus* in Texas seen by Prof. Long (Syn. Known Phalloids, p. 40; also Myc. Notes, p. 407). In Mycological Notes, pp. 586 and 647, Lloyd reports *L. Mokusin* from hothouses at Chico, California, where it was probably introduced from the Orient.

Anthurus borealis Burt

We take the following description from Burt (Mem. Boston Soc. Nat. Hist. 3: 504. 1894):

"Solitary or subcaespitose. Stipe white, clavate, divided above into 6 erect, narrowly lanceolate, hollow arms incurved above, and with pale, flesh-colored backs

PLATE 2

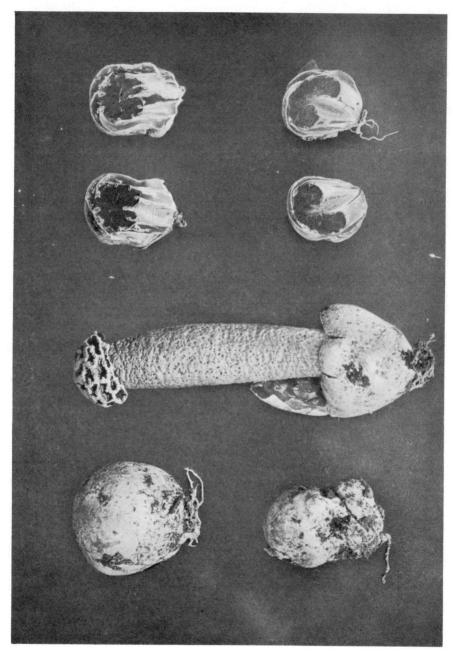

Simblum sphaerocephalum. No. 5917

PLATE 3

SIMBLUM SPHAEROCEPHALUM. No. 1426

which are traversed their entire length by a shallow furrow having its surface continuous with the surface of the stipe; cavity of the stipe nearly closed at the base of the arms by a thin diaphragm opening above into a closed chamber with dome-shaped wall even on its inner surface and adherent to the arms for about one-sixth their length; gleba brownish olive-green, supported upon the dome and closely embraced by the arms; spores simple, olive-green, ellipsoidal, 3–4 x 1.5μ, 5–8 on septate and constricted basidia.

"Total height of plant 10–12 cm.; arms one-sixth of this; greatest diameter of stipe 15 cm."

As Lloyd supposes, this species is almost certainly introduced from the tropics or south temperate regions.

The basidia as described by Burt are most remarkable. They are constricted at intervals so as to appear like a row of beads, a form apparently unknown in other Basidiomycetes. Individual plants vary greatly in size: in those we have seen, the arms in the dry state varying from 1 to 3.6 cm. in length. In addition to plants seen which are cited below, the species has been reported from Ohio, Connecticut, Massachusetts, England and Germany. (See Lloyd, Myc. Notes, pp. 183, 219, 386, 515; Beardslee, Ann. Rept. Ohio St. Acad. Sci. 9: 19. 1901; Sumstine, Ohio Naturalist 6: 474. 1906; Stockberger, Ohio Naturalist 6: 517.)

Lloyd thinks it very probable that *L. australiensis* (see figure by Rea in Trans. Brit. Myc. Soc. 2: pl. 3, fig. A. 1904), *L. Clarazianus* and *L. Gardneri* are all the present species (Myc. Notes, p. 594).

A variety of this species (*Klitzingii* Hennings) has been described from Germany (Hedwigia 41: 167. 1902), differing only in paler color and absence of green in the gleba (see Rea, as cited under the genus).

Illustrations: Burt. l.c., pls. 49 and 50.
　　Lloyd. Myc. Notes, p. 386, fig. 219; p. 513, fig. 510.
　　Volkert. Mycologia 4: pl. 68, fig. 8. 1912.

New Jersey. Ramsay. In a flower garden. Lutz, coll. (N. Y. B. G. Herb.).
New York. Columbia University campus. Griffiths, coll. (N. Y. B. G. Herb.).
　　Blackwell's Island. In a mushroom bed. Dr. Baker, coll. (N. Y. B. G. Herb. and U. N. C. Herb.).
　　New York Botanical Garden. In a flower bed. Boynton, coll. (N. Y. B. G. Herb.).
Pennsylvania. Sumstine, coll. (Herb. Carnegie Mus., Pittsburgh, Pa., and U. N. C. Herb.).

MUTINUS Fr.

Receptaculum formed of a distinct, delicate, hollow stalk as in *Simblum*, but differing in the spore slime being borne on the outside of the upper part of the stalk itself, which is smooth and more or less pointed, the tip often perforated. Color rosy red above (under and below the deep olive slime), fading downward. Volva soon collapsing against the base of the stalk.

For literature see under the family and species.

Mutinus Ravenelii (B. & C.) E. Fischer

Plates 1, 4 and 105

Plants about 6–8 cm. high, the ample volva 2.5–3.5 cm. long; stalk up to 1.3 cm. thick in center and typically tapering a little downward, again nearly cylindrical, the spore-bearing part about 2–2.5 cm. of the apex, more or less abruptly marked off from the sterile part by the narrower, radially elongated, definitely one-layered compartments of the wall.   Color bright rosy red above (under and below the slime), fading downwards; apex with or without a small opening; odor strong and offensive.   Wall of the stalk about 3 mm. thick in center and 1.5 mm. thick near base; that of the spore-bearing part about 2 mm. thick below and 1 mm. thick above; walls of the stalk compartments 55–75μ thick, with 3–4 layers of cells, those of the spore-bearing part 90–95μ thick, with about 5–7 layers of cells.

Spores (of No. 741) smooth, elliptic, 1.6–2.2 x 3.7–4.8μ.

This is more common with us than *M. Curtisii*.   For treatment of its development see Burt in Ann. Bot. **10**: 343, pls. 17, 18.   1896; see also Bambeke, Mém. Acad. Roy. Belgique, 2nd. ser., **2**: 1.   1910.   Lloyd considers *M. Ravenelii* as different from *M. caninus*, both occurring in the eastern United States (Myc. Notes No. 24: 300; No. 26: 325; Syn. Known Phal., p. 28).   Burt considers the two species the same (l. c., p. 344). Lloyd's interpretation would probably refer the left hand plant on our pl. 4 to *M. caninus*, the two right hand plants to *M. Ravenelii*.   We cannot find any important difference in structure among the forms we have collected.   *Mutinus caninus* is common in Europe.

Illustrations: Long.   Journ. Myc. **13**: pl. 104 (as *M. caninus*).   1907.
    Lloyd.   Myc. Notes No. 24, fig. 135; No. 28, fig. 183.
    Marshall.   Mushroom Book, pl. opposite p. 136 (as *M. caninus*).
For illustrations of the European *M. caninus* see:
    Fischer.   l. c., fig. 142 A–E.
    Hollos.   l. c., pl. 1, figs. 3–11.
    Long.   l. c., pl. 104, fig. 9.
    Nees von Esenbeck.   Syst. Pilze Schw., pl. 36b, fig. 260.   1817.
    Sowerby.   Engl. Fungi, pl. 330.

22a.   By stone wall near Battle's Park, October 24, 1902.   Spores 1.4–2 x 3.7–4.4μ.
24a.   Old Chapel Hill collection without label.   Spores smooth, 1.6–2.2 x 3.7–4.8μ.
741.   On ground near stream, September 12, 1913.
1312.   Near brook just above Meeting of the Waters, September 17, 1913.   Spores 1.2–2.2 x 3.7–4.6μ.
1729.   In low place by branch, September 10, 1915.
1925.   In grass in front of Davie Hall, October 25, 1915.   Spores 1.6–2.2 x 3.7–4.8μ.

Pennsylvania.   Buck Hill Falls.   Mrs. Delafield, coll. (N. Y. B. G. Herb., as *M. elegans*).
Also collection from Pennsylvania by Sumstine.   (Herb. Carnegie Mus., Pittsburgh, Pa., as *M. caninus*, and U. N. C. Herb.)

Mutinus Curtisii (Berk.) E. Fischer
    M. bovinus Morgan
    M. elegans Mont.

Plates 5, 6 and 105

Plant about 10–17 cm. high, the white volva at first spherical then elongating and on rupturing at the apex collapsing against the stalk which is almost cylindrical for the first third and up to 2.5 cm. thick, then tapers gradually upward to the blunt point; spore-bearing (slimy) part composing about 3–5 cm. of the apical end, similar in superficial appearance to the rest of the stem except for the slime; color bright rosy red under and below the slime, gradually fading to watery white or flesh color below; apex perforated by a small opening; volva rooted by a strong cord; odor of the brownish slime very strong and offensive.

PLATE 4

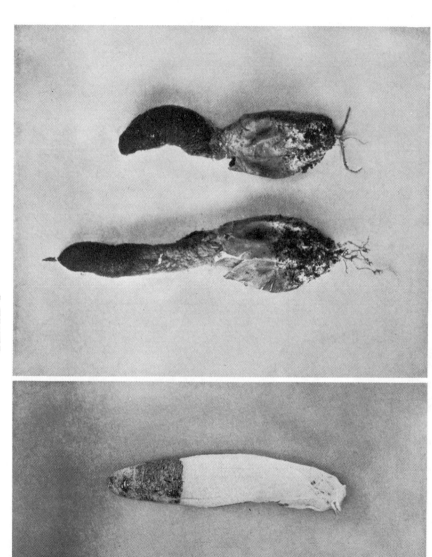

MUTINUS RAVENELII
No. 22a [left]; No. 1925 [right]

PLATE 5

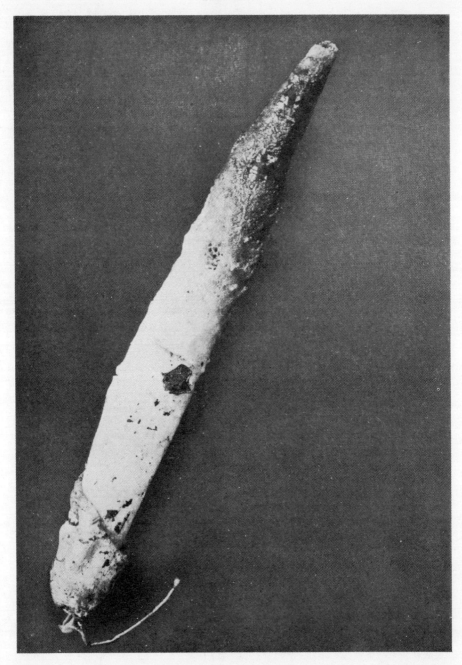

MUTINUS CURTISII. No. 2421

Spores (of No. 5113) smooth, elliptic, 2–3 x 4–7μ. Wall of the very hollow stem about 2–3 mm. thick and composed of one or two layers of small thin-walled chambers which are irregularly isodiametrical below and change gradually to radially elongated and definitely to a single layer in the slime-bearing part. Walls of the chambers of the stalk 90–95μ thick, with only 3–4 layers of cells; of the spore-bearing part 55–75μ thick with 3–4 layers of cells.

The plants usually appear singly in woods or groves.

Illustrations: Hard. Mushrooms, pl. 56 and fig. 453.
James. Bull. Torr. Bot. Club 15: pl. 86. 1888.
Lloyd. Syn. Known Phalloids, fig. 24 (as *M. elegans*).
Lloyd. Myc. Notes No. 28: fig. 182 (as *M. elegans*).
Morgan. Journ. Cin. Soc. Nat. Hist. 11: pl. 3 (as *M. bovinus*). 1889.

2421. In wood mold, Battle's Park, July 24, 1916. Spores smooth, elliptic, 2–2.8 x 4–7μ.
5113. In rotting leaves, May 16, 1922.

Asheville. Beardslee.
Blowing Rock. Seen by the authors.

ITHYPHALLUS Fr.

Volva and stalk as in *Mutinus*, but the spore slime is borne on the outside of a thin, pendent, campanulate membrane or cap which is free from the stem except at the tip. Between this cap and the stalk above and between the volva and the stalk below another delicate, white membrane or veil is obvious (at least in *I. Ravenelii*).

We are following Fischer and Atkinson in placing in this genus *Phallus Ravenelii*, *P. impudicus*, and *P. rubicundus*. Atkinson has shown that the membranous veil of this genus is not homologous with the veil-like indusium of *Dictyophora*.

For literature see under the family and species.

Ithyphallus Ravenelii (B. & C.) E. Fischer
Dictyophora Ravenelii (B. & C.) Burt.

Plates 7–9 and 105

Stalks usually 10–16 cm. high, tapering gradually upward or nearly equal, about 1.7–2.5 cm. thick, springing from an ovate egg or volva, which is pinkish, tough, thick, wrinkled below and connected with the earth and with other eggs by purplish pink strands or roots which grow out from the base. The eggs are large and just before rupturing may reach a height of 5 cm. and a thickness of 3.5 cm. The cap or pileus is conical and is attached around the raised white ring which terminates the stem. The upper part of the membranous veil is concealed beneath the cap while the lower half remains in the volva around the base of the stem. At times parts or rings of the veil may be torn loose in expanding and cling to the stalk so as to be visible beneath the cap. Surface of the cap minutely granular, not veined or honeycombed, covered at first by the dark, bad-smelling slime of the deliquescent gleba.

Spores (of No. 41a) smooth, elliptic, 1.2–1.8 x 3.7–4.4μ.

This interesting species is generally found growing in soil containing rotten wood such as old wood piles and rotting trash piles and often appears in large numbers from one colony. For discussion of sclerotia in this species, see Overholts, Mycologia 17: 109, pl. 11, figs. 5, 6. 1925.

Illustrations: Atkinson. l. c., pl. 2; pl. 3, fig. 7; pl. 4, fig. 10; pl. 6, fig. 14.
    Hard. Mushrooms, figs. 447–449.
    Lloyd. Syn. Known Phalloids, figs. 7 and 8.
    Lloyd. Myc. Notes No. 28: fig. 168.
    Overholts. As cited above.
    Patterson and Charles. U. S. Dept. Agric. Bull. 175: pl. 36, figs. 2 and 3 (as *Dictyophora*). 1915.
    Peck. Bull. Torr. Bot. Club. 9: pl. 25. 1882.
    Scofield. Minn. Bot. Survey 2: pls. 29–31. 1900.

41a. Chapel Hill. No other data.
618. In pile of chips and trash in road, October 24, 1912.
649. Same spot as No. 618, October 31, 1912.

Asheville. Beardslee.

New York. New Rochelle. Seaver, coll. (N. Y. B. G. Herb.).

Ithyphallus impudicus (L.) Fr.

Plate 10

This is a rare plant east of the Mississippi and, except for doubtful early records, as Schweinitz and Curtis, seems to have been recorded only twice in that territory. The American form seems to have consistently a pink volva which is elongated or egg-shaped and may be best considered as *I. imperialis* or as a variety of *I. impudicus*. The latter is said by some to have in Europe a round, white volva (see Lloyd, Myc. Notes, p. 327 and 328, also p. 508), but Rea (British Basidiomycetae, p. 23) says the volva is round or oval and Hollos shows one with an oval, very pink volva. We have not seen the plant alive and take the following measurements from Dr. W. B. McDougall.

Buttons oblong or egg-shaped, pinkish, much like those of *I. Ravenelii*, 3–4.5 x 3.5–6 cm.; expanded plant 7.5–15 cm. tall; cap up to 4.5 cm. long, deeply reticulated with large chambers, which are at first filled with olivaceous slime, apically attached (in the plant we have) to a broad (1.3 cm.) white expansion of the stem apex which is not perforated; a thin, membranous, non-perforated veil is present between the cap and the stem and a thicker basal portion surrounds the stem attachment in the volva base. Odor very putrid.

Spores (of plant from Urbana, Ill.) color of the slime, 1.4–1.7 x 3–3.7μ, short-elliptic, smooth. Spores of a typical plant from England in the New York Botanical Garden (Kew Gardens; Murrill, coll.) are 1.3–2 x 3.2–4.2μ.

Illustrations: Bambeke. Bull. Acad. Roy. Belgique, No. 6, pls. 1–2. 1914.
    Bambeke. Mém. Acad. Roy. Belgique, 2nd. ser., 2: pls. 1–3. 1910.
    Dumée. Nouvel Atl. Champ., 2nd ser., pl. 59.
    Fries, Th. C. E. Sveriges Gasteromyceter, fig. 2. Arkiv für Botanik 17: 1921.
    Hollos. Pl. 1, figs. 1–2, 12–15.
    Lloyd. Myc. Works, pl. 114.
    McDougall. Trans. Ill. Acad. Sci. 15: fig. 4. 1922.
    Nees von Esenbeck. Syst. Pilze Schw., pl. 36. 1817.
    Patterson and Charles. U. S. Dept. Agric. Bull. 175: pl. 37, fig. 2. 1915; also Farmer's Bull. 796, fig. 19. 1917.
    Schaeffer. Der Gichtschwamm mit grünschleimigem Hute, pls. 1–5. 1760.
    Schaeffer. Fung. Bavar., pls. 196–198.
    Tulasne. Fungi Hypogaei, pl. 21, fig. 10.

PLATE 6

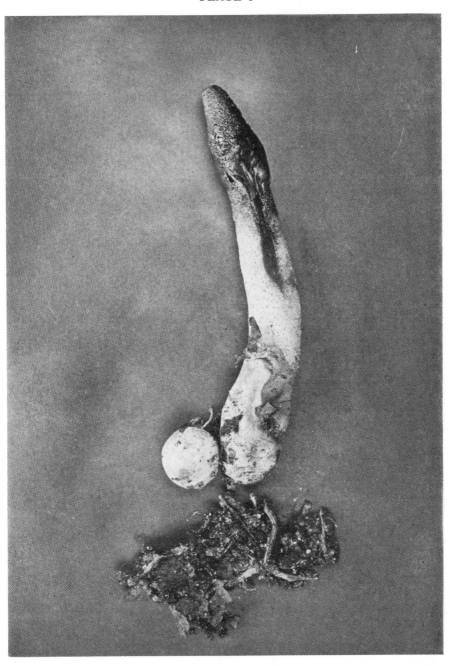

Mutinus Curtisii. No. 5113

PLATE 7

ITHYPHALLUS RAVENELII. No. 649

Illinois. Urbana. McDougall, coll. (U. N. C. Herb.).
Colorado. Seaver, coll. (N. Y. B. G. Herb., as *P. imperialis*). Seaver says this rosy plant is common
in the West and is a rosy form of *I. impudicus*.
Minnesota. Elk River. Baitey, coll. (U. S. Nat'l. Herb., as *P. Ravenelii*).
Kansas. Lawrence. Det. by Underwood. (U. N. C. Herb.)

Ithyphallus rubicundus (Bosc) E. Fischer

We have not seen this and adapt the following from Long (l.c., p. 109):

Eggs white, solitary or in groups of 2–6 individuals from a common mycelium,
when in groups usually one large plant surrounded by small ones, ovate to globose,
2–3 cm. tall by 1–3 cm. thick. Stipe cylindric-fusiform to fusiform, hollow, scarlet,
9–15 cm. tall by 1.5 to 2.5 cm. in diameter, walls of several chambers thick, which open
onto outer and inner surfaces of stipe as pits; chambers isodiametric, pseudo-parenchymatous; apex perforate or imperforate, but usually perforate as the plant ages, by
scarlet top of apex falling entirely off of plant; joined to pileus by a narrow irregular
scarlet collar or ring. Pileus conic, smooth or rugose, scarlet, sometimes extending
below gleba into a narrow sterile border, whose edges are finely crinkled to dentate,
pseudo-parenchymatous, 1–2 cm. wide to 2–3 cm. tall. Gleba at first isabella color,
becoming a dirty yellowish brown when deliquescing, odor very foetid. Veil wanting
or when present, membranous floccose, white beneath pileus or in bands or patches on
the stipe or clinging to stipe within volva as in *I. impudicus*. Spores oblong, 2 x 4μ.
In lawns and open grassy places, Austin, Tex., April, May, and Nov., 1900, or in old
sandy fields near rotting oak stumps and along fences in sandy soil. Denton, Tex.,
Nov. to Jan., 1902 and 1903.

Lloyd thinks that *Phallus aurantiacus* Mont. is the same as this (Myc. Notes, p.
330 and Syn. Known Phalloids, p. 14).

Illustrations: Bosc. Mag. Gesell. Naturf. Freunde, Berlin, **5**: pl. 6, fig. 8. 1811.
Long. Journ. Myc. **13**: pl. 104, fig. 5; pl. 105. 1907.
Lloyd. (Copied from Long.) Syn. Known Phalloids, fig. 5.
Lloyd. (Copied from Long.) Myc. Works, pl. 116, figs. 1–3.

South Carolina. Bosc, coll. Type locality.
North Carolina. Reported by Curtis.

DICTYOPHORA Desv.

With the characters of *Ithyphallus* except that there is a large campanulate, veil-
like, netted indusium that is attached to the stem tip under the cap and extends far
below it. Atkinson has shown (l. c.) that this indusium is a distinct organ and not
homologous with the short, membranous veil of *Ithyphallus*. The species here included
is the only one known in the United States.
For literature see under the family.

Dictyophora duplicata (Bosc) E. Fischer

Plates 11–14 and 105

Our largest and most massive Phalloid, arising from a large egg which is subspherical, ovate or sometimes flattened, about 4–4.5 x 4.5–5 cm., when flattened up to 7 cm.
broad and 5 cm. high, white and plicate below as in a peeled orange, the upper half
smooth, pale flesh color to deep fleshy brown; in the center below is given off a large,

fleshy root, and sometimes one or two smaller, more lateral ones.   The expanded plant may reach a height of 17 cm. with the fertile, pendent, apical cap about 5 cm. long and broad, its outer surface strongly chambered by anastomosing plates, over which the brownish olive slime is spread.   Between the cap and the stem, and hanging from the top, is a beautiful net-like veil (technically the indusium) of a light rosy pink color that extends below the cap for about 3–5 cm., the perforations being rather regular and about 1–2 mm. broad except towards the margin where they become much smaller. Stalk about 4.5 cm. thick, nearly cylindrical, very hollow and with chambered walls; between its base and the volva is a thick, brownish yellow slime which is separated from the stem by a thin membrane.   The odor of the dark spore slime above is offensive but not nearly so much so as in the species of *Mutinus*, being weaker and not so distressingly fetid.

Spores (of No. 5195) smooth, elliptic, 1.2–1.8 x 3.7–4.4μ.

Not rare in Chapel Hill, occurring usually in a scattered colony of several in woods mold in deciduous woods.   *Dictyophora phalloidea* (*Phallus indusiatus*) is a closely related tropical species.   Fischer considers it the same as the above (l. c., 1890).   See this paper for a long list of synonyms of *D. phalloidea*.

Illustrations: Atkinson. l. c., figs. 6, 7, 11, 13, 16.
    Hard.   Mushrooms, pl. 55.
    Lloyd.   Syn. Known Phalloids, fig. 16.
    Murrill.   Chart of Edible and Poisonous Mushrooms, fig. 34.
    Nees von Esenbeck.   Syst. Pilze Schw., pl. 35, fig. 258.   1817.
    Patterson and Charles.   U. S. Dept. Agric. Bull. 175: pl. 35, fig. 1.   1915.
    Rau.   Bot. Gaz. 8: pl. 4 (as *Phallus togatus*).   1883.   See Farlow, ibid., 8: 258.

836a.   On lawn of president's house, October 22, 1911.
2286.   On a ditch in woods, June 28, 1916.
5195.   In rich woods, June 20, 1922.
5343.   In deciduous woods near Forest Theater, July 8, 1922.   Plant 12 cm. long.

    Asheville.   Beardslee.

Alabama.   Winston Co.   Underwood, coll. (N. Y. B. G. Herb.).
New York.   New York Botanical Garden.   Miss Eaton, coll. (N. Y. B. G. Herb.).
    Syracuse.   Underwood, coll. (N. Y. B. G. Herb.).
Massachusetts.   Middlesex Falls.   Underwood, coll. (N. Y. B. G. Herb.).
Indiana.   Greencastle.   Underwood, coll. (N. Y. B. G. Herb.).

PLATE 8

ITHYPHALLUS RAVENELII. No. 649

PLATE 9

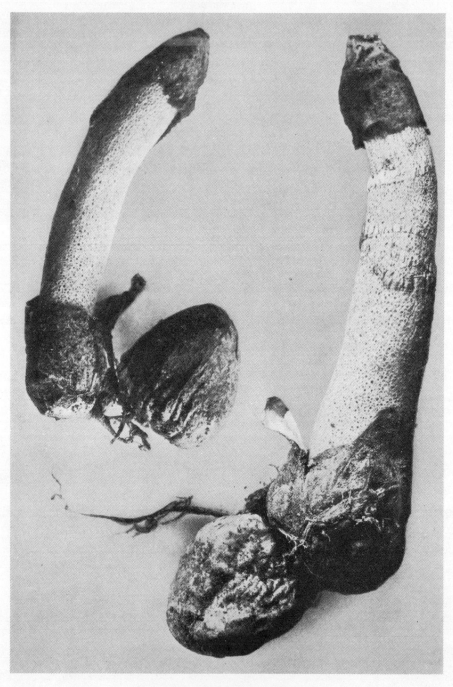

ITHYPHALLUS RAVENELII. No. 618
Reduced. Largest plant 7¾ in. long

HYSTERANGIACEAE

Fruit bodies usually subterranean (in *Phallogaster* and *Protophallus* exposed), tuberous to pyriform or spherical, the mycelium basal from a central point or with several scattered fibrils; peridium simple, thin, not intimately connected with the tramal plates, in some cases disappearing by maturity; gleba very irregularly chambered, the walls more or less obviously radiating from a sterile base which extends upward and outward into plates and strands that do not extend into the peridium; texture toughish, subgelatinous, after maturity deliquescing into a glutinous mass. Basidia elongated; spores 2–8, apical, rough or smooth.

Of the few genera of this family, *Phallogaster* and a species each of *Gautieria* and *Hysterangium* are the only ones heretofore reported east of California. We are adding *Hysterangium clathroides*, a species not before found in the East, and a new species of *Gymnomyces*. There is no doubt that many other species of this and related families await discovery in the eastern United States. On account of its peculiar interest we are including *Protophallus* from Jamaica.

The following genera have been described since Fischer's treatment in Pflanzen-familien:

Martellia Mattirolo. Malpighia **14**: 78. 1900. See Saccardo, Syll. **16**: 252.
Clathrogaster Petri. Malpighia **14**: 125. 1900. See Saccardo, Syll. **16**: 250.
Torrendia Bres. Atti dell' R. Acad. di Sc. Lett. ed Arti degli Agiati in Roveredo, 3rd. ser., **8**: 132. 1902. See Saccardo, Syll. **17**: 241.
Dendrogaster Bucholtz. Beitr. Morph. Syst. Hypog., p. 148. 1902. See Saccardo, Syll. **17**: 240.
Jaczewskia Mattirolo. Reale Accad. d. Sci. d. Torino, 2nd. ser. **63**: 213. 1912.
Protophallus Murrill. Mycologia **2**: 25. 1910. See our treatment.
Gallacea Lloyd. Lycoperdaceae of Australia, p. 37: Myc. Notes, p. 1201. See also Cunningham, Trans. Brit. Myc. Soc. **9**: 193, pls. 9 and 10. 1924. The hollow structure of the mature plant is shown by Cunningham not to exist in the younger condition but to be due to gelatinization and collapse toward maturity.
Phallobata Cunningham. Trans. New Zealand Institute **56**: 73, pls. 12, 13. 1926.

KEY TO THE GENERA

Peridium ephemeral, entirely or almost absent from the mature fruit body.
    Spores melon-shaped, with longitudinal ridges...............................*Gautieria* (p. 21)
    Spores spherical, rough to spiny.......................................*Gymnomyces* (p. 23)
Peridium present at maturity
    Fruit body not stalked, buried or only partly exposed....................*Hysterangium* (p. 17)
    Fruit body entirely exposed
        Fruit body stalked...*Phallogaster* (p. 16)
        Fruit body not stalked and with the exact appearance of a Phalloid "egg"
                                        Protophallus (Jamaica) (p. 15)

PROTOPHALLUS Murrill

Characters of a true Phalloid except for the entire absence of a stalk, the gleba remaining permanently enclosed in the volva until its liberation as a slime by irregular rupture. A monotypic genus known at present only from Jamaica.

Protophallus jamaicensis Murrill

Plates 15 and 105

Sessile on very rotten wood; nearly spherical, 2–3.5 cm. thick, whitish, quite smooth and glabrous, attached by a single, strong basal strand as in Phalloids, and the whole with exactly the appearance of a Phalloid "egg." Peridium (volva) single, tough and pliable, membranous, about 0.5 mm. thick, internally lined by a hyaline gelatinous sheath, 1–2.5 mm. thick, which extends inwards as plates between the deep brown, fertile tissue which forms rather narrow, elongated, irregular masses, connecting in center to a distinct, slender, subgelatinous columella, which extends up to about the center. At maturity the sheath, plates, and columella break down into a homogeneous slime like white of an egg, in which the unchanged fertile tissue floats. Dehiscence by rupture of the peridium, probably by bursting from internal pressure.

Spores 1.5–1.8 x 3.5–4.8μ, smooth, short-elliptic. Basidia subcylindrical, 3–3.7μ thick at the enlarged end.

This remarkable plant is obviously nearest *Protubera* from Brazil, but is distinctly more Phalloid in appearance, the smooth, even, spherical egg being indistinguishable from that of a typical Phalloid. The gleba also has almost exactly the appearance of that in the egg of *Dictyophora*. We have here in fact a Phalloid in every respect except the absence of a stalk. It is a beautiful connecting link between *Phallogaster*, *Jaczewskia*, *Protubera* and the true Phalloids.

Doctor Murrill found the type collection in 1909 (Mycologia **2**: 25. 1910) in the same general locality from which our plants were taken nine years earlier. Although extra-limital, we include this plant because of its great interest and because no illustrations of it have heretofore been published.

Jamaica. Cinchona. 1900. Coker, coll. (U. N. C. Herb.).

PHALLOGASTER Morgan

We take the following from Thaxter (Bot. Gaz. **18**: 120. 1893):

"Mycelium fibrous, branching. Peridium spherical to pyriform, stipitate or substipitate, consisting of a single layer covered by an evanescent cortex and coarsely reticulated through the presence of numerous irregular thin areas which become perforate at maturity, the perforation commonly associated with a general terminal dehiscence of the peridium into several divergent lobes. Gleba irregularly lobed, the lobes continuous with slight prominences from the surface of the peridium from which they are elsewhere separated by a gelatinous layer continuous with a central gelatinous axis which penetrates the gleba and separates its lobes. The entire contents deliquescent at maturity, adhering in distinct masses to the inner surface of the ruptured peridium."

Phallogaster saccatus Morgan

We can add nothing of importance to Thaxter's description and take the following from him (Bot. Gaz. **18**: 120, pl. 9. 1893):

"Solitary or rarely subcespitose. Peridium spherical to pyriform, 20–50 x 10–25 mm., stipitate or nearly sessile, the surface smooth, slightly uneven, whitish stained with dull flesh-color at maturity, becoming coarsely clathrate from the formation of irregular perforations, the perforation usually associated with a terminal dehiscence of the peridium into from three to five divergent lobes; the dark sage-green gleba adhering in definite masses of irregular size and shape to the inner face of the peridial wall. Spores

PLATE 10

ITHYPHALLUS IMPUDICUS. Urbana, Illinois

greenish, subcylindrical, 4–5.5 x 1.5–2μ, 6–8 on each basidium." The spores are smooth; basidia elongated, club-shaped.

Phallogaster Whitei, described by Peck (Bull. N. Y. St. Mus. 116: 31. 1907) from Connecticut, was based on small plants which in the opinion of Lloyd are a depauperate form of this species.

Illustrations: Fitzpatrick. Ann. Myc. 11: pl. 4, figs. 8 and 9; and text figs. 1, 3, and 7. 1913.
  Lloyd. Syn. Known Phalloids, figs. 93 and 94.
  Mattirolo. Reale Accad. d. Sci. di Torino, 2nd ser., 63: figs. 9–12. 1912.
  Morgan. Journ. Cin. Soc. Nat. Hist. 15: pl. 2, 1892.
  Thaxter. As cited above.

Pennsylvania. Ohiopyle. Murrill, coll. (N. Y. B. G. Herb.).
  Buck Hill Falls. Mrs. Delafield, coll. (N. Y. B. G. Herb.).
New York. West Park. Earle, coll. (N. Y. B. G. Herb.).
  Onondago Co. Underwood, coll. (N. Y. B. G. Herb.).
Connecticut. West Goshen. Underwood, coll. (N. Y. B. G. Herb.).
Wisconsin. Blue Mounds. (Univ. Wis. Herb. and U. N. C. Herb.)
Reported also from Massachusetts, Ohio, Kentucky, West Va., Iowa. See Lloyd, Myc. Notes, p. 1327, and Martin, Iowa Acad. Sci. 32: 222. 1925.

HYSTERANGIUM Vitt.

Fruit body subterranean or partly exposed, subglobose, not stalked; peridium thin and easily removable at maturity; gleba tough and elastic, finally deliquescing into a slime; cavities irregular, elongated radially, extending to and abutting on the peridium, with which the tramal plates are not continuous. Spores elongated, slightly or distinctly rough, and in all of our species furnished with a basal cup.

LITERATURE

Setchell and Watson. Some Ecological Relations of the Hypogaeous Fungi. Science 63: 313. 1926.

KEY TO THE SPECIES

Plants 3–15 mm. thick, surface fibrous and sandy or trashy; rooting by a bunch of fine fibers; basidia mostly 2-spored
  Gleba distinctly olive; spores pointed at the distal end...................*H. clathroides* (p. 17)
  Gleba not greenish; spores rounded at the distal end.....................*H. pompholyx* (p. 19)
Plants 1–2.5 cm. thick, surface smooth and even; rooting by a single basal cord; spores pointed at the distal end; basidia mostly 3-spored............... *H. stoloniferum* var. *americanum* (p. 20)

Hysterangium clathroides Vitt.

Plates 16 and 105

Fruiting bodies spherical to subspherical, 3–14 mm. wide by 4–11 mm. high, sessile or partly buried, rooted by a more or less branched bunch of fibrils, some of which may pass up on the side of the plant as in *Rhizopogon;* mycelium fibrous and obvious in the soil. Peridium surface myceloid with numerous minute particles of earth and trash adherent, rarely nearly smooth above, at times slightly areolate, whitish when young with tints of flesh color, becoming buff to clay colored when maturing, consisting of a single layer 145–190μ thick, composed of much entangled, closely packed threads which in section appear like closely packed parenchyma cells; easily separable from the gleba. Gleba tough-cartilaginous when young, becoming somewhat mucilaginous upon deliquescing, usually with a more or less central, branched columella which arises from the base and from which the tramal plates radiate. Color at first pale greenish, becoming darker and finally about dark Saccardo's olive (Ridgway). Tramal plates with a gelatinous hyaline appearance which persists even in mature plants; quite variable in thickness from one hundred to several hundred microns; cavities of the gleba labyrinthiform, long, and narrow, nearly closed with spores when fully mature.

Spores (of No. 7416) 5–6.2 x 12–15.5μ, subelliptic, often narrowed toward the distal end, smooth under low power, but appearing minutely punctate under oil immersion, with a distinct cup at the mucro end (appearing under ordinary power as two prongs), subsessile on the basidia. Basidia long cylindrical, 5.5–6.6 x 30–42μ, usually with somewhat sinuous walls, bearing two spores, rarely four.

Odor quite variable: fresh unripe plants with a very faint not unpleasant odor; deliquescing plants when first collected with a very strong odor suggesting that of *Clathrus;* while deliquescing plants kept covered in the laboratory give off an odor like that of fermenting wine. Taste of fresh plants slightly sweet, not unpleasant.

It seems that this species, from the literature we have at hand, has been reported only from Europe, North Africa and California. Our plants agree well with the descriptions of both Vittadini and Tulasne. The former author describes his plant as varying from about the size of a pea to a hazel nut, rarely larger, with a closely fitting but separable peridium, from the base of which numerous fibrils extend, some of which run over the surface of the ground. The odor is described as being strongly nauseous, much like that of *Clathrus.* He reports his plants as being found deeply buried in humus, and occurring in the months of March and April. With the latter author's description and elaborate notes and figures, our plants agree in all essential characters. Tulasne described two varieties which differ from each other in size and in the fact that in one the peridium was much more easily separable from the gleba than in the other. Our plants vary enough in size to include both of his varieties, while in our specimens the separability of the peridium seems to be dependent on the age of the plant, the peridium being separable, but with some difficulty in young specimens, while it often breaks and slips off in collecting mature plants.

We have examined plants identified by C. Torrend (No. 90) as *H. clathroides,* and find that his plants agree with ours in practically all characters, the only difference being that the spores of his plants are slightly smaller than in ours.

Of the six other species of *Hysterangium* described or recorded by Tulasne, four: *H. nephriticum, H. Thwaitesii, H. fragile,* and *H. stoloniferum,* while showing certain points of superficial resemblance, have spores too large for our present plant and show differences in other characters. Of the other two species noted by Tulasne, *H. membranaceum* is admittedly very close to *H. clathroides,* but differs in having smaller spores according to Hesse's measurements; while *H. pompholyx* differs in odor and in having spores which are argillaceous in color. The peridium of *H. clathroides* is described by Hesse as being composed of pseudoparenchymatous cells, a structural character with which our Chapel Hill plant is in agreement, while the peridium of *H. pompholyx* according to Hesse is without pseudoparenchymatous cells in the peridium. Of the three new species described by Hesse, *H. rubricatum* differs in being larger, in having a much thicker peridium, and in the clay colored gleba; *H. coriaceum* differs in having a much thicker reddish peridium and much smaller spores; *H. calcareum* differs in having the peridium covered with a grayish white, silky flocculence and in slightly smaller spores.

PLATE 11

DICTYOPHORA DUPLICATA. No. 2286
Much reduced (actual length 18.5 cm.)

PLATE 12

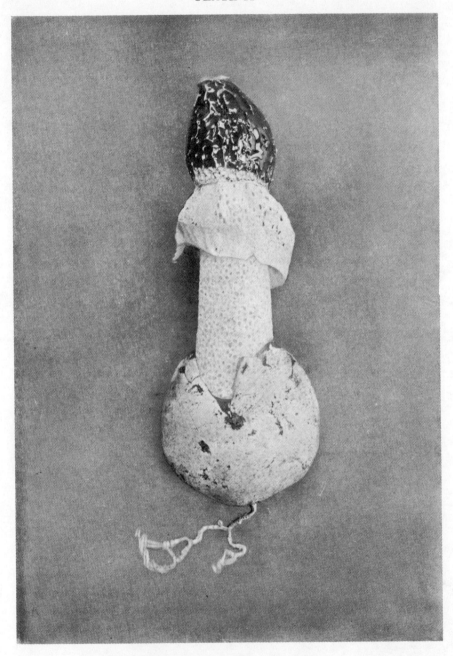

DICTYOPHORA DUPLICATA.   No. 5343

The only other record of *Hysterangium* in the eastern United States is *H. stoloni-ferum* var. *americanum* Fitzpatrick. We have compared material sent us by Dr. Fitzpatrick with our Chapel Hill *H. clathroides* and find that the two disagree in size, peridial structure, and in the much more myceloid basal attachment of the latter plant.

For a detailed comparison see notes under Dr. Fitzpatrick's plant.

Illustrations: Bucholtz. Beiträge zur Morphologie und Systematik der Hypogaeen (Tuberaceen und Gastromyceten), pl. 1, fig. 16. 1902.
  Fries, Th. C. E. Sveriges Gasteromyceter, fig. 9.
  Hesse. Die Hypogaeen Deutschlands 1: pl. 1, figs. 1–14; pl. 7, fig. 19.
  Rehsteiner. Bot. Zeit. 50: figs. 7–11. 1892.
  Tulasne. Fungi Hypogaei, pl. 2, fig. II–II₄.
  Vittadini. Monog. Tub., pl. 4, fig. 2.

7416. On very rich, nearly bare soil by Bowlin's Creek, July 15, 1924.
7435. On soil near Meeting of Waters, July 19, 1924.
7490. Under soil and humus by branch, Aug. 9, 1924.
7496. On soil by Fern Walk, Aug. 10, 1924.
7501. Under beech trees, Aug. 14, 1924. Spores elliptic with distal end often pointed, 5.5–6.8×14–20μ, with prongs at the proximal end.

Hysterangium pompholyx Tul.

Plate 105

Largest plants up to 1.5 cm. thick, subspherical, rooted by branched fibrils. Peridium 180–260μ thick, not readily separable from the gleba, covered externally with a white myceloid layer to which particles of sand and trash adhere in abundance, giving the surface a mottled appearance; in section composed of an inner layer made up of parenchyma-like cells and the outer myceloid part of loosely woven, clamp-connected threads, 3–7μ thick, which are heavily encrusted with triangular or rosette-shaped crystals. Gleba toughish-pliable, pale buff when young, becoming darker and finally brown upon maturity; quite often with a fairly distinct, hyaline, sterile base which passes up irregularly toward the center, branching out into the hyaline tramal plates. Cavities rounded to elongated, often sinuous.

Spores 6.6–7.4×13–14.8μ, blunt-elliptic, rounded at the distal end and with a distinct cup at the proximal end. Wall very remarkable in structure: the outer and inner layers becoming separated from each other as the spores mature, leaving the adjacent surfaces of the walls irregularly rough. The outer wall is usually attached to the distal rim of the cup while the base of the cup rests on the inner wall. Spores buff to brownish in mass without any tint of green. Basidia 6–7.6×16–23μ; 2-spored, club-shaped.

Our only collection of this plant occurred along with the plant with greenish gleba which we are calling *H. clathroides*. The present species seems quite distinct from the latter in glebal color and structure, and in peridial, basidial and spore structure: the color of the gleba in the species here described is buff to brown without any tint of green and the chambers are pouch-like and only slightly elongated, while in our collections of *H. clathroides* the gleba always has a greenish tint and the chambers are usually elongated and narrow; in the present plant the peridium is covered with flocculent threads which are covered with crystals, while in our specimens of *H. clathroides* the flocculence, though usually present, is nothing like so evident as in the present plant. The basidia in the present plant are two-spored while in *H. clathroides* they are 2–4-

spored; the shape and color of the spores furnish the sharpest distinction of all.   In the present plant they are blunt-elliptic, rounded at the distal end, and buff to brown colored, while in *H. clathroides* they are subelliptic, distinctly pointed at the distal end, and always with a greenish tint.

Of the species described by Tulasne, the present plant seems closest to *H. pompholyx*, especially in the appearance of the gleba in structure and color.   Tulasne states (p. 84) "when one cuts this fungus vertically, a crowd of chambers is found in section, and their transparence makes it easy to see the argillaceous color of the spores accumulated on the walls.   One could believe, in this case, in the existence of short tubes, of little fertile sacks, joined together by an agglutinative substance."   The spores agree well enough in size and some of Tulasne's figures agree in shape, being rounded at the distal end; others however show a distinctly pointed distal end.   Tulasne does not mention or figure any peculiarity in the spore wall, if it did exist, and he figures all of the spores as smooth.   We have found in all specimens examined that the spores under high magnification present a more or less rough appearance.   It is quite possible that Tulasne in working under rather low magnification overlooked any peculiarity in structure which might have been present.

Though this slight difference in the spore shape renders our determination somewhat unsatisfactory, it seems better, with the rather limited first hand information on the group, not to multiply names.

Illustrations: Tulasne.   Fungi Hypogaei, pl. 2, fig. 3; pl. 11, fig. 6.

7490a.   Under soil and humus by branch in woods, August 9, 1924.

Hysterangium stoloniferum var. **americanum** Fitzp.

Plate 105

We adapt the following in condensed form from Fitzpatrick's description (Ann. Myc. 11: 130. 1913).   In addition the article contains an account of the development of the fruit body in this plant and in *Phallogaster* and *Gautieria* as well as a discussion of their relationships and the derivation of the Phalloids.

Fruit bodies subterranean, gregarious, 1–2.5 cm. in diameter, usually globose and with a basal depression from which a thick, cord-like rhizomorph attaches the plant; peridium at first snow white, later mottled with dingy brown, not changing color on exposure, easily separable even in youth, fleshy to cartilaginous, in age tough and papery and scaling off the gleba; only 0.3–0.4 mm. thick, but composed of two layers, a thicker, pseudoparenchymatous, large-celled one and a thin fibrous inner one.   Gleba elastic and cartilaginous, olive green in section, the surface bluish just under the peridium; sterile base and columella distinct, with radiating, anastomosing branches extending to the peridium; chambers minute, irregular, elongated.   At maturity the gleba softens and the columella and radiating plates become gelatinous, and a not unpleasant odor resembling gasoline is given off.   In alcohol the peridium turns red-brown.

Spores smooth, narrowly ellipsoidal, tapering at both ends, the base with a short stalk up to 1μ long, olive green in mass, 5–6 x 14–17μ, at maturity with gelatinous walls. Basidia long, irregularly cylindrical, 3-spored.

PLATE 13

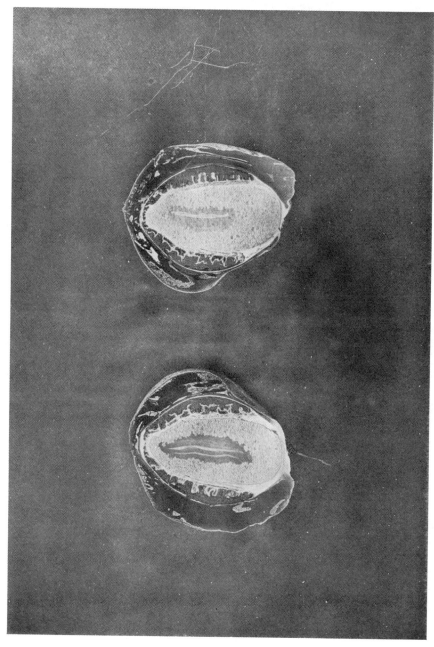

DICTYOPHORA DUPLICATA. No. 5374

PLATE 14

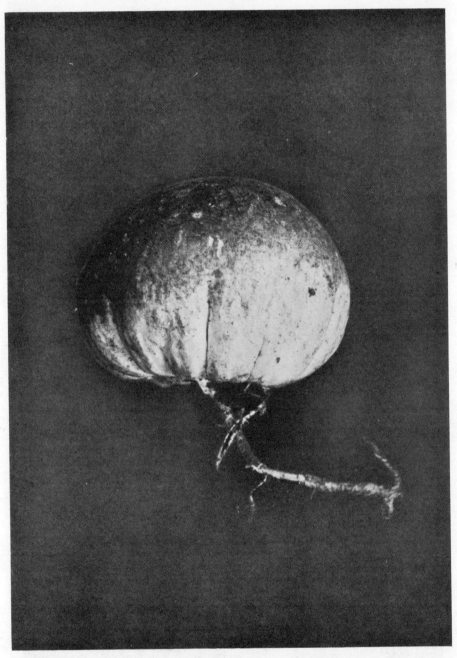

DICTYOPHORA DUPLICATA, "EGG." No. 2286

The variety differs from the type in the olive green and less firm gleba, thinner peridium and smaller spores; differs from var. *mutabile* Bucholtz in smaller spores, and white peridium which does not become reddish in age or on handling.*

It seems after a careful comparison of the present plant with Vittadini's, Tulasne's and Hesse's descriptions of *H. clathroides* and with European material of *H. clathroides* determined by Torrend and with Tulasne's description of *H. stoloniferum* that this plant should stand as a variety of the latter. Fitzpatrick's plant varies from 1–2.5 cm. in diameter, while *H. clathroides* according to Vittadini, Tulasne, and Hesse varies from the size of a pea to a hazel-nut, seldom larger. The great majority of the examples we have seen are about 5–8 mm. thick. The presence of a single, thick, white, cord-like rhizomorph at the base of each fruit body which is very persistent and in most cases is unbranched for an inch or more from the fruit body, together with the smoothness of the surface of the peridium are structural characters of the most fundamental importance with which Vittadini's, Tulasne's, and Hesse's figures and descriptions of *H. clathroides* are in total disagreement. In the microscopic structure of the peridium the two plants disagree: The peridium of Fitzpatrick's plant is composed of large pseudoparenchymatous cells which, cut at any angle or even teased apart, present practically the same appearance, and there is no outer flocculent layer; while in our study of *H. clathroides* we have found that the peridium presents a pseudoparenchymatous cell structure only when cut at certain angles and when cut at other angles or teased apart it presents a filamentous structure and there is present in our specimens of *H. clathroides* an outer flocculent layer (Tulasne and Hesse report the same condition). In the color of the peridium and gleba the two plants agree fairly well according to Fitzpatrick's description, but in a specimen which he sent us the gleba is deep brown with an extremely faint tint of olive. In basidial and spore characters the two plants are practically inseparable (Fitzpatrick reports three spores to a basidium but we find a few with two and some with four).

It is a noteworthy fact that the peridium of Dr. Fitzpatrick's plant has a striking resemblance in structure to that of *Protophallus jamaicensis* Murrill. It is also obvious that in the more globular form and single cord-like root, this species approaches nearer the Phalloids than any other species of *Hysterangium*.

Illustrations: Fitzpatrick, l. c., pl. 4, fig. 10; pl. 6; also text figs. 2 and 6.

New York. Ithaca. In humus under leaves in dense woods. Fitzpatrick, coll. (U. N. C. Herb.).

GAUTIERIA Vitt.

Plants subterranean or partly so, subglobose to tuberous; peridium thin and disappearing entirely or in large part by maturity so as to expose the gleba and some of the cavities; base attached by one or more strands, columella and radiating plates present or absent; glebal cavities not filled at any stage. Spores shaped like an oblong cantaloupe with longitudinal ridges and grooves.

Seven species have heretofore been described, two of which are doubtful. Of the five good species three occur in America and two of these in the eastern states. *Gymnomyces*, in which the peridium is thin and often entirely or partly lacking, is distinguished by the very different spores.

---

* Note below that in the plants sent us, preserved in formaldehyde, there is practically no green color, while in all conditions of *H. clathroides* the gleba is a clear olive.

LITERATURE

Zeller and Dodge. *Gautieria* in North America. Ann. Mo. Bot. Garden 5: 133, pl. 9. 1918.
See other citations under the species.

KEY TO THE SPECIES

Odor strong and offensive; cavities small..*G. graveolens*
Odor not offensive; cavities large..*G. morchelliformis*

Gautieria graveolens Vitt.

We copy the following description from Zeller and Dodge:

"Fructifications globose, 1–2 cm. in diameter, light ochraceous-buff to Prout's brown; stipe slender and fragile, up to 1 cm. long, 1 mm. thick; columella frequently reaching the center of the fructification, forking; odor very strong, suggestive of decaying onions; peridium thin, composed of delicate, thin-walled, loosely woven hyphae, soon rupturing and disappearing; gleba ochraceous-tawny to cinnamon-brown; cavities globose or elongated, minute, empty; septa 40–80μ thick, composed of small hyphae, compact; cystidia clavate to subfusiform, hyaline, often obscured by the spores; paraphyses linear, septate; basidia broadly clavate, 2-spored, 12–16 x 8–9μ, with long filiform sterigmata; spores ochraceous-tawny, usually with 10 prominent striations, the latter smooth or nearly so, apex rounded, base pedicellate, 18–19 x 11–12μ, often with a large oil globule."

"Deeply buried under leaf mold. Europe and North America. Summer."

Illustrations: Bucholtz. Ann. Myc. 1: pl. 5. fig. 14. 1903.
    Chatin. La Truffe, pl. 15, fig. 4.
    Corda. Icon. Fung. 6: pl. 7, fig. 63.
    Fischer in Engler & Prantl. Die Nat. Pflanzenfam. 1. 1**: 304.
    Fitzpatrick. Ann. Myc. 11: pl. 4, fig. 11; pl. 7, figs. 29–39, also text figs. 4 and 5.
    Hesse. Hypog. Deutschl. 1: pl. 2, figs. 5–9; pl. 7, figs. 4–6.
    Vittadini. Monog. Tuberac., pl. 4, fig. 3.

New York. Ithaca. Fitzpatrick, coll.

Gautieria morchelliformis Vitt.

We copy the following description from Zeller and Dodge:

"Fructifications globose to oblong, 1–3 cm. in diameter, with a basal stalk-like rhizomorph, usually much branched; columella rudimentary, merely a subglobose summit of the rhizomorph; peridium thin in early stages, quickly evanescent; gleba ochraceous-tawny to hazel; cavities 1–6 mm. in diameter, subglobose to irregular; septa white when broken, hyaline to cream-colored under the microscope, composed of a stupose mat of hyphae, about 75μ broad; basidia about as large as the spores, hyaline, granular, 2–3-spored; sterigmata filiform, as long as the spores; cystidia in the upper cavities of the fructification, not prominent; paraphyses clavate, septate, hyaline; spores fusiform to citriform, ochraceous, longitudinally striate, with 8–10 usually smooth striations, 1–2-guttulate, pedicellate, 12–24 x 8–12.5μ."

"In clay soil. Europe and United States. Spring and summer."

Illustrations: Bucholtz. Ann. Myc. 1: pl. 5, figs. 12 and 13. 1903.
    Corda. Icon. Fung. 6: pl., 7, fig. 62.
    Bail in Nees v. Esenbeck. Syst. d. Pilze 2: pl. 27, figs. 1–4.

PLATE 15

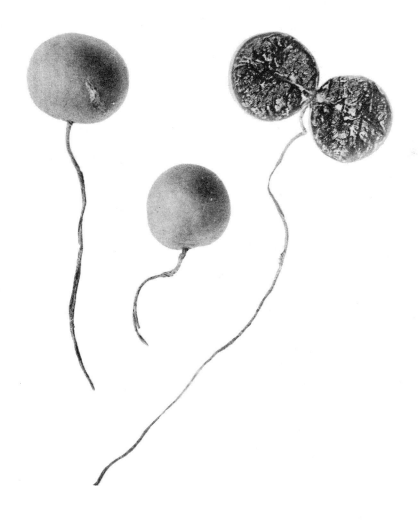

PROTOPHALLUS JAMAICENSIS. From Jamaica

PLATE 16

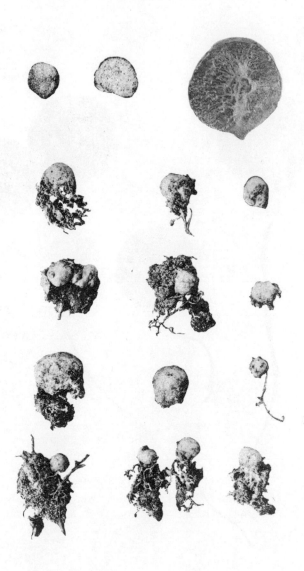

GYMNOMYCES VESICULOSUS. No. 7470 [two small plants in upper left corner]
HYSTERANGIUM CLATHROIDES. No. 7490 [upper right] × 3; No. 7416 [below]

Vittadini. Monog. Tuberac., pl. 3, fig. 6.

Klotzch in Dietr. Fl. Boruss. (Fl. Konigr. Preuss.) 7: pl. 764.

New York. Washington Co., Hudson Falls. Burnham, coll.

GYMNOMYCES Massee & Rodw.

Fruit body subglobose to irregular, peridium delicate or entirely wanting. Gleba fleshy, rather pale; cavities box-like to labyrinthiform; septa not scissile, composed of delicate hyphae or bladdery cells. Basidia forming a distinct hymenium, lining the empty cavities, sterigmata 2–4. Spores hyaline to pallid brown, globose, echinulate to rugose-reticulate.

Three species have so far been described, one of which is from the United States (California), and we are adding a fourth from Chapel Hill. The genus is distinguished from *Gautieria* by the rough, spiny, spherical spores; from *Arcangeliella*, by the absence of milk; and from *Macowanites* by the absence of a stalk.

Our Chapel Hill plant described below is clearly marked and is very peculiar in the friable texture of the tramal plates.

Literature

Zeller and Dodge. *Arcangeliella, Gymnomyces,* and *Macowanites* in North America. Ann. Mo. Bot. Gard. 6: 49, text figs. 1–3. 1919.

Gymnomyces vesiculosus n. sp.

Plates 16, 17 and 105

Fruiting body subspherical, about one cm. thick when fresh, drying to about half size, the base attached by a few basal fibrils which spring from a narrow depression; light buff yellow (about Naples yellow); odorless. Peridium nearly absent at maturity, some of the chambers being exposed, others separated from the air only by the tramal plates and visible as small depressions, the whole giving the surface a spongy look; gleba pallid gray brown (pale earthy buff), firm, but pliable, not tough or elastic, about like a potato; chambers rather large and box-like, empty, about 0.4–0.8 mm., walls thick, about 0.17–0.2 mm. including the hymenial layers which are about 30μ thick; structure of the walls remarkable, composed of large bladdery cells about 20–40μ thick except for a very thin layer under the hymenium where the cells are small. Peridium, where present, composed of a very thin layer of delicate, loosely woven, yellowish threads. A sterile base and radiating plates are entirely lacking.

Spores color of the gleba under a lens, darker under the microscope, spherical, 7.5–10μ thick including the strong, blunt spines, often stuck together in groups of 4. Basidia short and thick, the 4 sterigmata nearly half as long as the spore diameter.

We take the name from the peculiar cells of the tramal plates, which are different from those of any other Gasteromycete we have seen. They remind one of the flesh of a *Russula*, and the friable texture of the plant is a reflection of this structure. The texture is not at all tough or elastic or subgelatinous.

Gautieria Trabuti from California (N. Y. Bot. Gard. Herb.; Parks, coll., and apparently correctly determined) has vesiculose cells just beneath the hymenium, but the central region of the trama is composed of filamentous threads as in most species and the cavities are much more tortuous. The spores are entirely different, having the surface characteristic of *Gautieria*, longitudinally ridged, 9–11 x 11.5–20μ.

7470. Found exposed on soil in frondose woods after a hard rain had washed away the humus, August 4, 1924.

HYMENOGASTRACEAE

Plants produced underground or on the surface, more or less globular or irregular. Peridium connected intimately with the tramal plates which form the irregular, elongated to more or less box-like chambers which in most cases are empty in youth, with or without a distinct hymenium; at maturity partly or completely filled with spores. Basidia clavate with 1–8, more or less stipitate or sessile spores of a great variety of size, shape and structure. Capillitium none; sterile base or column in some species obvious, again practically absent. At maturity not dehiscing but rotting slowly, the gleba not becoming powdery but (in our species at least) deliquescing inside to a dark slimy mass or slowly undergoing a viscid disintegration from above downward.

Four of the genera have been reported from the eastern United States and we are adding *Sclerogaster* and *Melanogaster*.

LITERATURE

For special literature on this family see Fischer, Harkness, Hesse, Massee, Tulasne, and Vittadini as cited on p. 194.

Cavara.   Sur la Morphologie et la Biologie d'une Espèce Nouvelle d'*Hymenogaster*.   Rev. Myc. **16:** 152, one plate.   1894.   Also published in Italian.
Cavara.   Nuov. Giorn. bot. ital. **7:** 126.   1900.
Fischer.   Mykologische Beitrage 25.   Jugendstadien des Fruchtkörpers von *Leucogaster*.   Naturf. Ges. Bern, Mitt. 1921: 301.   1922.
Lloyd.   The Hymenogastraceae.   Myc. Notes, p. 1138, figs. 2152–2176.   1922.
Zeller and Dodge.   *Arcangeliella*, *Gymnomyces*, and *Macowanites* in North America.   Ann. Mo. Bot. Gard. **6:** 49, text figs. 1–3.   1919.
Zeller and Dodge.   *Leucogaster* and *Leucophlebs* in North America.   Ann. Mo. Bot. Gard. **11:** 389, pl. 11.   1924.

KEY TO THE GENERA

Fruit bodies very small, white; gleba chambers very minute......................*Sclerogaster* (p. 25)
Not as above
    Spores strongly angled and lobed ....*Nigropogon* (p. 37)
    Not as above
        Fruit bodies veined with superficial fibers; spores elliptic, smooth.........*Rhizopogon* (p. 26)
        Fruit bodies attached by scattered fibrils; superficial veins short or absent; cavities box-like, nearly or completely filled at maturity; spores smooth; basidia irregularly distributed, not forming a distinct hymenium ....*Melanogaster* (p. 38)
        Fruit bodies attached by one or a few fibrils, superficial veins present or absent; cavities mostly polyhedral, when young filled with tissue which later gelatinizes and embeds the spores; spores pale, usually spherical to oval, rough or pitted but surrounded by a smooth, hyaline, gelatinous sheath; basidia irregularly distributed, not forming a distinct hymenium..*Leucogaster* (p. 42)
        Fruit bodies without obvious vein-like fibers running over the surface and attached only at one place
            Spores not spherical, in our species surrounded by a bladder.......*Hymenogaster* (p. 45)
            Spores spherical, reticulated or warted........................ ....*Octaviania* (p. 47)

PLATE 17

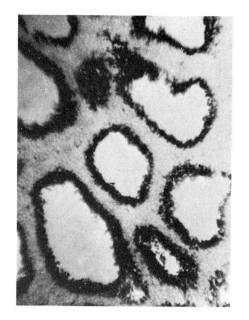 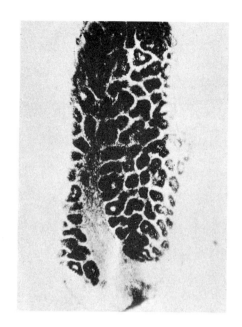

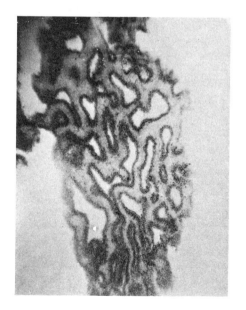 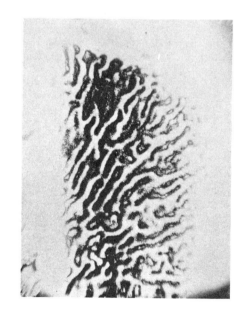

GYMNOMYCES VESICULOSUS. No. 7470. × 130
[above]

HYMENOGASTER FOETIDUS. No. 7473. × 50
[below]

SCLEROGASTER MINOR. No. 7474. × 25
[above]

HYMENOGASTER FOETIDUS. No. 7473. × 15
[below]

PLATE 18

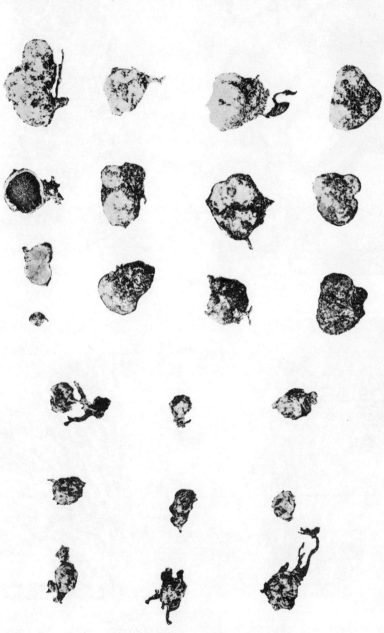

SCLEROGASTER Hesse

Fruiting bodies white, subglobose, small, rooted by several fibrils; peridium soft, flocculent, but persistent, often connecting with byssoid mycelium which runs about conspicuously through the substratum; cavities very minute, round to oblong, becoming nearly completely filled with spores; hymenium disappearing, being replaced by spores; septa very inconspicuous at maturity; spores abundant, spherical, warted, yellow.

The genus was established by Hesse to contain the plant called *Octaviania compacta* by Tulasne and up to the present no other species has been added. Our plant is the first record of the genus in America outside of California.

Tulasne, recognizing the striking distinctness of the species *O. compacta*, reluctantly placed it in the genus *Octaviania* saying, "This species differs much from all the hypogenous fungi which we have seen, and it is with doubt that we place it in the genus *Octaviania*. In fact it has none of the sterile base, or large, lacunate, sessile chambers of *O. asterosperma*, differing from it in its compactness and in that its chambers become nearly entirely filled with spores. It should perhaps rather be placed with *Hydnangium*, after *H. liospermum* or *H. hysterangioides;* but it differs from these fungi by its mycelium which is much like that of *Hysterangium*."

Sclerogaster minor n. sp.

Plates 17, 18 and 106

Fruiting bodes small, about 0.3–1 cm. wide by 0.3–0.7 cm. high, subglobose, often irregularly lobed; buried 2–4 cm. under cedar humus, often more or less covered with a pure white byssoid mycelium which extends through the humus, covering twigs and cedar berries so that the latter may often be mistaken for the fruiting bodies themselves; usually with several considerably branched, mycelioid fibrils extending out from the base or sides of the plants, often connecting two or more plants. Odor faintly earthy. Peridium pure white on young fresh plants, changing only slightly on drying, 0.3–0.45 mm. thick, composed of two layers: an outer, very thin, byssoid layer made up of delicate threads which are in places continuous with the mycelium, and the thick inner layer which in young fresh plants is composed of chains of large bladder-like cells, but which in mature plants appears to be composed of large parenchymatous cells; peridium readily separable from the gleba in areas. Gleba pure white when young and fresh, becoming pale buff and finally deep ochraceous yellow when the spores ripen. Tramal plates, 60–185μ thick composed of septate, branched threads 3–5μ thick, continuous with the peridium, continuous also (when it is present) with a sterile plug-like area which may be basal or lateral, and also with a more or less central columella. The plates become very inconspicuous as the cavities and space occupied by the hymenial layer become filled with spores. Cavities 37–100 x 74–300μ, varying from nearly spherical to long and narrow, becoming almost or completely filled with spores. Scattered throughout the plant are numerous crystals. Hymenium forming a distinct layer lining the cavities, obvious only in young plants while the spores are forming, disappearing entirely upon their formation, the space occupied by the hymenium being filled with spores; composed of basidia and long, slightly acuminate cells; basidia long, irregularly cylindrical, 4–7.4 x 28–40μ, bearing 1–5 spores, three being the commonest number, sterigmata quite conspicuous, thick and of equal diameter throughout their length, part or all of the sterigmata remaining on the spore as a distinct stalk which varies in length from a very small fraction of the diameter of the spore to about as long as half the spore's thickness.

Spores 7.4–9.5μ thick, spherical, at first smooth, becoming covered with conspicuous warts upon maturing, often with a pedicel.

The present plant presents some points in structure which show the difficulty in separating the families Hysterangiaceae and Hymenogastraceae. In the former the tramal plates arise from a sterile, more or less conspicuous base and hence the peridium is readily separable from the gleba, an excellent type of this order being *Hysterangium clathroides*. In the latter family the tramal plates arise from the peridium, and hence the latter is more or less inseparable from the gleba. In the present plant tramal plates usually arise entirely from the peridium but there is quite often a fairly distinct sterile base or central columella from which the tramal plates also originate and in sections, of a few young specimens, small spaces have been observed where the gleba was not even in contact with the peridium. But since the sterile base and columella, when present, are almost always continuous in all directions with the peridium, and since it is separable only with difficulty from the gleba, we are considering our plant as belonging in the Hymenogastraceae. It seems clearly a *Sclerogaster*, as shown by the presence of numerous mycelial strands which often extend out into byssoid mycelial plates, the minute glebal chambers, the hymenium with long, irregularly cylindrical basidia and the accompanying slightly acuminate, sterile cells (which may be young basidia), and the spherical, warted spores with short stalks. Our plant differs from *S. compactus* (Tul.) Sacc. (=*Octaviania compacta* Tul. and *S. lanatus* Hesse) in smaller size, larger spores, and fewer spores to the basidium. We have examined the spores of an authentic specimen of *Octaviania compacta*, through the kindness of the Director of Kew Gardens, and find them to be subspherical, warted but not strongly so, pale olivaceous under the microscope, $4.5–6\mu$ thick. They are much less rough than is shown in Tulasne's drawings, but possibly immature. Aside from microscopic characters the present plant can readily be distinguished from other hypogenous fungi, which we have observed, by its very small size, white color, minute chambers, and by the very obvious byssoid mycelium.

7474.   Buried in humus mixed with cedar leaves and twigs, August 5, 1924. An ample collection of about 100 plants.

RHIZOPOGON Fr.

Fruit body subglobose, growing on the surface of the ground or buried up to several inches in humus or soil. Peridium tough, its surface more or less netted or lined with adherent vein-like fibrils which fuse below into one or several threadlike rhizomorphs; gleba attached to peridium, composed of small crumpled or box-like chambers which are lined by a distinct hymenium and contain an empty cavity in youth, but which at maturity may or may not be stuffed with spores. After maturity the gleba deliquesces slowly into a deep brown slime which escapes by the decay of the peridium or its rupture by insects. Basidia subclavate to nearly cylindrical, thin-walled, collapsing after the spores are formed; spores smooth, elliptic, 2–8 on a basidium, the sterigmata short or none, sometimes represented by a little cup which remains attached to the spore.

Tulasne says that the spores are sessile in *Rhizopogon*, and in all species we have studied except *R. parasiticus* the sterigmata are very short or absent. Zeller and Dodge speak of and illustrate long sterigmata in several cases, but where we have been able to check these we find the usual short sterigmata. Their fig. 2 on pl. 3, of *R. roseolus*, we are confident is an erroneous interpretation of their material, both in the length of the sterigmata and the gelatinized basidial walls. The gelatinized cells there shown are other cells of the hymenium, and the supposed sterigmata are probably the collapsed basidia lying among them. In all species we have seen the basidia are very delicate and soon collapse.

A very peculiar species is *R. parasiticus*, which grows as a parasite on the rootlets of pine. It is the only one of our subterranean Basidiomycetes which is certainly known to be a parasite. *Rhizopogon graveolens* has been reported by Zeller and Dodge from Alabama (Earle, coll.). Through the kindness of Dr. C. L. Shear we have seen a good plant of this collection and find that it agrees well with our *R. rubescens*, No. 1932.

LITERATURE

Lloyd. The Genus *Rhizopogon*. Myc. Notes, p. 1170, figs. 2312–2322. 1923.
Zeller and Dodge. Ann. Mo. Bot. Garden **5**: 1. 1918.

KEY TO THE SPECIES

Parasitic in clusters on the roots of pine; plants small........................*R. parasiticus* (p. 27)
Not noticeably parasitic; plants larger
  Spores without a cup and not appearing truncate
    Peridium composed of a single layer
      Cavities only partially filled with spores at maturity
        Fibrils few; peridium in section reddish brown to black when treated with 7% KOH
          Peridium when cut turning pink or rosy throughout; spores 2–2.7 x 5.5–7.4μ
                                     R. rubescens (p. 28)
          Peridium when cut turning rosy in inner part only, outer part remaining citron
             yellow; spores 3–3.7 x 6.4–8.5μ....................*R. roseolus* (p. 32)
        Fibrils many; peridium turning distinctly purplish in section when treated with 7%
             KOH; plants deep sordid brown to black when dry......*R. nigrescens* (p. 30)
      Cavities filled with spores at maturity; fibrils many
        Surface woolly; septa 60–90μ thick; odor unpleasant..............*R. luteolus* (p. 33)
        Surface not woolly; septa 74–111μ thick; odor pleasant............*R. piceus* (p. 34)
    Peridium double; many of the cavities filled with spores at maturity.... *R. maculatus* (p. 35)
  Spores with a vague cup which is often extended into a collapsed filament (a part of the basidium),
    but spores scarcely truncate, 3.7–4.6 x 8–11μ........................*R. luteolus* (p. 33)
  Spores with an open cup on the proximal end and thus appearing truncate; glebal chambers very
    small and barely visible without a lens
  Spores 3–3.7 x 7.4–8.5μ..*R. atlanticus* (p. 35)
  Spores 3–4.4 x 6.8–7.2μ..*R. truncatus* (p. 36)

Rhizopogon parasiticus Coker and Totten

Plates 19 and 20

Fruit body up to 1.5 cm. broad and high, though usually much smaller, the great majority about 2–5 mm., sometimes almost evenly globose but more often lobed and convoluted; attached at any point to one or several branching, flocculent, rhizomorphous threads which run in the humus and connect the fruit bodies on different roots; rarely some of these branching threads may run along and cohere with the surface of the fruit body; color of both mycelium and the fruit body varying from a light ochraceous salmon to a warm buff at all ages until decay sets in. Peridium of mature plants duplex, 50–130μ thick, the outer layer a spongy mass of loosely woven threads that collapse when the plant is cut or bruised or when decay sets in; the inner layer more closely woven, lighter in color and intimately connected with the internal hyphae; threads of the peridium soft and delicate, 2.6–10.4μ thick, in young plants more closely woven.

Gleba when fully formed containing many cavities that are minute, irregular,

20-200μ broad, hollow and lined with the hymenium. Septa 40-115μ thick, delicate and intimately connected with the peridium, the threads that compose them much branched, segmented, thin-walled, without clamp connections, 2.6-10.4μ thick and having much the appearance of those of the peridium. The hymenium contains no obvious specialized cystidia, but certain cells among the basidia are of more fusiform shape and these have not been seen to bear spores.

Spores brown, fusiform, smooth, 3-3.5 x 7.8-10.4μ. Basidia short-clavate, 5 x 17μ, 2-4-spored, with slender sterigmata, which are 2.5-3.5μ long.

Gregarious and often crowded in large numbers in connected colonies in humus just under or at the surface, and parasitic on rootlets of pine in damp places.

Illustrations: Totten.   Journ. E. M. Sci. Soc. **39**: pls. 1-7.   1923.

3990.   On roots of *Pinus echinata* and *Pinus taeda*, by branch south of Pritchard's, January 10, 1920.
5383.   Same place as No. 3990, July 22, 1922.
6051.   Roots of *Pinus taeda*, edge of swampy place north of cemetery, January 19, 1923.
6057.   Same place as No. 3990, January 28, 1923.

Rhizopogon rubescens Tul.

Plates 21, 22 and 106

Plants above ground or partly or completely buried; single plants up to 5.7 cm. broad by 4 cm. high (one cluster almost fused into a single plant 7 x 6.5 cms. by 4.5 cm. high), irregularly subglobose, not rarely lobed, surface nearly smooth except for ridges, channels and depressions, usually somewhat flattened above; not viscid; young underground plants pure white when fresh, turning a distinct rosy pink when bruised; exposed plants pure white at first, then yellowish with a tint of olive above (about citron yellow, amber yellow or buffy citrine of Ridgway with russet areas where bruised), remaining whitish below, becoming darker in age and an earthy tan with brown or black areas on drying.   Fibrils very few, usually absent above, innate-appressed on the sides, becoming free below, and passing into one or several more or less conspicuous rhizomorphs; underground plants usually without any fibrils and with more or less conspicuous myceloid rhizomorphs which may be attached to the top, sides or base of the plant.   Peridium single, 0.4-0.6 mm. thick, pure white when fresh, turning fleshy pink or rosy red throughout when cut, not viscid, composed of closely packed threads 4-9μ thick, and numerous brownish amorphous crystals which do not change color upon the application of 7% KOH.   Gleba pure white when fresh, becoming pinkish when bruised (often changing when simply cut with a sharp knife), after some hours losing the pink color and becoming dull brown where cut, drying with a pale olive tinge; texture rather tough and firm.   Cavities irregularly flattened, 2-3 to a mm., not rarely up to 1 mm. long, labyrinthiform; septa 85-100μ thick, composed of threads which become gelatinized; becoming very scissile upon maturing.

Spores (of No. 7204) light brownish yellow, oblong-elliptic, smooth, 2-2.7 x 5.5-7.4μ.   Basidia more or less obscure, clavate, 4.8-6.8 x 16-35μ; thin-walled, often extending out beyond the hymenium, collapsing more or less completely after the spores are formed; bearing 4-8 sessile spores; associated with the basidia in the hymenium are numerous cells which become slightly gelatinized.

Taste and odor at first practically none; plants drying without deliquescing are nearly odorless, deliquescing plants becoming fragrant with an odor much like that of strawberry preserves or scuppernong grapes, or decaying apples, in which condition the plants are infested with numerous fruit flies.

This species can be distinguished from *R. luteolus* as represented by a European

PLATE 19

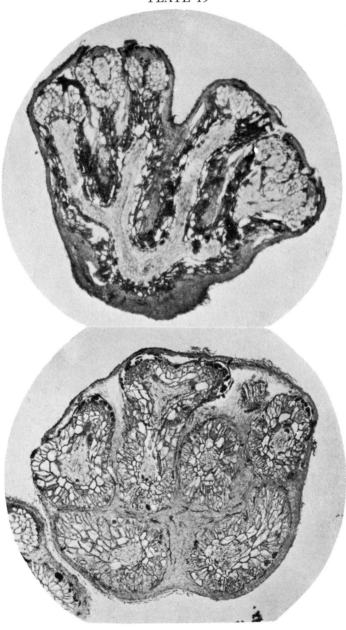

Rhizopogon parasiticus. × 40

PLATE 20

Fig. 1. Fungal threads attacking cortical cells of the pine.   The threads force their way between and
        over the pine cells which are the unshaded areas in the figure.   × 690.
Figs. 2 and 3. Basidia with nearly mature spores.
Fig. 4. Young basidia.   × 1290.
Fig. 5. Mature spores.   × 1290.
Fig. 6. Tramal thread, showing nuclei.   × 1290.
Fig. 7. Trama and hymenium of mature plant, some of the basidia with two, others with four sterigmata.
        × 1290.

Figs. 4–6 stained to show nuclei.

PLATE 20

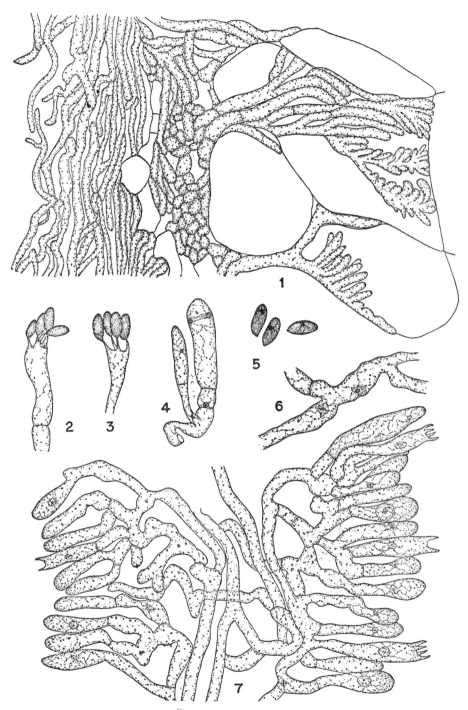

RHIZOPOGON PARASITICUS

specimen (Höhnel, Krypt. exs. No. 1607) by the more numerous fibrils, tawny colored peridium and distinctly larger spores of the latter, which in mass and under the microscope are decidedly more colored.

The present plant can also be distinguished from *Rhizopogon nigrescens* (see below) by the peridium of the latter, which is viscid when fresh and which dries a much darker color, becoming inky black in most specimens, by the slender but numerous fibrils, and by the pleasant but weak odor of the latter plant. A section of the peridium of the present plant when put in a 7 per cent solution of KOH changes its color only slightly if at all, while the peridium of *nigrescens* becomes a distinct orange lavender when so treated. For differences between this species and *R. roseolus*, see that species.

This is not at all rare with us in fall and winter, growing on bare soil or in thin grass and always near or under pines or cedars; rarely found completely buried to a depth of several inches. It agrees best with *R. rubescens* among the species described by Zeller and Dodge, but has a thinner peridium in the dry state, distinctly smaller spores, and a strong and pleasant fragrance. In *R. rubescens* the odor is said by Tulasne to be weak or almost none. The variety *Vittadini* has spores as small (3×6–8μ) as in our plants, but is said to have a thicker peridium when dry and not to redden so distinctly when bruised. Tulasne gives the spores as 3×7–9μ and Hesse as 3–4×6–9μ. The simple peridium is in section dull yellow or rosy when cut in the fresh state and sordid brown or reddish brown, or blackish in areas when dry. We have examined Ravenel's specimen in his Fung. Car. 1: No. 75, labelled *R. rubescens* Tul. with *R. luteolus* Vitt. and *R. albus* Schw. given as synonyms (Herb. Dept. Agric., Washington). Our plants are certainly the same, agreeing in all structural characters. The spores of the Ravenel plant are elliptic, smooth, 1.8–2×4.4–6.2μ. Dr. Dodge has seen some of our plants and thinks it best to retain them in *R. rubescens* for the present. The strong odor and small spores is a discrepancy, and it is obvious that this group is not yet in a satisfactory state. If the sterigmata are as long as stated by Zeller and Dodge, that would be a further discrepancy. The plant from Hartsville (*R. atlanticus*) differs conspicuously in the separable peridium which is white in section when dry, in the much smaller chambers, larger spores with cupped base, and in not turning rose when rubbed.

We have made over 20 collections of this species around Chapel Hill from 1911 to date. Excellent lots of material have been collected for three successive years during the fall and early winter from the same location in a pine grove near Chapel Hill. The spores are very consistent in size in different collections, e.g., 2.2–2.6×5.5–7.4μ in No. 6003, 1.6–2.3×5.5–7.5μ in No. 58.

Collections number 7450, 7457, 7499, and 7563 differ in certain particulars from the typical pleasant smelling plants such as 6003 and 7565, though two of the first mentioned collections, 7450 and 7563, came from the same location as 6003. The peridium in No. 7450 has a basic color of about tawny with a tint of vinaceous, in places Rood's brown or burnt umber, and not rarely with black areas, whereas in No. 6003, etc., the peridium has a basic color of sordid buff to clay with brown or blackened areas. In the odor of the deliquescing plants the two sets of collections differ in that the former plants (No. 7450, etc.) usually have an odor of decaying Irish potatoes when kept covered in the laboratory for several hours while the odor of No. 6003 is very pleasant. In the texture of the dried plants the two sets of collections show some differences. Numbers 7450, etc., are all hard and brittle when dry while many of the plants in No. 6003, etc., have a texture only slightly harder and firmer than a raisin; many plants of No. 6003, however, are bony hard when dry. The above mentioned plants agree in all characters except the ones mentioned above, and we are therefore retaining numbers 7450, etc., under *R. rubescens* as a color form.

North Carolina. Chapel Hill. Nos. 58, 1444, 1932, 6003, 6043, 6049, 7199, 7203, 7204, 7212, 7213, 7218, 7223, 7450, 7457, 7499, 7563, 7564, 7565, 7567, 7570, 7573, 7579, 7583.

    Saxapahaw. Coker, coll. August 1922. No. 5503. On ground under cedars. Strongly parasitized internally by a mold with large, spherical, spiny, golden yellow spores, 18–22μ thick. These spores were so abundant as to give their color to the entire gleba, but the spores of the host had also matured and were like those of our collections. There were no external signs of a parasite, the surface being to all appearances normal.

    Asheville. Beardslee, coll.

South Carolina. Sandy soil in pine and oak woods, just under loose surface leaves, about 7 miles above Georgetown, Dec. 29, 1926. Coker, coll. (U. N. C. Herb.). Spores 2.–2.8 x 6–8.5μ.
Alabama. Auburn. Earle, coll. (Path. and Myc. Herb., as *R. graveolens*).

Rhizopogon nigrescens n. sp.

Plates 23 and 107

    Fruiting body above ground, about 2–6 cm. wide by 1.5–3 cm. high, subglobose, pure white when young and fresh, becoming mottled with several colors when maturing, about light cadmium (Ridgway) beneath, shading to russet on top, turning orange below or reddish brown above when rubbed and later almost black; becoming chestnut to bay or inky black upon drying; fibrils numerous but slender, quite conspicuous in fresh plants, innate-appressed above, becoming more conspicuous below, passing into several rhizomorphous strands, reddish when fresh, becoming concolorous with the peridium and so inherently appressed above and on the sides on drying as to be quite inconspicuous, usually remaining free and conspicuous below. Fresh peridium slightly sticky, about 290–400μ thick, simple, filled with a bright red or orange amorphous material which gives a strong color to a section and which seems to cause the surface color when rubbed; color changing slowly to a deep purple upon the application of 7% KOH; in old specimens in which deliquescence has proceeded far the peridium may be very thin or even absent in places; threads of peridium septate, only slightly branched 1.8–4μ thick. Gleba pure white when fresh, turning light clay color, sometimes with a tint of olive on drying; cavities labyrinthiform, up to 0.5 mm. long, not filled with spores; septa 80–110μ thick (fresh) but varying much in the same collections and sometime even in the same plant, only slightly if at all scissile.

    Spores 2.4–3 x 6–9μ, smooth, long-elliptic, 2-guttulate, 4–8 on each basidium, and usually remaining attached even after the basidium has collapsed. Hymenium 22–30μ thick; basidia 5–7.4 x 28–38μ, with thin, non-gelatinized walls; basidia extending out considerably beyond the hymenial surface, collapsing more or less completely after the spores are formed. In the hymenium are numerous more or less cylindrical cells which along with the tramal threads become very much gelatinized as the plant deliquesces. Sterigmata very short and inconspicuous.

    Plant nearly odorless when fresh, deliquescing plants fragrant, the odor faintly suggesting wine or candy; the quality of the odor the same but diminishing in strength on drying.

    In fresh condition the distinctive characteristics of the plants are the peridial colors and the abundant slender fibrils. In the dried condition the peridium becomes very dark, sordid brown to a dull or shiny black and the fibrils, so conspicuous in the fresh condition, usually become so innately appressed above as to appear as though there were none, while below and occasionally on the sides they remain free and conspicuous. The pleasant wine-like odor is also distinctive.

The present species seems close to *R. roseolus* and we were at first inclined to refer our plant to that species, but upon comparing a specimen of the latter plant kindly sent us by Dr. Fitzpatrick (from Dept. Pl. Path. Herb., N. Y. State Coll. Agric. at Cornell Univ.; Whetzel, No. 598) and determined as *R. roseolus* by Zeller and Dodge with our collections of the present plant, they were found to differ in the following ways: In color the peridium of *R. roseolus* is citron yellow to olive brown with blackish areas when dry and the fibrils are very few, innate-appressed and black when dry; the peridium of the present plant is chestnut to bay or inky black upon drying, and the fibrils are very numerous and conspicuous. The peridium of the present plant is viscid when fresh while in Chapel Hill collections of *R. roseolus* the peridium is not at all viscid. In section the peridium of *R. roseolus* is more or less reddish brown and does not change color upon the application of 7% KOH, whereas the peridium of the present plant contains a red or orange amorphous material which changes to a purplish orange upon the application of 7% KOH. In the macro- and microscopic characters of the gleba the two plants agree except for the somewhat larger spores of *R. roseolus*.

In some respects the present plant resembles *R. provincialis* but the hairlike threads making up the peridium of the latter plant and the much thinner scissile septa seem to separate the former from the latter plant.

The species differs from *R. rubescens* in having a very slight though pleasant odor, while the latter is very fragrant while deliquescing and retains the odor for several months after drying. The almost total absence of fibrils in *R. rubescens* also serves to distinguish that plant from the present species, in which the fibrils are quite numerous and conspicuous in the fresh state and are usually quite obvious in the dried condition. The present plant turns black with rather inconspicuous reddish black areas on drying, while *R. rubescens* becomes light to dark earthy tan (or dull black on crushed places) on drying. In section the two plants are quite distinct: (1) the peridium in *R. rubescens* having brownish, amorphous, crystalline material which does not change color on the application of 7% KOH, the present plant having embedded in its peridium a bright red or orange amorphous material which changes slowly to a purplish orange on the application of 7% KOH; (2) in *R. rubescens* the septa are slightly scissile in the fresh and very much scissile in dried plants, while in the present plant the septa are usually not at all scissile in either the fresh or dried plants.

From *R. piceus* which is also blackish when dry *R. nigrescens* easily differs in the smaller, more densely packed chambers, the absence of purple color in the peridium and in the more regular spores.

Attention has already been called to the peculiarities of the basidia in the present plant, a condition found in young fresh specimens of Nos. 7372 and 7569. In older specimens such as No. 1910 no plump basidia could be found at all, whereas conditions such as those represented in fig. 7 (showing collapsed basidium) are fairly common, but could be made out only after crushing a section of the gleba under the cover glass. It was only after studying young fresh material which showed the different stages in the development of the basidia that we were able to account for the extreme difficulty in finding basidia in the old dried specimens. It seems probable that, since Zeller and Dodge were studying dried specimens on the hymenia of which the spores are usually so abundant as to render such delicate objects as sterigmata, even when present, extremely hard to see, the long prongs figured and described by them (especially in *R. roseolus*) as sterigmata are nothing more than the remains of the collapsed basidia (fig. f).

591. On bank of a brook, Oct. 18, 1912.   Spores 2.2–2.8 x 6–7.5μ.
1011. Under cedars, Oct. 21, 1913.
7177. On rocky ground in pine woods, Sept. 30, 1923.   Spores 2.5–3.2 x 6.5–9μ.
Also Nos. 976, 1031, 1910, 7198, 7210, 7227, 7372, 7478, 7566, 7569, 7582, 8139, 8168.

South Carolina. About 7 miles above Georgetown, Dec. 29, 1926. Coker, coll. (U. N. C. Herb.).
        Spores 1.8–2.6 x 5–7.6μ.
Alabama. Spring Hill. Nov. 9, 1902. (Univ. Wis. Herb., as *R. rubescens*, and U. N. C. Herb.)

Rhizopogon roseolus (Corda) Hollos

Plates 24 and 107

Plant irregularly subglobose, usually flattened above, not rarely flattened laterally to about kidney-shaped, 0.5–2.5 cm. thick, nearly white when young and fresh, turning reddish or purplish red (nearly Hessian brown of Ridgway) where bruised, becoming citron yellow to olive brown with blackish areas when dry; fibrils inconspicuous, absent above and appearing as innate ridges below, blackening upon drying, passing into one or more conspicuous and considerably branched rhizomorphs. Peridium when fresh 0.4–0.6 mm., not rarely up to 1 mm. thick; outer part citron yellow, glabrous above, thinly felted below, composed of loosely packed, only slightly entangled hyphae, 4.4–11μ thick when fresh, septate, without clamp connections, encrusted with pale olive-colored granules; inner part rosy salmon in section when fresh, composed of more closely packed and much entangled hyphae with reddish granules intermingled; when dry more or less reddish brown throughout and not changing color in 7% KOH; 200–300μ thick. Gleba pallid white at first, drying warm buff, not changing when cut, rather tender when fresh, becoming quite brittle upon maturing; tasteless, odor faintly farinaceous; cavities averaging 2–4 to the millimeter, labyrinthiform, not rarely up to 2 mm. long in section, empty; septa 90–110μ, averaging about 100μ thick, occasionally scissile, hyphae loosely packed, much entangled and branched. When dry the peridium is only about 200–300μ thick, the outer part 30–80μ, the inner 110–230μ thick.
    Spores (of No. 7207) elliptic, smooth, with two conspicuous droplets, 3–3.7 x 6.4–8.5μ. Basidia 6–9 x 18–30μ, with thin, nongelatinized walls; extending out considerably beyond the hymenial surface, collapsing more or less completely after the spores are formed. On the hymenium are numerous more or less cylindrical cells which along with the tramal threads become very much gelatinized as the plant deliquesces.

    We have compared our plants with a specimen of *R. roseolus* studied by Zeller and Dodge (Whetzel, No. 598; N. Y. State Coll. of Agric. at Cornell Univ.), kindly sent us by Dr. Fitzpatrick and find that they agree in all respects except for the size of the spores which in the plant from Ithaca are somewhat larger (measuring 3.6–3.9 x 8.1–11.1μ) than those of the Chapel Hill plants.
    This plant is closest to *R. rubescens* and epigeal forms of the latter might easily be confused with the present plant since the exposed surface of *R. rubescens* is quite often more or less citron yellow. The citron yellow color when present, however, in the

PLATE 21

RHIZOPOGON RUBESCENS. No. 7199 [two top plants and one on left just below]; No. 7213 [all others].

PLATE 22

RHIZOPOGON RUBESCENS. No. 7565

latter, usually extends throughout the thickness of the peridium; while in the present plant the yellow color is limited to the outer part, the inner part being a distinct rosy salmon. The two plants are quite distinct in the color changes in the gleba, the present plant showing no change in the gleba upon cutting, while in *R. rubescens* the cut surface of the gleba changes to a distinct, rosy pink. Furthermore, the cavities of the gleba in *R. roseolus* are larger than in *R. rubescens*, and the septa are considerably thicker, more gelatinized and much less scissile.

7207. On very damp, moss-covered earth, mixed wood, November 11, 1923.
7212a. On mossy ground in old road, pine woods, near No. 7212, November 13, 1923.
7214. On damp grass and moss covered earth, open place in thin mixed woods, November 17, 1923.
7229. On ground, partly under pine needles, near New Hope Creek, December 11, 1923.

New York. Ithaca. On ground in moss. Whetzel, coll. (N. Y. St. Coll. Agric. Herb., No. 598, and U. N. C. Herb.).

Rhizopogon luteolus Fries & Nordholm emend Tulasne

Plate 106

We have not found this species in North Carolina but have studied a piece of a plant preserved in formalin kindly sent us by Dr. Fitzpatrick from Ithaca, N. Y. This same collection was examined by Zeller and Dodge and included under this species. These authors give the size of the spores as 3–5 x 7–16μ, while our measurements are 3.7–4.6 x 8–13μ. They give the basidia as 9–10 x 12–13μ, with sterigmata as long as the spores, while we find the basidia about 5.5μ thick in the uncollapsed half by 24–28μ long, and the spores nearly sessile, as is the case in most species we have seen. In this material the thin-walled basidia had collapsed in the distal half or throughout, but often were easily recognizable from the 2, 3 or 4 spores attached to the end. We find the great majority of the cavities to be completely filled with spores.

We have examined also a European specimen distributed by von Höhnel as *R. luteolus* (Krypt. exs. No. 1607; U. S. Nat'l. Herb.), and find the surface to be distinctly netted below, the peridium thin; chambers stuffed with spores; no olivaceous color obvious in the gleba. Basidia 5.5–9 x 20–30μ, with 4–8 subsessile spores which are 3.2–4.4 x 5.5–8μ, rarely up to 11μ, mostly elliptic but some bent or angular. As usual in *Rhizopogon*, the basidia are thin-walled and collapse after maturing the spores, and the hymenium is also furnished with numerous elongated cells with highly gelatinized walls. This plant differs from *R. luteolus* from Dr. Fitzpatrick in the size and numbers of spores on the basidia and in the presence of gelatinized cells in the hymenium of the European plant, but because of other resemblances and the scanty material we are including both under this species.

Krombholz's figure (Abbild. Schwamme, pl. 60, fig. 15) shows a green gleba, and Hesse notes the gleba as becoming olivaceous. Tulasne rejects Krombholz's figure as not being his interpretation of *R. luteolus*.

The following description except for the italicized parts, which are ours, is from Zeller and Dodge (Ann. Mo. Bot. Gard. **5**: 11. 1918):

Fructifications subglobose to oblong and often pear-shaped, diameter up to 3 cm. when dry, color warm buff to mummy brown when dry: odor weak at first and later stercoreus (Tulasne); fibrils numerous but not prominent, fine, elastic, about the same color as the peridium or darker, composed of septate hyphae, innate-appressed above and not very prominent below; peridium thick, 240–400μ, simplex, context meshy and quite loose, stupose, ochraceous-buff to ochraceous-tawny under the microscope; gleba white at first, then yellowish when dry; cavities narrowly labyrinthiform, empty or filled with spores where the cavities are small; *septa 60–90μ thick*, made up of hyaline, branched hyphae mostly extending parallel with the surface of the hymenium, becoming scissile early; *basidia almost entirely collapsed, a few were seen which were completely collapsed only in the distal half, the uncollapsed part about 5.5μ thick; the length of the basidia 24–28μ.* Spores acrogenous, distinctly colored, ochraceous tawny, *usually ellipsoidal, but often irregularly bent or angular, 3.7–4.6 x 8–11μ rarely up to 13.2μ,* smooth, *with a vague cup which is often extended into a collapsed filament (a part of the basidium) but spores scarcely truncate.*

In sandy coniferous woods. Cosmopolitan.

Illustrations: Hesse. Die Hypogaeen Deutsch., pl. 2, figs. 1–4; pl. 5, figs. 5–7; pl. 7, fig. 26; pl. 9, fig. 26.
    Tulasne. Fungi Hypogaei, pl. 1, fig. 5; pl. 11, fig. 5.
    Zeller and Dodge. Ann. Mo. Bot. Gard. 5: pl. 1, fig. 4.

New York. Ithaca. Reddick, coll. (Dept. Pl. Path. Herb., 7359, in N. Y. State Coll. Agric. at Cornell
    Univ. and U. N. C. Herb.).
Reported by Zeller and Dodge also from Massachusetts and North Carolina.

Rhizopogon piceus B. & C.

Plate 107

Plants irregularly globose, up to 1.5 cm. thick, glabrous, greenish yellow when first dug, soon sordid yellowish and then brown to blackish on exposure and handling; fibrils abundant and netting the surfaces all over, inherent and only sparingly free below, dark brown, several entering the ground and there branching and holding a ball of earth. Peridium 300–500μ thick, single, mottled with dark and light areas, in microscopic section composed of densely packed, small threads about 3.7μ thick, and of dark colored, subspherical to oblong or irregular bodies up to about 10μ long which turn reddish brown in large part when fresh upon the application of 7% KOH. When dry a section in KOH becomes largely black, mottled with pale areas. Gleba brownish yellow, toughish and elastic, the chambers small, 70–300μ broad or long (most about 100–200μ), irregular, but less so than in other species, remarkable in being blocked out into small groups by obvious plates; empty at first, becoming densely filled with spores at maturity, lined with a hymenium; septa not scissile or very slightly so, 74–111μ thick, the context composed of densely packed, much-entangled hyphae about 2–3.7μ thick. Odor distinct but not nearly as strong as in *R. rubescens* (No. 6049, etc.), pleasant and suggesting walnuts or wine.

Spores brown in mass, pale olivaceous when single, smooth, subelliptic with two oil drops, very peculiar in that a good many are slightly to considerably bent and less often deviating to irregular and even subtriangular, occasionally slightly constricted, 2.9–3.7 x 7.2–8μ, not rarely up to 11μ. Basidia totally collapsed in dried specimens; in the hymenium are numerous highly gelatinized thick-walled cells.

According to Dr. Dodge our plants are just like the co-type in the Curtis Herbarium (Hong Kong), including the abundant and conspicuous bodies in the peridium. A note with the Curtis plants says, "Germinating beneath the surface, and by its expansion causing small areas of a hand-breadth size to cleave off. Black or brown after exposure."

PLATE 23

Rᴀ ɪᴢᴏᴘᴏɢᴏɴ ɴɪɢʀᴇsᴄᴇɴs. No. 7210 [above]; No. 591 [below]

PLATE 24

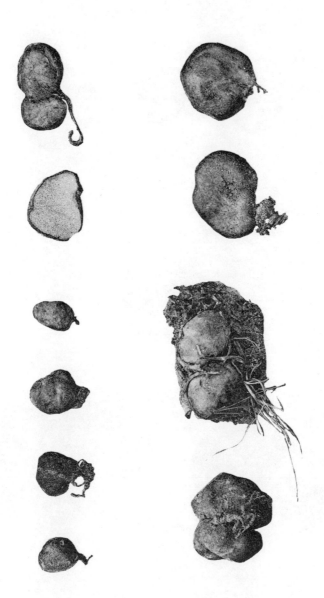

RHIZOPOGON ROSEOLUS.   No. 7207

From *R. luteolus* which is somewhat similar in color of fresh plant, abundant fibrils and irregular spores, this species differs in the abundant dark bodies in the peridium, giving to the dried plants a blackish color, by the smaller and more densely packed spore chambers and the plates which divide the gleba into larger areas, each containing several spore chambers. This last peculiarity is the rule in *Melanogaster* and indicates an affinity to that genus. For a comparison with *R. nigrescens* see that species.

6059. Under pines in upland woods near a branch, rooted in sandy soil under several inches of rotting humus, Jan. 30, 1923.

Rhizopogon maculatus Z. & D.

Plate 107

Plants subglobose, ovoid, oblong, or irregularly lobed, flattened, 0.6–1 cm. high by 1–2 cm. broad, becoming much smaller upon drying; sordid yellow to deep brown and mottled with lighter colored areas; attached to the earth by one to several conspicuous, dark brown fibers which are free from the peridium below, anastomosing to form a loose web which is innate-appressed laterally and which branches into little fibrils that are sparse and inconspicuous above. Peridium 70–140μ thick, composed of two layers: the outer one 30–80μ thick, made up of hyaline, densely entangled hyphae; the inner layer 35–60μ thick, consisting of brown, much entangled hyphae and brown bodies. The outer peridial layer may become worn off or mashed down so as to expose the inner dark layer. Gleba dark grayish to brown, tough, elastic when fresh, becoming hard upon drying; cavities of gleba labyrinthiform, appearing long (up to 1 mm.) and narrow in section, many of them filled with spores at maturity; tramal plates 45–80μ thick, composed of the two hymenial layers which are about 20μ thick and a non-scissile layer of hyphae which are about 3.7μ thick.

Spores smooth, elliptic, regular, rounded at both ends, 3–3.7 x 5.5–7.4μ. Basidia clavate without gelatinized walls, 4–5 x 10–14μ, with 4–8, usually 8, nearly sessile spores.

Of the species of *Rhizopogon* studied by us this plant is nearest *R. piceus*, but differs from that in the more loosely attached and more conspicuous fibers, in the shorter, elliptic spores which are not angular, in the much smaller basidia without gelatinized walls, and in the double-layered and much thinner peridium. It may also be separated from *R. atlanticus*, with which it agrees in having a double peridium, by the much more numerous and conspicuous fibers, by the absence of the peculiar cups on the end of the spores, and by the thinner peridium. Our description has been drawn from material preserved in formalin. For a comparison of *R. maculatus* with others nearly related, see Zeller and Dodge, l. c., page 5.

South Carolina. Hartsville. Coker, No. 955. On the surface of damp soil near a branch in a pasture, November 27, 1913.

Rhizopogon atlanticus Coker and Dodge n. sp.

Plates 25 and 106

Plants subglobose, oblong or irregularly lobed, 1–4 cm. thick; young plants pure white then dull yellow toward maturity, not turning rose when rubbed, becoming pinkish cinnamon or sordid yellow-brown upon drying; odor of fresh plants faintly of woods mold, odor of deliquescing plants fragrant like *Calycanthus* blossoms; superficial veins few, not conspicuous, innate appressed, darker colored than the peridium usually attached at base by a single small strand which is not conspicuous, separating very easily from the substratum. Peridium when fresh 300–450µ thick, when dried and resoaked 250µ thick, simple, composed of loosely interwoven, much entangled, encrusted hyphae, pale under the microscope, if dried in the fresh state, except for an outer, thin, brownish crusty area; easily separable from the gleba which is covered with a continuous white layer of the same tissue which separates the chambers. Gleba white when young, becoming Isabella color to buffy brown, shrinking considerably upon drying and not rarely separating from the outer peridial layer; cavities very small, almost invisible to the naked eye, about 5–8 to a mm., slightly larger toward the center, narrowly labyrinthiform, hollow at first, then only partly filled with the brown spores; tramal plates 45–95µ thick, hyaline, composed of a narrow central region made up of a few gelatinized hyphae (3–3.9µ thick) and the two hymenial layers.

Spores 3–3.7 x 7.4–8.5µ, blunt-elliptic, brown in mass under the low power of the microscope, furnished at the base with a large empty cup, formed by a continuation of the spore wall. Basidia inconspicuous, 5.5–7.8µ thick, collapsing early, bearing 4–8 sessile spores on the ends, the lower part of the spore becoming the empty chamber.

This species is near *R. truncatus* described by Linder in Rhodora 26: 196, 1924, from a single specimen collected by him under hemlocks in New Hampshire. Mr. Linder has kindly furnished us with a section of his plant. The peridium of *R. truncatus* is described as being 120µ thick and composed of a single layer, while the peridium of the present plant is 300–450µ thick when fresh and up to 250µ thick when dried and resoaked, and is composed of two layers. The tramal plates of the present plant are much thicker than those of *R. truncatus*, but have the same arrangement and general appearance. The cavities between the plates are exceptionally small in both plants. The basidia are alike except for a slight difference in thickness. The spores of the two plants are remarkable for the genus in being the only spores with apparently truncated ends. If the spores of *R. truncatus* are examined under an oil immersion objective they can easily be seen to be provided with the same empty chamber formed by a continuation of the spore wall as in the spores of the present plant, a point not mentioned by Linder. The cup-like extensions are not so conspicuous as in the southern species where they are easily visible under a high dry objective. The spores of our plant are also longer, narrower and paler than those of *R. truncatus*. This cup on the spore giving it a broadly truncate base distinguishes these two species from all other Rhizopogons. A similar cup is found in *Hysterangium* and *Melanogaster*.

South Carolina. Hartsville. Coker, No. 5999 (type). In damp pine woods just below the surface of humus, or a few with upper part exposed, December 25, 1922. (U. N. C. Herb.)
Florida. Eustis. At foot of a long leaf pine. Thaxter, coll. 1897.

Rhizopogon truncatus Linder

Plates 26 and 106

This species has recently been described from New Hampshire (Camp Algonquin in Holderness; moist birch woods with scattered hemlocks) and a slide of the type has been kindly sent us by Mr. Linder. The species is closely related to our *R. atlanticus*, which see for a comparison.

We translate the following from the original Latin description (Rhodora 26: 196, pl. 148, figs. 3, 5–7. 1924).

"Fructifications subglobose and irregular, measuring 3 cm. in diameter, a beautiful citrine when fresh, odor not strong, when dry like *Phallus duplicatus,* chamois or honey yellow (Ridgway); funiculi attached, mummy brown (Ridgway) when dry; peridium thin, 120μ thick, simple, byssoid, context of slender hyphae, maize yellow (Ridgway); gleba when dry cinnamon buff (Ridgway); cavities globose or irregular, empty; septa $16-27\mu$ thick, context of hyaline hyphae; basidia broadly clavate, 7 x $13-15\mu$, hyaline, with sterigmata which are $3-4.5\mu$ long; spores truncate, broadly ellipsoid, creamy, $3-4.4$ x $6.8-7.2\mu$, smooth."

In a letter Mr. Linder calls attention to the fact that the cavities grow larger toward the center.

Illustrations: Linder. As cited above.

New Hampshire. Holderness. Linder, coll. (Farlow Herb.).

NIGROPOGON Coker and Couch, n. gen.

As in *Rhizopogon* except adherent superficial fibers entirely lacking, peridium and tramal plates composed almost entirely of pseudoparenchymatous cells, and the spores strongly angular.

Nigropogon asterosporus n. sp.

Plate 108

Fruit body hypogeal, subglobose, 11 mm. thick when fresh, shrivelling and drying to a little more than half its original size; peridium when fresh nearly pure white, drying tawny or amber brown; rooting by an entangled network of very delicate black, hairlike fibrils; adherent, vein-like fibrils entirely lacking on the surface. Peridium $100-220\mu$ thick, of one layer composed of large parenchymatous cells and delicate threads. Gleba pure white at first but soon becoming pale vinaceous russet or pecan brown (Ridgw.) as the spores are formed, drying sayal brown. Cavities up to 1.5 mm. wide by 120μ deep, sinuous, remaining empty. Tramal plates quite variable in thickness, $80-200\mu$ thick, usually about 110μ thick, composed of thin-walled pseudoparenchymatous cells and threads, continuous with the peridium. Hymenium composed of short, more or less rectangular cells which elongate to form basidia. Basidia collapsing in the distal half immediately after the spores are formed, the proximal half persisting; $7.5-9\mu$ thick in the proximal half, $5.5-6.5\mu$ in the distal half by $26-38\mu$ long; usually with 4 (rarely 2) nearly sessile spores. Odor when fresh slightly like an old Irish potato but not unpleasant; on drying becoming like that of ham, faintly nitrous or phosphorous.

Spores color of gleba, very peculiar in shape, strongly angular, usually with four angles showing in optical section, the most acute angle being at the mucro end, $8.3-9.8$ x $11.5-12\mu$.

This remarkable species belongs in the Hymenogastraceae, close to *Rhizopogon.* It is clearly distinct from that genus, however, in peridial and tramal plate structure and in the shape of the spores. In the present species the peridium and tramal plates are composed of pseudoparenchymatous cells and a few threads, while in *Rhizopogon* the peridium and tramal plates are composed of threads which usually are rather delicate; also the spores of this plant are angular while the spores of *Rhizopogon* are invariably elliptic and smooth. The rhizomorphs, the empty glebal chambers, and the structure and development of the basidia suggest a close relationship to *Rhizopogon.*

The development of the basidia in this species is very peculiar. The hymenium is composed of cells which are almost as thick as they are long. These cells elongate at the distal end to form a narrower tube and on the end of this tube the spores are borne. Since there is no cross wall between the cell and the tube and since both empty their entire contents into the spores, both together must be considered the basidium. After the spores are formed the tube collapses. A somewhat similar condition has been found and is described here for certain species of *Rhizopogon* and *Octaviana purpurea*.

8271. Under deep layer of decaying oak and dogwood leaves, slightly buried in the soil, Oct. 22, 1927.

MELANOGASTER Corda

Fruiting bodies rounded or irregularly lobed with branched fibrils springing from any part of their surface. Peridium tough, fleshy, not readily separable from the gleba. Gleba with rounded to polygonal chambers which are larger towards the center and become nearly or completely filled with spores. Tramal plates directly continuous with the peridium, bearing the numerous basidia which are not arranged in a definite hymenial layer but are irregularly distributed throughout a broad peripheral zone which may nearly fill the cavity. Basidia club-shaped, 2-8-spored; spores usually apical on the basidia but not rarely somewhat laterally placed, elliptic, smooth, furnished with a cup at the proximal end. At maturity the gleba breaks down into a slimy mass and escapes by the final rupture of the peridium.

The irregularly distributed basidia and the nearly solid interior at maturity gives this genus a superficial approach towards *Scleroderma*. The essential structure is, however, quite different as the chambers are not really stuffed solidly at all stages and the basidia are not surrounded by a ground tissue which nourishes and matures the spores. The distribution of the spores in a slime and not a powder is also a fundamental difference. *Rhizopogon* seems the nearest relative.

We are including four species, two from New York State and two from North Carolina.

KEY TO THE SPECIES

Spores less than 11μ long and the distal end not pointed
    Peridium 300–600μ thick, composed of irregularly swollen hyphae 7.4–33μ thick
        Odor strong and nauseous: basidia long, club-shaped................*M. nauseosus* (p. 39)
        Odor not strong; basidia short and thick........................*M. rubescens* (?) (p. 40)
    Peridium 50–320μ thick, composed of threads 3–7μ thick..................*M. variegatus* (p. 38)
Spores over 11μ long and the distal end pointed............................*M. ambiguus* (p. 41)

Melanogaster variegatus Vitt.
    M. mollis Lloyd

Plate 109

Part of a collection of this plant preserved in formalin was sent us by Dr. Fitzpatrick from Cornell University. From this collection the following descriptive notes have been made:

Fruiting bodies up to 3.7 cm. in diameter, irregular in form; attached at base by elaborately branched rhizomorphs. Peridium simple, composed of closely packed, much entangled, clamp-connected threads, 3–7μ thick; surface of peridium covered with numerous, thick-walled, swollen, club-shaped cells; peridium deep brown in section, quite variable in thickness, 50–300μ thick. Tramal plates directly continuous with

PLATE 25

PLATE 26

RHIZOPOGON TRUNCATUS. Type [above]
CALVATIA ELATA. No. 2843H [below]

the peridium, concolorous with it in places but usually appearing white (?) to the naked eye or hyaline under the microscope; 74–148μ thick. Threads of the tramal plates 2–6μ thick, separate, considerably branched and much entangled, highly gelatinizable. Glebal chambers quite variable in size, 0.3–2 mm. long, elongated or polygonal basidia irregularly disposed.

Spores black in mass, dark brown under microscope, 3.5–4 x 7–10.4μ, elliptic, smooth, with a distinct hyaline cup (the remains of the short stalk which attached the spore to the basidium) at the proximal end. Basidia irregularly arranged, 4.2–5 x 12–18μ, club-shaped, usually with four spores, rarely with three or only two.

The spores of the present plant have been compared with type material kindly sent us by Dr. Dodge from the Sprague Herbarium at Cambridge. The spore sizes of the type vary from 3.7–4.5 x 7–9μ, rarely 10μ long, and have rather indistinct prongs (rings) at the proximal end. The spores of the present plant, while agreeing with the type in size, differ from the latter in having the proximal end extended into a rather long and fairly conspicuous cup-like stalk. These cup-like extensions while present on the proximal end of the type spores are much less conspicuous than in the present plant. The threads composing the tramal plates and peridium of the type material are so collapsed that it is very difficult to make out their structure. The present plant agrees with material kindly given us by the New York Botanical Garden which was collected and identified by Dr. Hollos in Hungary (Krypt. Exs. No. 1812) except that the spores of the latter plant are slightly thicker and without such a distinct stalk. The slight differences in spore size and structure do not seem sufficient to exclude the present plant from *M. variegatus.*

The present species is distinct from the Blowing Rock plant No. 5804, described below, in size, in peridial structure and in spore color and size.

Illustrations: Bucholtz. Beitr. Morph. und Syst. der Hypogaeen (Tuberaceen und Gastromyceten), pl. 1, fig. 19.
Fries, Th. C. E. Sveriges Gasteromyceter, fig. 36.

New York. McLean, near Ithaca. J. H. Miller, coll. August 17, 1924. (Cornell Univ. Herb., No. 12657.) Two specimens collected together and attached at base by rhizomorphs.
Canada. Dearness, coll. Reported by Lloyd, Myc. Notes, p. 1064.

Melanogaster nauseosus n. sp.

Plates 27 and 108

Fruiting bodies gregarious, subglobose; up to 3 cm. wide by 2 cm. high, most about 2 cm. wide by 1.5 cm. high. Peridium light cinnamon brown when fresh, becoming darker, about russet; outer part turning reddish upon being cut or bruised or eaten by insects. Fibrils rather large below, few and very inconspicuous above, darker than the peridium. Peridium, 300–600μ thick, single; composed of large, subglobose to elongated vesicular cells usually about 20μ thick, often up to 33 x 46μ; on the outer side are occasional patches of septate irregular threads with clamp connections. Gleba at first white, then becoming light tan and auburn as the spores mature and finally black in the dried plants, except for the yellowish tramal plates; more or less firm and solid when fresh and young, but changing upon maturing into a slimy gelatinized mass. Glebal chambers 1–3 mm. wide, polygonally shaped, loosely filled from the first with hyaline hyphae. In these are developed one to several "pockets" of spores. Chambers without a distinct hymenial layer, basidia irregularly disposed. Basidia elongated, club-shaped, 4.6–5.8μ thick, with 4–8, usually 6 or 7, nearly sessile spores. Basidia gelatinizing and early disappearing. Odor very strong, penetrating and peculiar, quite unpleasant, nauseous, but with a somewhat fruity element like decaying apples and very attractive to fruit flies, even in the dried condition.

Spores smooth, elliptic, 3.9–4.2 x 7.4–8.4μ, with a hyaline cup at the proximal end.

This species seems close to *M. variegatus* in certain characters, but it can be easily distinguished in the fresh condition by the very striking and unpleasant odor. In *M. variegatus* the spores are 2–5 on a basidium and are larger than in the present species. The shape of the basidia is also quite distinct as shown by Tulasne's figures. The name of *M. odoratissimus* suggests this plant but the odor of that is described as pleasant while the odor of this is decidedly otherwise; the basidia of that plant are short and distinctly swollen at the distal end, and the spores have a distinct long stalk (Hesse).

The most important characters in distinguishing the present plant are the brownish colored peridium which becomes red on being wounded, the large vesicular cells of the peridium, and the exceedingly strong unpleasant odor.

This species is nearest the plant treated tentatively as *M. rubescens*, but careful comparison shows them to be distinct. In section the dried gleba appears much alike in the two plants except that in the Chapel Hill plant the tramal plates are much more distinct. Sections, however, when soaked in water so that they regain approximately the size when fresh show striking differences: in the Blowing Rock plant the "cavities" are invariably stuffed with spores and the tramal plates are thin and rather inconspicuous, while in the Chapel Hill plant the cavities are only partially filled, leaving the plates broad and conspicuous. The structure of the tramal plates at maturity is quite different: in the plant from Blowing Rock they are composed of entangled hyphae which are partly gelatinized and which do not break apart easily when crushed; in *M. nauseosus* they are composed of highly gelatinized hyphae which break apart when crushed into separate units much like the cells in the subhymenial layer in *Crucibulum*. Furthermore the spores in *M. nauseosus* are slightly larger and the basidia of the two plants are quite different in shape.

8281.   On and under beech leaves and humus, Nov. 4, 1927.

? **Melanogaster rubescens** (Vitt.) Tul.

Plate 109

During the summer of 1922 we collected in the mountains a single specimen of this interesting plant. Unfortunately no notes were made on the fresh state. Our plant in the dried condition is decidedly shrunken, subglobose, 11 mm. thick; surface dark bay-brown, finely rivulose as if wrinkled in drying and marked on the lower half by a few inconspicuous veins. Peridium simple, 320–450μ thick, composed of irregularly swollen hyphae about 7.4–25μ thick and nearly hyaline under the microscope. Gleba very hard, black and solid, with no cavities; when cut showing a shining surface with faint whitish lines of the tramal plates outlining very large areas up to 1.5 mm. wide, which are not sinuous, but box-shaped like parenchyma cells. These chambers are solidly filled with the hard, black spore-mass, a condition different from species we are referring to *Rhizopogon*. Tramal plates 35–110μ thick.

Spores smooth, black in mass, light brown under the microscope, subelliptic, 3.4–4.2 x 5.5–8.8μ, the more mature ones showing the pale cup-like base as in *M. variegatus*. Basidia short and thick, 7–9 x 12–15μ, 4–8-spored, the sterigmata short.

Zeller and Dodge have referred to *Rhizopogon* several species in which the glebal chambers are solidly filled with black contents at maturity. Of these *R. pachyphloeus* seems nearest our plant, and Dodge seems inclined to put it provisionally in that species. To us, however, it differs strikingly in the far greater development of superficial fibers, its much thicker peridium, thinner tramal plates and very much smaller glebal chambers. From *R. diplophloeus*, also with solid contents, our plant differs in the simple peridium, larger glebal cells, smaller basidia and larger spores. We think the plant is best treated as a *Melanogaster*, but with only one plant and no notes on the fresh condition, we think the specific name somewhat doubtful.

After referring to *M. variegatus*, Dr. Dodge in a letter says, "There is much closer resemblance between your material and *Melanogaster rubescens* (Vitt.) as interpreted by M. A. Curtis. He so determined (Ms. note in his copy of Schweinitz, specimen from Schweinitz Herb. in Curtis Herb.) material collected by Schweinitz and referred by Schweinitz to *Rhizopogon aestivus* Wulfen ex Fries.* The peridium of the Schweinitzian specimen is about ½ the thickness of your No. 5804 but it has a somewhat collapsed appearance as do many of the older specimens which were repeatedly poisoned by the old methods. The spores are much the same but darker than in your specimen. I have never seen any authentic material of this species, so do not know whether Curtis's interpretation is correct or not. Apparently Peters got the same thing in Alabama. Your material has much lighter spores than anything I have ever seen in *Melanogaster*, but I am not quite sure whether that is significant as in some other groups spores do not assume their full color until late. For the present I am inclined to leave the specimen in *Rhizopogon pachyphloeus* Z. & D. until I have had further opportunity to study *Melanogaster*."

The relationship to *M. rubescens* is indicated by the basidia, which are similar to those shown in Tulasne's figure, and by the appearance of the peridium.

Blowing Rock. Coker and party, No. 5804. Exposed on humus under chestnut and rhododendron, August 26, 1922.

Melanogaster ambiguus Tul.

Plate 109

Dr. L. H. Pennington has kindly sent us a section of a plant found by him in New York and reported by Lloyd as *M. ambiguus* (Myc. Notes, p. 1065, fig. 2005).

The dried section of the plant is slightly over a centimeter thick and has a considerably wrinkled blackish bay peridium. In section the peridium is simple; about 300μ thick in dried condition and about 600μ thick when fresh (from prepared slide of Pennington); composed of very irregularly interwoven threads with numerous bladder-like swellings. Gleba jet black, the chambers rounded and filled with spores, 0.5–2 mm. wide; tramal plates very narrow, cream colored, contrasting strikingly with the black spore mass.

Spores 7.7–10.4 x 13–18μ, most about 8.5 x 15.9μ, broad-elliptic, more or less pointed at both ends, with a distinct cup-like prolongation at the proximal end, deep brown in color under the microscope. Basidia 8.5–11.8 x 22–26μ, club-shaped, with 2–4 sessile spores; cavities filled with interwoven threads, 3–3.7μ thick, which give rise here and there to basidia.

* Probably not in the sense of modern authors who use this name as an older name of *Rhizopogon rubescens* Tul.

"Odor strong and penetrating, somewhat like that of onions" (Pennington).

This plant in the dried condition shows considerable resemblance to *M. variegatus* but can readily be separated from that by the much larger spores.

Illustrations: Bucholtz. Beitr. Morph. und Syst. Hypogaeen (Tuberaceen und Gastromyceten), pl. 1, figs. 22–24.
Hesse.   Hypog. Deutsch., pl. 4, figs. 6–9; pl. 5, fig. 4; pl. 6, fig. 2.
Lloyd.   Myc. Notes, fig. 2005.
Massee.   Brit. Gastromycetes, pl. 1, fig. 5.
Smith.   Brit. Basidiomycetes, p. 488, fig. 141.
Tulasne.   Fungi Hypogaei, pl. 2, fig. 5; pl. 12, fig. 5.

New York.   Syracuse.   Pennington, coll. (Herb. N. Y. St. Coll. Forestry).

LEUCOGASTER Hesse

We have been able to study only one species of this genus, and take the generic as well as other specific descriptions from Zeller and Dodge, who have recently monographed the American species, five of which they record from the eastern United States (Ann. Mo. Bot. Gard. **11**: 389–408.   1924).

"Fructifications globose to irregular, hypogaeous to emergent, fleshy or waxy; fibrils sometimes present, leading to rhizomorphs; columella, stipe, and sterile base absent; peridium usually thin and fragile, sometimes rupturing at maturity; cavities frequently polyhedral, usually filled with spores embedded in a gelatinous mass; septa homogenous, with or without a distinct trama, often gelatinizing at maturity; basidia from subglobose to ovoid and subcylindric, mostly 4-spored, sometimes 3- or 5-spored; spores hyaline or slightly colored, with various surface markings embedded in a gelatinous spherical mass."

KEY TO THE SPECIES

Peridium double, thin, 60–80μ thick, white spotted with yellow, becoming reddish on drying; basidia linear-oblong...*L. luteomaculatus* (p. 42)
Peridium single, although sometimes with flocculent patches, then much thicker
    Peridium thin (under 180μ when dry)
        Tramal plates 40–50μ thick; spores globose, 8–11μ.....................*L. araneosus* (p. 43)
        Tramal plates 70–150μ thick; spores subglobose, 8.5–11 x 11–14μ........*L. carolinianus* (p. 43)
    Peridium thick (over 200μ)
        Septa thin, 60–120μ thick; basidia clavate, 22 x 8μ; spores 11–13μ in diameter, sterigmata short...*L. anomalus* (p. 44)
        Septa thick, 150–200μ thick; basidia pyriform
            Basidia 20–24 x 12μ; spores 12–16μ in diameter; sterigmata short.......*L. badius* (p. 44)
            Basidia 7–8 x 5–6μ, pedicellate; spores 8–10μ in diameter, sterigmata long
                                                 L. fulvimaculosus (p. 44)

Leucogaster luteomaculatus Z. and D.

"Fructifications globose, 2.5 x 1 cm., drying 1.5 x 0.8 cm., chalk-white with yellow flecks (Thaxter's field notes), becoming ox-blood red to garnet-brown on drying, surface uneven, shining; fibrils anastomosing, free in places, black, shining; peridium 60–80μ thick, duplex, outer layer readily separating from the inner, leaving patches 20–30μ thick, of large, septate, olive-brown hyphae, inner layer 40–55μ thick, of slender, reddish brown, granular, closely woven hyphae; gleba milk-white when fresh, drying cinnamon or clay-color; cavities globose to polyhedral, filled; septa thin, 50–60μ, hyaline, of large, parallel, thin-walled, hyaline hyphae, scissile; basidia hyaline, 7 x 12μ, narrowly

PLATE 27

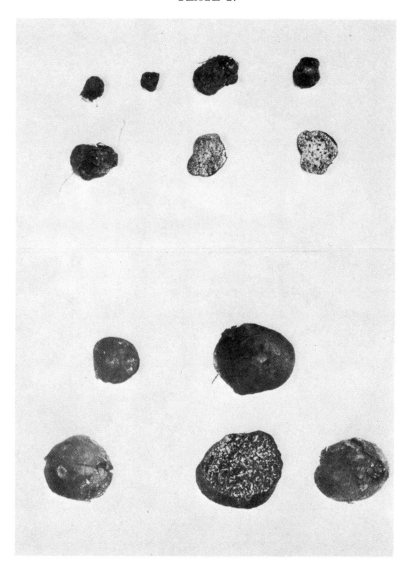

LEUCOGASTER CAROLINIANUS. No. 8262 [above]. Dried plants
MELANOGASTER NAUSEOSUS. No. 8281 [below]. Fresh plants

PLATE 28

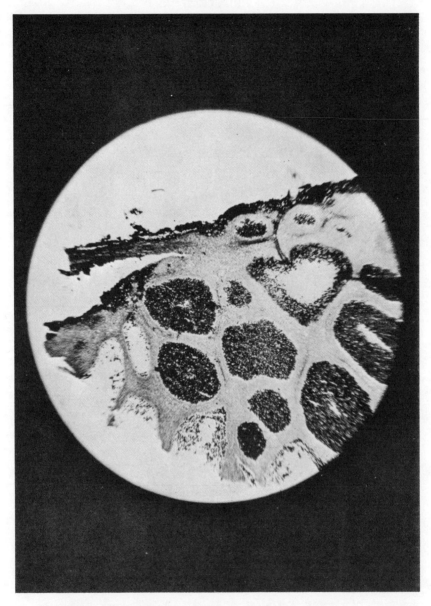

LEUCOGASTER CAROLINIANUS.   No. 8262.   × 44

oblong, 2-spored; sterigmata 2–4μ long; spores light olivaceous under the microscope, globose, minutely verrucose with a gelatinous sheath, 7–9μ in diameter.

"Under leaf mould in beech forests. Europe and North America. Summer. "The duplex character of the peridium, the color both when fresh and upon drying, as well as the very thin peridium, should serve to distinguish this species from other members of the genus."

Reported from Cranberry, North Carolina.

Leucogaster araneosus Z. & D.

"Fructifications globose, 0.6 cm. in diameter in preserved material, snuff brown to bister; fibrils large but not prominent, few, half-immersed, somewhat branched; peridium 130–180μ thick, simplex, of closely woven, very slender, light brown hyphae; gleba white with tawny spots; cavities subglobose, filled; septa thin, 40–50μ thick between hymenia, compact, of 3 layers, the middle layer being light brown, the other 2 layers hyaline; hymenial layer arachnoid; paraphyses none; basidia hyaline, granular-guttulate, 8–10 x 6–8μ, pyriform, on pedicels up to 300μ long, 4-spored; spores hyaline, globose, alveolate-reticulate, angles of alveoli projecting as blunt spines, in a gelatinous sheath, 8–11μ in diameter."

North Carolina. Summer.

Leucogaster carolinianus n.sp.

Plates 27, 28 and 108

Fruiting bodies hypogeal; subspherical, lobed, 5–17 mm. in diameter. Rooted by several delicate, branched fibrils which may arise from either the top, sides or bottom of the fruiting body. Mycelium fibrous and abundant in the soil, white. Peridium 50–220μ thick when fresh, about 60μ thick when dry, single, composed of threads 2.1μ thick which soon collapse; nearly white in the young condition when first dug up, becoming antimony yellow or clay color or ochraceous buff or tawny in spots upon maturing or drying; peridium disappearing in small areas, either being worn away or sloughing off, thus exposing the whitish gleba; peridium in the young condition continuous and homogeneous with the septa. Gleba pure white when fresh, becoming cream color upon drying, composed of the numerous polygonal or subglobose sacs which are surrounded by the tramal plates and filled when young with a gelatinous fluid in which the spores are later embedded; upon ripening and drying some of the sacs come to contain a large cavity, the walls of which are lined with the white spores, most of the sacs, however, are filled with spores. Tramal plates, not measuring hymenium, 70–150μ thick, usually about 100μ thick, composed of the central region of densely packed, irregular threads which, cut at the right angle, give the appearance of pseudoparenchymatous cells, quite variable in thickness, bordered on both sides by layers of irregular threads, the walls of which become thickened and highly gelatinized as the plants mature. Basidia arising from the layers which become gelatinized, long clavate, much swollen at the distal end, 8.2–9.4μ thick at the end; apparently without a basal septum, entire stalk 100–150μ long or perhaps longer; basidia not forming a definite hymenial layer; sterigmata about 2μ long.

Spores 4 on a basidium, ovoid, rarely globose, heavily reticulated, covered with a smooth layer of gelatinous material, 8.5–11 x 11–14μ (measuring sheath), very rarely abnormally large ones 14.7 x 16.8μ, these being 2 on a basidium.

Taste faintly sweet, pleasant; odor slight, not unpleasant, faintly nutty, becoming like machine oil as the fungus matures.

This species appears to be nearest *L. araneosus* Zeller and Dodge, which plant was found by Dr. Thaxter in the mountains of North Carolina. Our plants are larger on the general average than the size given by Zeller and Dodge, 6 mm. being their only measurement, while ours are from 5–17 mm. thick. Their single measurement, however, comes within our range. In the color and the gross and minute structure of the peridium the plants also agree. In the thickness and color of the tramal plates and the size of the basidia and spores the plants are distinct. Zeller and Dodge give the tramal plates as 40–50μ thick between hymenia while ours are 70–150μ thick, averaging about 100μ thick. In both plants the tramal plates are composed of three layers not including the hymenium. In *L. araneosus* the middle of these three layers is light brown while in our species it is white. The tramal plates in our plants are often scissile. The basidia of *L. araneosus* are 6–8μ x 8–10μ; ours are 8.2–9.4μ thick and apparently without a basal septum. The spores of *L. araneosus* are globose, 8–11μ in diameter; while those of the present species are subglobose, rarely globose, 8.5–11 x 11–14μ. Dr. Dodge has compared a specimen of our plant with his and thinks that there is no question but that our species is new.

8262. Under deciduous leaves and earth, upper Laurel Hill, Oct. 19, 1927.

Leucogaster anomalus (Peck) Z. & D.

Hymenogaster anomalus Peck

"Fructifications globose to irregular, 1–2.5 cm. in diameter, cinnamon-buff, clay-color, and tawny olive to Mikado brown above, Hay's russet and liver-brown below, 'glabrous, slightly lacunose, often with a root-like strand of mycelium at the base, ... sterile base obsolete or nearly so, odor slight, not disagreeable,' (Peck); peridium 240–520μ thick, grenadine to English red near the surface to hyaline within, composed of very slender interwoven hyphae; gleba amber-brown to Sudan brown, sometimes lighter; cavities large, mostly more than 1 mm. in diameter, subglobose to irregular, empty; septa 60–120μ, composed of very closely woven, hyaline hyphae, not scissile; cystidia none, paraphyses clavate, granularly guttulate; basidia clavate, 22–24 x 8μ, hyaline, 4-spored; spores almost sessile, dilute cream-colored to hyaline, globose, 11–13μ in diameter, uninucleate, surface pitted, giving the appearance of hexagonal reticulations, surrounded by a hyaline, gelatinous sheath.

"Hypogaeous, in woods. District of Columbia. August to September."

Leucogaster badius Mattirolo

"Fructifications subglobose, 1 cm. in diameter, raw sienna to raw umber, surface pitted, glabrous; stipe very slender, from a very slight, inconspicuous, sterile base; peridium 200–340μ thick, ochraceous-buff, stupose, composed of very slender hyphae; gleba raw umber; cavities polygonal, filled with spores in a gelatinous mass due to deliquescence, 0.7–1.0 mm. in diameter; septa 160–200μ thick, composed of compactly woven, gelatinous, cream-colored hyphae; cystidia none; basidia hyaline, pyriform, 20–24 x 12μ, 4-spored, guttulate; spores almost sessile, subglobose, 12–16μ in diameter, cream-colored, surface pitted, giving the appearance of hexagonal reticulations, surrounded by a hyaline, gelatinous sheath.

"On the ground, under leaves. Italy and New York, July and August."

Leucogaster fulvimaculosus Z. & D.

"Fructifications globose, 2.0–2.5 cm. in diameter, drying cinnamon-buff, spotted with tawny; fibrils not prominent, few, con-colorous; peridium 375–425μ thick, simplex, compact, of closely woven, slender hyphae; gleba warm buff or lighter; cavities globose or polyhedral, half filled; septa 150–180μ thick, hyaline, of closely woven slender hyphae, not scissile; basidia hyaline, 7–8 x 5–6μ, pyriform, on pedicels about 90μ long, 3-spored; sterigmata conical, 2μ long; spores hyaline in preserved material, brown in dry material, spherical to ovoid, verrucose to reticulate, leaving a pore where detached rom the sterigma, inclosed in a gelatinous sheath, 8–10μ in diameter.

"Damp woods. New York. Summer.

"The peridium of this species appears to be variable in thickness, new cavities seeming to form in the inner layer as the fructification increases in size, with the hyphae next the basidia-bearing hyphae gelatinizing and finally disappearing. A study of young material is very desirable for further interpreting this phenomenon."

HYMENOGASTER Vitt.

Subterranean or partly exposed; peridium without superficial veins, not easily removable, in our species white or nearly so; glebal chambers empty at first, sometimes stuffed at maturity; spores oval, lemon-shaped or elliptic, in most cases pointed at the distal end and rough, in some species rounded at the distal end and smooth, but inclosed in a hyaline sac. The spores seem to be the only generic character of any value and they are of two distinct types (if descriptions can be trusted).

Except for *H. anomalus* Pk., which Zeller and Dodge have transferred to *Leucogaster*, only one species has been reported from the eastern United States. This was determined by Lloyd as *H. decorus*, but we are transferring it to *H. Thwaitesii*. We are herewith adding one other.

KEY TO THE SPECIES

Odor very strong, not pleasant; spores 6.5–7.4 x 10–13μ, surrounded by a sac . . . .*H. foetidus*
Odor slight; spores 13–15 x 24–28μ . . . .*H. Thwaitesii*

Hymenogaster foetidus n. sp.

Plates 17, 18 and 110

Plants partly or entirely buried in soil under humus, single or cespitose or often fused, 0.3–1.3 cm. wide by 0.3–0.7 cm. high, when fresh, shrinking to about two-thirds this size on drying, rooting by several basal rhizomorphic strands; subspherical or lobed, fleshy, odor when fresh very strong and persistent, not pleasant, to some suggesting aniline oil, to others witch hazel. Peridium 0.5–0.8 mm. thick, simple but often partly covered with white byssoid mycelium, whitish when fresh, changing to creamy buff on drying, not changing color when cut or wounded; tender and fragile when fresh, becoming only slightly toughish on drying; smooth and without ridges or fibrils, but often encrusted with sandy particles, becoming wrinkled on drying; composed of much entangled, densely packed, thin- and thick-walled threads, the latter often terminating in large spherical swellings 37–55μ thick, which strikingly resemble the oogonia of certain species of *Cystopus*, except that the swellings are usually empty. Gleba whitish at first, changing to pale green and then to light brown with a greenish tint, and finally blackish brown on drying; without any signs of a sterile base. Tramal plates arising from the peridial wall and passing inwards in a more or less radial fashion, in some uniting in the center to form a fairly distinct columella. Cavities of the gleba subrotund in the central region, up to 0.6 mm. wide, becoming narrow and radially elongated toward the peripheral region; empty at first, becoming nearly or completely filled with spores. Hymenial layer concolorous with the tramal plates; composed of young and old basidia 3–7 x 16–25μ long, which, when young, are cylindrical but which collapse after the spores are formed.

Spores 2–4 to a basidium, smooth, elliptic, deep brown under the microscope, 6.5–7.4 x 10–13μ (not counting the utricle), with an open cup on the proximal end (at first appearing like two prongs), the spore body surrounded at some distance by a very thin, hyaline, bladdery utricle, which is in contact with the spore only at the cup end. The surface of the utricle is faintly rugulose.

This plant clearly belongs in the Hymenogastraceae in the obvious origin of the tramal plates from the peridium. Of the genera in this order it seems closest to *Hymenogaster* in the absence of fibrils from the sides and top of the plants and in the structure and shape of the spores, a utricle being present in several species of that genus. However, the appearance of the gleba is more like that of *Hysterangium*, with its long, radially elongated chambers, stuffed or nearly so at maturity, radiating in many cases from a distinct, subgelatinous, central column. The complete continuity of the tramal plates with the peridium, however, is so striking that the plant cannot be placed in the family Hysterangiaceae.

We have carefully examined the descriptions of the thirty-four species of *Hymenogaster* listed in Saccardo, Vol. 19, and find that our plant can be separated from each of them by obvious characters. In the color of the gleba, the shape of its cavities and the shape and size of the spore body, our plant resembles *H. utriculatus* Harkness, but that can be separated easily by the chocolate brown peridium and the fact that the utricle of the spore is winged or angled. Moreover, no mention is made by Harkness of any odor, while that of our plant is so strong and distinct as to be easily noticed by the most casual observer. So penetrating in fact is the odor that the plants, if partly uncovered by rain, can be located in the woods before being seen (10 or 15 feet away). A pitcher of water put in the ice box with a dish of these plants was so impregnated with the odor as to be nauseating. The present species is apparently nearest *H. Thwaitesii* Berk. and Br., in that both species are externally white and internally brown, and the spores of both plants are covered by a utricle. The two plants, however, can be separated by the distinct difference in the shape and structure of the spores. Those of *H. Thwaitesii* are larger and the proximal end is without a cup. Moreover, the utricle is attached at both ends of the spore instead of only one end as in our plant. Also, no mention is made of odor in *H. Thwaitesii*. The New York plants which we are referring to *H. Thwaitesii* differ strikingly from the present species in the thinner peridium, the empty chambers of different shape, and much lighter color of the gleba.

Among our plants the present species can be easily recognized when fresh by the peculiar and intense odor and in all conditions by the distinct utricle covering the small spores. *Hymenogaster decorus* Tul. also has spores with a rounded distal end or very obscurely pointed and surrounded by a utricle, but it is a much larger plant, has much larger spores and is nearly odorless. *Dendrogaster connectens* Bucholtz (Hedwigia **40:** 316. 1901) is easily different, as shown by the brown surface, yellow gleba, more extensive sterile tissue, and much larger spores. No odor is mentioned.

7467.   Partly buried in soil by branch under beech trees, by old Hillsboro road about 4 miles from Chapel Hill, July 30, 1924.
7473.   Buried in soil under humus or partly unearthed by heavy rain around the base of a tulip poplar, by branch behind athletic field, August 4, 1924.

PLATE 29

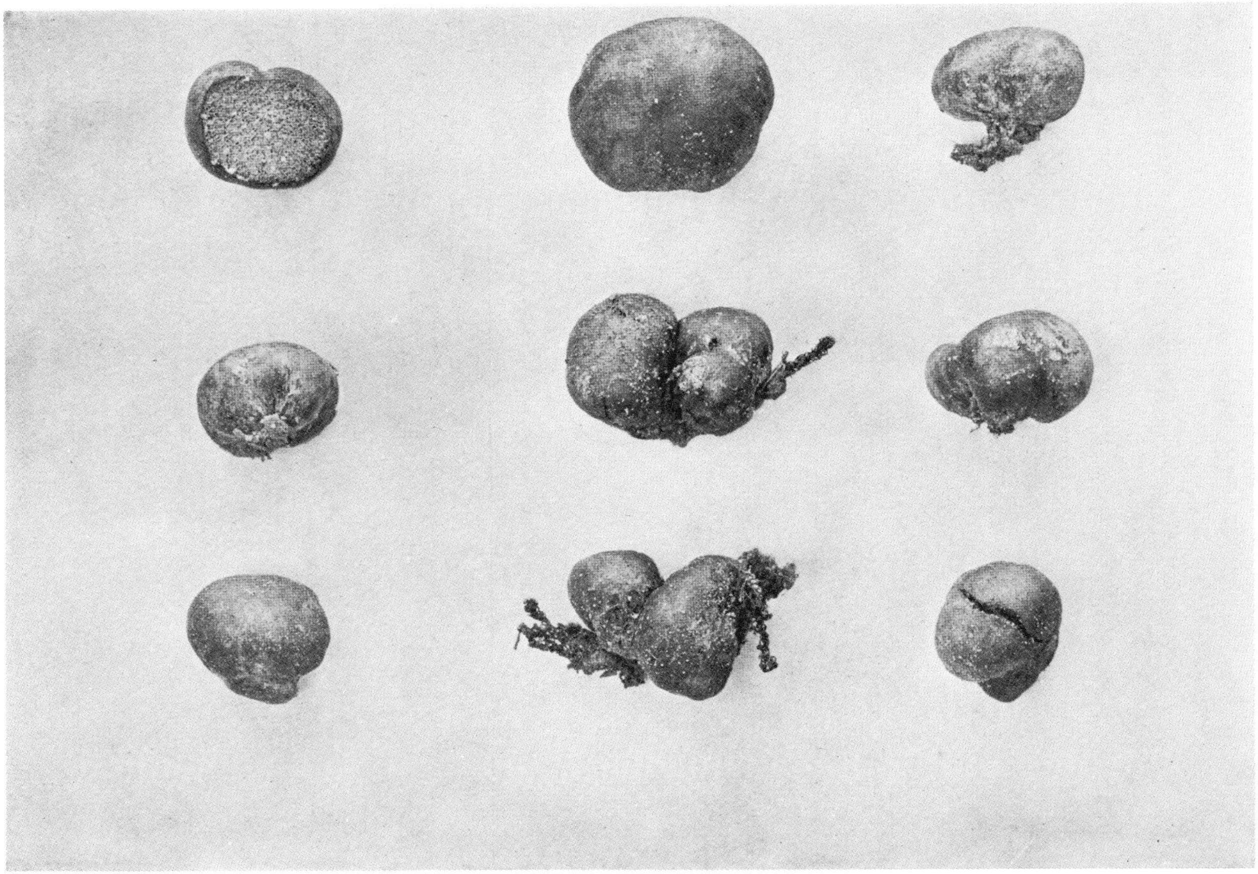

OCTAVIANIA RAVENELII. No. 6009

PLATE 30

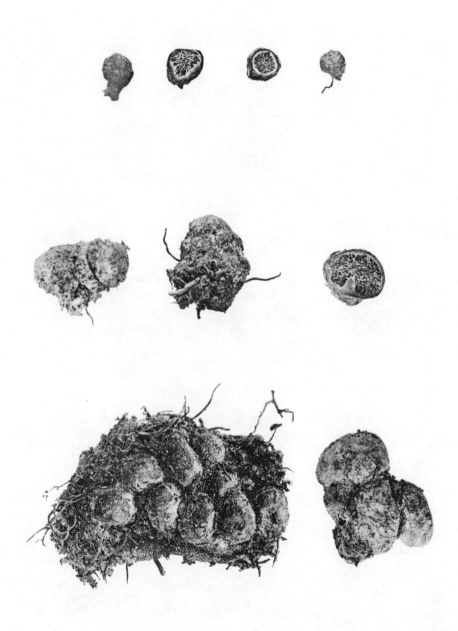

Octaviania purpurea. No. 7456 [top]; No. 7468 [below]

7469. On damp soil by Battle's Branch, August 4, 1924.
7580. By a tulip poplar, Nov. 27, 1924. One of the plants in section showed a distinct, hyaline, central columella.

Hymenogaster Thwaitesii Berk. and Br.

Plate 109

A plant collected by Mr. A. H. W. Povah among roots of sedges at Syracuse, New York, has been determined and reported by Lloyd as *Hymenogaster decorus* (Myc. Notes, p. 1166). We have a bit of this collection and on comparing it with Tulasne's original description we are convinced that it is not that species but rather an American form of *H. Thwaitesii*, a plant described from England and which has apparently not been found since.

The New York plants are very small, in the dry state about 3 mm. or less. The interior is not at all purplish but sordid ochraceous. The chambers are comparatively large, about 3–4 to a mm. and rounded and largely empty. Surface glabrous, pallid ochraceous or paler, much wrinkled on drying.
Spores oval to subelliptic, with distal end rounded or somewhat pointed, surrounded by a hyaline sheath, the body of the spore 9.2–11 x 11–17.3μ.

The spores agree very well both in size and structure with those of the type of *H. Thwaitesii*, a preparation of which was kindly sent us by the Director of Kew Gardens. We find the latter to be 8.5–11 x 14–20μ, not counting the irregularly crumpled, hyaline sheath surrounding them, more or less pointed at each end. The English plant has spores prevailingly more pointed than the American, as will be seen from our figures, but the general characters are so similar that the American plant had best be considered only a form. The original description of *H. Thwaitesii* gives the spores as globose, but this is not the case. Tulasne's figures also taken from the type are drawn somewhat more globose than we find them to be. The spores of *decorus* are much larger and the gleba is purplish. Also the plant itself is much larger.

Illustrations: Tulasne. Fungi Hypogaei, pl. 10, fig. 11.

New York. Syracuse. Povah, coll. "Among the roots of sedges in oak woods within an inch of the surface of the ground."

OCTAVIANIA Vitt.
(Including HYDNANGIUM Wallr.)

Fruiting bodies subglobose, oblong or lobed; exposed or underground. Peridium thin, nearly smooth, not netted with veinlike strands. Gleba fleshy, elastic, intimately connected with the peridium and not separable from it; cavities rather large, hollow (at least when young); sterile base present or absent. Basidia 1–4-spored; spores spherical or subspherical, with warted to reticulated walls.

Two species have been reported from the eastern United States and we are adding a new one. To separate this genus from *Hydnangium* has proved practically impossible. We agree with Lloyd (Myc. Notes, p. 269; also p. 1139) that it is best to unite them and have done so in the above description. In this last publication Lloyd reunites the genera and treats all the species known by him.

For cytology of spore formation in *Hydnangium carneum* see Rhuland (Bot. Zeit. **59:** 187. 1901). In this plant Rhuland finds basidia in a single fruit body to have 2, 3 or 4 spores. There are 4 nuclei in each basidium. In the two-spored cases each spore may contain two nuclei or one may contain one and the other three. In the four-spored cases each one contains a single nucleus. In the spores further division of the nuclei may take place producing nuclei up to six. Bausch (Bot. Zeit. **18:** 352. 1926) states that this behavior of nuclei, that is more than one entering a single spore from the basidium is the only case proven. For *Hydnangium carneum* also see further Bambeke, Mém. Acad. Roy. Sci. Belgique **54:** 1903 and Klika, Mykologia **2:** 143, 3 text figs. 1925. See also Patouillard, Note sur trois espèces d'*Hydnangium* de la flore du Jura, Bull. Soc. Myc. France **26:** 199, figs 1–3. 1910.

KEY TO THE SPECIES

Plants bay or red-brown..*O. Ravenelii* (p. 48)
Plants purplish on exposure...*O. purpurea* (p. 50)
Plants gray to bluish green...*O. asterosperma* (p. 51)

Octaviania Ravenelii (Berk.) Lloyd

Hydnangium Ravenelii (Berk.) Curtis
Hydnangium Stephensii var. *Ravenelii* Berk.
Octaviania Stephensii var. *Ravenelii* (Berk.) De Toni

Plates 29 and 110

Plants superficial or partly underground, gregarious and often crowded, subglobose to oblong-lobed, usually flattened when large, 1–3 cm. wide, 0.6–1.5 cm. high; bay red to chestnut or Sanford's brown when fresh, paler and more or less plicate underneath; surface quite smooth, dull (not flocculent); rooting by a small white myceloid base, no fibrils present; peridium wall simple, 130–150μ thick, its context reddish brown under microscope, consisting of much tangled, closely packed hyphae. Gleba creamy white, becoming pale rose when cut, exuding a white, tasteless milk which also becomes faintly rose colored and more watery upon exposure to air; cavities of the gleba large, about 0.3–1.5 mm. long or wide, labyrinthiform, quite hollow until deliquescence and easily visible without a lens; septa 110–190μ thick, consisting of (a) closely packed, irregular hyphae, 3.7–6.2μ thick, (b) elongated, laticiferous sacs, and (c) the two conspicuous hymenial layers which are 40–50μ thick and without cystidia. Odor when fresh rather faintly aromatic and very like that of a certain group of Lactarias, e. g., *L. theiogalus*, as also noted by Berkeley for *H. Stephensii*. When rotting the odor is mildly fetid and moderately strong, not at all like the pleasant odor of *Rhizopogon rubescens*.

Spores spherical, 11.8–16μ thick, with a short mucro and large oil drop, the surface set with irregular, imperfectly reticulated warts and ridges almost exactly as in certain species of *Russula* and *Lactarius*. Basidia clavate or spindle-shaped, 8–13 x 45–65μ counting the sterigmata, which are 7.5–14μ long and only two in number.

Not rare in Chapel Hill on sandy soil mixed with moss and grass in low open woods among pines. The plants are seated on the surface and never more than about one-third submerged. After maturity the plants do not deliquesce as in *Rhizopogon*, but begin slowly to decay, the gleba and peridium becoming water-logged, the former getting much darker and usually spotted or covered with a blackish brown mold, the gleba not changing color, slowly the tramal plates break down and the gleba becomes a tough and elastic jelly, the disorganization proceeding gradually from the top and sides. Fissures next appear in the top of the peridium and collapse begins as the jelly is slowly dissolved out by the rains. Even when the plant is half rotted off above and shrunken like a dried plum, the structure of the gleba is still obvious below and all the plant remains tough and elastic. Weeks and probably months are required to complete the disorganization.

Reported from North and South Carolina, Florida and Alabama.

Though Ravenel's plant was described as white by Berkeley (Grevillea **2**: 33. 1873, as a var. of *H. Stephensii*) we have no doubt that our plant is the same. We have compared a collection labelled *Octaviania Ravenelii* from Alabama by Earle (N. Y. Bot. Gard.), who notes that the color was "uniform terra cotta red, after exposure the tops bleach to a dirty white." He also notes that the plants were growing singly on the ground in a pasture and were usually 1–2 cm. broad (up to 3 x 4 cm.). Our plants are the same as these in all characters, including the spores which we find to be in Earle's plants 11–14μ, rarely up to 16.6μ, including the tubercles. *Hydnangium Stephensii* Berk. and Br. (Ann. & Mag. Nat. Hist. **13**: 352. 1844) was transferred to *Octaviania* by Tulasne, but the characters that distinguish these two genera are very obscure. (See note under the genus.)

The American plant is closely related to *H. Stephensii*, but the spores easily separate the two species. The spores of *H. Stephensii* are short-elliptic and with slender, sharper spines and are not reticulated. Our fig. 7 on pl. 110 is drawn from a slide, which was generously prepared for us by Miss Wakefield from the type at Kew. Tulasne and Massee draw the spores as elliptic, but with the spines more prominent than they appear to us. Quélet (Champ. Jura et Vosges, pt. 3, p. 18, pl. 1, fig. 9) shows the spore as subspherical (13μ thick) with small spines. It is interesting that he gives the color of the plant as whitish, the very character that made Berkeley describe the American plant as a variety of his "dark rufous" *H. Stephensii*. This suggests a similar fading in age. Corda shows the spores of *O. Stephensii* as quite spherical and with short, sharp spines, not reticulated (**6**: pl. 7, fig. 67). Patouillard's drawing of spores (Bull. Soc. Myc. France **26**: 201, fig. 1. 1910) of what he calls a form of *Stephensii* (*Hydnangium galathejum*) are as he notes just like those of the type of *Stephensii*. He further notes that in the type as in the form the basidium has but one sterigma. This makes a further distinction between *Octaviania Ravenelii* and *O. Stephensii*. In the fresh state a section of our plant showed a narrow, plug-like sterile base about 1–2 mm. thick. From this base two or three lines (in section) radiated and were plainly visible for about half way to the surface. When cut the milk exuded much more abundantly along these lines and from the sterile base. There is no sign of splitting in the tramal plates. In his original description of *H. Stephensii*, Berkeley does not describe the juice as turning red then yellowish on exposure as stated by Rea (British Basidiomycetae, p. 28) but says, "substance when cut and exposed to the air soon acquiring a red tinge, which is not however permanent and in young specimens vanishes almost entirely in drying, in which state the hymenium is cream colored." This is exactly the color change in our plants.

Since writing the above we have seen notes on this species in the fresh condition by Prof. Povah of Alabama (Lloyd Myc. Notes, p. 1140. 1922). His observations are in close agreement with ours in regard to milk and color changes. The odor he describes as "suggesting to some strawberries, to another the odor of a freshly dug sweet potato." The odor of the sweet potato is not very different from the *Lactarius* odor noted by us.

1445a.   Beside a low place near Mason Farm, Oct. 28, 1914.
6026, 6042.   On damp ground in pine woods on Durham road, Jan. 7 and 12, 1923.
6061.   On ground in pasture near pines, Feb. 9, 1923.
Also Nos. 6002, 6009, 7200.

South Carolina.   Santee Canal.   Ravenel, No. 883; Curtis, No. 2576.   (Curtis Herb.)
   Society Hill.   Curtis, coll. (Curtis Herb.).
   Also from South Carolina by Ravenel in Fungi Car. Exs. No. 71 (Philadelphia Acad. Herb., as
      H. Stephensii var. *Ravenelii*).
Alabama.   Auburn.   Earle.   (N. Y. B. G. Herb. and U. N. C. Herb.)
   Also collected in Alabama by Povah, as noted above.
New York.   Ithaca.   Whetzel, coll. (Cornell University Herb. and U. N. C. Herb.).   Spores 11–16.6μ
   thick, with an imperfect reticulum.   Basidia 2-spored.

Octaviania purpurea n. sp.

Plates 30, 31 and 111

Fruiting bodies hypogeal, single or cespitose, subglobose, often irregularly lobed; fresh plants 0.6–1.8 cm. high by 0.6–2.5 cm. wide, drying to about two-thirds that size, fleshy; rooting by numerous mycelioid, branched fibrils which extend out from several points of attachment on the base.   Peridium white throughout when young, turning vinaceous to deep vinaceous when exposed or wounded; retaining the vinaceous tint on drying; 1–2 mm. thick when fresh, drying to about one-quarter this thickness; composed in large part of small thin-walled, densely packed and considerably entangled threads 3–4μ thick, and a few much larger thick-walled threads, 11–16μ thick, which often terminate in large globose cells.   Gleba pure white when young, acquiring an olive tint as the hymenium and spores begin to develop, passing through olive brown to deep blackish brown as the spores mature.   Tramal plates pure white, becoming only slightly discolored upon maturity and contrasting strikingly with the nearly black spores and the more or less deep purple peridium; arising from the peridium and composing in the young state by far the greater part of the gleba, persisting in mature plants as very thin white byssoid plates.   Cavities of gleba first arising as narrow, pouch-like spaces which by growing and anastomosing, form labyrinthiform spaces, which, in section, often appear in clusters, 3–8, separated by rather wide tramal plates, thus presenting the appearance of several small cavities within a large one; cavities becoming only partially filled with spores.   Odor of fresh plants faintly like an Irish potato.   Plants kept covered in the ice box for several days gave an odor strongly suggestive of oysters. Taste not unpleasant.

Spores subsessile, subspherical, sometimes considerably elongated at the proximal end, angular-warted, 9.5–12.5μ thick, with a pedicel about as long as the diameter of the spore.   Hymenial layer, lining the cavities, composed of young and old basidia which are very peculiar in that in the young state they are thick, rather short cells, 7.4–11.2 x 20–25μ, which by elongating into a narrow tube, 4.4–5.5μ thick, more than double their length; mature basidium 5.5–7.8 x 30–44μ, jug-shaped, bearing one apical spore; collapsing after the spores are formed.

Suitable material being at hand, it was thought of interest to study the nuclear behavior in this single-spored basidium for comparison with that of the normal four-spored basidium.   The material for this study was prepared as follows: small slices about a half millimeter thick of the youngest plants were cut and put in Flemming's weak chrom-acetic acid where they were allowed to remain over night.   The material

PLATE 31

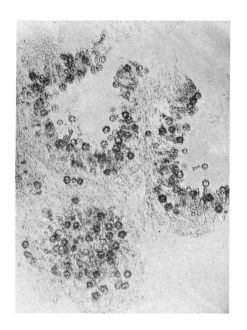 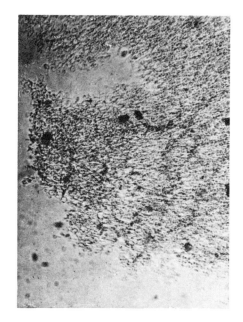

OCTAVIANIA PURPUREA.   No. 7468. × 400
   [above]
GEASTER VELUTINUS. × 36 [below]

ASTRAEUS HYGROMETRICUS. No. 7441. ×
   100 [above]
DISCISEDA CANDIDA.   No. 7507. × 100
   [below]

was dehydrated and infiltrated in paraffin in the usual manner for very delicate objects. Sections were cut 5 microns thick and stained with Haidenhain's iron alum haematoxylin and by Gram's method, the latter giving much better results.

It was found that the nuclear behavior agreed in the essential details with that described for typical Basidiomycetes with four-spored basidia except that three of the nuclei remain in the basidium and degenerate, the fourth entering the spore which is always uninucleate.

In the young basidium, which has not developed the elongated, tubular process, there were quite often seen two nuclei which might be located near the base or in center or in position as shown in figure 4. Numerous stages were seen in which the two nuclei were apparently fusing. When the basidium is in a somewhat later stage of development (fig. 5) it is usually found to be uninucleate, the nucleus now being considerably larger than either of those shown in figure 4. This large nucleus soon becomes somewhat vesicular in structure, the linin threads with chromatin granules on them showing up conspicuously (fig. 6). A comparatively large spindle is formed on which the chromatin granules arrange themselves (fig. 7). The first mitosis seems to be followed immediately by the second in which the spindle is considerably smaller and the chromosomes much less distinct (fig. 8).

Four nuclei are thus formed from the original fusion nucleus (fig. 9). Meanwhile the basidium has sent out a tubular process into which the nuclei and some cytoplasm migrate. At the tip of this tubular process a bud is formed which enlarges to form the spore. One of the four nuclei passes into the spore (fig. 10). In later stages as shown in figure 11, the spore is seen to be uninucleate; the three supernumerary nuclei left in the basidium can hardly be distinguished—so poorly do they absorb the stain. They are doubtless degenerating.

Our plant is evidently nearest *Hydnangium monosporum* Boud. and Pat. (See Boudier; Icon., pl. 193, and Patouillard; Tab. Fung. No. 692) as shown by the strongly cespitose habit and single-spored basidia with rough spores. That is easily separated by ochraceous color, larger size, and minutely spiny spores. *Gallacea Scleroderma* (Cooke) Lloyd (= *G. violacea* (Cooke & Mass.) Lloyd), a violet plant from New Zealand and related to *Hysterangium*, has recently been examined microscopically by Cunningham, and is quite different from our *O. purpurea* (Trans. Brit. Myc. Soc. 9: 193, pls. 9 and 10. 1924).

The genus *Leucophleps* Harkness (*Leucophlebs*, as the spelling was corrected by Roumeguère) contains a species *L. magnata* which, in its one-spored basidia, resembles our plants, but which can be easily separated by the partial absence of the peridium and the smooth spores. Appearances are against *Leucophleps* being a good genus.

7456. Plants partly or entirely buried in damp soil by Battle's Branch below Forest Theater, July 25, 1924.
7468. Abundant on washed soil by Battle's Branch, Aug. 4, 1924.
7508. On ground and slightly buried under a sweet gum tree near Meeting of Waters, Aug. 27, 1924.

Octaviania asterosperma Vitt.

Plate 110

Dr. Fitzpatrick has kindly sent us a single plant of this species from Ithaca (entered below), mentioned by Lloyd in Mycological Notes, p. 1141. We find it to agree with the descriptions by Tulasne and Boudier so far as can be seen from specimen kept in formalin.   The peridium is irregularly areolate, salmon colored, usually about 100μ thick, composed of densely packed tangled threads.   Tramal plates continuous with the peridium, considerably thinner than the peridium and much lighter colored, appearing almost white; glebal chambers rounded or elongated, usually filled with spores, 0.5–1.5 mm. wide.   Spores round, 13–17μ thick, light brown under the microscope, very dark brown in mass, conspicuously set with large pyramidal spines and often with a short pedicel.

The following description is from Boudier, Icon. Myc. **4**: 97:

"Peridia white, rounded, solitary or cespitose, and more or less irregular, covered with a light tomentum which is separated into small, tomentose, flattish warts, white at first, then turning smoky gray; cortex turning more or less bluish green by cold or exposure to air; the peridia are attached to the earth by root-like, mycelial filaments which form a very visible base.   The gleba is full, firm, formed of rounded chambers, filled with spores and separated from each other by the whitish plates which seem to arise from the basal portion, and which are colored equally green by cold.   The spores are perfectly round, echinulate, brownish drab when seen one at a time, and purplish brown when seen in mass, which makes a section of this species appear finely marbled with white by the plates; they have a large internal oil drop often divided, and are often furnished with a pedicel; they measure 15–18μ in diameter with the spiny warts."

"This species seems rare; I have found the specimens which I have figured in damp woods of the forest of Montmorency in Sept.; it was there in numbers under the leaves at the foot of a clump of ash trees."

Illustrations: Boudier. Icon. Myc., pl. 191.
    Fries, Th. C. E.   Sveriges Gasteromyceter, fig. 3 (in error as *O. asterospora*).
    Lloyd.   Myc. Works, pl. 205, fig. 2168 and fig. 2169 (copied from Boudier).
    Tulasne.   Fungi hypogaei, pl. 11, fig. 1.

New York. Ithaca. Fitzpatrick, No. 9969.   (Reported by Lloyd in Myc. Notes, p. 1141.)

SECOTIACEAE

Fruit body above ground and with a short or long stalk which extends as a columella entirely through the peridium and is connected with it above; gleba chambered, the tramal plates arising like the gills in an agaric and growing into a gill chamber, anastomosing and crumpling to form numerous irregular cavities which are lined on the inner side by a typical agaricoid hymenium; tramal plates persisting after the maturation of the spores; capillitium absent. Dehiscence ventral around the stem with subsequent expansion and in some cases longitudinal cracking, or there may be no true dehiscence (as in *Rhopalogaster*), the very thin peridium disappearing more or less by collapse. Basidia clavate with distinct apical sterigmata.

The family as above described is so modified from that of Fischer as to include only the genera *Secotium* and *Rhopalogaster* (possibly also *Macowanites*). We are following Fischer in not considering *Elasmomyces* as distinct from *Secotium*. This is about as suggested by Cunningham (l. c., p. 223). A very interesting family with characters suggesting the agarics and apparently connecting them with the Hymenogastraceae, which they resemble in later stages of glebal development. Only two genera have been found in the eastern United States. It is interesting to compare here the peculiar genus *Rhacophyllus* B. & Br. (Trans. Brit. Myc. Soc. 11: 238. 1926) from the tropics, which externally has the exact appearance of a small, delicate agaric with conic cap. Petch has recently been able to study the plant in all stages. Instead of gills there are borne on the underside of the cap more or less linear groups of bulbils which germinate easily and are the only reproductive bodies. These bulbils arise separately inside a delicate fundamental tissue. They may be at first hollow, soon becoming solid through growth of the palisade-like central tissue. This tissue produces on the inside subspherical cells in rows. It is not stated from what cells of the bulbils hyphal threads originate in germination.

KEY TO THE GENERA

Peridium tough and persistent..*Secotium*
Peridium very delicate and disappearing in part at maturity........................*Rhopalogaster*

SECOTIUM Kunze

Peridium above ground with a long or short stalk, which extends entirely through the sporiferous portion as a stout columella which is continuous above with the peridium. Gleba spongy, cellular; tramal plates arising from the peridium wall and also connected with the top or greater part of the columella and filling the space between them, somewhat lamellate, very sinous with a more or less horizontal direction suggesting an unopened agaric with sinuous gills; capillitium not present. Dehiscence basal and longitudinal, the peridium usually separating slightly from the stem below and in some cases expanding more or less, after the manner of a young agaric. Basidia clavate with 2–4 apical, stipitate, smooth or rough spores.

For a good drawing of the hymenium of *S. krjukowense*, a European species with rough spores, see Bucholtz, l. c., pl. 3, fig. 4.

53

The genus seems to be particularly abundant in Australia and New Zealand, from which Cunningham (l. c.) reports 16 species. He adds the following facts to our knowledge of the cytology:

"The hyphae of the columella, stipe and peridium are invariably binucleate. The basidia at first are binucleate, these nuclei fuse, and a slightly larger fusion-nucleus is formed. This takes up a position in the distal end of the basidium; there it divides twice. The first division precedes the formation of the sterigmata, the second succeeds their appearance. When the sterigmata are about half their normal length, spores begin to appear on them, and when they are full length, the spores are about half size. When the spores are about one-quarter their normal size, a nucleus migrates into each, divides mitotically, and the spores become binucleate, a character constant in each of the numerous species examined. The spore attains its full size before it changes colour; at maturity the epispore becomes coloured some shade of brown, the depth of colour depending on the species.

"Clamp connections are abundant in the tissues of the stipe and partial veil. . . . .

"On germination a germ tube protrudes, usually from the end of the spore opposite to that by which it was attached to the sterigma; this branches repeatedly to form a mycelium, the cells of which are septate and binucleate."

Conard and Cunningham, working on different species disagree as to the presence of a veil, Conard claiming the presence of universal veil and absence of a partial one and Cunningham stating just the reverse.

LITERATURE

Conard. The Structure and Development of *Secotium agaricoides*. Mycologia **7**: 94, pl. 157 and 1 text fig. 1915.
Cunningham. A Critical Revision of the Australian and New Zealand Species of the Genus *Secotium*. Proc. Linn. Soc. of New South Wales **49**: 97, pls. 12–15. 1924.
Cunningham. The Structure and Development of Two New Zealand Species of *Secotium*. Trans. Brit. Myc. Soc. **10**: 216, pls. 11 and 12. 1925.
Lohwag. Entwicklungsgeschichte und systematische Stellung von *Secotium agaricoides* (Czern.) Holl. Österr. Bot. Zeitschr., 1924, p. 161, pl. 2.
Setchell. Two New Hypogaeous Secotiaceae. Journ. Myc. **13**: 236. 1907.

Secotium agaricoides (Czern.) Hollos
   S. acuminatum Montagne
   S. Warnei Peck
   S. rubigenum Harkness

Plates 32 and 111

Fruit bodies epigeal, solitary or gregarious, usually distinctly heart-shaped, rarely subglobose, with a distinct conical or rounded stalk which tapers into a thick strand and anchors the plant in the ground; very variable in size and shape, 1–5.5 cm. wide by 1.5–6 cm. high. Peridium nearly pure white when young and fresh, turning straw color to cinnamon-buff or leather color upon maturing and drying; single-layered, 1–3 mm. thick, nearly smooth in very young specimens, covered at maturity with inherent scales which may resemble fish scales or may be very irregularly arranged; fleshy and tender when young, becoming rather tough and fibrous upon drying. Gleba nearly pure white when young, becoming yellow and finally brown; glebal chambers somewhat labyrinthiform, varying in width from a fraction of a millimeter up to 1 mm. Tramal plates

PLATE 32

SECOTIUM AGARICOIDES. No. 7091 [two small plants]; No. 7119 [others]

PLATE 33

CALVATIA RUBRO-FLAVA. Nos. 7154, 7163 and 7107

about 75μ thick, persisting in the mature and dried specimens, forming lamella-like folds. Odorless when young; taste sweet and nutty like that of *Boletus edulis*. Edible when young.

Spores (of No. 7091) smooth, ovate, yellow under the microscope, 5.5–6.8 x 6.6–8μ, a few irregular, larger ones. Hymenium 25–30μ thick; basidia club-shaped, 4-spored, 7.4–9.3μ thick, no cystidia.

This is the first record so far as we can find of this fungus in the southeastern states, but at the New York Botanical Garden we find a collection from Virginia by Dodge (as *S. acuminatum*). The only record we find of its occurrence in the Atlantic states is from Pennsylvania (Barnett, as *S. Warnei;* Peck, l. c., 1882). It is apparently not rare in the Mississippi Valley and westward, and is reported from Alabama and Texas. This is the same as the plant described by Peck from Wisconsin as *Lycoperdon Warnei* (Bull. Torr. Bot. Club **6:** 77. 1876) and later transferred to *Secotium* (Ibid. **9:** 2. 1882).

We have examined and compared specimens and spores of *S. Warnei* from Nebraska (N. Y. Bot. Gard. Herb.; H. J. Webber, coll.) and specimens and spores of *S. agaricoides* from Hungary (N. Y. Bot. Gard. Herb., determined by Hollos) and find that they both agree with our Chapel Hill plants. We agree with Hollos that *S. rubigenum* Harkness (Bull. Cal. Acad. Science, 1886, p. 257) is the same as the present species. A specimen at the New York Botanical Garden from California, collected by Harkness himself, has spores smooth, oval-elliptic, variable in size, 4.8–6.8 x 7–10.5μ.

Secotium arizonicum Shear and Griffiths (Bull. Torr. Bot. Club **29:** 450. 1902) seems to be a good species, as shown by the much larger spores (7.2–12 x 8.5–15μ) of the type material in Washington (pl. 111, fig. 14), and by the short, often aborted columella (see note by Lloyd, Myc. Notes, p. 149). *Secotium tenuipes* Setchell (Journ. Myc. **13:** 239, pl. 107, figs. 4–8. 1907) and *S. russuloides* (Setchell) Lloyd (published as *Elasmomyces*) are also good species, growing entirely concealed under leaves in California. At the New York Botanical Garden is an abundant collection of the former by Harper from Berkeley, California (type locality). The plant (when dry) is small, blackish red with a slender stem and a deep reddish brown gleba. The spores are deep brown, smooth, ovate, 8.5–10.2 x 12–16μ. *Secotium australe* Lloyd (Myc. Notes, p. 788) is also apparently a good species, as the spores are said to be only 4–5μ thick. Lloyd has seen the types of *S. decipiens* Peck (Bull. Torr. Bot. Club **22:** 492. 1895) and thinks it the same as the European *Gyrophragmium Delilei* (Myc. Notes, p. 150). Later he uses the name *G. decipiens* and calls it the western form of the European species (Myc. Notes, p. 196).

Illustrations: Bucholtz. Beitr. Morph. und Syst. der Hypogaeen (Tuberaceen und Gasteromyceten), pl. 4, fig. 19.

Fries, Th. C. E. Sveriges Gasteromyceter, fig. 7.

Hollos. l.c., pls. 3, 4, 5, 6, and pl. 29, figs. 33–35.

Lloyd. Myc. Works, pl. 13 (as *S. acuminatum*).

Lloyd. The Genera of Gasteromycetes, pl. 3, fig. 25 (as *S. acuminatum*).

McDougall. Trans. Ill. St. Acad. Sci. **15:** fig. 3 (of McDougall article).

Peck. Bull. Torr. Bot. Club **9:** pl. 9, figs. 6–11 (as *S. Warnei*). 1882.

Shear. Asa Gray Bull. **6**, No. 6: 95, fig. 1, A-E. (as *S. Warnei*). 1898.

Sorokine. Rev. Myc., 1890, pl. 27, fig. 367; pl. 31.

Trelease. Morels and Puff-Balls of Madison, pl. 8, fig. 7 (as *S. acuminatum*).

7091.   On ground in a pasture near Chapel Hill, August 24, 1923.
7119.   Same location as above, September 11, 1923.

Virginia.   C. F. Dodge, coll. (N. Y. Bot. Gard. Herb.).
Indiana.   Lafayette Co.   J. C. Arthur, coll. (N. Y. Bot. Gard. Herb., as *S. Warnei*).
Dakota.   October, 1908.   Braendle.   Fungi Dakotensis No. 49.   (N. Y. Bot. Gard. Herb., as *S. acuminatum*.)
Wisconsin.   Madison.   Cheney, coll. (U. N. C. Herb.).   Spores 5.5–6.6 x 8–9.7μ.

For other localities see Lloyd, Myc. Notes No. 14: 139.   1903.

RHOPALOGASTER Johnston

Johnston has shown (Proc. Am. Acad. Arts and Sciences **38**: 61, one plate. 1903) that the following species, commonly known as *Cauloglossum transversarium*, cannot be retained in that genus which is really a synonym of *Podaxon*.   He proposes for the species the monotypic genus *Rhopalogaster*.   Johnston defines the genus as follows:

"Fruiting body clavate, stipitate, traversed by a firm subgelatinous axil columella continuous with the stipe.   Stipe firm, erect with naked base.   Peridium simple, continuous with the stipe below and with the columella at the apex, more or less evanescent-indehiscent.   Gleba persistent.   Tramal plates extending from the columella toward the peridium.   Basidia clavate, in groups, 4-spored, spores simple, borne on well-developed sterigmata."

Rhopalogaster transversarium (Bosc) Johnston.
Cauloglossum transversarium (Bosc) Fr.

Plates 41 and 111

This plant of the southeastern Gulf states was first collected in the Carolinas but was not well known structurally until the work of Johnston (l. c.).   It has been found at Wilmington in abundance by Curtis and by Wood, and we have a collection from Nag's Head, N. C.   As our dried plants are not in good condition we copy the following description from Johnston's paper, which see for much fuller structural detail and discussion of synonomy:

"Narrowly to broadly club-shaped, 3–7 cm. high; the distal end of the columella appearing at or near the apex, either as a shallow orbicular depression, or a slight protuberance.   Peridium dirty brownish or buff yellow.   When young the gleba is dirty gamboge yellow; when exposed by injury becoming dirty olive brown, eventually dark.   Stem nearly white when fresh.   Spores ovate-elliptical, 3.6–4.3 x 5.8–7.2μ, yellow brown, borne on long slender sterigmata.   The plants grow out of the bases of living or dead trees or upon rotten wood, stumps or fallen logs, or among rubbish on the ground close by in wet pine lands.   September–November.   S. Carolina (Bosc, 1811, Curtis, 1857?); Santee Canal, S. C. (Ravenel); Wilmington, N. C. (Wood, November, 1880, Curtis, November, 1846); Carolina (Berkeley, 1873); Gainsville, Fla. (Ravenel, 1878); Eustis, Fla. (Thaxter, October, 1897); Tuskegee, Ala. (Beaumont, aestate, 1853)."

The specimen labelled *Cauloglossum transversarium* in the Philadelphia Herbarium (Ravenel, Fung. Car. Exs. 79) is not this species but *Sphaeria herculea* Schw., according to Ravenel.

Illustrations: Johnson. As cited above.
Lloyd. Myc. Works, pls. 12 and 40.

North Carolina. Wilmington. (Curtis Herb.)
Nag's Head. Around roots of black gum at edge of fresh water, Sept. 18, 1927. Coker and
Braxton, colls. (U. N. C. Herb., No. 8261).
South Carolina. Santee Canal. Ravenel, coll. (Curtis Herb.).
Alabama. Tuskegee. Beaumont, coll. (Curtis Herb.). Also from Alabama (in sphagnum swamp)
by Earle. (N. Y. Bot. Gard. Herb. and U. N. C. Herb.)

LYCOPERDACEAE

Fruit bodies exposed at all stages or subterranean until just before maturity. Peridium consisting of more than one layer (very obscure in *Calvatia rubro-flava*, and in some Lycoperdons where the outer layer may consist of only scattered particles or flakes). Gleba at maturity breaking down into a dry powder which contains the spores. Capillitium always present but sometimes (as in *Disciseda*) obscured by fragmentation after maturity. Basidia borne in a distinct hymenium surrounding small chambers or (in *Disciseda*) scattered in irregular groups without a distinctly organized hymenium or chambers. Basidia club-shaped with four (rarely fewer) spores borne on apical sterigmata; spores growing to full maturity on the basidia.

It will be noticed that this description does not include the genus *Arachnion*. We have found it impossible to retain it and have any character left to determine the Lycoperdaceae.

The lower part of the fruit body is often sterile and persistent and composed of larger compartments than the fertile part above. The former is called the subgleba and from it may extend up into the fertile tissue a more or less well developed column of sterile tissue called the columella. In most species the spores escape from a single, definite apical pore in the inner peridium. In *Myriostoma* there are several mouths, in *Disciseda* a basal mouth and in *Calvatia* no definite mouth, the whole upper part of the peridium flaking away. The family includes all the well known puffballs and earth stars. The larger puffballs when young and white (before the spores begin to ripen) are not only edible but very palatable and they should be much more used as food.

For literature see under the order (p. 194) and genera.

KEY TO THE GENERA

Fruit bodies small, densely clustered on a common, leathery subiculum covering the substratum
Diplocystis (West Indian) (p. 143)

Not as above
  Outer peridium (cortex) thin, mostly peeling off in flakes or wearing away; inner peridium thick, firm and corky when dry, opening from above by irregular flaps and fissures; capillitium of separate threads with thorny prickles and a few short branches..*Mycenastrum* (p. 101)
  Outer peridium thin, mostly peeling off in flakes; inner peridium opening by an apical pore, firm and resilient, retaining its form for some time after maturity; capillitium of smooth, separate threads with slender, pointed branches; mature plants loosened from place of growth and rolled about by the wind (the tumblers)...............*Bovista* (p. 97)
  Outer peridium thick or thin, scaling off in flakes or particles or wearing off by degrees or more or less persistent; inner peridium usually flaccid and collapsing or breaking up as the spores emerge; plants normally remaining attached to place of growth
    Capillitium of separate threads with slender, pointed branches............*Bovistella* (p. 94)
    Capillitium of long interwoven threads that are not separable into unbroken units (in the case of *Calvatia* breaking up into short pieces except in some specimens of *C. elata*)
      Peridium opening by a definite mouth...........................*Lycoperdon* (p. 69)
      Peridium irregularly ruptured by the scaling off of fragments above; plants large (at times small in *C. rubro-flava*). ....*Calvatia* (p. 59)

58

Outer peridium thick, splitting at maturity into star-like rays from above downward and remaining attached to the inner peridium by their united bases

Inner peridium with a single, apical mouth..............................*Geaster* (p. 102)

Inner peridium with several mouths and several pedicels..............*Myriostoma* (p. 138)

Outer peridium splitting horizontally around the middle, the upper part with the inner peridium attached breaking away and leaving the lower part in the ground as obscure fragments or an obvious cup..*Disciseda* (p. 139)

CALVATIA Fries

Plants large to very large, globose, flattened or pyriform, etc., with or without a thick, stalk-like, sterile base; cortex thin, even or areolated (absent in *C. rubro-flava*); inner peridium thin, delicate, not opening by a pore but falling away irregularly in scales and plates from above downward and exposing the densely woven capillitium composed of long, much branched threads which at maturity in most species are easily broken into short pieces; sterile base (nearly absent in *C. maxima*) concave above, persisting a long time as a cup-shaped remnant, easily distinguished from *Lycoperdon* by the irregular scaling away of the peridia at maturity, and in most species by the fragility of the capillitium.

The sterile base is in most species sharply delimited by a diaphragm, and in this case is obviously cellular. In *C. rubro-flava* and *C. maxima* there is no diaphragm and the sterile base is homogeneous at maturity.

The genus includes the large puffballs, one species (*C. maxima*) reaching the enormous width of three feet or even more. They are important sources of food and should be used whenever found in the young condition with white interior, but note that the edibility of *C. rubro-flava* is not known. A neighbor of ours had some cooked and reported that they were too bitter to eat. They may be poisonous. In regard to the edibility of puffballs, it is interesting to note that Porcher (Resources of Southern Fields and Forests, 2nd ed., p. 699. 1869) quotes a letter from Ravenel as follows:

"It has been mentioned by medical writers that the spores of the puffballs have narcotic properties, and it is an anaesthetic agent, acting somewhat like chloroform when inhaled, but I have never experienced any effects of the kind from its use as a vegetable. However, Dr. Harry Hammond, of Beech Island, S. C., writes to me, 'since writing to you, I and a number of others have made several meals on *Lycoperdon*, and I think I have discovered in myself well marked evidences of a narcotic influence— and two other experimenters have described similar sensations to me. I recollect also to have heard from Mr. Mahan that a friend of his, a physician in Georgia, had been seriously affected in this way by too large a meal on *Lycoperdon*.'"

From the context it would seem that the puffball referred to is not *C. maxima*, as stated, but *C. cyathiformis*, as the spores are spoken of as purplish. This note need not deter one from eating these puffballs, as they are among the most esteemed of edible fungi. The ripe contents of the larger puffballs have long had a reputation for stopping the flow of blood (see, e.g., Lind, Danish Fungi as Represented in the Herbarium of E. Rostrup, p. 401).

LITERATURE

Cunningham. Gasteromycetes of Australasia. The Genus *Calvatia*. Proc. Linn. Soc. N. S. W. **51:** 363, pls. 23, 24. 1926.

Lloyd. French Collections of *Calvatia*. Myc. Notes, p. 264. 1906.

Lloyd. Japanese Collections of *Calvatia*. Myc. Notes, p. 548. 1916.

Morgan. Journ. Cin. Soc. Nat. Hist. **12:** 165. 1890.

For other literature, see p. 194.

KEY TO THE SPECIES

Peridium apparently single, the outer peridium being represented by only a delicate furfurescence,
very thin; subgleba homogeneous at maturity; all parts turning yellow when bruised before
maturity; spores yellow-ochre in color.............................*C. rubro-flava* (p. 60)

Peridium single, or at least not separable into two distinct layers, thick; gleba bright olivaceous
*C. pachyderma***

Peridium double, outer layer thick, inner layer thin
Gleba olivaceous yellow...*C. lepidophorum***
Gleba purplish brown...*C. cretacea* (p. 66)

Peridium double and separable at maturity into a thin outer and a thicker inner layer; subgleba, if
present, chambered at all ages; not turning yellow when bruised; spore color purplish or brown
or olivaceous yellow
Plants very large, almost entirely filled with the gleba; sterile base nearly absent; mature gleba
greenish yellow...*C. maxima* (p. 62)
Plants rather small; subgleba nearly absent; mature gleba dark purplish; spores nearly smooth
C. fragilis (p. 64)

Plants large or moderately small; sterile subgleba large and persistent
Spore powder dark purplish; plants large; spores strongly warted......*C. cyathiformis* (p. 63)
Spore powder brown; plants rather small; spores minutely warted...........*C. elata* (p. 65)
Spore powder dull or bright olivaceous yellow; spores smooth or nearly so
Capillitium threads about as thick as the spores and with circular holes in them; spores
very small...*C. craniformis* (p. 67)
Capillitium threads much thicker than the spores and with long linear pits; spores larger
C. caelata (p. 68)

Calvatia rubro-flava (Cragin) Lloyd
C. aurea Lloyd

Plates 33, 34 and 112

Plants subglobose, flattened on top, 2–10 cm. wide by 1.5–5 cm. high, strongly
plicate beneath, usually with a short, abruptly pointed stalk which is centrally attached
by one or more slender root-like strands; usually nearly white when fresh and immature
with a faint tint of pink or lavender but varying to pinkish leather color, all parts
turning at once to brilliant yellow (about chrome yellow) upon rubbing or cutting,
drying orange or yellow orange to orange red or bay, in age becoming a metallic brown.
Peridium about 125–160μ thick when fresh, becoming very thin and papery on drying,
practically single layered, the outer layer being represented by only a delicate furfurescence, becoming smooth and shiny on exposure to weather, cracking up into irregular areas and falling away after drying. Gleba pure white when young and lined
with a hymenium as in *Lycoperdon;* the cavities very minute, up to about 0.2 mm.

* *Calvatia pachyderma* (Peck) Morgan and *C. lepidophorum* (Ellis) Lloyd are two western species which are sometimes
confused. Both have thick peridia but may easily be distinguished by the following characters: In the former the pale peridium
is smooth or with thin adherent, white patches and there are no separable layers, although the entire peridium is apt to be scissile
like short-cake; spores (in plant from type locality, collected by Pringle and determined by Peck) oval to elliptic, very finely
warted under high power (x 2160), 3.5–4 x 4.2–6μ, with a mucro or short pedicel; capillitium threads fragmented, strongly olivaceous yellow under microscope, irregular in thickness, rather frequently branched, pitted, up to 11μ thick in swollen places;
mature gleba bright olivaceous. In *C. lepidophorum* the outer peridium has an extremely thin, glazed surface marked with
inherent patches or rounded "bosses" but this is not separable. Beneath the thick outer peridium, unlike any other American
Calvatia, the gleba is covered by a thin, papery membrane and this is the character which most easily determines the species.
Spores spherical, distinctly warted, 4.2–6μ. Capillitium threads slender, fairly even, up to 5μ thick, brown, occasionally branched,
and not so sinuous as in *C. pachyderma*. The plant Morgan described as *C. pachyderma* is *C. lepidophorum*, as noted by Lloyd,
and not Peck's species. Lloyd proposed the genus *Hypoblema* for Ellis's *Lycoperdon lepidophorum* (Myc. Notes, p. 140) but later
reduced it to a subgenus of *Calvatia* (Footnote 13 to Index to vol. 2).

PLATE 34

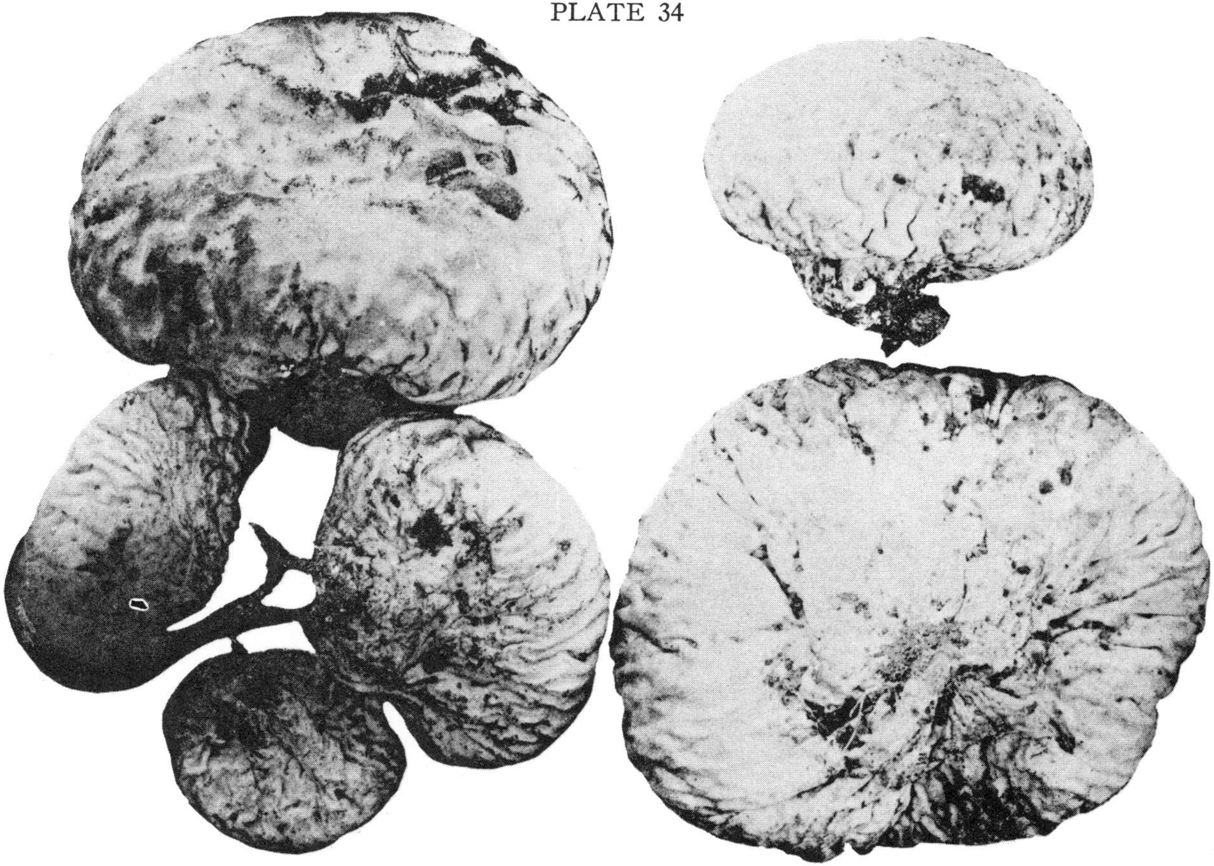

CALVATIA RUBRO-FLAVA. No. 7163

long in section, labyrinthiform, becoming larger and more indistinct as they pass into the subgleba, the cavities of which are up to about 1 mm. long, empty when young, but becoming loosely filled with soft, woven threads toward maturity so as to obscure their outlines. At full maturity this growth has in most cases entirely obliterated the outlines of the chambers and the subgleba is homogeneous. At times the original chamber wall may still be noticed, although the cavity is stuffed. This last condition is shown in one of the plants on pl. 33. Subgleba occupying a comparatively small part of the peridium, about 3 mm. to 2.5 cm. thick below, depending on the size of the stalk, but running as a thin layer far up around the sides of the gleba. Gleba and subgleba changing when cut or wounded from a pure white to a brilliant yellow, the color change appearing first in the subgleba and slowly spreading over its surface and then over the surface of the gleba. Gleba changing to honey yellow or Isabella color when fully ripe, the subgleba more brownish and often with a tint of chocolate. Glebal chambers usually incompletely breaking down, particularly in the region just beneath the peridium so that erosion is very slow, the gleba remaining as a soft, spongy mass like a powder puff for a long time after exposure. Taste pleasant and odor weak when fresh; a decidedly strong odor of old ham on drying.

Spores (of No. 7163) nearly yellow ochre, between that and buckthorn brown of Ridgway, spherical, very minutely rough even under high power (x 2160) with a hyaline outer membrane and a colored inner one, $3–4.4\mu$ thick, with a short pedicel. Basidia subglobose, about $6–8\mu$ thick, with 2–4 sterigmata. Capillitium threads up to 4.4μ thick, considerably septate, moderately thin-walled and remarkable in the frequent occurrence of distinct holes, $1–3\mu$ in diameter, in the walls, sinuous, usually breaking into short pieces when put under a cover glass.

This is certainly *C. aurea* Lloyd (Myc. Notes, p. 11) and it is probably true as Lloyd thinks that *C. rubro-flava* is the same (Myc. Notes, pp. 32, 90, 149). We have not seen any authentic material of the latter, but the description agrees. The species differs sharply from all other Calvatias in the single layered peridium and homogeneous subgleba at maturity. These characters are probably of enough importance to entitle the plant to a genus of its own. The long persistence of the soft gleba makes these very clean puffballs to handle, and is in sharp contrast to the easily fragmented and dirty habit of *C. caelata*, etc. A homogeneous subgleba at maturity is, so far as we know, found in no other puffball except *C. maxima*, *C. candida* and *Lycoperdon polymorphum* (*L. cepaeforme*). The present plant is in fact very closely related to *C. candida*, and Cunningham reduces it to a variety of that species. The striking color and the remarkable color change of fresh plants when injured lead us to retain it as a species, at least until more is known of *C. candida* in the fresh condition. The latter is not known to occur in America. A peculiarity of the color change when a fresh young plant is rubbed is that the bright yellow color persists only for a few minutes, then fades away to the original tint.

The species seems confined in our country to cultivated soil, and this suggests that it is an introduction, probably from South America. It is reported by Lloyd from Alabama, Missouri, Ohio, Indiana, Washington, D. C., and Connecticut, and we are adding several other stations. Cragin's plant was found in Kansas. Our record is the first for this state. It is also reported from Brazil, Bolivia, Australia, and Japan.

Illustrations: Lloyd. Myc. Illustrations, No. 22 (as *C. aurea*).

7107. On a lawn, Sept. 2, 1923. Spores minutely rough, $3.5–4.4\mu$.
7154. Under an arbor among flowers, The Rocks, Sept. 26, 1923. Spores $3–4.2\mu$ thick.

7163. On the ground in a corn field, Sept. 27, 1923.

7242. Same location as No. 7163, Feb. 15, 1924. This winter collection was less red than the others.

Louisiana. (N. Y. B. G. Herb. No data or name).

Virginia. Blacksburg. Murrill, coll. (N. Y. B. G. Herb.).

New York. New York Botanical Garden, in a dahlia bed. Miss Eaton, coll. (N. Y. B. G. Herb.).

Illinois. Urbana. McDougall, coll. (U. N. C. Herb.).

Missouri. St. Louis. Trelease, coll. (N. Y. B. G. Herb., as *Lycoperdon delicatum*). Spores nearly smooth, 3.5–4μ thick, often with a short pedicel. Capillitium threads slender, 2–3.7μ thick with holes in the walls.

Jamaica. Cinchona. On a dry bank. Murrill, coll. (N. Y. B. G. Herb.).

Brazil. Rick, coll. (U. N. C. Herb.). Spores apparently smooth, 3.4–4μ, with a mucro.

Calvatia maxima (Schaeff.) Morgan
>   *Lycoperdon giganteum* Batsch
>   *Lycoperdon bovista* Linn.

Plate 112

We take the following description from Morgan (l. c., p. 166):

"Peridium very large, globose, depressed-globose or obovoid, with a thick cord-like root. Cortex a flocculose or nearly smooth continuous layer, very thin and fragile, white or grayish, changing to yellowish, drying up and becoming brown, remaining closely adherent to the inner peridium or sometimes peeling off in patches; inner peridium thin and very fragile, after maturity gradually breaking up into fragments and falling away. Subgleba very shallow or quite obsolete, when present said to be compact and not cellular; mass of spores and capillitium greenish yellow, then brownish olivaceous; the threads very long, frequently septate, branched, the primary branches much thicker than the spores, the ultimate ones more slender; spores globose, even or sometimes very minutely warted, 3.5–4.5μ in diameter, often with a minute pedicel."

We have examined a specimen from Madison, Wisconsin, and find the spores to be smooth, subspherical, 3.5–4μ thick, with a short pedicel and a distinct oil drop; capillitium threads easily fragmented, occasionally branched, about 5.5μ thick.

It is surprising that we have not found this huge puffball in Chapel Hill, nor has Beardslee found it at Asheville. Both Schweinitz and Curtis report it, the former saying that it may reach a breadth of three feet, but his finding it in this state is doubtful as the *Bovista gigantea* of his herbarium is *Calvatia cyathiformis* (also noted by Lloyd, p. 396). It occurs in meadows and is excellent food. In American Naturalist (**18**: 530. 1884) Professor C. E. Bessey records a specimen of the giant puffball found by Professor R. E. Call in Herkimer County, N. Y., in 1877, that was 5 ft. 4 in. x 4 ft. 6 in. x 9½ in. This, says Professor Bessey, is by far the largest on record. Buller (Researches on Fungi, p. 85) has estimated that a large fruit body of this species (40 x 28 x 20 cm.) contained over seven trillion spores.

The species is said by Dearness to be fairly common in Ontario.

Illustrations: Batsch. Elench. Fung., pl. 29, fig. 165.
>   Berkeley. Ann. Sci. Nat., 2nd ser., 12: pl. 2, figs. 7–14. 1839.
>   Boudier. Icon. Myc., pls. 188 and 189 (as *Lycoperdon bovista*).
>   Gibson. Our Edible Toadstools and Mushrooms, pl. 34. 1895.
>   Hard. Mushrooms, pl. 57 and fig. 455.

PLATE 35

CALVATIA CYATHIFORMIS. No. 550. About four-fifths natural size

PLATE 36

CALVATIA CYATHIFORMIS.   No. 7162

Hollos. l. c., pl. 12, figs. 4–6.
Krieger. Nat. Geog. Mag. 37: 415. 1920.
Murrill. Mycologia 6: pl. 126. 1914.
Nees von Esenbeck. Syst. Pilze Schw., pl. 11, fig. 124C.
Patterson and Charles. U. S. Dept. Agric. Bull. 175: pl. 38, fig. 2 (as *C. gigantea*). 1915; also
  Farmers' Bull. No. 796, fig. 18 (as *C. gigantea*). 1917.
Schaeffer. Fung. Bavar., pl. 191.
Sorokine. Rev. Myc. 1890, pl. 26, fig. 360.
Taylor. Food Products I, fig. 11. 1894.

Wisconsin. (Univ. Wis. Herb. and U. N. C. Herb.) Spores smooth, subspherical, 3.5–4μ, with a short
pedicel. Capillitium fragmenting, occasionally branched, frequently pitted, up to 5.5μ.

Calvatia cyathiformis (Bosc) Morg.
Lycoperdon cyathiforme Bosc
Bovista lilacina Berk. & Mont.

Plates 35, 36 and 112

Plants nearly globose or turbinate, 7.5–15 cm. thick, attached below by a short
root; cortex smooth or slightly scaly, the upper part often cracking into areas. Inner
peridium thin and delicate, at maturity scaling away by degrees together with the
cortex to expose the dark purple interior; lower, sterile part (subgleba) remaining intact
as a persistent, dark, cup-like base which may remain in place over winter. Gleba at
first white, then changing through yellow to deep purple brown as the plant matures.
Spores (of No. 550) globose, with numerous distinct spines, 4.4–6.5μ thick, excluding the spines. Capillitium threads up to 4.3μ thick, very long, sparingly branched,
interwoven, considerably septate and breaking into sections at the septa, walls with
minute pits which are not easily visible except under high power.

The species is common in Chapel Hill from July to late autumn in open places,
uncultivated fields, lawns and orchards. When it is young and the inside white it is
excellent food when fried like an egg plant.

Some interesting facts concerning this *Calvatia* have been brought out in a study by
Shantz and Piemeisel (Journ. Agric. Research 11, No. 5: 191. 1917). They find that
the so-called "fairy rings" caused by this fungus advance about 24 cm. a year. One
ring has been found which is estimated to be 420 years old. The grass is stimulated
just behind the fruiting bodies of the ring, and forms a deeply colored, luxuriant growth,
whereas it is dry, often dead over the mycelium of *Agaricus tabularia* and *Marasmius
oreades* and shows a luxuriant growth on both sides. When disturbed, as by being
plowed up, the rings cease to fruit, and cannot be detected in vegetation, while in the
closely related species, *C. polygonia*, they continue to grow and fruit, as is also the case
with *Agaricus tabularia*.

Cunningham considers *C. novae-zelandiae* Lév. an additional synonym for this
species (Trans. N. Z. Inst. 57: 191. 1926).

Illustrations: Cunningham. Trans. N. Z. Inst. 57: pl. 2, fig. 3 (as *C. lilacina*). 1926.
  Hard. Mushrooms, pl. 58 and fig. 457 (as *C. lilacina*).
  Hollos. l. c., pl. 13, pl. 14, figs. 1–5, pl. 29, fig. 7.
  Krieger. Nat. Geog. Mag. 37: 416. 1920.
  Lloyd. The Lycoperdaceae of Australia, etc., pl. 35, fig. 1.
  Murrill. Mycologia 1: pl. 15, fig. 1. 1909.
  Sweetzer. Univ. Oregon Leaflet, Bot. Ser. No. 9, fig. 3.

550. On campus, Oct. 10, 1912.

556. On a lawn, May 18, 1912.   Spores distinctly warted but still immature, 4–5.5μ thick.

672. Among broomsedge on a hillside, Sept. 18, 1908.

3229. In a pasture, Feb. 25, 1919.   Plant practically gone except for the sterile base.   Spores distinctly spiny, 4.4–6μ.

6044. In open, grassy place, Jan. 10, 1923.   Plant with no sterile base.   Spores with distinct warts, 4.8–6.2μ thick.

   Asheville.   Beardslee.

Florida.   Weber, coll. (U. N. C. Herb.).

Alabama.   Auburn.   Earle, coll. (N. Y. B. G. Herb.).

Kentucky.   Crittenden.   Lloyd, coll. (N. Y. B. G. Herb.).

Virginia.   Blacksburg.   Murrill, coll. (N. Y. B. G. Herb.).

District of Columbia.   Cook, coll. (U. S. Nat'l. Herb.).

New Jersey.   Newfield.   Ellis, coll. (N. Y. B. G. Herb.).

New York.   Peck, coll. (N. Y. B. G. Herb.).

Wisconsin.   Vilas Woods.   (U. N. C. Herb.)   Spores apparently immature, some distinctly warted others less so, 4.4–4.8μ, often up to 6.8μ.

South Dakota.   Huron.   Miss Crouch, coll. (N. Y. B. G. Herb.).   Spores distinctly warted, 4.5–6.2μ thick, sometimes pedicellate.   Capillitium threads up to 5.5μ thick, sometimes irregular and up to 10μ thick in swollen places, fragmented with ends often closed.

Canada.   Melbourne, London, Vauxhall Bridge.   Dearness, coll. (Dearness Herb.).   Said by Dearness to be common in Ontario.

Calvatia fragilis (Vitt.) Morgan

Plates 37 and 112

Fruit body obovate, up to 5.5 cm. thick (in our collections), the base abruptly contracted to a blunt point; cortex thin, separable, brownish to straw color, the surface minutely felted to smooth and usually areolated or pitted (in a form quite smooth), the larger depressions usually with a central flat, purplish brown scale with the edges more or less free; inner peridium deep purplish brown in section, about 0.7 mm. thick, brittle and breaking away by degrees in irregular fragments from the top downward. Gleba at maturity deep purplish brown, soft but not very powdery and not falling out easily as in *C. caelata*.   Subgleba often almost absent, at times more obvious when the base is pointed, brown, the cavities very small and obscure.

Spores (of No. 4783) dark brownish purple, spherical, smooth or minutely warted, 3.7–4.6μ, rarely 5.4μ thick.   Capillitium of short segments, irregular, sinuous, 3.5–6μ thick, pits very minute and not easily visible except under high power (just like the capillitium of *C. cyathiformis*).

This species is distinguished from *C. cyathiformis* by its small base with very little subgleba, the smaller size of the plants, and the nearly smooth spores which are of smaller average size.   *Calvatia caelata* is of course separated by its gleba color and by the much thicker and peculiarly pitted capillitium.   The surface appearance of the typical form of the present species is almost exactly like Lloyd's figs. 2 and 4 and, in part, fig. 3 of plate 36 of *C. caelata* and form, but that is, of course, excluded by the purplish spores of our plants.

Calvatia pachyderma differs distinctly in the olive brown or buffy brown gleba, homogeneous but scissile peridium of uniform color throughout and without a sharply contrasting cortex, and in the average larger size of the capillitium.

PLATE 37

CALVATIA FRAGILIS. Urbana, Illinois [above]; London, Can. [below]

PLATE 38

CALVATIA ELATA. Connecticut

Our description is from the Canadian plants listed below. A plant from Colorado is quite similar to these, except that the areolations above are very pronounced, so that the tendency is for each areolation to break away separately, bringing its part of the inner peridium with it. The smooth form mentioned above is represented by plants from Kansas and Nebraska entered below. The peridium is quite smooth, tan to brownish tan; all forms are otherwise the same.

Illinois. Urbana. McDougall, coll. (U. N. C. Herb.). Spores minutely warted, 3.5–4.5μ.
Kansas. Rooks Co. On open prairie. Bartholomew, coll. (U. N. C. Herb.).
    Also a Kansas plant from Cragin, No. 522. (N. Y. B. G. Herb. and U. N. C. Herb.) Spores minutely rough, 4.5–5.8μ.
Nebraska. Long Pine. Bates, coll. No. 486. (N. Y. B. G. Herb. and U. N. C. Herb.) Spores smooth with a mucro, 4–5.5μ. Capillitium threads sinuous, 2–4μ thick.
Colorado. Bethel, coll. (N. Y. B. G. Herb., as *C. pachyderma*, and U. N. C. Herb.). Spores purple, minutely warted, 4.5–6μ thick. Capillitium threads about 5μ thick, in fragments with ends usually closed.
Wyoming. Pitchfork. Davis, coll. (U. N. C. Herb. from N. Y. B. G. Herb., labelled *C. lilacina* var. *occidentalis*). Spores nearly smooth, 4–5.5μ, rarely up to 7μ, no pedicel.
Canada. London. Dearness, No. 4783 Font. (Dearness Herb. and U. N. C. Herb.) Also another collection by Dearness from London. (N. Y. B. G. Herb. and U. N. C. Herb.) Spores nearly smooth, 3.7–4.5μ thick.

Calvatia elata (Massee) Morgan

Plates 26, 38 and 112

Plants small for this genus, with a distinct, usually long, subcylindrical, often pitted stalk up to 4 cm. thick and 8.5 cm. long (rarely longer) and a subglobose head about 3–6 cm. thick; color when mature pale brown to leather color; cortex only a very thin granular or powdery, persistent layer that is almost absent on the stalk below; inner peridium thin and at maturity very fragile, soon cracking up into fragments and falling away or adhering for awhile to the capillitium. Gleba brown; the subgleba of the stalk with distinct empty chambers of fair size.

Spores (of plant from Litchfield, Conn.) spherical, very minutely warted, short-pedicellate, 3.5–4.4μ. Capillitium threads much fragmented, moderately pitted, up to 5μ thick.

The species was described by Massee as *Lycoperdon elatum* from New England plants in the Berkeley Herbarium, where it was included as *L. saccatum*. We have seen a good example of *C. saccata* from England (N. Y. Bot. Garden, from Cooke) and find that the spores are larger and rougher than in our *C. elata* (distinctly warted, 4.5–5.5μ), thus confirming Morgan's statement to that effect. As in so many other cases, these differences are hardly more than in regional forms of the same species. Hollos considers *C. elata* a variety of *C. saccata*.

The two Canadian plants entered below are like each other in every particular except that the capillitium in one plant was unbranched, in the other freely branched. In both plants the capillitium was less fragmented than in other specimens we have seen. One of the plants had previously been sent to Lloyd and determined by him as *C. saccata*.

This species is in the *craniformis* group, and seems nearest that species. It differs in smaller size, a proportionately longer stem, darker color of mature gleba, and in larger and minutely roughened spores. It seems also near *L. muscorum* and in certain respects resembles *L. gemmatum*. See these species for further discussion.

Illustrations: Hollos. l. c., pl. 17, figs. 3–5.
    Lloyd. Genera of Gasteromycetes, pl. 10, fig. 48.
    Massee. Journ. Roy. Mic. Soc., 1887, pl. 13, figs. 13–15.
    Morgan. Journ. Cin. Soc. Nat. Hist. 12: pl. 16, fig. 7.
Illustrations of *C. saccata:* Hollos. l. c., pl. 16.
    Krombholz. Abbild., pl. 30, figs. 11, 12.

New York. Peck, coll. (N. Y. B. G. Herb., as *L. saccatum*).
Connecticut. Litchfield. Miss White, coll. (N. Y. Bot. Gard. Herb. and U. N. C. Herb.).
Massachusetts. Waltham. Reported by Lloyd in Genera of Gasteromycetes, p. 12.
Ontario. Byron. Dearness, coll. Two plants. No. 2843 H. (U. N. C. Herb.). Spores minutely
    warted, short-pedicellate, 3.7–5μ. Capillitium threads not breaking up into short pieces,
    pitted, sinuous in places, up to 9μ thick. No. 4825/2843. (Dearness Herb.).

Calvatia cretacea (Berk.) Lloyd
    Lycoperdon cretaceum Berk.
    C. borealis Th. Fries

Plate 112

Peridium subglobose to flattened, plicate below, the base pinched to a small point
which is lightly attached by white mycelium, 2.5–5 cm. broad; cortex conspicuous, white
then buffy to ochraceous, composed of a continuous coat which consists above of thick
compound warts with connivent tips, becoming smoother downward and fading to a
mealy furfurescence below, or in some cases much smoother above and resembling the
smoother forms of *Scleroderma aurantium;* in all cases cracking into irregular areas or
groups of warts much as in *Lycoperdon marginatum* and falling away by degrees to expose
the thin, shining, silvery brown to chocolate colored inner peridium which falls away in
flakes from above downward.   Gleba passing through golden olive to chocolate brown,
the subgleba small, chocolate brown or the basal part white, the chambers obvious,
but not large.

Spores (of plant from Lapland) spherical, greenish yellow under the microscope,
minutely but distinctly warted, the warts embedded in a hyaline coat, 4.2–5.5μ, rarely
6.8μ, with one strong oil drop and sometimes a mucro.   Capillitium threads fragmented,
color of spores, often wavy, rarely branched, much pitted, 3–7μ thick.

This arctic species is strongly characterized by its thick, deciduous cortex and
purplish brown gleba.   It was first described from Bellot Island, and has since been
reported from Lapland by Th. C. E. Fries (as *C. borealis;* Zur Kenntnis der Gasteromyceten flora in Torne Lappmark, p. 238.   1914) and from Herschel Island, Kay
Point, Mackenzie River Delta, and Bernard Harbor by Mr. John Dearness (Rept.
Canadian Arctic Exp. 1913–18, 4, Part C: 17.   1923).   We have two good collections
from Lapland made by us in 1921, and these show the variation in the cortex mentioned
above.   Lloyd (Myc. Notes, p. 650) suggests that *C. arctica* Ferdinandsen and Winge
(Meddelelser om Groenland **43:** 144, pl. 9.   1910; see Saccardo, Sylloge **21:** 480)
may be the same and in this he is followed by Fries (Arkiv f. Botanik **17**, No. 9: 23.
1921).   We think it very probable that this supposition will finally prove to be correct.
The illustrations of *C. arctica* show stouter warts than are recorded for *C. cretacea*
(up to 8 mm. thick at least in one plant) and little or no chocolate color is shown in the
gleba.   However, in the discussion Ferdinandsen says the gleba is "grayish chocolate-
brown."   The larger warts may easily be a variation within the species.   The long
sterigmata described in *C. arctica* are a remarkable peculiarity, but this does not

PLATE 39

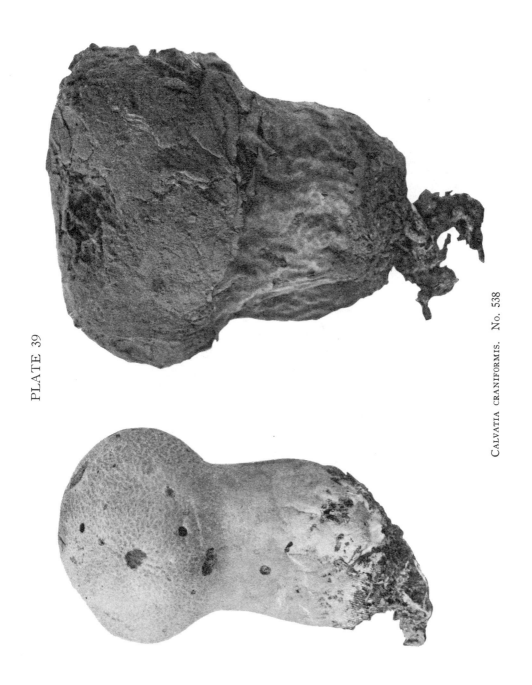

CALVATIA CRANIFORMIS.   No. 538

PLATE 40

CALVATIA CAELATA. Pawling, N. Y.

exclude *C. cretacea*, as its basidia have not been studied. Our material does not show them.

Illustrations: Fries. As cited above.
  Lloyd. Myc. Notes, p. 650, fig. 929.

Canadian Arctic. Bernard Harbor. Johansen, coll. (Dearness Herb. and U. N. C. Herb.) Spores
  distinctly warted, 4.2–6.5μ. Capillitium threads up to 11μ thick.
Swedish Lapland. Abisco. Coker, coll. (U. N. C. Herb.). One of these two collections had spores
  very minutely warted, less so than in the other, apiculate, spherical to subspherical, 4.5–6μ.
  Capillitium threads up to 7.5μ thick.

Calvatia craniformis (Schw.) Fr.
  Lycoperdon delicatum B. & C. (Not *L. delicatum* Berk.)
  L. Missouriense Trelease

Plates 39 and 112

Plant large, up to 9 cm. thick, obovoid or top-shaped, the thick, stalk-like base rounded below and attached by fibrous strands; cortex very thin, papery, smooth, nearly glabrous to delicately furfuraceous, pale tan or grayish in color, at maturity scaling off in areas; inner peridium also thin and fragile, yellowish to reddish, the upper part cracking into plates and scaling off after the cortex peels. Subgleba occupying the stalk-like base, of honeycomb structure and quite spongy, concave above and long persistent. Gleba white, then greenish yellow or soiled ochraceous in color.

Spores (of No. 538) spherical, smooth, with a distinct mucro or short pedicel, 2.8–3.9μ thick. Capillitium slightly branched, sparingly septate, walls with numerous pits, possibly holes in them which are 1–3μ in diameter, easily breaking up, usually at these pits; average thickness of main threads 3.5μ.

Unlike *C. cyathiformis*, this species inhabits wooded places or shrubby borders of paths or walls, and is much less abundant, though not at all rare. It, too, is a palatable and valued food. It is easily distinguished by the greenish yellow rather than purple spore mass. The type in the Schweinitz Herbarium is a fine example of the species. The spores are smooth, 3.2–3.6μ thick.

In referring to *C. craniformis* on p. 100, Hollos is confused. The *L. delicatum* that Lloyd says is the same as *C. craniformis* is evidently from the context the *delicatum* of Berkeley and Curtis from Pennsylvania, not of Berkeley from India, etc. (*L. Berkeleyi* De Toni). In his reference to *L. delicatum* on p. 153 of Myc. Notes, Lloyd makes the double error of confusing Morgan's treatment of what he took to be *L. delicatum* Berk. with the B. & C. species and further of accusing Morgan of having no conception of *L. delicatum* B. & C., when Morgan stated thirteen years earlier (Journ. Cin. Soc. of Nat. Hist. **12**: 171. 1890) the same thing that Lloyd here announces in italics, i.e., that *L. delicatum* B. & C. is the same as *C. craniformis*. It seems well established that *L. Missouriense* Trelease (see Sacc. Syll. **9**: p. 277) is also the same as *C. craniformis*, (Morgan, l. c.). For explanation of Cooke's mistake in thinking it *C. lilacina* see Lloyd, Myc. Notes, p. 308.

Illustrations: Hard. Mushrooms, pl. 60 and fig. 461.
  Krieger. Nat. Geog. Mag. 37: 419. 1920.
  Marshall. Mushroom Book, pl. opposite p. 126.

538. Near rock wall in Episcopal churchyard, October 9, 1912.
676. Battle's Park, just east of campus, September 19, 1908.
1535. In woods, Battle's Park, summer of 1915. Spores smooth, 3–3.8μ.

Alabama.   (Curtis Herb.)
      Auburn.   Earle, coll. (N. Y. B. G. Herb.).
Texas.   Long, coll. (N. Y. B. G. Herb.).
Virginia.   Blacksburg.   Murrill, coll. (N. Y. B. G. Herb.).
Maryland.   Agric. College.   James, coll. (U. S. Nat'l. Herb.).
Delaware.   Mt. Cuba.   Commons, coll. (N. Y. B. G. Herb.).
Pennsylvania.   (Curtis Herb.)
      Also Gentry, coll. (N. Y. B. G. Herb.).
New Jersey.   Ballou, coll. (N. Y. B. G. Herb.).
New York.   (Curtis Herb.)
Wisconsin.   (Curtis Herb.)
Ohio.   Morgan, coll. (N. Y. B. G. Herb.).
Illinois.   Urbana.   McDougall, coll. (U. N. C. Herb.).   Spores smooth, 3.2–3.8μ.

Calvatia caelata (Bull.) Morg.

Plates 40 and 112

Plant large to very large, sterile base ample, either long and cylindrical or shorter and tapering to the pointed base; cortex a flocculent layer which is thicker above and there usually areolated into more or less prominent warts, thinner downward, but with a tendency throughout to form more or less stellate, flattish areas; color whitish, then pallid yellowish to brownish.   Inner peridium thin, breaking up into fragments at the top, then downward, exposing the bright olivaceous gold to brownish olivaceous gleba, which is very fragile and powdery.   Sterile base persistent, up to 9.5 cm. thick and 10 cm. high, furrowed below and pinched to a point; the chambers of the subgleba distinct, empty and moderately large, extending up the sides for several centimeters as a tapering margin to the cup.

Spores (of the plant from Pawling, New York) spherical, smooth, with a short mucro and distinct oil drop, 3.8–4.5μ.   Capillitium threads up to 17μ thick, usually 7–11μ, somewhat branched, easily breaking up at maturity; walls with narrow (about 1μ wide), linear, sinuous pits.

This is a northern and middle western species and so far as we know has not been collected in the southeastern states.   Specimens we have seen are from New York and Canada.   Curtis reports *Lyc. caelatum* from this state (Cat'l., p. 110), but there is no reason to think that his plant was correctly determined.   *Calvatia caelata* is not represented in his herbarium, but *C. craniformis*, which he does not report, is found there under the name of *L. delicatum* B. & C.   The species is well marked and very easily recognized by the fibrous or flocculent covering, separated into warts or stellate areas, and by the very characteristic thick capillitium with its conspicuous, linear pits.   For treatment of this species see Morgan, Journ. Cin. Soc. Nat. Hist. **12**: 169; also Lloyd, Myc. Notes, p. 166 and Lycoperd. Austr., p. 35.   Lloyd's magnified figure of the cortex is good.

The plant is most like *C. craniformis* in size, shape, and color of gleba, and in the northern states it seems largely to take the place of that species; in the south *C. craniformis* is very common, while in the north it is certainly rare.

Cunningham gives the following list of synonyms for this species: *L. Fontanesii* Dur. et Mont.; *L. favosum* Bon.; *L. Sinclairii* Berk.; *C. favosa* (Bon.) Lloyd.   (Trans. N. Z. Inst. **57**: 190.   1926.)

For cytological information by Maire covering this and other species, see under *Scleroderma aurantium*.

Illustrations: Bulliard. Herb. Fr., pl. 430.
  Cunningham. Trans. N. Z. Inst. **57**: pl. 1, fig. 1. 1926.
  Hollos. l. c., pl. 15, figs. 1–12.
  Krombholz. Abbild., pl. 30, figs. 7–10.
  Lloyd. Myc. Works, pl. 36.
  Lloyd. Lycoperdaceae of Australia, etc., fig. 39.
  Lloyd. Photogravure of Am. Fungi, No. 22.
  Schaeffer. Fung. Bavar., pl. 189.

New York. Pawling. Dr. H. S. Robinson, coll. (N. Y. Bot. Gard. Herb. and U. N. C. Herb.).
Wisconsin. Sheboygan. Brown, coll. (N. Y. Bot. Gard. Herb.).
Dakota. Huron. Miss Crouch, coll. (N. Y. Bot. Gard. Herb.).
Colorada. Denver. Bethel, coll. (N. Y. B. G. Herb.).
Canada. Ontario. Ottawa Valley. Dearness, coll. (Dearness Herb., No. 4783 od'l).

LYCOPERDON Tourn.

Plants comparatively small, globose, obovoid, top-shaped or pyriform; the base in nearly all of our species filled with a sterile, honeycomb tissue (subgleba); cortex sometimes smooth but usually composed of a coat of spines, scales, warts, or scurf, the spines frequently converging at their apices to form stellate groups. Inner peridium thin, papery and flaccid, opening by a definite apical mouth and collapsing more or less as the spores escape. Gleba composed of minute chambers which are lined with the hymenium, white when young, changing as the plant ripens through yellowish or olive to brown or purplish. Capillitium well developed, composed of long, branched or unbranched interwoven threads which are continuous with the inner peridium and the subgleba. From the center of the subgleba the threads may extend upward in such a thick fascicle as to form a more or less conspicuous column called the columella. Subgleba in most species obvious and "cellular" in structure, that is, composed of small or rather large empty chambers. Spores globose or rarely elliptical, commonly warted or spiny, in most species with a short or long pedicel. Basidia short and plump with four slender, apical sterigmata that are usually of unequal length (2–3-spored forms are said to occur).

In *L. polymorphum*, the subgleba is not cellular but formed of homogeneous tissue. In *L. pusillum* it is lacking. In some species a distinct homogeneous diaphragm very similar in structure to the inner peridium separates the subgleba from the fertile tissue; in other cases the two may merge imperceptibly into each other. For the development of *Lycoperdon depressum* in the diaphragm group, see Rabinowitsch (l.c.); for the group without diaphragm, see Bonorden. In his paper on the development of *L. depressum* (l. c.) Cunningham says:

"About the time of the commencement of the breaking-up of the tramal plates, hyphae from the endoperidium (of the capillitium type, being thick-walled and sparingly branched) grow out from the endoperidium into the cavity of the gleba, following for the most part the inner portions of the glebal plates. They develop in large numbers, so that soon the whole cavity of the gleba becomes filled with them."

Though he does not say so in so many words, it is evident that he means that these are the capillitium threads and that such is their origin. So far as we know this has not been brought out before. As to the cytology, he finds that the cells of the fruit body are probably binucleate, that there is a nuclear fusion followed by two divisions in the basidium, one going into each of the spores and there dividing, so that the mature spores are binucleate.

A genus of numerous species of small plants that grow on earth or rotten wood, or rarely on moss or the bark of living trees. Unless found in large groups, which often happens with *L. pyriforme*, the plants are too small to be of much value as food. In addition to the species treated, *L. muscorum*, which Hollos thinks is the same as *L. pseudoradicans* Lloyd, should be found here in dense moss beds, as Lloyd's plant has been collected in Virginia. In a group by itself is the very remarkable *Lycoperdon sculptum* found by Harkness in the mountains of California. It is covered with massive pyramidal warts up to 4 cm. broad and 3 cm. high (see Bull. Cal. Acad. Sci. **3**: 160, pl. 1. 1885).

LITERATURE

Bambeke.   De la valeur de l'épispore pour determination et le groupement des espèces du genre *Lycoperdon*. Bull. Soc. Myc. Fr. **22**: 1. 1906.
Bonorden.   Die Gattungen *Bovista, Lycoperdon* u. ihr Bau. Bot. Zeit. **15**: 593, 609, 625. 1857.
Cunningham.   Development of *Lycoperdon depressum*. New Zealand Journ. Sci. and Tech. **8**: 228, figs. 1–7. 1926.
Cunningham.   Lycoperdaceae of New Zealand. Trans. N. Z. Inst. **57**: 187. 1926.
Cunningham.   The Genus *Lycoperdon*. Proc. Linn. Soc. N. S. W. **51**: 627. 1926.
Hollos.   l. c., p. 90.
Lloyd.   The Genus *Lycoperdon* in Europe. Myc. Notes No. 19. 1905.
Lloyd.   The Lycoperdons of the United States. Myc. Notes No. 20. 1905.
Massee.   Monograph of the Genus *Lycoperdon*. Journ. Roy. Mic. Soc., p. 701, pls. 12, 13. 1887.
Massee.   l. c., p. 66.
Morgan.   Journ. Cin. Soc. Nat. Hist. **14**: 5. 1891.
Peck.   New York Species of *Lycoperdon*. Rept. N. Y. St. Mus. **32**: 58. 1879.
Peck.   United States Species of *Lycoperdon*. Trans. Albany Inst. **9**: 285. 1879.
Petri.   Flora Italica Cryptogama (Gasterales), Fasc. 5, p. 34. 1909.
Rabinowitsch.   Beiträge zur Entwickelungsgeschichte der Fruchtkörper einiger Gastromyceten. Flora **79**: 385, pls. 10 and 11. 1894.
Trelease.   Morels and Puffballs of Madison, Wis. Trans. Wis. Acad. Sci., Arts and Letters **7**: 105. 1888.
Tulasne, L. R. and Ch.   De la Fructification des *Scleroderma* comparée a celle des *Lycoperdon* et des *Bovista*. Ann. Sci. Nat., 2nd. ser., **17**: 5, pls. 1, 2. 1842.

KEY TO THE SPECIES

Mature spore-mass with a purplish tint (grayish purple or purplish brown)
  Cortex composed of very slender hairlike spicules among granules........ *L. atropurpureum* (p. 71)
  Cortex composed of very long spines convergent in groups at their apices
    Spines pale at maturity and, on falling off leaving the inner peridium smooth and unreticulated
      L. pulcherrimum (p. 72)
    Spines dark brown at maturity and, on falling off leaving the peridium reticulated with minute granules..*L. echinatum* (p. 73)
  Cortex a smooth, continuous layer which breaks up into very thin scales....*L. rimulatum* (p. 75)
  Cortex thick with spongy patches on a granular membrane which peels off at maturity
      L. subvelatum (p. 76)
  Cortex a scurfy or granular, persistent coat, at times mixed with very fine spines
      L. umbrinum (p. 76)
Mature spore-mass olive-brown
  Growing on the bark of living trees or rarely on logs; plant very small.....*L. acuminatum* (p. 78)

Growing on dead wood (rarely on earth)

 Plants pyriform, usually crowded, surface nearly smooth..............*L. pyriforme* (p. 79)

 Plants subglobose, rarely touching; the surface of the peridium becoming marked with distinct pits like a thimble.....................................*L. subincarnatum* (p. 80)

Growing among mosses in meadows and pastures

 Plants distinctly stalked, cortex of minute granular warts and particles..*L. muscorum* (p. 81)

Growing on the ground or rotting leaves (rarely on rotten wood)

 Plants of medium size, rarely below 2 cm. thick; subgleba usually well developed; plants not crowded

  Subgleba at maturity apparently homogeneous, the minute chambers invisible except with a lens...*L. polymorphum* (p. 92)

                  and *L. coloratum* (p. 93)

  Subgleba with obvious chambers

   Cortex of stout, terete, separate spines, mingled with shorter wart-like ones; surface reticulated when larger spines fall................*L. gemmatum* (p. 82)

   Cortex of pyramidal spines up to 1.5 mm. long which are arranged in groups with the tips united, and which in our form are lavender when fresh; spores without a long pedicel, 3.7–4.4μ thick......................*L. Peckii* (p. 84)

   Cortex of very slender spines which are single or grouped and convergent at the apex, and which fall away with age and leave a smooth, shining surface to the inner peridium

    Spines up to 1 mm. long, rather pale; spores with a long persistent pedicel, 4–5 times as long as the diameter of the spore...*L. pedicellatum* (p. 85)

    Spines up to 1 mm. long, brown to deep brown at maturity; spores elliptic, 4.3–5 x 5–6.5μ...............................*L. eximium* (p. 86)

    Spines up to 0.5 mm. long, deep brown to black at maturity; easily falling off; spores spherical, 4–4.8μ thick....................*L. fuscum* (p. 87)

   Cortex a dense coat of short, sharp spines which largely cohere in groups at their tips, the soft tissue supporting them breaking up at maturity into large flakes which fall away above, exposing the inner peridium, which is dull and furfuraceous with minute scales until weathered

                 L. marginatum (p. 87)

   Cortex as above, but each fascicle of spines falling off singly or in small groups from above downward.................*L. marginatum*, form of woods (p. 87)

   Cortex of minute spinules and granules or scurfy scales which slowly wear away

                 L. umbrinum (p. 76)

 Plants small, rarely up to 2 cm. thick; subgleba scanty or almost absent

  Cortex of rather persistent, crowded spines; plants often crowded.....*L. Curtisii* (p. 89)

  Cortex a thin, whitish, scurfy coat, remaining as persistent scales or minute warts upon the pale brown surface of the inner peridium

   Spores short-elliptic to subglobose, smooth....................*L. oblongisporum* (p. 91)

   Spores globose, minutely asperulate or varying to smooth..........*L. pusillum* (p. 91)

Mature spore-mass brown or gray-brown, etc., with no distinct tint of purple or olive (this includes certain specimens of species included in the other two sections).

 Growing on the ground; cortex of minute, soft granules and spicules........*L. umbrinum* (p. 76)

 Growing on wood (very rarely on earth); cortex of minute, harsh warts......*L. pyriforme* (p. 79)

Lycoperdon atropurpureum Vitt.

Plates 42 and 112

 Plants up to 3.5 cm. in diameter, depressed-globose or nearly pyriform, plicate below in large squat individuals, and often with a distinct, pointed root. Subgleba large, occupying a third or sometimes nearly a half of the body. Surface light tan, turning brownish tan, covered with very delicate, hairlike spicules and granules with the spicule tips usually free from each other. These are quite persistent but in old plants are partly worn away at the top, thus exposing the light brownish gray shining surface below. When the plants are exposed to the weather after maturity the granules and spicules may be worn away over the entire plant, leaving it perfectly smooth, as in our No. 3230. Pore apical and small.

Spores (of No. 498) deep smoky purple when fully mature (but apparently going through an olivaceous stage which may be found in herbaria, with the possibility of confusion as to the real spore color), spherical, 4.4–5.5μ thick (counting spines), covered with small blunt spines about 1μ long, pedicellate, the greater length of the pedicels being broken off and intermixed with the spores, the part remaining attached to a spore about half as long as the diameter of the spore. Capillitium composed of long, brown, unpitted, branched fibers attenuated at the ends and about 5–7.5μ thick in the larger parts.

The typical form of this species as described above seems to run into forms approaching *L. echinatum* with longer, stellate spines, and Peck treated the latter as var. *stellare* of *atropurpureum*.

Illustrations: Lloyd. Myc. Works, pl. 42; pl. 57, figs. 1–6; pl. 123, figs. 7–12.
    Peck. Bull. N. Y. St. Mus. 150: pl. 121, figs. 6–10. 1910.
    Petri. l. c., figs. 19, 20.
    Quélet. Champ. Jura Vosg. 3: pl. 2, fig. 10. 1875.
    Vittadini. Monog. Lycoperd., pl. 2, fig. 6. 1842.

498. Near Battle's Branch, October 4, 1912.
934. Under cedars east of campus, Oct. 17, 1913. Spores 3.7–4.8μ thick, not counting spines which are up to 1.5μ long.
1019. Among leaves in woods, Nov. 26, 1913. Spores 4.4–6μ thick, covered with blunt spines which are surrounded by a hyaline substance which gives the appearance of a halo.
7143. On ground in mixed woods, Sept. 26, 1923. Spores densely covered with blunt spines, 4.4–5.5μ thick.
Also Nos. 498a, 1005, 3230, 7147, 7430.

Asheville. Beardslee, coll.
Blowing Rock. Coker, coll. (U. N. C. Herb.).
Nantahala. Alma Holland, coll. (U. N. C. Herb.). Spores 3.8–5.5μ.

Wisconsin. (Univ. Wis. Herb. and U. N. C. Herb.) Spores rather strongly warted and with hyaline material between the warts, 5.5–6.5μ, with many long pedicels broken off and mixed with the spores.
Canada. London. Dearness, coll. (Dearness Herb.). Spores distinctly warted, often mucronate, 3.7–5μ.
Ottawa. Macoun, coll. (N. Y. B. G. Herb.).

Lycoperdon pulcherrimum B. & C.
    L. Frostii Pk.

Plates 43, 44 and 112

Plant 1.8–4.5 cm. broad and about the same height, tapering below to a slender root, covered at first with very long, slender, pure white then pale tan spines, which are united into groups by their tips and which finally fall away from the upper part of the plant, leaving the smooth shining deep brown, purplish brown or silvery brown surface of the inner peridium exposed and not reticulated. Gleba white then passing through

PLATE 41

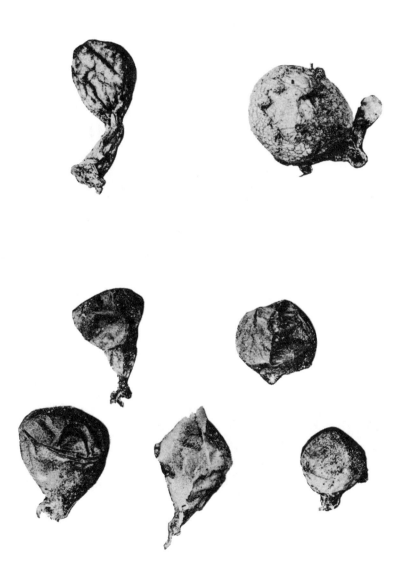

RHOPALOGASTER TRANSVERSARIUM. Alabama [upper left]
LYCOPERDON SUBVELATUM. No. 7263. Florida [upper right]
LYCOPERDON RIMULATUM. No. 7264. Florida [below]

PLATE 42

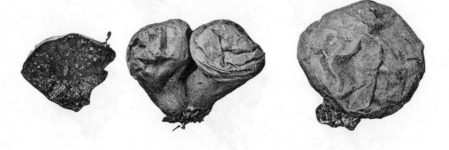

Lycoperdon fuscum, cupricum form. No. 5719 [above]
Lycoperdon atropurpureum. No. 498 [below]

olivaceous to dark purple-brown; subgleba occupying about one-third or slightly more of the plant. Odor when maturing distinctly aromatic, somewhat like that of *L. marginatum*, but not nearly so offensive.

Spores (of No. 477) with a large oil drop and no obvious stalk, globose, set with short blunt spines, 4–4.8μ thick, not counting the spines, average about 5μ with spines. Capillitium much branched, long and tapering, the lesser branches about the size of the spores, the main branches up to 8.6μ in diameter in places.

This is a beautiful species and notable for its very long white spines. While hardly rare, we never find it in abundance, and often only a single specimen at a time. For a comparison with *L. echinatum* see that species.

Illustrations: Hard.' Mushrooms, figs. 463 and 464.
Hollos. l. c., pl. 17, figs. 15–17.
Lloyd. Myc. Notes No. 20: pl. 55. 1905.
Lloyd. Photogravure of Am. Fungi, No. 19.
Morgan. Journ. Cin. Soc. Nat. Hist. **14**: pl. 1, fig. 3.

477. At edge of woods, October 2, 1912.
979. Under cedars in woods, October 21, 1913. Spores covered with blunt, colorless spines which are less than 1μ long, 3.7–5.5μ thick, omitting spines.
1683. On soil under white oak tree, September 14, 1915.
7560. On campus under a tree, Oct. 8, 1924. Spores minutely but distinctly warted, 4–5μ, usually without a pedicel. Capillitium threads irregular, frequently branched, pitted, about 4μ thick.

Asheville. Beardslee.

Maryland. Agric. College. James, coll. (U. S. Nat'l. Herb.).
Pennsylvania. Bethlehem. (Schw. Herb., No. 2259, as *L. echinatum*.)
Vermont. Brattleboro. Frost, coll. (N. Y. B. G. Herb., as *L. Frostii*).
Ohio. Morgan, coll. (N. Y. B. G. Herb., as *L. Frostii*).
Illinois. Urbana. McDougall, coll. (U. N. C. Herb.).
Kansas. Stockton. Bartholomew, coll. (N. Y. B. G. Herb.).

Lycoperdon echinatum Pers.
L. constellatum Fr.

Plates 45 and 112

Plants about 2.5–4 cm. broad not counting the spines, usually flattened, the base pinched to a slender root; cortex of long (2–5 mm.) fascicled spines, with the tapering points approximated; when young creamy white, in age deep brown and falling off, leaving the shining, light or dark brown inner peridium reticulated with minute scurfy particles. Gleba purplish brown to dull brown; subgleba small, with very small chambers, brown to golden. Odor in drying like that of old ham.

Spores (of No. 7421) spherical, distinctly and rather regularly warted, with hyaline material between the warts, 4.8–6μ, often with long pedicels attached but these are usually broken off. Capillitium threads up to 7μ thick, rarely or rather frequently branched, set with rather numerous knobs, pitted, slightly sinuous and irregular.

The species seems to be confined to deciduous woods and is apparently rare in this section. It was not reported from North Carolina by Schweinitz or Curtis. In addition to our Chapel Hill plants, we have examined plants from Asheville, N. C., and from Wisconsin, and plants from Scarboro, England (New York Botanical Garden), also plants from Watlington, England, from Denmark, and from France. These last three were kindly furnished by Kew Gardens, Romell, and Patouillard, respectively.

The spines vary considerably in length and delicacy: in our No. 7421 they are much longer than in the Asheville plants or in any others we have seen. The spines of the European plants are much shorter than in the Chapel Hill ones, and are stouter than in any American specimen met with. Lloyd also notes the more slender spines of the American form (Myc. Notes, p. 208). When the spines of our plants were fresh they also were stout below, but in drying they shrank greatly. The spores of the plant from Scarboro (Massee, coll.) are distinctly warted, 4.2–5.8μ; those of the plant from Montmorency, France, 4.2–6.2μ, with a distinct oil drop; those of the Asheville plants, 4.2–5.5μ thick with pedicels usually broken off but sometimes with long ones present.

In regard to *L. echinatum*, Romell writes that since Fries gives the spores of the plant from Denmark as "6–7μ" thick, he thought it might be different, but on receiving a Denmark plant from Rostrup he found the spores to be no larger than in other specimens, for example, one from Persoon's herbarium which were 4.5–6μ. These measurements we can confirm for the Rostrup plant, which is the one sent us by Romell.

The gleba color and the spore characters are about the same as in *L. pulcherrimum*, but from that the present species is easily separated by the dark brown to blackish spines at maturity, and the paler color and reticulated surface of the inner peridium when the spines fall off, the reticulations being due to the minute granular particles left around the bases of each fascicle of spines. *Lycoperdon echinatum* has also a strong tendency to a more flattened shape. The color of the immature plant has rarely been noted. Rea says that the young plants are white. In our collection the spines on the basal half of freshly opened plants were pale creamy brown at the tips, cream colored at the base, and those at the very top dark brown.

There is an odd contrast in the color changes in the present species and in *L. pulcherrimum*. Both are light colored when young; in the last species as the plants mature, the inner peridium soon becomes deep brown long before the spines fall off, the bases of the spines in some areas becoming brown at times, but the tips remaining white. In *L. echinatum* the opposite is the case, the tips of the spines soon become brown, the bases and inner peridium remaining cream colored, in fact the peridium remains cream colored for some little time after the spines fall off, turning brown gradually on exposure, in some cases remaining very pale. The scurfy dots that later form the reticulum are deep brown even in young stages.

Peck seems to have treated the present species as *L. atropurpureum* var. *stellare*, as shown by a plant so determined by him at the New York Botanical Garden. A good collection from New Zealand, labelled *L. echinatum* (gift of Mr. G. H. Cunningham), looks exactly like our plants, but has distinctly smaller spores (3.5–4μ thick) and less warted than in ours.

Lycoperdon compactum Cun. is a New Zealand species with similarly reticulated peridium, but differing otherwise (Lycoperdaceae, etc., p. 195).

Illustrations: Dufour. Atlas Champ., etc., pl. 74, No. 169.
    Fries. Th. C. E. Sveriges Gasteromyceter, fig. 14.
    Hollos. l. c., pl. 17, figs. 11–14 and 18–24.
    Leuba. Champ. Comest., pl. 52, figs. 1–6.

PLATE 43

Lycoperdon pulcherrimum. No. 477

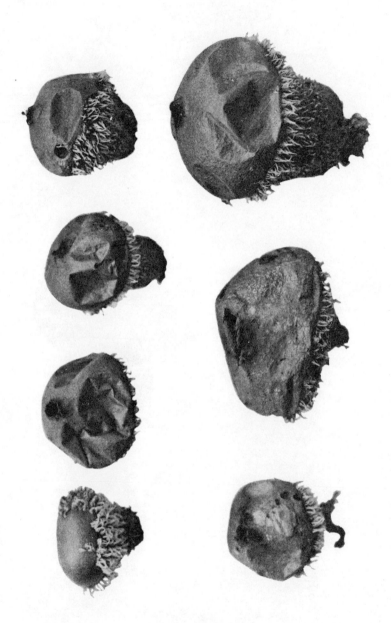

PLATE 44

LYCOPERDON PULCHERRIMUM. No. 979

Lloyd. Myc. Works, pl. 41.
Morgan. Journ. Cin. Soc. Nat. Hist. 14: pl. 1, fig. 5. 1891.
Rolland. Champ. France, pl. 110, fig. 251.
Trelease. Morels and Puffballs of Madison, Wisconsin, pl. 9, fig. 4 (as *L. constellatum*).

7421. On deciduous leaf mold, upland woods near Fern Walk, July 18, 1924.

Asheville. On mats of old leaves. Beardslee, coll.

New Jersey. Newfield. Ellis, coll. (N. Y. B. G. Herb., as *L. atropurpureum* var. *stellare*).
New York. Newcomb. House, coll. (Herb. N. Y. St. Mus. and U. N. C. Herb.) Spores apparently not mature.
Wisconsin. Madison. Aug. 29, 1924. (Univ. Wis. Herb. and U. N. C. Herb.)
    Manson. July, 1909. (Univ. Wis. Herb., as *L. cepaeforme* Bull., and U. N. C. Herb.) Spores distinctly warted, 5–6.5μ, no pedicel.
Reported also from Kentucky, Ohio, Michigan, New York. Schweinitz's record from Pennsylvania (No. 2259) is *L. pulcherrimum*.

Lycoperdon rimulatum Peck.

Plates 41, 46, 47 and 112

Plants 1–5 cm., generally 2–3 cm. broad, depressed-globose, conspicuously plicate below and narrowing quickly to a slender pointed root. Cortex light gray at first, turning a deeper gray and often in age with reddish brown colors. Almost as smooth as kid at first, but sooner or later the cortex becomes minutely dotted and cracked and in age wears away irregularly and incompletely as very thin scales. When young the surface may appear minutely fibrous-granular or almost completely smooth. In exposed areas the inner peridium is seen to be smooth and shining, brownish gray and often tinted with the spore color. Gleba changing from light yellow to gray, purplish gray and then deep ferruginous brown or chocolate brown (auburn to chestnut brown of Ridgway). Subgleba small, occupying only the lower fifth or sixth of the plant and composed of large papery cells. When fully grown but still immature plants are cut, water exudes from the surcharged peridium and escapes as drops, and this excess water often water-soaks areas of the surface when the plants are brought in to dry; in these respects behaving exactly like *Bovistella radicata*, which it further resembles in the long pedicellate spores. Lloyd does not place this species in *Bovistella*, but it would seem to belong there if his extension of the genus is adopted.

Spores (of No. 715) when mature a deep chocolate brown with faint tint of purple, globose, covered with warts embedded in a clear, amorphous substance, some of the warts extending slightly beyond this substance, giving the appearance of an outer wall with radial pits, 5.5–6.8μ thick, with one conspicuous oil drop and a stalk about twice, or rarely nearly thrice, the length of the spore diameter. Frequently the stalk is broken off. When KOH is applied the clear material surrounding the spore swells considerably. Capillitium of simple or moderately branched, somewhat irregular and knotted threads tapering at both ends and about 4–5μ wide in middle, occasionally 7μ wide at knotted places. Rarely a short branch is observed on a thread. At a certain stage it can be seen that threads are formed from the sclerotic thickening of certain selected parts of the trama. These were not simple threads at first, but the branches that came from them did not become hard and went to pieces with the spore mass at maturity. The points where these branches joined the capillitium may be detected as knots or short stubs.

Illustrations: Hollos. l. c., pl. 18, figs. 36–38.
    Lloyd. Myc. Notes No. 20: pl. 56, figs. 1–9. 1905.
    Morgan. l. c., **14**: pl. 1, fig. 6.

715. On Dᵣ. Wagstaff's lawn, September 8, 1913.
811. In old road to Rocky Ridge Farm, September 10, 1913.
7059. On wet ground in deciduous woods in Emerson's swamp, August 5, 1923. Spores dull brown under the microscope, spherical, warted, 5.8–7.2μ thick, often with a very long pedicel, up to 3 times the length of the spore. Capillitium threads 3.5–4.8μ thick, pitted.
7160. On lawn among elms, September 27, 1923. Smallest plants about 1 cm. broad. Spores distinctly warted and with hyaline material, 5.5–7μ, often with a long pedicel.
7165. On ground in swamp of Emerson Farm, September 28, 1923. Largest plants up to 5 cm. wide.

Florida. Alachua Co. Couch, coll. June 24, 1924. (U. N. C. Herb., Nos. 7261, 7252, 7262, 7264.)
New Jersey. Newfield. Ellis, coll. (N. Y. B. G. Herb., as *L. cupricum* var.).

Lycoperdon subvelatum Lloyd

Plates 41 and 112

Plant depressed-globose, 3 cm. broad and about 1.5 cm. thick in the dried state; base pinched to a short stalk, ending in a stout cord which in our one collection branches under ground to bear two fruit bodies; cortex thick, superficially areolated into appressed, spongy patches on a granulated membrane, the whole peeling back from the top in strips, some of which have fallen off. The inner peridium is glabrous, shining, light grayish brown, without the scales which form the conspicuous furfurescence on the denuded inner peridium of *L. marginatum*. Mature gleba deep brownish purple; subgleba nearly white, occupying only the stalk, the chambers obvious.

Spores (of No. 7263) distinctly warted, 4.8–6μ thick, furnished (in the dry state) with long pedicels up to three times the diameter of the spores, but these pedicels fall off when put into water. Capillitium threads irregular in size, wavy, encrusted in places, up to 6.5μ thick.

This agrees in every respect with Lloyd's species (Myc. Notes, pp. 224 and 274). It differs from *L. rimulatum* in the thick, continuous cortex which peels off in pliable patches and strips. This peeling off in good sized patches recalls *L. marginatum*, but the resemblance between the two is entirely superficial. We have four collections of typical *rimulatum* from the same section of Florida, which is good evidence that the present plant is not merely a regional form of that species.

Illustrations: Lloyd. Myc. Notes, p. 274, figs. 120 and 121; and pl. 56, figs. 10 and 11.

Florida. Alachua Co. Couch, coll. On sandy soil, July 28, 1924. (U. N. C. Herb., No. 7263.)

Lycoperdon umbrinum Pers.
L. hirtum Mart.
L. glabellum Peck

Plates 48 and 113

Plants depressed-globose with an abrupt base or pear-shaped with a tapering base; up to 3.5 cm. broad and 4.5 cm. high, usually about 3 cm. high; white or light brownish gray before maturity, turning to tawny buff or brownish buff or light grayish tan, or rarely golden yellow. Surface lightly covered with a fine scurfy or granular stuff mingled with minute, slender spines that are separate and erect or, especially on the lower half, flattened toward each other in patches. These spines are often absent in places. This superficial material is very persistent and is only partly worn away in old age to show the shining inner peridium. Subgleba occupying the stalk-like or tapering base and extending in a thin layer up to the widest part of the plant, with chambers of moderate

PLATE 45

LYCOPERDON ECHINATUM, Asheville, N. C. [upper four]
LYCOPERDON MUSCORUM, No. 676 [lower left]. West Albany. Type [other two]

size. Gleba pale olivaceous then darker olivaceous brown at maturity, varying considerably in color in different collections. It may be Isabella color (nearly old gold) or Brussel's brown with a faint tint of purple or rarely a distinct purplish brown.

Spores (of No. 679) very small, spherical, about the color of the mature gleba, 3.7–4.5μ thick and with a short pedicel, minutely asperulate; after soaking in water appearing to have a thick, hyaline wall, the spines showing as darker striations in the hyaline material. Capillitium threads more or less uneven, with numerous or scattered distinct pits in the walls, frequently branched, tapering to a point, averaging about 3.9–4.3μ in the larger threads, in places rarely up to 7μ thick.

Our collections have been compared with a good plant of *L. umbrinum* from Bresadola's herbarium (labelled *L. hirtum*). The spinules on the top of this specimen are somewhat larger than on any American plant we have seen, but otherwise the differences are trivial. The spores are minutely but distinctly warted, 4–5.5μ, rarely with a mucro; capillitium threads knobbed and strongly pitted. Our plants also agree well with descriptions of *L. glabellum* by Peck and Morgan except that the spore color is given as purplish brown and the spores as described are too large. However, we have examined a plant from the type locality (West Albany), collected by Peck and possibly a part of the type, and find that it agrees in these spore details and not with published descriptions. Peck gives the spores as purplish brown, 5.1–6.3μ thick, but in his plant we find them to be brown with little or no purplish tint and 4–4.8μ thick, including warts. Peck's specimen agrees further in showing the distinct pits in the capillitium, a character that we find most useful in determining this species. The threads are also of the same thickness and irregularity, up to 4.2μ thick.

We cannot find any good difference between the present species and *L. Turneri* as treated by Morgan (l. c., p. 17) and Lloyd (Myc. Notes, p. 236). The original description of *L. Turneri* E. & E. (Journ. Myc. 1: 87. 1885) was unfortunately based on two different lots of plants, one, the true type from Labrador, and another smaller and different plant from the eastern United States. This last we cannot distinguish from *L. glabellum*. The type from Labrador is represented in the New York Botanical Garden and is a larger plant with much larger and rougher spores and with the capillitium threads unpitted (see pl. 113, figs. 4 and 5). One supposed difference between *L. glabellum* and *L. Turneri* is the purplish spores of the former, but this does not hold, as most specimens of *L. glabellum* found in herbaria, including some of Peck's own, as stated above, have brown to olivaceous gleba.

Lloyd considers *L. glabellum* a synonym of *L. umbrinum* (Myc. Notes, p. 225), while Hollos treats it as a variety. The species is treated as *L. glabellum* by Morgan (l. c., 14: 10). Lloyd thinks that *L. elegans* Morgan is the same. This is the plant determined by Ellis as *L. molle* Pers., and Lloyd also considers the latter the same as *L. glabellum* (Myc. Notes, p. 209). In a plant of *L. molle* from the Persoon Herbarium, now at the New York Botanical Garden, the gleba is Isabella color and the spores 3.4–3.8μ thick, faintly warted to smooth, smaller and less rough than in American *L. umbrinum* (pl. 113, fig. 6).

Illustrations: Fries, Th. C. E. Sveriges Gasteromyceter, fig. 15.
    Hollos. l. c., pl. 18, figs. 23–29; pl. 29, fig. 5.
    Lloyd. Myc. Works, pls. 43 and 58.
    Morgan. Journ. Cin. Soc. Nat. Hist. **14**: pl. 1, fig. 7.

679. In grass on shaded lawn, Oct. 4, 1908.

1001. In pine woods, Sept. 15, 1913. Spores olivaceous, 3.7–4.6μ thick. Subgleba in some plants purple.

1027. Under cedars near campus. The plants in this collection were fully mature and were a pale earth color (gray brown) outside; the spores and capillitium somewhat deeper earth color within, and with a slight tint of olive. Spores 3.7–4μ thick, smooth, spherical. Capillitium delicate, branched, diameter of spores and tapering at the ends.

7215. On ground in pine woods, Nov. 17, 1923. One plant in this typical lot was strong golden yellow on one side shading to brownish yellow on the other.

Also Nos. 1003a, 1004, 1026, 1762, 3233, 5921, 7103, 7148.
>   Asheville. Beardslee, coll.
>   Blowing Rock. Coker, coll.
>   Hendersonville. Alma Holland, coll. (U. N. C. Herb.). Spores 3.5–4μ.

Virginia. Warrenton. Coker, coll. (U. N. C. Herb.)

Florida. Alachua Co. Couch, coll. June 22, 1924. (U. N. C. Herb. Nos. 7253 and 7254.)

New York. West Albany. Peck, coll. (Albany Herb.). Also other New York plants from Peck at N. Y. B. G.

Wisconsin. (U. N. C. Herb. from Univ. Wisconsin Herb.) Spores minutely but distinctly warted, 3.7–4.2μ, no pedicel.
>   Eagle Heights. Sept. 1903. (Univ. Wis. Herb. and U. N. C. Herb.) Spores distinctly rough, 4.2–5μ, no pedicel.

Canada. London. Dearness, No. 915. (Dearness Herb. as *L. molle.*) Spores nearly smooth, with a short pedicel, 3.4–4μ.

Lycoperdon acuminatum Bosc

>   *L. leprosum* Berk. & Rav. in Peck
>   *L. calyptriforme* Berk.

Plates 49 and 113

Plants very small, 3–9 mm., shaped like an inverted top or long, pointed egg, with a small apical pore in age; cortex composed of a thin, spongy or granular scurf which very slowly wears away exposing the dull inner peridium or in rare cases the cortex may assume the form of short fascicled spines up to 1 mm. long above (as in plants from Cincinnati and Newfield entered below); color whitish or pale tan, inner peridium yellowish to gray or pale gray-brown in color. The entire peridium wall is very thin and delicate. Gleba pale brown with a slight olivaceous tint. Subgleba none.

Spores (of No. 680) pale olivaceous, then dirty gray, globular, 3.3–4μ thick, smooth, walls fairly thick, a large oil drop and a short mucro. Capillitium simple, about the color of the spores, up to 10.8μ in diameter, averaging about 5.5–6μ.

This is the smallest known puffball and it is remarkable in its habit of growing on mossy places on the bark of living tree trunks at some distance (usually 4–15 feet) from the ground. Others give the habitat as on old logs or around the mossy bases of living trees, but with us it always grows on living trunks. We have never found it near the ground. It has exactly the same habits and preferences for cold weather that *Geaster leptospermus* shows, and may often be found associated with it. This is the same as *L. leprosum* in the sense of Ravenel, Peck, and others, as shown by plants from their herbaria. The capillitium of Peck's plants shows slight branching, whereas in our plants it is simple or very rarely branched, agreeing with Lloyd's description.

PLATE 46

LYCOPERDON RIMULATUM.   No. 715

PLATE 47

LYCOPERDON RIMULATUM. No. 7165

Illustrations: Hollos. l. c., pl. 22, figs. 1–7.

Lloyd. l. c., pl. 64, figs. 1–4. 1905.

Morgan. l. c., **14:** pl. 2, fig. 8.

680. On oak trees among moss about 5 or 6 feet from the ground, September 19, 1908, and on *Cupressus* trees in a yard, Oct. 9, 1908.

975a. In moss on a cedar tree, Dec. 9, 1913. Spores as usual, 3.2–3.6μ thick.

3221. On trunks of oak and hickory, Jan. 22, 1919. Spores smooth, spherical, 3–3.7μ, with a distinct oil drop and often a short mucro.

7513. On bark of living white oak, Sept. 18, 1924.

Asheville. Beardslee.

Yadkin College. On branch of *Ulmus alata*, Sept. 16, 1922. Coker, coll. (U. N. C. Herb.).

Hillsboro. (Curtis Herb.)

South Carolina. Aiken. Ravenel, Fungi Amer. Exs. No. 14 (N. Y. B. G. Herb. as *L. leprosum*).

New Jersey. Newfield. On mossy stump. Ellis, coll. (N. Y. B. G. Herb., as *L. leprosum?*).

Ohio. Cincinnati. (N. Y. B. G. Herb. from Morgan Herb., as *L. calyptriforme* Berk.)

Missouri. Perryville. Demetrio, coll. Rabenhorst-Winter, Fungi europaei, No. 3535, as *L. leprosum* (N. Y. B. G. Herb.).

Lycoperdon pyriforme Schaeff.

Plates 49, 50 and 113

Plants pyriform, often crowded, up to 4.5 cm. broad and 4.5 cm. high, usually much smaller; color red-brown when dry or old, paler when fresh; cortex composed of minute warts, spines and granules which are very persistent and rough to the touch like a file; sometimes cracked into distinct areas. The apical pore is very slow to form, often taking three weeks or a month to appear after full size is reached. The plants are connected with the wood and with each other by conspicuous, pure white strands of mycelium. Gleba changing through greenish yellow to deep olive-brown at maturity; subgleba rather small, occupying only the constricted base, the chambers very small.

Spores spherical, smooth, with a large oil drop, deep olive-brown when fully mature, 3.3–4.3μ in diameter. Capillitium branched, brownish olivaceous, main threads from 3.5–5.5μ in diameter, averaging about 3.7μ, tapering to the tips.

The spores and capillitium of our plants have been compared with those of Peck's collections, and were found to agree. The species is often found in immense quantities on rotten logs and stumps and rarely in the ground. The entire plant is very persistent and after maturing in the fall may pass the winter with little change, and be found in good condition in the spring. It is edible and when found is abundant enough to be of use.

Illustrations: Dufour. Atlas des Champ. Comest. et Ven., pl. 74, No. 170. 1891.

Gillet. Champ. Fr. (Gasteromycetes), pl. 14.

Hard. Mushrooms, pl. 62 and fig. 470.

Hollos. l. c., pl. 20, figs. 4–12.

Krieger. Nat. Geog. Mag. **37:** 418, 419. 1920.

Lloyd. l. c., pl. 48. 1905.

Marshall. Mushroom Book, pls. opposite pp. 125 and 134.

Michael. Führer f. Pilzfreunde **2:** No. 200. 1918 (2nd ed.).

Murrill. Mycologia **6:** pl. 127. 1914.

Patterson and Charles. U. S. Dept. Agric. Bull. 175: pl. 34, fig. 1. 1915; also Farmers' Bull. 796, fig. 17. 1917.

Vittadini. Monog. Lycoperd., pl. 2, fig. 9. 1842.

633. On stump of dead beech tree in Battle's Park, October 24, 1912.
917. Scattered in large numbers over several yards on earth and in and by the brick drain and in grass just east of the Alumni Building, October 15, 1913. This colony of plants was interesting in being apparently unconnected with wood. The mycelium could be traced as white strands for some distance into the rather poor earth and then was dissipated into invisible fibers. All characters exactly as in plants on wood. The plants were fully grown a month before the apical pores appeared.
1046. On exposed dead root in Bowlin's Creek swamp, December 6, 1913.
Also Nos. 665, 935, 998, 1469.

Asheville. Beardslee.
Blowing Rock. Coker and party, August 1922.

South Carolina. Ravenel. Fungi Car. Exs. No. 72. (Phil. Acad. Herb. and N. Y. B. G. Herb.)
   Aiken. Ravenel. Fungi Amer. Exs. No. 469. (N. Y. B. G. Herb.)
Georgia. Harper, coll. (N. Y. B. G. Herb.).
Florida. Clark's Run. Calkins, coll. (N. Y. B. G. Herb.).
   Marion County. On dead wood. Couch, coll. (U. N. C. Herb.). Spores smooth, 3.4–3.8μ thick.
New York. Alcove. Shear, coll. Ell. & Ev., Fungi Columb. No. 106 and N. Amer. Fungi No. 2906. (N. Y. B. G. Herb.).
Pennsylvania. Buck Hill Falls. Mrs. Delafield, coll. (N. Y. B. G. Herb.)
Ohio. Cincinnati. Lloyd, coll. (N. Y. B. G. Herb.).
Illinois. Urbana. McDougall, coll. (U. N. C. Herb.).
New Zealand. Cunningham, coll. (U. N. C. Herb.). Spores smooth, 3.5–4.2μ thick, often with a mucro.
Also from Venezuela, Ecuador, and Europe in N. Y. B. G. Herb.

Lycoperdon subincarnatum Peck

Plates 51, 57 and 113

Plants small, about 1–2.5 cm. thick, depressed-globose, almost or quite sessile, growing on logs or stumps and attached by byssoid strands; color when young reddish brown, at maturity becoming dark brown or dull leather brown; covered with minute, separate, brown warts or with little pointed spines in groups with united tips, their bases connected by a smooth thin tissue of the same color; after full maturity these warts or spines and tissue slowly wearing away and leaving exposed the paler brown, dull inner peridium, which is very firm and tough and is marked all over with small pits outlined by acute ridges, appearing under a lens exactly like a thimble. This reticulated surface is assumed after maturity, in any case, whether the outer peridium falls away or not and is obvious through the outer peridium which accommodates itself to it. Subgleba scanty or practically absent, composed of small pale chambers. Gleba peculiar in the distinctly radiating tramal plates which, before maturity, give a section very much the appearance of a *Geaster;* color at maturity grayish purple. In some specimens there is a very distinct columella, thus increasing the resemblance to *Geaster.*

Spores (of No. 3171a) dull brown, spherical, when dry appearing distinctly warted, when in water appearing spiny under high power, 3.8–5μ thick, counting the spines. Capillitium of long, simple or sparingly branched, very pale threads (much paler than the spores) up to 6.5μ thick, the walls irregularly thickened in places, sometimes closing the lumen.

This species is a strongly marked one and is easily distinguished by the small deep pits, growth on wood, sessile habit and peculiar capillitium. In most of our collections

PLATE 48

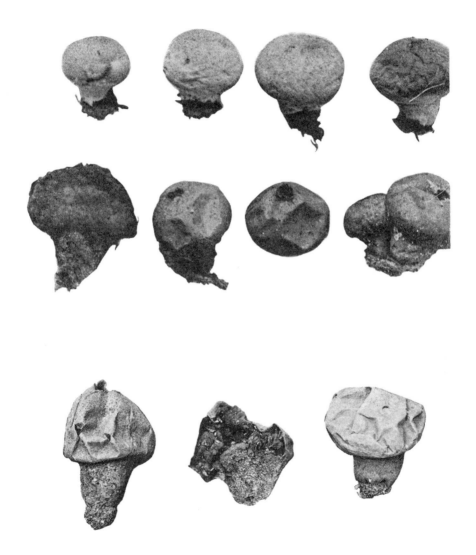

LYCOPERDON UMBRINUM. No. 1004 [above]; No. 679 [below]

the peridium is much more rigid and leathery than in most puffballs, but in our No. 3171a from Chapel Hill it is more pliable, though still thick and leathery. In this lot too, the outer peridium is more scurfy than warty and has not become at all worn off though the plants are old, and the spores have slightly longer spines. The surface has, however, assumed the pitted appearance in about the same fashion as other lots. All other characters are the same.

Illustrations: Cunningham. Proc. Linn. Soc. N. S. W. **51**: pl. 46, figs. 4, 5. 1926.
  Lloyd. Myc. Works, pl. 63, figs. 5–9.
  Morgan. Journ. Cin. Soc. Nat. Hist. **14**: pl. 2, fig. 6.

3171a. On very rotten wood, Aug. 13, 1918.
7030. On rotten wood, Handcock's swamp, Aug. 3, 1923. Spores spherical, spiny, 4–4.8μ with a distinct oil drop and a pedicel usually about one-half as long as the diameter of the spore.

  Blowing Rock. Coker and party, Aug. 1922. No. 5556. On small pieces of rotten deciduous wood and bark. No. 5641. On rotting deciduous log. Spores minutely spiny, 3.7–4.6μ thick. No. 5775. On very rotten chestnut stump. Also collection by Coker, Sept. 3, 1924. Spores minutely warted, 3.5–4.2μ thick.
  Linville Falls. Coker and party, Aug. 1922. No. 5754. On a rotting log in rich deciduous woods.
  Asheville. Beardslee, coll. (U. N. C. Herb.). Spores spiny, 3.7–4.6μ.
  Buncombe Co. Harvey, coll. (U. N. C. Herb.). Spores minutely warted, 3.5–4μ.

Pennsylvania. Buck Hill Falls. Mrs. Delafield, coll. (N. Y. B. G. Herb.).
New York. Sand Lake. Peck, coll. (N. Y. B. G. Herb.).
  Arkville. Murrill, coll. (N. Y. B. G. Herb.).
Maine. White, coll. (N. Y. B. G. Herb.).
Wisconsin. Devil's Lake. (Univ. Wis. Herb. and U. N. C. Herb.) Spores minutely but distinctly warted, 3.6–4.2μ, with no pedicel.

Lycoperdon muscorum Morgan
  L. pseudoradicans Lloyd
  L. polytrichum Lloyd

Plates 45 and 113

We copy the following from Morgan's original description (Journ. Cin. Soc. Nat. Hist. **14**: 16. 1891):

"Peridium turbinate, globose or depressed-globose above, contracted below into a stem-like base, with a filamentous and fibrous mycelium. Cortex a thin white or yellowish coat of minute spinules with intermingled granules, which are coarser towards the apex; these wither or shrivel with age and are mostly persistent on the smooth olive-brown, shining surface of the inner peridium. Subgleba occupying little more than the stem-like base; mass of spores and capillitium greenish yellow, then brownish olivaceous; spores minutely warted, 4–4.5μ in diameter.

"Growing among mosses, especially *Polytrichum*, in old meadows and pastures. New York, Peck. Peridium one-half to one and one-third inches in diameter and 1–3 inches in height. This is *L. molle* of Peck's U. S. Species of Lycoperdon."

Peck calls attention to the resemblance of this plant in the immature state to *Calvatia elata*. The mature plant is easily distinguished from the latter by the apical mouth, and the average size is smaller.

Dr. House has kindly sent us two plants of the type collection of *L. muscorum* from West Albany (Peck, as *L. molle*, l. c., p. 310). The spores are spherical, minutely warted, 4–5.5μ with a short pedicel; capillitium threads about 3–4μ thick, pitted, easily broken up.

Hollos considers this the same as *L. polytrichum* Lloyd and *L. pseudoradicans* Lloyd. Lloyd states that his *L. polytrichum* grows only in hair cap moss, but he refers to that species a collection from Maine by Beardslee, a part of which at least was not growing in *Polytrichum*. Three plants of this collection seen by Lloyd and returned to Beardslee show no *Polytrichum*, but a much smaller moss attached, and Beardslee writes that the plants did not all grow in *Polytrichum*. The individual of this lot figured by Lloyd (pl. 67, fig. 7) has a moss plant attached that looks like *Polytrichum*. We find on examination of Beardslee's plants that the spores are like those of the type, faintly warted or many smooth, usually with a mucro, 3.8–5μ, rarely 6μ; capillitium easily fragmented by slight pressure on the cover glass, pitted, often encrusted, up to 5μ thick. It is to be noted that the resemblance to *Calvatia elata* in general appearance is further emphasized by the breaking up of the capillitium into short joints under slight pressure. This fragmentation is found in all or nearly all Calvatias. It does not occur in any other *Lycoperdon* we have seen. As to *L. molle* of Persoon, this cannot be that species, as the plant in his herbarium, which may be considered the type, has smaller spores, and according to the original description grows in oak woods. Fries says it grows in mossy fields.

Illustrations: Hollos. l. c., pl. 29, figs. 1 and 2.
Lloyd. Myc. Notes No. 9, figs. 50 and 51 (as *L. pseudoradicans*); also pl. 67, figs. 1–5 (as *L. muscorum*) and figs. 6–10 (as *L. polytrichum*).
Lloyd. Genera of Gasteromycetes, pl. 10, fig. 45 (as *L. muscorum*, later changed to *polytrichum*).

Connecticut. Miss White, coll. (N. Y. B. G. Herb.). Two plants on *Polytrichum*, one on *Leucobryum glaucum* (det. by Mr. R. S. Williams).
Maine. West Harpswell. Beardslee, coll. No. 676. (U. N. C. Herb.)
Ohio. Foerste, coll. (N. Y. B. G. Herb., as *L. glabellum*). On *Polytrichum*.

Lycoperdon gemmatum Batsch
 L. excipuliforme Scop.
 L. macrogemmatum Lloyd

Plates 52, 53 and 113

Plants 3–7.5 cm. high and 2.5–6 cm. broad, obovoid to turbinate with a distinct base which is comparatively large and often elongated and stalk-like; growing on mouldy woods earth or from decaying wood or leaves. Cortex made up of intermingled long and short terete spines or warts, the short ones being considerably more numerous than the long ones and all becoming smaller and more uniform downward and fading to scurfy granules toward the base; the color grayish tan to buff or leather color, the longer spines often darker. The large spines fall off first and leave pale smooth spots that are very obvious and characteristic; the other warts fall very slowly, if at all, and even in quite old collapsed plants only the top is free from them in areas so as to entirely expose the smooth, straw-colored inner peridium. Gleba at maturity dull ochraceous brown with a tint of olive or in some old plants brown with a tint of purple. Subgleba occupying the stem-like base which is usually a third to more than a half of the whole, its chambers up to 1 mm. wide.

PLATE 49

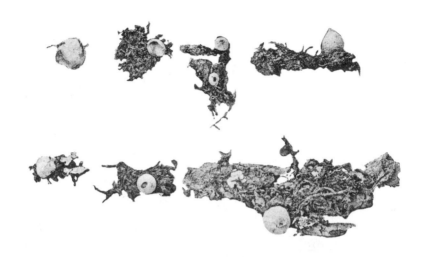

Lycoperdon acuminatum. No. 3221 [above]
Lycoperdon pyriforme. On chestnut log at Blowing Rock, N. C. [below]. Much reduced

PLATE 50

LYCOPERDON PYRIFORME. No. 935

Spores (of No. 3159) color of the gleba, usually smoky brown with a tint of olive, spherical, very minutely asperulate, 3.7–4.4μ thick. Capillitium of long, sparingly branched, brownish threads, about 5.5μ in thickest places, tapering to about 2μ, heavily encrusted in places, frequently pitted, the color about that of the spores, appearing lighter when the spores are knocked out.

The plant is peculiar in the variation shown in fragility in various collections. Some are as fragile as *Calvatia elata*, and the peridium easily breaks up into small fragments; in others the peridium is pliable and toughish as is usual in *Lycoperdon*. Except for the characteristic warts, the more fragile collections could easily be referred to *Calvatia elata*. Furthermore, in some specimens of that species the capillitium does not fragment so readily as in other Calvatias. For cytological information by Maire covering this and other species, see under *Scleroderma aurantium*.

Morgan (l. c., p. 13) treats *L. perlatum* as distinct, but Lloyd thinks he misunderstood that species. Hollos considers them the same. Figures by Tulasne (Ann. Sci. Nat. **17**: pl. 2, fig. 11), as *L. perlatum*, do not show any roughness on the spores. Under the name *L. nigrescens*, Lloyd treats an American plant that he considers "really a form of *gemmatum* excepting that the stiff spines are not consolidated" (Myc. Notes, p. 229). The European plant with blacker warts he refers to on pages 212 and 338 (see his plates 47, 60, and 123), and in his last reference he considers it less like *L. gemmatum* than he had formerly supposed. The American plants above mentioned as *L. nigrescens* may be the same as those we refer to *L. Peckii*. It seems clear that the original *L. excipuliforme* Scop. is only a form of *L. gemmatum*, as treated by Fries and Lloyd. The name has also been applied, apparently without reason, to a form of *L. pyriforme* and apparently to a form of *Calvatia saccata*. A European plant (Herbarium of Klotzsch), received from Ryks Herbarium at Leiden as *Lycoperdon gemmatum* (No. 58), has the external appearance of that plant, but is peculiar in having very small, smooth spores, 2.3–3.2μ thick. We have found one cespitose group of plants very much like this: spores nearly as small (2.8–3.7μ) and nearly smooth (Linville Falls, No. 8221).

Illustrations: Dufour. Atlas des Champ. Comest. et Ven., pl. 74, No. 167. 1891.
    Fries. Sverig. Atl. Svamp., pl. 73, fig. 2. 1861.
    Gibson. Our Edible Toadstools and Mushrooms, pl. 34.
    Gillet. Champ. Fr. (Gasteromycetes), pl. 12.
    Hard. Mushrooms, pl. 61.
    Hollos. l. c., pl. 19, figs. 14–25.
    Krieger. Nat. Geog. Mag. **37**: 414. 1920.
    Lloyd. Myc. Works, pl. 46; also Lycoperdaceae of Australia, etc., fig. 35. 1905.
    Micheli. Nova Plant. Gen., pl. 97, fig. 1.
    Michael. Führer f. Pilzfreunde **1**: No. 79. 1918 (2nd ed.).
    Sweetzer. Univ. Oregon Leaflet, Bot. Ser. No. 9, fig. 1.
    The figure by Murrill in Mycologia **1**: pl. 15, fig. 3, 1909, is not this species.

500. On a piece of rotting wood, Oct. 4, 1912. Spores minutely warted, 3.5–4.4μ thick.
502. Around and on roots of a cedar tree, Oct. 5, 1912. Spores in this collection slightly rougher than in others.
1403. In rich damp places in the edge of woods, Oct. 22, 1914. Spores 3.7–4.5μ thick, rarely with a short pedicel.
1784. Among dead leaves on Lone Pine Hill, Sept. 14, 1915. Spores 3.5–4.2μ thick.
Also Nos. 554, 677, 678, 731, 2990, 3159.

Asheville. Beardslee, coll.

Blowing Rock. Coker and party, August 1922. Common. No. 5669. On chestnut leaves. Stalk 5 cm. long, 2.5 cm. thick above; head 4.5 cm. wide. 5670. Among frondose leaves in woods. No. 5806. In leaves in deciduous woods. Spores very minutely rough, 3.4–3.9μ.

Linville Falls. Coker, coll. (U. N. C. Herb., No. 8221).

Salem. Schweinitz. (Schw. Herb., as *L. excipuliforme.*)

Winston-Salem. Schallert, coll. Oct. 1, 1922. (U. N. C. Herb.)

Alabama. Earle, coll. (N. Y. B. G. Herb.).

Virginia. Mountain Lake. Murrill, coll. (N. Y. B. G. Herb.).

Pennsylvania. Bethlehem. (Schw. Herb., as *L. perlatum.*)

Buck Hill Falls. Mrs. Delafield, coll. (N. Y. B. G. Herb.). Spores minutely rough, 3.5–4μ with a distinct oil drop and often a short pedicel.

West Chester. Jackson, coll. (N. Y. B. G. Herb.).

New York. Alcove. Shear, coll. (N. Y. B. G. Herb.).

Osceola. House, coll. (Herb. N. Y. St. Mus. and U. N. C. Herb.). Spores 3.5–4μ.

Massachusetts. Jamaica Plains. (N. Y. B. G. Herb., as *L. perlatum.*)

Wisconsin. (Univ. Wis. Herb. and U. N. C. Herb.) Spores faintly warted, 3.2–3.8μ.

Illinois. Urbana. McDougall, coll. (U. N. C. Herb.).

Washington. Langley. Grant, coll. (U. N. C. Herb.). Spores very minutely warted, 3.6–4.2μ, no pedicel. Capillitium threads up to 6μ thick, strongly pitted.

Canada. Manitoba. Victoria Beach, May 24, 1926. Bisby, coll. (U. N. C. Herb.).

Swedish Lapland. Abisco. Coker, coll. (U. N. C. Herb.). Spores olivaceous brown, minutely warted, 3.5–4μ rarely with a mucro. Capillitium threads irregular, strongly pitted, about 5μ thick.

Lycoperdon Peckii Morgan. A form

Plates 53 and 113

Plants shaped as in *L. gemmatum*, the distinct stalk up to 3 cm. long; the mycelium ropy; peridium about 1.5–3.8 cm. broad, covered with tapering spines about 1–1.5 mm. long, which as the plant grows split at base into 2–4 parts which remain united at their tips and are easily rubbed off, leaving pale, smooth, circular spots which are surrounded by minute granular warts and dots; color of the longer spines in youth and until near maturity a delicate and pretty purplish lavender, at maturity changing to buffy brown. Toward the base the spines become more slender and hairlike and are more obviously intermingled with granular matter. Except for the lavender color of the upper half, the plant until near maturity is nearly white. Subgleba composed of rather small cells and occupying about a third of the plant.

Spores (of No. 5749) olivaceous brown, spherical, 3.6–4.4μ thick, with a small oil drop and a short pedicel, the wall obscurely dotted (pitted or minutely warted) and appearing faintly striate radially in optical section; surrounding the spore is the thin hyaline layer that is found in most *Lycoperdon* species. Capillitium threads very slightly branched, up to 6μ thick and tapering to delicate tips.

We have compared our plants with a collection in the Albany Herbarium from Forestburg, N. Y., collected and determined by Peck and find them the same in appearance, surface characters, spores and capillitium. The species (at least in so far as our collections go) is easily distinguished in the fresh state before maturity by the lavender color, a character not mentioned by others; in the mature and dry state it is distinguished by the ochraceous or buff color, by compound spines with flaring bases and delicate, cohering tips, by granular matter between the spines, and by the small, dotted (not obviously warted) spores with distinct pedicels. When the spines fall away they

PLATE 51

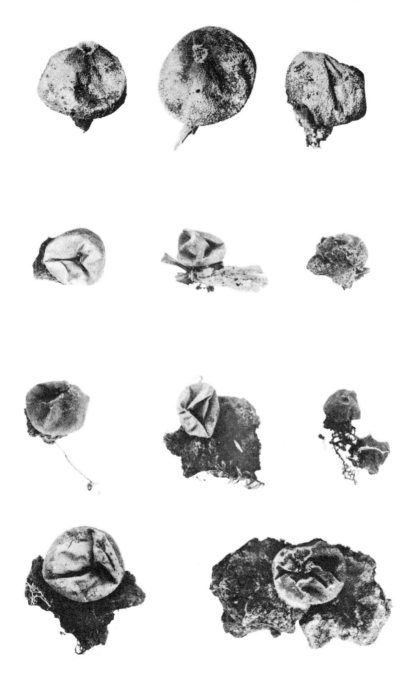

LYCOPERDON SUBINCARNATUM. Asheville, N. C. [top row]. Photograph by Beardslee. No. 5754 [all others]

leave smooth circular spots surrounded by minute granules, thus giving a spotted or reticulated appearance to the surface as in *L. echinatum* and *L. gemmatum*. According to Morgan (Journ. Cin. Soc. Nat. Hist. **14**: 15. 1891) this is the *L. echinatum* of Peck's United States Species of *Lycoperdon*, while the true *L. echinatum* is treated as *L. constellatum* by Peck and by Trelease. In the Ellis collection at the New York Botanical Garden are plants from Peck (N. Y.) labelled *L. echinatum* which are *L. Peckii*. (See Morgan, above cited, and Lloyd, Myc. Notes, p. 223.) *Lycoperdon Peckii* is not recognized by Lloyd, but we cannot reconcile our plant with any other species and refer it to *C. Peckii* as it seems to agree well with Morgan's description and with the above-mentioned plants from Peck. To all appearances this might represent the *L. nigrescens* of Europe to which it might be referred except for the light color which is retained at all ages (see Lloyd, Myc. Works, pl. 123, figs. 1–6). It differs from *L. echinatum* in the shorter pale spines and much smaller olivaceous spores; from *L. pulcherrimum* in the much shorter spines, the pale surface of the inner peridium and the smooth, olivaceous spores; from *L. eximium* in stouter, longer spines and the smaller, spherical spores; from *L. fuscum* in the paler, stouter, longer spines with granular or scurfy material between. The most important differences between the present species and *L. gemmatum*, which is nearest, and of which this might be treated as only a variety, is the tapering fascicled spines with tips united, and the smooth spores. In these characters it agrees with the plants from Peck above-mentioned, which are also similar in the small, dot-like warts between the spines. As *L. Peckii* is described as having a smooth surface (not spotted) after the spines fall off, a divergence from our plant in this respect is indicated; Peck's specimens above-mentioned are, however, like ours. A difference in age of plants might easily account for such a discrepancy. Our oldest plants were found soon after opening and only a part of the upper surface was denuded.

North Carolina. Blowing Rock. Coker and party, August 1922. No. 5654. On rotten chestnut wood. No. 5655. Among frondose leaves in woods. Spores smooth or nearly so, 3.5–4.2μ with a short pedicel. No. 5801. Under white pines. (U. N. C. Herb.)
Linville Falls. Coker and party, August 1922. No. 5749. Among leaves under rhododendron, chestnut, etc. (U. N. C. Herb.)
Pennsylvania. Buck Hill Falls. Mrs. Delafield, coll. (N. Y. B. G. Herb.).
Canada. Ontario. Dearness, No. 3026 c. (U. N. C. Herb.) Spores olivaceous in mass, smooth or nearly so, 3.2–3.8μ.
Newfoundland. Waghorne, coll. (N. Y. B. G. Herb., det. by Peck). Spores smooth or nearly so, 3.4–3.8μ thick.

Lycoperdon pedicellatum Pk.

L. caudatum Schroet.

Plate 113

Plants depressed-globose, plicate below, sessile or with a small stem, attached by delicate fibers. Cortex pale, grayish then ochraceous to rather light ochraceous brown, composed above of rather stout spines about 0.5-1 mm. long, single or arranged in fascicles with the incurved tips united and the bases separated by a thin, glabrous cortex of the same color. The spines fall off singly and each carries its own area of the thin cortex, thus exposing the pale brown, smooth and shining, inner peridium which is faintly pitted or wrinkled, or in a form distinctly reticulated. Subgleba very scanty in nearly sessile forms or more obvious when there is a distinct stalk.

Spores (of No. 5668) dull brown at full maturity, subspherical to short oval, 3.7–4.8μ thick, minutely rough, furnished with a long persistent pedicel which is about

4–5 times as long as the spore.   Capillitium threads up to 6.6μ thick, pitted, sparsely branched, ochraceous under transmitted light.

Growing in humus or on logs in deciduous woods, and apparently northern in its range except for the higher southern mountains (reported by Atkinson from Alabama). It has not before been reported from our state.   The species is easily recognized by the rather long, deciduous spines, the pale, shining, inner peridium and particularly by the very characteristic smooth spores with very long persistent pedicels.   Lloyd includes this species in his expansion of the genus *Bovistella* (Myc. Notes, p. 282), but we are not including in *Bovistella* plants with the capillitium of *Lycoperdon*.

Illustrations: Hollos. l. c., pl. 20, figs. 44–47.
    Morgan. l. c., 14: pl. 2, fig. 2.

North Carolina. Blowing Rock. Coker and party, August 1922. No. 5668. On rotting wood of a deciduous tree.

New York. Center. (N. Y. B. G. Herb.) Spores oval, smooth, 3.2–3.6 x 3.5–4μ, with slender, persistent pedicels up to 30μ.

Wisconsin. Parfrey's Glen. (U. N. C. Herb. and Univ. Wis. Herb.) Spores oval, smooth, 3.4–3.8 x 3.7–4.5μ, with slender pedicels up to 35μ long.

    Homewood. (Univ. Wis. Herb. and U. N. C. Herb.) Spores oval, smooth or nearly so, 3.5–4 x 4–5μ, with slender pedicels up to 35μ long.

Lycoperdon eximium Morgan

Plates 54 and 113

Plants up to 4 cm. broad, turbinate, distinctly stalked, even or plicate beneath. Cortex composed of slender spines about 1 mm. long which often curve and converge at the apex, and gradually decrease in length downward until they are mere granules at the base of the stalk; color tan, brownish tan or deeper brown, and in age the spines become very deep brown.   After maturity the spines begin to wear away, so that in age they are reduced to granular dots, or even these may be worn off in areas, so as to expose the tan or light brown shining layer beneath.   The mouth is a torn, irregular opening of rather tardy appearance.   Gleba greenish yellow, then brownish olivaceous and at full maturity deep brown with a tint of purple, about bister of Ridgway.   Subgleba of honeycomb structure, occupying all of the stalk and extending with a thin expansion to the broadest part, occupying in all about one-third to one-fourth of the body.

Spores (of No. 1002) purplish brown, elliptic or oval, with a thicker, clear inner wall and a darker outer wall which is dotted with minute warts, surrounded by a hyaline coat, distinctly stalked, 4.3–5 x 5–6.5μ.   Capillitium of long, sparingly branched, deep brown threads that are almost the diameter of the spores, and taper to slender tips.

Recognized by its densely set, regular spines, dark color in age and rather large oval spores.   It does not seem to have been reported from this state before, and has been known only from South Carolina and Alabama.   The species is described by Morgan as having brownish olivaceous spores, but in our fully mature plants with open mouths the spores are deep purplish brown.   Only a slight difference in maturity would make this difference in color.

Illustrations: Lloyd.   Myc. Works, pl. 59, figs. 6–8.
    Morgan.   Journ. Cin. Soc. Nat. Hist. 14: pl. 2, fig. 3.

1002. In a pine grove, Sept. 28, 1913.

1762. In pine woods, Sept. 12, 1915. Spores minutely punctate, 4.4–4.8 x 5.5–6.3μ.

7144. On the ground in mixed woods, Sept. 26, 1923. Spores oval, minutely warted, 3.8–4.2 x 4.4–5.4μ, all with a short pedicel.

Also Nos. 501, 553, 588, 7150.

    Asheville. Beardslee.

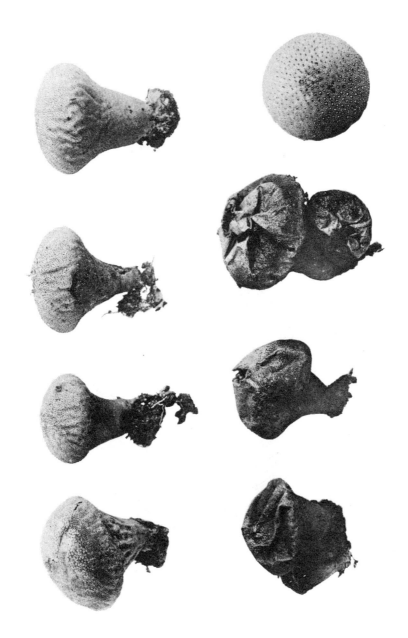

PLATE 52

LYCOPERDON GEMMATUM. Nos. 500 and 554

PLATE 53

Lycoperdon gemmatum. No. 5570 [plant on left]
Lycoperdon Peckii. No. 5655 [middle]; No. 5654 [small plants]

Lycoperdon fuscum Bonorden

Plates 42 and 113

Plants, in our collections, broadly top-shaped or pyriform or subglobose, about 1.8–3.5 cm. broad, with a short stalk; covered with slender, delicate, dark brown to blackish spines about 0.5 mm. long which are either single or grouped in fascicles of several with the tips usually incurved, and which are long persistent; they are not intermixed with other granular or scurfy material and on falling away finally they leave the dark brown inner peridium quite smooth and shining. Subgleba small, in the present form occupying only about a sixth of the body, in one form nearly absent (see below); chambers of moderate size.

Spores (of No. 5525) dusky olivaceous, spherical, 4–4.8μ thick, distinctly dotted with warts which project through the hyaline coat. Capillitium threads slightly branched, up to 3.7μ thick, with thick, pitted walls.

The plant described above is the dark-colored, often large form with dark brown inner peridium and persistent spinules. We also have the form known as *L. dryinum* and one approaching the form *L. cupricum*. The former is a small plant with very short black spinules, silvery brown inner peridium, and little or no subgleba (No. 5777). The latter is a plant of moderate size with slender, rather scattered, black spinules and a golden brown to coppery brown inner peridium (No. 5719). All forms are separated from related species by the very slender spines which soon turn dark brown to black and which are so openly placed as to clearly show the smooth surface of the inner peridium between them. These spines are the only covering of the inner peridium and are not intermingled with scurfy or granular material. The resulting appearance in the fresh plant is remarkably like that of a baby's head, set with thin dark hair. All forms grow in deciduous woods on leaves or rotting wood.

Illustrations: Hollos. l. c., pl. 21, figs. 1–7 and 18.
Lloyd. Myc. Works, pl. 45 (back), figs. 1–7.

North Carolina. Blowing Rock. Coker and party, August 1922. No. 5525. On bark of dead frondose tree near ground. No. 5642. In thick humus on a mossy rock. Spores minutely warted, pedicellate with ends of pedicels broken off and mixed with the spores, 4.4–5.5μ. No. 5777. On leafy mold, deciduous woods (*L. dryinum* form). No. 5779. Among frondose leaves. Typical; spores pedicellate, faintly dotted, 4.4–5μ. (U. N. C. Herb.)
Linville Falls. Coker and party, August 1922. No. 5719. Among leaves in deep frondose woods (*L. cupricum* form). (U. N. C. Herb.) Spores pedicellate, 4–4.8μ, faintly warted and surrounded by a hyaline coat.
Washington. Langley. Grant, coll. (U. N. C. Herb.). This is a form with minute dark warts instead of spines. Spores minutely warted, 4.2–5.5μ, with a small, dark mucro. Capillitium branched, up to 5μ thick, distinctly pitted.

Lycoperdon marginatum Vitt.

L. papillatum Schaeff. in sense of Hollos
L. cruciatum Rostk.
L. separans Peck
L. calvescens B. & C.

Plates 55, 56 and 113

Plants 1.2–4.5 cm. broad and nearly always broader than tall; narrowing below to a short stem and root. Cortex pure white, then a little discolored or pinkish, becoming clay colored or deep brown in age, composed of densely set, sharp, erect warts which are short, thick and simple or more slender and fascicled with their tips cohering, at maturity breaking up into large or small flakes (see below), usually beginning in a median line between the stem and top, but often rupturing at every point or at many points at once (see below for woods form).   The lower third, covering the stem and lower part of the body, does not fall away.   Inner peridium strong to pale olivaceous brown when first exposed, even, or in one of our collections (Warrenton, Va.) obviously pitted, much as in *gemmatum*.   It is peculiar in having beneath the spines a covering of a minute brown furfurescence which disappears rather slowly and leaves the surface paler and shining.   This furfurescence is different from that of any other plant we know.   It is composed of little flat scales, the prevailing shape of which is spherical to oblong, varying to irregular and angled, the majority elongated and up to 60 x 100μ.   Subgleba ample, composed of distinct, rather large compartments, occupying the stem and lower part of the body and persistent after the top has disappeared, remaining as a dark brown pedicel with a thin, collapsed margin.

Spores (of No. 482) spherical, smooth, 3.6–4.1μ thick, with one oil drop.   The spores have mixed with them about an equal number of small rods like bacilli, that average about twice the length of the spore's width.   Basidia (of No. 5225) 6.6–7.4μ thick, usually 4-spored.   Capillitium composed of yellowish brown fibers very little branched, about as thick as the spores as a rule, but up to 5μ in diameter, attenuated at the ends.

The spores and capillitium of our plants have been compared with Peck's collections of *separans* and are the same.   One of the most characteristic qualities of the plant is its strong odor when ripening or fading like that of horse urine, a distinction it shares with *L. gemmatum*.   It is a very common plant with us in open places and cultivated ground, and less often in woods.   The spines are very variable, in some cases very thick and short and not split up into fascicles, in others slender and moderately short or long, and in groups of several with their tips united.   In Chapel Hill there are two rather distinct forms; in one (typical) of cultivated or open ground the cortex falls off in larger flakes and more irregularly and the spores have a little mucro left after the pedicel breaks off; in the other one of woods each group of spines with its underlying tissue is apt to fall off singly or with a small group of others, and the denudation is more regular, proceeding from the top downward.   In this form the spores have no mucro.   The scales on the denuded surface are just like those of the typical form.   This character alone is sufficient to distinguish the species.   For general discussion of the species see Lloyd (Myc. Notes, pp. 214 and 231).

It seems certain that *L. cruciatum* is *L. marginatum*, as Rostkovius's good figure could not be referred to anything else.   Spores of three specimens labelled *cruciatum* in Bresadola's herbarium (sent by Romell) are not those of the present species.   This is true also of a specimen labelled *marginatum* in the same herbarium   We have seen European material of true *L. marginatum*, as *L. cruciatum* (Herb. Hasskarl & Herb. Klotzsch), received from the Ryks Herbarium in Leiden.   They show the same spores and peridial scales as in our specimens (spores 3.6–4.5μ).   The capillitium is not colorless but of about the same tint as in ours.   We have compared capillitium of plants just maturing in our No. 482 with other mature ones of the same collection and find that the capillitium does not change after the spores are mature.

A bit of the inner peridium and spores and capillitium of *L. calvescens* B. & C. from the Curtis Herbarium (Wright, No. 6366, co-type), kindly sent us by Dr. Thaxter, shows it to be *marginatum*.   The peridial scales and the spores are the same as in the typical form of *L. marginatum*.   *Lycoperdon pratense* Pers. is also considered a synonym

PLATE 54

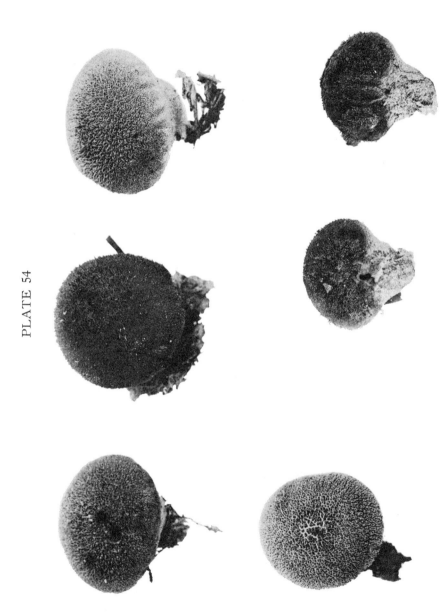

Lycoperdon eximium. Nos. 501 and 553

by Hollos, but Lloyd thinks that the typical *pratense* does not occur in the United States. A specimen from New Zealand determined as *L. pratense* by Lloyd does not look like our *L. marginatum*, as the spines are much shorter and the denuded peridium shows no obvious furfurescence. The spores are slightly smaller and both they and the capillitium are paler than in our plants.

From the description and illustration, *L. abscissum* R. E. Fries from Bolivia and Argentina is nearest *L. marginatum*. It is remarkable in the comparatively large size of the subgleba which occupies most of the fruit body.

Illustrations: Hard. Mushrooms, fig. 467.
    Hollos. l. c., pl. 20, figs. 17–22; pl. 29, fig. 6 (as *L. papillatum*).
    Lloyd. Myc. Works, pl. 51 (as *L. cruciatum*). 1905.
    Lloyd. Photogravure of Am. Fungi, No. 3 (as *L. separans*).
    Morgan. l. c., **14**: pl. 2. fig. 1.
    Murrill. Mycologia **1**: pl. 15, fig. 7 (as *L. Wrightii*). 1909. The three plants on right may be true *L. Wrightii*.
    Rostkovius in Sturm. Deutsch. Fl. Pilze **1**: pl. 8 (as *L. cruciatum*). 1813.
    Vittadini. Monog. Lycoperd., pl. 1, fig. 11. 1843.

  99. On ground in cemetery, October 27, 1911. Spores spherical, smooth, 3.6–4µ thick, with a very distinct oil drop.
  482. Glen Burnie meadow and on campus, October 3, 1912.
  922. In mixed woods, September 13, 1913.
1762b. In pine woods, September 12, 1915.
5225. In a lowground pasture, June 23, 1922.
7194. In mixed woods, October 14, 1923. Spores 3.7–4.2µ thick, with pedicels entirely broken off.

    Haywood County. In mold in semi-open place by Pigeon River, Aug. 9, 1926. Coker, coll. (U. N. C. Herb., No. 8131).

South Carolina. Ravenel. Fungi Car. Exs. No. 73. (Phil. Acad. Herb. and N. Y. B. G. Herb., as *L. gemmatum*.)
Florida. Couch, coll. (U. N. C. Herb., Nos. 7266–7272).
Alabama. Auburn. Earle, coll. (N. Y. B. G. Herb.).
Virginia. Mountain Lake. In moist woods. Murrill, coll. (N. Y. B. G. Herb.). This is exactly like our woods form No. 7194.
    Warrenton. Coker, coll. (U. N. C. Herb.). Spores faintly rough, 3.5–4.2µ. Woods form.
District of Columbia. Cook, coll. (U. S. Nat'l. Herb., as *L. cruciatum*).
New Jersey. Newfield. Ellis, coll. (N. Y. B. G. Herb., as *L. Wrightii* and as *L. pedicellatum*).
New York. Sand Lake. (N. Y. B. G. Herb., as *L. separans*.)
    Newcomb. House, coll. (Herb. N. Y. St. Mus. and U. N. C. Herb.). Spores smooth, 3.7–4.2µ. Scales on inner peridium as usual.
Connecticut. Miss White, coll. (N. Y. B. G. Herb.).
Ohio. Lloyd, coll. No. 2655. (Bres. Herb., as *L. separans*, and U. N. C. Herb.)
    Cleveland. Beardslee, coll. (Bres. Herb., as *L. separans*, and U. N. C. Herb.). Spores 3.6–4.2µ.
Wisconsin. La Crosse. (Univ. Wis. Herb. and U. N. C. Herb.). Spores smooth, 3.5–4µ, sometimes with a mucro.

Lycoperdon Curtisii Berk.
L. Wrightii B. & C.

Plates 57 and 113

    Plants small, globose or depressed-globose, 0.7–2.3 cm. (rarely 3.5 cm.) thick, averaging about 1 cm., with a distinct tendency to cespitose growth, generally sessile or with a very abrupt, short stem; surface thickly set with white or whitish, rather persistent spines, which are usually convergent at their tips in stellate groups. With age these fall away in part from the top of the plant, but the powdery scurf between them wears away more slowly so that the pale brown inner peridium becomes very tardily smooth. Gleba greenish yellow, then light brownish yellow to brown with a tint of olive. Subgleba quite small but distinct, the compartments of moderate size.

Spores (of No. 552) small, spherical, minutely asperulate, 2.6–3.7μ in diameter, averaging about 3.3μ. Capillitium of almost hyaline, sparingly branched, flaccid, septate threads, 3–7μ in diameter, averaging about twice the diameter of the spores.

This little plant has almost the external appearance when immature of *L. marginatum*, but averages much smaller and also differs in a strong tendency to crowded growth. The cortex does not flake off as in *L. marginatum*, but this difference cannot be made out until full maturity. The plants of No. 539 were thought at first to be *L. marginatum* and were watched for two weeks. As no cracking occurred they were brought in and found to differ from *L. marginatum* in the color of the spores and the character of the capillitium. In the herbarium at Albany some of Peck's collections labelled *L. Wrightii* are *L. marginatum*. As Morgan points out (as *L. Curtisii*), the thin-walled, collapsing capillitium is a peculiar character. We have examined the co-type of *L. Curtisii* No. 197 and find the spores to be spherical, minutely rough, 3–3.7μ thick. Morgan treats both *L. Wrightii* and *L. Curtisii*, the latter being the plant as we have it. What plant Morgan treated as *L. Wrightii* we do not know (see Lloyd, Myc. Notes, p. 153). *Lycoperdon Wrightii* is in reality a synonym of the present species, as shown by the co-type in the Curtis Herbarium (Wright, No. 7; Curtis, No. 5633). The spores are spherical, minutely warted, 3–3.6μ thick. Another collection so labelled in the Curtis Herbarium from New York (Peck) looks like *L. pusillum*, while still another from New Jersey (Austin) looks like *L. marginatum* (*L. cruciatum*), as Lloyd says (Myc. Notes, p. 153). For the distribution of this species see R. E. Fries, l. c., p. 8.

We have examined a specimen of *L. candidum* Pers. from Persoon's herbarium, kindly sent us by Miss Cool. The appearance of the cortex is like that of *L. Curtisii*, and the spores agree in size (3–3.8μ) but run smoother (pl. 113, fig. 23). The plant seems to be not quite mature, and this may account for the difference. The *Lyc. candidum* of Schweinitz Herbarium as represented in the Michener Herb. (No. 2747) is *Bovista plumbea*. *Lycoperdon candidum* (Rostk.) Bon. is a different plant, now put under *Calvatia*.

Illustrations: Hard. Mushrooms, fig. 468 (as *L. Wrightii*).
　　Lloyd. Myc. Works, pl. 63, figs. 1–4 (as *L. Wrightii*).
　　Morgan. Journ. Cin. Soc. Nat. Hist. 14: pl. 2, fig. 4.

552. In grass on the campus, Oct. 10, 1912.
1718. On bare earth in a yard, Sept. 10, 1915.
7546. On bank of a ditch in the Arboretum, Oct. 1, 1924.
7549. In manured grass on campus, Oct. 2, 1924.
Also Nos. 539, 984, 7151.

　　Asheville. Beardslee.
　　Linville Falls. Coker and party, Aug. 1922. No. 5760. On ground in a pasture. (U. N. C. Herb.)

PLATE 55

LYCOPERDON MARGINATUM. No. 482

PLATE 56

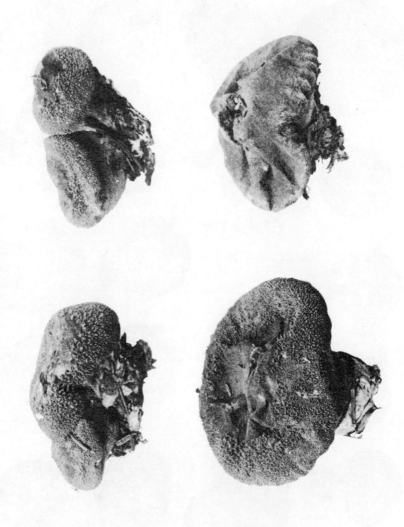

LYCOPERDON MARGINATUM. Woods form. No. 7194

District of Columbia. Lloyd, coll. (U. S. Nat'l. Herb.).

New York. Unionport. Harper, coll. (N. Y. B. G. Herb.).

Wisconsin. Eagle Heights. (Univ. Wis. Herb. and U. N. C. Herb.) Spores subspherical, nearly
smooth, 3–3.8μ. Capillitium very pale and easily collapsing.

Lycoperdon oblongisporum B. & C.

Plates 58 and 113

Plants globose or depressed-globose, with a distinct cord-like root. Cortex of
minute appressed fibers arranged in groups so as to form whitish, scurfy spots on the
pale, dull brown surface of the inner peridium, which is tardily exposed. Gleba olivaceous to dark olive brown; subgleba none.

Spores (of No. 497) oval to subspherical, deep olive brown, smooth, 3–4 x 4.3–5.5μ,
with a large oil drop and a prominent mucro about 1μ long. Capillitium threads long,
delicate, branched, up to 6.5μ thick, considerably pitted in places.

This little plant was originally described from Cuba, and is quite rare in this
country, only a few scattered collections having been noted before and none from this
state. However, it agrees so well with the descriptions of both Morgan and Lloyd for
this species that we feel quite sure our determination is correct. The plants look like
Lloyd's figures, and the spores are shaped like those shown on his plate 65, figs. 9–12.
The species shades into *L. pusillum* by intermediate forms. We are entering No.
5312 as this species on the ground of its absolutely smooth spores that are not perfectly
spherical. No. 5211, which we are entering under *L. pusillum*, is also intermediate.

Illustrations: Hollos. l. c., pl. 21, figs. 36–41.
Lloyd. As cited above.

497. In poor soil on campus and in Arboretum, Oct. 1, 1912.

5312. In a field of Sudan grass, July 8, 1922. Plants up to 2.3 cm. thick; subgleba none; gleba gray-
brown; the spores themselves brown with a faint olive tint, smooth, spherical to slightly subspherical with the proximal end pointed, 2.8–4μ thick. Capillitium threads pitted, up to 6μ
thick.

7116. On ground in a pasture, September 9, 1923. Spores 3.4–3.7 x 4–4.4μ.

Asheville. Beardslee, coll.

Lycoperdon pusillum Batsch

Plates 58 and 113

Plants subglobose or flattened, small, rarely up to 2 cm. broad, pinched to a cord-
like root; surface variable, usually almost smooth to naked eye, but with a lens it is
seen to be covered with a fine fibrous flocculence that seems to flatten down like drying
suds and separates into very small patches, giving a maculated or areolated appearance, or rarely this flocculence takes the form of small soft spines; again the surface
may be entirely covered with a delicate powder or more rarely minute compact warts.
Color when young pure white, then clay color or dull olivaceous yellow, and often
dark brown in age. Gleba passing through yellow to greenish yellow, becoming at full
maturity brownish olive or grayish olive-brown to deep coffee-brown without a tint of
olive, filling the entire peridium; that is, there is no subgleba. The peridium before
maturity is thick, up to 15 mm., but rapidly becomes extremely thin as it dries during

maturation. There is no breaking away of a superficial part. At maturity a small apical pore is formed.

Spores color of the gleba, spherical, 3.2–4.3μ thick, with rather thick wall, a distinct, small mucro and a large oil drop, quite smooth in some plants, in others with the walls faintly warted or pitted, appearing radially striate. Outside of the main brownish wall a faint hyaline coat may be seen under high power. Basidia (of No. 5211) short-clavate, stout, 4.5–5.5 x 9–11μ, with 4 or in many cases only 2 long sterigmata visible at one time. Capillitium color of the gleba and composed of long, delicate, branched threads that are attenuated at the ends and are about the width of the spores, some up to 6.5μ thick; walls more or less pitted, the larger threads usually more pitted than the smaller ones.

This is a rather common little plant in Chapel Hill in open places, fields and yards. It is a puzzling species due to variation in the spores which is not associated with any other character we can make out, such as size, subgleba or surface. The capillitium is the same in all. None of our plants has a subgleba.

Some collections that we are retaining in *L. pusillum* are intermediate between that and *L. oblongisporum*, as No. 5211, which has spores that are mostly oval and pointed toward the mucro, smooth to very minutely punctate.

98. In grass on ground in cemetery, Nov. 10, 1911. Spores minutely asperulate.
2209. On bare soil under cedars, June 23, 1916. Spores 3.2–4.3μ.
5202. On ground among grass and moss, June 19, 1922. Spores 3.2–4.2μ thick, all minutely spiny and only a few with a mucro.
5390. Sandy old field, July 23, 1922. Spores appear smooth in water even when magnified 2160 times; warted, however, under same magnification when nearly dry.
Also Nos. 1003, 1025, 3268, 5211.

Asheville. Beardslee, coll.

South Carolina. Ravenel, coll. (N. Y. B. G. Herb.). Spores smooth, 3.4–4μ thick.
Florida. Gainesville. Couch, coll. (U. N. C. Herb., Nos. 7256–7259, 7264, 7265). Spores (of No. 7259) smooth or nearly so, 3.5–4.2μ thick, with a mucro.
New Jersey. Newfield. Ellis, coll. (N. Y. B. G. Herb. and U. N. C. Herb.). Spores spherical, minutely warted, 3.5–3.8μ.
New York. Newcomb. House, coll. (Herb. N. Y. St. Mus. and U. N. C. Herb.). Spores minutely rough, 3.6–4μ.
Wisconsin. Blue Mounds. (Univ. Wis. Herb. and U. N. C. Herb.) Spores smooth or nearly so, 3.4–3.8μ.
North Dakota. Kulm, Aug. 1909. Brenckle's Fungi Dakotenses No. 93 (Path. and Myc. Herb., as *L. cepaeforme*). In size some of these specimens approach *L. cepaeforme*, but there is no subgleba. Spores spherical or subspherical, 3.5–3.8μ, smooth, usually with a mucro. Capillitium rather pale and irregular, encrusted, up to 7.4μ thick.
Pacific Coast near Canadian boundary. Dearness, No. 5550. (U. N. C. Herb.) Spores minutely warted, 3.5–4.2μ.

Lycoperdon polymorphum Vitt.

L. cepaeforme Bull.

Plate 113

Plants subglobose, often contracted into a stalk-like base, and characteristically with a conspicuous, stout root which may ramify in the earth and connect individuals of a group; size variable, 1.3–3.5 cm. broad and up to 4.5 cm. high. Peridium in the

PLATE 57

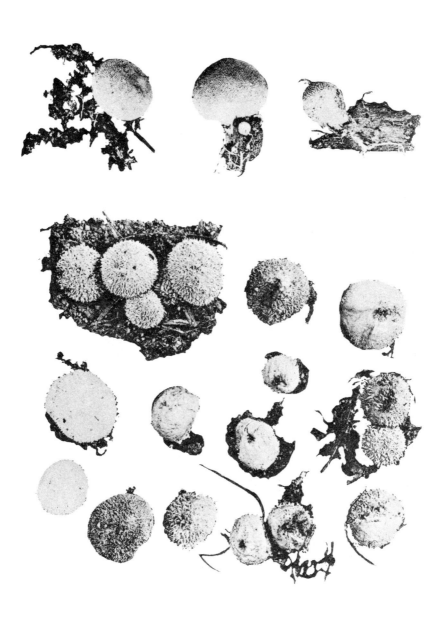

LYCOPERDON SUBINCARNATUM. No. 5556 [above]
LYCOPERDON CURTISII. No. 552 [below]. $\times$ 1 1/3

PLATE 58

LYCOPERDON OBLONGISPORUM. No. 5312 [above]
LYCOPERDON PUSILLUM. No. 3268 [below]

dry state dull brown to olivaceous brown, varying to a brighter reddish yellow, thin and papery, in the Wyoming plant noted below, really divided into two extremely thin layers, the outer of which may or may not scale off in part; the surface dotted with minute, scattered, persistent flecks or nodules or varying to more closely placed granular particles. Gleba dull olivaceous brown at maturity; subgleba obvious to large, filling the stalk-like base, about the same color as the gleba and remarkable in its compact structure with chambers so small as to be invisible, thus easily separating this species from all other American species of *Lycoperdon* (*Calvatia rubro-flava* has no chambers at maturity).

Spores (of plant from Wyoming) smooth or rarely faintly dotted, spherical, 3.4–4µ, with a conspicuous oil drop and sometimes a short pedicel. Capillitium threads branched, averaging about 3.7µ thick.

Gregarious on earth in open places. We have not found it in North Carolina, but it is reported from a number of eastern states, and the *cepaeforme* form is said by Lloyd to be common. This last form is the more spherical one without a stalk-like base. In plants we have from Wyoming, kindly sent us by Mr. Simon Davis, both forms are well represented and apparently from the same collection. One of the plants has as distinct a stalked base as that from Europe shown by Lloyd on his plate 52, fig. 4. We have a good European specimen from Romell (Sweden) which agrees with the Wyoming plants in every particular except that the peridium does not divide into two papery layers in age (spores smooth, 3.6–4µ); also one from Torrend (Portugal) which is similar (spores smooth, 3.5–4.2µ, rarely with a short pedicel).

This species is closely related to *L. pusillum*, and Lloyd thinks that they intergrade. With us *L. pusillum* is a very common little plant without subgleba, and it does not vary here to the larger forms of the above description. Its root is distinctly more slender than in *L. polymorphum* of the same size. Its spores are indistinguishable. Lloyd shows forms of this species from Australia with several plants of a colony connected by underground rhizomorphs (Myc. Notes, p. 730, fig. 1096). It is interesting to note that some of our plants from Wyoming show this character clearly.

Cunningham gives the spores of the present species as 4.5–5.5µ. Other characters agree well with the above. It is supposed by some authors, as Hollos, that *L. polymorphum* is the same as *L. furfuraceum* Schaeff., a species which is insufficiently known.

Illustrations: Bulliard. Herb. Fr., pl. 435, fig. II (as *L. cepaeforme*).
  Cunningham. Trans. N. Z. Inst. **57**: pl. 5, fig. 12. 1926.
  Hollos. l. c., pl. 21, figs. 19–23 (as *L. furfuraceum*).
  Lloyd. Myc. Works, pl. 34, figs. 1–6; pl. 52; pl. 53, figs. 1–4 (as *L. cepaeforme*); pl. 65, figs. 1–7 (as *L. cepaeforme*).
  Morgan. Journ. Cin. Soc. Nat. Hist. **14**: pl. 2, fig. 9 (as *L. cepaeforme*).
  Vittadini. Monog. Lycoperdaceae, pl. 2, fig. 7.

Wyoming. Pitchfork. Simon Davis, coll. (U. N. C. Herb.).
Reported also from many other states (see Lloyd, Myc. Notes, p. 234).

Lycoperdon coloratum Peck

Plants subglobose, up to 3 cm. thick, pinched in at base, firmly attached either by one conspicuous strand or by more numerous white fibers which may often be seen to connect beneath the surface small sclerotia-like initials. Color from first appearance until near maturity a brilliant golden yellow; surface dotted with minute, harsh, discrete warts or nodules which during maturity become dark brown to nearly black and slowly wear away separately, exposing the shining bright brown peridium. Young gleba white then passing through yellowish to dull dark brown at maturity; subgleba very small, with small but distinct cavities under a lens. Odor while maturing strong and fragrant.

Spores (of No. 8044) spherical, nearly smooth but not quite, 3.5–4μ thick. Capillitium (of No. 8108) irregular, main branches 4–5.5μ thick; color dull brown with a tint of vinaceous under the microscope, no obvious pits in the walls.

Until dulled by maturity, this striking plant is by far the most brilliant of our puffballs. No description by others suggests the brilliant orange of our mountain plant, though Peck speaks of the species as conspicuous. While the plant may be only a form of *L. polymorphum*, it is so conspicuous and distinctive in itself that it will do no harm to retain Peck's name for it. In the mountains of western North Carolina, *L. pusillum* grows in pastures, and *L. coloratum* in the woods. They are strikingly different.

Illustrations: ? Morgan. Journ. Cin. Soc. Nat. Hist. **14**: pl. 2, fig. 10.
     ?Trelease. Morels and Puffballs of Madison, pl. 2, fig. 2.

North Carolina. Haywood County. On ground in mixed woods by Crawford's Creek, Aug. 2, 1926. Coker, coll. (U. N. C. Herb., No. 7995). Under rhododendron and hemlock by Cold Creek, Aug. 6, 1926. Coker and Totten, colls. (U. N. C. Herb., No. 8044). Woods mold by Cold Creek, Aug. 8, 1926. Coker, coll. (U. N. C. Herb., No. 8108).

BOVISTELLA Morgan

Plants subglobose and permanently attached by a rooting base; inner peridium thin, flaccid, opening by a definite, apical pore, and collapsing as the spores escape; capillitium as in *Bovista*, of distinct units with all the ends tapering and not connected with the peridium; but in some cases very slender and not abundantly branched; spores oval or subglobose, smooth (at least in American species), and with long pedicels.

Separated from *Lycoperdon* by the discrete, branched units of the capillitium; from *Calvatia* by this character and by the torn mouth; and from *Bovista* by the collapsing inner peridium, and by the permanent attachment to the soil. The above is essentially the conception of the genus by Morgan who established it (see below), except that we are including species without a sterile base, as does Lloyd. We are not following Lloyd in including plants with long, intertwined capillitium fibers which arise from the periphery as in *Lycoperdon*. Without this character we would not know how to separate the latter. Lloyd would extend the limits of the genus as follows (Myc. Notes No. 23: 277. 1906).

"Peridium flaccid, with or without a sterile base, opening by a definite mouth. Capillitium of short, separate threads or long, intertwined threads. Spores pedicellate." Note that the flaccid peridium is the only character in this definition that would exclude species of *Bovista*. However, in his discussion, Lloyd makes the further distinction of the breaking away from the base in *Bovista* and the permanent attachment of Lycoperdae, including *Bovistella*. He says that frequently the characteristic capillitium and pedicellate spores are associated in the same plant, but not always, and he would "embrace in the genus *Bovistella* all plants of the tribe Lycoperdae that have *either* or *both* of these characters."

PLATE 59

BOVISTELLA RADICATA. No. 537

LITERATURE

Cunningham. The Genera *Bovista* and *Bovistella*. Proc. Linn. Soc. New. South Wales **50**: 367, pl. 37. 1925.
Lloyd. As cited above.
Morgan. Journ. Cin. Soc. Nat. Hist. **14**: 141. 1892.
Petri. Flora Italica Cryptogama (Gasterales), Fasc. **5**: 58. 1909.

KEY TO THE SPECIES

Plants of moderate size; sterile base obvious...*B. radicata*
Plants small; sterile base none
    Plants epigeal; capillitium units very slender, the main branches only about 6–7µ thick...*B. echinella*
    Plants subterranean until maturity; main threads of the capillitium up to 18.5µ thick
                         See *Bovista minor*

Bovistella radicata (Mont.) Pat.

Bovistella ohiensis Ell. & Morg.

Plates 59 and 114

Plants globose or broadly top-shaped, up to 7 cm. broad usually, but rarely as large as 14.5 cm., often plicate below; attached by a firm, thick, tapering root; cortex composed over the upper half or more of soft, pyramidal warts which are often fused at their tips into fascicles as in species of *Lycoperdon*, these fading towards the base to a dense soft scurf; white at first, then dull ochraceous when dry and wearing away irregularly and incompletely to expose the thin, papery, inner peridium which is metallic buff or silvery buff or ochraceous in color, rupturing at maturity by an apical pore or slit which extends by fission on exposure and finally by collapsing and incurling leaves the entire subgleba exposed in age. Subgleba large, broad, occupying about one-third to one-half the plant, the edges extending up the sides of the peridium to form a cup-shaped base which is long persistent. Gleba at first white and cheesy, then passing through yellowish to brown (about Brussels brown of Ridgway); chambers of the young gleba 25–250µ wide, hollow. Before ripening begins, a section of the peridium shows that the scurfy and warty superficial coat is an extension of a thick, compact, pulpy, tender layer about 450µ thick of bladdery cells beneath which lies the thin, very tough inner peridium about 130µ thick, composed of densely woven, slender filaments about 3.7µ thick.

Spores oval, smooth, 3.5–4.5 x 4.3–5.2µ, with one large oil drop and long, hyaline, persistent pedicels which average about 11µ long. Basidia short, 6.6µ thick, with 4 long sterigmata which break off with the spores. Capillitium threads free, short, 3–5 times branched, the main stem 7–12µ thick, the branches tapering to about 3.5µ thick near the ends.

At Hartsville, S. C. (see below), we have collected a very robust form reaching 14.5 cm. broad, which is considerably larger than the form figured by Lloyd (cited below). The species is common in Chapel Hill and prefers cultivated soil and open places. When quite fresh and white the taste is sweetish and pleasant and the odor slight, but as the color begins to change the odor becomes rather strong and nitrous.

As represented in Torrend's Fungi Selecti Exs. No. 77, *Bovista radicata* is the same as our plant and confirms Patouillard's conclusion (accepted by Hollos) that our American plant is *B. radicata*. The type was described from northern Africa (Syll. Crypt., etc., Paris, 1856). Plants from California distributed by McClatchie as *B. ammophila* Lév., a European species, now included in *Bovistella*, are considered by Lloyd as *B. plumbea* (Myc. Notes, p. 88).

Illustrations: Hard. Mushrooms, fig. 473.
   Lloyd. Myc. Works, pl. 86.
   Marshall. Mushroom Book, pl. opposite p. 128.

   79. In a corn field, October 12, 1909.
3903. In pine woods, Nov. 11, 1919.
5200. Strowd's pasture, June 17, 1922. Spores 3.7–4.2 x 4–5μ, with pedicels about 12μ long.
5919. On ground in pasture, Nov. 22, 1922. Spores 3–4 x 4–5.5μ. Capillitium threads up to 5.5μ thick.
Also Nos. 537, 1018, 1428, 1520, 2438, 3010, 5361, 6094.

   Asheville. Beardslee.
   Flat Rock. Memminger, coll. (N. Y. B. G. Herb.).

South Carolina. Hartsville. Coker, No. 1545. In a sandy cow pasture, June 12, 1915. A very stout
   form, up to 14.5 cm. broad, but the spores and all other characters just as in the Chapel Hill
   plant.
   Georgetown. Coker, No. 6015. In sandy woods pasture near Silver Hill, Dec. 29, 1922.
Florida. Couch, coll. (U. N. C. Herb., No. 7276). Also collections by Weber and Walker.
   Clearwater. Rousseau, coll. (U. S. Nat'l. Herb., as *B. ohiensis*).
Alabama. Auburn. Earle, coll. (N. Y. B. G. Herb., as *B. ohiensis*).
New York. Botanical Garden. Murrill, coll. (N. Y. B. G. Herb., as *B. ohiensis*).
Indiana. Gentry, coll. (N. Y. B. G. Herb., as *B. ohiensis*). Main threads of capillitium about 11μ
   thick. Spores oval, smooth, 3.4–4.2 x 3.7–5.5μ, with a pedicel up to 10μ long.

Bovistella echinella (Pat.) Lloyd

Plate 114

   Plants small, subglobose, 5–8 mm. thick, attached by a short, blunt, sandy pad;
when young, white with a thin, continuous, felt-like or granular cortex, at maturity
becoming dark brown and papery with scattered white flecks, in age practically decorticated. Mouth apical, definite, becoming fimbriated or toothed. Mature gleba
olivaceous brown, glebal chambers minute and irregular; subgleba practically none.
   Spores (of plant from Lapland) subspherical, 4.2–5.5μ, apparently smooth but with
radial lines showing in the wall, furnished with slender, tapering pedicels up to 8.5μ
long. Capillitium of separate units, but threads long and slender and less frequently
branched than in most species of this genus or of *Bovista;* main threads about 5.5μ
thick.

   This little species has been collected in a number of widely separated places. The
original collection was from Ecuador, and we have specimens from North Dakota and
Lapland. Dr. R. E. Fries has also reported it from Lapland, and Lloyd reports it from
Michigan. This last is the only record, so far as we know, from the eastern United
States.
   We have examined a part of the original collection from Ecuador, kindly sent us by
Patouillard himself, and find it to be just like our collection from Lapland. The capillitium is of long, slender branched units with main threads only about 6.5μ thick; spores
subspherical, 4–5.2 x 4.8–5.8μ with slender pedicels up to 12.8μ long, the walls of the
spores showing faint radial lines. Patouillard describes the spores as echinulate, but
we see only faint lines with no projection in optical section.
   Lloyd describes from Massachusetts *Bovistella Davisii* (Myc. Notes, p. 286, pl.
89), which from the description can hardly be distinguished from the present species.
We have not seen an authentic specimen.

Illustrations: Fries, Th. C. E. Sveriges Gasteromyceter, fig. 21.
  Lloyd. Myc. Works, pl. 89, figs. 1 and 2.

North Dakota. Anselm. On mossy sod in sand hills. Brenckle and Stevens, colls. (N. Y. B. G. Herb. and U. N. C. Herb.). Spores 3.6–4.4µ, with a slender pedicel up to 8.2µ long. Capillitium of long, branched units, about 4.8µ thick in largest places, olivaceous under the microscope.

Michigan. Reported by Lloyd.

Swedish Lapland. Abisco. On grassy railroad embankment, summer, 1921. Coker, coll. (U. N. C. Herb.).

BOVISTA Pers.

Plants spherical, attached centrally at the base, the outer peridium thin, fragile, flaking off at maturity and leaving exposed the smooth, thin, distended, metallic-looking inner peridium which opens by an apical pore, becomes detached from the ground, and is blown about like a light ball, puffing out the spores. Capillitium not connected with the peridium, but composed of separate units which branch dichotomously or irregularly and end in tapering points. There is no sterile base. Spores dark brown or purplish brown, in one of our species with a well developed pedicel.

The genus is remarkable in its tumbling habit (shared by *Mycenastrum* and to a less extent by *Disciseda**) and the inner peridium is especially adapted to this end by the retention of its shape as an inflated ball and by its firm, parchment-like, resilient texture. These balls are rolled about by the wind and the spores shaken out by degrees through the apical mouth or slit. They are very durable and in mountain pastures old plants of the preceding year may still be found in good condition.

Lloyd considers *B. montana* Morgan the same as *B. pila*.

LITERATURE

Bonorden. Die Gattungen *Bovista, Lycoperdon* u. ihr Bau. Bot. Zeit. **15**: 593, 609, 625. 1857.
Cunningham. The Genera *Bovista* and *Bovistella*. Proc. Linn. Soc. N. S. W. **50**: 367, pl. 37. 1925.
Lloyd. The Bovistae. Myc. Notes No. 12: 113. 1902.
Massee. A Revision of the Genus *Bovista*. Journ. Bot. **26**: 129. 1888.
Morgan. Journ. Cin. Soc. Nat. Hist. **14**: 144. 1891.
Petri. Flora Italica Cryptogama (Gasterales), Fasc. **5**: 60. 1909.
Rolland. Observations sur le *Mycenastrum corium* Desv. et sur le *Bovista plumbea* Pers. Bull. Soc. Myc. Fr. **22**: 109. 1906.
Tulasne, L. R. and Ch. De La Fructification des *Scleroderma* comparée à celle des *Lycoperdon* et des *Bovista*. Ann. Sci. Nat., 2nd. ser. **17**: 5, pls. 1 and 2. 1842.

KEY TO THE SPECIES

Fruit bodies above ground, of moderate to large size
  Spores spherical with a short pedicel...*B. pila* (p. 97)
  Spores oval with a long pedicel.. *B. plumbea* (p. 99)
Fruit bodies subterranean until exposed by rains, etc., small; spores oval with a long, wavy pedicel
                                                                          B. minor (p. 99)

Bovista pila B. & C.

Plates 60 and 114

Plants globose or subglobose and irregularly pinched and lobed downward, 6–9 cm. in diameter, attached abruptly below by a single, small cord which breaks at

---

* *Disciseda* does very little tumbling, the flat shape with one side heavier not adapting it well to that habit. It is, however, detached from its place of growth at maturity and knocked about by rain.

maturity; outer peridium thin (0.25 mm.), pure white, tending to become alutaceous or pinkish when handled, surface delicately furfuraceous, becoming rivulose, flaking off in patches at maturity; inner peridium when exposed smooth and shining, more or less bronze colored and splotched with blackish or gray areas, the effect being quite metallic-looking like burnt copper or tin, soon opening at the top by an irregular pore or by more extensive fissures and flaps.

Spores deep brown, thick-walled, smooth, spherical with a very short pedicel or mucro, 3.5–4.3μ thick. Capillitium dark purplish brown at maturity, much branched; branches long, gradually tapering to a point; main hyphae mostly about 11μ thick, rarely up to 13μ. Immature gleba white, showing very small irregular chambers under a lens; basidia (of No. 7999) short-clavate, 8–10.5 x 14–18μ, with 4, rarely 3, unequal sterigmata 4–7.4μ long.

The co-type of *B. pila* in the Curtis Herbarium agrees with the usual interpretation. The spores are spherical, smooth, 3.7–4.5μ thick. This species seems to be the American representative of *B. nigrescens* of Europe, and Lloyd seems to be right in concluding that the latter does not occur in this country. Early records in this country, as by Schweinitz and Curtis, have since proved to be based on *B. pila* or *B. plumbea*. The two species, *B. pila* and *B. nigrescens*, can easily be distinguished by the spores (as noted by Hollos and Lloyd), the latter having somewhat oval spores with a long pedicel. (In a specimen from Bresadola, Cavelante, August, 1898, the spores are 3.8–4.8 x 4–5.2μ, with a long tapering pedicel.) The spores of *B. nigrescens* (pl. 114, fig. 12) are much more like those of *B. plumbea*, which are oval with a long pedicel, but those of the latter that we have seen are distinctly larger. Th. Fries gives the spores of *B. nigrescens* as 5–6μ in diameter. If this variation exists, the plants should hardly be separated. The spores of Schweinitz's "*B. nigrescens*" arc those of *B. pila*, spherical, usually sessile, sometimes with a short mucro, 3.7–4.5μ thick.

Illustrations: Lloyd. Genera of Gasteromycetes, pl. 9, figs. 43 and 44.
    Lloyd. Myc. Works, pl. 2.

North Carolina. Black Mountain. At summit on grassland frequented by cattle. Holmes, coll. (U. N. C. Herb., No. 5359).
    Boone. Coker, coll. Aug. 22, 1922. The photograph shows this collection but the plants were lost.
    Asheville. Beardslee.
    Haywood Co. Piney Mountain (alt. 5700 ft.), open pasture, July 31, 1926. Coker, coll. Also Cold Spring Mountain, by barn, immature state, Aug. 3, 1926. Totten, coll. (U. N. C. Herb. No. 7999).
Virginia. Apple Orchard Mountain. Murrill, coll. (N. Y. B. G. Herb.).
Pennsylvania. Buck Hill Falls. Mrs. Delafield, coll. (N. Y. B. G. Herb.). Spores smooth or nearly so, 3.8–4.4μ, with a pedicel and very distinct oil drop. Capillitium much branched, main threads up to 17μ.
New York. Arkville. Murrill, coll. (N. Y. B. G. Herb.).
Vermont. Middleburg. Burt, coll. (Bres. Herb.). Spores spherical, usually with a short mucro, 3.7–4.4μ.
Wisconsin. Madison. Trelease, coll. (N. Y. B. G. Herb.).
    Algonia. Dodge, coll. (Univ. Wis. Herb. and U. N. C. Herb.). Spores smooth, 3.7–5μ, often with a short pedicel.
Wyoming. Pitchfork. Davis, coll. (U. N. C. Herb.). Spores smooth or nearly so, 3.8–5μ, with a short pedicel.
Washington. Langley. Grant, coll. (U. N. C. Herb.). Spores subspherical, smooth, 4–5.5μ, with a short pedicel. Main threads of capillitium up to 12μ thick.

PLATE 60

BOVISTA PILA.   Boone, N. C.

PLATE 61

BOVISTELLA DEALBATA. LLOYD HERB. [above]
CRUCIBULUM VULGARE. No. 1534. Magnified

Canada. London. Dearness, coll. (U. N. C. Herb.). Spores smooth, spherical, 3.8–4.5μ, with no obvious pedicel.

Bovista plumbea Pers.

Plate 114

Plants small, 2–3 cm. thick, nearly globose and attached by a clump of fibrous mycelium; cortex thin, whitish, at maturity shelling off in plates over the upper half or over most of the surface. Inner peridium thin, smooth, mouse gray to deep mouse gray of Ridgway, dehiscing at the apex by a rather large, nearly circular mouth.

Spores (of No. 5358) oval with long, pointed, hyaline pedicels up to 13μ long, very minutely rough, with a halo around the spore; wall two-layered, outer layer thinner and dark, inner one thicker and lighter, 4.5–6 x 5.5–7μ, with one large oil drop. Capillitium ochraceous brown, loose, the threads several times branched, main stems 16–22μ thick, branches tapering to a point. According to Rolland (see below), the basidia are 4-spored with rather long sterigmata.

Our plant agrees well with Morgan's description. *Bovista ovalispora* Cooke and Massee is probably the same plant (Ann. Bot. **4**: 62. 1889). Lloyd states (Myc. Notes No. **12**: 115) that in *B. plumbea* "most spores are not truly globose, but have a tendency to oval form. There is, however, a wide range in this respect." See under *B. pila* for comparison with *B. nigrescens*.

Illustrations: Berkeley. Ann. Sci. Nat., 2nd ser., **12**: pl. 2, figs. 15–18. 1839.
    Corda. Icon. Fung. **5**: pl. 6, fig. 47. 1837.
    Dufour. Atlas des Champ. Comest. et Ven., pl. 75, No. 171. 1891.
    Hard. Mushrooms, fig. 472.
    Lloyd. Myc. Works, pl. 1.
    Massee. Ann. Bot. **4**: pl. 4, fig. 63.
    Rolland. Bull. Soc. Myc. Fr. **22**: pl. 22, figs. 12–15. 1906.
    Sorokine. Rev. Myc., 1890, pl. 12, figs. 342, 343; pl. 25, fig. 352.
    Tulasne. Ann. Sci. Nat., 2nd ser., **17**: pl. 2, figs. 1–3. 1842.

North Carolina. Asheville. Beardslee. (U. N. C. Herb., No. 5358.) Spores oval, with faintly striated walls, 4.5–6.5 x 5.5–8μ.
South Carolina. Ravenel. Fungi Car. Exs. No. 81, as *B. nigrescens*. (Phil. Acad. Herb.)
New York. Albany. Peck, coll. (Curtis Herb.). Also others from New York as *B. nigrescens*.
Massachusetts. Boston. Sprague, coll. (Curtis Herb., as *B. nigrescens*).
Ohio. Hayden, coll. (Curtis Herb., as *B. nigrescens*).
    Cincinnati. Lloyd, coll. (Bresadola Herb. and U. N. C. Herb.). Spores dark, oval, faintly rough, 4.5–6.8 x 5.5–7.4μ, with a pedicel up to 13μ long. Capillitium as usual, dark, thick-walled, up to 22μ thick.
Wisconsin. Blue Mounds. (Univ. Wis. Herb. and U. N. C. Herb.) Spores oval with long tapering pedicels, 4.2–5.2 x 5.5–7μ.
    Eagle Heights. (Univ. Wis. Herb. and U. N. C. Herb.) Spores oval, with walls faintly lined, 4.8–6 x 6–7.5μ, with pedicels up to 16μ long.
Wyoming. Pitchfork. Davis, coll. (U. N. C. Herb.). Spores oval, minutely rough, 4–5.5 x 5.5–7μ, with long pedicels.

Bovista minor Morgan

Plate 114

Plant subglobose, about 1.5 cm. broad (1.3–1.8 cm., according to Morgan), sub-terranean until exposed by rain, etc., the surface at first entirely covered with earth held on by a rather inconspicuous mycelial felt, this wearing away slowly and exposing the pale grayish, then reddish brown, flaccid inner peridium, except for a basal remnant as an earthy point or disc, opening tardily by a small, apical mouth.   Gleba olivaceous, then brownish; subgleba none.

Spores (of No. 2416) oval, smooth, 3–3.7 x 3.8–5μ, with long, wavy pedicels up to 15μ long.   Capillitium of branched units as in its relatives; main threads up to 22μ thick, with thick walls.

This rare plant was described by Morgan from Ohio and Nebraska and is doubtfully reported from Massachusetts by Lloyd.   We have drawn the above description from two Canadian plants noted below and kindly sent us by Dearness.   One of these plants is still covered all over with the thin sand case except for spots here and there; the other is clean of dirt, the cortex remaining only as a basal disc.   This last has the inner peridium deep red-brown, while in the former it is grayish where exposed.   The spores and capillitium in both plants are identical.   The thin, papery peridium would seem to indicate a close approach to the genus *Bovistella*.

Hollos (l. c., p. 126) reduces both this species and *Bovistella dealbata* Lloyd (Myc. Notes, p. 86) to *Bovista tomentosa* (Vitt.) De Toni of Europe.   We have examined an authentic specimen of *Bovistella dealbata* (pl. 61 and pl. 114, fig. 14) and find it quite different from the plant described above.   It is an epigean species exposed throughout the entire growth of the fruit body and in this way differing sharply from what we are taking to be *B. minor* and also from Morgan's description of that species.   The spores of the Lloyd specimen are larger than in the Dearness plants and are as Hollos said furnished with minute warts (x 2160).   They are spherical to subspherical, 4.3–5.5 x 5–6.3μ (rarely 6.8μ), with pedicels 6–12.5μ long, usually about 8μ long.   Capillitium threads up to 10μ thick, moderately branched into long, slender, tapering branches. We have also examined a specimen of *B. tomentosa* from Bresadola's herbarium from Andola, collected and determined by him, and find that it agrees well with Hollos's description and figures except that the spores are practically smooth (3.5–4.2 x 4–5.5μ). The plants are the same size as *B. dealbata*, but seem to be darker at all stages, the spores are somewhat smaller, and the capillitium threads are thicker and more branched. Without further evidence we prefer to keep the two species separate.   As the European species is obviously epigean we cannot see how it could be *Bovista minor*.   We have not seen an authentic specimen of the latter, but as both Morgan's (Journ. Cin. Soc. Nat. Hist. **14**: 147) and Lloyd's (Myc. Notes, p. 117) descriptions agree in every respect, we use the name for the Canadian plants.

Plants in the U. S. National Museum from Nevada de Toluca, Mexico, determined by Lloyd as *B. brunnea* Berk., are, in appearance, spores and capillitium, like those of specimens of *Bovistella dealbata* from the Lloyd Herbarium, sent us by Lloyd.   *Bovista brunnea* Berk. was originally described from New Zealand, and plants from that country sent us by Cunningham under that name are distinctly olive-brown in the immature condition and otherwise look somewhat different from the others.   The spores and capillitium are, however, the same.   Lloyd thinks that *B. brunnea* is the same as *B. tomentosa* and not the same as *B. dealbata*.

Illustrations: Lloyd. Myc. Works, pl. 3, figs. 3–5.
    Morgan. Journ. Cin. Soc. Nat. Hist. **14**: pl. 5, figs. 10–12.

Canada. London. On clay bank by spring. Dearness, coll. (Dearness Herb. and U. N. C. Herb. No. 2416).

MYCENASTRUM Desv.

Fruit body epigeal, breaking from its attachment after maturity; peridium thick and tough, splitting irregularly above. Capillitium of short, free threads which are furnished with short prickles. Spores brown, spherical (said to be sessile and 2–4 to a basidium in *M. radicatum*). According to Hollos there is only one species, though a good many have been described.

The genus is easily distinguished from all others here included by its prickly capillitium.

LITERATURE

Desvaux. Sur le genre *Mycenastrum*, du groupe des Lycoperdées. Ann. Sci. Nat., 2nd. ser., **17**: 143. 1842.

Mycenastrum corium Desv.

M. spinulosum Peck

Plates 62 and 114

Plants seated on the ground, subglobose, depressed or obovate, often irregular, more or less plicate or pitted below and attached by a point to the fibrous mycelium; size various, usually about 4–10 cm. thick; cortex a soft, felted, whitish coat which dries down irregularly and wears away slowly, parts remaining here and there as inherent scales; inner peridium deep brown on surface and in section, about 2 mm. thick, tough and corky, splitting tardily from above downward into unequal and irregular flaps which may separate slightly or at least open widely. Gleba without a sterile base, dark brown to purplish brown at maturity, not very powdery.

Spores (of a plant from the Lloyd Herbarium) dark brown, spherical, thick-walled, minutely but, under high power, distinctly marked with a more or less perfect reticulum of linear warts, 8.5–12μ thick. Capillitium of separate, short threads with a few short branches, and peculiar in the thorn-like spines with which they are more or less thickly set.

This species is abundant in the west, but rare in the eastern states. Lloyd reports it from Illinois (Myc. Notes, p. 120) and from Florida (Letter 62, note 441). (See also Myc. Notes, p. 1173, where an error is corrected.)

The plant much resembles a *Scleroderma* in general appearance, but it is easily distinguished by the spiny capillitium threads. It differs also in its habit of breaking loose from its attachment when mature and adopting a tumbling habit like *Bovista*. The separate threads arising freely in the gleba also recall *Bovista*. For numerous synonyms see Hollos.

Illustrations: Cunningham. Trans. N. Z. Inst. **57**: pl. 9, figs. 25 and 26. 1926.
    Fischer. Engl. & Prantl. Pflanzenf. 1¹: fig. 165 B.
    Hollos. l. c., pls. 24–26; pl. 29, fig. 31.
    Lloyd. Myc. Works, pl. 5, figs. 1–11.
    Lloyd. Photogravure of Am. Fungi, No. 18.
    Morgan. Journ. Cin. Soc. Nat. Hist. **14**: pl. 5, figs. 13–14.
    Petri. l. c., fig. 35.
    Sorokine. Rev. Myc., 1890, pl. 25 (101), fig. 354 (as var. *Kara-Kumianum*); pl. 27 (103), fig. 365; pl. 29–30 (105) (figs. 371–372 as var. *Kara-Kumianum*).

New Jersey. Newfield. Ellis, coll. (N. Y. B. G. Herb., as *M. spinulosum*). Spores dark, reticulated, 9.3–11.2μ. Capillitium threads of branched, spiny units about 12.5μ thick in main threads.

Wyoming. Pitchfork. Oct. 1912. Simon Davis, coll. (U. N. C. Herb.).

Canada. Eastern Ontario. Dearness, coll. (N. Y. B. G. Herb.).

Also specimens seen from Kansas, Nebraska, North Dakota, Colorado, Texas.

GEASTER Mich.

Plants at first subglobose and with or without an apical beak; either just buried in the soil, trash, or moss they grow in and with or without a fine flocculence all over which binds the substratum to the surface, or in some species seated on the surface of rotting wood, trash, or earth and attached only at the base (epigeal). Outer peridium at maturity splitting from the apex into few or many rays which expand more or less in a stellate way, or even recurve strongly and are composed typically of three layers, the surface one a delicate, interwoven coat of flocculence or tomentum that in some species is scarcely obvious, but in others forms a more or less perfect membrane which remains attached to the next layer on expansion, or becomes more or less detached from it, and in some cases is completely stripped off and remains as an empty sac in the ground when the rest of the plant is lifted out by the recurving lobes of the next layer. This next inner layer, called the fibrous layer, is thicker and tougher and is formed of closely woven, homogeneous fibers. Lining this layer and splitting with it is a third layer of turgid, fleshy tissue which dries out and shrinks after opening, either remaining attached to the inner side of the fibrous layer as a continuous or much cracked cartilaginous-looking membrane, or peeling off and disappearing in places or throughout. Sometimes a part is separated and remains as a kind of collar around the center. For the microscopic structure of peridia, see under *G. velutinus*. Inner peridium (spore sac) thin, tough, membranous, pliable, stalked or sessile, opening by a single, apical mouth that is simply a small torn hole or an elevated pore which may or may not be surrounded by a circular area (peristome) of different texture, and more or less sharply circumscribed outline. In one group of species this area is prettily and regularly fluted (sulcate). Gleba pure white when young, composed of tramal fibers and plates which radiate straight from the columella to the peridium, and which enclose the very narrow, much elongated, almost tubular cavities which are lined with the basidia. The glebal chambers are not visible in longitudinal section and barely so in cross section. Basidia thick, elliptic to pyriform, borne on very slender hyphae, 4–8-spored. Spores spherical or subspherical, usually warted or asperulate. Capillitium abundant, composed of simple, rarely-branched threads which arise from the walls and also from the more or less prominent (in some species vague or absent) columella.

An interesting genus of numerous species that are popularly known as "earth stars." The dry spores puff out of the mouths as in puffballs, leaving the persistent capillitium behind. A peculiar, long-stalked species (*G. stipitatus* Solms) is recorded from Java (Fischer, Hedwigia **32**: 50, pl. 5. 1893). Before opening it has much the appearance of *Lycoperdon muscorum* but has a short point. Another peculiar plant should be mentioned here, although not found in America. It is *Trichaster melanocephalus* from Europe. It is like a large *Geaster fornicatus* in general appearance except that the inner peridium wall very soon disappears. It differs also in the very large, globose, hard columella around which the capillitium forms a matted mass filled with spores. There is a specimen in Washington under the name of *G. fornicatus* (Myc. and Path. Herb.; Petrak, Fl. Bohemiae et Moraviae exs. No. 1498). It is just like Lloyd's figures (Myc. Notes, p. 189, pl. 17) and has all the characters of the species. The spores are about like those of *fornicatus*, distinctly warted, 3.8–4.5μ. The plant is said to be quite

PLATE 62

MYCENASTRUM CORIUM. LLOYD HERB. [above]
Pitchfork, Wyoming [below]

epigean, and this is borne out by the plant just mentioned, as the outer layer has not been stripped off and is furthermore free of trash.

In attempting to find a natural classification for the species of *Geaster*, one meets with difficulties and with differences of opinion among authors. What are the characters expressing the most fundamental relationships; and those of lesser degrees of importance? All arrangements heretofore proposed have in certain sections obviously violated, it seems to us, the true relationships. De Toni (Rev. Mycol. **9**: 64. 1887. See also Sacc. Syll. **7**¹: 70, and Hollos, l.c., p. 51) divides the true Geasters first into a fornicate and a cupulate group (Fornicati and Cupulati) and the remaining species which are subdivided into the sulcate-striate group (Striati) and the fimbriate group (Fimbriati). As a result of the first two groupings there are thrown together the very dissimilar *fornicatus* and *radicans*, while the near relatives *fornicatus* and *rufescens*, and *coronatus* and *minimus* are separated. The third group is a natural one, but the last should be rearranged.

Morgan's two main groups, Depelliti and Pelliculosi, are in part natural, but are unnatural in having species with sulcate-plicate peristomes in each. His two subgroups under Depelliti are unnatural for the same reason. He does not make the mistake of making the hygroscopic character a leading one. In Lloyd's last outline of the Geasters (Myc. Notes, p. 317), as well as in The Geastrae, he first divides them into the Rigidae and the Non-rigidae, the latter with six groups. This throws together such distantly related plants as *mammosus* and *Drummondii* and separates species with sulcate peristomes.

Of the six groups of Lloyd's Non-rigidae, the first and last are natural in their inclusions, though *Hariotii* is excluded from the first. The other three groups are in our opinion unnatural to a greater or less degree. That the hygroscopic character is not the most fundamental one seems obvious. Both hygroscopic and non-hygroscopic species are found in the very natural group with sulcate peristomes, as well as in the non-sulcate group. In related species and even in the same species at times the intensity of this character is very variable and in individuals may practically disappear. For example, in *arenarius* the rays while hygroscopic are usually pliable and thin, while in the very closely related *floriformis* they are much more rigid. In *asper* individuals appear rarely without any hygroscopic tendency at all, though the species is markedly hygroscopic.

Within certain limits the structure of the mouth area is the most dependable character. The sulcate group is a natural one and there are no confusing intermediates connecting it with the non-sulcate group. So-called intermediates like *Morganii* are not troublesome, as their crumpled mouths rarely bear any real resemblance to a truly sulcate peristome. In the non-sulcate group the distinction between the definite and indefinite peristome, while adequate enough as a rule, is in some cases obscured by variation. This is particularly true in *floriformis* and *arenarius*. In constructing the key we have used the characters in the order of their importance as it seems to us, and the key is therefore as natural a grouping of the species as we can arrange at present.

LITERATURE

Cunningham. Species of the Genus *Geaster*. Proc. Linn. Soc. New South Wales **51**: 72, pls. 2–7. 1926.

Cunningham. The Development of *Geaster velutinus*. Trans. Brit. Myc. Soc. **12**: 12, 9 text figs. 1927.

Destrée, Caroline. Révision des *Geaster* observés dans les Pays-Bas. Neederlandsch Kruidkundig Archief, 2nd. ser., **6**: 488. 1895.
De Toni. Revisio monographica generis Geasteris, Mich. Rev. Myc. **9**: 61, 125, pl. 2. 1887.
Lloyd. The Geastrae, figs. 1–80. Cincinnati, 1902.
Lloyd. New Notes on the Geasters. Myc. Notes No. 25: 309, figs. 144–149 and pls. 94–101. 1907.
Morgan. The North American Geasters. Amer. Nat. **18**: 963, figs. 1–12. 1884.
Morgan. New American Geasters. Journ. Myc. **1**: 7. 1885. Condensed from above paper.
Morgan. Journ. Cin. Soc. Nat. Hist. **12**: 12, pls. 1, 2. 1889.
Morgan. The Genus *Geaster*. Amer. Nat. **21**: 1026, figs. 1–2. 1887.
Petri. Flora Italica Cryptogama (Gasterales), Fasc. **5**: 67. 1909.
Rea. British Geasters. Trans. Brit. Myc. Soc. **3**: 351, pls. 17–19. 1911.
Rick. Die Gattung *Geaster* und ihre Arten. Bot. Centralb. **27**, Abt. II: 375, figs. 1, 2. 1910.
Scherffel. Bemerkungen über *Geaster*-Arten. Ber. d. Deutsch. Bot. Ges. **14**: 312, pl. 19. 1896.
Smith. Two species of *Geaster*. Grevillea **2**: 35, pls. 13 and 14, fig. 1. 1873.
Smith. British Geasters. Grevillea **2**: 76, pls. 13–17 and 19–20. 1873.
Tulasne, L. R. and Ch. Sur les genres *Polysaccum* et *Geaster*. Ann. Sci. Nat., 2nd. ser., **18**: 129. 1842.
Woodward. An essay towards an history of the British stellated Lycoperdons. Trans. Linn. Soc., London **2**: 32, 323. 1794.

KEY TO THE SPECIES

Peristome not truly sulcate, i.e., not regularly ridged and grooved throughout the extent of the peristome; irregularly wrinkled and crumpled only in G. *Morganii*
Mouth area distinct as a silky zone of different texture and often of different color, but not outlined by a sharp narrow groove (in G. *subiculosus* the mouth area is scarcely distinct); spore sac without glistening particles and, if stalked, the stalk short and thick; button exposed or, if submerged, the outer coat not holding earth or trash to any extent and the mycelium attached only by the center of the base; expanded plant saccate or convex below or imperfectly to typically fornicate
Rays not hygroscopic, i. e., not incurved over or around the spore sac when dry or expanding when wet
Outer surface smooth and glabrous or with the texture of soft leather (rarely scaly); button with a distinct, narrow point
Outer layer of rays tending to crack into longitudinal strips or less often into irregular plates, slightly if at all separating from the middle layer; base saccate or plane or less often concave below; mouth not wrinkled........G. *triplex* (p. 106)
Outer layer of rays stripping off on the central region and over the proximal part of the rays and remaining convex below, the inner layer arching upward and elevating the spore sac (pseudofornicate); mouth not wrinkled
G. *limbatus* (p. 107)
Outer layer and shape of plant as in G. *triplex*, but outer layer tending to peel off in irregular flakes; mouth irregularly wrinkled or crumpled (pseudosulcate)
G. *Morganii* (p. 109)
Outer layer soft, not cracking into strips, but with some tendency at times to peel from the rays; mouth not wrinkled; plants small (at least in the N. American form)
Spores 3.4–4.8μ thick.....................................G. *saccatus* (p. 110)
Spores 2.2–3.5μ thick..................Northern form of G. *saccatus* (p. 111)
Outer surface pale buff, nearly or quite glabrous, with the texture of leather; peristome scarcely distinct; dry button blunt, with a low broad umbo, or the top umbilicate; spores smooth, 2–3μ....................G. *subiculosus*, sense of Lloyd (p. 118)
Outer surface not glabrous, but tomentose, strigose or spongy; button not pointed
Plants medium to large; outer surface minutely felted-tomentose, rather harsh, pale
Expanded plant saccate; spores 2.5–3.3μ.................G. *velutinus* (p. 113)
Expanded plant fornicate; spores 3.8–4.8μ...............G. *radicans* (p. 115)

Plants small, the base pinched to a point; cespitose or gregarious in numbers from a conspicuous, superficial white mycelium which binds together the twigs and leaves of the substratum; outer surface strongly tomentose to strigose, at least when young

Plants not saccate; spore sac and fleshy layer blackish.......*G. Lloydii* (p. 123)

Plants saccate; spore sac and fleshy layer not blackish

Spores 3.4–4µ......................................*G. mirabilis* (p. 116)

Spores 3–3.6µ.......................................*G. trichifer* (p. 118)

Rays hygroscopic

Plants of medium size; outer peridium clean of dirt even in the button

G. mammosus (p. 119)

Plants small, covered with sand all over at first.................*G. arenarius* (p. 120)

Mouth area not distinct, at least without a definite boundary (at times the color is paler or darker, and a depressed zone may be present in *G. floriformis*); button quite submerged; outer surface covered with flocculent mycelium holding trash or sand; plants saccate or fornicate or intermediate

Rays not hygroscopic

Spore sac asperate with stiff hairs............................*G. Hieronymi* (p. 123)

Spore sac not asperate

Outer peridium with center elevated to expose the spore sac, which is short-stalked or sessile

Mycelial (outer) layer adhering to the center and rays..... *G. rufescens* (p. 121)

Mycelial layer remaining in the ground and forming a hollow cup with the strongly reflexed rays attached to its margin (fornicate)

G. fornicatus (p. 124)

Outer peridium saccate and enclosing the sessile spore sac like a bowl

G. fimbriatus (p. 125)

Rays hygroscopic

Surface of spore sac spongy...................................See *Astraeus* (p. 185)

Surface of spore sac not spongy

Spores about 3.5–4.5µ..........................A form of *G. arenarius* (p. 121)

Spores about 5–7µ..................................*G. floriformis* (p. 127)

Mouth area very distinct, silky and outlined by a narrow groove; buttons quite submerged until dehiscence, and the outer layer covered with earth or trash; expanded plants concave below and often truly fornicate; spore sac with a slender stalk and covered when fresh with minute, glistening particles; rays not hygroscopic

Plants of small to medium size, growing on the ground or on humus; spores dark brown

G. coronatus (p. 129)

Plants small to very small, growing on mossy trunks of living trees; spores very pale

G. leptospermus (p. 131)

Peristome truly sulcate with regularly arranged ridges and grooves composing the peristome; all U. S. American species (at least) with buttons submerged until dehiscence

Not hygroscopic, the rays bent backward, the base concave below; spore sac stalked or sessile

Peristome not black

Plants of medium size, stalk long, lower part of spore sac often striate radially; spores about 4.2–5.5µ..................................*G. pectinatus* (p. 132)

As above but spore sac not striate and having a flaring collar pendent around its lower side..*G. Bryantii* (p. 133)

Plants small; stalk short; spores about 3.7–4.4µ.................*G. Schmidelii* (p. 134)

Peristome black or nearly so; spore sac sessile........................*G. Hariotii* (p. 135)

Hygroscopic, the rays bent inward (typically) when dry, spreading when wet

Spore sac covered with rather coarse, wart-like particles, short-stalked......*G. asper* (p. 135)

Spore sac minutely furfuraceous, smooth in age, sessile

G. umbilicatus, sense of Morgan (p. 136)

Spore sac minutely spiny to pulverulent-granular, sessile...........*G. Drummondii* (p. 137)

Geaster triplex Jung.

G. Michelianus W. G. Smith

Plates 63 and 115

Plants large, pointed before opening, the point up to 12 mm. long, the inner peridium subspherical, up to 2.7 cm. thick, quite sessile, gray-brown when fresh, becoming reddish brown with age; mouth fibrillose and becoming lacerated, surrounded by a more or less definitely outlined, broadly conical area which may or may not be paler. Outer peridium splitting into 6–8 segments with long acuminate tips which expand or become revolute under the convex, flat or less often arched base; fleshy layer thick, in our plants mostly remaining intact as a moderately thick, reddish brown, cracked crust on the fibrous layer, the central region in some plants breaking loose from the part on the rays to form a broad collar or cup around the inner peridium; outer layer usually nearly free of dirt or trash, but with a few small particles sticking to any part, firm, glabrous, dull yellowish, mostly adnate, but cracking into radial strips or irregular areas; mycelium basal and leaving a scar at point of attachment when the plant is lifted; button supposed normally to be sunk in the substratum, but its surface does not hold the trash as in *G. fimbriatus*, *G. rufescens*, *G. fornicatus*, and most other subterranean species (for rare exception see note under Alabama entry below).   Columella about 1 cm. long, clavate, and persistent.

Spores (of No. 5886) deep smoky brown, distinctly warted, spherical, 3.7–4.4μ, most about 3.9μ thick.   Capillitium threads unbranched, about 5μ, up to 6μ thick, not sinuous, concolorous with the spores.

Geaster lageniformis, as suggested by Morgan (see Lloyd, The Geastrae, p. 38), is a small form of *G. triplex*. The cracked surface, definite mouth, pointed button, and spores are all the same. A typical-looking plant of *G. lageniformis* from London, Canada (N. Y. Bot. Gard., labelled *G. saccatus*), has spores distinctly verrucose, 3.5–4.2μ. Another from the same place and in the same herbarium is Ellis & Ev., N. Am. Fungi, No. 2735 (as *G. triplex*). Our plants are like the *G. triplex* of Thümen's Mycotheca Universalis No. 1410 from Holland, which has spores distinctly papillate, 3.6–4.2μ. Plants from Hungary at the New York Botanical Garden correctly labelled *G. lageniformis* are the same, with spores verrucose, 3.4–4μ thick. Similar plants from Hungary also labelled *G. lageniformis* are in the Herbarium of the Museum of Paris. Another example from Charlottenburg in the same herbarium (P. Sydow, coll., as *G. fimbriatus*) has spores distinctly verrucose, 3.7–4.5μ. In American herbaria one often finds under *G. lageniformis* plants that we are referring to *G. saccatus*, northern form.

Illustrations: Clements. Minnesota Mushrooms, fig. 89.

    Cunningham. Trans. N. Z. Inst. **57**: pl. 11, figs. 35, 36.

    Cunningham. Proc. Linn. Soc. N. S. W. **51**: pl. 2, figs. 3, 4.

    Destrée. l.c., pl. 9, fig. A.

    De Toni. l.c., pl. 63, fig. C.

    Hard. Mushrooms, pl. 66.

    Hollos. l.c., pl. 11, figs. 1–6 (these figs., if correct, represent a very coarse form); pl. 29, fig. 17.

    Lloyd. The Geastrae, figs. 47–49. Also pl. 94, figs. 1–5.

    Massee. Ann. Bot. **4**: pl. 1, fig. 27 (as *G. Michelianus*).

    Micheli. Nova Plant. Gen., pl. 100, fig. 1.

    Morgan. Amer. Nat. **18**: fig. 2. 1884.

Illustrations of the form *G. lageniformis*:

    Hollos. l.c., pl. 10, figs. 13 and 14. Figs. 11 and 12 more nearly represent what we are calling
        G. triplex.

    Lloyd. The Geastrae, figs. 76 and 77.

PLATE 63

GEASTER TRIPLEX. No. 682

PLATE 64

GEASTER LIMBATUS
Burlington, Wisconsin [lower right]; Kansas, No. 8252 [other three]

Smith. Grevillea 2: pl. 20 (as *G. saccatus*).
Vittadini. Monog. Lycoperd., pl. 1, fig. 2.

682. Chapel Hill, December 1908. Old collection with no other data.
5886. On mossy oak stump, October 17, 1922.
7483. Under cedars, Aug. 7, 1924.

Asheville. Beardslee.

South Carolina. Ravenel. (Curtis Herb., as *G. fimbriatus*, No. 3025, and as *G. saccatus*, No. 1600; Path. and Myc. Herb., as *G. saccatus*, Fung. Car., No. 77.) Another folder of this No. 77 is a smaller plant with softer felted outside and tapering lobes and looks like our *G. saccatus* from Asheville.

Florida. Alachua Co. Weber, coll. Spring of 1924. (U. N. C. Herb., No. 7445). Also collection by Walker.

Gainesville. Weber, coll. (U. N. C. Herb. and Univ. Florida Herb.). *Lageniformis* form. Spores distinctly warted, 4–5.5μ thick, often with hyaline material. Also another collection which is remarkable in its thin, soft, papery peridium.

Alabama. Spring Hill. Bertolet, coll. (Lloyd Herb.). Some of these have clean surfaces, while in others the surface is as dirty and trashy as in *G. rufescens*. Mouth very definite.

Maryland. Smith, coll. (U. S. Nat'l. Herb., as *G. saccatus*).

New Jersey. Pennsville. Sept. 1891. Ellis and Everhart, N. Am. Fungi, No. 2736. (N. Y. Bot. Gard. Herb., as *G. fimbriatus*.) This is good *G. triplex*. (Path. and Myc. Herb., Washington, as *G. striatus*.)

Pennsylvania. New Garden. (Michener Herb., as *G. rufescens*.)

Ohio. Loveland. James, coll. 1880. (Path. and Myc. Herb., as *G. saccatus*.) Outer surface mottled as in Rick, No. 261.

Cincinnati. Spurlock, coll. (Path. and Myc. Herb., as *G. lageniformis*). Also collection by James in the same herbarium.

Illinois. Urbana. McDougall, coll. (U. N. C. Herb.).

Missouri. St. Louis. Trelease, coll. (Farlow Herb.). *Lageniformis* form.

Wisconsin. Algonia. Dodge, coll. (Univ. Wis. Herb. and U. N. C. Herb.).

Madison. Trelease, coll. (Farlow Herb.). A small, papery form.

Washington. Seattle. Murrill, coll. (N. Y. Bot. Gard. Herb., No. 208). With a long single root 2–3 mm. thick, attached to center of base and branched below.

Canada. London. Dearness, coll. (Path. and Myc. Herb., U. N. C. Herb., also Ellis and Everhart, N. Am. Fungi, No. 2735 in N. Y. Bot. Gard. Herb.).

Mexico. Colima. Murrill. January 1910. Several buttons show a small point with top collapsed around it; surface hard and glabrous, in some cases with flat, more or less inherent scales like *Scleroderma vulgaris*, nearly clean; peristome distinct. Such a form is shown by Lloyd, Myc. Notes, p. 339, fig. 166.

South America. Paraguay. Balansa, coll. (N. Y. Bot. Gard. Herb., unnamed). Spores 3.7–4.2μ.

Brazil. Rick, coll. Fungi Austro-Americani, No. 261. (Path. and Myc. Herb., Washington.) Exactly like *G. triplex* except that the outer surface is cracked and mottled to remind one of a giraffe, a form closely approached by the plant from Ohio cited above. Spores 3.5–4.1μ thick, surface as in *G. triplex*. Also 4 plants from Rick. (U. N. C. Herb.)

Venezuela. Fendler, coll. (N. Y. Bot. Gard. Herb., as *G. saccatus*). Looks exactly like *G. triplex*. A large plant with spore sac 2.5 cm. thick; rays long and taper-pointed. Spores distinctly warted, 3.7–4.4μ thick.

England. Surrey and Ascot. (N. Y. Bot. Gard. Herb. from Massee Herb., as *G. Michelianus*.)

New Zealand. Cunningham, coll. (U. N. C. Herb.). Spores distinctly warted, 4.2–5.5μ thick.

Geaster limbatus Fr. Sense of Bresadola.

Plates 64, 115 and 116

Plants large and resembling *G. triplex* in most important characters. The following description refers to the dried plants: Outer peridial surface firm, glabrous, nearly clean of trash except at base, mycelium attached only at a central point below; rays reflexed, the long tapering tips usually revolute; outer layer not cracked into strips or flakes, but separating as a rule from the central region and the proximal part of the rays, and remaining convex below while the inner layer arches upward and elevates the spore sac (pseudofornicate).   Spore sac subglobose with a more or less obvious apophysis, brown, nearly glabrous and with a short, thick, often flattened stalk; peristome definite, silky, often paler than the sac, broadly conical, the mouth fimbriate.   Fleshy layer brown, rather thick, mostly adnate and not cracking.   Columella subspherical, about 4–5 mm. thick.

Spores (of plant from Wisconsin) spherical, distinctly warted, 3.7–4.8μ, most about 4μ thick.   Capillitium threads straight, not branched, concolorous with the spores, up to 7μ thick.

This plant is evidently nearly related to *G. triplex* as shown by long-pointed lobes (indicating a pointed button), absence of flocculence on the outer surface, which is clean and glabrous in large part, and in the definite mouth and similar spores.   It differs from *G. triplex* in the splitting away of the outer layer over the central region and the arching up of the middle layer.   The stalk is probably no more obvious than it would be in *G. triplex* if it were to assume such a position.

There is much confusion among authors and in herbaria as to the identity of *G. limbatus*.   This is the only American plant labelled *G. limbatus* in American herbaria which cannot be referred to *G. triplex* or *G. rufescens* or *G. pectinatus*.   Most of the collections at the New York Botanical Garden labelled *G. limbatus* are *G. rufescens*, e.g., from Alabama, Kentucky, Ohio, Missouri, Indiana, Colorado and Canada.   All the material in the Path. and Myc. Herb. at Washington as *G. limbatus* is *G. rufescens*, as Ellis, N. Amer. Fungi, No. 1309, and others from Ohio and Colorado.   Morgan figures a plant as *G. limbatus* (N. Amer. Geasters, fig. 6) which is probably *G. rufescens*, as noted by Lloyd and Hollos.   A plant in the Curtis Herbarium from Alabama as *G. limbatus* (Peters, No. 934) is *G. rufescens* with a short stalk.   We are adopting the name of *G. limbatus* for the present species as it is so determined by Bresadola, as shown by a European specimen from him in the Lloyd Herbarium.   This has exactly the habit of the American plant described above, the outer surface clean and separated from the fibrous layer over the center and proximal part of the rays.   Another plant from Bresadola so labelled has the outer surface earthy and not separated in part.   The mouth is distinct in both.   Our plants described above are also the *G. limbatus* of Lloyd, at least in so far as the American specimens are concerned, as shown by a number of plants in his herbarium.   Among Lloyd's illustrations of *G. limbatus* (The Geastrae, figs. 42–46), figs. 45 and 46 represent the species as we have it.   His three other figures are probably not the same.   Figure 42 of a plant from Rea (England) and fig. 44 of a plant from Hollos (Hungary) apparently represent the dark species noted below and considered *G. limbatus* by English authors and by Hollos.

It is certain that the *G. limbatus* of Hollos and of Massee and Berkeley and to all appearances that of Elias Fries* is not our plant, and we have never seen anything like it in this country.   It is a large, usually very dark plant (blackish brown; some forms are paler and glaucous) with a short thick stalk, a large, definite, fimbriate mouth of

---

* In the Curtis Herbarium are two plants from E. P. Fries (Upsala) labelled by him *G. limbatus*, but they are really of *pectinatus*.   Worthington G. Smith gives a figure (Grevillea 2: pl. 17, fig. 2) as *G. limbatus* which has all the appearance *G. G. pectinatus* except that grooves are not shown on the peristome.

more brownish tint and with a universal flocculent covering that holds earth tightly as in *G. rufescens*. In fact, the appearance is very much that of *rufescens* except for the blackish and more glabrous spore sac and more definite mouth. It is beautifully shown in Hussey's Illustrations, pl. 2. Good plants from Hollos in the Farlow Herbarium and from Massee (determined by Berkeley) in the New York Botanical Garden Herbarium are alike. The former has spores which are distinctly warted, 4–5.2μ thick, and with which those of the latter agree (4.2–5.5μ). Another plant from Massee (Chiselhurst) so labelled is the same. Plants from Germany (Berlin; Magnus, coll.) labelled *G. rufescens* by the collector are also the same: nearly black, mouth distinct. The outer surface of this blackish plant of Northern Europe is quite different from that of our plant, and it does not peel off. Neither Hollos nor any other European author mentions the separation of the outer layer in *limbatus*. The spores as given by Hollos are 4–5, often 6μ thick, which is too large for our plant. *Geaster pseudo-limbatus* is represented from Hollos in Lloyd's Herbarium and apparently does not agree with either idea of *limbatus* discussed above.

Illustrations: Fries, Th. C. E. Sveriges Gasteromyceter, fig. 29 (spores).
    Lloyd. The Geastrae, figs. 44 and 45.

New York. Syracuse. Oct. 1888. Underwood, coll. (N. Y. Bot. Gard. Herb; also a small form as
    G. Schaefferi).
Massachusetts. South Hadley. 1888. Hooker, coll. (N. Y. Bot. Gard. Herb.).
Kansas. Bartholomew, coll. (N. Y. Bot. Gard. Herb., No. 2215; U. N. C. Herb., No. 8252). Spores
    of No. 8252 are 3.4–4μ thick.
Wisconsin. Burlington. (Univ. Wis. Herb. and U. N. C. Herb.)
Minnesota. Miss Hone, coll. (N. Y. Bot. Gard. Herb. and Lloyd Herb.). Spores dark, distinctly
    warted, 3.5–4.2μ, most about 4μ.
Colorado. Brandegee, coll. (N. Y. Bot. Gard. Herb.).
Canada. Macoun, coll. (N. Y. Bot. Gard. Herb.).
    London. Dearness, coll. (U. N. C. Herb.). Spores 3.6–4.2μ.

Geaster Morganii Lloyd

Plate 115

Button broadly bulb-shaped with a short to rather long point (up to 6 mm.), yellowish, the base flat; mycelial attachment from a central basal point, the surface nearly or quite clean, buffy alutaceous, dull, felted to minutely spongy; rays about 7–10, taper-pointed, pliable, the outer layer tending to crack and peel off in irregular flakes (more separable than in typical *triplex* or *lageniformis*); fleshy layer dark brown to blackish, cracking and at times forming a collar as in *G. triplex;* spore sac sessile, subspherical, usually compressed when dry, minutely granular-felted, wearing glabrous, brown; peristome rather vaguely outlined, forming a narrowly conical papilla (typically) with the sides crumpled toward the top or almost all over, forming a pseudo-sulcate peristome with lacerated tip.

Spores (of a plant from Ohio; Underwood, coll.) spherical, distinctly warted, 3.4–4.1μ thick. Capillitium threads wavy, up to 7μ thick.

The plant seems common in the middle west, less so elsewhere. We know of no record for the southern states, but there is in the Curtis Herbarium a plant from Alabama (Peters, No. 198) as *G. saccatus* that we believe to be this species. The mouth is very long and narrow and not at all like *triplex*, but is not crumpled. Lloyd mentions such a mouth as occurring. The nearest relative seems *G. triplex*, which differs in even

mouth and smooth outer surface.   Lloyd now considers his *G. Morganii* a synonym of
G. Archeri Berk. (Hooker's Fl. Tasm. **2**: 264, pl. 183, fig. 9 bis. 1860) but compared
with American *G. Morganii*, the lobes of *G. Archeri* are more slender and tapering, and
the outer surface differs in not being cracked.   The fleshy layer looks quite different
and has a hard, cartilaginous appearance with few cracks, instead of the softer, more
leathery appearance of the rimose fleshy layer in *G. Morganii*.   The spores are the same.
The type material of *G. Archeri* at Kew consists of two separate mounts of one open
plant each, both from Tasmania (Archer, coll.).   The plants have long, tapering and
twisted lobes, rather pliable; fleshy layer thin, continuous; outer layer with texture of
leather, not cracked in radial lines; spore sac deep brown, glabrous, mouth apparently
as in *G. Morganii*, but somewhat obscured by pressure.   Spores (of No. 28) spherical,
regularly warted, 3.4–4µ thick (pl. 116, fig. 14).

Illustrations: Lloyd. The Geastrae, figs. 31–36.
   Morgan. North Amer. Geasters, fig. 3 (as *G. striatus*).

Delaware. Commons, coll. (N. Y. B. G. Herb.).
New York. Chippewa Bay. Phillips, coll. (Path and Myc. Herb.).   Spores minutely warted, 3.4–4µ
   thick.
Massachusetts. Peabody. Mackintosh, coll. (Lloyd Herb.).   Fine lot with buttons.
Ohio. Underwood, Morgan, Lloyd and James, colls. (All in N. Y. B. G. Herb.).
   Columbus. Brewer, coll. (Lloyd Herb.).
   Cincinnati. Lloyd, coll. (Lloyd Herb.).
   Dinwood. Lloyd, coll. (Lloyd Herb.).
Indiana. Underwood, coll. (N. Y. B. G. Herb.).
Illinois. Urbana. McDougall, coll. (U. N. C. Herb.).

Geaster saccatus Fr.

Plates 65, 115 and 117

   Buttons gregarious, not caespitose or crowded, 7–12 mm. thick, 7–14 mm. long,
including point, when fresh, entirely subterranean or half exposed, abruptly pointed by a
short small mucro about 1.5 mm. long; surface nearly clean, tomentose to spongy-felted,
ochraceous to buff.   Rays about 5–7, upright or revolute, the base strongly saccate.
Fleshy layer when fresh pallid, faintly or distinctly pinkish, about 0.8 mm. thick.
Spore sac light or dark drab, glabrous, dull; peristome, broadly conical, definite, surrounded by a paler depression or much paler all over (at times nearly pure white);
mycelium attached only as a basal strand, the submerged part of the plant, which is
more often all in the button, not binding trash to it, but coming up nearly clean, the
mycelium forming a powdery-looking, mouldy layer about 1 cm. from the surface.
   Spores (of No. 7350) spherical, minutely asperulate, 3.5–4.3µ.

   In Chapel Hill we find this only under cedars, but the Florida collection was under
oaks, though otherwise exactly like the others, the whiter peristomes being matched in
some of our collections.   Our plants are very small, only 6–15 mm. wide when open in
the dry state, and they look most like *G. mirabilis*.   That is separated by the strictly
epigeal and crowded habit, absence of point, strigose surface and entirely different
mycelium.   The tropical form of *saccatus* may run much larger than ours, but there are
intermediate sizes.   What we are calling the northern form of *saccatus* runs somewhat
larger than ours and has much smaller spores.
   There is still some doubt as to what the true *G. saccatus* is.   As Fries described it,

PLATE 65

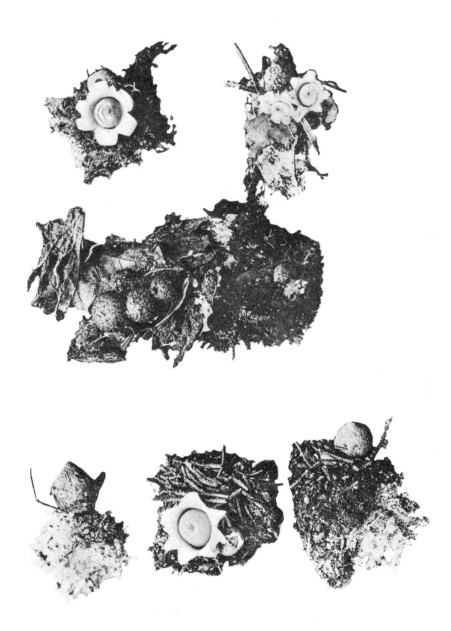

GEASTER MIRABILIS.   No. 7331 [above]
GEASTER SACCATUS.   No. 7350 [below]

PLATE 66

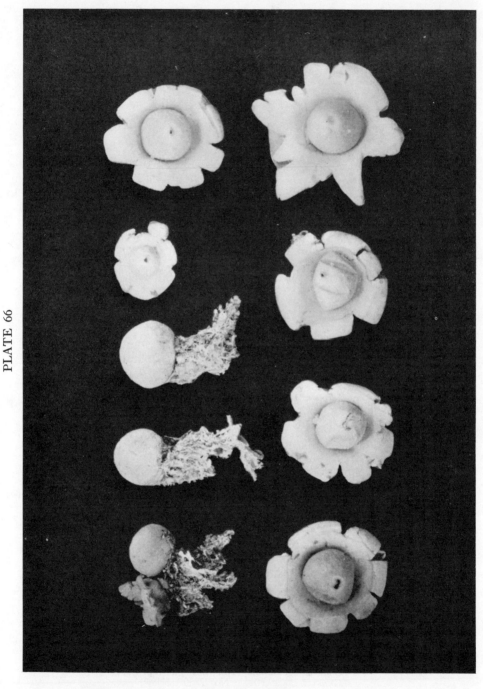

it is obviously in the *G. triplex* rather than in the *G. fimbriatus* series, as indicated by the radicating, basal mycelium and the clean or trashy, adnate, soft, leather colored outer surface, and long, narrow points of the rays. Authors and collectors have referred to *G. saccatus* both *G. triplex* (including the *lageniformis* form) and *G. fimbriatus*, as well as the plant that we are calling *G. saccatus*. Lloyd confuses the latter two in America and has also referred the *lageniformis* form of *G. triplex* to *G. saccatus* (see plants at the New York Botanical Garden, sample box). Morgan distinguishes them properly by the difference in the mouth, but fails to call attention to the difference in the outer surface which is at least as important. Rick has distributed from Brazil as *G. saccatus* two quite different plants; one (Fungi Aus.-Amer., No. 330) which looks just like *G. fimbriatus*, with flocculent trashy outer surface and indefinite mouth. The spores, however, are distinctly larger than in *G. fimbriatus*, faintly warted, 3.8–4.6μ thick. Another (Fungi Aus.-Amer., No. 261) is just like our *G. triplex*, except that the outer surface is cracked in a mottled way rather than in radial lines (spores 3.5–4.1μ). This mottled cracking may also be noted in U. S. American *G. triplex* (as plant from Loveland, Ohio, noted under that species). Rick's figure of *G. saccatus* (Broteria **5**: pl. 2, figs. 6 and 8) shows a little plant with distinct mouth and clean surface that looks just like the plants we are calling by that name. What Spegazzini distributed from Argentina as *G. saccatus* (Dec. Myc. Arg., No. 44) is a hygroscopic plant with an indefinite mouth and about the size of *G. mammosus*. It is evidently not the Friesian species. (This is noted also by Lloyd.)

7173. Under cedars, buttons covered up, The Rocks, Sept. 26, 1923. Peristome very pale. Spores 3.2–4.1μ.
7441. Under cedars in Mrs. Kluttz's yard, July 20, 1924. Spores 3.5–4.5μ.
7475. In humus under cedars, Aug. 5, 1924. Spores 3.5–4.2μ.
Also Nos. 7350, 7415, 7479, 7506.

Florida. Columbia Co. On lake bank under oaks, June 28, 1924. Mouth (of all four open plants) nearly pure white, contrasting strongly with the dark drab sac. Spores minutely spiny, 3.4–4μ.
Alachua Co. Walker, coll. (U. N. C. Herb.). Spores very dark, subspherical, distinctly warted, 3.8–4.8μ thick.
New Smyrna. Sams, coll. (Lloyd Herb.).
Gainesville. Among leaves in moist woods, Aug. 16, 1926. Erdman West, coll. (U. N. C. Herb.). Spores 3.5–4.2μ.
Mexico. Botteri, coll. (Curtis Herb., as *saccatus*).
Porto Rico. Stevenson, coll. (N. Y. B. G. Herb.). Spores minutely warted, 3.4–3.7μ.
Bahamas. New Providence, Sept. 1904. Mrs. Britton, coll. (N. Y. B. G. Herb.).
Jamaica. New Haven Gap, 5600 ft. elevation. Murrill, coll. Jan. 1909. (N. Y. B. G. Herb.) Spores 3.7–4.8μ.
Cuba. Wright. (Curtis Herb., as *G. saccatus*, No. 668 and 870, and as *G. fimbriatus*, the latter with a clean, pointed button.)
Bolivia. January 1902. R. S. Williams, coll. (N. Y. B. G. Herb.). Spores spherical, minutely but distinctly warted, 3.4–4μ thick.

Geaster saccatus Fr., Northern Form

Plate 115

The following is drawn up entirely from dried plants:

Plants saccate, of medium size or rather small, the expanded rays with a spread of 2.5–4 cm. (see note on a larger form below); buttons subglobose with a point up to 4 mm. long, or rarely with only a rounded umbo. Mycelium strictly basal and radicating by flocculent strands from a central basal point; outer surface felted or nearly smooth, almost clean or at times with a few bits of rotten wood or leaves, not cracking, with some tendency for outer layer to separate on the rays which are 6–9, pliable, thin, expanded, with the tapering rips revolute; fleshy layer reddish brown, thin, adnate, somewhat cracked. Spore sac 10–13 mm. broad, sessile, surrounded below by the saccate base, smooth, brownish drab to gray-drab; peristome silky, paler or nearly concolorous, distinctly or rather vaguely limited. Columella not obvious.

Spores (of plant from Asheville) spherical, dark, minutely but clearly warted, 2.2–3.3μ, distinctly smaller than in the southern form. Capillitium threads about the color of the spores or paler, 5–7.5μ thick.

Gregarious on leaves of deciduous trees with a tendency to crowding, which is more or less obvious in most collections. Apparently rare. We have not found it at Chapel Hill.

Neither this nor the southern form can be distinguished from *G. triplex* by. the absence of point on the buttons, as there is a point or umbo present both when fresh and dry. Buttons in the same collection may vary from slightly umbonate to pointed like our photograph of the Asheville collection. Hollos, Morgan, Trelease, and Lloyd include our U. S. American plant in *G. saccatus*. Hollos separates it correctly from *G. lageniformis* by its soft outer peridium which is usually free from trash. It is further separated from that species which has a firm, hard outer surface by the absence of longitudinal surface cracks that are usually present in the latter, and, in the northern form, by the smaller and less rough spores. Hollos is wrong in considering *G. velutinus* the same as *G. saccatus*. The former is very easily distinguished from *G. saccatus* by its larger size, firmer, harsher, paler, more spongy-looking and more separable surface layer.

At the New York Botanical Garden is a collection that we take to be this (Gentry, coll. Two buttons and an open plant; no data). The buttons are larger than in the others, 2.2 cm. thick and up to 2.6 cm. tall including the point, which in one is about 1 cm. long, in the other about 4 mm. Surface layer soft and felted, very clean except on the base, separating in places from the middle layer; mycelium attached to a basal point. Spore sac sessile, mouth very distinct. Spores spherical, minutely warted, 3–3.6μ thick.

In the Lloyd Herbarium there are two collections of *G. saccatus* from Berlin (Magnus, coll.). They are like the American plants, with surface nearly or quite clean, peeling off to some extent from the tips of the rays.

Illustrations: Hollos. l. c., pl. 10, fig. 19.
  Lloyd. The Geastrae, fig. 75b.
  Rick. Broteria 5: pl. 2, figs. 6 and 8.

North Carolina. Asheville. Beardslee, coll. 1917. (U. N. C. Herb.)
Maryland. Plummer's Island. P. L. Ricker, coll. 1922. (Path. and Myc. Herb., Washington.)
Ohio. Lloyd. (N. Y. B. G. Herb., 2 colls.) Spores of one minutely rough under high power, 2.3–3.1μ thick; in the other, 3–3.5μ thick. Also E. & E., North Amer. Fungi, No. 3417. (Path. and Myc. Herb.)
  Cincinnati. Aiken, coll. (Lloyd Herb.).
Kansas. Fort Scott. On leaf mold, July 1902. Garrett, coll. (N. Y. B. G. Herb., no name). Cespitose, small, soft, surface felted. Exactly like Lloyd's plant from Ohio.
Missouri. St. Louis. Glatfelter, coll. (Lloyd Herb.).
Canada. London. Dearness, coll. (U. N. C. Herb.).

Geaster saccatus var. Walkeri

Buttons subspherical with or without a small blunt point, gregarious to subcespitose, 1–1.5 cm. thick, epigean and basally attached to an obvious floccose mycelium, surface felt-like, not strigose, very dark brown (verona brown of Ridgway), splitting into 6 or 7 bluntish rays which extend only about one-third to one-half the distance and confine the spore sac to a deep cup, outer layer not at all separable. Fleshy layer when dry varying from dark brown to much paler. Spore sac grayish brown, the mouth without a peristome, fimbriated about as in *G. fimbriatus.*

Spores minute, faintly rough, 2–3.2μ.

The plant differs from *G. fimbriatus* in entirely different habit (basal attachment of exposed buttons and inseparable spongy surface) and from *G. saccatus* and its relatives in absence of peristome and very dark color. The plants are larger than any species of the *saccatus* group except *saccatus* itself. The spores are smaller than in any of the *saccatus* group except what we have called the small-spored northern form. Miss Walker writes that "All of the colors had a beautiful rosy tint to them in the fresh condition."

Nebraska. Lincoln. Fall of 1926. Miss Leva B. Walker, coll. (U. N. C. Herb. No. 4).

Geaster velutinus Morg.

G. Readeri Cooke and Massee
Cycloderma ohiensis Cke.

Plates 31, 66, 67 and 115

Unopened plants seated on the substratum (not embedded in it) and therefore attached to the mycelium only at the base, ovate and bluntly pointed at the top, up to 2.7 cm. broad and long. Surface dull and finely felted-tomentose, very much like the surface layer of *Lycoperdon leprosum.* It is flesh color, becoming creamy yellow or buff color on drying. Outer peridium splitting into about 7 reflexed or expanded segments which are a pretty flesh color on the inner (upper) surface when fresh. As these dry they split more or less into two thin, fibrous, persistent layers, a characteristic habit, and usually curl backward under the basal part which remains convex or flat below. Inner peridium smooth, appearing minutely felty under a lens, dark brown or sometimes light gray (when collected perfectly fresh), subglobose, attached by a broad or rather narrow base, almost or quite sessile; mouth small, fibrillose and later lacerated, surrounded by a distinct, radially fibrous, broadly conical, silvery gray or light to dark brown area which is about 5 to 8 mm. in diameter. Columella obvious and clavate in the button; slender and more obscure in the mature plant.

Spores (of No. 4095) spherical, 2.5–3.3μ thick, most about 3μ thick, distinctly asperulate and with a halo, deep smoky purplish brown. Capillitium threads rather large, up to 11μ thick, often branched near the tapering tips.

In an unopened button of average size, a microscopic section of the peridia showed the following: outer peridium composed of four distinct regions, (1) a surface layer about 350–400μ thick in which the threads are large, irregular, entangled and approximately perpendicular to the surface of the plant; (2) a very thin layer 50–65μ thick in which the threads are small, regular and extend approximately parallel to the surface of the plant; (3) a slightly thicker layer 130–150μ thick in which the threads are small, regular and much entangled; and (4) a very thick (1.5 mm.), fleshy region composed of large parenchymatous cells. Inner peridium composed of a single very thin layer made up of delicate threads that run approximately parallel to the surface.   The threads of the four layers of the outer peridium pass into each other, but at maturity the fleshy layer and the two outer layers (which are an inseparable unit) are easily removed from the third layer.   The columella, inner peridium, and all the layers of the outer peridium are continuous with each other at the base.

In this species Cunningham finds (l. c.) that the basidia are uninucleate and the plant appears to be haploid throughout its development.   The nucleus divides to form nuclei for each spore, usually four.   Clamp connections were not found in any part of the plant.   All attempts to germinate the spores were unsuccessful.

A rather common, large plant that prefers pine woods.   It is easily distinguished from its relatives of similar habit by the larger size and minutely felted-tomentose, not hairy, outer peridium which splits into two persistent layers.   In many individuals there is plainly to be seen on the under side a circular scar marking the area of attachment.   From a part of the type collection of *G. Readeri* from Australia (Grevillea **16**: 73.   1888), at the New York Botanical Garden, it is shown that it is the same as *G. velutinus*, the plants not being distinguishable from the American ones in any way, the surface pale, velutinate, peeling off in part; peristome distinct, size and shape of plant the same; spores spherical, very minutely warted, 2.8–3.3μ thick.   There are two other plants mounted in the same herbarium that are also marked "type specimens." These have some sand on the outer surface, but the spores are the same, 3–3.5μ thick. The plant was first named *G. australis* by Reader, a name previously used by Berkeley. A plant from New Zealand determined as *G. Readeri* by Massee (N. Y. Bot. Gard. Herb.) is not the same.   It has the surface more strigose-tomentose and not peeling off, and the spores are distinctly different, warted, 3.8–5μ.   The plant distributed by Rick in Fungi Austro-Amer., No. 13, as *G. triplex* is *G. velutinus*.   We have a plant from Brazil (Murrill, coll.) which seems intermediate between *velutinus* and *subiculosus*. The silky peristome is very distinct, and the button has almost the same surface as *G. velutinus;* the mature plant is nearly smooth.   The spores are minutely warted, 2.5–3.6μ thick.

Illustrations: Cunningham.   Trans. N. Z. Inst. **57**: pl. 10, fig. 33; pl. 11, fig. 34.   1926.
    Hard.   Mushrooms, fig. 489.
    Lloyd.   The Geastrae, figs. 62–71.   Also pl. 101, figs. 1–2.

846.   In pine woods, October 13, 1913.
1260.   Under pines in woods, September 24, 1914.   Spores 2.7–3μ thick, minutely asperulate.   Capillitium threads 3–5.5μ thick, minutely roughened.
7133.   In rotting leaves under shrubs in Arboretum, September 22, 1923.   Buttons exposed, subspherical, not umbonate when fresh.
Also Nos. 999, 1000, 1381, 4095, 7114, 7164, 7219, 7442, 7503.

    Statesville.   Coker, coll. In pine needles, Aug. 1922.   (U. N. C. Herb., No. 5499.)
    Asheville.   Beardslee, coll.

Florida.   Gainesville.   Walker, coll. (U. N. C. Herb.).
Alabama.   Auburn.   Baker, coll. (N. Y. B. G. Herb.).
Cuba.   Wright, No. 254.   (Curtis Herb., no name.)   Button and open plant.
Porto Rico.   J. R. Johnson, coll. (N. Y. B. G. Herb.).   The plant, though saccate, has slipped entirely out of the sheath.

PLATE 67

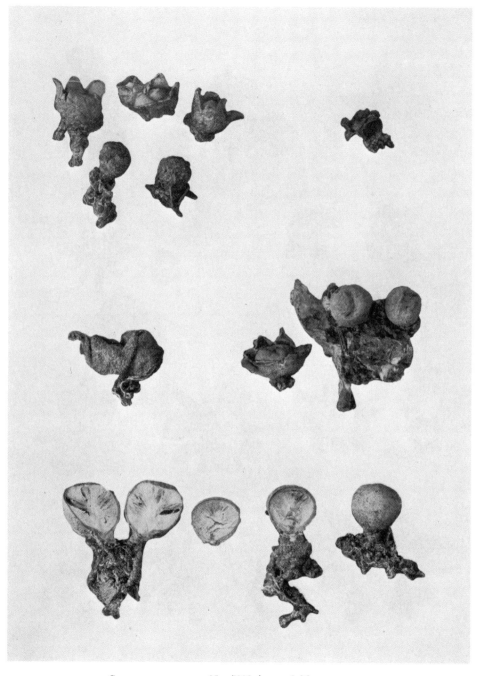

GEASTER MIRABILIS. No. 7208 [upper left]
GEASTER CAESPITOSUS. Ohio [upper right]
GEASTER TRICHIFER. Morce's Gap, Jamaica [middle left]
GEASTER SUBICULOSUS. No. 184 [middle right]
GEASTER VELUTINUS (BUTTONS). No. 7219 [below]

PLATE 68

[Top row] GEASTER HARIOTII.   Brazil (left); Porto Rico (middle); British Honduras (right)
[Second row] GEASTER CAESPITOSUS. Type (left)
          GEASTER ARENARIUS. Type (right)
[Third row] GEASTER FLORIFORMIS. Grasmere, Florida (three tiny plants); Denton, Texas
          (2 larger plants in middle); North Dakota (one plant on right)
[Bottom row] GEASTER ASPER. Long Pine, Nebraska

Brazil. Rick. (Path. and Myc. Herb., Washington.) Also reported by Sydow (Ann. Myc. 5: 353. 1907).

Mt. Corcovado. Murrill, coll. (N. Y. B. G. Herb. and U. N. C. Herb.).

Africa. Uganda. 4000 ft. elevation. Dümmer, coll. (Lloyd Herb.). These are buttons which look exactly like the American ones.

New Zealand. Cunningham, coll. (U. N. C. Herb.). Spores minutely rough, 2.5–3.6μ thick.

Geaster radicans B. & C.

Plates 115 and 116

The co-types of *G. radicans* (Grevillea 2: 49. 1873) in the Curtis Herbarium (as *G. Curtisii*) show it to be closely related to *G. velutinus*. In so far as the appearance goes, it is only a fornicate form of that species, as Lloyd says (Myc. Notes, p. 155; The Geastrae, p. 31). There are two mounted plants with basal cups gone and one perfect plant in a box, all Ravenel, No. 953. Ravenel's ms. notes accompany the last specimen. The velutinate outer surface and the felted spore sac are exactly as in *G. velutinus*. A microscopic examination, however, reveals a difference in the spores, which are larger than in *G. velutinus*, 3.5–4μ thick, and more distinctly rough. We have examined the plants from Florida (Sarasota, on a cedar stump) in Washington, one of which was photographed by Lloyd (The Geastrae, fig. 57), and find them exactly like the types, the spores 3.4–4μ thick. The basal cup is a strong, pliable membrane, free from earth, and in no way like the delicate, submerged cup of *G. fornicatus* and *G. coronatus*. We find at the New York Botanical Garden a specimen of this plant from Bermuda, which extends its known range. The spores of this plant are spherical, distinctly warted, 3.8–4.8μ, most about 4.1μ thick. The species is reported as new to Europe by G. Lind in "Danish Fungi as Represented in the Herbarium of E. Rostrup," p. 401, 1913 (no description). Rick figures a plant as *G. radicans* from Brazil (Broteria 5: pl. 5, fig. 9) that is not fornicate and looks exactly like *G. triplex* with a large collar. He had earlier reported this as *G. triplex*, and says that Bresadola referred his plant to *G. radicans*. It may be *G. velutinus*, but cannot be accepted as *G. radicans*. Lloyd thinks that *G. Welwitschii* (from Spain) is the same as the American plant (Myc. Notes, p. 315, pl. 101, fig. 3).

The Cuban plants reported in the original description as *G. radicans* are represented in the Curtis Herbarium as Wright, No. 873. These three plants are all buttons and are not *G. radicans*. They were entirely submerged and are covered with humus held on by a flocculence as in *G. rufescens;* a single stout basal strand is attached to buttons in two cases; not pointed.

The types were sent to Berkeley by Curtis, who received them from Ravenel, who also sent notes and added that if a new species then "it is *G. Curtisii*," wishing to honor Curtis. Berkeley, however, ignored this wish of Ravenel's and named it *G. radicans* B. & C. (See Lloyd, Myc. Notes, p. 171.) Ravenel in his notes says "with a sulcate-plicate mouth," but the mouth is not truly so as we are defining that character. The best specimen has the mouth pinched into a few crumples, but the others do not show this.

As the usual form and spores distinguish *G. radicans* from *G. velutinus*, we think it well to retain the name, though it would be better to reduce it to a variety.

Illustration: Lloyd. As cited above.
    Patterson and Charles. U. S. Dept. Agric. Bull. 175: pl. 36, fig. 1. 1915.

South Carolina. Ravenel, No. 953; Curtis, No. 3041. (Curtis Herb., as *G. Curtisii* Rav., co-types;
    also in Farlow Herb. from Ravenel.)
Florida. Sarasota. On a cedar stump. (Path. and Myc. Herb.)
Bermuda. Millspaugh. (N. Y. Bot. Gard. Herb.)

Geaster mirabilis Mont.

G. caespitosus Lloyd
G. lignicola Berk.

Plates 65, 67, 68, 115 and 116

Densely cespitose to single in considerable numbers, and arising from an obvious white mycelium which binds together the leaves and twigs. Buttons spherical, not pointed, but a few with a small umbo when dry, 0.8–1.2 cm. thick, strigose-tomentose, reddish brown to ochraceous buff, a few blackish; mycelium basal, the buttons quite exposed or partly covered with loose trash (completely covered in No. 7173). Expanded plants 1.4–2.2 cm. wide; lobes usually 6 or 7, expanded (tending to become elevated when dry), the basal half bowl-shaped and holding the completely sessile inner peridium which is 6–9 mm. thick, subspherical, gray, with a delicately felted surface; peristome distinct, silky, more or less elevated, conical, immediately after exposure pale from a granular-looking, minute pubescence, with a darker line around the base, soon darker than the peridium; mouth fimbriated, not sulcate. Fleshy layer when first exposed about 0.5 mm. thick, smooth, light flesh color, soon darker and drying to a thin, adnate, continuous, gray-brown membrane.

Spores (of No. 7077) very dark, minutely warted, 3.2–3.8μ, most about 3.6μ. Capillitium threads sinuous, thick-walled (practically no lumen), much paler than the spores, about 3.4μ thick, the tapering ends smaller.

From *G. saccatus* the present species is distinguished by cespitose habit, much smaller size, hairy surface, less pointed buttons when dry and larger spores. Both have the habit of growing exposed (epigeal).

The species was originally described from French Guiana and is known also from Brazil, Africa, and the Orient.

Our plants are the same as plants received through the kindness of M. Patouillard and collected in Brazil by Rick. The young buttons have the same strigose-tomentose surface; the older ones more felted-tomentose; spores exactly as in our plants, faintly warted, 3.4–4μ thick, not like the smooth and smaller spores of what we are calling *G. subiculosus*. Rick considers *G. trichifer* the same (see Myc. Notes, p. 804), but Lloyd thinks it different (see that species). In our No. 7077, some of the plants are apparently as strigose as *G. trichifer* (which see), while others show only a matted tomentum, exposure to weather having a considerable effect.

The species is represented in the Kew Herbarium by five cards of material: three from Cuba (Wright), two from Ceylon (G. H. K. T.), and one from Uganda, Africa, (Dümmer, No. 1462). All these have the spores of *G. mirabilis*, and in appearance are the same as the Chapel Hill and Brazilian specimens except that none shows quite so strigose a surface. The spores of the plant from Ceylon, No. 184, are 3.2–3.8μ thick, minutely rough. The African plants connect up directly with *G. papyraceus*, with outer peridium more papery-looking than in the others. The spores of this collection are 3.5–4.2μ thick, with surface as in the others.

Geaster papyraceus B. & C.   (Proc. Amer. Acad. Arts and Sciences **4**: 124) in the Curtis Herbarium from Japan and Bonin Islands (authentic, but not type) is closely related if not the same.   The Japanese plants are all open; peridium extremely thin and papery, pliable, pale creamy straw color, outer surface with a concolorous coat of very thin soft weft in places.   Mycelium membranous; fleshy layer almost all gone; inner peridium broken or worm eaten, peristome not shown.   The Bonin Island plants are strigose-hairy outside; two cespitose buttons, one grown button apparently torn open at the top, and one open plant; even the last is strigose.   These look like *G. mirabilis*. Fleshy layer intact and rays much stiffer than in the Japanese plants.   Peristome distinctly silky.   A microscopic examination, however, shows the spores to be identical in the two collections.   In the Japanese plants they are spherical, finely but distinctly warted, 3.5–3.8μ thick, with a very distinct and shiny oil drop.   In the Bonin Island plants they are 3.6–4μ thick, surface and oil drop as in the others.   We can confirm Lloyd's opinion (Myc. Notes, p. 181) that *Coilomyces Schweinitzii* B. & C. is an unopened *Geaster* related to, if not the same as, *G. mirabilis*.   The plants in the Curtis Herbarium have spores exactly like our Chapel Hill *G. mirabilis*, spherical, minutely warted, 3–4μ thick (pl. 116, fig. 15).

Geaster caespitosus is apparently the same, with the usual slight variations which are to be expected.   The ample type collection in the Lloyd Herbarium has the exact appearance of our plants except that the strigose character is not so obvious.   The surface is softly felted, becoming smoother; peristome silky, sharply defined by a ridge; the plants attached by a pointed base to the abundant mycelium.   Spores slightly smaller than in our collections, very minutely warted, 2.3–3.4μ.   We find at the New York Botanical Garden a box of miscellaneous material without names but labelled Ohio, Lloyd, No. 255, in which, mixed with three other species, is a dense clump of small plants that are *G. caespitosus* and just like the types.   The type of *G. lignicola* Berk. (Journ. Linn. Soc. Bot. **18**: 386.   1881) at Kew from Rockingham, Australia (Thozet, No. 908), is apparently not different from *G. mirabilis*.   There are two crushed buttons and one open plant on fragments of plant material.   Mycelium not very obvious; surface of both buttons and mature plants nearly smooth.   Spore sac dark brown with fimbriate mouth.   Peristome characters not obvious on account of the way the plant is pressed and glued down.   Spores spherical, minutely warted, 3.2–4μ thick.

Illustrations: Lloyd.   Myc. Works, pl. 100, figs. 2 and 3; also figs. 6–9 (as *G. caespitosus*). Rick.   Broteria **5**: pl. 4, fig. 3.   1906.   Freshly opened plants.

7077.   On trash and leaves of deciduous trees and a few pine needles, wooded hillside, August 10, 1923.
7208.   In rich, rocky soil near cedars, November 11, 1923.
7502.   In humus in mixed woods (mostly deciduous), Aug. 14, 1924.
Also Nos. 7331, 7413, 7414.

Virginia.   Warrenton.   Upland frondose woods, Sept. 6, 1926.   Coker, coll. (U. N. C. Herb.)
Ohio.   Lloyd.   (N. Y. Bot. Gard. Herb., unnamed.)
Kansas.   Cragin, coll. (N. Y. Bot. Gard. Herb., as *G. saccatus*).   Outer surface clean, tomentose;
      spread when expanded 1.8 cm.   Spores minutely warted, 3.5–4.2μ.
Cuba.   Wright, No. 696.   (Curtis Herb.)   Button very small, strigose to tomentose.
Jamaica.   Bancroft.   Ellis, coll. (Farlow Herb.).
Brazil.   Rick, coll. (U. N. C. Herb.).

Geaster trichifer Rick

Plates 67 and 115

Plants gregarious to cespitose; buttons exposed, subspherical to oblong, pinched below to a point and attached to ropy mycelium, slightly umbonate above, buffy straw color, covered with more or less fascicled hairs about 1 mm. long; rays about six, splitting to or below the middle and tending to remain upright or with tips spreading; outer layer showing a distinct tendency to peel off the rays as in *velutinus*, but less so; fleshy layer leather color, thin, adnate.   Spore sac subglobose, sessile in the cup-shaped base, grayish brown, glabrous; peristome very distinct, flat with elevated center, mouth becoming fimbriate.

Spores very minutely rough, 3–3.6µ thick.

Murrill's notes on the fresh condition say,"Outside with long, stiff hairs, ferruginous-fulvous, shaggy-setose . . . fleshy layer dirty white; spore sac flattish acorn-shaped, avellaneous. . . . Spread 5 cm., center 2 cm." One of the largest plants is now broadly spread and reaches 4 cm., the smaller ones if spread would be about 3 cm. The plants are growing on leaves and twigs and have the habit and shape of *G. mirabilis*, which differs from the Jamaica collection in being much smaller, less strigose, with outer layer not peeling, and in the smaller spores.

The original plants were collected by Rick in Brazil.   He now considers it a form of *G. mirabilis*, while Lloyd thinks it different.   The plants shown in Lloyd's photographs are not larger than *G. mirabilis*, and in fig. 1251 the surface does not appear more shaggy than in *G. mirabilis*.

Illustrations: Lloyd. Myc. Notes, p. 314, figs. 147, 148, and p. 804, fig. 1251.

Jamaica.   Morce's Gap.   Murrill, coll.   No. 739.   (N. Y. Bot. Gard. Herb. and U. N. C. Herb.)

Geaster subiculosus Cooke and Massee (sense of Lloyd)

Plates 67, 115 and 116

Plants with the habit of *G. mirabilis*, crowded and springing from copious, white, felted mycelium which binds together the leaves, twigs, and sticks on which they grow. Buttons 9–11 mm. broad, completely exposed, obovoid, pinched below to a point connecting with the mycelium; apex concave by collapse (when dry), not pointed. Surface pale buff, wrinkled, glabrous, but with the soft appearance of leather; tardily opening by 6 or 7 rays, the sinuses extending into about a third of the peridium, leaving the basal part unchanged as a deep cup enclosing the sessile spore sac.   Fleshy layer drab brown, thin, adherent, not cracked except across the bottom of the rays.   Spore sac 1 cm. broad, subspherical, glabrous, brown.   Peristome not distinctly outlined or distinctly silky, fading into the sac surface about as in *G. fimbriatus*, sometimes sunken and then more distinctly outlined; mouth scarcely elevated, the opening fimbriate.

Spores (of Jamaica plant) spherical, smooth, 2–3µ thick.

This is clearly distinguished from *G. mirabilis* Mont. by larger size, absence of tomentum, obscure peristome, and smooth and much smaller spores.   Even very young buttons are practically glabrous and nearly white.   The plant described above is certainly the same as that illustrated by Lloyd in Lycoperd. Australia, etc., fig. 19, and Myc. Works, pl. 100, figs. 4 and 5.   He refers to it as *G. subiculosus*, which he considers a form of *G. mirabilis*.   From the description of *G. subiculosus* (Grevillea 16: 97.   1887) one would hardly refer the present plant there, as it is described as furfuraceous and wood colored on the outside, with spores 4μ thick, but the types at Kew from Trinity Bay, Australia, are essentially like our plants from Jamaica. There are two open plants and several more or less crushed buttons. The best specimen shows a spore sac about 7 mm. thick, dark brown; peristome not outlined by a groove or ridge but paler and fibrous. Surface of buttons minutely spongy, of older plants nearly glabrous. Largest button 1.1 cm. thick. Subiculum white, membranous. Spores spherical, practically smooth, some finely dotted, $3–3.8\mu$.

Lycoperdon pusio B. & C. is apparently a *Geaster*. The co-types in the Curtis Herbarium, No. 253 (Cuba), are all buttons, but they look just like another collection so labelled, also from Cuba (Wright), in which the plants are open. These last are small Geasters looking very much like *G. subiculosus*, with pale, smooth surface, and conspicuous mycelium. The spores, however, are not those of any member of this group, but are $3.8–4.8\mu$ thick, with distinct, blunt warts.

Illustrations: Lloyd. As cited above.

Jamaica. Hope. Earle, coll. (N. Y. Bot. Gard. Herb., No. 184).

Geaster mammosus Fr.

G. corallinus (Batsch) Hollos
G. lugubris Kalch.
G. argenteus Cooke

Plates 115 and 116

Button bulb-shaped with a distinct tapering point about 3–4 mm. long when dry, covered all over with a finely felted, thin, soft, buffy yellow coat which is usually quite clean of dirt except at the base and apparently exposed. Mycelium basal; outer scurf wearing off gradually and exposing the glabrous shining copper brown or darker, fibrous layer of the rays, which are about 8–12 in number, of unequal width and strongly hygroscopic; fleshy layer thick, adnate, smooth, at first gray-brown then darker brown to blackish. Inner peridium 5–15 mm. thick, subglobose to compressed, very finely puberulent, sessile, grayish to brown then darker; peristome distinctly outlined by a depressed border, plane, silky-strigose, the mouth elevated and papillose-fimbriated. Expanded plants up to 5.5 cm. broad.
Spores (of a Canada plant) spherical, minutely warted, $3–3.7\mu$.

Easily defined in the hygroscopic section by the clearly outlined silky-fibrous, plane and non-sulcate peristome. The above description was mostly drawn from a fine collection from Canada, containing one button and plants of various ages and sizes (N. Y. Bot. Gard. Herb., no data except Canada).

Plants in the Lloyd Herbarium from Paris (L. Rolland) are like American specimens, with a spongy, yellow, nearly clean superficial layer peeling off in flakes; the mouth distinct. Plants in the same herbarium from Tucuman, Argentina (Leon Castillon, coll.), are like the United States and European plants except that the outer layer when present is covered with sandy earth.

Geaster argenteus Cooke (Grevillea **17**: 75. 1889) is represented at Kew by three sets on the same sheet, all from Fort Carlton, Saskatchewan (one lot not named). The plants of the upper lot with pasted label giving fullest data, we take as the types. The plants have the appearance of *G. mammosus* with outer superficial layer weathered off, showing the whitish, fibrous layer and blackish fleshy layer; spore sac sessile and largely enclosed by the strongly hygroscopic lobes.   The mouth area is obvious as a silky zone, the center more or less elevated and lacerate.   The spores, which are spherical, distinctly warted, 3.7–4.5μ (pl. 116, fig. 13) are distinctly those of *mammosus* and not of *floriformis*, which are larger (5–7μ).   Hollos considers *G. argenteus* the same as *G. floriformis*, but he apparently had not seen authentic specimens.

Geaster argentatus Cooke and Massee from Brisbane, Australia, is closely related. A part of the type collection is at the New York Botanical Garden.   It has a definite silky peristome; spread of rays 3 cm., the outer surface scurfy and ochraceous at first, then smooth and gray to buffy gray; fleshy layer reddish brown; spore sac 12 mm. thick, finely furfuraceous to sub-granular, gray-brown to reddish brown, sessile.   Spores dark, mostly spherical but some irregular, 4.5-6μ (pl. 116, fig. 17).   Other plants from Kew Herbarium labelled *G. argentatus* Cooke from Victoria, Australia (not types), now pasted on the same sheet with *G. argenteus*, are quite different from the types, and we take them to be *G. Drummondii*, which they resemble in all important respects: mouth sulcate, spore sac granular to subasperate.

Illustrations: Destrée.   l. c., pl. 9, fig. B.
   De Toni.   l. c., pl. 2, fig. 0 (as *G. lugubris*).
   Hollos.   l. c., pl. 10, figs. 1–3 (as *G. corallinus*).
   Kalchbrenner.   Gasteromycetes novi vel minus cogniti, pl. 5, fig. 3 (as *G. lugubris*).   1884.
   Lloyd.   The Geastrae, figs. 16, 17.   Also pl. 98, figs. 7–11.
   Micheli.   Nov. Pl. Gen., pl. 100, fig. 3.
   Smith.   Grevillea **2**: pl. 19, fig. 1.   (Reproduced from Gardener's Chronicle.)
   Vittadini.   Monog. Lycoperd., pl. 1, fig. 9.

North Carolina.   Flat Rock.   Memminger, coll. (Lloyd Herb., as *G. floriformis*).
New Jersey.   Ellis, coll. (Lloyd Herb.).
Ohio.   Cincinnati.   Lloyd, coll. (Lloyd Herb.).
Wyoming.   Cody.   Davis, coll. (Lloyd Herb.).
   Pitchfork.   Davis, coll. (U. N. C. Herb.).   Spores 3.8–5μ.
Iowa.   Iowa City.   Teeters, coll. (Lloyd Herb.).
Colorado.   Clements, coll. (Path and Myc. Herb.); also Demetrio, coll. (N. Y. Bot. Gard. Herb.).
North Dakota.   Fargo.   Brenckle, coll. (Path. and Myc. Herb., Lloyd Herb., and U. N. C. Herb.).
   Note in Lloyd Herb. says "epigean."   The plants show pointed buttons with yellow, spongy surface and some adhering humus; mouth distinct.   Spores (of No. 254) minutely warted, 3.6–4.4μ.
Canada.   (New York Bot. Gard., as *G. umbilicatus*.)
   London.   Dearness, coll. (Lloyd Herb. and U. N. C. Herb.).
   Nova Scotia.   Halifax.   Crossland, coll. (Lloyd Herb.).

Geaster arenarius Lloyd

Plates 68, 115 and 116

Lloyd describes *G. arenarius* (The Geastrae, p. 28) as follows:

"Exoperidium subhygroscopic, cut to five to ten segments; drying usually with segments incurved.   Mycelial layer closely adnate with adhering sand.   Fleshy layer closely adnate, light color, not rimose.   Inner peridium subglobose, with a very short but distinct pedicel in some specimens, in others appearing sessile.   Mouth even, conical, acute, definite and usually darker colored than the remainder of inner peridium. Columella indistinct.   Spores globose, rough, 3–4μ."

PLATE 69

GEASTER RUFESCENS. No. 985

PLATE 70

GEASTER FORNICATUS.   Smith's Island
GEASTER FIMBRIATUS.   No. 7093 [middle four dry plants];
No. 7097 [lower three fresh plants]

The abundant type collection from Jupiter, Fla. (Culbertson, coll.), shows this to be a remarkable plant intermediate between *G. coronatus* and *G. floriformis*. In some the rays are distinctly revolute with the center elevated, in others the rays are closed in over or entirely under the sac. Though some of the rays are pliable they are distinctly hygroscopic, expanding quickly in water. Spore sac very faintly felted to glabrous, not at all granular-dotted as in *G. coronatus*, about 1 cm. thick, practically sessile; peristome varying from sharply outlined by a groove (about as in *G. coronatus*) to a less emphasized boundary as in *G. mammosus;* mouth apparently brown in the fresh condition, washing out pale and becoming lacerate. The outer layer of sand is thin and the flocculence holding it is very delicate and obscure. Spores minutely and irregularly warted, 3.2–3.8μ thick. Mixed with the types is a good specimen of *G. coronatus*, and this is almost certainly the plant referred to by Lloyd in his footnote as being an exception.

From the appearance of the rays of *G. arenarius*, which are acute, but not acuminate, the button is probably little if at all pointed. At the New York Botanical Garden there are two plants from Florida labelled *G. fimbriatus* (Underwood, coll., No. 1801a) that are almost certainly this species, though the mouth is only vaguely if at all determinate. The plants are small, hygroscopic, covered with sand on the outside; peristome vague, spore sac nearly glabrous; spores minutely warted, 3.7–4.5μ thick, just like those of Lloyd's plant and smaller than in *G. floriformis*.

The species is very near *G. floriformis* (see Lloyd, Myc. Notes, p. 143) and this approach is further emphasized by the vague peristome of the Underwood plants, which have the same spores as Lloyd's plants. The rays of *G. arenarius* are distinctly less rigid than in *G. floriformis*, but the smaller spores of the former are now the principal character separating the two species.

The extreme variation of Geasters is well shown by what appears to be a giant form of *G. arenarius* that is represented in the New York Botanical Garden by two very large plants from Greencastle, Indiana (as *G. rufescens*). They are 3.5–4 cm. thick with the rays closed over the spore sac. The peristome is vague, but the spores are like those of *G. arenarius*, minutely warted, 3.5–4μ thick, much smaller than in any other related species. Another interesting case is that of plants from Lake Titicaca, noted under *G. floriformis*.

Illustrations: Cunningham. Proc. Linn. Soc. N. S. W. **51**: pl. 5, figs. 24, 25.
    Hollos. l. c., pl. 29, figs. 19, 20.
    Lloyd. The Geastrae, figs. 53 and 54.

Florida. Lloyd. (U. N. C. Herb.) Another collection by Underwood. (N. Y. Bot. Gard. Herb., as *G. fimbriatus*.)
    Lake Helen. Mrs. Noble, coll. (Lloyd Herb.) Mouth distinct.
    Grasmere. Baker, coll. (Lloyd Herb.).
Texas. Denton. Long, coll. (Lloyd Herb.). Mouth distinct. This is variable in its hygroscopic character.

Geaster rufescens Pers.

Plates 69 and 115

Plants large, the button subspherical, not pointed, entirely buried until dehiscence, when open 5 to 8 cm. wide; the thin outer mycelial membrane covered with earth or trash and tending to split away in patches from the fibrous layer which is flesh colored when fresh; rays splitting about half way to the base into about 7–9 lobes, or only shallowly into many more, the lobes when fresh are expanded or recurved, when dry recurved or the tips incurved, the unsplit basal portion convex above (vaulted beneath) as in the fornicate group.   Fleshy layer of outer peridium very thick when fresh, up to 5 mm.; when dry forming a thinner crust with a felted-looking, brown surface on the face of the fibrous layer.   Spore sac up to 4 cm. thick, depressed-globose, the base usually constricted into a short thick stalk, not rarely with a low apophysis around the lower side of the spore sac some distance from the stem; color when fresh varying from pale flesh color to grayish flesh or deep brownish gray, when dry brown to gray brown, the surface not glabrous but covered with very minute, inherent scurfy dots (granular-velvety).   Mouth slightly elevated, fibrous and becoming fimbriated, without a definite peristome (indeterminate).   Columella large and subglobose, up to 1.5 cm. thick, the basal part with a peripheral extension as far as the apophysis.

Spores (of No. 985) globose, deep brown when mature, 3–4.4μ thick, minutely warted or asperulate, with a halo.   Capillitium of simple threads which are about 3.5–4.8μ thick.

This fine species, which is not at all rare in America, grows usually around the bases of oak stumps and occurs in groups.   One of the most remarkable characters is the very pleasant and decided fruity fragrance of the unopened and just opened plants.   There has been considerable confusion regarding this plant and G. limbatus.   As understood in Northern Europe (Fries, Berkeley, Massee), the latter differs in the expanded, not reversed rays, the darker and smoother inner peridium, the thinner and less spongy fleshy layer, and the more obvious peristome.   For G. limbatus in the sense of Bresadola, in which sense we are using the name, see under that species.   European specimens of G. rufescens arc rare in American herbaria.   One from Bresadola in the Lloyd Herbarium is like our plants, with spores 3.6–4.2μ thick, minutely warted.   For comparison with G. triplex see that species.

Illustrations: Bulliard. Herb. Fr., pl. 471, fig. L.
    De Toni. l. c., pl. 62, fig. 1.
    Hollos. l. c., pl. 11, figs. 7, 8.
    Lloyd. The Geastrae, figs. 38–41. Also pl. 97, figs. 6–8.
    Morgan. North Amer. Geasters, fig. 11. 1884.
    Petri. l. c., figs. 45, 46.
    Rea. l. c., pl. 19.

  985. At base of an old oak stump, November 17, 1913.
2984. On old oak stump, December 4, 1917. Spores 3–4.4μ thick, apparently pitted in water, but
    upon application of KOH the surface appears spiny and with a halo.
7221. On damp clay soil, November 25, 1923. A small form; the spore sac only 1 cm. thick. Spores
    3.3–4μ.
Also Nos. 683, 1033, 6025, 6053, 6066.

Carolina. (Schw. Herb.; also in Michener Herb. from Schw. Herb.)
Alabama. Auburn. Under a rotting log, August 1897. Baker, coll. (N. Y. Bot. Gard. Herb., as
    G. limbatus).   Two folders, each with three buttons, which are up to 3 cm. broad, subspherical
    to compressed and completely covered with rotten wood held on by flocculence. Also a col-
    lection from Alabama by Peters. (Curtis Herb., as G. limbatus.)   This is typical G. rufescens
    with a short stalk; outer surface covered with earth held on by flocculence.
New York. Botanical Garden. Williams, coll. (N. Y. Bot. Gard. Herb.).

Ohio. Dayton. Foeerste, coll. Ellis, N. Am. Fungi, No. 1309, as *G. limbatus*. (N. Y. Bot. Gard.
    Herb. and Path and Myc. Herb.)
    Norwood. Lloyd, coll. (Lloyd Herb.).
    Chillicothe. Hard, coll. (Lloyd Herb.).
    Preston. Morhan, coll. (Lloyd Herb., labelled *G. limbatus* by Morgan).
Missouri. Saint Louis. Hedgecock, coll. (Lloyd Herb.).
Wisconsin. Milwaukee. Brown, coll. (Lloyd Herb.). Buttons.
    Cedarburg. Panly, coll. (Lloyd Herb.).
Ontario. Regina. Willing, coll. (Lloyd Herb.).
Mexico. Ross and Painter, coll. (U. S. Nat'l. Herb.).
Japan. Sapporo. Miyabe, coll. (Lloyd Herb.).

Geaster Hieronymi Hennings

Plate 116

Buttons embedded in the substratum, apparently slightly pointed; outer surface covered at first with sandy earth or trash which may later strip off in part as a layer. Rays expanded or the tips incurved, pliable, about 5–8 in number, center concave below; fleshy layer adnate, thin and brown. Spore sac 1.5–2 cm. broad, subsessile or with a short stalk, dark brown, harshly asperate with short, setose hairs. Peristome rather indefinite (not sulcate), silky, mouth fimbriate.

Spores (of plant from Jalapa, Mexico), small and minutely warted, 2.6–3.6μ thick, often seeming slightly angular.

Except for the asperate spore sac the plant is very like *G. rufescens* or *G. fimbriatus* and seems certainly to belong to their group.

We have seen the type collection of *G. Hieronymi* in the Lloyd Herbarium, and find that it agrees closely with the Mexican plants. There are also two other lots in the Lloyd Herbarium labelled *G. Hieronymi* from Brazil (Rick, coll.). One of these is as described above and like the type; the other is something different, with a sulcate mouth.

Illustration: Lloyd. Myc. Works, pl. 229, fig. 2347.

Mexico. Jalapa. Moist forest, alt. 5000 ft., Dec. 1909. Murrill, No. 244. (N. Y. Bot. Gard. Herb.)
Brazil. Rick, coll. (Lloyd Herb.).
Argentine. Hieronymus, coll. (Lloyd Herb.; type).
South Africa. Miss Duthie, coll. (Lloyd Herb.).

Geaster Lloydii Bresadola

Plate 117

Buttons evidently subterranean or nearly so (submerged in humus), about 1.5 cm. thick when dry, spherical, not pointed, woolly felted all over or with spots where the softer wool has collapsed between the stiffer groups of hairs; largely covered with bits of leaves and trash, in some places nearly clean; the central point below attached to obvious mycelial strands. Rays six or more, thin but rather rigid; center concave below usually; the thin tomentose outer layer with a strong tendency to peel off except at tips, as in *G. limbatus* (sense of Bresadola); fleshy layer deep reddish brown to nearly black, rimose, adherent. Spore sac sessile, thin, collapsing, dark brown with paler areas at times or rarely pale all over, surface dull, minutely granular velvety, almost exactly the color and surface of our *G. fornicatus;* mouth large, fimbriate; peristome not defined, concolorous. The peeled off outer layer is delicate and pliable, and is usually torn into strips. As it pulls away from the fibrous layer it leaves a narrow, root-like core projecting downward from the central point where the mycelium was attached. (This core is lacking in No. 8702 from Porto Rico.)

Spores (of No. 7436) sometimes faintly angular as well as minutely warted, 3.5–4.2μ thick. Capillitium threads up to 7.4μ thick, strongly encrusted.

We have not seen the types, but as our plants agree almost perfectly with the description of *G. Lloydii*, we refer them to it with confidence (see Myc. Notes, p. 50. 1901). Lloyd, who collected the types in Samoa, later merged the species with *velutinus* (Geastrae, p. 35). If our determination is correct, we think this a good species.

The species is in the *rufescens-fornicatus* group and almost exactly intermediate between them in habit. The outer layer separates, not as in *velutinus*, beginning at the tips, but as in *fornicatus*, *radicans*, and *limbatus*, beginning at the center. It is distinguished from *fornicatus* by the imperfectly fornicate habit and by the strigose and much less trashy surface. The spores are larger than in *G. Hieronymi* and the spore sac is not asperate; *G. fimbriatus* differs in more saccate base, smaller spores, entire absence of hispid hairs, and in usually lighter color. In an ample collection from Florida, consisting of 8 buttons and 12 open plants, all but one open plant were very dark; another collection of a single plant from the same section was pale brown.

This species, as well as *G. fimbriatus* and *Astraeus hygrometricus*, shows that in some, if not all, Geasters with so-called universal mycelium, the true mycelium is really only basal and the felted "mycelial layer" only an outgrowth from the button. Expanded plants of *G. fornicatus* often show a hole in the bottom of the sac-like base as if it had been pulled away from a firmer basal attachment.

Florida. Gainesville. On an old stump. Weber, coll. 1923. (U. N. C. Herb., No. 7436, and Univ. of Florida Herb.)
Porto Rico. Seaver and Chardon, colls. (N. Y. B. G. Herb. and U. N. C. Herb.). Outer tomentose layer almost entirely stripped off but fragments present. Spores dark, minutely warted, 3.5–4μ. Capillitium threads paler than the spores, up to 7.5μ thick.

Geaster fornicatus (Huds.) Fr.
G. marchicus Hennings

Plates 70 and 115

Plants of medium to large size, the outer peridium splitting beyond the middle into four (usually) to five (rarely more) lobes which bend strongly backward and downward, the tips remaining attached to an equal number of shorter lobes on the margin of a membranous cup, sunken in the earth and trash, which, as the outer layer of the button, was stripped off from the middle layer when evagination occurred. This cup is always completely covered with adhering trash and earth due to the flocculent mycelium wefting it. Rays firm, the fleshy layer dark brown and adherent or partly peeled off, in old plants worn away; the exposed fibrous layer whitish tan. Inner peridium seated on a distinct, whitish, short stalk about 2–3 mm. long (in our plants), subglobose or urn-shaped to depressed, constricted near the base so as to form a ring; surface dark brown, finely velvety; mouth large, slightly elevated, fibrous lacerated, wrinkled, without a distinct peristome, but the paler brown fibers in older plants have a distinct limit exactly as in *G. limbatus* (sense of Hollos), which is very near. Columella not large, about 3 or 4 mm. high and 2.5 mm. broad (in the Smith's Island plant).

Spores spherical, blackish brown, distinctly warted under high power with rather regular, blunt warts, 3.7–4.5μ thick. Capillitium threads 3–7.5μ thick, about as dark as the spores; walls roughened.

This is a rare plant in the United States and is reported by Lloyd only from Texas and Catalina Island. In the rest of the world it is supposed to be of wide but erratic distribution (Lloyd, Lycoperdaceae of Australia, etc., p. 21). The report by Curtis that it is common in this state (Catl. 'Plants of North Carolina, p. 110) almost certainly refers to what we now call *G. coronatus*, as all the plants in his herbarium under *G. fornicatus* are the latter species. Our single collection from this state consists of three plants in fine condition that grew under cedar, but the species is reported as growing under both conifers and frondose plants. It is easily distinguished from *G. coronatus* by the absence of an outlined peristome and the entirely different surface of the inner peridium. The species is really most nearly related to *G. rufescens* which is very similar in fundamental characters, as mouth, surface of inner peridium, separating layers of the outer peridium, and concave base when expanded. The spores, too, are very similar. The two species, however, are not forms of the same thing, but are easily distinguished by the fornicate habit, fewer and more rigid lobes, and darker and more densely velvety inner peridium of *G. fornicatus*. *Geaster marchicus* is usually considered a synonym of *G. fornicatus*, and plants so determined by Hollos in the U. S. National Herbarium are certainly this species, as are also those determined by him and represented by No. 950 of J. Wagner's Kryptogamae exsiccatae. Spores of the latter are dark, minutely warted, 3.6–4μ. For other supposed synonyms, see Hollos, p. 154.

Illustrations: Batsch. Elench. Fung., pl. 29, fig. 168.
    Corda. Icon. Fung. 5: pl. 4, fig. 43.
    Destrée. l. c., pl. 6, fig. B.
    Hollos. l. c., pl. 8, figs. 9–18; pl. 29, fig. 26.
    Lloyd. Myc. Works, pl. 96, figs. 1–3 (fig. 2 was first published as *G. fenestratus* in Myc. Notes, p. 70, fig. 33).
    Massee. Brit. Fungi and Lichens, pl. 35, fig. 5.
    Petri. l. c., fig. 44, 2.
    Rea. l. c., pl. 17.
    Smith. l. c., pl. 15, fig. 2.
    Sowerby. Eng. Fungi 2: pl. 198.

Smith's Island. In a dense bed of cedar twigs under a cedar in sandy soil, December 29, 1921. Couch and Grant, colls. (U. N. C. Herb.).

Geaster fimbriatus Fr.
    G. tunicatus Vitt.

Plates 70 and 115

Plants small, in our collections up to 3 cm. wide when freshly expanded; inner peridium about 9–14 mm. thick when fresh, subglabrous to minutely dotted, pale or dark brown, sessile in and surrounded by the concave lower half of the outer peridium; mouth on a more or less elevated, concolorous or paler cone, but without a definitely outlined area around it, the margin fibrous-flocculent and at times lacerate, not sulcate. Outer peridium splitting about half way down into 5–8 lobes which when freshly expanded are strongly recurved around the margin of the bowl-shaped base, usually remaining recurved in the dry state, not hygroscopic. Mycelial layer very thin with wefted surface, pale tan or buff to soaked ochraceous when fresh, tending to peel away in part from the rays but as a rule not nearly so much so as in *G. velutinus*. Fleshy layer pallid (nearly white to pale smoky tan; not pinkish) and about 2 mm. thick when fresh, drying down to an extremely thin, smooth or finely cracked up, brown or ochraceous membrane or scurf which disappears only after much exposure. Buttons quite spherical, not pointed, completely covered by humus and trash and retaining trash over the whole or most of the surface after opening. Columella in the mature plant represented by a small, subspherical, pale core some distance from the base.

Spores (of No. 7093) dark smoky brown, spherical, very minutely asperulate, many appearing smooth except under high power, 2.2–3.4μ, most about 3μ. Capillitium threads unbranched, about 5μ thick, sometimes up to 7μ, usually lighter than the spores, but varying in color in plants of the same colony.

This small *Geaster* grows usually in groups of several, not truly cespitose (rarely crowded in twos or threes), in partly rotten leaves and trash under cedars or in mixed woods. As is to be expected, specimens are found (rarely) that are not saccate but have the outer peridium concave below. It also happens occasionally that the outer layer may peel off completely. For both of these variations see plants from Lynn, England (Plowright, coll.), at the New York Botanical Garden.

In American herbaria this is often referred to *G. saccatus*. Lloyd thinks that *G. fimbriatus* does not occur in America (The Geastrae, p. 37), though reported by Morgan and others. However, as our plants agree clearly with this species in all important points (indeterminate mouth, splitting of the outer peridium into two layers in part, etc.), we see no reason not to refer them to it. In cases where the paleness of the mouth area is most pronounced as in plants from Buck Hill Falls, Pa. (see below), some authors might be inclined to call it definite, but there is no structural boundary and except for color the mouth is exactly as in other forms. The European plant also has a tendency to a paler mouth area. As Lloyd says, the mouth is no more fimbriate than in some other species. The true European *G. fimbriatus* is represented by plants in Washington (Path. and Myc. Herb.) from lower Austria collected by Zahlbrückner and determined by Keissler. They are just like our plants. We have received from Patouillard another typical European specimen (Jura) with spores minutely warted, 2.5–3.5μ thick. Still a third (N. Y. Bot. Gard. Herb. from Herb. of Thümen) has spores a trifle larger (3.4–4μ) but is otherwise identical. It grew in coniferous woods and still shows fir leaves attached.

A European collection from Sydow (Flora Marchica, Charlottenburger Schloss-garten, P. Sydow, coll.) labelled *G. fimbriatus* and now at the New York Botanical Garden is not the plant we here describe, but *G. lageniformis* with much rougher spores and determinate mouth. Our plants agree with Rea's description of *G. fimbriatus* except in size of spores which he gives as 4–5μ. It is very likely that *G. triplex* (with *G. lageniformis*) and *G. fimbriatus* have been often confused.

Geaster rufescens is the nearest relative of *G. fimbriatus*, and large plants of the latter might easily be referred to it. The thinner fleshy layer, more saccate form, and smaller average size distinguish *G. fimbriatus*, but there may be connecting forms. *Geaster tunicatus* as represented in Saccardo, Mycotheca italica, No. 1625 (Mendola; Bresadola, coll.), is *G. fimbriatus*. The mouth is indefinite, the base saccate. The two species are also treated as synonyms by Hollos.

Illustrations: Berkeley. Outlines Brit. Fung., pl. 20, fig. 4.
  Cunningham. Proc. Linn. Soc. N. S. W. **51**: pl. 6, fig. 36.
  Destrée. l. c., pl. 10, fig. A.
  De Toni. l. c., pl. 63, fig. P.
  Fries, Th. C. E. Sveriges Gasteromyceter, fig. 31.

Hollos. l. c., pl. 10, figs. 17 and 18.
Lloyd. The Geastrae, fig. 74.
Michael. Führer f. Pilzfreunde 2: No. 202, figs. a and b. 1918 (2nd ed).
Morgan. North American Geasters, fig. 8.
Petri. l. c., fig. 42.
Rea. l. c., pl. 19.
Rolland. Champ. France, pl. 110, fig. 252.
Schmidel. Icon. Plant., pl. 50, figs. 1–4. 1747.
Smith. Grevillea 2: pl. 17, fig. 2.
Sowerby. Engl. Fungi, pl. 80.

1291. In cedar twigs and oak leaves mixed at the base of a cedar tree, September 30, 1914. Spores minutely asperulate, up to 3.7μ thick.
7092. Under cedar tree, August 24, 1923. Spores 2.8–3.7μ. Capillitium threads thick-walled, nearly hyaline, up to 6.6μ thick.
7093. In rotting frondose leaves, August 24, 1923. Spores dark under the microscope, surface as usual, 2.2–3.4μ thick.
Also Nos. 4096, 7097, 7135, 7439, 7476, 7480.

Statesville. Beardslee, coll. (Lloyd Herb., as *G. saccatus*).

South Carolina. Society Hill. (Curtis Herb., as *G. fimbriatus*, No. 3833.)
Tennessee. Unaka Springs. Murrill, coll. (N. Y. Bot. Gard. Herb.).
Pennsylvania. New Garden. (Michener Herb., as *G. minimus*.)
New Hampshire. Shelburne. Farlow, coll. (Farlow Herb.).
Wisconsin. Eagle Heights, near Madison, August 26, 1903. No distinct peristome. Spores very faintly spiny, 3–3.7μ thick. (U. N. C. Herb.)
Ohio. Miami Valley. Morgan, coll. (N. Y. Bot. Gard. Herb.).
Colorado. Minnehaha. Clements, Crypt. Form. Colo., No. 194, as *G. limbatus* (in part). (Farlow Herb.)
Denver. Bethel, coll. (N. Y. Bot. Gard. Herb.).
Ontario. Sarina. Bertolet, coll. (Lloyd Herb., as *G. saccatus*). Also collection from Canada by Dearness. (U. N. C. Herb.)

Geaster floriformis Vitt.
G. delicatus Morg.

Plates 68, 115 and 116

Plants (typically) small, with a spread when expanded of 2–2.5 cm., submerged until mature; rays about 8–10, unequal, hygroscopic and expanding quickly when put into water, covered at first with sandy earth held on by mycelium, this flaking off by degrees to leave the surface smooth and pale after exposure; fleshy layer dark brown, adnate, continuous then rimose; inner peridium about 6–8 mm. thick, subglobose or depressed, sessile, pale, covered at first with fine granules or furfuraceous particles which soon wear away in large part; mouth only a puncture or slit with short radiating fissures with no defined or silky area around it as a rule, after a time the margin becoming fimbriate.

Spores (of Clements, No. 613) distinctly warted, spherical, 5–7μ thick, or slightly elongated and about 6.5 x 7.4μ. Capillitium threads straight, thick-walled, up to 7μ thick.

The American plants are like those of a good collection from Hollos (Hungary) sent us through the kindness of Patouillard. In these plants the peristome is indefinite, rays strongly hygroscopic, spores spherical or somewhat irregular, distinctly warted, 5–7 x 6–8μ. Similar plants from Hollos have been seen by us in the Lloyd Herbarium.

Good collections of this species from San Diego, California, in Washington and New York show an interesting variation in the mouth. In the plants at the New York Botanical Garden the two plants with mouths visible show a depressed zone around the mouth but the surface of the zone is not silky as in most Geasters, but of the same texture as the remainder of the surface. In one of the plants the mouth was an elevated papilla in the center of this zone; in the other it was a plane opening. For a similar variation see plants from Florida and North Dakota entered below. The plants in Washington show a plane opening without a depressed zone. In most herbarium material the spore sac is nearly smooth or faintly powdery. The granules when present are not so large as in *G. asper*. The rays when dry are either folded over the top of the inner peridium or are curved in more abruptly with their tips under it, or they may take any intermediate position. The species grows in sandy soil and in this country is apparently confined to the western states, occurring also in Europe and Africa. A large form of this with the spore sac 2 cm. thick (in the pressed condition) is represented in the Herbarium of the Museum of Paris from western Africa. Except in size they do not differ apparently from the American plants. The spores are distinctly warted, 5–6.5 x 6–7μ. An interesting plant that seems referable to this as a variant is represented in the Farlow Herbarium from Lake Titicaca, Bolivia (Mrs. Shepard, coll.). The rays are thick, strongly hygroscopic, covered with sand; spore sac densely furfuraceous, nearly white, peristome vaguely defined by a low ridge, fimbriate; spores spherical to irregular, distinctly warted, 4–5μ thick or up to 6μ long.

In his treatment of *G. delicatus* (The Geastrae, p. 11), Lloyd makes the mistake of referring to *G. lageniformis* when he should have said *G. floriformis* (see Hollos, p. 67).

Illustrations: Cunningham. Trans. N. Z. Inst. **57**: pl. 11, fig. 37. 1926.
  De Toni. l. c., pl. 1, fig. O.
  Hollos. l. c., pl. 10, figs. 20–25; pl. 29, figs. 29, 30.
  Lloyd. The Geastrae, figs. 14, 15 (as *G. delicatus*) and fig. 78; also pl. 98, figs. 12–18.
  Morgan. The Genus Geaster, fig. 2 (as *G. delicatus*).
  Petri. l. c., fig. 43.
  Vittadini. Monog. Lycoperd., pl. 1, fig. 5. 1842.

Florida. Grasmere. Baker, coll. (Lloyd Herb.). Mouth indistinct. Two other boxes of same show
    very minute plants, many not over 4–5 mm. in diameter when closed; many with depressed
    mouth area.
  Alachua Co. Couch, coll. (U. N. C. Herb., No. 7274).
Texas. Denton. Long, coll. (Lloyd Herb.). Columella cylindrical, about 4 mm. long.
California. San Diego. Orcutt, coll. (Path. and Myc. Herb. and N. Y. Bot. Gard. Herb., as *G.
    delicatus*). Spores subspherical, about 5–6.8μ thick.
  Catalina Island. Mrs. Trask, coll. (Lloyd Herb.).
South California, 32–36° N. Lat. Parry, coll. (Curtis Herb., as *G. rufescens*).
Colorado. Yuma. Clements, No. 613. (N. Y. Bot. Gard. Herb.) Spores sacs distinctly granular.
North Dakota. Brenckle, coll. (Path. and Myc. Herb. and U. N. C. Herb., No. 152 of Sydow, Fungi
    Exot. Exs.). Spores spherical or somewhat elongated, 4.2–5 x 5–7μ. In Lloyd's Herbarium
    plants from N. Dakota (Brenckle, coll.) show a more or less definite, depressed area around the
    mouth.
Nebraska. Lincoln. Webber, coll. (N. Y. Bot. Gard. Herb.; also in Path. and Myc. Herb. as Ell.
    & Ev., N. Am. Fungi, No. 1941).
Washington. Cheney. Mrs. Tucker, coll. (Lloyd Herb.). Lloyd has a note saying, "Mrs. Tucker
    writes me that this species proves quite a pest in flower beds."

PLATE 71

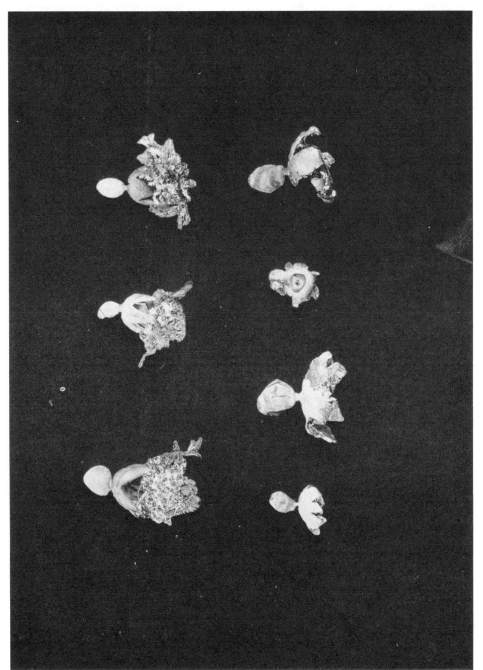

GEASTER CORONATUS. No. 75 [above]; No. 684 [below]

PLATE 72

GEASTER CORONATUS. No. 3881
Fresh condition

Canada.   London.   Dearness, coll.   (U. N. C. Herb.).
Transvaal.   Pretoria.   Evans, coll.   (Lloyd Herb.).
New Zealand.   Rangitata.   Barker, coll.   (Lloyd Herb.).

Geaster coronatus (Schaeff.) Schroet.
  G. minimus Schw. (not *Geastrum minimum* Chevallier)
  G. marginatus Vitt.
  G. quadrifidum Pers.
  G. Cesatii Rabenhorst

Plates 71, 72, 115 and 116

Plants when expanded 1.5–3.5 cm. broad and up to 3.3 cm. tall excluding the basal
cup when present; outer peridium splitting into 4–8 strongly recurved or rarely horizontal lobes, the mycelial layer often being stripped off and remaining as an obscure
weft which holds together a hollow mass of earth or trash out of which the plant was
lifted, the tips of the rays attached to its margin (typical or fornicate form); in other
cases the mycelial layer with the adhering trash is lifted with the plant and forms a
more or less persistent coat on the outer surface (form *minimus*); fleshy layer brown,
cracking and often seceding in large part from the rays, the central part most persistent
and at times forming a low collar around the base of the stalk.   Inner peridium ovoid
to oblong, 4–14μ thick, brown to umber or slate color, the surface, except when weather-
worn, powdered with minute glistening particles; stalk distinct, about 1.5–2.5 mm.
long and expanding above into a ridge which in some specimens may have an acute rim
like a little collar.   Mouth delicately fimbriated, not sulcate, low, abruptly or gradually elevated from a nearly flat, sharply defined silky area which is outlined by a groove.
Columella in mature plant not obvious.
Spores (of No. 3881) dark smoky purplish, distinctly rough, 4–5.1μ thick, most
about 4.5μ.   Capillitium threads up to 6μ thick, not sinuous and branching rarely if
at all.

This species has been confused with *G. fornicatus* both in Europe and America
and it is treated under the latter name by Morgan.   We are following Lloyd and Hollos
in using the name *G. coronatus* for the present species.   The true *G. fornicatus*, as now
understood, is usually larger and is easily distinguished by the absence of a well defined
mouth area, the different surface of the spore sac, and by the smaller and less strongly
warted spores.
The type of *G. minimus* in the Schweinitz Herbarium is just like the usual *G.
minimus* of herbaria; the spores distinctly warted, 3.7–4.4μ thick.   Another authentic
specimen of *G. minimus* from Schweinitz, now in the Michener Herbarium in Washington, is just like the form that we are calling *G. minimus*.   Lloyd has seen the plant in
the Schweinitz Herbarium and says that it is the same as the *minimus* form.   We find
it impossible to distinguish between *G. coronatus* and *G. minimus*.   If the mycelial
layer with its trash remains attached and is lifted when the rays bend back we have
the *minimus* form, if not it is the *coronatus* form, and both forms with intermediates
may occur in the same colony.   Smaller size does not distinguish *minimus*, as we have
seen the fornicate form with the inner peridium less than 5 mm. thick.
In several plants in our collections the ridge around the expanded top of the stem,
which is often obvious in stalked species, is terminated by a distinct, fimbriated frill,
recalling the broader frill of *G. Bryantii*.   The last mentioned is distinguished by its
sulcate and more narrow and elevated mouth, by the distinct columella and by the

broader frill. Both forms of *G. coronatus* are widely distributed in the United States and are not uncommon. In Europe the *minimus* form seems much rarer. The European plant is represented in Torrend's Mycotheca Lusitanica No. 79 (*in pinetis*), also in Cesati's Herbarium Mycol., No. 1634 (as *G. Cesatii*. Both in Path. and Myc. Herb., Washington). In *G. Cesatii* the spores are distinctly warted, 3.8–4.5μ thick.

Geaster granulosus is an extreme form or variety of *G. minimus* with distinctly larger granules on the spore sac and in some cases covering it almost solidly with a white crust, at least as much so as in *G. calceus* as shown by Lloyd's fig. 9, pl. 95. We have studied authentic specimens of *G. granulosus* from Austria (Fuckel, coll.) and find the spores to be larger and rougher than in *G. minimus*, 4.2–5.6μ thick, often with an angular appearance from the irregular warts (pl. 116, fig. 12). A plant from Ymala, Mexico, has the exact superficial appearance of *G. granulosus* and the spores approach those of that species, with the same irregularity, but are somewhat smaller, 3.8–5μ. They have the form of spores of *G. minimus* shown on pl. 115, fig. 24, and are only slightly larger. *Geaster calceus* Lloyd (Myc. Notes, p. 311) from South Africa is very near the last, but with smaller spores (3.5–4.2μ), of regular, spherical shape and with equal warts (pl. 116, fig. 11).

A peculiar plant is represented in the Path. and Myc. Herbarium by three specimens from Waste Land, South Dakota (Wilcox, coll.). It looks like a small, nearly sessile specimen of *G. minimus* but the spores are distinctly larger and irregular (4.8–5.5 x 6.4–7.5μ), with large, unequal warts (pl. 116, fig. 16). The plant bears the ms. name of *G. terreus* Ellis, n. sp., with description in ms. attached. It may be a new species, but is more probably an extreme variant of the *minimus* type. Macbride describes as a new species, *G. juniperinus*, a plant from Iowa, very close to *G. coronatus*. It seems scarcely more than a form (Mycologia **4**: 84. 1912).

Noack (cited below) reports this fungus, which he calls *G. fornicatus*, as forming mycorrhizas on the roots of conifers.

Illustrations: De Toni. l. c., pl. 63, fig. H and fig. I (as *G. marginatus*).
  Fries, Th. C. E. Sveriges Gasteromyceter, fig. 28 (as *G. quadrifidum*).
  Hard. Mushrooms, fig. 482 (as *G. minimus*).
  Hollos. l. c., pl. 7, figs. 11–14 (as *G. coronatus*); pl. 10, figs. 8–10; pl. 29, fig. 28.(as *G. minimus*).
  Lloyd. The Geastrae, figs. 50–52 (as *G. minimus*); figs. 58–61 (as *G. coronatus;* fig. 59 was first
    published as *G. fornicatus*, Myc. Notes, p. 71, fig. 36). Also pl. 95, figs. 1–7 (as *G. minimus*).
  Macbride. Mycologia **4**: pl. 62, fig. 2 (as *G. marginatus*) and fig. 3 (as *G. minimus*). 1912.
  Morgan. North Amer. Geasters, fig. 1 (as *G. fornicatus*) and fig. 7 (as *G. minimus*).
  Nees von Esenbeck. Syst. Pilze Schw., pl. 12, fig. 128 (as *Geastrum quadrifidum*). 1817.
  Noack. Bot. Zeit. 47: pl. 5, fig. 1 (as *G. fornicatus*). 1889.
  Petri. l. c., fig. 37, No. 1 (as *G. minimus*); fig. 44, No. 4 (as *G. coronatus*).
  Schaeffer. Fung. Bavar., pl. 183.
  Schmidel. Icon. Plant., pl. 37 figs. 1–3 (as *G. coronatus*). 1747.
  Vittadini. Monog. Lycoperd., pl. 1, fig. 6 (as *G. marginatus*). 1843.

  75. On mossy shaded ground under cedars, November 10, 1911. Fornicate form. Spores 3.7–4.4μ,
      most about 3.9μ thick. Capillitium threads sinuous, up to 5.5μ thick.
3881. By a decaying oak stump in Strowd's low grounds, December 13, 1919. Fornicate form and
      minimus form mixed in same colony.
6065. By a cedar stump in a pasture, February 12, 1923. Fornicate form. Spores distinctly warted,
      4–5.3μ, most about 4.6μ thick. Capillitium threads straight, apparently unbranched, up to
      5.1μ thick.

6091. On the ground by a decaying oak stump, May 20, 1923. Fornicate form. Spores distinctly warted, 4–5.1μ thick. Capillitium threads straight, apparently unbranched, up to 7μ thick. Also Nos. 684, 5903, 6076, 6077, 7403, 7484.

Raleigh. Wells, coll. (U. N. C. Herb.).
Smith's Island. Couch and Grant, coll. No. 5965. In sandy soil, December 29, 1921. *Minimus* form. Spores minutely warted, 4–5μ.

"Carolina." Pine woods. (Michener Herb. from Schw. Herb., as *G. fornicatus* and *G. striatus*.) Also in Schw. Herb., No. 2247, as *G. quadrifidum*.
South Carolina. Aiken. Ravenel, coll. (Path. and Myc. Herb., as *G. minimus*, Fung. Am. Exs., No. 472). Also Fung. Car. Exs., No. 74. (Phila. Acad., as *G. minimus*.)
Society Hill. (Curtis Herb., as *G. fornicatus*, No. 2301.)
Also a collection from South Carolina by Ravenel in Michener Herb., as *G. minimus*.
Florida. DeFuniak Springs. Fisher, coll. (Lloyd Herb.). These plants have a distinct apophysis with a distinct edge as in one or more of our Chapel Hill collections, but is not exactly typical *G. coronatus* as the sac particles are dull and look more like specks of dust.
New Jersey. In very sandy soil. Ellis, coll. (N. Y. Bot. Gard. Herb.). Lobes varying from 4–8; an imperfect cup attached in some, in others not.
New York. Mohawk. Mrs. Lobenstein. (N. Y. Bot. Gard. Herb., as *G. fornicatus*.)
Massachusetts. Boston. Sprague, No. 42. (Curtis Herb., as *G. minimus*.) There are also two typical specimens of *minimus* from Schweinitz Herb. in the Curtis Herb.
Ohio. Lloyd, coll. (N. Y. Bot. Gard. Herb., as *G. minimus*, and U. N. C. Herb.). Spores distinctly warted, 3.8–5.5μ thick. Capillitium threads straight, up to 5.5μ thick.
Michigan. Agricultural College. Wheeler, coll. (Path. and Myc. Herb., as *G. minimus*).
Wisconsin. (Univ. Wis. Herb., as *G. minimus*, and U. N. C. Herb.) Spores distinctly warted, 3.7–4.4μ thick.
Texas. Wright, No. 326. (Curtis Herb., as *G. fornicatus*.)
California. Pasadena. McClatchie, coll. (N. Y. Bot. Gard. Herb.).
Canada. Macoun, coll. (N. Y. Bot. Gard. Herb., as *G. minimus*, and U. N. C. Herb.). Minute plants of both forms. Lobes varying from 4–8, revolute, the earth mass attached in some.
Jamaica. A. E. Wright, coll. (Farlow Herb., as *G. limbatus*). One is covered with coarse white particles like Lloyd's *G. calceus*.
Mexico. Ymala. (Path. and Myc. Herb.) *Minimus* form with large granules like *G. granulosus*. Spores 3.8–5μ.
Ecuador. Mille, coll. (Lloyd Herb.).
Japan. Sapporo. Miyabe, coll. (Lloyd Herb.).
New Zealand. Cunningham, coll. (U. N. C. Herb.). Spores strongly warted, 4.2–5.5μ thick.

Geaster leptospermus Atk. & Coker

Plates 73 and 115

Inner peridium nearly globular, 2.5–5 (rarely 6.5) mm. thick, pale gray to pale tan in color, minutely dusted with fine whitish particles which also cover the inner surface of the freshly opened rays; mouth very small, minutely fibrous, surrounded by a conical, white disc which is distinctly outlined and radially fibrous (not sulcate). Fibrous layer of the outer peridium splitting into 3–6 rays about half way down or more, the rays recurving and the base becoming arched up (vaulted beneath), leaving the delicate, fibrous, mycelial layer as a distinct, membranous, white cup beneath, with its margin also rayed by slits, the rays attached to the rays of the plant above (typically fornicate). Inner surface of the rays when freshly opened covered with a succulent, pale buff, fleshy layer, which when dry forms the thin, tan or light brown, smooth and nearly complete membrane over the fibrous layer; underside of the rays white and smooth. Columella not obvious.

Spores (of No. 2028) minute, spherical, 2–3µ, usually appearing under high power as if very minutely punctate or asperulate. Capillitium threads unbranched, about 3µ thick. Both spores and capillitium very pale yellow-brown (whitish).

This is a very distinct and well marked little species and is the smallest known *Geaster*, the inner peridium of a full-grown plant seldom reaching over 5 mm. in diameter. They have the unique habit of growing in moss on tree trunks, as cedar, hickory, elm, etc., and usually from about four feet from the ground up, most of our collection coming from a height of ten to twenty feet. It is not at all uncommon in Chapel Hill, which is the only known station, and is distinctly a cold weather species, appearing in mild wet spells in winter and early spring and often associated with *Lycoperdon acuminatum*. The flocculent white mycelium penetrates the old bark and extends itself abundantly between the planes of cleavage. The species is distinguished from *G. coronatus*, which is nearest, by the much smaller average size, smaller and nearly white spores, and capillitium, and peculiar habitat. For the original description, see Bot. Gaz. **36**: 306. 1903.

681, 1085, 1479, 1537, 2028, 2029, 2466, 3222, 3231, 6052, 7586. All on mossy bark of living elm, hickory or cedar during winter or early spring.

Geaster pectinatus Persoon
　G. multifidum var. *a* Pers.

Plates 74, 75 and 115

Mycelium universal and forming a soft, flocculent coat that holds trash to the entire outer surface of the plant as in *G. rufescens;* rays few to numerous, typically reflexed but the tips often incurved, central region concave below and elevating the spore sac; mycelial layer with attached earth tending to peel off after expansion as is also the brown fleshy layer, so that the thin, pale fibrous layer may be left almost naked in old specimens; spore sac subglobose to urn-shaped, with or without an apophysis, the lower part with radial lines or ridges that in some cases may be quite faint; stalk slender, typically rather long, up to 5 or 6 mm., often with a collar or ring near center or base; surface when fresh covered with a fine powder which is whitish against the spore sac and brown without so as to give the spore sac a whitish bloom where it is thin and a brown-drab color where it is thicker. Mouth long, narrowly conical, prettily sulcate-striate, brown.

Spores (of plant from Jamesville, N. Y.) very dark, with large blunt warts, 4.2–5.5µ thick. Capillitium threads up to 7µ thick.

A rare plant apparently, and Schweinitz's record is so far the only one from North Carolina. The length of stalk is very variable, e.g., in one good lot from Surrey, England, at the New York Botanical Garden Herbarium (as *G. limbatus*), the stalk is only 2 mm. long. The species runs into two extremes that are most conveniently treated as species, though intermediates occur. The smallest of these is *G. Schmidelii*, which also approaches *G. Smithii* (*G. ambiguus*, sense of Hollos). The other is *G. Bryantii* which is distinguished by a deflexed collar around the base of the spore sac. Specimens of *G. pectinatus* (Upsala) in the Curtis Herbarium are labelled *G. limbatus* by E. P. Fries.

A part of the type collection of *G. biplicatus* (Proc. Am. Acad. Arts and Sciences **4**: 124. 1860) in the Curtis Herbarium (Bonin Isles) is so pressed as not to show the base of the spore sac; peristome truly sulcate; spore sac reddish brown with a grayish

PLATE 73

GEASTER LEPTOSPERMUS. No. 2466

PLATE 74

GEASTER PECTINATUS, North Island, S. C.

powder; outer surface covered with humus held by flocculence. Spores distinctly warted, 3.8–4.8μ, rarely up to 5.2μ thick. Other plants from the type collection in Washington are similar with inner peridium blackish brown with a grayish powder. We have a fine specimen from New Caledonia sent us by Patouillard (as *G. plicatus* = *G. biplicatus*) with strongly sulcate base to the spore sac, the stalk about 4 mm. long; spores spherical to a little irregular, distinctly warted, 4–6μ thick; capillitium straight, up to 6.5μ thick. It is probable that *G. plicatus* and *G. biplicatus* are the same, as Patouillard thinks, and both are certainly very near *G. pectinatus*. The deep and regular sulcations on the base of the spore sac are a striking character that we have not seen exactly duplicated in *G. pectinatus*. We have seen Lloyd's abundant specimens of *G. plicatus* from Australia and South Africa, but have not seen the type.

Illustrations: Cunningham. Trans. N. Z. Inst. **57**: pl. 9, fig. 27. 1926.
  Cunningham. Proc. Linn. Soc. N. S. W. **51**: pl. 3, figs. 7, 8.
  Fries, Th. C. E. Sveriges Gasteromyceter, fig. 30.
  Lloyd. The Geastrae, figs. 19–22 (fig. 19 was first published as *G. tenuipes* in Myc. Notes, p. 72, fig. 37).
  Lloyd. Gen. Gastromycetes, pl. 8, fig. 38.
  Petri. l. c., fig. 37, 4–5 and fig. 40.
  Rick. Broteria **5**: pl. 1, figs. 14–15.
  Schmidel. Icon. Plant., pl. 37, figs. 11–14. Edition of 1793. These are referred to by Persoon.
  Smith. Grevillea **2**: pl. 17, fig. 1 (as *G. limbatus*). Ridges on mouth obscure.

North Carolina. Salem. (Schw. Herb.) Plant as large as usual in the species; stalk short and rather thick.
South Carolina. North Island. Under cedars. Coker and party, colls. (U. N. C. Herb.).
New York. Jamesville. Mrs. Goodrich, coll. (N. Y. Bot. Gard. Herb.).
  Pompey. (N. Y. Bot. Gard. Herb., as *G. Bryantii*.)
Ohio. (N. Y. Bot. Gard. Herb., from Lloyd Herb.)
Reported from Florida and Pennsylvania by Lloyd.
Ontario. Hamilton. Dearness, coll. (U. N. C. Herb.). Spores strongly warted, 4.5–6μ.

Geaster Bryantii Berk.

Plate 115

Like *G. pectinatus* except that around the base of the spore sac at some distance from the stem there hangs a collar-like ring with an acute edge. This character alone would hardly entitle the plant to more than varietal rank.

Spores of a plant from Massee (England [?], N. Y. Bot. Gard. Herb.) are spherical, distinctly warted, very dark, 4–5.5μ, most about 4.8μ. In another plant from Europe (Rabenhorst and Winter, Fungi europaei, No. 2639, N. Y. Bot. Gard. Herb.) the spores are smaller and less distinctly warted, 3.8–4.8μ thick. The plant is also well represented in Sydow's Mycotheca germanica, No. 1449 (Path. and Myc. Herb., Washington).

The plant is rare in America and is not reported from the southeastern states. Lloyd reports it from Maine and Texas, and Morgan from New York.

Illustrations: Berkeley. Grevillea **2**: pl. 16, fig. 2.
  Bryant. An Historical Account, etc., fig. 19. 1782.
  Cunningham. Proc. Linn. Soc. N. S. W. **51**: pl. 3, fig. 10.
  De Toni. l. c., pl. 1, fig. D.
  Hollos. l. c., pl. 9, figs. 1–4.
  Lloyd. The Geastrae, figs. 23–26.
  Morgan. North Amer. Geasters, fig. 5.
  Rea. l. c., pl. 18.

Geaster Schmidelii Vitt.

  G. Rabenhorstii Kunze

Plates 75 and 115

Like *G. pectinatus*, except smaller arid with a short stalk and less separable mycelial layer and smaller spores. A typical lot of this form is No. 5020 of E. Bartholomew's Fungi Columbiana (Calloway, Nebraska; J. M. Bates, coll.). These have 5–6 reflexed rays with trashy mycelial layer attached, the thin brown fleshy layer also present; spore sac suboval, very short-stalked, smooth, dark brown, mouth elevated, strongly sulcate. Spores medium dark, minutely warted, spherical, 3.7–4.4μ, with a visible oil drop.

Another lot of Bates' plants from Nebraska are in the New York Botanical Garden (from Lloyd Herb.). The outer surface is covered with sand, the spore sac blackish with a whitish or brown powder. A less typical lot is from New Jersey (Newfield; Earle, coll., at N. Y. Bot. Gard. Herb.). This lot has the rays slightly hygroscopic and in one of the plants the spore sac is yellowish buff color. Another plant of this lot is the one shown by Lloyd in his Geastrae, fig. 27 a. The spores of this particular plant are like those noted above, minutely warted, 3.7–4.5μ. A plant about intermediate between *pectinatus* and *Schmidelii* is at the New York Botanical Garden Herbarium (Underwood, coll.; Kirkville, N. Y.). The spore sac is buffy and the stalk very short. European *G. Schmidelii* as distributed by Torrend (Mycotheca Lusitanica, in Path. and Myc. Herb., Washington) is like our American plant and like the types of *G. Rabenhorstii*. Three plants sent us for examination by Patouillard (Herb. Mus. Paris; Barla, coll.) as *G. Schmidelii* are somewhat worn specimens of the *minimus* form of *G. coronatus*. The spores are spherical, warted, 3.7–4.6μ.

In freshly opened plants collected by us in Warrenton, Va., the fleshy layer was nearly white; spore sac drab. On drying the fleshy layer turned brown and cracked considerably.

Spores of the type material of *G. Rabenhorstii* (Fungi selecti exs., No. 10, in Path. and Myc. Herb., Washington) are spherical, distinctly warted, 3.8–5μ, a few up to 5.5μ. *Geaster elegans* Vitt. is very near *G. Schmidelii*, the only obvious difference being the entirely sessile spore sac and larger spores of the former. These characters are shown by plants in Torrend's Mycotheca Lusitanica, No. 78 (Univ. Wis. Herb. and U. N. C. Herb., as *G. elegans*), and in his Fungi selecti exs., No. 79 (in the same herbarium, as *G. minimus*); also in the Herbarium of the University of Paris (from Tulasne Herb.). The spores of the last mentioned are minutely but distinctly rough, 4.2–5.5μ thick (pl. 116, fig. 2). The plant is not known from America.

This would seem to run into a saccate form, apparently quite sessile as shown by a distribution of 11 good plants by J. Kunze, Fungi selecti exs., as *G. striatus* DC., from the same place as his *G. Rabenhorstii* and also like that in growing in *Picea excelsa* needles; mouth, peridium and all else same except that the outer peridium is saccate or flat and inner peridium with no obvious stalk.

Illustrations: Destrée. l. c., pl. 7, fig. B.
   Lloyd. As cited above.
   Petri. l. c., fig. 37, 3.
   Trelease. l. c., pl. 7, fig. 3 (as *G. Rabenhorstii*).
   Vittadini. Monog. Lycoperd., pl. 1, fig. 7.

PLATE 75

[Top] GEASTER PECTINATUS.   Small plant, London, Canada, No. 3023;
larger, Webster's Falls, Canada, No. 4235
[Middle] GEASTER SCHMIDELII. Newfield, N. J.
[Bottom] GEASTER UMBILICATUS. Newfield, N. J. (left)
GEASTER RABENHORSTII. Type material (right)

PLATE 76

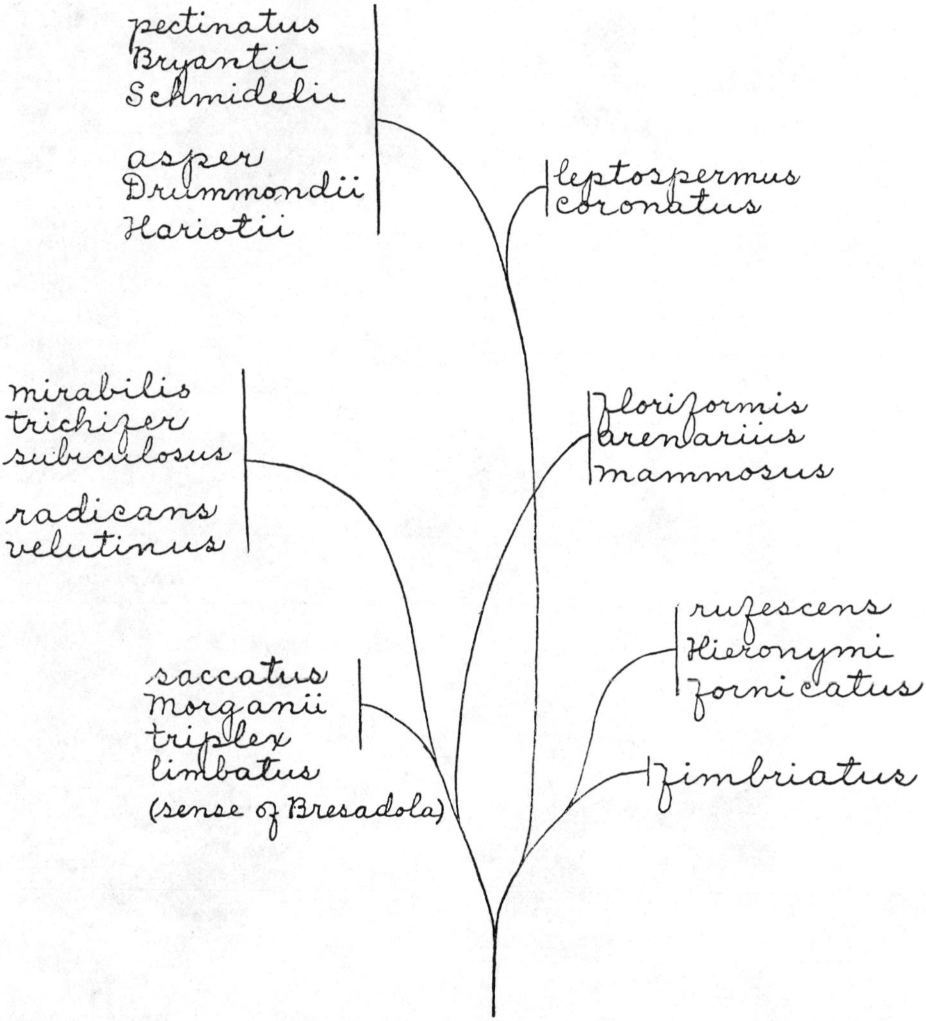

pectinatus
Bryantii
Schmidelii

asper
Drummondii
Hariotii

leptospermus
coronatus

mirabilis
trichifer
subiculosus

radicans
velutinus

floriformis
arenarius
mammosus

rufescens
Hieronymi
fornicatus

saccatus
Morganii
triplex
limbatus
(sense of Bresadola)

fimbriatus

SUGGESTED RELATIONSHIPS OF THE GEASTERS

North Carolina. Salem. Schweinitz, coll. (Curtis Herb., as *G. pectinatus*). Spore sac practically sessile.

Virginia. Warrenton. In upland frondose woods, Sept. 6, 1926. Coker, coll. (U. N. C. Herb.). Spores minutely warted, 3.4–4μ.

New Jersey. Newfield. Ellis, coll. (N. Y. Bot. Gard. Herb.).

Nebraska. Bates, coll. (N. Y. Bot. Gard. Herb., from Lloyd Herb. and Path. and Myc. Herb., Washington, as Bartholomew, Fungi Columb., No. 5020).

Texas. Denton. Long, coll. (Path. and Myc. Herb., Washington; Ellis and Everhart, Fungi Columb., No. 1620, as *G. pectinatus*). Mixed with these is a plant with strongly granular spore sac like *G. asper* except that the outer peridium is not hygroscopic but like the others.

Cuba. Wright, No. 694. (Curtis Herb., as *G. tenuipes* Berk.). Spore sac apparently sessile, slate color with a dusting of grayish powder.

Geaster Hariotii Lloyd

Plates 68 and 115

Rays about 8, spreading about 3 cm., pliable, not hygroscopic, revolute or in part expanded, the center concave below and elevating the spore sac; outer surface entirely covered with earth or trash held on by flocculent mycelium which may in time be partially shed in flakes. Fleshy layer dark brown, cracking and seceding in places. Spore sac 1.5 cm. broad, subglobose, sessile, dark brown to black, distinctly pitted and rough to asperate with small points, but not truly warted or tomentose. Peristome truly sulcate, mouth elevated and becoming fimbriate.

Spores (of plant from Porto Rico) spherical, dark, faintly rough under very high power, 3.5–4μ thick.

As Lloyd does not mention a rough surface to the peridium (Myc. Notes, p. 311), we had referred our plant to this species with some doubt until the recent receipt from Patouillard of a specimen from Brazil that had been seen by Lloyd and which Patouillard designates as an "original specimen." This is exactly like our plant except that the surface is somewhat less conspicuously rough; rays not rigid; spores spherical, nearly smooth, 3–3.6μ thick, often with a visible oil drop. Capillitium threads straight, encrusted, up to 6.5μ thick. Under *G. Archeri* Lloyd has two collections, one from Ceylon (Petch, coll.) and one from Victoria (Winkler, coll.). They are not that species, but pale forms of *G. Hariotii*. The mouth in each case is darker than the granular or spongy peridium; peridium clay-brown to brown; mouth truly sulcate; outer surface densely flocculent and with trash as in *G. Hariotii*.

Illustrations: Cunningham. Proc. Linn. Soc. N. S. W. **51**: pl. 4, fig. 12.
Lloyd. Myc. Works, pl. 99, figs. 7–9.

Porto Rico. March 1923. Seaver, coll. (Seaver Herb., No. 840, and U. N. C. Herb.).
British Honduras. M. E. Peck, coll. (N. Y. Bot. Gard. Herb.). Spores smooth, 3–3.7μ thick.
Brazil. (U. N. C. Herb. from Patouillard.)
 Rio. In leaf mold, March 1894. Murrill, coll. (N. Y. Bot. Gard. Herb.).
Dutch Guiana. Samuels, coll. (N. Y. Bot. Gard. Herb.).

Geaster asper (Mich.) Lloyd
 G. pseudomammosus Henn.
 G. campestris Morgan

Plates 68 and 115

Plants submerged until mature, the mycelium universal; rays with a spread of 2.5–3.5 cm. (up to 5 cm., Morgan), hygroscopic, rigid, 8–10, rarely more, involute or spreading when dry, outer surface covered at first and rather persistently with sandy earth mixed with flocculent mycelium, this slowly flaking off or wearing away on exposure, leaving the surface pale and smooth; fleshy layer adnate, usually continuous, dark brown to blackish; base concave below and elevating the spore sac which is sub-globose with a short thickish stalk, the surface gray to brown and covered with wart-like particles; mouth strongly and prettily sulcate, seated in a depressed zone, con-colorous or darker, at times nearly black.

Spores (of a plant from Lincoln, Nebraska), spherical, distinctly warted, 4.5–6.5μ. Capillitium threads straight, up to 5μ thick.

A plant of the Mississippi valley and westward, seeming to prefer sandy soil. It is well marked by the conspicuous granules on the spore sac, which are much coarser than the fine powdery particles on the sac of *G. coronatus* and *G. leptospermus*.

This species varies to a form with lax and pliable outer peridium like that of *G. mammosus* and *G. Schmidelii*. See, for example, one plant among a typical lot of *G. asper* from Dakota at Washington (Brenckle, Fungi Dakotensis, No. 35, in Path. and Myc. Herb.); also in the same herbarium a plant from Texas, mixed with *G. Schmidelii* (Ell. & Ev., Fungi Columb., No. 1620; Long, coll.).

Illustrations: Cunningham. Proc. Linn. Soc. N. S. W. **51**: pl. 2, fig. 1; pl. 3, figs. 13, 14; pl. 7, fig. **41**
    (as *G. campestris*).
  Hollos. l. c., pl. 9, figs. 12–14, 21, 22; pl. 29, figs. 24, 25.
  Lloyd. Myc. Notes No. 7: fig. 34; Geastrae, figs. 28–30.
  Micheli. Nov. Plant. Gen., pl. 100, fig. 2.
  Morgan. The Genus *Geaster*, fig. 1 (as *G. campestris*).
  ?Rick. Broteria **5**: pl. 1, fig. 13 (as *G. asper*, but does not look much like ours).

Nebraska. Long Pine. Bates, coll.
    Lincoln. Webber, coll. (N. Y. Bot. Gard. Herb. and U. N. C. Herb.).
North Dakota. Kulm, coll. (N. Y. Bot. Gard. Herb. and U. N. C. Herb., as Sydow, Fungi exot.,
    No. 151).
Wyoming. Pitchfork. Davis, coll. (U. N. C. Herb.).
Kansas. Bartholomew, coll. (Path. and Myc. Herb.). In this lot the mouth is nearly black, con-
    trasting strongly with the nearly white peridium.
Utah. Fort Douglas. Clements, coll. (Farlow Herb.). Granules on spore sac inconspicuous, but
    appearance and spores as in *G. asper*. Spores spherical, irregularly warted, 4.4–5.5μ, rarely
    up to 6μ thick.
Texas. Denton. Long, coll. (Ell. & Ev., Fungi Columb., No. 1825; Path. and Myc. Herb., as *G. striatus*).

Geaster umbilicatus Fr.   Sense of Morgan
    G. striatulus Kalch.   Sense of Lloyd
    ? G. Smithii Lloyd
    G. ambiguus Mont.   Sense of Hollos in part

Plates 75 and 115

Plants small, hygroscopic, the button subterranean and when first expanded covered completely without by sandy earth; rays about 7–10, unequal in breadth, the delicate, flocculent outer layer intimately mixed with earth and gradually wearing away to leave the rays smooth and glabrous and pale brown to pallid tan, scarcely shining and not as metallic-looking as in *G. mammosus;* fleshy layer rather thin, smooth or more or less rimose, brown to blackish. Spore sac 7–12 mm. thick, sessile, pale tan to dark brown, minutely furfuraceous until old; peristome prettily and regularly plicate-sulcate, strongly furfuraceous, particularly below, when fresh, the mouth usually elevated and conical or at times flattened in a depressed zone.

Spores (of plants from New Jersey, Ellis, No. 3472) spherical, faintly warted, 3.5–4μ thick. Capillitium threads wavy, up to 6.5μ thick.

A plant of sandy soil in Europe and America and evidently rare. It is the plant distributed by Ellis as No. 110 in his North American Fungi (as *G. mammosus*), and a letter to Ellis from Morgan at the New York Botanical Garden states this to be the same as his *umbilicatus*. The species is known from New Jersey (Ellis) and from Florida (Lloyd). Morgan thinks that *G. Smithii* Lloyd (Geastrae, p. 21) is the same, but Cunningham does not agree with this. It should certainly occur on our North Carolina coast.

The rays in this species while distinctly hygroscopic are more delicate and pliable than in *G. mammosus* and much more so than in *Astraeus*. From *G. Drummondii* (*G. involutus*) and *G. asper* the plant is easily separated by the delicately and softly furfuraceous, not warted or asperulate spore sac, and by the smaller spores. From *G. Schmidelii*, which is very near, it is separated by its hygroscopic and not revolute rays and by the sessile spore sac. The spores of the two are very nearly alike. Lloyd has seen the type of *G. ambiguus* and thinks it different from *G. striatulus*, to which he refers the present plant (Myc. Notes, p. 311).

Geastrum minimum Chev. (Fl. Gen. Env. Paris 1: 360, pl. 10, fig. 3. 1826) does not look much like this species. It has a distinct, slender stalk, though short, and that is why Chevallier considered it new. He gives the sessile *G. badium* Persoon under his species as a form *alpha*. Hollos considers *G. badium* and *G. umbilicatus* the same as *G. elegans* Vitt. (which see under *G. Schmidelii*). From the description there is no reason to think that *G. striatus* var. *minimus* Wallroth (Fl. Crypt. Germaniae 2: 400 (No. 2274)) is the same as our American plant above described. He refers to Chevallier's *G. minimum* as the same.

Illustrations: Hollos. l. c., pl. 9, figs. 15–17 (as *G. ambiguus*).
    Lloyd. Myc. Notes, p. 71 (as *G. striatulus*). Also copied on pl. 98, figs. 3, 4.
    Morgan. North Amer. Geasters, fig. 4.

Florida. Mrs. Sams, coll. (Lloyd Herb., as *G. Smithii*).
New Jersey. Newfield. Ellis (N. Am. Fungi, No. 110. Also several other collections by Ellis at the
    N. Y. Bot. Gard. Herb., as *mammosus* or *umbilicatus*).

Geaster Drummondii Berk.
    G. involutus Massee
    G. Schweinfurthii Hennings

Plates 115 and 116

At the New York Botanical Garden Herbarium are two good plants from Brisbane, Australia (Herb. Massee) which appear to truly represent this species. The plants are:

Hygroscopic, rigid; fleshy layer blackish; outer surface covered with sandy humus; **spore sac small, subglobose, sessile.**

One plant has the inner peridium 12 mm. broad, spiny-granular; mouth blackish, 12-ridged. Spores faintly rough, spherical, 5.4–6.5μ.

The other has the inner peridium 9.5 mm. broad, pulverulent-granular; mouth creamy gray, 19-ridged.   Spores faintly rough, 4.5–6.5μ.
Inner peridium of both creamy gray (pale leather color).

Type plants of *G. involutus* from St. Domingo at the New York Botanical Garden show that no important difference can be made out to distinguish it from *G. Drummondii*.   The appearance is identically like that of the plant with spiny peridium, except that the mouth is not dark.   The spores are the same, minutely warted, 4–5μ thick.   The inner peridium is asperate and the mouth beautifully sulcate with 12 or 14 ridges.   Hollos gives *G. avellaneus* Kalch. as a synonym of this species, and both as synonyms of *G. ambiguus* Mont.   The former was published only as a figure, with no written description.   The spore sac is shown as white and not dotted; the outer peridium evidently hygroscopic, in one case folded over the spore sac, its outer surface ochraceous with some earth attached; mouth truly sulcate.

Illustrations: Berkeley.   Journal of Bot. for 1845, pl. 1, fig. 4.
　　　Cunningham.   Proc. Linn. Soc. N. S. W. **51:** pl. 4, figs. 17–18.
　　　Fries, Th. C. E.   Sveriges Gasteromyceter, fig. 27.
　　　Hennings.   Engler's Bot. Jahrb. **14:** pl. 6, fig. 7.
　　　Lloyd.   Lycoperd. of Australia, etc., fig. 8 (types of *G. Drummondii*).

St. Domingo.   Part of type of *G. involutus* at N. Y. Bot. Gard. Herb.
Australia.   Victoria.   (Kew Herb., as *G. argentatus*).

MYRIOSTOMA Desv.

Outer peridium as in *Geaster*, coriaceous, pliable, splitting in a stellate way with segments expanded or reflexed; inner peridium with several short stalks (rarely one by coalition), membranous, papery, opening by several to many mouths (rarely one). Columellas several, slender.   Capillitium threads free, simple or nearly so.

There is only one species of this genus known, as it has been shown by Patouillard that *Geaster columnatus* Lév. is a synonym (see Lloyd, Myc. Notes, p. 156).

Myriostoma coliformis Corda

Plate 117

Plants subterranean until dehiscence, lobes usually 5–7, acute; fleshy layer thin, brown, adherent at first but wearing away; outer layer nearly smooth, usually with adherent sand or trash.   Inner peridium subspherical to compressed, 1.5–5 cm. broad, roughened by minute points and lines, silvery brown.   Mouths small, fibrous to lacerate.
Spores (of plant from Lloyd Herbarium) spherical, strongly warted with irregular pale warts, 4–6μ thick, rarely abnormal ones up to 8μ.   Capillitium threads long, slender, tapering at both ends, entirely free from the peridium and columella, about 2–5μ thick, with a thick wall which often closes the lumen.

This species has a wide but erratic distribution in this country and in Europe. It is not known from the Carolinas, but has been found in both the northern and southern states.

Illustrations: Destrée.   l. c., pl. 6, fig. A (as *Geaster*).
　　　Hollos.   l. c., pl. 7, figs. 1–10; pl. 8, fig. 8; pl. 29, fig. 18.
　　　Lloyd.   The Geastrae, figs. 1–4.
　　　Petri.   Flora Ital. Cryptogama (Gasterales), fasc. 5, figs. 49 and 50.

PLATE 77

ASTRAEUS HYGROMETRICUS

Smith's Island [4 large plants]; No. 685 [middle above]; No. 73 [right above]

PLATE 78

DISCISEDA CANDIDA.   No. 5969

Florida. Eldorado. Underwood, coll. (N. Y. B. G. Herb.).
    Also collection by Mrs. Sams. (N. Y. B. G. Herb. from Lloyd).
Ohio. Sandusky. Schaffner, coll. (N. Y. B. G. Herb.).
Ontario. Point Abino. Cook and Underwood, coll. (N. Y. B. G. Herb.).
Reported from Dakota and Colorado.
Also from South America in the New York Bot. Gard. Herb.

DISCISEDA Czern.

Fruit bodies growing just beneath the surface or partially exposed; outer peridium thickish and volva-like, composed of two layers, an outer of loosely interwoven white threads which grow around and enclose many particles of sand and trash and a much thicker inner layer which is watery and subtranslucent when fresh and composed of large, thin-walled, parenchyma cells which dry up and collapse at maturity to form a thin coat on the inside of the outer peridium, the lower part of the outer peridium splitting away at maturity and remaining in the ground, the upper part with the thin, firm, inner peridium attached, breaking away and becoming free; inner peridium opening by a small basal mouth to liberate the spores, which are spherical and warted. Gleba composed of very minute, irregular, anastomosing chambers which are separated by clusters of basidia and a very little trama; basidia much as in *Lycoperdon*, with four slender sterigmata; capillitium threads extending inward from the inner peridium, sparingly septate and slightly branched, at maturity breaking up into small sections. Subgleba none.

Up to the present the internal structure of this genus has not been known, so that its proper position in the system was obscure. It is now apparent, it seems to us, that the genus is a highly specialized member of the Lycoperdaceae. The best evidence to this effect are the basidia, which are obviously of the *Lycoperdon* and *Bovista* type and quite different from the *Astraeus* and *Calostoma* type. Moreover, while the chambers are very small and the hymenium poorly defined, there is an obvious resemblance to the Lycoperdaceae in these characters also.

Three species are known from the southeastern states. Several others are known from the West. Lloyd extends the genus to include several species without the peculiar dehiscence and inverted mouth (Myc. Notes, p. 121, pls. 6 and 7; Myc. Notes, p. 1167).

A new genus, *Abstoma*, has been established by Cunningham (Lycoperdaceae, etc., p. 206) to cover a single endemic species from New Zealand. It is very near *Disciseda*, differing from it essentially only in the absence of a definite mouth, both peridia wearing away gradually from the attrition of wind-blown sand, etc.

KEY TO THE SPECIES

Spores without a pedicel, or rarely with a short one
    Spores $3.6–5\mu$ thick...*D. candida*
    Spores $5.5–9.5\mu$ thick...*D. subterranea*
Spores with a pedicel up to 12.5μ long or rarely longer.............................*D. pedicellata*

Disciseda candida (Schw.) Lloyd

    Disciseda circumscissa (B. & C.) Hollos
    Bovista circumscissa B. & C.
    Catastoma circumscissum (B. & C.) Morgan

Plates 31, 78, 79, 99 and 118

Plants single or cespitose, compressed globose, with a single rhizomorph-like root when young and fresh; 0.5–2 cm. thick, 2–3.5 cm. wide before maturation; 0.8–1.5 x

1.5–2.5 cm. when dry; growing in the soil and partly exposed when fully grown; surrounded until maturity by a thickish cortex (outer peridium) the upper and thicker part of which remains attached to the inner peridium by a layer of spongy fibrous material, the lower part tearing irregularly from the upper and separating more or less completely from the inner peridium and remaining in the ground as broken and inconspicuous fragments. The upper part with the inner peridium attached is now free and is easily knocked out of the cup-like lower part by rain, etc., turning over so that the exposed part of the inner peridium is now above. A small torn hole now appears at the place of attachment of the stalk, in the center of this upturned base, and the spores begin to escape. The cortex is a sand case held together by the woven white mycelium. The inner peridium is rather firm and rigid, pale brown then silvery gray to slate gray in age, minutely granular or scurfy on the exposed (lower) part, densely scurfy above under the cortex. This thick spongy tissue above and thin granular layer below are the remains of a watery translucent layer, 0.6–1 mm. thick which lay between the more fibrous layers in youth. The inner peridium is very indistinct in sections when fresh, becoming conspicuous on maturing and drying. The whole plant shrinks to scarcely more than half its original size upon drying. Glebal chambers extremely minute, 5–25µ wide, but often longer; no definite tramal plates are formed, as in *Lycoperdon* and *Scleroderma*, but the basidia arise from irregularly anastomosing strings of threads and the chambers are very irregular. Gleba white when fresh, changing as the plant matures through yellowish olive to brown, at times faintly purplish. There is no sterile base.

Spores (of No. 5967) brown, at times with a tint of purple, globose, 3.6–4.4µ thick, warted, and with a short pedicel (mucro). Capillitium threads 3–5µ thick, irregular, not rarely branched, extending inwards from the walls of the peridium; after maturity breaking up into short pieces. Basidia (of No. 6092) short-pyriform, 6–7.4 x 9–14µ, usually with 4 slender apical sterigmata of equal length.

This little plant is easily recognized by its peculiar habit of dehiscence and reversal. It is not at all rare in pastures, the fresh, nearly mature plants appearing in mid-summer, the liberated plants obvious in fall and winter. The earthy color makes the plant inconspicuous and it has seldom been reported.

The type of *Bovista candida* Schw. in the Schweinitz Herbarium is this species, as Lloyd says (Myc. Notes, p. 93), but it is so pasted on its sheet as to obscure its characters, and the spores, while of the same size, are less rough than in our plants and in the co-type of *B. circumscissa* B. & C. The spores are 3.7–4.4µ, nearly smooth. The plant may have been collected before fully mature. The capillitium threads are unmistakably those of this genus, made up of irregular fragments, 3.3–4.6µ thick, rather rarely branched. We have some Chapel Hill specimens (as No. 6092) with spores less warted and approaching those of the type of *Bovista candida*. The co-type of *Bovista circumscissa* in the Curtis Herbarium (Blake, No. 164) is like our No. 7115. The spores are warted 3.9–4.6µ thick.

The form we have described above is the Chapel Hill plant which is typical as described by Hollos for the European plant, though running smaller than Morgan's drawings. We have a collection from Asheville (Beardslee) which are 2.5 cm. broad, counting the open cup. They are a brighter brown than our plants, about snuff-brown, but the spores and other characters are the same.

Illustrations: Clements. Minnesota Mushrooms, fig. 88 (as *Catastoma*).
    Hollos. l. c., pl. 22, figs. 25–27; pl. 29, fig. 37.
    Lloyd. Genera of Gastromycetes, fig. 33.

Lloyd. Myc. Works, pl. 6, figs. 1–7.
Massee. Journ. Bot. 26: pl. 282, fig. 6 (as *Bovista*). 1888.
Morgan. Journ. Cin. Soc. Nat. Hist. 14: pl. 5, figs. 4–9. 1892.

5967.   On mossy bank of branch, November 6, 1922.
6092.   In pasture below Cobb Terrace, partly submerged, June 14, 1923.   In fresh, nearly grown condition; basidia in various stages of development.
7117.   On ground in the drug garden, Sept. 10, 1923.   Spores warted, 4–4.8µ thick.
7246.   On ground in Arboretum, March 18, 1924.   Very small specimen, only 5 mm. wide.
Also Nos. 5969, 5974, 5980, 6007, 7109, 7115, 7507, 8151.

Asheville.   Beardslee, coll.
"Mountains."   Buckley, coll. (Curtis Herb.).

South Carolina.   Greenville.   Sept. 1926.   Coker, coll. (U. N. C. Herb.).   Spores 3.8–4.2µ.
Virginia.   White Post.   Dodge, coll. (N. Y. B. G. Herb.).
New Jersey.   Newfield.   Ellis, No. 3600.   (N. Y. B. G. Herb.)   Spores minutely warted, 3.7–5µ.
Ohio.   Norwood.   Lloyd, coll. (N. Y. B. G. Herb.).   Spores 3.8–4.4µ, sometimes with a short pedicel.
Nebraska.   Atkinson, coll. (N. Y. B. G. Herb.).   Spores 3.6–4.5µ.

Disciseda subterranea (Peck)

Plates 80 and 118

We have not seen this in the immature condition and have collected it only once. As it appears in herbaria, it is usually of larger size than *D. circumscissa*, but individuals may be smaller than the average in that species.   The size of the plant is therefore not a constant distinguishing feature, and the larger spores (5.5–9.5µ) must be finally relied on for determination.   The present species was described from Dakota and seems to be common in the middle and far west (see Lloyd, Myc. Notes, p. 122; Morgan, l. c., p. 143).   We have a good specimen from Denver, Colorado (Bethel, coll.), and have also seen a specimen from Canada kindly sent us by Dearness.   These plants are about 1.8–2.8 cm. broad, subspherical or depressed; in the Canadian plant the outer peridium covering about one-half of the inner; in the Denver plants forming only a disk opposite the mouth.

Our collection from North Island, South Carolina, is apparently the first collection from the southeastern states.   As this station invades the territory of *D. pedicellata*, which was plausibly separated from this species by the different regional distribution and pedicellate spores, confidence in a real specific difference is distinctly reduced. We can now make out no difference between the last two except the presence of a conspicuous and persistent pedicel on the spores of *D. pedicellata*.   The North Island plants are smaller than the Denver and Canadian specimens and, like the former, are not at all or scarcely depressed and retain only a small, sandy, basal pad representing the outer peridium.   Both the Denver and South Carolina specimens, as well as Ravenel's No. 15 (*D. pedicellata*) at Philadelphia, show several small openings in the inner peridium in addition to the apical one.   These may be due to insects but appear natural.

As Petri gives the spores as only 4.5–5.3µ, it is doubtful if he had this species. *Disciseda verrucosa* Cun. (Lycoperdaceae, etc., p. 205) should be compared with this species.   From the description it is very close if not the same.

Illustrations: Hollos. l. c., pl. 22, figs. 20–24; pl. 29, fig. 36 (all as *D. Debreceniensis*).
    Lloyd.   Myc. Notes, p. 263, fig. 98; pl. 7, figs. 1–3 (as *Catastoma*).
    ?Petri.   Flora Italica Cryptogama (Gasterales), fasc. 5, figs. 51, 52.

South Carolina.   North Island.   In sand dunes under cedars.   Coker and party, colls. (U. N. C.
    Herb.).   Plants only 1.2–1.4 cm. thick.   Spores strongly and irregularly warted, 7–9.5μ
    thick.
Colorado.   Denver.   Bethel, coll. (U. N. C. Herb.).   Spores spherical, strongly warted, 6–8.5μ
    thick, with traces of a halo.
    Yuma.   Clements, coll.   Crypt. Form. Coloradensium.   (N. Y. B. G. Herb., as *Catastoma candida*.)
        Spores minutely rough, 6–8μ thick, often with a short pedicel.
Wyoming.   Pitchfork.   Davis, coll. (U. N. C. Herb.).   Spores 5.5–7μ, sometimes with a short pedicel.
Canada.   Dorchester.   Dearness, No. 2841.   (Dearness Herb.)   Spores strongly warted, 6–7.5μ
    thick.   Capillitium threads broken up into bits, 3.2–4.5μ thick, wavy and irregular, with thick
    walls.

Disciseda pedicellata (Morg.) Hollos
Catastoma pedicellatum Morgan

Plates 80 and 118

Plants somewhat flattened, about 2–3 cm. broad; outer peridium not thick, usually
reduced to a small basal pad when collected; inner peridium purplish brown or pallid
grayish brown, soft and pliable.   Spore mass ashy brown at full maturity.
    Spores (of Hartsville plant) spherical, strongly warted, 6.5–8μ thick with a pedicel
about 2–9μ long [the short ones may have been broken].   Capillitium threads wavy,
fragmented, about 4μ thick.

We have collected this plant at Hartsville, S. C., and have compared it carefully
with Ravenel's *Bovista nigrescens*, No. 15, as represented in the Herbarium of the
Academy of Natural Sciences of Philadelphia (*ex* Herb. Geo. Martin).   Morgan established the species on a South Carolina specimen of this series from Ravenel.   The
Ravenel plant has spores irregularly warted, spherical, 7–9μ thick with pedicels up to
6μ long, in all respects like those mentioned above; capillitium threads fragmented,
sinuous, up to 5μ thick, with thick walls.

A plant received from Lloyd without locality data differs from South Carolina
plants in somewhat larger spores (7.4–9μ) with more cylindrical warts and distinctly
longer pedicels (12–20μ).   Otherwise the differences are inconspicuous and probably
represent a regional variety.   For comparison with *D. subterranea* see that species.
For references see Lloyd, Myc. Notes, p. 121; also Letter 42 and Letter 62, Note 433;
Morgan, Journ. Cin. Soc. Nat. Hist. **14:**   143.

Illustrations: Lloyd. Myc. Works, pl. 7, figs. 4–7.

South Carolina.   Hartsville.   In bare soil in a garden.   Coker and party, colls. (U. N. C. Herb.)
Alabama.   Auburn.   Underwood, coll. (N. Y. B. G. Herb. and U. N. C. Herb.).   Spores spherical,
    strongly warted, 7–9μ thick, with a pedicel up to 12.5μ long.

PLATE 79

DISCISEDA CANDIDA. No. 6092. Fresh condition

PLATE 80

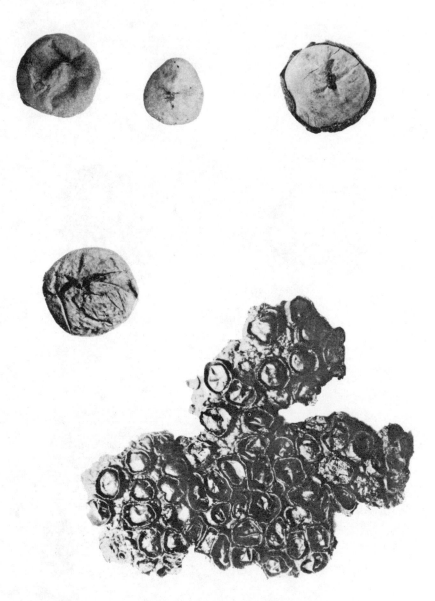

DISCISEDA SUBTERRANEA. Denver, Colo. [upper left]
DISCISEDA SUBTERRANEA. No. 2841. Ontario [upper right]
DISCISEDA PEDICELLATA. Hartsville, S. C. [center]
DIPLOCYSTIS WRIGHTII. Bahama Islands [Below]

Diplocystis Wrightii B. & C.

Plates 80 and 117

Fruit bodies small, crowded together in large numbers on a common, firmly leathery stroma about 1–2 mm. thick which superficially covers the substratum. Individual fruit bodies touching each other or here and there as much as 4 mm. apart; about 6–10 mm. thick, flattened above; at maturity the flattened top becoming pale and cracking into pieces which fall away, leaving the firm, deep brown, leathery sides to form a cup only slightly lower than the puffball within. Inner peridium paler brown, thin, pliable, opening by a small apical pore, collapsing gradually as the spores escape and finally settling into the bottom of the cup.

Spores yellowish brown under the microscope, spherical, minutely warted, 4–5.5μ, sometimes with a small mucro visible. Capillitium very scarce, pale, threads long or fragmented, branching, thick-walled with lumen almost closed, usually surrounded by remnants of collapsed threads, about 4.8–11μ thick, with a rough wall.

The type is from Cuba and it is also known from the Bahamas (Inagua, Andros, Long Island) and Guadaloupe.

As Lloyd mentions, the mouth is not protruding as shown in Fischer's figure. Our specimens, while ample, do not show stages young enough to determine the internal structure in youth, but the arrangement of the capillitium in a mount suggests that there were chambers. We therefore place the genus provisionally in the Lycoperdaceae.

Illustrations: Fischer. Engler and Prantl, Pflanzenfamilien 1¹: 323, fig. 167 D.
Lloyd. Myc. Works, pl. 15.

Bahamas. On bare earth on hillside, Clarence Harbor, Long Island. Coker, coll. (U. N. C. Herb.).

Broomeia. The North American (Albany) record for this little known genus, as given in Saccardo, is a mistake, as noted by Lloyd, the plant really being found in the district of Albany at the Cape of Good Hope (Léveillé; Ann. Sci. Nat., 3rd ser., 9: 129. 1848). This leaves the type species, *B. congregata*, known only from South Africa. Of the other two described species, *B. guadalupensis*, is almost certainly *Diplocystis Wrightii*. For discussion and reference to figures of *Broomeia* see Lloyd, Myc. Notes, p. 917. The genus *Broomeia* is distinguished from *Diplocystis* by a universal volva covering a crowded group of small peridia which are seated on a more or less elevated, common base.

ARACHNIACEAE

Fruit bodies exposed; peridium single, very thin, crumbling at maturity. Gleba with distinct chambers lined by the hymenium, these chambers forming at maturity a mass of minute, separate, hollow peridioles which crumble and escape like grains of sand. Capillitium and sterile base none.

This family is most nearly related to the Lycoperdaceae, from which it differs in the simple peridium, absence of capillitium, and presence of peridioles. The peridioles in *Pisolithus* are of a very different nature, being solid masses at all stages and without a hymenium. We are including in the family only the genus *Arachnion*, as *Arachniopsis* and *Holocotylon* are not yet well enough known to be placed. If the former genus is good and Long's description is accurate, it is very different from *Arachnion*, and if Lloyd is right in thinking it the same as *Arachnion* (Myc. Notes, p. 1134) it need not be considered. *Holocotylon* may be related to *Arachnion*, and if so the family description will have to be modified by the omission of peridioles.

ARACHNION Schw.

This genus is characterized by the peculiar nature of the contents of the peridium at maturity. It is filled not with the typical gleba consisting of capillitium and spores that are found in the Lycoperdons, but with a mass of granular particles like grains of sand. They are grayish or ash-colored, and look like a mass of sandy earth. These granules are peridioles or little sacks containing the spores. Each particle consists of a woven web of hyphae enclosing a minute chamber around the walls of which are borne the basidia pointing inwards, thus showing a close relationship to *Lycoperdon*. In youth the structure is like that of *Lycoperdon*, the empty chambers being separated by tramal plates of delicately woven hyphae. The peridium is smooth, not double, very thin and fragile, and breaks easily into small particles at maturity, exposing the granular contents. There is no sterile base. Originally there was only one species recognized, *A. album*, described by Schweinitz from this state in 1822, but other tropical and austral species have since been added. Long has described a genus *Arachniopsis* from Texas as closely related to *Arachnion* (Mycologia 9: 272. 1917), but Lloyd, who saw the types, thinks they are not different. *Holocotylon* from Mexico and southern Texas is a genus apparently related (Lloyd, Myc. Notes No. 21: 254, pl. 73, figs. 5–8. 1906. Also No. 22: 271. 1906).

LITERATURE

Lloyd. The Genus *Arachnion*. Myc. Notes No. 21: 252. 1906; No. 46: 643. 1917. Also Myc. Notes No. 66: 1133. 1922.
Lloyd. The Lycoperdaceae of Australia, etc., p. 39. 1905.
Long. Notes on New or Rare Species of Gasteromycetes. Mycologia 9: 271. 1917.
Saccardo. Syll. Fung. 7: 150. 1888.

For other literature see p. 194.

PLATE 81

ARACHNION ALBUM.   No. 730.   Enlarged one-fourth

PLATE 82

SPHAEROBOLUS STELLATUS. No. 7530 [above]
SCLERODERMA GEASTER. Stafford Co., Va.
From Doctor Howard A. Kelly. Reduced

Arachnion album Schw.

Plates 81 and 118

Plants with the fruiting body above ground, irregularly spherical with a more or less pointed base which extends into a small toughish root, lower surface more or less grooved or pitted, surface smooth, dull white until maturity then buffy when dry, or yellowish if water-soaked. Peridium thin, 0.5 mm. thick or less, the same thickness all around, toughish. Gleba pure white then gray or brownish olive at maturity, composed of a large number of minute empty chambers lined by a hymenial layer, apparently made up only of basidia, the context between the chambers consisting of a loose weft of delicate, interwoven hyphae. At maturity this loose tissue breaks down and leaves the chambers as distinct granular particles which contain the spores and fall apart like sand at maturity or decay into a sordid mass in wet weather. This structure indicates a close affinity to *Lycoperdon*. The peridium has no definite opening but falls to pieces slowly by decay or usually by the attacks of grubs (the larvae of the fire-fly playing a large part). Odor none until ripe, then decided and nitrous, resembling somewhat that of *Bovistella radicata* and some Lycoperdons. There is no capillitium or columella or sterile base.

Spores (of No. 730) brown under the microscope, smooth, short-elliptic, with a decided mucro or short stalk about 1μ long, though sometimes twice the length of the spore, $3.2-4.3 \times 4.3-5.5\mu$. Basidia clavate, $3.7 \times 11\mu$, apparently bearing only one mature spore at a time though two or four sterigmata may be seen in the young state; sterigmata very peculiar, a long, very slender part remaining attached to the basidium and a shorter, stouter part falling off with the spores as its stalk.

It was from this state that Schweinitz first described this interesting plant. It is plentiful in Chapel Hill in summer and seems to prefer cedars, but it also grows in deciduous groves and in open places and we have found it in abundance in flower beds. We have also found it at Hartsville, S. C. It is widely distributed in the eastern United States and, according to Lloyd, in other parts of the world. It has been found only once in Europe (Italy).

Illustrations: Lloyd. l. c., pl. 16, pl. 73, figs. 1–3 and Myc. Notes No. 46: figs. 917, 918.
    Schweinitz. Syn. Fung. Car. Sup., pl. 1, fig. 2.

  730. In grass under hickory, September 9, 1913. Spores $3-4.8 \times 3.7-5.5\mu$.
2364. Under cedars at The Rocks and on Rosemary Street, July 5, 1916.
3115. On damp soil in Strowd's lowgrounds, June 29, 1918.
5209. On sandy soil, June 22, 1922. Basidia $3.7 \times 11\mu$, 2-spored.
5224. On ground in Arboretum, June 23, 1922.

    Salem. (Schw. Herb., No. 2221, type).
    Hillsboro. Curtis, coll. (Curtis Herb.).

South Carolina. Ravenel. Fungi Car. Exs. No. 75. (Phil. Acad. Herb.).
    Society Hill. Curtis, coll. (Curtis Herb.).
    Hartsville. Coker, coll. In sandy soil in an apple orchard, June 1913.
Alabama. Earle, coll. (N. Y. B. G. Herb.).
Ohio. Berlin. Morgan, coll. (N. Y. B. G. Herb.).

SPHAEROBOLACEAE

Characters of the Genus *Sphaerobolus*

SPHAEROBOLUS Tode

Minute plants, growing on rotting wood (common form), on earth (Alabama) and on dung of herbivorous animals (Mississippi, Africa). Fruit bodies subspherical when on wood, breaking through without an exposed mycelium or less often seated on the wood and surrounded and covered when young by the white mycelium. Peridium of several layers, an outer, thick layer of woven hyphae, much like the mycelium; next a pseudoparenchymatous, gelatinous layer (lacking in *S. iowensis*), a thin filamentous layer, and, finally a thick highly specialized inner layer of long, densely packed, prismatic cells radially arranged. This last is sometimes called the receptaculum. The spore-bearing gleba is an inner ball of fertile tissue which at maturity is indistinctly divided into areas by thin sterile plates. In youth these areas may be hollow and lined with a distinct hymenium or stuffed and without a distinct hymenium, depending on the species. However, even in species with stuffed chambers, the basidia are not indiscriminately scattered, but are arranged in definite groups. This with the obvious chambers of *S. iowensis* clearly indicates a relationship with the Lycoperdaceae, rather than the Sclerodermataceae, as pointed out by Miss Walker. The dark, shining and viscid glebal ball is shot out with force at full maturity by the sudden evagination of the receptaculum. Spores smooth, sessile on the oblong basidia. Gemmæ capable of sprouting are also found in the gleba.

This is the only genus of the family. About eight species have been described but the validity of several of them is doubtful (see Saccardo, Syll. **7**, p. 46, and **17**, p. 216. For *S. impaticus* Boud. see Hollos, p. 185).

KEY TO THE SPECIES

Gleba without chambers or well defined hymenium; gelatinous layer present in peridium
S. stellatus and var. *giganteus*
Gleba before maturity with chambers lined with hymenium; gelatinous layer lacking in peridium
S. iowensis

LITERATURE

Corda. Icon. Fung. **5**: 66, pl. 6, fig. 48. 1842.
Cunningham. *Sphaerobolus stellatus* Tode. N. Z. Journ. Sci. & Tech. **6**: 16, figs. 1–6. 1923.
Fischer. In Engler and Prantl's Pflanzenfamilien 1¹: 346, fig. 182. 1900.
Fries. Systema Mycologicum **2**: 309. 1823.
Fries, Th. C. E. Sveriges Gasteromyceter, fig. 43.
Gillet. Champ. Fr. (Gasteromycetes), pl. 2.
Hollos. Die Gasteromyceten Ungarns, p. 139, pl. 28, figs. 27–30.
Lloyd. Myc. Notes, p. 431, figs. 245–247; also pl. 111.
Massee. Ann. Bot. **4**: 60, pl. 4, figs. 55–55c (mostly from Fischer, Bot Zeit. **42**: 1884). 1889.
Micheli. Nova Plantarum Genera, p. 221, pl. 101. 1729.
Nees von Esenbeck. Syst. Pilze Schw., pl. 11, fig. 122.
Pillay. Zur Entwicklungsgeschichte von *Sphaerobolus stellatus* Tode. Jahrb. der Phil. Fakultät II der Universität Bern **3**: 197–219. 1923.
Pitra. Zur Kenntnis des *Sphaerobolus stellatus*. Bot. Zeit. **28**: 681, 697, 713. 1870.

Petri. Flora Italica cryptogama (Gasterales), fasc. 5: 135, fig. 83. 1909.
Quélet. Champ. Jura et Vosg., pt. 2, pl. 3, fig. 2. 1873.
Rabinowitsch. Beitr. zur Entwickelungsgeschichte der Fruchlkörper einiger Gastromyceten. Flora 79: 385–418. 1894.
Schroeter. In Cohn's Krypt.-Fl. Schlesien 3, pt. 1: 688. 1889.
Sowerby. Engl. Fungi 1: pl. 22 (as *Lycoperdon carpobolus*).
Walker and Andersen. Relation of Glycogen to Spore-ejection. Mycologia 17: 154, pl. 18. 1925.
Walker. Development and Mechanism of Discharge in *Sphaerobolus iowensis* n. sp. and *S. stellatus* Tode. Journ. E. M. Sci. Soc. 42: 151, pls. 16–25. 1927.

Sphaerobolus stellatus Tode
S. carpobolus (L.) Schroeter
Carpobolus stellatus (Mich.) Desm.

Plates 82 and 117

Plants arising from within the soft wood or bark and pressing through to expose its upper surface or the greater part; subspherical, about 1.5–2 mm. thick, at first dull ochraceous from the surface color, then whitish from the cracking of this superficial layer into flakes; soon after exposure the little sphere opens at the top in most cases by four to seven stellate lobes and the outer, translucent-white layer (receptaculum) of the gleba suddenly reverses itself outward and throws the little central flattish ball containing the spores to a distance of several feet (Miss Walker reports a height throw of over 14 feet). The reversed and evaginated receptaculum now appears as a watery white sphere sitting on the lobes of the outer peridium. The ejected ball is slippery, smooth and very dark chestnut brown, looking like a miniature horse chestnut seed. Within it is divided into sections by delicate walls and in these areas are borne the oblong basidia, 4–4.8μ thick, with four to six, rarely eight (up to nine in Pillay's form), sessile spores. According to Miss Walker, these areas are never cavernous in their development, and there is no definite hymenium. She gives the following cytological facts for *S. stellatus*. All cells of the fruit body are binucleate; the two nuclei fuse in the young basidium; the fusion nucleus divides to form 4–8; the nuclear walls disappear; the chromatin center of a nucleus enters each spore, and where there are less than 8 spores, some of these granules are left behind; the young spores are uninucleate, the older ones may be binucleate.

Spores smooth, unevenly oblong, 3.7–4.8 x 7.4–10μ. Mixed with the spores are certain irregular densely filled cells (gemmae) formed by the hyphae which are also capable of sprouting to form new threads. The entire ball of the gleba is said (Fischer) to sprout without breaking up, sending out many hyphae from the gemmae and spores within. For references to illustrations and literature see under the genus.

Misses Walker and Andersen give evidence that the discharge of the bolus in *Sphaerobolus* is due to the rapid transformation of glycogen into sugars, followed by a great increase in osmotic pressure in the cells of the peridium. Miss Walker has grown four forms of *Sphaerobolus* in pure culture and obtained abundant fruiting. Her last paper gives further details of structure and behavior and proposes a new variety of *S. stellatus* and a new species. We are including her descriptions of these below.

5112. On decaying oak log, May 16, 1922.
5204. On rotten deciduous wood, June 22, 1922.
7530. On decorticated pine board, Sept. 23, 1924.

Asheville. Beardslee.

"Carolina." (Schw. Herb.).
Pennsylvania. Bethlehem. (Schw. Herb.).

Sphaerobolus stellatus var. giganteus Walker

"Basidiocarps having the color, structure, and appearance of *S. stellatus* but being much larger—up to 4 mm. in diameter (usually about 3 mm.) of unopened basidiocarps and 5–6 mm. from tip to tip of peridium in opened basidiocarps.   Spores globular with a slight apiculus, 5–7 x 6–8μ, mostly 6 x 7μ."

Type locality: Starkville, Miss., on dung (horse?).

Sphaerobolus iowensis Walker

"Unopened basidiocarps 1–1.5 mm. in diameter.   Peridium breaking stellately at the apex into 3–8 parts (usually 4–5), the tips becoming only slightly recurved so that the peridium of the opened fruit-body is somewhat cup-shaped.   Interior of peridium cadmium yellow when first opened, glebal mass raw umber when first exposed, soon becoming almost black.   Peridium separating into two regions, an outer and an inner. Outer peridium during its development and at maturity composed of two layers, an outer filamentous and an inner pseudoparenchymatic.   Inner region of a layer of tangential hyphae and a palisade layer.   Gleba containing during its development many definite chambers lined with basidia.   Wall of glebal mass firm, composed of cells 6–15μ in diameter.   Contents of glebal mass soft and gluey, never drying hard.   Spores oval, 5–6 x 6–10μ (usually 5.6 x 8μ)."

It is to be noted that Cunningham (l. c., p. 16), speaking of Australian plants that he refers to *S. stellatus*, described the gleba as having "several" cavities separated by thin walls and says that these cavities are lined with hymenium.   Whether by several he means many is not indicated by the figures.   However, as his plant has the gelatinous layer in the peridium, it does not agree fully with *S. iowensis*.

Type locality: Hunters, Iowa, on old coniferous boards.

TYLOSTOMATACEAE

Plants formed underground, emerging at maturity and consisting of a tough, fibrous, stalk bearing the globular spore sac, the outer wall of which (in *Tylostoma*) consists of a thickish, sandy layer which either breaks up and falls away soon in flakes or persistently adheres and slowly wears away. The inner layer is a thin, tough, rather firm, persistent membrane which contains the unchambered homogeneous gleba without tramal plates; the spores escaping by a definite apical mouth (at times several) or by an irregular or circumscissile dehiscence. Capillitium present, of varied character, arising from the entire surface of the inner peridium. Basidia club-shaped with 4, irregularly scattered, nearly sessile spores.

The outer peridium in *Queletia* has not been described in detail. Lloyd (Myc. Notes, p. 135) says that it is "apparently a thin white coat that breaks up into granular particles and mostly disappears." Six genera are included in the family by Miss White, five of which are from America. Only two of these, *Tylostoma* and *Queletia*, are known east of the Mississippi. *Chlamydopus* has been found in New Mexico and Washington, *Dictyocephalos* in Colorado, *Battarrea* in several western states, and *Sphaericeps* is known only from Angola in western Africa. See Miss White for descriptions of these. For convenience we include in the key all the genera of the family. With some changes it is copied from Miss White.

KEY TO THE GENERA

Peridium opening by an apical mouth
    No free volva present; stem not flaring above...........................*Tylostoma* (p. 149)
    Free volva present; stem flaring above..*Chlamydopus*
Peridium circumscissile
    Peridium nearly plane below, dehiscing around the basal margin....................*Battarrea*
    Peridium spherical, dehiscing at the equator.....................................*Sphaericeps*
Peridium opening irregularly
    Peridium easily separating from the stem; capillitium not embedded in a tissue..*Queletia* (p. 158)
    Peridium firmly attached to the stem; capillitium embedded in a tissue...........*Dictyocephalos*

TYLOSTOMA Pers.

Mycelium subterranean, composed of delicate, white, much branched strands which bear here and there white, sclerotium-like balls of various sizes, these developing (apparently slowly) into the full sized buttons. Peridium composed of an outer sandy case formed of delicate flocculence holding the earth,—in which in the button stage is also included the unextended stem,—and an inner, very thin layer formed of delicate, interwoven hyphae which, without apparent change, turn inward and continue as the elements of the gleba. Stalk cylindrical, tough and firm, with a central column of delicate soft, white, cottony tissue; surface usually brown and more or less marked with scales and fibers. Capillitium abundant, arising from the entire inner surface of the peridium, including the base, pale to nearly hyaline, frequently septate, much branched, not rarely with cross bar connections as if anastomosing had occurred (but probably only a method of branching); with walls irregular in thickness in the same thread, in places closing the lumen; tapering tips lacking, the ends appearing abrupt as if broken.

Basidia short-clavate, usually 4-spored, peculiar in having the spores scattered over the surface.   There is no trace of a hymenium or of tramal plates, the basidia being distributed equally on the interwoven threads of the homogeneous gleba.   Spores spherical or subspherical, rust colored to cinnamon, warted or smooth.

The genus is distinguished from others of the family by the smaller size and (except in *Chlamydopus*) by the definite, circular, smooth or fimbriated apical mouth (or mouths) by which the inner peridium opens to liberate the spores.   Miss White reports seventeen species from North America, eight of which are described as new.   *Tulostoma* is the spelling used by some authors, and *Tulasnodea* Fr. is a synonym.

In the unexpanded button the stem is a short plug enclosed in the outer peridium. When the expanded plant dries the stem shrinks considerably in thickness and draws away from the outer peridium which surrounds it above.   This leaves a space between the two, and the descending margin of the outer peridium which is often acute is the so-called collar around the stem apex.   If moistened after drying the stem swells back to its original size and fills the collar again.   The spores are often somewhat collapsed when dry so that even those that were smooth when fresh may appear angular or nodulated.   In such cases they should be plumped out by an application of KOH or lactic acid.

LITERATURE

Bessey.   Growth of *Tulostoma mammosum*.   Amer. Nat. 21: 665.   1887.
Lloyd.   Myc. Notes, p. 133, pls. 10 and 11 and text figs. 66, 67.   1903.
Lloyd.   The Tylostomeae, figs. 1–6 and pls. 20 and 74–85.   1906.
Morgan.   Journ. Cin. Soc. Nat. Hist. 12: 163, pl. 16, figs. 1–5.   1890.
Petri.   Sul valore diagnostico del capillizio nel genere "*Tylostoma*" Pers.   Ann. Myc. 2: 412, pl. 6.   1904.
Petri.   Flora Italica Cryptogama (Gasterales), Fasc. 5: 115.   1909.
Schroeter.   Ueber die Entwickelung und die systematische Stellung von *Tulostoma* Pers.   Cohn's Beitrage sur Biologie der Pflanzen 2: 65, 1 text fig.   1877.
White.   The Tylostomaceae of North America.   Bull. Torr. Bot. Club 28: 421, pls. 31–40.   1901.

For other literature see p. 194.

KEY TO THE SPECIES

Mouth projecting as a circular glabrous tube with a sharp edge
    Spores nearly smooth . . . .*T. mammosum* (p. 151)
    Spores distinctly warted
        Spore sac not warted . . . . $\begin{cases} T.\ simulans & (p.\ 151) \\ T.\ floridanum & (p.\ 153) \end{cases}$
        Spore sac warted . . . .*T. verrucosum* (p. 153)
Mouth less projecting, sometimes not at all so, edge not composed of a fibrous roll; often elliptical or linear; more than one mouth often present
    Spores smooth, minute, 2–3μ . . . .*T. Finkii* (p. 154)
    Spores smooth, larger, 4.2–5.5 x 5–7.4μ . . . .*T. volvulatum* (p. 155)
Mouth appearing in the center of a slightly elevated fibrous mat, its edge eroded and fibrous unless much worn
    Spores smooth
        Spore sac pale . . . .*T. poculatum* (p. 155)
        Spore sac reddish brown, stem very long . . . .*T. Lloydii* (p. 156)
    Spores minutely warted . . . .*T. campestre* (p. 156)
    Spores distinctly warted . . . .*T. Berkeleyii* (p. 157)

Tylostoma mammosum Fr.

  T. pedunculatum (L.) Schroeter
  T. brumale Pers.

Plates 83 and 119

Spore sac 0.6–1 cm. thick, tan to buff or slightly darker; outer peridium thin, wearing away gradually, leaving the inner peridium quite smooth or with persistent particles except around the base where an adherent ring remains. Mouth cylindrical, elevated, smooth, with a sharp edge, concolorous or often distinctly darker. Stem 1–2 cm. long, slender, brown, superficially spongy to slightly scaly, wearing away slowly to expose the paler layer beneath; basal mat small.

    Spores (of plant from North Dakota) spherical, very faintly warted, 3.8–4.5 x 4–5.5μ. Capillitium threads somewhat irregular, occasionally branched and septate, up to 8μ thick.

Lloyd thinks that the typical European form of this species does not occur in America, but we find plants with dark mouths and exactly the microscopic characters of the European plant. They differ from *T. simulans* and *T. floridanum* in the darker mouth area and much smoother spores. We have examined a typical specimen of *T. mammosum* from Europe with a dark mouth area (A. Vill, Fungi bavarici, No. 926) and find that it agrees almost perfectly with the American plant: the spores are almost smooth, 4–5.5μ thick, and the capillitium threads agree. Another plant like it (Schlesien; Dresler, coll., as *T. brumale*) at the New York Botanical Garden has similar spores.

Illustrations: Batsch. Elench. Fung. 2: pl. 29, fig. 167 (as *Lyc. pedunculatum*).
    Gillet. Champ. Fr. (Gasteromycetes) pl. 7.
    Greville. Scott. Crypt. Fl. 6: pl. 340 (as *T. brumale*). 1828.
    Hollos. l. c., pl. 11, figs. 18–20; pl. 12, fig. 1.
    Lloyd. Myc. Works, pl. 78, figs. 5–8.
    Morgan. Journ. Cin. Soc. Nat. Hist. 12: pl. 16, fig. 1.
    Nees von Esenbeck. Syst. Pilze Schw., pl. 12, fig. 130.
    Sorokine. Rev. Myc. 1890, pl. 98, fig. 346; pl. 103, fig. 366.
    Sowerby. Engl. Fungi, pl. 406 (as *Lyc. pedunculatum*).

North Dakota. Brenckle, coll. (N. Y. Bot. Gard. Herb. and U. N. C. Herb.). Mouth dark and spore
    sac quite smooth and clean over most of its surface.
Wisconsin. Eagle Heights. (Univ. Wis. Herb. and U. N. C. Herb.) Spores spherical to oval,
    minutely warted and ridged, 4–5.5 x 4.5–6μ.
Kansas. Rooks Co. Bartholomew, coll. (N. Y. B. G. Herb.).

Tylostoma simulans Lloyd

Plates 84, 85 and 119

Spore case subglobose, 0.7–1.8 cm. thick, reddish brown when fresh, but so covered with sand and earth as to obscure the color; over this sandy coat is a delicate flocculent coat of clean white wool which persists only in places as the plant emerges from the ground and is soon shed. The sandy cortex is persistent for a long time and slowly wears away above and even more slowly below to expose the brown or whitish inner peridium which opens by a single, small, apical mouth with a smooth edge, at the top of a little tubular elevation which in a few of our plants is surrounded by a slightly darker area.

Stem 1.5–3 cm. long, 3–4 mm. thick when fresh, 1.5–2.5 mm. thick when dry, the base slightly enlarged by the soft, white, cottony mycelium which brings up a little earth; surface often nearly covered with reddish brown lacerate scales which wear away gradually on exposure and in age are represented only by the inherent parts; in some plants of the same colony the reddish brown cortex instead of being lacerated may be more even and adhesive and form a cracked and mottled outer layer of the stem which may persist for a long time; color under the scales buffy brown, becoming dull dark brown with age; body of the stem longitudinally striate when dry, deeply inserted in the outer peridium and on drying shrinking away from the peridium and leaving the usual collar which may or may not have a thin, free margin.   Context of stem white, fibrous, brittle when dry, containing a central cylinder that is partly filled with delicate, silky fibers.

Spores (of No. 87) globose to subglobose, yellowish cinnamon in color, closely set with thick, coarse, pale warts, 4.2–6 x 4.5–6.8μ thick counting the warts, which are up to a fraction over 1μ long; in KOH solution appearing spinulose with a hyaline material between the spines.   Capillitium threads buff, moderately branched, septate, somewhat swollen at the joints, 4.5–6.5μ thick.

This species is reported by Lloyd from Ohio and Texas.   It may be considered the southern form of *T. mammosum*, from which it is separated by the more persistent outer peridium and by the strongly warted spores.   There is also much less tendency to a dark mouth area, though in our No. 87 there is a somewhat darker diffuse area around the mouth.   For a comparison with *T. floridanum* see that species.   The present species is peculiar in the paleness of the warts on the spores and their vagueness in surface view.   This seems to be due to the abundance of the nearly colorless amorphous material which makes up the greater part of the warts and in places fills the space between them.

Examination of *T. mammosum* in Ellis and Everhart's North American Fungi, No. 2734, shows it to be exactly like the Chapel Hill plants.   The spores are 4–6μ thick, distinctly rough, subspherical; capillitium threads 3–6μ thick, thin- to thick-walled, swollen at the septa.   Their *T. pedunculatum* (Fungi Columbiani, No. 1888) is not different.   Spores 4–6μ thick, subspherical, distinctly rough.   Capillitium threads 3–7μ thick, thin- to thick-walled, swollen at the septa.   The *T. mammosum* of Curtis' list is probably this species.

Illustrations: Lloyd. Myc. Works, pl. 79, figs. 2 and 3

87. On a dry, pebbly hillside among cedars, April 1903, and April 1904.
5930. Same location as No. 87, Dec. 9, 1922. Spores yellowish cinnamon, subspherical, distinctly warted, 5.5–6.5μ thick.
7134. In grass under cedars, Sept. 22, 1923. Capillitium threads swollen at the joints. Spores 4.4–5.1μ thick, distinctly warted.
Also Nos. 5913, 7504, 7554.

Salem. Schweinitz, coll. (Curtis Herb., as *T. brumale*).
Asheville. Beardslee.

South Carolina. North Island. Coker and party, colls. (U. N. C. Herb.).
Florida. Gainesville. Weber, coll. (U. N. C. Herb.). Spores rather pale, coarsely warted, 4.2–6μ thick.
Alabama. Peters, coll. (Curtis Herb., as *T. mammosum*).

PLATE 83

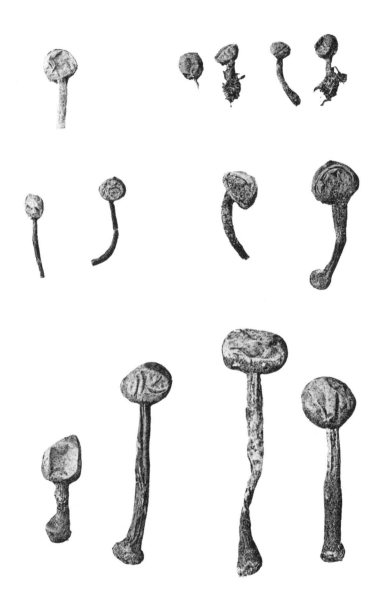

TYLOSTOMA MAMMOSUM. North Dakota [upper left] Wisconsin [upper right]
TYLOSTOMA FLORIDANUM. Type [center left]
TYLOSTOMA BERKELEYII. Folly Is., S. C., and Wilmington, N. C. [center right]
TYLOSTOMA CAMPESTRE. Colorado, Canada and Wisconsin [left to right below]

PLATE 84

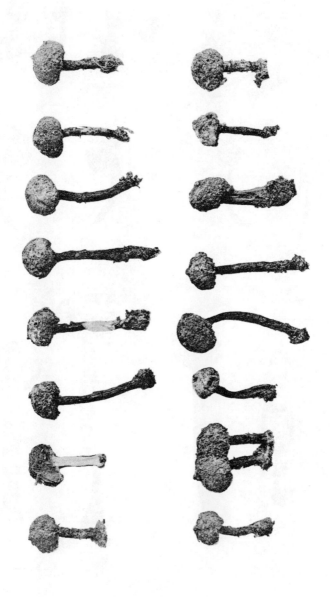

Tylostoma simulans.   No. 5913

Iowa. Iowa City. Macbride, coll. Ell. & Ev., N. Amer. Fungi, No. 2734, as *T. mammosum*. (Path.
& Myc. Herb.)

Kansas. Stockton. Ell. & Ev., Fungi Columbiana, No. 1888, as *T. pendunculatum*. (Path. & Myc.
Herb.)

Tylostoma floridanum Lloyd

Plates 83 and 119

We have examined specimens of the type collection of this species from the Lloyd
Herbarium. The plants are small and slender; spore sac about 5–7 mm. thick. We
find the spores to be spherical to oval or irregular, 4–6 x 4.8–6.8μ, distinctly warted
with elongated, irregular warts. Capillitium threads irregular, septate, branched,
up to 8.5μ thick with thickened walls.

Lloyd's description follows (The Tylostomeae, p. 18):

"Peridium dark castaneous color, with a small, tubular, circular, protruding mouth.
Cortex separating imperfectly, particles adhering to the peridium, thickened and subpersistent below. Stem slender, dark reddish brown, subsmooth, substriate with no
trace of scales, white within, hollow with central fibrils. Capillitium subhyaline, sometimes wavy [written waxy, in error?] with septa both swollen and even. Spores 5μ,
strongly asperate."

This plant is nearest *T. simulans*, from forms of which it can hardly be distinguished. The spores, while warted in about the same way as in *T. simulans*, show the
warts much more clearly in surface view. Other characters mentioned by Lloyd, as
slender, dark stem and colored peridium can be nearly or quite matched in *simulans*
or *mammosum*. Lloyd has described another species, *T. pygmaeum*, from Florida
(The Tylostomaceae, p. 16, pl. 78, figs. 3, 4) which, from the description, differs from
T. floridanum only in the unimportant character of color.

Illustrations: Lloyd. Myc. Works, pl. 80, figs. 1 and 2.

Florida. Lloyd. (Lloyd Herb., type, and U. N. C. Herb.)

Tylostoma verrucosum Morg.

Plate 119

This rare species has been found but a few times. Morgan described it from Ohio,
and Lloyd reports it from Texas (Long, coll.). We have seen authentic specimens
collected by Lloyd and determined by Morgan, and find the spores to be spherical to
irregular, distinctly warted, 4–6μ thick. Capillitium threads up to 8μ thick, irregular,
swollen at septa, walls irregularly thickened.

The original description by Morgan is as follows (Journ Cin. Soc. Nat. Hist. **12**:
164):

"Peridium depressed-globose, thickish, becoming firm and rigid, with a dense
brown cortex of minute persistent scales and warts; the mouth small, circular, prominent,
entire. Stipe long, slender, with a surface of brown lacerate scales, internally white,
with a central pith of long loose fibers; the mycelial bulb large, irregularly depressed-
globose. Threads of the capillitium long, slender, about as thick as the spores, hyaline,
branched; spores irregularly globose, minutely warted, pale brown, 5–6μ in diameter.

"Growing on the ground in rich soil in woods."

Lloyd says that the species is very close to *T. squammosum* of Europe, from which it differs in verrucose cortex and more robust habit.

Illustrations: Lloyd. Myc. Works, pl. 76, figs. 3–5.
    Morgan. Journ. Cin. Soc. Nat. Hist. **12:** pl. 16, fig. 2.
    Petri. Ann. Myc. **2:** p. 424 (text fig.). 1904.

Ohio. Lloyd, coll. (N. Y. Bot. Gard. Herb.).

Tylostoma Finkii Lloyd

Plates 85 and 119

Spore case depressed-globose, 0.7–1 cm. high by 0.9–1.4 cm. wide, color when fresh ochraceous to tan where not covered with sand, fading when dry to a mouse-gray with a tint of salmon (under the sand); outer peridium consisting of a rough sandy cortex which slowly wears away above and is even more persistent and somewhat thicker below where it may appear with an obscure margin like a cup after the wearing away of most of the upper part; mouth or mouths (1–4 in number) circular or elongated and irregular, elevated (up to 0.8 mm. high) or scarcely so, concolorous with the peridium or slightly lighter, the margin eroded or nearly smooth, and not surrounded by a fibrillose pad. Stem 1.8–2.7 cm. long by 3–3.6 mm. thick when fresh, 1.5–3.2 mm. thick when dry and then with longitudinal furrows, of equal diameter throughout or slightly tapering toward the base which ends in a small myceloid swelling; surface minutely and evenly lacerate scaly (the scales concolorous with the body of the stem and running horizontally around it and often with remnants of the gray, myceloid, outer peridium attached; context solid except for a small central strand of loose fibers; collar irregular, about 1 mm. distant from the dry stem, in contact with it when fresh, concolorous with the top of the stem.

Spores very minute, 2–3μ thick, smooth, spherical or slightly angled with a minute mucro, spores cinnamon color (Ridgway) in mass, pale under the microscope. Capillitium threads lighter colored than the spores, irregular, wavy, sparingly septate, 3.8μ thick, considerably swollen at the joints and at the ends which may be up to 12μ thick.

In one of our plants there are four scarcely elevated mouths in a row and all elliptic to elongated, in another there are two circular mouths and in two others there is a single circular mouth.

As *T. Finkii* (Lloyd; Myc. Notes, p. 1169, pl. 225, fig. 2307) agrees with our plant in its very characteristic spores, distinctly smaller than in any other species except in *T. Longii,* described by Lloyd as a form of *T. albicans,* which is white and has large rough spores, and as there are no essential disagreements we refer our plants to it. The multiple and somewhat elongated mouths in some of our specimens point to group 6 of Lloyd's Tylostomeae as its proper location. Lloyd's specimens having only single tubular mouths, he refers them to group 1. *Tylostoma kansense* and *T. americanum* (Lloyd thinks these the same) and the two new species proposed by Miss White (*T. gracile* and *T. minutum*) that if good might fall in the same group, are all easily separated by their much larger spores. In *T. Lloydii* Bres. (in Petri, Ann. Myc. **2:** 423. 1904) the spores are smooth and small but distinctly larger than in the present species, and the cortex is said to separate perfectly above, the mouth to be fibrillose until weather-worn. We have looked through the species represented in the Schweinitz and Curtis Herbaria, as well as in Washington and New York, and find nothing that agrees with our plant.

Illustrations: Lloyd. As cited above.

6060. By white oak tree in pasture, upland woods, Feb. 9, 1923.

Tylostoma volvulatum Borsch. in Sorokine.   Slender form

Plate 119

Peridium up to 1 cm. thick, covered until age with a rather thin, brown, sandy coat which wears away slowly and about equally over the surface, exposing the nearly white inner peridium.   Mouth plane, not regularly circular, margin clean and smooth, single in all nine plants of our collection.   There is no cortical cup at the base of the peridium. Collar short, fimbriate.   Stem 2–3 cm. long, 1.5–3 mm. thick, with a brown, more or less scaly but not conspicuously lacerate surface, cespitose at times, in which cases the peridia may be fused.

Spores subspherical, irregular, somewhat angled, practically smooth (even under oil immersion), 4.2–5.5 x 5–7.4μ.   Capillitium threads very irregular, nearly hyaline, paler than the spores, up to 5μ thick, with walls of varying thickness.

This agrees very well with *T. volvulatum* as treated by Lloyd (Tylostomeae, p. 19, pl. 81) except for more slender aspect.   The mouth is almost exactly like that of our No. 6060 (*T. Finkii*), as well as of the *T. volvulatum-cespitosum-americanum* group.

Illustrations. Lloyd. As cited above.
   Sorokine.   Revue Myc., 1890, pl. 98, figs. 347, 348; pl. 101, fig. 353a.

Porto Rico.   Seaver and Chardon, colls.   No. 142.   (N. Y. B. G. Herb. and U. N. C. Herb.)

Tylostoma poculatum White

Plate 119

Miss White reports this species from Alabama (l. c., p. 431).   We have examined what appears to be a true example of the species from Calloway, Nebraska (Bates, coll.; E. & E., Fungi Columbiani, No. 1889).   The spores are quite smooth, irregularly subglobose, 4–5μ thick, with the contents precipitated or fragmented into irregular particles which at first sight give somewhat the appearance of wrinkles on the surface. We find no actual wrinkles as figured by Miss White.   *Tylostoma obesum* Cke. & Ell. is so close that we hardly see how the two can be separated.   The spores of the Ellis plant at N. Y. Botanical Garden, mentioned by both Miss White and Lloyd, have been examined by us and found to be exactly like those of *T. poculatum* in size, shape, and surface, the contents differing somewhat in being less coagulated (pl. 119, fig. 12). *Tylostoma granulosum* of Europe is also very close.   As represented by D. Saccardo (Mycotheca italica, No. 424) the spores are smooth and just like those of the American plants mentioned above, spherical to slightly irregular, 3.7–4.4μ thick (pl. 119, fig. 13). Lloyd gives the spores of *T. granulosum* as granular and Hollos gives them as warted. Miss White's description of *T. poculatum* follows (Bull. Torr. Bot. Club **28**: 431. 1901):

"Peridium globose, somewhat depressed, 1–1.5 cm. high, 1–2 cm. in diameter, smooth, fawn-colored, membranaceous; outer peridium scaly, but more persistent than in most species, remaining in the shape of a cup-like involucre round the base of the peridium, mouth slightly raised, fimbriate, mostly large: collar entire, inconspicuous:

stem 1–3 cm. long, 3–6 mm. in diameter, cylindrical, firm, slightly bulbose, hollow or stuffed, often with considerable remnants of the outer peridium attached: capillitium lightish yellow, sparingly branched, septate, swollen at joints, 4–7μ wide, rather thick-walled: spores ferruginous, subglobose, smooth, or irregularly ridged in the older specimens, owing to the shrinking of the inner substance, short pediceled, 4–5μ in diameter."

Illustrations: Lloyd. Myc. Works, pl. 83, figs. 1–2.
    White. 1. c., pl. 34, figs. 4–6.

Tylostoma Lloydii Bres.

This species, known only from Cincinnati, Ohio, is near *T. poculatum*, from which it seems to be distinguished only by its dark color and long stem.   We have not seen it and give below the original description by Bresadola (in Petri, Ann. Myc. **2**: 423. 1904; see also Lloyd, The Tylostomeae, p. 22):

"Outer peridium membranaceous, brown, soon falling away in pieces and leaving a concolorous zone at the base; inner peridium subglobose, papery, smooth, pale, sub-cinereous, flattened at the base and deeply umbilicate, about 1 cm. broad, 8–9 mm. high, mouth white, oblong, 2 x 1½ mm., slightly protruding, like a subfimbriate, tomen-tose circle, about 0.5 mm. broad, defined; stem hollow, fibrous-subwoody, brown, covered all over with rather thickly set, at length deciduous scales, apex tapering and sunken in the cup of the peridium and free from it on the sides, considerably thickened below and furnished with a pale, subvolviform, fimbriate membrane at the base, 6–7.5 cm. long, 2.5–3 mm. thick at top, 4–5 mm. at base, white within; gleba subochraceous; spores smooth, often inequilateral, 3.5–4 x 3.5μ; threads of the capillitium thick-walled, not easily separating into joints, hyaline, 3–9μ thick."

Illustrations: Bresadola in Petri. Ann. Myc. 2: pl. 6, fig. 4, and one text figure. 1904.
    Lloyd. Myc. Works, pl. 82, figs. 5–8.

Tylostoma campestre Morg.

Plates 83 and 119

Spore case subglobose, about 1–1.8 cm. thick; outer peridium a sandy coat which wears away except for a basal disk exposing about two-thirds or three-fourths of the pale grayish to pale brownish, smooth or somewhat pitted, inner peridium.   Mouth area a distinct, spongy, somewhat elevated disk which opens in the center by a circular or lacerate mouth to liberate the spores.   Stalk 1.7–5.5 cm. long and 3–4.5 mm. thick, usually longitudinally sulcate when dry, and shrinking away from the outer peridium so as to leave a distinct collar around its apex; surface layer dark brown, lacerate-scaly over most of the area, white within and with a central cottony cylinder as is usual in the genus; base expanding into a sandy bulb of moderate size.
Spores (of No. 861 Ip) pale, spherical or slightly oval, minutely warted, 4.5–6.8μ or if elongated rarely up to 7.2μ.   Capillitium threads septate and slightly swollen at the joints, irregular and constricted at places with the lumen closed by the thickening of the walls, 3–6.5μ thick.

This species is a northern and western plant, and we have not seen specimens of it from east of the Mississippi.   However, as it occurs on the shores of Lake Erie in Canada we include it as eastern American.   As Lloyd says, this is the American representative of *T. granulosum* Lév. of Europe, of which *T. fimbriatum* Fr. is a probable synonym.   We have carefully examined the spores of two typical examples of *T.*

PLATE 85

TYLOSTOMA SIMULANS. No. 7504 [above]
TYLOSTOMA FINKII. No. 6060 [below]
Second plant from left moistened and swollen; others dry

PLATE 86

Scleroderma geaster.. No. 657

granulosum represented in D. Saccardo's Mycotheca italica, No. 424, and find them to be smaller and smoother than those of the American plant. In one plant (Path. & Myc. Herb.) the spores are spherical to slightly irregular, smooth or nearly so, 3.7–4.4μ thick; in the specimen at the New York Botanical Garden the spores are spherical to oval, 3.7–4.2μ thick or if oval up to 5.5μ long.

The southern representative of *T. campestre* has been named *T. Berkeleyii* by Lloyd, and while the differences are not great we are retaining the name (see that species for comparison). Lloyd is right in considering *T. punctatum* Pk. only a form of *T. campestre*. A part of the type collection at the New York Botanical Garden, noted below, is similar and with identical spores, minutely roughened, 5–6.5μ thick.

Illustrations: Morgan. Journ. Cin. Soc. Nat. Hist. 12: pl. 16, fig. 4.
    Petri. Ann. Myc. 2: p. 433 and p. 434 (text figs., the latter as *T. punctatum*). 1904.
    Petri. Flora Italica Cryptogama (Gasterales), fasc. 5, fig. 76.

District of Columbia. Braendle, coll. (U. N. C. Herb. and N. Y. B. G. Herb.). Spores warted but
    not reticulated, 5–6.8 x 5.5–7.2μ.
Wisconsin. (Univ. Wis. Herb. and U. N. C. Herb.) Spores 4.8–6 x 5.5–8.2μ.
South Dakota. Chamberlain, coll. (Univ. Wis. Herb., as *T. granulosum*, and U. N. C. Herb.).
Nebraska. Long Pine. Bates, coll. Ell. & Ev., N. Amer. Fungi, No. 3514. (Path. & Myc. Herb.)
    Also Bates, No. 499. (N. Y. Bot. Gard. Herb.) Spores spherical or elongated, minutely rough,
    6–7.4μ thick.
Colorado. Harkness, coll. (N. Y. Bot. Gard. Herb., as *T. fimbriatum*). Spores nearly spherical,
    minutely warted with elongated warts, 5–7.2μ thick. Capillitium threads septate, swollen
    at the joints, usually up to about 6μ thick, up to 8μ or 9μ at the joints: walls irregularly
    thickened, closing the lumen in places.
Canada. Ontario. Dearness, coll. No. 2394 Pe. In sand by shore of Lake Erie, Oct. 5, 1922. No.
    861. Port Frank on Lake Huron. Spores minutely but distinctly warted, 4.5–6.5μ thick.
    No. 861 Ip. On shore of Lake Huron. No. 2394/861. London, Sept. 27, 1895.

Tylostoma Berkeleyii Lloyd

Plates 83 and 119

Spore case subglobose, 1–1.7 cm. thick; outer peridium as in *T. campestre*, wearing away slowly but with traces nearly always remaining as small, inherent flecks on the grayish to ochraceous tan inner peridium; the basal portion persistent as a closely applied, sandy cup. Mouth as in *T. campestre*. Stem about 2.5–3 cm. long, rather slender, with a deep brown spongy or flaky superficial layer, not so scaly as in *T. campestre*, apparently smooth in No. 8707 from Porto Rico, sulcate when dry, base with a small bulb.

Spores (of plant from Folly Island, S. C.) spherical to oval, distinctly warted and partially reticulated, 4.5–6μ thick or if oval up to 7.2μ long. Capillitium sparingly septate, swollen at the joints, branched, irregular, 4–9μ thick, larger at the swollen joints.

This is the southern representative of *T. campestre*. The spores of the present species differ only in having slightly more prominent warts which are distinctly more elongated so as to form a partial reticulum. The stem is less scaly (in plants seen); there is more color in the denuded inner peridium, and the size averages smaller.

Illustrations: Lloyd. Myc. Works, pl. 84, figs. 8 and 9.

North Carolina. Chapel Hill. No. 5908. On bank of branch in a pasture, Nov. 20, 1922. Spores irregularly spherical, 4.4–6μ thick, warted and often distinctly reticulated.

    Wilmington. Dr. F. F. Wood, coll. (N. Y. Bot. Gard. Herb. and U. N. C. Herb.). Spores spherical to oval or irregular, 5–6.5μ or if elongated up to 7.4μ long, warted and often partially reticulated.

    Salem. Schweinitz, coll. (Schw. Herb., No. 2267, as *T. squammosum*). Spores distinctly warted and often with a partial reticulum, 5–6.5μ or rarely 6.5 x 7.8μ.

South Carolina. Folly Island. Small and Bragg, colls. (N. Y. Bot. Gard. Herb. and U. N. C. Herb.).

    Hartsville. In sandy loam in a vegetable garden, Dec. 24, 1925. Coker, coll. (U. N. C. Herb.). Spores distinctly warted and often with a partial reticulum, 4.5–6.5 x 5.4–7.4μ. These are the largest plants we have seen, the case varying from about 1.2–1.7 cm. thick and with a base with a very large sand bulb.

    Also from South Carolina in Ravenel's Fungi Car. Exs. No. 80, as *Tulasnodea fimbriata*. (N. Y. Bot. Gard. Herb., Phil. Acad., and U. N. C. Herb.) The spores of the plant in New York are distinctly warted and with partial reticulum, 5–6.5 x 6–7.4μ; capillitium threads frequently septate, 3–7.4μ or up to 11μ thick at the swollen joints.

Florida. Gainesville. Ravenel. Fungi Amer. Exs. No. 137 as *T. mammosum*. (Path. and Myc. Herb. and U. N. C. Herb.) Mouth opening surrounded by a thick, felted, chestnut colored mat; upper part of inner peridium quite clean. Spores strongly reticulated, 4–6.6μ thick.

Alabama. Auburn. Earle, coll. (N. Y. Bot. Gard. Herb. and U. N. C. Herb.).

QUELETIA Fries

We give below a translation of the original description (Öfvers. K. Vetesnk.-Akad. Förh. 28: 171. 1871):

"Peridium simple, membranous, smooth, fragile, furnished at the basal margin with a membranous collar and discrete from the stem, at length dehiscing irregularly. The apex of the stem extending into the peridium supports a rudimentary columella. Capillitium flocculent, scarce, attached to the peridium on all sides, continuous, contorted, branched, hyaline. Spores very plentiful, in masses, short-pediceled, globose, verrucose-echinulate. Stem strong, fleshy-fibrous, loosely broken up externally in a peculiar way into fibrous shavings. Only one species known: *Queletia mirabilis*."

The genus differs from *Tylostoma* in larger size and absence of a definite mouth or mouths, the inner peridium cracking and breaking up irregularly. There is no volva, but the structure and behavior of the outer peridium are not well known. In speaking of the capillitium as scarce, Fries seems to have been in error, as Miss White says it is abundant (see below). For references to Lloyd's observations see under the species.

Queletia mirabilis Fr.

Plate 119

We take the following description from Miss White, l. c., p. 441:

"Peridium globose, 2.5–3.5 cm. high, 3–4 cm. in diameter, fragile, easily separating from the stem, rupturing irregularly, of a reddish brown color; collar irregular, of the same substance as the peridium; stem 6.5–8 cm. long, 1.5 cm. wide at the top, 2 cm. at the base, fascicular, reddish brown, within and without, like the peridium, solid, lacerate, fibrillose, particularly at the base; capillitium very abundant and interwoven, forming with the spores a felt-like mass, reddish brown, single threads whitish yellow, thick-walled, hollow as shown by the truncated ends, septa rare or wanting, 5–9μ wide, branches rather short, free ends rounded and recurved; spores subglobose, coarsely warted, 4–6μ in diameter, some short-pediceled, inner portion breaking up and issuing from the thin-warted coating which is then hyaline and shrivelled."

A rare and interesting plant of curious distribution and habits. Lloyd in Myc. Notes, p. 185, refers to the four places that the plant had been found up to that time. He later refers to another find in France (Myc. Notes, p. 337) and there gives structural details of young plants. There is only one American record, on tanbark at Trexlertown, Pennsylvania, where it was collected by Dr. Herbst, who found it three years in succession.

We have examined the capillitium and spores of one of Dr. Herbst's plants from the Pennsylvania station (now in the New York Botanical Garden) and do not find the spores behaving in the way described by Miss White. They are strongly and ir- regularly warted, 6–9μ thick, often with a short pedicel. The capillitium is peculiar in fragmenting up at the joints into fairly long contorted sections with closed ends. They may of course be broken at other places to allow the entrance of air or water, but the completely closed sections are characteristic.

For other references by Lloyd, see Myc. Notes, pages 135, 217, 323.

Illustrations: Fries.   Öfversigt Kongl. Vetens. Akad. Förhandlingar, Stockholm, pl. 4.   1871.   Copied
    by Fischer in Pflanzenfamilien 1¹: 343, fig. 180.
Lloyd.   Genera Gasteromycetes, pl. 3, fig. 23.
Lloyd.   Myc. Works, pl. 10, figs. 5–7; pl. 122.
Quélet.   Champ. Jura, etc., part 2, pl. 3. fig. 8.
White.   Bull. Torr. Bot. Club 28: pl. 38.   1901.

Pennsylvania.   Trexlertown.   On tanbark.   Dr. Herbst, coll. (N. Y. B. G. Herb. and U. N. C.
    Herb.).

SCLERODERMATACEAE

Plants more or less globular, usually partly or wholly exposed above ground at maturity (but at times entirely embedded);* peridium thick or thin, tough or fragile at maturity, rupturing irregularly and tardily, or splitting at maturity into stellate lobes, or, in *Pisolithus*, flaking off in fragments from above downward; gleba divided irregularly by thin or thick sterile tramal plates into areas which from the first are stuffed full of the fertile tissue containing the irregularly arranged basidia. At maturity both plates and fertile tissue break down into a powder at times by slow degrees. Plants attached below by a thick mass of mycelial plates and fibers and sometimes stalked. Basidia swollen, pyriform to subspherical; spores spherical, echinulate and sometimes also reticulate, brown; capillitium none or rudimentary.

A closely related family is Podaxaceae, a long-stalked group of large plants not represented in eastern United States. *Podaxon* and *Phellorina* occur in the western states.

Key to the Genera

Walls of the gleba chambers very thin and not forming distinctly outlined or complete chambers, disorganizing throughout at maturity, together with the fertile tissue, to form a flocculent or powdery mass containing the spores..*Scleroderma*
Walls of the gleba chambers thick, forming distinct peridioles which slowly pulverize from above downward after maturity and exposure..*Pisolithus*

SCLERODERMA Pers.

Characters of the family and distinguished from *Pisolithus* by the absence of distinct and persistent peridioles in the gleba. The plants are sessile except for a root-like attachment of plates and fibers mixed with earth. The brownish or purplish or olive-brown spores are echinulate or in several species obviously reticulated. In some cases there is visible regularly or at times (before much exposure) a peculiar veil or halo connecting the tips of the spines or reticulum. This effect is probably the result of a hyaline material which covers the spore between the spines. The spores of this genus show a remarkable peculiarity in their development. In 1889 it was shown by Beck (l. c.) that in *Phlyctospora fusca* Corda (*Scleroderma fuscum* (Corda) E. Fischer) the spores when somewhat more than half grown become surrounded by a sheath of cells which grow in from surrounding hyphae or much less often from the basidia. This sheath persists until the maturity of the spores and as the basidia have disappeared when the sheath is formed, the remaining growth and maturation of the spores is made possible by nourishment derived from the sheath. The sheath in most species is not so prominent as in *S. fuscum*, but in essentials the development of the spores is the same in all species investigated. We have studied *S. lycoperdoides* through these stages and find that the basidia disappear when the spores are only half grown and quite colorless. See details under that species.

---

* Zeller has recently described a peculiar *Scleroderma* from Oregon that is normally quite subterranean and that is still more remarkable in having a deliquescent gleba. (Mycologia 14: 193. 1922.) *Scleroderma pteridis* is also subterranean (see p. 162).

The plants are firm or even hard until mature, and while probably not harmful so far as known are not of much value as food. McIlvaine says (American Fungi, p. 615) that all the Sclerodermas are edible when young and never poisonous. Marshall says (Mushroom Book, p. 134) that *S. aurantium* (*S. vulgare*) has been eaten without harm, but is pronounced very unattractive. According to Bulliard it is claimed that *S. verrucosum* is deadly if eaten, but it is pronounced good by McIlvaine (at least the plant he discusses as such). The spiny spores are distinctly irritating to the eyes.

LITERATURE

Bambeke. Bull. Soc. Roy. Belgique 43: 104, figs. 1–4. 1906.

Beck. Über die Sporenbildung der Gattung *Phlyctospora* Cda. Ber. Deutsch. Bot. Ges. **7**: 212, one figure. 1889.

Lloyd. The Genus *Melanogaster*. Myc. Notes, p. 1064. 1921.

Petri. Flora Italica Cryptogama (Gasterales), Fasc. 5: 93. 1909.

Rabinowitsch. Beiträge zur Entwickelungsgeschichte der Fruchtkörper einiger Gastromyceten. Flora 79: 385, pls. 10 and 11. 1894.

Sorokine. Développement du *Scleroderma verrucosum*. Ann. Sci. Nat., 6th ser., 3: 30, pls. 5 and 6. 1876.

Tulasne, L. R. and Ch. De la Fructification des *Scleroderma comparée* à celle des *Lycoperdon* et des *Bovista*. Ann. Sci. Nat., 2nd ser., 17: 5, pls. 1 and 2. 1842.

KEY TO THE SPECIES

Plant large (4–10 cm. thick), the peridium thick and scaly and splitting at maturity into several more or less stellate and recurved lobes....................................*S. geaster* (p. 161)

Plant smaller (2–5.5 cm. thick), the peridium thinner (from very thin up to 1 mm. when dry) and less stellate in dehiscence

Peridium straw-colored before opening, smooth except for coarse cracks; spores not reticulated
S. flavidum (p. 162)

Peridium yellowish, nearly smooth or finely areolated; spores strongly reticulated
S. bovista (p. 163)

Peridium ochraceous or brownish, thick when fresh, thin when dry, the surface cracked into distinct, inherent scales about 1–3 mm. wide, which are with or without a stout central wart; spores strongly reticulated.....................................*S. aurantium* (p. 165)

Peridium leather or bay color, thick when fresh, thin when dry, the surface only delicately cracked into areas and in large part smooth; spores not reticulated.............*S. cepa* (p. 167)

Peridium light brown or yellow-brown, dotted over with minute, dark brown, inherent scales; thin when fresh and very thin when dry

Spores spiny, not reticulated...................................*S. lycoperdoides* (p. 168)

Spores reticulated..............................*S. lycoperdoides* var. *reticulatum* (p. 170)

Scleroderma geaster Fr.

Sclerangium polyrhizon (Gmel.) Lév.

Stella americana Mass.

Plates 82, 86 and 120

Peridium about 4–13.5 cm. thick when closed and up to 15 cm. broad when open, subglobose, depressed and often irregular and lobed; sessile and entirely embedded until nearly mature, often remaining more than half buried; connected beneath with diffused plates and strands of floccose mycelium; peridium hard and rigid, up to 5 mm. thick when fresh, about 1–2 mm. thick when dry, nearly white, then yellow or dull yellowish clay or straw color, rough and more or less cracked into areolations and scales; splitting up irregularly at maturity into a varying number of lobes which curl back as they dry and expose the dark spore mass which is deep brown when fully mature.

Spores deep brown with a slight tint of purple, globose, asperulate, not rarely with an imperfect reticulum, 5–10μ (most about 6.5–8μ) thick, including the spines which are up to about 0.5–1μ long.

This species gets its name from the way in which it cracks up, which is more or less stellate like the dehiscence of the outer peridium in the genus *Geaster*. It is a common plant in Chapel Hill, and is found from September through the winter in hard ground, preferring clay. The plants open in the fall and persist a long time, becoming blackened and empty with age. They often appear on the clean, newly eroded pure clay sides of gullies, a most remarkable choice for a home. *Scleroderma pteridis* Shear (Bull. T. B. C. **29**: 451. 1902) does not seem to differ essentially from *S. geaster*. The type was collected 2–4 feet below the surface of the ground and attached to dead rhizomes of *Pteris aquilina*. The spores are given as 6–8μ and the peridium as 3–8 mm. thick, and the author states that the species differs from *S. geaster* in the thicker peridium and smaller spores. In our numerous collections of the latter the great majority of the spores come within these limits, and the peridium thickness is almost exactly 3–8 mm. in moist, unopened specimens. A plant from the type collection kindly sent us by Dr. Shear is unopened, as were all his plants, and most of the spores are immature. We find, however, a few that are like those of *S. geaster*, about 7.7–10μ thick, with surface spines. Dr. Shear writes (Nov. 27, 1923) that he is "now inclined to think that this may be merely a form or variety of *S. geaster*."

Illustrations: Boudier. Icon. Myc., pl. 186.
　　Hard. Mushrooms, pl. 65.
　　Lloyd. Myc. Notes No. 9: fig. 47. 1902; also pl. 30, figs. 1–3. 1905.
　　Massee. l. c., pl. 2, figs. 35–35a.
　　Murrill. Mycologia 2: pl. 17, fig. 9. 1910.
　　Vittadini. Monog. Lycoperd., pl. 2, fig. 11; pl. 3, fig. 14. 1842.

　674.　In woods, top of Lone Pine Hill, and along roadside in fields, Sept. 20, 1908.
　973.　In hillside pasture, Nov. 11, 1913. Spores 6–8.3μ thick.
1014.　In a clay gully, Oct. 22, 1913. Spores 5–8.6μ, including spines, not rarely with an imperfect reticulum.
2938.　Unearthed in digging trenches (depth not known), Nov. 1, 1917. Spores asperulate, 6.7–9μ thick, omitting spines.
7571.　Under cedars, Oct. 29, 1924.
Also Nos. 657, 660, 920, 978, 1029, 1761, 7106.

　　Asheville. Beardslee.

South Carolina. Hartsville. Coker, coll. (U. N. C. Herb., No. 6014). In Bermuda grass lawn, Dec. 26, 1922. Spores warted and with a faint sign of a reticulum, 7.2–11μ thick.
　　Ravenel. Fungi Car. Exs. No. 76. (Phil. Acad. Herb.)
　　North Island. Coker and party, colls. (U. N. C. Herb.). Spores scurfy-warted, 7–10μ thick.
Florida. Gainesville. Weber, coll. (U. N. C. Herb., No. 7576). Stalked form. Spores very dark, strongly warted and partly reticulated, 7.4–11.2μ.

Scleroderma flavidum E. & E.

Plates 87, 88 and 120

Plants gregarious, at times crowded, 2–4 cm. broad, subglobose, compressed, sessile, plicate below around the thick basal attachment which holds the earth firmly;

PLATE 87

SCLERODERMA FLAVIDUM.   No. 675

PLATE 88

Scleroderma flavidum. No. 5857

surface rather light straw-yellow, more or less cracked above and on the sides into small to large, inherent, flat areas like dried mud or in a more one-sided way to give a shingled appearance (in some specimens the greater part not cracked); peridium tough, thin, only 0.5–1 mm. thick (dry), splitting above into several persistent lobes that open up irregularly (stellate, incurved or erect) to expose the spore mass, which varies remarkably in color in our collections, as fuscous then mummy brown (Ridgway) at full maturity in No. 5857, while in No. 675 it is Saccardo's umber.

Spores (of No. 675) spherical, 7.4–12.9μ, including the stout spines which reach a length of 1.5μ and not rarely show faint traces of a halo around their tips. They are mixed with numerous threads of the persistent trama which under the lens are nearly hyaline, branched, and 2.5–4.5μ thick.

This is a good species and easily separated from *S. geaster*, its nearest relative, by the smaller size, much smoother and thinner peridium and the larger spores with longer spines. Before opening the plants are partly or almost completely buried in the earth. The spore color of No. 675 is nearly the same as our *S. bovista* (sense of Bresadola), but the spores of the latter are entirely different, much larger and with a conspicuous and perfect reticulum. Smooth forms of the present species approach *S. cepa* in appearance, but that can be separated from this by the thinner, more flexible, and generally darker peridium.

We have studied an authentic specimen of this species (E. & E., N. Amer. Fungi, No. 1698, 2nd ser.) and find the spores to be spherical or nearly so, spiny-warted, 8–12μ thick.

660. On ditch bank at side of road west of Carrboro, Nov. 3, 1912. Spores 7.8–14μ counting spines, which are rarely up to 3μ long, usually shorter.

3109. Pasture by New Hope Creek, June 23, 1918. Spores spherical, 7.8–14.8μ thick counting spines, which are rarely up to 3μ long.

7562. In poor soil on campus, Oct. 14, 1924. Spores spiny, 8–11μ.

Raleigh. L. R. Detjen, No. 1889. Near an old stump in a yard, Oct. 9, 1915. Spores 8–11μ, excluding the spines which are up to 2μ long.

Asheville. Beardslee. Sept. 18, 1918. Spores 7.5–13μ thick, counting spines, which are not rarely up to 3μ long. This plant agrees perfectly with our Chapel Hill plants.

Mecklenburg Co. On sandy bank, July 21, 1924. Couch, coll. (U. N. C. Herb., No. 7444).

Bladen Co. In sandy loam, Sept. 6, 1924. Alma Holland, coll. (U. N. C. Herb., No. 7509). Spores very dark, strongly spiny-warted, 9.7–14.8μ, with a halo.

South Carolina. Hartsville. Coker, No. 675. Sandy soil on Coker College campus, Nov. 1908. No. 1962. In Bermuda grass lawn, Oct. 23, 1915. Spores 9.3–11μ thick, distinctly spiny. No. 5857. Again on Coker College campus, Aug. 30, 1922. Spores 7–10.5μ, excluding the spines which are up to 1.2μ long; hyaline threads mixed with the spores. No. 6022. On Coker College campus, Dec. 26, 1922.

Florida. Mell, coll. (N. Y. B. G. Herb.).

Alabama. Reported as common. (Bull. Ala. Agric. Exp. Sta. **80**: 268. 1897).

Mississippi. Biloxi. Tracy, coll. (N. Y. B. G. Herb.).

Wisconsin. Palmyra. (Univ. Wis. Herb. and U. N. C. Herb.)

Scleroderma bovista Fr.   Sense of Hollos

Plates 89 and 120

Plants roughly spherical, usually flattened horizontally, at times lobed, about 1.5–4 cm. broad, narrowly or rather broadly attached to earth by a thick or slender root which diffuses at once into mycelial plates and fibers; surface when young smooth, dull, remaining smooth or less often becoming cracked up toward maturity over part of the top into rather small, flattish areas about 1–3 mm. broad.   Color buffy yellow to buffy when young, then leather color or sordid brown, the top tending to become blackish after maturity, and with black spots often present on paler plants.   Peridium when fresh only 0.7–1 mm. thick, pure white in section and not changing when cut or rubbed, hardly more than 0.5 mm. thick when dry, at maturity splitting irregularly at the top; the spore mass soon becoming very dark blackish brown with a tint of chocolate. Tramal plates obviously yellow and until full maturity or after very distinct and perfect, the threads of the plates peculiar in that they swell and regain their form in water and can be distinctly seen to have clamp connections.

Spores (of No. 725) about blackish brown of Ridgway, spherical, in most cases reticulated, but only imperfectly so in some, with a halo about the reticulum, 9–15.5μ thick, including the reticulum which is up to 3μ high.

There are in herbaria two plants passing for *S. bovista*, the one here described (our No. 725, etc.) and the following (our No. 5920).   The first is in almost full agreement with Hollos's description and figures and we are considering it the species in his sense. Both plants are found in Bresadola's herbarium under the name *S. bovista*.   The one here described is represented there by plants from Cincinnati, Ohio, sent by Lloyd, and illustrated by him as *S. Texense* (cited below).   Lloyd's plant is the exact form as ours in every detail.   The other form is represented by a European plant collected by Bresadola which is exactly like our No. 5920.   It is larger than No. 725, has a longer and stouter rooting mass, a more yellow color, much thicker peridium, distinctly paler and larger spores, and tramal plate cells which do not regain their form when put in water.   The English plant figured by Lloyd in Myc. Notes No. 8, fig. 43 is like our No. 5920 in appearance, and he says he has the same thing from Falmouth, Mass., growing in clear beach sand, exactly the kind of habitat of our No. 5920.

Which of these two plants is the *S. bovista* of Fries we do not know, but think it likely that the species is truly represented by our No. 725 and Lloyd's plants from Cincinnati; and that our No. 5920 and the plant from Bresadola (and probably Lloyd's plant from Massachusetts) represent another species that has not been correctly understood.   Petri's treatment of *S. bovista* Fries apparently covers this plant.

Illustrations: Hollos. l. c., pl. 23, figs. 16–20.
　　Lloyd.   Lycoperdaceae of Australia, pl. 31, figs. 2–5.   1905.
　　Massee. l. c., pl. 2, fig. 36 (the spore drawn here does not show the reticulum).
　　Petri. l. c., fig. 54, No. 2.

600a. On cinder track with clay underneath, October 13, 1911.
　725. On damp ground in Arboretum, September 8, 1913.
5880 and 5885. On damp soil on bank of New Hope Creek, October 8, 1922.
7113. On ground in Arboretum, September 10, 1923.   Spores 9.7–14.8μ thick, usually reticulated.
8150. Grassy pasture on Glen Burnie farm, Oct. 11, 1926.   Spores strongly reticulated, 9.5–13.5μ thick.
Ohio. Cincinnati. Lloyd, coll. (Bresadola Herb.).

Scleroderma bovista Fries.   Sense of Bresadola

Plates 90 and 120

Fruit body irregularly globose; depressed above, deeply and widely plicate beneath, 3–5 cm. thick; sordid yellow, the peridium rigid and brittle when dry and about 1 mm. thick, very slightly to considerably squamulose, the very small inherent scales being

PLATE 89

SCLERODERMA BOVISTA.   Sense of Hollos.   No. 7113

PLATE 90

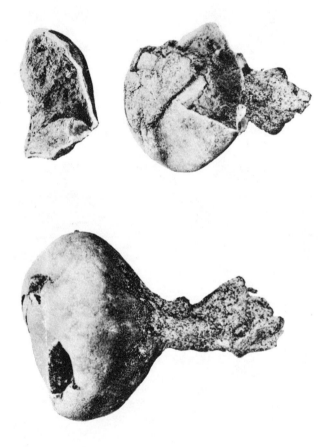

SCLERODERMA BOVISTA. Sense of Bresadola. No. 5920

formed by an irregular cracking of the outer surface of the peridium; rooted by a dense mass of entangled mycelioid cords, and opening when mature by irregular cracks and lobes. Gleba dark yellowish brown (sepia of Ridgw.); tramal plates yellow and quite persistent.

Spores (of plant from Smith's Island) spherical, 11–18.5μ (including the reticulum), the majority between 12.5μ and 14μ thick, with a coarse reticulum, surrounded by a semi-transparent, pale yellow substance; treated with KOH solution the spore becomes lighter, the reticulum clearer, and the gelatinous material swells considerably.

The distinguishing characters of the plant are its smooth to minutely areolated yellow surface, thick peridium (even when dry) which is white in section, long thick root, olive-brown spore mass mixed with yellow trama, and the large and coarsely reticulated spores. For a comparison with *S. bovista*, sense of Hollos, see that species. The species can readily be distinguished from *S. lycoperdoides* by the larger size, more yellow color, paler and far less conspicuous areolations, and by the strongly reticulated spores. *Scleroderma cepa*, which is about the same size and color, differs (when dry) in the thinner and less brittle peridium, more reddish spore mass and non-reticulated spores; *S. flavidum* differs in the much paler straw color, coarsely cracked surface, and non-reticulated spores; *S. aurantium* has a much rougher surface, and when dry a thinner and less brittle peridium.

We have compared our plant with a good example in Bresadola's herbarium collected by him in Europe, and find them just alike in appearance and spores, which are in the latter 9.3–14μ thick, not counting the reticulum which is up to 3μ high.

North Carolina. Smith's Island. No. 5920. In very sandy soil near the sea, December 28, 1921.
    (U. N. C. Herb.)
Canada. London. Dearness, No. 135B. (U. N. C. Herb.)
    Pelee. Dearness, No. 4826. (U. N. C. Herb.) Spores 12–25μ, most about 19μ, reticulated.

Scleroderma aurantium (Vaill.) Pers.
    S. vulgare Horn.

Plates 91 and 120

Fruit body about 2–5 cm. thick, subspherical and usually compressed horizontally, plicate below and rarely lobed, sessile and attached by a thick mass of fibers; peridium yellowish ochraceous or brownish, thick (about 2 mm.) when fresh and turning pink when cut (when dry less than 1 mm. thick), the surface cracked into distinct areolations which may or may not have a central wart, the warts and areolations often arranged in a beautifully embossed pattern; after maturity slowly cracking into irregular lobes which do not open in a stellate way. Gleba gray then nearly black, the tramal plates white.

Spores (of No. 5622) blackish brown, strongly reticulated, 8–11μ thick, not counting the reticulum which is 1.5–2μ high.

This is recognized by its verrucose and usually distinctly warted surface, thickish peridium which turns pink when cut in the fresh state, white tramal plates and reticulated spores. It is nothern in its range and in the south we have found it only in the mountains. It grows in either deciduous or coniferous woods, but seems to prefer mossy humus or very rotten wood under hemlock, spruce or pine. This is the species that is occasionally parasitized by a *Boletus* (*B. parasiticus*) and we have found a fine example of this condition at Blowing Rock (see Journ. E. M. Sci. Soc. **42**: pl. 48. 1927).

A plant from Bresadola's herbarium determined by him as *S. vulgare* is the same as *S. aurantium*, with spores 7–11.8μ thick.

Maire's cytological work on this species we quote below (Comp. Rend. **131** (2): 1247. 1900). It will be noted that he states the spore number to be four. Tulasne says they are "usually four, sometimes two, three or five," and he also states that their respective positions are very variable.

"The study of the basidium is especially interesting in *Scleroderma vulgare*. At the beginning of the prophase of the first division, the cytoplasm contains a certain number of granules which stain black in iron haematoxylin, around which radiate the microsomes. It seems clear that two of these granules become the centrosomes, for a little later only two from among them show as center of radiation; they are then placed on each side of the nucleus whose nucleolus and membrane soon disappear, while the chromatic reticulum is transformed into two irregular knotty clubs which represent two chromosomes and which extend almost from one centrosome to another.

"At the same time there is organized between the centrosomes a spindle; the two chromosomes contract while increasing in thickness, then divide into two *longitudinally*, while shaping themselves into a "V" until they are end to end parallel to the axis of the spindle. They are then directed toward the poles and there reunite into a chromatic mass which covers the centrosomes and from which seem still to radiate the astral rays. The spindle soon disappears and the second division begins almost immediately: there is formed around each nucleus a spindle with centrosomes and asters. All the granules of the cytoplasm are massed on the radiations of the asters, except some which remain in a parietal layer at the base of the basidium, in such a way that, except for this residue, everything that is visible in the cytoplasm is oriented with regard to the four centrosomes. The second division is like the first, since the events take place as if the four centrosomes determined the formation of the four spores; they disappear moreover on the arrival of the nuclei at the latter, to reappear only at the mitosis, which takes place in the spore some time after its formation."

Maire also makes the general statement in regard to this species, as well as all others studied [*Geaster hygrometricus, Lycoperdon caelatum, excipuliforme, gemmatum; Nidularia globosa, Cyathus hirsutus*]: "We have observed the fusion of only two nuclei in the young basidia. The subhymenial cells always contain two associated nuclei with conjugate mitoses. Many cells of the other tissues when they are old contain a more or less large number of nuclei, but these nuclei come from an amitotic fragmentation of the two primitive nuclei. The number of chromosomes is two in all species studied."

Illustrations: Bambeke. l. c., fig. 2.
    Boudier. Icon. Myc., pl. 145. This shows the condition parasitized by *Boletus parasiticus*.
    Bulliard. Champ. Fr., pl. 270.
    Fries, Th. C. E. Sveriges Gasteromyceter, fig. 37.
    Gillet. Champ. Fr. (Gasteromycetes), pl. 15.
    Hard. Mushrooms, pl. 64 and fig. 475.
    Hollos. l. c., pl. 23, figs. 8–15.
    Hussey. Ills. Brit. Myc., pl. 17.
    Marshall. Mushroom Book, p. 134.
    Massee. Brit. Fungi, pl. 35, fig. 6.

PLATE 91

Scleroderma aurantium.   No. 5506 [above] ; No. 5681 [below]

PLATE 92

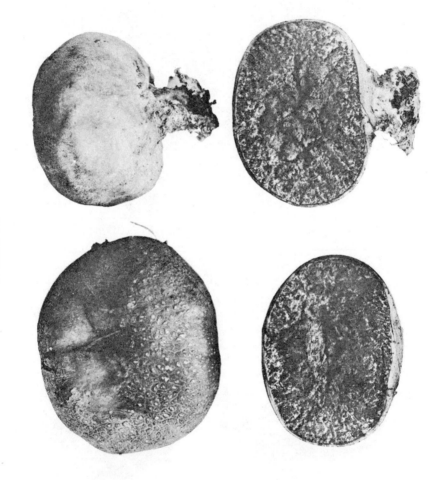

SCLERODERMA CEPA. No. 916. Dried plants

Michael. Führer f. Pilzfreunde 1: No. 82. 1918 (2nd ed.).
Petri. l. c., figs. 53, 54, No. 4 (both as *S. vulgare*).
Tulasne. Ann. Sci. Nat., 2nd. ser. 17: pl. 1. 1842.

North Carolina. Blowing Rock. Coker and party, August 1922. No. 5506. Under balsam and spruce on Grandfather Mountain. No. 5528. By a chestnut oak stump. No. 5622. On rotting wood and deep woods mold by Glen Burnie Falls. No. 5656. At foot of a chestnut. Spores 8–13μ thick not counting the spines which are up to 1.8μ long. No. 5681. In deciduous woods by roadside. Spores 8–14μ thick, with a distinct reticulum. No. 5686. In mossy humus under hemlock. Parasitized by *Boletus parasiticus*.
Pennsylvania. Buck Hill Falls. Mrs. Delafield, coll. (N. Y. B. G.).
New York. Cold Spring Harbor, L. I. Couch, coll. (U. N. C. Herb.).
Illinois. Urbana. McDougall, coll. (U. N. C. Herb.).
Wisconsin. Devil's Lake. (Univ. Wis. Herb. and U. N. C. Herb.) Spores reticulated, 9.5–12μ.
Canada. London. Dearness, No. 578F. (U. N. C. Herb.)
    Avon. Dearness, No. 578 Av. (U. N. C. Herb.)

Scleroderma cepa (Vaill.) Pers.

Plates 92, 93 and 120

Plants subglobose or lobed, often flattened, about 1.5–6 cm. broad, sessile or nearly so and attached by a thick mass of fibrous mycelium; surface nearly pure white when young, soon straw colored or yellowish ochraceous to dull leather brown, turning quickly deep vinaceous when rubbed, finely areolated, or covered over most of the surface with very small, inherent, concolorous scales, or in large part smooth; peridium up to 1.5 mm. thick when fresh, less than 0.5 mm. thick when dry, firm, not very brittle, much thinner and less brittle than in *S. flavidum*, white in section at first then turning vinaceous on exposure; spore mass watery white until at least half grown, then rapidly becoming nearly black with a purple tint and finally less dark, varying from Saccardo's umber to sepia (Ridgway) depending on the time collected; odorless.

Spores (of No. 916) globose, strongly spinulose, 7–11.4μ thick, including the sharp spines which not rarely are up to 2μ long; not at all reticulate and with or without a halo connecting the spine tips. Tramal plates only partly reswelling in water, heavily encrusted with yellow crystals.

Smooth forms of this plant resemble *S. bovista* (in sense of Hollos) in surface appearance, but can be distinguished from the latter by the less rigid and less brittle peridium, less dark spore-mass (if mature) and the smaller, spiny spores which are without a reticulum. Young plants are separated by the paler color and purplish color change of the peridium. Rough forms approach *S. flavidum* in appearance, but that is easily separated by the thicker, more brittle and paler peridium.

Illustrations: Bambeke. l. c., fig. 4 (spores).
    Fries, Th. C. E. Sveriges Gasteromyceter, fig. 38.
    Hollow. l. c., pl. 23, figs. 3–7.
    Lloyd. Myc. Works, pl. 31. 1905.
    Petri. l. c., fig. 54, No. 1 and fig. 55.

916. In grass on campus, Oct. 15, 1913.
7112. In sandy soil by campus path, Sept. 10, 1923. Fresh plants distinctly tinted lavender when bruised.
7201. In swamp of Bowlin's Creek, Oct. 26, 1923. Spores 10–12.5μ thick, counting the spines which are long, sharp and triangular; no reticulum.

7515. Under a hawthorn bush in the Arboretum, Sept. 2, 1924. Spores dark, spiny-warted, 8–12μ with a halo. In this collection the peridium had apparently grown more after the maturity of the gleba, leaving the latter as a loose ball inside.
Also Nos. 5394, 5998, 6093, 7547, 7561.

Wisconsin. Burlington. (Univ. Wis. Herb., as *S. verrucosum*, and U. N. C. Herb.) Spores warted, 7–10μ.

Scleroderma lycoperdoides Schw.

Plates 94 and 120

Gregarious or cespitose; body 0.8–5 cm. (most about 1.5–2.5 cm.) broad, usually broader than thick; surface light brown or yellowish brown and dotted all over with minute darker brown or reddish brown, separated, inherent scales; becoming blackish on long exposure; smooth or minutely roughened; flat below and abruptly rooted by a stout embedded stalk of varying length which is soon dissipated into a few strong, stout strands and plates or into many smaller fibers. Peridium thin, when fresh and immature 0.5–0.7 mm. thick, becoming thinner and on the inside obscurely defined, the inner layer becoming fibrous like the trama and continuous with it and wearing away so as to leave in age only a very thin outer layer of a more leathery texture. Glebal chambers very small, about 0.2–0.5 mm., the plates very thin and composed of delicate rather straight hyphae about 2.5–3.5μ thick. Spore mass when very young watery cream color, then deep brown and faintly purplish, changing to paler grayish brown with or without a faint tint of olive after maturity; the delicate threads and plates of the trama are not quickly disintegrated but remain as a decided matrix for the exposed spores as they are slowly dissipated. There is no distinct dehiscence, but after much delay there appears an irregular worn opening in the tip and there are often other pores made by grubs. In age the stalk and all the basal part of the body are left as an empty saucer.

Spores deep brown, spherical, asperulate, not reticulated, very variable in size of body and length of spines in the same plant: in No. 5201 they are 7.5–18.5μ (most about 11–14μ) thick excluding the spines which vary from a length of 2μ (rarely) to scarcely more than pointed warts (all from one fully mature plant). In No. 3488 a halo was noticed connecting the spine tips over a part of the spore surface in many cases. Basidia (of No. 5253) 7–8.5μ thick with 4–8 sessile spores.

While still half grown and before the gleba has a tint of brown the spores are formed and the fertile tissue stuffing the chambers, including the basidia, has undergone a disintegration into a translucent almost structureless mass surrounding and embedding the spores, which at this time are hyaline, smooth and only about half the size they attain later. It seems certain that the spores are nourished by the surrounding matrix and undergo growth and maturation after separation from the basidia, as in *S. fuscum* (see under the genus).

This is our commonest *Scleroderma* in Chapel Hill. It prefers damp, shaded places on bare ground or in thin grass or moss, but is often found on rotten logs in swamps. It appears every year in the same places. The correct name has been in much doubt. In American herbaria and literature it appears as *S. verrucosum* (Bull.) Pers., or *S. tenerum* B. & C. (Cuban Fungi, No. 512). It is certainly near *S. verrucosum*, as that species is now understood in Europe, and larger individuals pass for that species in America. In fact one meets rarely with small European specimens which cannot be distinguished from the typical American form. Such a plant is represented in Rathay's Flora Exs. Austro-Hungarica, No. 1559 (U. S. National Herbarium). We have always felt with Lloyd that the European name could hardly be applied to the present small species. A European plant from Bresadola's herbarium (as *S. verrucosum*) has spores

PLATE 93

SCLERODERMA CEPA.   No. 7515 [above] ; No. 7547 [below]

that can be matched by our plants, asperulate, 6.6–18μ, most about 11–14μ (pl. 120, fig. 12), but the surface, while cracked into areas, is not dotted with small separated scales of a different color. Lloyd uses *S. tenerum* for our U. S. American plant, and the Cuban plant certainly represents ours in the tropics. The types at Kew (kindly loaned us by the director) consist of two good plants. One has the surface of our plants; the other has more pronounced warts (pl. 95). The spores of both are the same and are like the American form except for the average smaller size, 8–11μ, most about 8.5–10μ (pl. 120, fig. 8). They are almost exactly the size of the spores of *S. cepa*. We have fortunately been able to find a good name for our form of the plant as proved by an authentic specimen of *S. lycoperdoides* in Michener's herbarium from the Schweinitz Herbarium. The specimen is in good condition and shows all the characters of our plants, the spores 10–15μ thick, covered with short or long, sharp spines which become clear only after a treatment of KOH has dissolved away the gelatinous, granular material between them. Lloyd did not find the species represented in the Schweinitz Herbarium in Philadelphia and so hesitated to use the name. There is, however, a fragment of this in the Schweinitz Herbarium which has the same spores as the plant above mentioned (10.5–13μ). There are also fragments from the Schweinitz Herbarium in the Curtis Herbarium labelled *S. lycoperdoides* which seem to be the same. The spore structure of *S. lycoperdoides* is as in *S. cepa* (No. 3109) except that the spores in the present species are considerably larger and more variable. For a supposed variety of this species see Peck, Rept. N. Y. St. Mus. **53**: 848, pl. B, figs. 8–12. 1899.

Illustrations: Hard. Mushrooms, fig. 476 (as *S. tenerum*).
    Lloyd. Myc. Notes No. 8: fig. 38. 1901 (as *S. verrucosum*).
    Trelease. Trans. Wis. Acad. Sci. Arts and Letters **7**: pl. 9, fig. 7. 1888 (as *S. verrucosum*).
For the European *S. verrucosum* see: Bigeard. Flore Champ. **1**: pl. 51, fig. 1.
    Bulliard. Herb. Fr., pl. 24.
    Gillet. Champ. Fr. (Gasteromycetes), pl. 15.
    Hollos. l. c., pl. 23, figs. 21–29.
    Hussey. Illustrations, pl. 17, fig. 1.
    Leuba. Champ. Comest., etc., pl. 52, figs. 7–11. 1887–90.

523, 726, 2396, 5253. All from damp soil in the Arboretum, June to October.
5395. On rotten logs in a swamp, July 24, 1922.
7000. On earth by Meeting of Waters branch, July 30, 1923. Some of these plants were mere shells,
    the spores having all been washed out.
Also Nos. 1013, 1785a, 5201.

    Asheville. Beardslee.
    Blowing Rock. Coker and party, August 1922. (U. N. C. Herb.)
        Also collection by Coker, Sept. 3, 1924. Spores spiny-warted, 10–14.8μ thick.
    Winston-Salem. Vogler. In moss and on ground, July 30, 1919. (U. N. C. Herb., No. 3488).
        This is also probably the type locality.

    Florida. Marion Co. Couch, coll. (U. N. C. Herb., Nos. 7278 and 7279). Spores (of No. 7278)
        irregularly spiny and granular with hyaline material, 8–12μ thick.
        Gainesville. Walker, coll. (U. N. C. Herb.).
    Alabama. Peters, coll. (Curtis Herb., as *S. vulgare*).
    Virginia. Falls Church. Murrill, coll. (N. Y. B. G. Herb.).
        Warrenton. Coker, coll. (U. N. C. Herb.).
    Pennsylvania. Buck Hill Falls. Mrs. Delafield, coll. (N. Y. B. G. Herb.).
    New York. Represented from various places in N. Y. B. G. Herb.

Connecticut. Redding. Underwood, coll. (N. Y. B. G. Herb.).

Massachusetts. Sprague, No. 737. (Curtis Herb., as *Lycoperdon gemmatum*.)

Wisconsin. Nelson's Woods near Madison. (Univ. Wis. Herb. and U. N. C. Herb.) Spores spiny-warted, 8–11μ.

Canada. Ontario. Dearness, coll. (U. N. C. Herb., several collections). Spores (of No. 3841b) spiny, 7.5–11μ thick.

Scleroderma lycoperdoides var. reticulatum n. var.

Size, habit and surface appearance about as in the species, from which it differs in distinctly olive colored spore mass at maturity and in the strongly reticulated instead of merely spiny spores and the more delicate, less massive roots. The color may run a little darker and the spots somewhat less conspicuous than is usual in the species, but these characters are too variable to be emphasized. The gleba color and spore differ-ence are very obvious, the latter being easily seen under moderate power. When the dark olivaceous spores are shaken out, the remaining matrix is bright olivaceous yellow.

Spores (of No. 8076) spherical, spiny but also strongly reticulated, 10–13μ.

North Carolina. In mixed woods by Pisgah Creek, Haywood Co., N. C., Aug. 7, 1926. Totten, coll. (U. N. C. Herb., No. 8076).

New York. Under shrubs in New York Botanical Garden, July 27, 1919. Coker, coll. (U. N. C. Herb.). Spores strongly reticulated as in No. 8076.

PISOLITHUS Alb. & Schw.

Distinguished from *Scleroderma* by the distinct peridioles or irregular bodies that with their separating walls make up the body of the gleba and contain the spores. A number of species have been described, but all those of the northern temperate zone are probably only forms of the one that occurs here. There is certainly nothing in the descriptions to separate them. Differences in form, as presence or absence of a con-spicuous, simple or complicated stalk, and surface color of peridium are all certainly worthless. The plant is a common one in Chapel Hill and all forms occur. The fresh young plants if unweathered are very obviously yellow, but this soon changes to shades of brown or blackish on exposure.

This has been widely treated as *Polysaccum*, a genus now known to be antedated by *Pisolithus*.

LITERATURE

Bambeke. Bull. Soc. Roy. Bot. Belgique **42:** 178. 1906.

Massee. Revision of *Polysaccum*. Grevillea **16:** 26, 76. 1887–88.

Petri. Flora Italica Cryptogama (Gasterales), Fasc. 5: 104. 1909.

Tulasne, L. R. and Ch. Sur les genres *Polysaccum* et *Geaster*. Ann. Sci. Nat., 2nd ser., **18:** 129 pl. 5, figs. 1–7. 1842.

Pisolithus tinctorius (Pers.)

P. arenarius A. & S.

Polysaccum pisocarpium Fr.

Polysaccum crassipes DC.

Plates 96, 97 and 120

Mycelium olivaceous yellow. Fruiting body irregularly globose or pear-shaped and up to 18 cm. high and 10.5 cm. broad, narrowing below to a stout, stem-like, ir-

PLATE 94

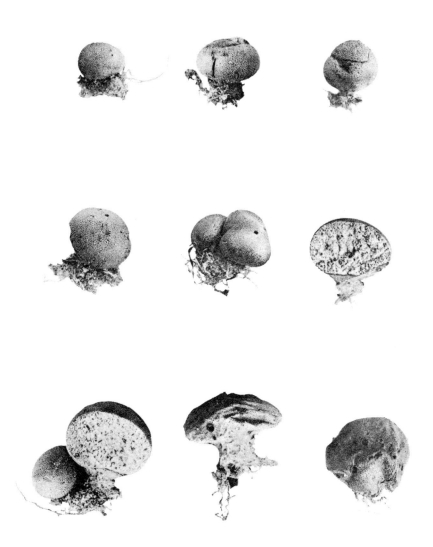

SCLERODERMA LYCOPERDÓIDES.   No. 523

PLATE 95

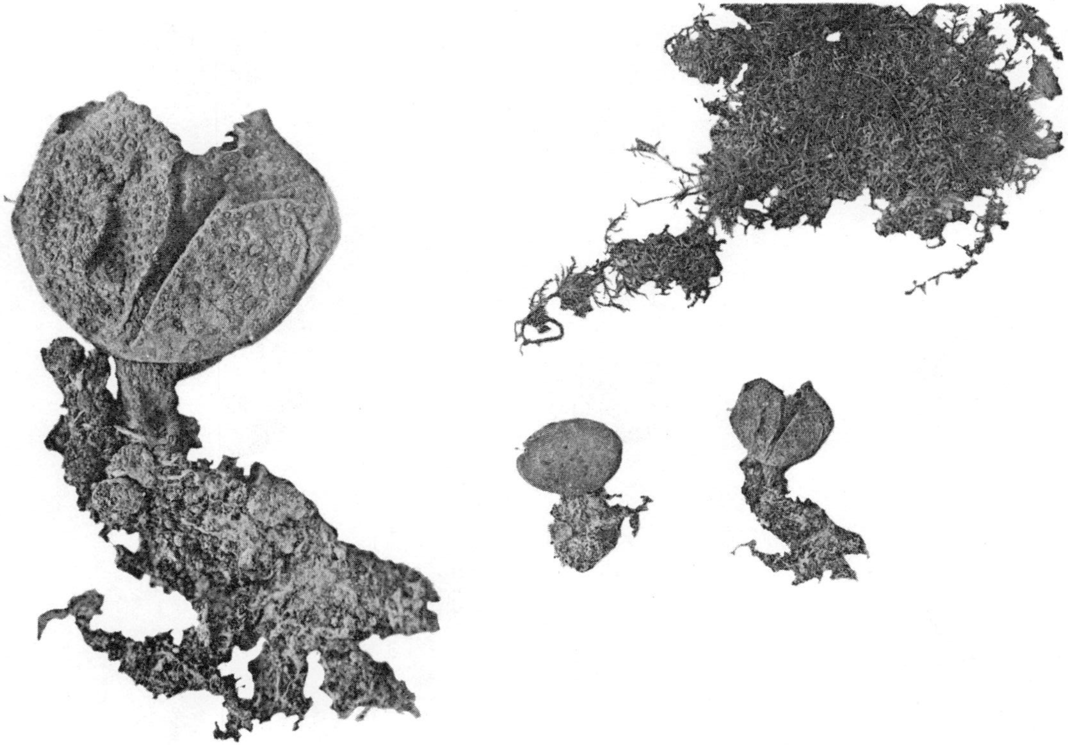

SCLERODERMA TENERUM. Type. Kew Herbarium. Plant on left × 3

regular base of very variable length and thickness, at times sessile and attached as in *Scleroderma;* solid and firm, at first olivaceous yellow but usually dull ochraceous when found, then brownish to blackish, the surface nearly glabrous; peridium very thin and at maturity becoming brittle and soon cracking into flakes above until the whole contents are exposed. Peridioles in section whitish or yellow, then watery vinaceous, then through darker vinaceous to nearly black, subspherical, irregularly angular, usually compressed, about 1–2 mm. thick and up to 4 mm. long, smaller toward the base; texture that of a firm elastic and translucent jelly until the desiccation of maturity. Peridioles separated by a nearly black jelly enclosing a densely woven mass of delicate threads with clamp connections.

Spore powder cinnamon brown; spores globose, spiny but with the spines covered with a gelatinous material that makes them look blunt when first put into water, 7–11.5μ thick, counting the spines which are up to 2μ long.

This peculiar plant is common in fall in well drained gravelly and sandy soil, as pastures, old fields, thin places in lawns, etc. The dry spore powder is scattered by the breaking down of the peridioles after the peridium cracks off. This disorganization proceeds by degrees and the lower peridioles are intact for some time while the upper part is being dissipated. The old, woody, discolored base remains intact for months.

The blackish jelly between the peridioles and the peridium also of this plant gets its color from a bright olivaceous yellow pigment which quickly stains cloth or paper and is hard to remove. It is said to be used for dye for cloth in France (Lloyd, Lycoperdaceae of Aus., p. 12). When put under the microscope this jelly itself is seen to contain most of the pigment, the threads being pale. The vinaceous purple color of the jelly in the peridioles is due to the maturing spores, the threads and jelly around them being colorless. If a ripening peridiole be put into water the purplish pigment in the spores will diffuse into the water and color it. The plant thus contains two distinct pigments, a yellow and a purple one. The purple tint of the spores is lost at full maturity, the dry spore powder being deep brown without purple. The very surface of the peridioles is covered with a thin weft of yellow fibers that are not gelatinized and contrast strongly with the jelly on each side. When fresh the very thin weft of fibers that make up the peridium is lined beneath by about one millimeter of the same black jelly that surrounds the peridioles. This is mottled with yellow plates as if the outer peridioles had been aborted.

The spores of *P. crassipes* as illustrated by Tulasne show thick, rounded warts rather than spines, but we do not take this to be evidence that the plants are different. When first put into water many of the spores have thick, rounded warts but these become sharper after standing awhile or on application of KOH.

As in the case of *Scleroderma* and the Nidulariaceae, it is obvious that the spores grow considerably after the basidia disappear by gelatinization. At the stage shown in fig. 17 the basidia have lost all their contents and are almost invisible, yet the spores are only about two-thirds grown. Figure 18 shows the mature spores at the same magnification.

As Persoon's Synopsis Fungorum is now generally accepted as the starting point for the nomenclature of the Gasteromycetes, there is no reason why his specific name (based on Micheli's plate) should not be applied to this plant. Though Lloyd suggests this, we cannot find that the combination we use has ever been published before. For other synonyms, see Hollos, p. 179.

Illustrations: Albertini and Schweinitz. Consp. Fung., pl. 1, fig. 3.
  Boudier. Icon. Myc., pl. 185.
  Bruns. Beitrag zur Kenntniss der Gattung *Polysaccum*. Flora 78: 67. 1894.
  Hollos. l. c., pl. 27 and pl. 28, figs. 1–6.
  Lloyd. Lycoperdaceae of Australia, pl. 29. 1905.
  Michael. Führer f. Pilzfreunde 3: No. 345. 1919 (2nd ed.).
  Micheli. Nova Plant. Gen., pl. 98, fig. 1.
  Nees von Esenbeck. Syst. Pilze Schw., pl. 13, fig. 131 B.
  Sowerby. Engl. Fungi, pl. 425 (as *Lycoperdon capsuliferum*).
  Vittadini. Monog. Lycoperd., pl. 2, fig. 8 and pl. 3, fig. 13.

  663. By path northeast of athletic field, November 26, 1912.
  974. Among scattered pines on hillside pasture, Nov. 11, 1913.
  4903. On ground in a yard, October 17, 1921. Spores spherical, densely but rather bluntly spiny, 7–9.5μ thick, rarely 11μ.
  7090. In clay soil by road west of President's house, August 23, 1923. Plant 18 cm. high and 10.5 cm. thick when gathered.
Also Nos. 686, 687, 723, 902, 2219, 5402, 7125, 8170.

South Carolina. Marion Co. Sandy soil near Little Pee Dee River. Coker, coll. (U. N. C. Herb. No. 8136). This seems to be an immature or conditional form. The spores are bluntly warted instead of spiny.
Florida. Gainesville. In sandy pine woods. Weber, coll. (U. N. C. Herb.). Spores spiny-warted, 8.5–11.5μ.
Alabama. Tuskegee. Beaumont, coll. (Curtis Herb.).

PLATE 96

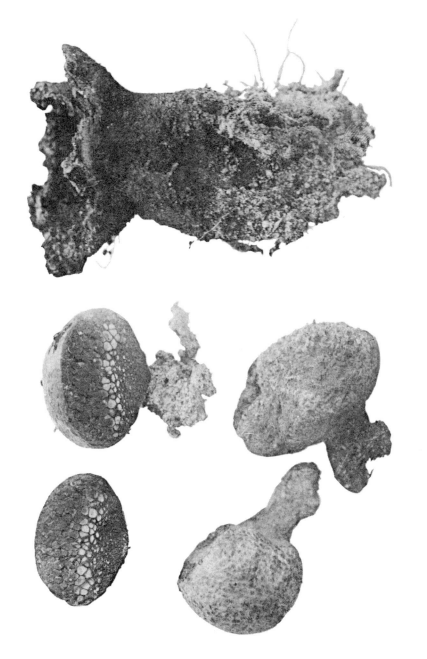

PISOLITHUS TINCTORIUS. No. 723 [left]; No. 974 [right]

PLATE 97

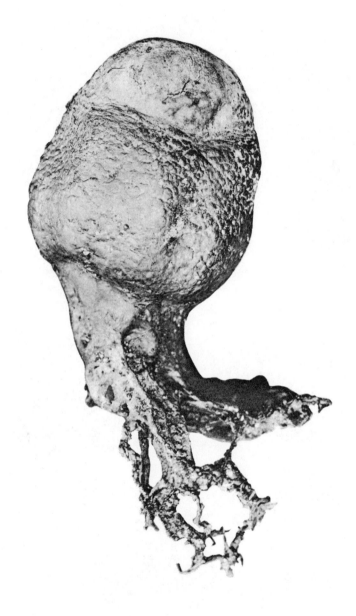

PISOLITHUS TINCTORIUS. No. 5402

NIDULARIACEAE

Plants small, growing on the ground, on dead vegetable matter or on dung; cup-shaped or goblet-shaped or globular; the mouth in two genera closed until maturity by a membrane (the epiphram); gleba in the form of separate, lens-shaped bodies (the periodioles) of easily visible size, which contain a number of large, smooth spores and are covered by a dark, hard, protective coat which is with or without an obvious superficial, white, thinner layer (the tunic). Basidia clavate, with 2–8 smooth, sessile or stipitate, apical or scattered spores, forming in *Crucibulum* a definite hymenial layer near the center, but in *Cyathus* occupying irregularly, together with sterile threads, a large central area of the peridiole. Spores smooth, usually flattened, binucleate in the species studied. Capillitium lacking.

The peridioles do not open of their own accord, but liberate the spores only when eaten by insects (or when decayed?). The tunic is thick and removable in *Crucibulum*, very thin and obscure in *Cyathus* (Lloyd thinks it entirely absent in *C. stercoreus*). The hard wall of the peridioles is only superficially black or brown, and composed almost entirely of very irregular, branching and knobbed, very thick-walled sclerotic cells, which, when a peridium is crushed, are found scattered abundantly among the spores. In nature they retain their position and are not mixed with the spores. These cells are only remotely, if at all, homologous to the capillitium of other genera. Next within this hard layer comes the spore-bearing tissue which may or may not form a definite hymenial layer. See under the different genera for details on this point. The spores have been made to germinate in water and in culture media and have produced fruit bodies in pure culture (Walker, Hesse, Eidam). On account of the peculiar resemblance to little nests with eggs, these plants are popularly known as "bird's-nest fungi." So far three of the four genera have been found in the eastern states. In two of these the peridioles are connected on their under side to the wall of the peridium by a cord (the funiculus), which is elastic when wet and brittle when dry. In *Crucibulum* it is usually very obscure after maturity and often disappears from gelatinization. In *Cyathus*, the funiculus, while much more conspicuous, may be rarely entirely lacking from some of the upper peridioles (Miss White, Lloyd). In the other they are free from the wall, but embedded in a mucus. The spores are hyaline, and are elliptic or subglobose. They vary a great deal in size from the comparatively small ones of *Crucibulum vulgare* to the immense ones of *Cyathus melanospermus*. They also vary considerably in the same collection and at times in the same peridiole, and they are much more abundant in the small-spored species than in those having large spores. In 1902 Miss White (l. c.) brought together in convenient form the species known from North America and established a new genus, *Nidula*, with two species from the western states and Canada. Lloyd (l. c.) adds a third species (the *Cyathus emodensis* of Berkeley, Kew Journ. Bot., p. 204. 1854) and extends the geographical range of the genus. For the structure of the peridioles, see Tulasne, Walker, Lloyd, or Fischer, as cited below. Fischer suggests that the family may have descended from the Hymenogastraceae, mentioning *Octaviania*, but the origin of this group is certainly very obscure. Lohwag (cited on

p. 194) expresses the surprising opinion that these plants are related to *Tylostoma* and represent a compound group of *Tylostoma* fruit bodies enclosed in a common sheath.

LITERATURE

Andrews. Notes on a Species of *Cyathus* common in Lawns at Middleburg, Vermont. Rhodora 2: 99, pl. 17. 1900.
Brefeld. Botanische Untersuchungen über Schimmelpilze 3: 176. 1877.
Cunningham. A Revision of the New Zealand Nidulariales, or "Birds-nest Fungi." Trans. New Zealand Institute 55: 59, pls. 3 and 4. 1924.
Eidam. Die Keimung der Sporen und die Eutstehung der Fruchtkörper bei den Nidularieen. Cohn's Beiträge der Pflanzen 2: 221. 1877.
Fischer. l. c., in Pflanzenfamilien, p. 324, which see for other literature.
Fries, R. E. Om utvecklingen af fruktkroppen och peridiolerna hos *Nidularia*. Svensk bot. Tidskr. 4: 126, one plate. 1910.
Fries, R. E. Ueber die cytologischen Verhältnisse bei der sporenbildung von *Nidularia*. Zeitschr. Bot. 3: 145, pls. 1 and 2. 1911.
Hesse. Keimung der Sporen von *Cyathus striatus* Willd., einer Gastromycetenspecies. Jahrb. Wiss. Bot. 10: 199. 1876.
Lloyd. The Nidulariaceae, figs. 1–20 and pls. 102–111. Cincinnati, 1906
Maire. Recherches cytologiques et taxonomiques sur les basidiomycètes. Bull. Soc. Myc. France 18: 178 (of supplement), pl. 6. 1902.
Martin. Basidia and Spores of the Nidulariaceae. Mycologia 19: 239, pls. 22, 23. 1927.
Mollaird. Le cycle de développement du *Crucibulum vulgare* Tul. et de quelques Champignons supérieurs obtenu en cultures pures. Bull. Soc. Bot. France 56: 91. 1909.
Sachs. Morphologie des *Crucibulum vulgare* Tulasne. Bot. Zeit. 13: 833, pls. 13, 14. 1855.
Tulasne, L. R. and Ch. Recherches sur l'organisation et le mode de fructification des Champignons de la tribu des Nidulariées. Ann. Sci. Nat., 3rd ser., 1: 41. 1844.
Walker. Development of *Cyathus fascicularis*, *C. striatus*, and *Crucibulum vulgare*. Bot. Gaz. 70: 1, pls. 1–6 and 3 figs. 1920.
White. The Nidulariaceae of North America. Bull. Torr. Bot. Club 29: 251, pls. 14–18. 1902.

KEY TO THE GENERA

Peridioles (or most of them) attached by cords to the cups
    Peridium cup-shaped with a thick wall composed of a single layer; peridioles whitish from the thick
        white tunica..*Crucibulum* (p. 181)
    Peridium bell-shaped or goblet-shaped, with walls of three obvious layers; peridioles gray or nearly
        black; tunica thin or wanting.....................................*Cyathus* (p. 174)
Peridioles not attached by cords, but embedded when fresh in a mucus
    Peridium thin, spherical, falling into fragments..........................*Nidularia* (p. 183)
    Peridium thick, cup-shaped, opening at the top................................*Nidula*

CYATHUS Haller

Plants distinctly bell-shaped or goblet-shaped; the tough peridium composed of three distinct layers, in expanding towards maturity exposing a thin, pale, usually almost smooth epiphram which is stretched across the top and which disappears with age. Peridioles attached by a cord, black or dark brown, in some cases covered with a very thin tunica, which, however, does not completely hide their dark color. Basidia not forming a distinct or homogeneous hymenium, but scattered at irregular heights throughout a large central area and intermingled with numerous delicate threads which at maturity have their cell walls greatly thickened and gelatinized to form a solid horny matrix, throughout which the spores are unevenly scattered. At the time the spores are growing, this matrix is not horny but gelatinous, becoming horny at maturity.

Under ordinary powers of the microscope the almost closed lumens of these thick-walled threads have the appearance of delicate filaments running among the spores. Minute, amorphous granules are also found in abundance. The hyaline, sclerotic layer, composing the greater part of the wall, is composed of crumpled and distorted cell units with very thick walls. In *Cyathus* these units do not separate when crushed but break up into irregular masses and bits of cells; in *Crucibulum* they separate in great part when crushed and the individual cells can be easily seen and drawn. For other differences in structure see under *Crucibulum vulgare*.

The spores of this genus show the remarkable peculiarity of carrying on a large part of their growth after the basidia that produced them have entirely disappeared. When the spores are about half grown or less, the basidia become empty and gelatinize, leaving the spores embedded in the gelatinous matrix mentioned above. As shown in several figures on plates 122 and 123, the threads producing the matrix can be seen to wrap about the spores in large numbers. It is obvious that these threads furnish the nutrition necessary for the post-basidial growth of the spores. This remarkable condition is found also to a somewhat less degree in *Pisolithus* and *Scleroderma*, which see.

At the Washington meeting of the Botanical Society of America (Dec. 1926). Prof. George W. Martin gave a paper on the basidia of the Nidulariaceae in which he brought out this fact. Our work on the subject had been completed two years earlier.

In addition to the species listed below, Miss White includes from our territory *C. intermedius*, referring to it a plant from Delaware. Other collections of this species are from the tropics, and from Miss White's description the Delaware plants could readily be referred to *C. striatus*. For *C. rufipes* see discussion under *C. stercoreus*.

KEY TO THE SPECIES

Cups distinctly striate inside but not outside; spores 8.3–10.4 x 15–20.5μ..........*C. striatus* (p. 175)
Cups distinctly striate both inside and outside, at least after removal of the hairy surface; spores 11–20.3
    x 22–40μ...*C. Poeppigii* (p. 177)
Cups even inside
    Outer surface covered with matted, woolly hairs
        Mouth hardly if at all fimbriate
            Spores 11.4–14.8 x 15–18.5μ (8–10 x 10–14μ, Miss White); outer surface of cup dark
                chestnut brown.................................*C. rugispermus* (p. 178)
            Spores 18–29 x 20–31μ; outer surface of cup soiled drab to paler; cup very slender
                                     C. Lesueurii (p. 179)
            Spores larger, 18–30 x 22–35μ; outer surface of cup tawny to gray brown or paler
                                       C. stercoreus (p. 177)
        Mouth strongly fimbriate; spores very large, 25–35 x 27–48μ......*C. melanospermus* (p. 179)
    Outer surface comparatively smooth, with fine appressed hairs; spores 5–7.4 x 8.6–12μ
                                         C. vernicosus (p. 180)

Cyathus striatus Willd.

    Cyathia hirsuta (Schaeff.) White

Plates 98, 99 and 121

Plants long goblet-shaped, with a short stem, 8–12 mm. high and 6–8 mm. broad, growing on twigs, branches, dead leaves, etc., with the stem sometimes attached to the substratum by a dark cinnamon-brown mycelial pad, as in several other species; outer surface tawny when quite fresh, becoming more brown, the darker specimens dark brown (raw sienna), covered with coarse shaggy hairs, often obscurely or when the hairs are worn off distinctly striate above; inner surface variable in color, pale to nearly black, glabrous, shining, distinctly striate; mouth closed by a thin, pale, smooth epiphragm that breaks and withers away at maturity. Peridioles confined to lower half of the cup, 1.5–2 mm. in diameter, usually attached to the cup by a strong, very elastic cord. Tunica very thin (11–30μ), often absent in places, but usually obvious, so that the peridioles appear gray or silvery brown; composed of light brown, collapsed threads; black layer thin (about 20μ), dense; sclerotic layer 110–365μ thick, its cells vaguely outlined and not separable as units on crushing.

Spores (of No. 2432) scattered as usual in the central horny tissue, elliptic, hyaline, rather thick-walled, 8.3–12 x 15–22μ. When young the wall is very thick, becoming thinner as the spores mature. Basidia long-clavate, 6.8–7.8μ thick, with 4 sessile spores.

Not rare on dead wood and other vegetable matter. The young plants have rounded hairy tips, the peridium expanding above and the hairs seceding so as to expose the thin diaphragm only a little while before full maturity.

For cytological information by Maire covering this and other species, see under *Scleroderma aurantium*.

Illustrations: Bolton. Hist. Fungi Halifax 3: pl. 102, fig. 2 (as *Peziza striatus*).
Dufour. Atlas des Champ. Comest. et Vén., pl. 71, No. 160. 1891.
Eidam. l. c., pl. 10, figs. 1–22.
Fries, Th. C. E. Sveriges Gasteromyceter, fig. 34.
Gillet. Champ. Fr. (Gasteromycetes), pl. 1.
Hard. Mushrooms, fig. 441.
Hesse. l. c., pl. 13.
Hollos. l. c., pl. 28, figs. 7–10.
Michael. Führer f. Pilzfreunde 2: No. 206. 1918 (Second edition).
Micheli. Nova Plant Gen., pl. 102, fig. 2.
Murrill. Mycologia 3: pl. 40, fig. 11. 1911.
Nees von Esenbeck. Syst. Pilze. Schw., pl. 13, fig. 132 A-B.
Walker. l. c., pl. 4, figs. 34–48.
White. Bull. Torr. Bot. Club 29: pls. 14 and 18. 1902.

68. In ravine northeast of Tenney's on twigs, October 4, 1911.
2432. On top of a rock wall by President's house on twigs and leaves, July 26, 1916.
5280. Deciduous wood in Arboretum, July 5, 1922. Spores 9.3–10.4 x 15–20.5μ.
Also Nos. 2987, 5367, 5911.

Asheville. Beardslee.
Blowing Rock. On log of deciduous tree, Aug. 1922. Coker, coll. (U. N. C. Herb., No. 5590).
Buncombe Co. Standley and Bollman, coll. (U. S. Nat'l. Herb., as *Cyathia hirsuta*).
Haywood Co. On rotting leaves, Aug. 2, 1926. Totten, coll. (U. N. C. Herb.). Spores 8–9.5 x 12.5–17μ.

Alabama. Mobile. Mohr, coll. (U. S. Nat'l. Herb.).
Tennessee. Elizabethtown. Murrill, coll. (N. Y. Bot. Gard. Herb.).
Virginia. Peaks of Otter. Murrill, coll. (N. Y. Bot. Gard. Herb., no name).
Pennsylvania. Trexlertown. Lloyd, coll. (N. Y. Bot. Gard. Herb.).
Ohiopyle. Murrill, coll. (N. Y. Bot. Gard. Herb.). Spores elliptic, 7–9.3 x 11.5–20μ.
New York. Green Co. On twigs. Wilson, coll. (N. Y. Bot. Gard. Herb.).
Massachusetts. Davis, coll. (N. Y. Bot. Gard. Herb. and U. N. C. Herb.). Spores 9.2–11.2 x 13–15μ.
Ohio. Lloyd, coll. (N. Y. Bot. Gard. Herb.).

PLATE 98

CYATHUS RUGISPERMUS. No. 7489 [above].   Upper row dry; lower moistened
CYATHUS STRIATUS.   No. 5367   [below]

PLATE 99

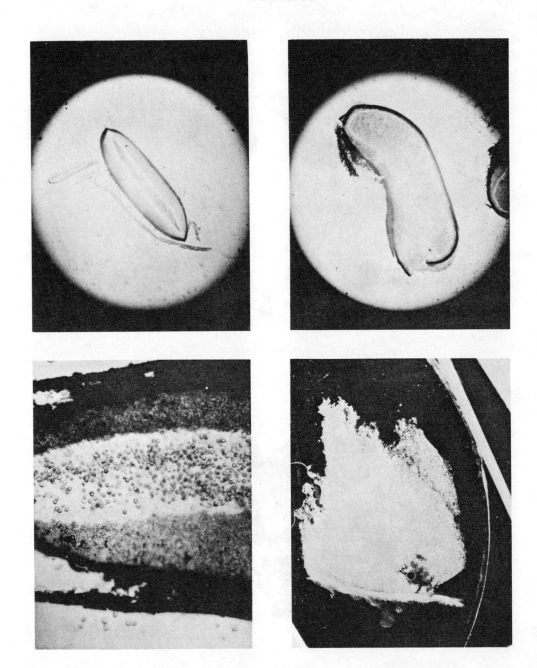

CRUCIBULUM VULGARE. No. 7462. × 70 [above]

CYATHUS STRIATUS. No. 5911. × 260 [below]

CYATHUS STRIATUS. No. 5590. × 70 [above]

DISCISEDA CANDIDA. No. 7507. × 6 [below]

Cyathus Poeppigii Tulasne

Plate 121

Cups 6–8 mm. high, goblet-shaped, the mouth up to 6 mm. wide, shrinking and crumpled when dry, dark brown (about sepia), felted and fibrous to shaggy; inner surface slate gray, shining, both surfaces strongly and closely striate-fluted in the upper half. Peridioles 1.6–2 mm. wide, flat, black, dull or a little shining, the funiculi conspicuous.
Spores short-elliptic, 11–20.3 x 22–40μ.

This species is easily distinguished from others of its group by its large spores and striated outer as well as inner surface. It is new to the United States, being known heretofore only from northern South America and the West Indies. There is at the New York Botanical Garden a collection of this marked "in bamboo pots" (Stevenson, coll.) with no other locality data given, but probably from the tropics. The spores are 18–37 x 22–55μ.

Illustrations: Lloyd. Myc. Works, pl. 105, figs. 1–5.
    Tulasne. Ann. Sci. Nat., 3rd ser., **1**: pl. 4, figs. 23–25; pl. 5, figs. 3–4. 1844.
    White. Bull. Torr. Bot. Club **29**: pl. 14, figs. 1–4. 1902.

Florida. Gainesville. On earth in a yard, July 1924. Couch, coll. (U. N. C. Herb., No. 7282).
St. Croix. A. E. Ricksecker, coll. (N. Y. B. G. Herb.).

Cyathus stercoreus (Schw.) De Toni
    Nidularia stercorea Schw.

Plates 100 and 121

Plants goblet-shaped, about 5–10 mm. high in our collections, almost sessile or with a short stalk, gregarious in large numbers and usually crowded so that a group of old plants looks very much like a wasp's nest; growing usually on manure or on earth where manure has been spread. The mycelium is rufous as in all other species we have seen except in *C. Lesueurii*, and it sometimes forms an obvious pad at the base of the cup. Outer surface tawny when young, then tan to buff or gray-brown, covered with thick, matted, woolly hairs, which with age become worn off, leaving the cups almost smooth; inner surface smooth, even (not striate), dark grayish brown to nearly black in age. On expanding above from the rounded, strigose stage of youth, the delicate epiphragm is exposed, only to break and disappear in a short time; mouth smooth, not fimbriate (the surface hairs that project above it soon after opening do not constitute a fimbriate mouth). Peridioles nearly black, without a tunica, 1.5–2.5 mm. in diameter, with a thick, hard wall, usually attached to the cup by funiculi, although often we find some of the upper peridioles in the cups which show no signs of a funiculus and which drop out of the cup when it is inverted (as noticed by Lloyd). Outer removable layer (tunica?) and denser layer below about 90–130μ thick; sclerotic layer about 37μ thick around the edge of the peridiole, about 165μ thick on the sides near the center.
Spores (of No. 39) almost hyaline, subglobose to oval, thick-walled, varying greatly in size, 18–30 x 22–35μ. Basidia (of No. 5916) club-shaped, distinctly swollen at the distal end, 9–12.5 x 28–44μ, bearing 4–8 sessile spores, only 2 or 3 of which mature. The spores may be attached to any part of the basidium, but are usually borne in a circle near the end. After the spores are formed the basidia collapse, finally leaving long threads among the spores, the layer just beneath the hymenium becoming sclerotic.

Not rare and often in large colonies on manured ground, dry manure, and much more rarely on decidedly rotten wood. In the large spores, the species approaches

C. melanospermus, but that has distinctly larger spores on the average, and a fimbriate mouth. Miss Andrews (l. c.) says that the spores of the type of *Nidularia stercorea* in Schweinitz's herbarium are 15.8–18.7μ, and thinks it perhaps the same as *C. Lesueurii* var. *minor* Tul. We find the spores of the type to be 16.5–22 x 18.5–27μ.

Illustrations: Andrews. l. c., pl. 17, figs. 2 and 6 (as *C. stercoreus*); figs. 1, 3, 5, and 7 (as *C. Lesueurii*).
    Hard. Mushrooms, fig. 443.
    Hollos. l. c., pl. 28, figs. 11–14.
    Lloyd. The Nidulariaceae, pl. 108.
    Marshall. Mushroom Book, pl. opposite p. 130 (in error as *C. vernicosus*).
    White. Bull. Torr. Bot. Club 29: pl. 15, figs. 17–20 and pl. 16, figs. 1, 2. 1902.

    39. On heavily manured ground in Arboretum, Nov. 4, 1908.
5916. On soil in pasture, Nov. 21, 1922.
7516. On rotten place in a live sugar maple, Sept. 23, 1924. Spores 22–30 x 27–35μ. This is just like
        plant on manure except in habitat.
Also Nos. 97, 377, 5417, 7494.

    Asheville. Beardslee.
    Linville Falls. Coker and party, No. 5728. On cow manure, August 24, 1922.
    Haywood Co. On sawdust by Crawford's Creek, Aug. 2, 1926. (U. N. C. Herb.)

Florida. Couch, coll. (U. N. C. Herb., No. 7284). Spores 24–32 x 28–36μ. Several of these plants
        had an obvious brown pad at the base.
Alabama. Auburn. Earle, coll. (N. Y. B. G. Herb.).
Mississippi. Underwood, coll. (N. Y. B. G. Herb.).
Virginia. Blacksburg. Murrill, coll. (N. Y. B. G. Herb.).
District of Columbia. Cook, coll. (U. S. Nat'l. Herb.).
New Jersey. (Schw. Herb.).
    Newfield. Ellis, coll. (N. Y. B. G. Herb.).
New York. Bronx Park. Murrill, coll. (N. Y. B. G. Herb.).
Ohio. Lloyd, coll. (N. Y. B. G. Herb.).
Illinois. Urbana. McDougall, coll. (U. N. C. Herb.). Spores 20–30 x 25–35μ.

Cyathus rugispermus (Schw.) De Toni

Plates 98 and 121

Cups short goblet-shaped, about 4–5 mm. high and up to 8 mm. broad, the mouth in youth convex, at maturity not flaring or fimbriate except that the outer spongy layer projects a little farther than the inner layer and is minutely eroded; base narrow the light brown mycelium holding firmly to a bit of earth; outer surface deep chestnut brown, felted-tomentose to moderately strigose; inner surface deep brown, shining, not at all striate. Peridioles 1.6–2 mm. wide, smooth, black, shining, not concave below, the funiculi represented only by a little central plug at the time found. Spores (of No. 7458) smooth, oval, thick-walled, 11.4–14.8 x 15–18.5μ, borne as usual in the genus.

While the spores of our plants run larger than in the type, as given by Miss White, other characters seem to fit well except for the darker outer surface of the former. The species is near *C. stercoreus*, and Lloyd thinks they are the same. In all of our collections of *C. stercoreus* the spores, though variable, run much larger than in the present species. Lloyd finds the spores of Japanese specimens to run as low as 16–24μ, while for American plants he gives the spores as 30–40μ. On account of the different habitat and smaller spores, we are for the present retaining *C. rugispermus* as a species. *Cyathus rugispermus* has been known only from the original collection in Pennsylvania.

Illustrations. White. l. c., pl. 16, figs. 3–6.

5911. On bank of branch, Nov. 20, 1922. Spores 11–14 x 14–18.5μ.
7458. On bare red clay soil by road, July 20, 1924.
7489. On sticks and bare clay, Aug. 8, 1924. Spores 11.2–15 x 15–21μ.

Cyathus Lesueurii Tul.

Plate 123

Plants very slender, about 6–8 mm. high and 3.5 mm. broad at the top, brownish drab below, dull gray above; upper part fibrous to strigose, lower part felted; mouth surrounded by long, scattered hairs. Inner surface smooth, blackish brown. Base without a pad, but the concolorous mycelium holding a ball of earth. Peridioles about 1.7 mm. broad, very thin, nearly black.

Spores (of No. 7281) subspherical, very large, 18–29 x 20–31μ.

Gregarious to crowded in fine, sandy soil. This seems to agree prefectly with *C. Lesueurii* except that the plants are not quite so large and grow on poor soil without obvious humus. The shape, however, is more that of the typical form than of the variety *minor*. Both Miss White and Lloyd, as well as Hollos, consider *C. Lesueurii* var. *minor* as a synonym of *C. stercoreus*, and in this seem certainly correct. The first two authors also consider *C. Lesueurii* as indistinguishable from *C. stercoreus*, and they are probably right in this also in so far that intermediates occur. As the present plants grew on sand, are more slender than in *C. stercoreus*, and have a peculiar appearance, we think it well to retain the name for the present.

Tulasne gives the spores of the variety, which he describes from "Carolina," as 17.5–19.8 x 22.3μ.

Illustrations: Tulasne. l. c., pl. 5, figs. 5–10.

Florida. In poor sandy soil by roadside (no obvious manure). Couch, coll. (U. N. C. Herb., No. 7281).

Cyathus melanospermus (Schw.) De Toni

Plates 100 and 122

Cups gregarious or crowded, distinctly infundibuliform, or sometimes somewhat long-campanulate, 9–12 mm. high by 6–8 mm. broad at the mouth, which is slightly flaring; outer surface shaggy-hairy, the hairs collapsing and largely disappearing on long exposure; color in our plants which are old, dark brown, about Mars brown of Ridgway, in some with a slight tint of purple; inner surface even, smooth, and about the same color as the outside. Mouth straight and distinctly fimbriate. Peridioles 1.8–2.3 mm. in diameter, almost black, with a rather thick outer layer of coarse, dark brown fibrils with dark granules between. When wet this coat is easily torn off with a needle, and underneath is a thin, dark, hard layer of densely packed threads and granules. Inside this is the much thicker layer of pale sclerotic cells and within this is the hymenium which is recognizable only in the young condition. The rather ample "cavity" in the center is filled with the immense spores lying in a horny (when dry), hyaline matrix formed of greatly gelatinized threads. Funiculus large, strong, and very elastic.

Spores hyaline, round to short-oval, very large and varying greatly in size, 24–35 x 28–48µ, some with very thick walls, 3–4µ thick.

The extremely large average size of the spores of this species is supposed to distinguish it from others of its group, and in our collection as well as in the type they do run larger than in *C. stercoreus*. The average length of ten spores of our No. 23 measured as one came to them was 34µ, while ten of *C. stercoreus* measured in the same way was 24.9µ.

The types in the Schweinitz Herbarium are a good lot of 16 plants densely set together, shape and appearance about as in *C. stercoreus*. The only egg well seen was smooth and black; spores subspherical to oval, 20–31 x 26–38µ, which is very little larger than in *C. stercoreus*. Miss White gives the spores of the type as 45–55 x 18–45µ. Lloyd considers the species as a synonym of *C. stercoreus* and says he "can find no difference in the general size of the spores from the type material of *C. stercoreus* and *C. melanospermus*. While in the latter there are many large spores, there are also small ones and some we note measure not over 20 mic." The distinctly fimbriate mouth in our No. 23 is probably of no specific importance, and in the type the mouth is smooth or slightly fimbriate. While we retain the species at present, Lloyd is probably right in regarding it as a form of *C. stercoreus*.

Illustrations: White. Bull. Torr. Bot. Club 29: pl. 15, figs. 1–4. 1902.

23. On soil and old male cones under pine trees, fall of 1908.

Asheville.   Beardslee.

Pennsylvania.   Bethlehem.   (Schw. Herb., types, and Curtis Herb. from Schw. Herb.)

Cyathus vernicosus De Candolle
  Cyathus olla (Batsch) Pers.
  Cyathia lentifera (L.) White
  Nidularia fascicularia Schw.

Plates 100 and 122

Cups long, goblet-shaped, or bell-shaped, 8–12 mm. high by 7–10 mm. broad at the moderately or widely flaring mouth. Outer surface when young tomentose spongy with appressed hairs, becoming nearly smooth in age; color when young brown to tawny, later becoming paler (grayish brown to dull gray); inner surface even, smooth, dark grayish brown to silvery brown. Mouth even, flaring, incurved and depressed when young. Peridioles large, disc-shaped, averaging about 2–3 mm. in diameter, about 0.5 mm. thick in center, concave above, convex below, attached to the cup by large, strong, whitish funiculi.
Spores (of No. 1688) hyaline, ovate to ovate-elliptic, 5–7.4 x 8.6–12µ.

Wall of the peridium composed as usual of a dark outer region of three parts: a surface layer (tunica?) about 20µ thick and composed of light brown filaments, mostly collapsed; a loose median area of many cavities and scattered, nearly hyaline, thick-walled filaments and numerous granules; an inner black layer about 37µ thick, composed of dark brown, thick-walled, densely packed threads and numerous granules. The pale, sclerotic, horny layer beneath is of the usual structure.

PLATE 100

Cyathus vernicosus. No. 1688 [above]
Cyathus melanospermus. No. 23 [center]
Cyathus stercoreus. No. 39 [below]

PLATE 101

CRUCIBULUM VULGARE. No. 3865

This plant is distinguished from all our other species by its smaller spores. We have studied the type of *Nidularia fascicularia* and find the spores to be oval, 6.5–8 x 8.5–12μ.

Illustrations: Andrews. l. c., pl. 17, figs. 4 and 8.
    Fries, Th. C. E. Sveriges Gasteromyceter, fig. 35 (as *C. olla*).
    Hard. Mushrooms, fig. 442.
    Lloyd. The Nidulariaceae, pl. 110, figs. 1–4. 1906.
    White. Bull. Torr. Bot. Club **29**: pl. 15, figs. 8–13. 1902.

1688. On soil under cedars in Arboretum, September 7, 1915.

    Asheville. Beardslee.

Tennessee. Elizabethtown. Murrill, coll. (N. Y. B. G. Herb.).
New York. Westchester Co. Howe, coll. (N. Y. B. G. Herb.).
Wisconsin. Madison. (U. N. C. Herb. and Univ. of Wis. Herb.) Spores 6–8 x 9–11.5μ.

CRUCIBULUM Tul.

    Plants cup-shaped or bell-shaped, sessile, gregarious on twigs and trash in general or on the bark of logs, or rarely on living trees. Wall composed of a single thick layer which in youth is velvety-tomentose externally, becoming almost smooth with age. Inside of the cup covered with a thin, pale lining and without striations; the mouth in youth covered with a thick, soft veil or epiphragm which disappears with maturity. Peridioles numerous, almost filling the cup and attached to it by simple funiculi. Tunica thick, white and quite conspicuous. The basidia forming a distinct and closely packed hymenium surrounding a narrow central area which at maturity becomes densely filled with spores. All the cells of the hymenium then become very thick-walled and fuse together into a solid, hyaline, subhorny tissue, which seems almost structureless under low power. The spores are not embedded in cellular tissue, but stick together by their surfaces and do not fall out when exposed. This organization of the fertile part of the peridiole is quite different from that in *Cyathus*, which see.

    There is but one species in the genus.

Crucibulum vulgare Tul.
    C. crucibuliforme (Scop.) White
    Nidularia Juglandicola Schw.

Plates 61, 99, 101 and 122

    Plants bell-shaped or cup-shaped, sessile, varying greatly in size, even in the same collection, from 3–7 mm. high by 4–8 mm. broad at top, but not so crowded as *Cyathus stercoreus*, growing on trash or twigs of various kinds, bark of decaying logs, or even on the bark of living trees; when young covered with an ochraceous tawny, velvety tomentum (much less coarse and shaggy than in *Cyathus stercoreus*), then becoming almost smooth, brownish, light tan or grayish with age. Inside of the cup smooth and sometimes shiny, and usually silvery gray to white. The epiphragm, which closes the cup until maturity, consists of two layers, the outer one felted-tomentose, colored like the cup, and made up of short, thick hairs with many short, stubby branches; the inner layer white and made up of an interwoven mass of slender, much branched filaments. In withering, the outer felted layer of the epiphragm sloughs off first, leaving the very thin layer which soon also tears and withers away. The peridioles are lenticular in shape, 1–2 mm. in diameter, attached to the cup by cords and covered with a rather thick white tunica which frequently ruptures.   Under the tunica is the thin black layer composed of slender filamentous dark brown cells mixed with a large amount of granular, amorphous material.   Beneath this is a thicker layer (95–115μ) composed of hyaline, thick-walled, sclerotic cells, hard and horny when dry but much softer when soaked for several hours.   Next comes the hymenium which is peculiar in that the old basidia and intermediate cells also become thick and sclerotic after spore formation (see fig. by Sachs, l. c., and our fig. 8).   The funiculus is composed of a delicate fascicle of long, thick-walled, hyaline threads which are rarely branched, and which have at intervals peculiar joints.   At maturity many of the funiculi may have disappeared, and the peridioles be held in only by a small amount of mucus.

Spores (of No. 647) hyaline, elliptic or oval-elliptic, and varying greatly in size, 3.5–5.5 x 4.3–8.6μ.   Basidia (of No. 5277) long-clavate, about 3.7μ thick at the swollen tip, with 2–4 spores on distinct, slender sterigmata.

A very common and widely distributed plant, growing on wood, twigs and other vegetable matter.   Referring to Lloyd's remark that it rarely if ever occurs on large logs, we have several collections from the bark of logs and living trees (Nos. 35, 1534, 2904, 2986 and 2987a).   One collection (No. 2904) is on sound bark from a large hickory log.   The cups of this collection are a little larger than the average, but agree in other respects.   Lloyd has seen the type of *C. fimetarius* DC. and considers it the same as *Crucibulum vulgare* (Myc. Notes, p. 291).

Illustrations: Eidam. l, c., pl. 10, figs. 23–30.
    Fries, Th. C. E.   Sveriges Gasteromyceter, fig. 33.
    Hard.   Mushrooms, fig. 444.
    Hollos.   l. c., pl. 28, figs. 23–26.
    Lloyd.   The Nidulariaceae, pl. 104.   1906.
    Lloyd.   Photogravure of Am. Fungi, No. 7.
    Micheli.   Nova Plant. Gen., pl. 102, fig. 3.
    Michael.   Führer f. Pilzfreunde **2**: No. 205.   1918 (2nd ed.).
    Murrill.   Mycologia **3**: pl. 40, fig. 12.   1911.
    Nees von Esenbeck.   Syst. Pilze Schw., pl. 13, fig. 133A-B.
    Sachs.   l. c., pls. 13, 14.
    Sturm.   Deutsch. Fl. Pilze **1**: pl. 23 (as *Cyathus crucibulum*).   1814.
    Walker.   l. c., pls. 5, 6.
    White.   l. c., pl. 16, figs. 10–15; pl. 18, figs. 7–13 and 16.

  35.   On dead bark of a live cedar tree about 2–3 feet from ground in Battle's Park, Jan. 15, 1909.
  647.   On pile of trash, Oct. 21, 1912.
2904.   On sound bark of hickory log, Oct. 10, 1917.   Spores 4–6.5 x 6.5–10μ.
7440.   On frondose twigs in Arboretum, July 20, 1924.
Also Nos. 67, 1534, 2986, 2987a, 3375, 3865, 5277.

    Salem.   (Schw. Herb., as *N. crucibulum*.)
    Asheville.   Beardslee.
    Pink Bed Valley.   Murrill and House, colls. (N. Y. B. G. Herb.).
    Blowing Rock.   Coker.   No. 5711.
    Waynesville.   Standley, coll. (U. S. Nat'l. Herb.).

Alabama.   Auburn.   Earle, coll. (N. Y. B. G. Herb.).
Virginia.   Mountain Lake.   Murrill, coll. (N. Y. B. G. Herb.).
Pennsylvania.   Bethlehem.   (Schw. Herb., as type of *N. Juglandicola*, and as *N. crucibulum*.)
    Ohiopyle.   Ricker, coll. (U. S. Nat'l. Herb.).
New York.   Murrill, coll. (N. Y. B. G. Herb.).

Ohio. Lima. Dawson, coll. (N. Y. B. G. Herb.).
Illinois. Urbana. McDougall, coll. (U. N. C. Herb.).
Wyoming. Pitchfork. (U. N. C. Herb.)
Washington. Langley. Grant, coll. (U. N. C. Herb.).
Also from many other states in N. Y. B. G. Herb. and U. S. Nat'l. Herb.

New Zealand. Wellington. Atkinson, coll. (U. N. C. Herb. from Cunningham Herb.). Spores smooth, oval-elliptic, 3.7–5 x 6.8–9μ.

NIDULARIA Fries

Plants subglobose, the peridium wall of one layer and without an epiphram, not opening regularly or forming a perfect cup, but thin and fragile and breaking up irregularly, leaving the peridioles in an exposed pile on the substratum. Peridioles (in our species) dark brown to reddish brown, shining, not attached by cords to the peridium wall, but embedded in a mucus when fresh, the mucus drying down and sticking the peridioles together after exposure.

Miss White uses the name *Granularia* Roth, but, as Fries and Tulasne use *Nidularia* and the latter clearly defines the genus as now used we retain the latter name. Both names antedate Persoon.

KEY TO THE SPECIES

Plants minute, sporangioles less than half mm. broad.................................*N. castanea*
Plants larger, sporangioles more than a half mm. broad.............................*N. pulvinata*

Nidularia pulvinata (Schw.) Fries
  Granularia pulvinata (Schw.) Kuntze
  Granularia pisiformis Roth
  Nidularia pisiformis (Roth) Zell.
  Nidularia alabamensis Atk.
  Nidularia globosa (Ehr.) Fr.

Plate 122

Plants subglobose, small, up to about 6 mm. thick in specimen seen, surface cinnamon brown, covered with a felted and somewhat powdery tomentum; peridium excluding the tomentum only one layer thick, that is, there is no thin inner layer that is stretched over the top as a diaphram before opening. Peridioles small, flattened, only up to 0.8 mm. wide, dark brown, wrinkled when dry, densely packed, destitute of a funiculus or other attachment to the wall, but embedded in a mucus when fresh and damp and lightly stuck together by this mucus when dry. The surface of the plants may be nodulated from the pressure of the peridioles within. After maturity the peridium ruptures irregularly and does not form a perfect cup as in the other genera.
Spores (of No. 7588) ovate to subelliptic, hyaline, smooth, 4.2–5.5 x 6–7.4μ, mixed with irregular, branched and nodulated, thick-walled cells. Basidia 4-spored (Maire, Comp. Rend. **131** (2): 1248. 1900; as *N. globosa*).

A rare plant but widely distributed, growing gregariously on wood. It was first described under this species name from North Carolina, but Lloyd is probably right in thinking it the same as *N. pisiformis* of Europe, which has also been described under many other names. We have examined the type of *Nidularia alabamensis* and find that it agrees in all respects with *N. pulvinata*. The spores are oval with one end distinctly pointed, 4–5.5 x 5–7.4μ.

For a long list of supposed synonyms, see Lloyd, l. c., p. 8. For other cytological information by Maire covering this and other species see under *Scleroderma aurantium.*

Illustrations: Fries, Th. C. E.   Sveriges Gasteromyceter, fig. 32 (as *N. pisiformis*).
Lloyd.   Myc. Works, pl. 102 (as *N. pisiformis*).
Massee.   l. c., fig. 37 (as *N. pisiformis*) and fig. 81 (as *N. confluens*).
White.   l. c., pl. 17, figs. 10–16, 20; pl. 18, fig. 19 (as *Granularia pulvinata*).

7588.   On old pine board fence near the power house, Feb. 4, 1925.

North Carolina.   Asheville.   Beardslee, coll.   On old logs.   (U. N. C. Herb.)
Alabama.   Peters, coll. (Curtis Herb.).
Auburn.   (N. Y. B. G. Herb., as type of *N. alabamensis*.)
Louisiana.   Langlois, coll.   On a decaying pine log.   (N. Y. B. G. Herb.)
New York.   Arkville.   Murrill, coll. (N. Y. B. G. Herb.).
West Park.   Earle, coll. (N. Y. B. G. Herb. and U. N. C. Herb.).   Spores oval, 4–5.5 x 5.5–7.5μ.
Connecticut.   Litchfield.   White, coll. (N. Y. B. G. Herb.).
Maine.   Piscataquis Co.   Murrill, coll. (N. Y. B. G. Herb.).

Nidularia castanea Ell. & Ev.
Granularia castanea (Ell. & Ev.) White

Plate 122

This interesting little plant, remarkable for its minute size, is known only from the original locality.   Careful search would probably discover it in other parts of the Atlantic seaboard.   The types at New York have been studied and agree well with Miss White's description.   The peridioles as we find them, are dark reddish brown, not "yellowish brown," and the spores are 4.5–7 x 6–9μ.

We take the following from Miss White (l. c., p. 276):

"Peridia small, elongate-globose, or subspherical, sessile, sometimes confluent, 0.5–2 mm. long, 0.5–1 mm. high; peridial walls very thin, and brittle at first, pale yellowish fawn-colored, gradually as the plant matures becoming grayish, and somewhat tuberculose from the inner pressure of the sporangioles, dehiscing irregularly, the outer covering often breaking away completely, leaving the sporangioles seated alone on the wood, barely visible without magnification; sporangioles yellowish brown, very numerous, crowded, circular, flattened above and below, barely 0.25 mm. in diameter, even or slightly creased under high magnification; spores subglobose, hyaline, thick-walled, 4–7μ long, 3–6μ wide.

"Gregarious on wood."

Illustrations: White.   Bull. Torr. Bot. Club 29: pl. 17, figs. 17–19; pl. 18, fig. 20.   1902.

New Jersey.   Newfield.   Ellis, coll.   July 1883.   (N. Y. B. G. Herb. Types.)

CALOSTOMATACEAE

Fruit body hypogean or partly so until maturity, attached by obvious basal strands; with or without a stalk. Peridium highly specialized and formed of several layers. Gleba without cavities or organized hymenium, separated into small blocks by delicate tramal plates or strands. Capillitium or its rudiments arising from the whole inner surface of the inner peridium. Basidia irregularly arranged, stout, club-shaped, bearing several, usually more than 4, spores irregularly scattered and sessile around its surface. Spore powder dry and escaping by an apical mouth.

ASTRAEUS Morgan

This genus, formerly included in *Geaster* and of the same general appearance, was established by Morgan on the following essential differences: no open chambers and therefore no organized hymenium; threads of the capillitium long, much branched and interwoven, scarcely different from the elemental hyphae of the peridium and continuous with them, in these respects agreeing with *Tylostoma*; columella entirely lacking; spores much larger than in any *Geaster*. The hygroscopic character of the rays is very marked, as is their hard and woody texture when dry.

There is but one species known.

Morgan and Burnap call attention to the apparent relationship of this genus to *Tylostoma* and *Calostoma* and Fischer puts it in the Calostomataceae, in which he has been followed by others. We are following this precedent, although it is far from clear that it belongs here rather than in the Tylostomataceae. It seems to us that it would be better to establish another family for it, as its presence in any recognized one makes the definition of that family awkward and unsatisfactory. Fischer's definition of the Calostomataceae includes the statement that the capillitium is well developed. This is not true of *Calostoma*, in which the rudimentary "capillitium" disappears entirely before maturity (see p. 189). Relationship to *Calostoma* is shown mainly in the organization of the gleba into stuffed areas and the stout basidia with a varying number of scattered, partly lateral spores, and the highly complex organization of the coats. Its relationship to *Tylostoma* is indicated by the absence of open chambers, the basidia and spore characters, though the latter has only 4 spores, and by the highly developed capillitium, which arises from the entire inner surface of the peridium.

Astraeus hygrometricus (Pers.) Morg.
Geaster hygrometricus Pers.
Geastrum fibrillosum Schw.
Geaster stellatus Scop.
Astraeus stellatus (Scop.) Fisch.

Plates 31, 77, 115 and 117

Plants of small to medium size, growing in colonies just beneath the soil or partially exposed, arising from a group of black, hairlike, basal rhizomorphs. Outer peridium thick and composed of several distinct layers (see below); surface hard, smooth (except when very fresh or very old), at maturity splitting into six to many rays which expand or recurve when wet and fold in again when dry, the inner layer soon becoming much cracked.   Inner peridium pliable, thin, sessile, depressed-globose, about 1.2–3 cm. broad, surface felted and when in good condition reticulate with fibrous lines, whitish, becoming gray or brownish, opening by an irregularly torn mouth which is without a defined peristome.   In the fresh condition the plant is tasteless and odorless.   Gleba pure white in youth, divided up into very small, more or less box-like regions by very thin tramal plates, each chamber closely packed with the fertile, practically homogeneous tissue; this mass being made up of branching threads and small fibers bearing more or less grape-like clusters of nearly spherical basidia, which are crowded amongst each other, leaving only small unoccupied spaces here and there.

Spores 4–8 to a basidium, sessile on its top and sides, reddish brown, globose, distinctly tuberculate, 7.4–10.8μ thick including the warts.   Basidia irregularly arranged in long strings of clusters, subspherical with a stalk, 11–15.5 x 18–24μ.   Capillitium threads arising from the entire inner surface of the peridium, including the base, very pale, long, interwoven, branched, 3–5.5μ thick, smooth or encrusted with granules and without any obvious tapering terminals; walls very thick, so as to leave no lumen in many places; no cross walls obvious.

The plant is very persistent.   Ripening in the fall, it may be found in good condition through the winter and spring and the shape is retained for more than a year of exposure.   Like many Geasters, it is loosened from the soil on expanding and may be rolled about by the wind when dry, the outer layer of the rays slowly wearing away in thin flakes.   The range and adaptability of the species is astonishing.   It is apparently world wide in distribution and almost universal in habitat.   Scores may be picked up on a short walk among the sand dunes of the seashore, and it is among the commonest fungi of the high mountains.   We know of no other plant of which this can be said, not even the fern *Pteris*.

In a fresh button practically fully grown but still with white gleba, a section shows the following characters: a very thin outer flocculent layer of delicate, loosely woven fibers, which as the plant approaches maturity or is exposed, collapses almost to invisibility and soon wears away; next a strong fibrous layer about 1 mm. thick, brownish toward the surface, whitish inward; next the horny layer which in immature buttons is very thin but thickens toward maturity to about 0.5–0.7 mm., translucent cartilage color and sharply contrasting; next a soft, pure white layer which is thickest of all (about 1.5–1.8 mm.), which splits in the middle at maturity and collapses down to a thin, scurfy layer on the inside of the rays and the softly felted, irregularly reticulated layer on the surface of the spore sac.   Under the microscope it can be seen that the outer part of this layer which goes to the rays is denser, firmer, composed of fibers running parallel to the surface which in the central region turn inward and become more loosely woven.   At the point where the turn is made the splitting takes place.   The part remaining on the rays forms very thin reddish flakes that soon fall off.   The innermost layer is very thin (about 0.1 mm.), translucent white, fibrous and tough; basal attachment of the spore sac 1.5 cm. wide, distinctly limited by the extent of the fleshy layer.   At the base all distinct layers disappear into a homogeneous white tissue which is about 0.7–1.5 cm. wide.   While the plant is often entirely subterranean until dehiscence, the mycelial attachment is confined to a basal disk one cm. or more broad, from which rather numerous, small dark fibrils extend into the soil.   These are very easily broken off, and after dehiscence they are usually represented only by dark collapsed lines over the region of attachment, giving this part a roughish appearance.

Microscopic structure of the peridia is as follows: the outer fibrous layer is composed of small and densely packed threads, which in the outer region run parallel to the surface and curving through a right angle continue through the horny layer perpendicular to the surface. In this last layer the threads are straight, almost perfectly parallel to each other and very densely packed; continuing into the spongy layer they at once become looser and much more entangled. The thin inner layer of the spore sac is not very different from the spongy layer, and from its surface the threads composing it pass into the gleba without obvious change to form the capillitium.

Maire makes the peculiar statement that the basidia are terminated by a "sort of single compound sterigma at the top of which the spores are borne on very short pedicels." He gets the number of spores right. Tulasne gives the basidial shape right, but the number of spores as four. As they are of considerable interest, we quote below in full Maire's observations on this species (Comp. Rend. 131 (2): 1248. 1900):

"*Geaster hygrometricus* shows basidia with 2–8 spores. The fusion nucleus undergoes two successive divisions; sometimes the divisions stop there, and there are formed 4 spores, each of which receives a nucleus. At other times one or two of the 4 nuclei divided again, from which result 5 spores and 5 nuclei or 6 spores and 6 nuclei; often the 4 nuclei divide and there result 8 spores and 8 nuclei. Sometimes the nucleus of the basidium undergoes only one division, whence two nuclei and two spores. The most usual case seems to be the 6-spored basidium. On the other hand, the formation of the spores is, up to a certain point, independent of that of the nuclei: it happens, for example, that a basidium having only 4 nuclei forms 5 spores, etc. These processes are very variable, quite as in the basidia of the Cantharellaceae which we are studying at this time. However that may be, in *Geaster*, the formation of the spores always takes place in the following manner: at the tip of the basidium is sent out a single prolongation, a sort of compound sterigma, at the summit of which the spores are formed on very short pedicels. The nuclei, of definite number, are drawn all together into the compound sterigma, to be separated afterwards, each in its spore. In *Geaster*, the centrosomes and the kinoplasm are scarcely visible."

For other cytological information by Maire, covering this and other species, see under *Scleroderma aurantium*.

Up to the present the attachment of this plant to the soil has been completely misunderstood. This is hard to understand as the basal rhizomorphs are so conspicuous. DeBary's figure (Fungi, Myc. and Bact., fig. 146) shows no basal attachment and he says the button is attached to a felted mycelium which often spreads in the soil for the distance of an inch all around. This description completely reverses the facts and the error has never been corrected. The delicate flocculence of the surface of the buttons is so little connected with the soil that they come up almost clean. This is entirely different from the intimate attachment to the soil of the mycelial surface layer of hypogeal Geasters. It will be noted that this is an additional character pointing to a relationship with *Calostoma* and *Tylostoma*.

We have examined the type of *Geastrum fibrillosum* in the Schweinitz Herbarium, and find that it is, as Lloyd says (Geastrae, p. 10), a weathered specimen of this species. It is the flaky roughness of the outer surface that Schweinitz referred to in his name, not the felted reticulations of the inner peridium, as stated by Lloyd. The spores of this specimen are roughened, 7.4–10µ thick. *Lycoperdon recolligens* Woodward (Trans. Linn. Soc. **2:** 58. 1794) seems to include both the present species and *Geaster mammosus*. He refers to Schmidel's plates 27 and 28 which are of *A. hygrometricus*.

Illustrations: Destrée. Cited on p. 104, pl. 10, fig. B.
    Hard. Mushrooms, fig. 483.
    Hollos. l. c., pl. 10, figs. 26–29.
    Marshall. Mushroom Book, pl. opposite p. 130.
    Michael. Führer f. Pilzfreunde 2: No. 204. 1918 (2nd ed.).
    Micheli. Nova Plant. Gen, pl. 100, fig. 6.
    Morgan. Journ. Cin. Soc. Nat. Hist. **12:** pl. 2, figs. 8–11; Amer. Nat. **18:** fig. 12.
    Nees von Esenbeck. Syst. Pilze Schw., pl. 12, fig. 127.
    Petri. Flora Ital. Crypt. (Gasterales), Fasc. **5:** figs. 80–82. 1909.
    Rea. Trans. Brit. Myc. Soc. **3:** pl. 17. 1912.
    Schmidel. Icon. Plant., pls. 27 and 28, figs. 19–31. 1793.
    Vittadini. Monog. Lycoperd., pl. 1, fig. 8. 1842.

   73. Mixed woods with cedars, Oct. 11, 1911.
  673, 685. Old collections (Chapel Hill). No data.
7237. Underground in open, sandy field, Jan. 14, 1923.
7441. Sandy soil in woods, July 19, 1924.

    Smith Island. Sandy soil, April 1918. Couch and Grant, colls. (U. N. C. Herb., No. 3007).
        Spores 7.7–9.3µ.
    Blowing Rock. Coker and party, Aug. 1922. Nos. 5786 and 5823.
    Pink Bed Valley. Murrill and House, No. 400. July 1908. (N. Y. Bot. Gard. Herb.).

South Carolina. Ravenel. Fung. Car. Exs. No. 75. (Philadelphia Academy.)
    North Island. Coker and party, colls. (U. N. C. Herb.). Plentiful among the sand dunes.
Florida. Alachua Co. Couch, coll. (U. N. C. Herb., No. 7301).

CALOSTOMA Desv.

    Young fruit bodies formed just beneath the surface and basally attached; at maturity pushed by the elongation of the very peculiar stalk which is composed of a large number of anastomosing, firmly gelatinous strands woven together to make a spongy, more or less cylindrical column. Before elongation the entire plant is enclosed in a gelatinous layer called the volva by Burnap which at maturity becomes so watery as to fall away, exposing the spore-bearing head. This is subspherical and is composed of the outer peridium, the inner peridium, and the spore sac. The former is composed of two layers, an outer thicker one which is much like the stalk in structure and in most species becomes strongly or moderately gelatinized, and a thinner, denser inner layer which does not gelatinize. This exoperidium breaks into pieces after the plant emerges and falls off completely or in part, exposing the thin, dense, tough, and, when dry, hard and horny inner peridium which remains inflated and is very permanent. On the top of the inner peridium are elevated folds, like a puckered mouth, arranged in a more or less radiating way into several lobes which open down their centers by narrow slits leading into the spore sac within. This chamber is formed from the thin, soft and papery innermost layer of the inner peridium which is at first in contact with the next outer layer, but which soon begins to dry and contract away from the adjoining layer except above, and gradually getting smaller while hanging pendent within the firmer outer case it forces the dry spores and fragmentary remains of the accompanying fibers out of the slits for dispersal. The gleba when young has a lobulated appearance and is composed of solid masses of fertile hyphae with the basidia borne irregularly

PLATE 102

CALOSTOMA CINNABARINA. No. 5521 [right]; No. 5615 [left]

PLATE 103

throughout; between these masses run loosely woven fascicles or plates of branched threads with broad annular thickenings that are not obviously connected with the fertile hyphae and which entirely disappear before the maturity of the spores (Burnap, p. 183). Basidia ovate or pyriform or short-clavate, irregularly arranged throughout the fertile tissue. Spores sessile, variable in number (5–12), irregularly placed on both ends and sides of the basidia (Burnap, p. 185), oblong-elliptic to globose, walls usually pitted.

This peculiar genus is complex in structure and very striking in appearance.

The ephemeral threads with annular thickenings suggest a capillitium and are almost certainly homologous to it. They are so-called by Fischer, but it seems best to us to reserve this term for the threads found in mature fruit bodies. To say, as he does, that *Calostoma* possesses a well developed capillitium is misleading. In the youngest plant we have (*C. cinnabarina*) which is unexpanded but with spores about mature there are only a few detached fragments of this earlier system. These fragments show much narrower thickenings than those shown by Burnap.

Rev. Edward Hitchcock has published a non-technical article under the head of Physiology of *Gyropodium coccineum* (Amer. Journ. Sci. and Arts **9**: 56, pl. 3. 1825), describing a *Calostoma*. He speaks of the genus and species as recently established by Schweinitz, but the latter does not seem ever to have published this name, as noted by Hitchcock farther on. It does not seem to be known how Hitchcock got the name from Schweinitz. The species he described is doubtful. Burnap thinks it *C. cinnabarina;* Saccardo, *lutescens*.

Mitremyces Nees is the same as *Calostoma*.

LITERATURE

Atkinson. A New Species of *Calostoma*. Journ. Myc. **9**: 14. 1903.
Burnap. Notes on the Genus *Calostoma*. Bot. Gaz. **23**: 180, pl. 19. 1897.
Fischer, in Engler and Prantl. Pflanzenfamilien **1¹**: 339, fig. 177. 1900.
Lloyd. Myc. Notes, p. 123, pls. 8 and 9. 1903.
Lloyd. The Genus *Mitremyces*. Myc. Notes, p. 238, pls. 68 and 69. 1905.
Massee. A Monograph of the Genus *Calostoma*. Ann. Bot. **2**: 25, pl. 3. 1888.
Morgan. Journ. Cin. Soc. Nat. Hist. **12**: 20, pl. 2A. 1889.
Webster. Notes on *Calostoma*. Rhodora **1**: 30. 1899.

KEY TO THE SPECIES

Spores 3.5–5 x 6–10...*C. microsporum* (p. 192)
Spores larger
    Spores elliptic; exoperidium on dehiscing falling away entirely, the outer part forming a thick soft jelly; entire inner surface of the exoperidium and outer surface of the endoperidium bright red when fresh...*C. cinnabarina* (p. 189)
    Spores elliptic (a few may be spherical); exoperidium not gelatinous, the inner layer remaining as scales on the endoperidium; red color confined to the mouth region. *C. Ravenelii* (p. 191)
    Spores spherical; exoperidium composed of a firmly gelatinous (not watery) outer layer and a corky inner layer, on dehiscing a large part remaining as a collar around the base of the endoperidium; red color confined to the mouth region.............*C. lutescens* (p. 190)

Calostoma cinnabarina Desv.

Plates 100 and 123

Rooting stalks stout, rooting, usually short and often scarcely lifting the peridium above ground, dull, sordid ochraceous and soft gelatinous. Exoperidium when fresh and wet composed of a thick, slimy, transparent outer coat and a thin, bright red, non-gelatinous inner coat, the whole breaking up together into large or small pieces which curl inward and soon fall completely away, looking like red seed in a gelatinous pulp, and leaving the thin inner peridium covered with a fine cinnabar red powder or scurf which as it gradually wears away leaves the peridium surface paler until in old specimens the red may be nearly gone. Mouth composed of about 5 elevated ridges which are deep red until very old. Spore sac light clear yellow.

Spores (of No. 5521) pale yellow (about cream color), very distinctly pitted (pits visible when x 670), oblong-elliptic, 6.3–8.5 x 14–20μ, rarely up to 24μ long.

Distinguished by short, bulky stalk, cinnabar red color of the endoperidium and inner layer of the exoperidium, completely deciduous exoperidium, and elliptic spores. This is a very abundant plant at higher elevations in the eastern United States, rare or absent in the coastal plain.

Illustrations: Burnap. Bot. Gaz. 23: pl. 19, figs. 3–10. 1897.
Lloyd. Myc. Works, pl. 8, figs. 1–10.
Marshall. Mushroom Book, pl. opposite p. 132.
Morgan. l. c., pl. 2A (as *C. lutescens*).

North Carolina. Hillsboro. (Curtis Herb.).
Blowing Rock. Coker and party, August 1922. No. 5521 and No. 5615. In earth by paths. Very common.
Little Switzerland. Miss Osborne, coll. No. 2835. Sept. 21, 1917.
Brevard. Miss Cornelia Love, coll. September 1922.
Hendersonville. Alma Holland, coll. (U. N. C. Herb.).
Winston-Salem. Schallert, coll. No. C-42. On soil in shady places.

Alabama. Montgomery. Burke, coll. (N. Y. B. G. Herb.).
Mississippi. Trice, coll. (Curtis Herb., as *M. lutescens*). Spores oblong in sketch.
Virginia. Apple Orchard Mountain. Murrill, coll. (N. Y. B. G. Herb.).
Pennsylvania. Buck Hill Falls. Mrs. Delafield, coll. (N. Y. B. G. Herb.).
Also represented in the Curtis Herbarium from the Schw. Herbarium. (No data.)

Calostoma lutescens (Schw.) Burnap

Plates 103 and 123

Rooting stalk long (up to 6 cm.), compactly woven, yellowish, firmly gelatinous when fresh, clearer light yellow when dry. Exoperidium composed of two layers, an outer, firmly gelatinous, fibrous-spongy one about 1 mm. thick when wet which is the color and consistency of the stalk and continuous with its surface, and an inner one a little less than 1 mm. thick which is clear pale yellow, opaque and much more compact and homogeneous (about like orange peel), the two layers separable without much difficulty, but dehiscing together and remaining united. After the elongation of the stem this outer peridium breaks into several (usually) irregular apical segments which fall away and into 5 or 6 or more irregular basal segments that curl outward and usually remain expanded about the base of the endoperidium like a fluted collar or less often break off close to the peridium and fall away. Endoperidium subglobose, pale orange-yellow (not red), smooth, dull, pliable when wet, horny when dry, 1–1.5 cm. in diameter. Mouth consisting of 5 or 8 elevated, tooth-like lobes which are bright red within when fresh, the outside paler red and the whole fading somewhat with age. Spore sac bright yellow.

Spores (of No. 1935) light yellow, globose, the walls thick and distinctly pitted, giving the spore the appearance of a golf ball, 6–8μ thick.

This is an elegant species and easily distinguished by the long stalk, light yellow color throughout except the red teeth, fluted collar, and round spores. The surface layer of the exoperidium is intermediate between that of the other two species, as it is quite obviously gelatinous but thin, and does not form a thick, clear, slimy jelly as in *C. cinnabarina.*

Schweinitz's material labelled *Mitremyces lutescens* consists apparently of two species. There are two lots of two plants. The upper two with long stems are fused and the spore sacs are largely broken off, with no spores to be found. These, so far as they go, look just like *M. lutescens.* The other two consist of a smaller plant with the top nearly gone and the upper part of another with perfect sac and spores. This looks just like *Ravenelii*, with warts on the surface of the sac, and, according to Lloyd (Myc. Notes, p. 395), with elliptic spores. We are glad to say, however, that the part of Schweinitz's plants taken by Michener and now in his herbarium in Washington is *C. lutescens* as generally accepted and agree with the description, the spores being spherical, pitted, 6.5–8.2μ thick. The round spores and yellow spore sac and spores of the description (Syn. Fung. Car. Sup. No. 345) indicate clearly the species as now generally accepted. Schweinitz's figures do not show the fluted collar which is one of the most marked characters of this species(though not always conspicuous) and they may really represent *C. Ravenelii.*

Atkinson reported this species from Blowing Rock (this Journal **9**: 85. 1892), but later said that his plant was *C. cinnabarina* (Mushrooms, p. 213).

Illustrations: Burnap. Bot. Gaz. 23: pl. 19, figs. 1, 2. 1897.
　　Corda. Anleitung, pl. D, fig. 41.
　　Lloyd. Myc. Works, pl. 9, figs. 1–3.
　　Marshall. Mushroom Book, pl. opposite p. 132.
　　Schweinitz. Syn. Fung. Car. Sup., pl. 1, figs. 1–6.

1935. In mixed woods, Oct. 25, 1915.
1995. Under oaks south of campus, Nov. 23, 1915.
　　Asheville. Beardslee.
　　Pink Bed Valley. Murrill and House, colls. (N. Y. B. G. Herb.).

Alabama. Moulton. Peters, coll. (Curtis Herb., as *Mitremyces*). Spores spherical.
　　Auburn. Underwood, coll. (N. Y. B. G. Herb.).
　　Mobile. Mohr, coll. (U. S. Nat'l. Herb., as *Mitremyces*).
West Virginia. A. H. Curtis, coll. (Curtis Herb., as *Mitremyces*).

Calostoma Ravenelii (Berk.) Massee

Plates 104 and 123

Rooting stem 2–5 cm. long, stout, rather compact, consisting of an interwoven mass of thick, gelatinous fibers of a soaked clay color; exoperidium light clay or straw color, not gelatinous at any stage, not obviously two-layered, surface spongy or fibrous looking, less than 1 mm. thick; on exposure breaking up into small pieces except for a larger, fluted, apical part which lifts up and falls away, the larger particles on the sides also falling away usually, but some of the smaller ones remaining attached to the peridium for a long time until slowly worn away. In addition to these fragments which are the full thickness of the exoperidium, the endoperidium is covered with much thinner and smaller scales which are parts of the inner layer of the exoperidium from which the outer part has broken away. These scales are very persistent and are found on almost all herbarium specimens. When the exoperidial cap falls off, that part of the inner surface which was touching the mouth ridges is seen to be red, other parts of the inner surface are a distinct light yellow, as is also the freshly exposed surface of the inner peridium, the color being due to minute, inherent, bran-like scales. These scales get larger downward and merge into the larger scales above mentioned. Endoperidium tan or clay color, at length brown, the exposed surface dull and somewhat glaucous-looking, 7–18 mm. in diameter when fresh, 5.5–11 mm. when dry; mouth composed of about 5 rays, bright red when fresh, fading with age. Spore sac white.

Spores (of No. 1488) white, clear, with one or two large oil drops, variable in size and shape, usually oblong-elliptic, a few nearly spherical, 6.5–7 x 10–17μ; surface appearing smooth except under high power, then seen to be very minutely and closely pitted, showing faint radial lines through the walls.

This species is easily distinguished by the non-gelatinous exoperidium, clay colored endoperidium spotted with scales and particles, and the very faintly punctate spores. *Mitremyces Tylerii* Lloyd (Myc. Notes, p. 240) is probably only a small form of this species. One finds at times very small plants without obvious stalks mixed with more typical ones.

Illustrations: Berkeley. Trans. Linn. Soc. 22: pl. 25 B.
   Lloyd. l. c., pl. 9, figs. 4–6; pl. 68, figs. 3–8.
   Marshall. Mushroom Book, pl. opposite p. 132 (good).
Massee. l. c. (1903), pl. 3, figs. 26–28.

58. Among moss on hillside in open mixed woods, Sept. 27, 1910. Spores 6.5–8 x 8.6–14μ.
1488. On ground in open woods, Dec. 7, 1914.
2872. By path in Battle's Park, Oct. 5, 1917. Spores variable in size and shape, distinctly pitted, 4.8–6.6 x 8.6–18μ.
Also Nos. 119a, 1518, 1519.

Asheville. Beardslee, coll. Aug. 1918. Spores 6.2–7.4 x 11–17μ.
Columbus Co. Barlow, coll. No. 49. July 1909.
Caesar's Head. Ravenel, coll. (Curtis Herb., co-types).

Alabama. Moulton. Peters, coll. (Curtis Herb., as *M. lutescens*) Spores oblong (as shown by sketch) and case warted.
   Mobile. Mohr, coll. (U. S. Nat'l. Herb., as *Mitremyces*).
Kentucky. Conway. B. Fink, coll. (N. Y. B. G. Herb.).
Delaware. Wilmington. Commons, coll. (U. S. Nat'l. Herb., as *M. lutescens*).
Pennsylvania. Center Co. Adams, coll. (N. Y. B. G. Herb.). Spores elliptic, obscurely pitted, 6–7.5 x 8–13μ.

Calostoma microsporum Atk.

The following description is from Atkinson (Journ. Myc. 9: 16. 1903):

"Plants 4–7 cm. high, foot stalk 3–6 cm. by 1–2 cm., cylindrical or ventricose or enlarged below, sometimes compressed, rarely two foot stalks joined throughout the entire length. Peridium oval, 10–15 mm. broad; teeth 5–7, prominent, vermilion colored on their inner faces; exoperidium separating into numerous small hard adherent warts, covering the middle and lower surface of the endoperidium, usually entirely separating from the upper surface, leaving a smooth area on the inner peridium around the mouth. Spores white, smooth, oblong, some rarely elliptical, 6–10 x 3.5–5μ. Protoplasm usually homogeneous, sometimes granular, often showing a tendency to be constricted at the middle, perhaps because of a clear area at this point."

PLATE 104

CALOSTOMA RAVENELII.   No. 1488

For a comparison between this species and *C. Ravenelii*, see Atkinson's discussion, which is rather long for quotation. The most important differences that seem to distinguish the two species are the longer stalk (on the average), the smaller spores and the vermilion color being confined to the inner faces of the stomal teeth in *C. microsporum*. We have not seen Atkinson's plants and cannot give an opinion on the validity of the species.

Tennessee. Rugby. Percival, coll. (Cornell Univ. Herb., type).

LITERATURE

Berkeley. Sur la fructification des genres *Lycoperdon, Phallus*, et de quelques autres genres voisins. Ann. Sci. Nat., 2nd ser., **12**: 160, pl. 2. 1839. There is a larger work on this group in Russian with a German resumé printed in Moscow and St. Petersburg in 1902.

Bigeard. Flore des Champignons 2: 513, pls. 36, 37, and pl. 38, fig. 1. 1913.

Bucholtz. Beiträge zur Morphologie und Systematik der Hypogaeen (Tuberaceen und Gastromyceten). Riga, 1902.

Bucholtz. Zur Morphologie und Systematik der Fungi Hypogaei. Ann. Myc. **1**: 152, pls. 4 and 5. 1903.

Corda. Icon. Fung. **5**: 22, 70, pls. 4, 6, 7, and pl. 8, fig. 51. 1842.

Cunningham. The Gasteromycetes of Australasia. Proc. Linn. Soc. N. S. W. **49**: 97. 1924; **50**: 245, 367. 1925; **51**: 72, 363, 627. 1926.

De Bary. Comparative Morphology and Biology of the Fungi, Mycetozoa and Bacteria, p. 308, Oxford, 1887.

Fischer in Engler and Prantl. Pflanzenfamilien 1, pt. 1: 276, figs. 126–182. 1900.

Fitzpatrick. A comparative study of the development of the fruit body in *Phallogaster, Hysterangium*, and *Gautieria*. Ann. Myc. **11**: 119, pls. 4–7. 1913.

Fries. R. E. Einige Gasteromyceten aus Bolivia und Argentinien. Arkiv. för Botanik **8**, No. **11**: 1, pls. 1–4. 1909.

Fries. Th. C. E. Sveriges Gasteromyceter, 44 text figs. Arkiv. för Botanik **17**: 1921.

Harkness. New Species of California Fungi. Bull. Cal. Acad. Sci. **1**: 29. 1884.

Harkness. Californian Hypogaeous Fungi. Proc. Cal. Acad. Sci., 3rd ser., **1**: 241, pls. 42–45. 1899. Also in Rev. Myc. **22**: 82. 1900.

Harvey. Contributions to the Gasteromycetes of Maine. Bull. Torr. Bot. Club **24**: 71. 1897.

Hesse. Mikroscopische Unterscheidungsmerkmale der typischen Lycoperdaceengenera. Jahrb. Wiss. Bot. **10**: 383, pl. 28. 1876.

Hesse. Die Hypogaeen Deutschlands. Halle a. S., 1890–94.

Hollos. Die Gasteromyceten Ungarns. Leipzig, 1904.

Kauffman. Outline of the Gasteromycetes of Michigan. Rept. Mich. Acad. Sci. **10**: 70. 1908.

Lloyd. Myc. Notes Nos. 7–9, figs. 30–56. 1901–2.

Lloyd. The Genera of Gastromycetes, figs. 1–14 and pls. 1–11. Cincinnati, 1902.

Lloyd. The Curtis Collection. Myc. Notes No. 15: 152. 1903.

Lloyd. The Lycoperdaceae of Australia, etc., pls. 25–39 and figs. 1–49. 1905.

Lloyd. Sur Quelques Rares Gastéromycètes Européen. Myc. Notes No. 22: 261, figs. 98–111 and pls. 28, 35, 72, 87–89. 1906.

Lloyd. The Gastromycetes of Schweinitz's Herbarium. Myc. Notes No. 30: 395. 1908.

Lloyd. The Lycoperdaceae of Vittadini. Myc. Notes No. 70: 1222. 1923.

Lohwag. Zur Stellung und Systematik der Gastromyceten. Verhandlg. der Zool.-Bot. Gesell. in Wien **74**: 38. 1924.

Lohwag. Zur entwicklungsgeschichte und morphologie der gasteromyceten. Ein beitrag zur systematik der basidiomyceten. Beih. Bot. Centralbl. abt. II, **42**: 177–334, pls. 1–2. 1926.

Long. Notes on New Or Rare Species of Gasteromycetes. Mycologia **9**: 271. 1917.

Lotsy. Bot. Stammesgeschichte **1**: 718. 1907.

Maire. Sur la cytologie des Gastéromycètes. Comp. Rend. 131 (2): 1246. 1900.

Massee. A Monograph of the British Gasteromycetes. Ann. Bot. **4**: 1, pls. 1–4. 1889.

Micheli. Nova Plantarum Genera. 1729.

Morgan. Gastromycetes. Journ. Cin. Soc. Nat. Hist. **11**: 141, pl. 3. 1889; **12**: 8, pls. 1, 2. 1889; **12**: 163, pl. 16. 1890; **14**: 5, pls. 1, 2. 1891; **14**: 141, pl. 5. 1892.

Petri.   Flora Italica Cryptogama (Gasterales), Fasc. 5.   1909.

Rea.   British Basidiomycetae, p. 21.   1922.

Rehsteiner.   Beitr. zur Entwickelungsgeschichte der Fruchtkörper einiger Gasteromyceten. Bot. Zeit. **50**: 761, 777, 800, 823, 843, 865.   1892.

Saccardo.   Sylloge Fungorum **7**: 1, 469.   1888; **9**: 262.   1891; **11**: 152.   1895; **14**: 254.   1899; **16**: 224.   1902.

Schroeter.   In Cohn's Kryptogamen Flora von Schlesien **3**, pt. 1: 689.   1888.

Trelease.   Morels and Puff-balls of Madison.   Trans. Wis. Acad. Sci. Arts and Letters **7**: 105, pls. 7-9.   1888.

Tulasne, L. R. and Ch.   De la fructification des *Scleroderma*, comparé à celle des *Lycoperdon* et des *Bovista*.   Ann. Sci. nat., 2nd. ser., **17**: 5.   1842.

Tulasne, L. R. and Ch.   Champignons hypogés de la famille des Lycoperdacées.   Ann. Sci. Nat., 2nd. ser., **19**: 373.   1843.

Tulasne, L. R. and Ch.   Fungi nonnulli hypogaei, novi vel minus cogniti.   Parlatore, Giorn. Bot. **2**: 55.   1844.

Tulasne, L. R.   Fungi Hypogaei.   Histoire et monographie des champignons Hypogés.   Paris, 1851.

Vittadini.   Monographia Tuberacearum.   Mediolani, 1831.

Vittadini.   Monographia Lycoperdineorum.   Mem. Accad., Torino, **5**: 145, pls. 1-3.   1843.   Reviewed by Tulasne in Ann. Sci. Nat., 2nd ser., **19**: 277.   1843.

Winter.   Gasteromycetes.   In Rabenhorst's Krypt.-Fl. Deutsch. **1**, Abt. 1: 864.   1884.

Zopf.   Die Pilze, p. 362.   1890.

PLATE 105

Fig.   1. *Clathrus columnatus.*   No. 4949.
Fig.   2. *Simblum sphaerocephalum.*   No. 1427.
Fig.   3. *Mutinus Ravenelii.*   No. 741.
Fig.   4. *Mutinus Curtisii.*   No. 5113.
Fig.   5. *Ithyphallus Ravenelii.*   No. 41a.
Fig.   6. *Ithyphallus Ravenelii.*   No. 649.
Fig.   7. *Dictyophora duplicata.*   No. 5195.
Figs. 8 and 9. *Protophallus jamaicensis.*   Cinchona, Jamaica.
Figs. 10 and 11. *Hysterangium clathroides.*   No. 7416.
Figs. 12–14. *Hysterangium pompholyx.*   No. 7490a.   Fig. 14 shows one of the flocculent threads on the peridium.
Figs. 15 and 16. *Hysterangium stoloniferum* var. *americanum.*   Ithaca, New York.
Figs. 17–19. *Gymnomyces vesiculosus.*   No. 7470.   Fig. 18 shows 4 spores held together by a sort of gelatine; fig. 19 shows cross section of a wall of the glebal chambers.
Fig. 20. *Gautieria monticola.*   California.

Figs. 1–5, 7, 9, 10, 12, 15, 18, 20 × 1620; figs. 6, 8, 11, 13, 16 × 1013; figs. 14, 17 × 810; fig. 19 × 188.

PLATE 105

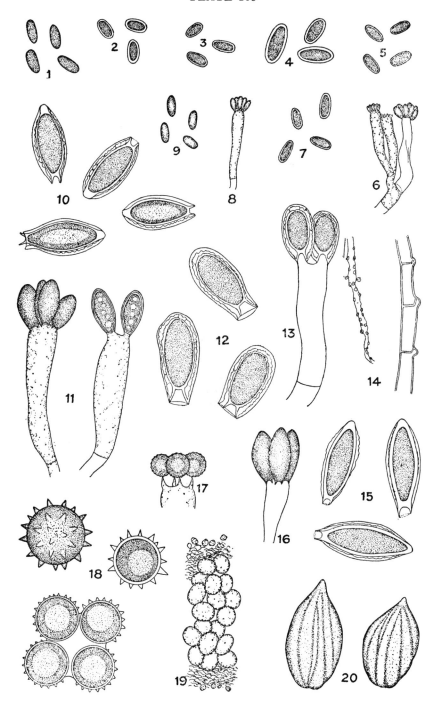

PLATE 106

Figs. 1–6. *Sclerogaster minor*. No. 7474.
Fig. 7. *Rhizopogon rubescens*. No. 6003.
Fig. 8. *Rhizopogon rubescens*. No. 7450.
Fig. 9. *Rhizopogon rubescens*. No. 7204.
Fig. 10. *Rhizopogon rubescens*. No. 58.
Figs. 11 and 12. *Rhizopogon atlanticus*. No. 5999.
Fig. 13. *Rhizopogon truncatus*. Type.
Figs. 14 and 15. *Rhizopogon luteolus*. No. 1607 (von Höhnel).
Figs. 16 and 17. *Rhizopogon luteolus*. No. 7359 (Fitzpatrick).

Figs. 1–5, 7–9, 11, 15, 17 × 1013; others × 1620.

PLATE 106

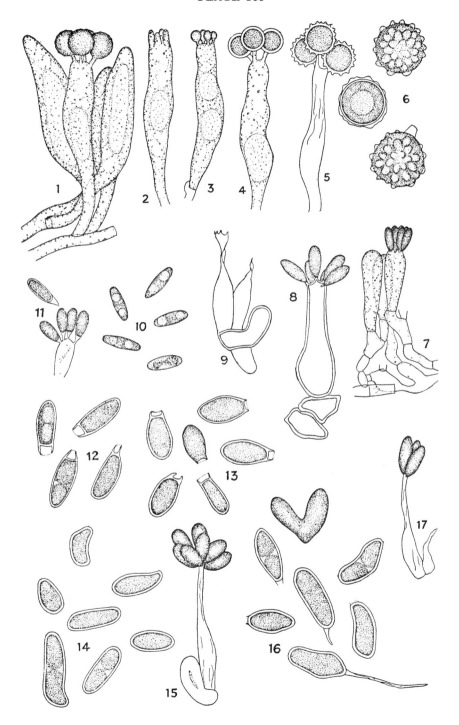

PLATE 107

Figs. 1–4. *Rhizopogon nigrescens.* No. 7582 (showing bits of hymenium and basidia).
Figs. 5 and 6. *Rhizopogon nigrescens.* No. 7372.
Fig. 7. *Rhizopogon nigrescens.* No. 1910.
Fig. 8. *Rhizopogon nigrescens.* No. 976.
Figs. 9–11. *Rhizopogon roseolus.* No. 7207.
Fig. 12. *Rhizopogon roseolus.* No. 598 (Whetzel).
Fig. 13. *Rhizopogon roseolus.* No. 7214.
Fig. 14. *Rhizopogon piceus.* No. 6059.
Figs. 15 and 16. *Rhizopogon maculatus.* No. 955.

Figs. 1, 2 × 825; figs. 3–7, 9, 10, 12, 13, 15 × 1013; Figs. 8, 11, 14, 16 × 1620.

PLATE 107

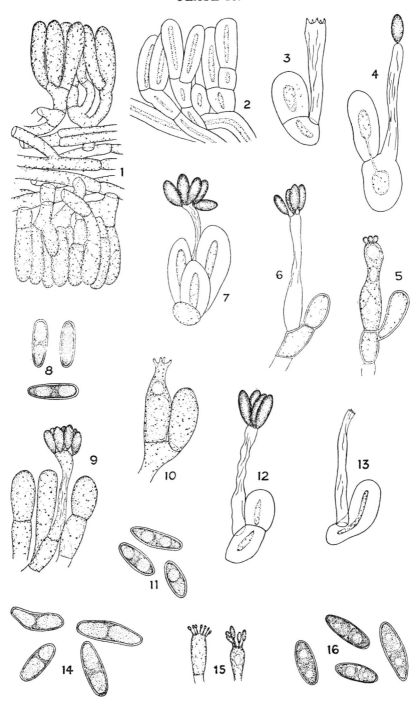

PLATE 108

Figs. 1 and 2. *Melanogaster nauseosus*. Sketch of a section showing peridium, tramal plates and cavities, some partly filled with spores and others with spores just beginning to form. × 34. Fig. 2, basidia with spores, basidia beginning to gelatinize. × 900.

Fig. 3. *Nigropogon asterosporus*. Sketch showing continuity of the tramal plates with the peridium. × 34.

Figs. 4–6. Sections of hymenium and subhymenium of the above, showing young basidia, basidia with spores and collapsed basidia. × 900.

Fig. 7. Spores of above. × 1440.

Fig. 8. *Leucogaster carolinianus*. Young and mature basidia. × 900.

Fig. 9. Mature spores of above, showing heavy reticulum. × 1440.

PLATE 108

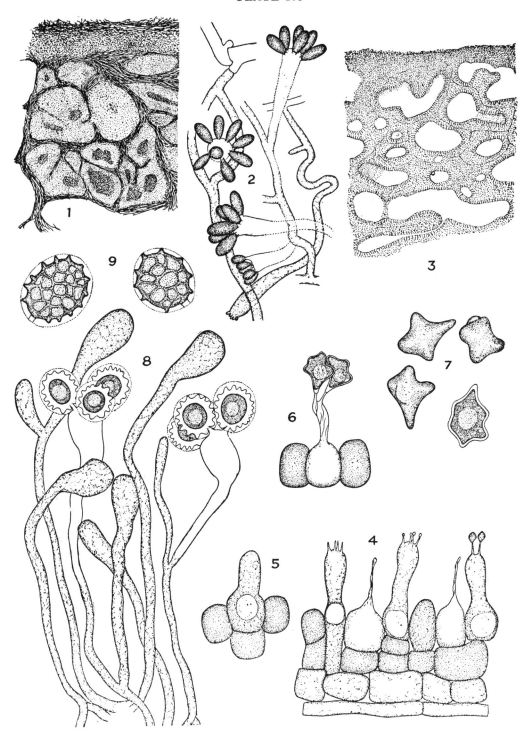

Figs. 1 and 2. *Melanogaster rubescens* (?). No. 5804.
Fig. 3. *Melanogaster variegatus.* Type.
Figs. 4 and 5. *Melanogaster variegatus.* Ithaca, N. Y.
Fig. 6. *Melanogaster variegatus.* Hungary (Hollos).
Figs. 7 and 8. *Melanogaster ambiguus.* Syracuse, N. Y.
Fig. 9. *Hymenogaster Thwaitesii.* Syracuse, N. Y. (Povah, No. 832).
Fig. 10. *Hymenogaster Thwaitesii.* Type.

Figs. 1, 4, 7 × 1013; others × 1620.

PLATE 109

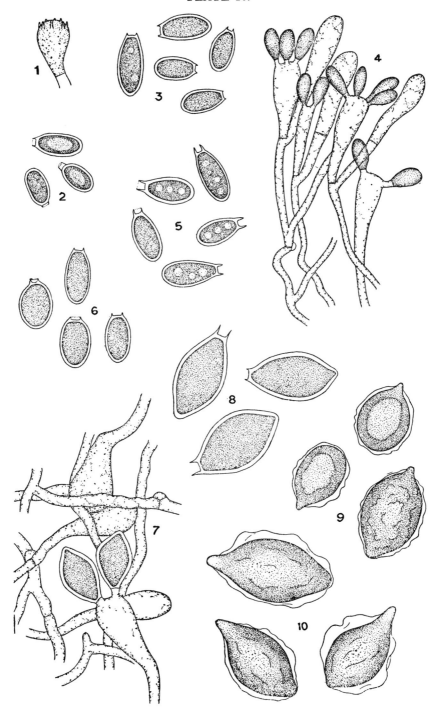

PLATE 110

Fig. 1. *Hymenogaster foetidus*.   No. 7473.
Figs. 2–4. *Hymenogaster foetidus*.   No. 7467.
Fig. 5. *Octaviania Ravenelii*.   No. 7200.
Fig. 6. *Octaviania Ravenelii*.   No. 6002.
Fig. 7. *Octaviania Stephensii*.   Type.
Fig. 8. *Octaviania asterosperma*.   Ithaca, N. Y.

Figs. 1 and 2 × 1013; figs. 4, 6 × 503; others × 1620.

PLATE 110

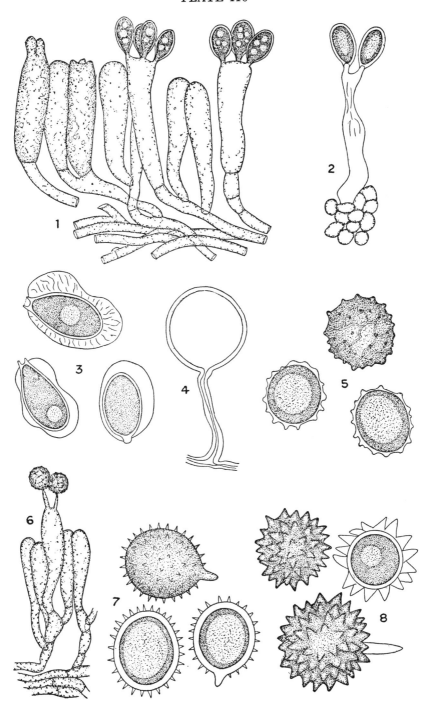

PLATE 111

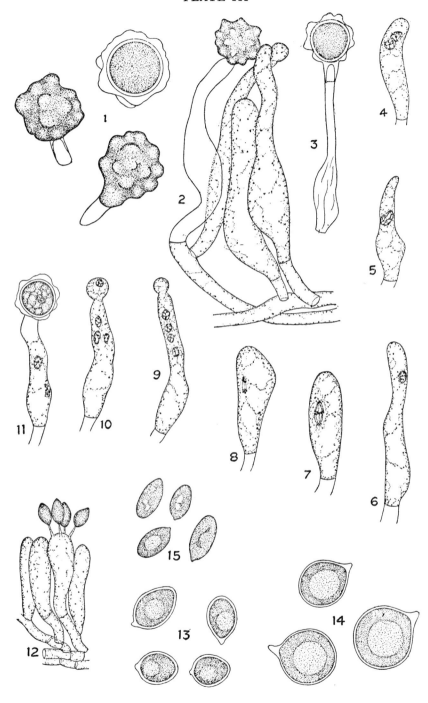

PLATE 112

Figs. 1–3. *Calvatia rubro-flava*. No. 7154 (showing basidia and capillitium thread with thin places in the wall).

Fig. 4. *Calvatia maxima*. Wisconsin.

Figs. 5 and 6. *Calvatia cyathiformis*. No. 550.

Figs. 7 and 8. *Calvatia elata*. No. 2843 H.

Fig. 9. *Calvatia cretacea*. Abisco, Lapland.

Fig. 10. *Calvatia fragilis*. No. 4783. Canada.

Figs. 11 and 12. *Calvatia craniformis*. No. 538.

Fig. 13. *Calvatia craniformis*. Type.

Figs. 14 and 15. *Calvatia caelata*. New York.

Fig. 16. *Lycoperdon atropurpureum*. No. 1019.

Fig. 17. *Lycoperdon pulcherrimum*. No. 7560.

Fig. 18. *Lycoperdon echinatum*. No. 7421.

Fig. 19. *Lycoperdon subvelatum*. No. 7263. Florida.

Fig. 20. *Lycoperdon rimulatum*. No. 715.

Figs. 1, 2, 11 × 1013; figs. 3–10, 12–20 × 1620.

PLATE 112

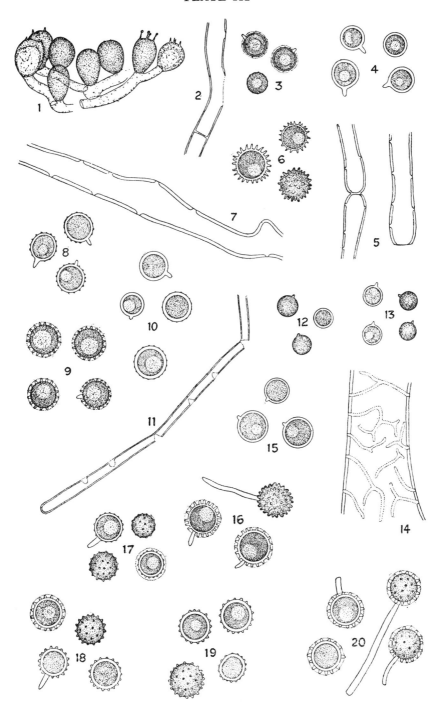

PLATE 113

Fig.   1. *Lycoperdon umbrinum.*   No. 1004.

Fig.   2. *Lycoperdon umbrinum.*   West Albany, N. Y.

Fig.   3. *Lycoperdon umbrinum.*   Bres. Herb. (as *L. hirtum*).

Figs.   4 and 5. *Lycoperdon Turneri.*   Type.

Fig.   6. *Lycoperdon molle.*   Persoon Herb. (now at N. Y. B. G. Herb.).

Fig.   7. *Lycoperdon acuminatum.*   No. 680.

Fig.   8. *Lycoperdon pyriforme.*   No. 998.

Fig.   9. *Lycoperdon subincarnatum.*   No. 5754.   Linville Falls, N. C.

Fig. 10. *Lycoperdon subincarnatum.*   No. 3171a.

Fig. 11. *Lycoperdon muscorum.*   Type.

Fig. 12. *Lycoperdon gemmatum.*   No. 3159.

Fig. 13. *Lycoperdon Peckii.*   No. 5749.   Linville Falls.

Fig. 14. *Lycoperdon pedicellatum.*   No. 5668.

Fig. 15. *Lycoperdon eximium.*   No. 1002.

Fig. 16. *Lycoperdon fuscum.*   No. 5525.   Blowing Rock.

Fig. 17. *Lycoperdon marginatum.*   No. 482.

Fig. 18. *Lycoperdon marginatum.*   No. 5225.

Fig. 19. *Lycoperdon calvescens.*   Co-type (Wright, No. 6366).

Fig. 20. *Lycoperdon Curtisii.*   No. 552.

Fig. 21. *Lycoperdon Curtisii.*   Co-type.

Fig. 22. *Lycoperdon Wriːhtii.*   Co-type.

Fig. 23. *Lycoperdon candidum.*   Persoon Herbarium.

Fig. 24. *Lycoperdon oblongisporum.*   No. 497.

Fig. 25. *Lycoperdon pusillum.*   No. 2209.

Fig. 26. *Lycoperdon pusillum.*   No. 1003.

Fig. 27. *Lycoperdon pusillum.*   No. 5390.

Fig. 28. *Lycoperdon pusillum.*   No. 5211.

Fig. 29. *Lycoperdon polymorphum.*   Pitchfork, Wyoming.

Figs. 1–17, 19–26, 29 × 1620; figs. 18, 28 × 1013; fig. 27 × 810.

PLATE 113

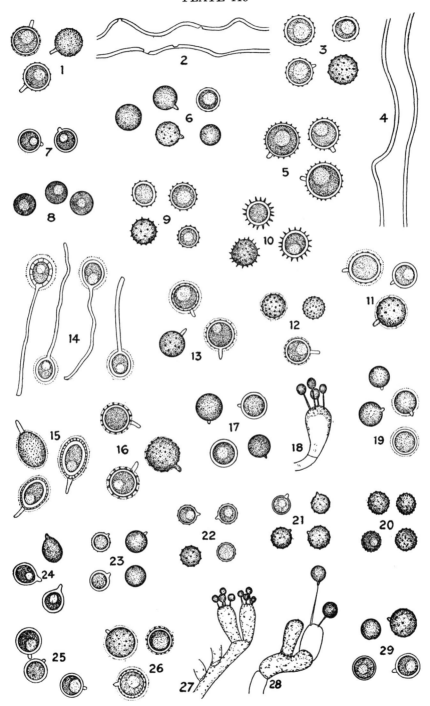

PLATE 114

Fig. 1. *Bovistella radicata*. No. 5919.
Fig. 2. *Bovistella radicata*. No. 5200.
Fig. 3. *Bovistella radicata*. Torrend, No. 77.
Fig. 4. *Bovistella radicata*. No. 1545. South Carolina.
Fig. 5. *Bovistella echinella*. Abisco, Lapland.
Fig. 6. *Bovistella echinella*. Type.
Figs. 7 and 8. *Bovista plumbea*. No. 5358.
Fig. 9. *Bovista pila*. No. 7999.
Fig. 10. *Bovista pila*. Co-type.
Fig. 11. *Bovista pila*. No. 5359.
Fig. 12. *Bovista nigrescens*. Cavelante. Bresadola Herbarium.
Fig. 13. *Bovista minor*. No. 2416. Canada.
Fig. 14. *Bovistella dealbata*. Lloyd Herbarium.
Figs. 15–17. *Mycenastrum corium*. Lloyd Herbarium.

Figs. 1, 3, 5, 6, 8, 10–14, 17 × 1620; figs. 2, 16 × 810; 4, 7 × 47; fig. 9 × 503; fig. 15 × 188.

PLATE 114

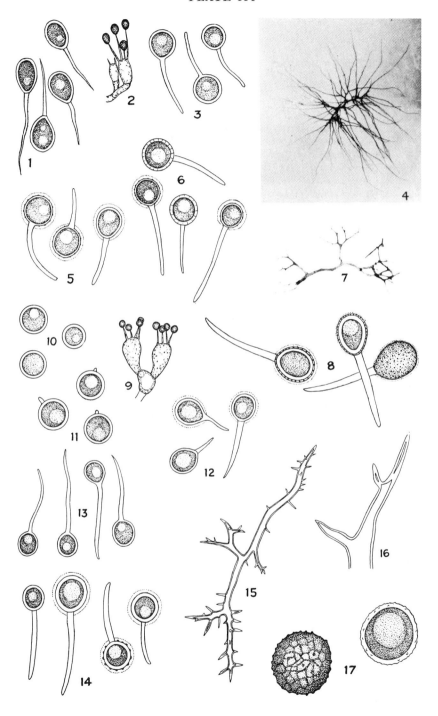

PLATE 115

Fig. 1. *Geaster triplex.* No. 682 (lower spore drawn in 7% KOH).

Fig. 2. *Geaster limbatus,* sense of Bresadola. Burlington, Wis.

Fig. 3. *Geaster limbatus,* sense of Hollos. England (?). N. Y. B. G. Herb. (Massee, coll.).

Fig. 4. *Geaster Morganii.* Ohio. N. Y. B. G. Herb. (Underwood, coll.).

Fig. 5. *Geaster saccatus,* northern form. Asheville, N. C.

Fig. 6. *Geaster saccatus.* New Haven Gap, Jamaica.

Fig. 7. *Geaster velutinus.* No. 4095.

Fig. 8. *Geaster Readeri.* Type.

Fig. 9. *Geaster radicans.* Co-type (Ravenel, No. 953).

Fig. 10. *Geaster mirabilis.* No. 7077.

Fig. 11. *Geaster papyraceus.* Kiu Siu, Japan (Curtis Herb.).

Fig. 12. *Geaster caespitosus.* Ohio. N. Y. B. G. Herb. (Lloyd, coll.).

Fig. 13. *Geaster trichifer.* Morce's Gap, Jamaica.

Fig. 14. *Geaster subiculosus.* Jamaica (Earle, No. 184).

Fig. 15. *Geaster mammosus.* Canada.

Fig. 16. *Geaster arenarius.* Florida (Lloyd, coll.).

Fig. 17. *Geaster rufescens.* No. 985.

Fig. 18. *Geaster fornicatus.* Smith Island, N. C.

Fig. 19. *Geaster fimbriatus.* No. 7097.

Fig. 20. *Geaster floriformis.* Colorado (Clements, No. 613.).

Fig. 21. *Geaster coronatus.* No. 75.

Fig. 22. *Geaster coronatus.* No. 684.

Fig. 23. *Geaster coronatus.* No. 3881.

Fig. 24. *Geaster minimus.* Type.

Fig. 25. *Geaster Cesati.* No. 1634 (Cesati; Path. & Myc. Herb.).

Fig. 26. *Geaster leptospermus.* No. 2028.

Fig. 27. *Geaster pectinatus.* Jamesville, N. Y.

Fig. 28. *Geaster plicatus.* France (Patouillard).

Fig. 29. *Geaster biplicatus.* Bonin Islands. Co-type.

Fig. 30. *Geaster Bryantii.* England (?). N. Y. B. G. Herb. (Massee, coll.).

Fig. 31. *Geaster Schmidelii.* Calloway, Nebraska (Bartholomew, coll.).

Fig. 32. *Geaster Rabenhorstii.* Type distribution.

Fig. 33. *Geaster Hariotii.* Brazil (Patouillard Herb.).

Fig. 34. *Geaster asper.* Lincoln, Neb.

Fig. 35. *Geaster umbilicatus.* Newfield, N. J.

Fig. 36. *Geaster Drummondii.* Brisbane, Australia.

Fig. 37. *Astraeus hygrometricus.* No. 685.

All figs. $\times$ 1620.

PLATE 115

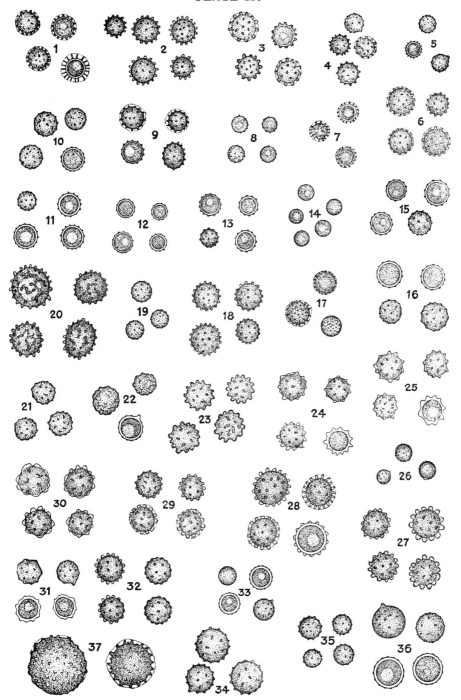

PLATE 116

Fig. 1. *Geaster limbatus*, sense of Bresadola. Kansas. No. 8252.
Fig. 2. *Geaster elegans*. France (?). Tulasne Herbarium.
Fig. 3. *Geaster radicans*. Sarasota, Florida.
Fig. 4. *Geaster caespitosus*. Type.
Fig. 5. *Geaster arenarius*. Type.
Fig. 6. *Geaster mammosus*. North Dakota. No. 254.
Fig. 7. *Geaster subiculosus*. Type.
Fig. 8. *Geaster lignicola*. Type.
Fig. 9. *Geaster Hieronymi*. No. 244. Jalapa, Mexico.
Fig. 10. *Geaster floriformis*. North Dakota. Sydow, Fungi exot. exs. No. 152.
Fig. 11. *Geaster calceus*. Type.
Fig. 12. *Geaster granulosus*. Austria (Fuckel, coll.).
Fig. 13. *Geaster argenteus*. Type.
Fig. 14. *Geaster Archeri*. Type.
Fig. 15. *Coilomyces Schweinitzii*. Co-type.
Fig. 16. *Geaster terreus*. Waste Lands, S. Dakota.
Fig. 17. *Geaster argentatus*. Type.
Fig. 18. *Geaster coronatus*, fornicate form. No. 6065.
Fig. 19. *Geaster coronatus, minimus* form. Ymala, Mexico.
Fig. 20. *Geaster involutus*. Type.

All figs. × 1620.

PLATE 116

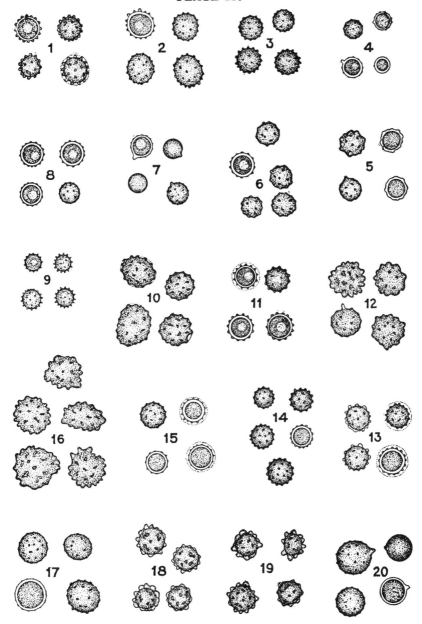

Fig.   1. *Geaster saccatus*.   No. 7350.
Fig.   2. *Geaster Lloydii*.   Florida.
Fig.   3. *Myriostoma coliformis*.   Lloyd Herbarium.
Figs. 4–7. *Astraeus hygrometricus*.   No. 7441.
Figs. 8 and 9. *Diplocystis Wrightii*.   Bahama Is.
Figs. 10–14. *Sphaerobolus stellatus*.   No. 5112.   Fig. 13 shows a gemma from the gleba.

Figs. 1–3, 8, 14 × 1620; figs. 4–6 × 810; figs. 7, 9 × 503; figs. 10–13 × 1013.

PLATE 117

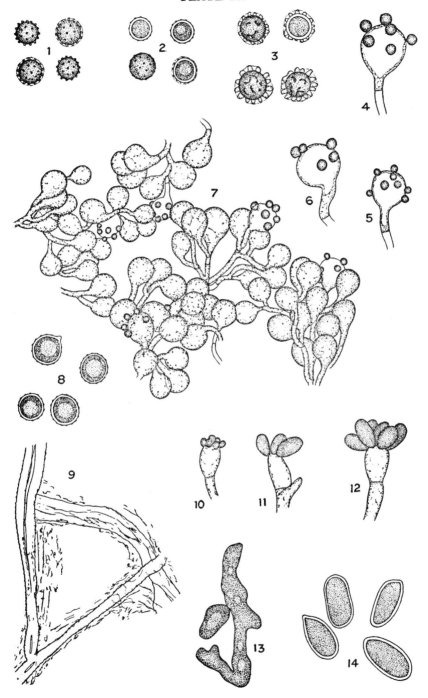

PLATE 118

Figs. 1 and 2. *Disciseda candida*. No. 6092.
Fig. 3. *Disciseda candida*. No. 7507 (showing section of trama with basidia).
Fig. 4. *Disciseda candida*. No. 5969.
Fig. 5. *Disciseda candida*. No. 7115.
Fig. 6. *Disciseda candida*. Co-type.
Fig. 7. *Bovista candida*. Type.
Fig. 8. *Disciseda subterranea*. North Island, S. C.
Fig. 9. *Disciseda pedicellata*. Hartsville, S. C.
Fig. 10. *Disciseda pedicellata*. No. 15 (Ravenel, as *Bovista nigrescens*).
Fig. 11. *Arachnion album*. No. 5209.
Figs. 12 and 13. *Arachnion album*. No. 5224.
Fig. 14. *Arachnion album*. No. 730.

Fig. 1, $\frac{3}{4}$ nat. size; figs. 2, 4, 11, 12 $\times$ 1013; fig. 3 $\times$ 466; figs. 5–10, 14 $\times$ 1620; fig. 13 $\times$ 298.

PLATE 118

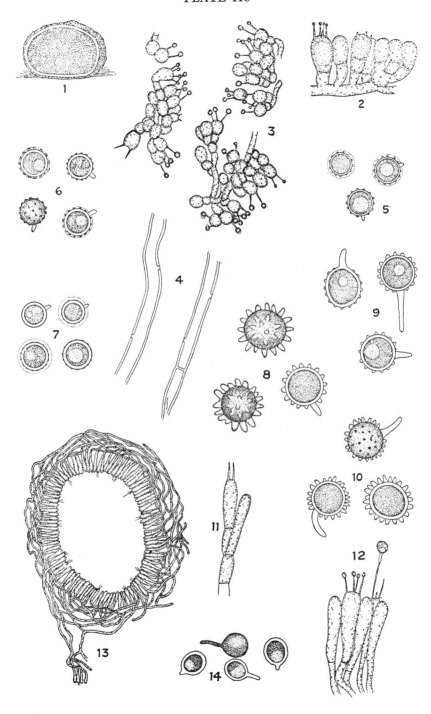

PLATE 119

Fig. 1. *Tylostoma mammosum.* North Dakota.
Fig. 2. *Tylostoma mammosum.* No. 926 (Fungi bavarici).
Fig. 3. *Tylostoma brumale.* New York Botanical Garden (Schlesien).
Fig. 4. *Tylostoma simulans.* No. 7504.
Fig. 5. *Tylostoma simulans.* No. 87.
Fig. 6. *Tylostoma floridanum.* Type.
Fig. 7. *Tylostoma verrucosum.* Ohio (Lloyd).
Figs. 8 and 9. *Tylostoma Finkii.* No. 6060.
Fig. 10. *Tylostoma volvulatum.* No. 142. Porto Rico.
Fig. 11. *Tylostoma poculatum.* No. 1889 (E. & E., Fungi Columbiana).
Fig. 12. *Tylostoma obesum.* Co-type.
Fig. 13. *Tylostoma granulosum.* No. 424 (Saccardo, Myc. italica).
Fig. 14. *Tylostoma campestre.* No. 861 Ip. Canada.
Fig. 15. *Tylostoma Berkeleyii.* Folly Island, S. C.
Figs. 16 and 17. *Queletia mirabilis.* Trexlertown, Pa. (Fig. 16 shows a bit of capillitium).

Figs. 1–3, 5–8, 10–15, 17 × 1620; fig. 4 × 1013; fig. 9 × 278; fig. 16 × 503.

PLATE 119

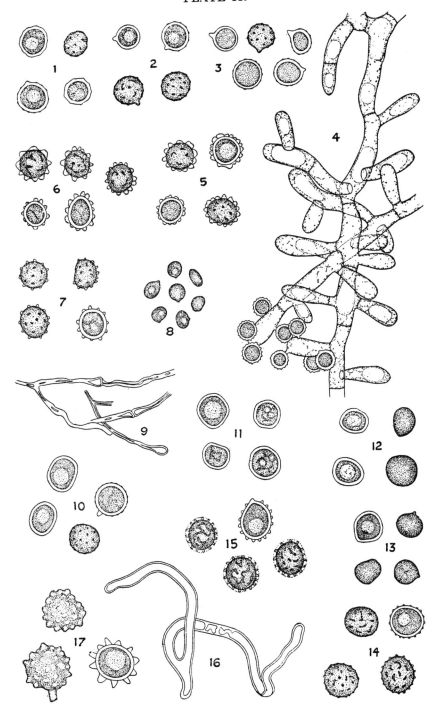

PLATE 120

Fig.   1. *Scleroderma geaster.*   No. 1761.

Fig.   2. *Scleroderma flavidum.*   No. 660.

Fig.   3. *Scleroderma flavidum.*   No. 1698 (E. & E.).

Fig.   4. *Scleroderma bovista,* sense of Hollos.   No. 725.

Fig.   5. *Scleroderma bovista,* sense of Bresadola.   No. 5920.

Fig.   6. *Scleroderma aurantium.*   No. 5622.

Fig.   7. *Scleroderma cepa.*   No. 916.

Fig.   8. *Scleroderma tenerum.*   Type.

Fig.   9. *Scleroderma lycoperdoides.*   No. 5201.

Fig.   10. *Scleroderma lycoperdoides.*   No. 5253.

Fig.   11. *Scleroderma lycoperdoides.*   Type.

Fig.   12. *Scleroderma verrucosum.*   Bresadola Herbarium.

Figs. 13–17. *Pisolithus tinctorius.*   No. 8170.

Figs. 18, 19. *Pisolithus tinctorius.*   No. 5402.   One spore in fig. 9 shows appearance when first put into water; the others after the gelatinous material has soaked off.

Figs. 1–9, 12 × 1013; figs. 11, 19 × 1620; figs. 10, 13–18 × 810.

PLATE 120

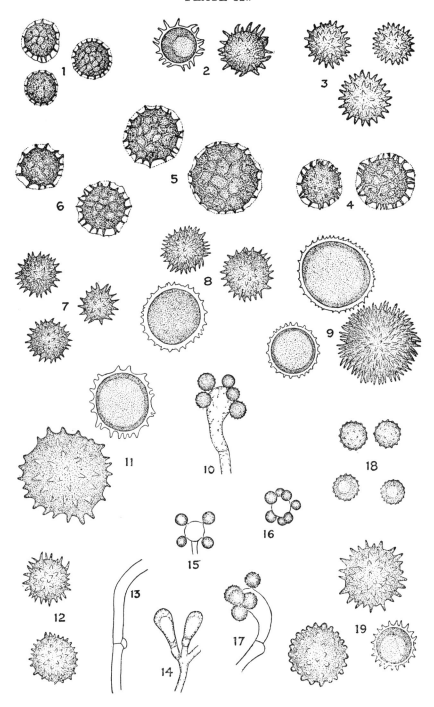

PLATE 121

Fig. 1. *Cyathus striatus.*   No. 5590.
Figs. 2–4. *Cyathus striatus.*   No. 5280.
Fig. 5. *Cyathus striatus.*   No. 2432.
Fig. 6. *Cyathus Poeppigii.*   No. 7282.
Figs. 7–12. *Cyathus stercoreus.*   No. 5916.   Fig. 12 shows section of wall of young peridiole: lower
     layer the tunic; middle, the sclerotic layer; upper, the hymenium with basidia and delicate
     threads.
Fig. 13. *Cyathus stercoreus.*   No. 39.
Fig. 14. *Cyathus stercoreus.*   No. 5417.
Fig. 15. *Cyathus rugispermus.*   No. 7458.

Figs. 1, 5, 6, 13–15 $\times$ 503; figs. 2–4 $\times$ 1013; figs. 7–11 $\times$ 810; fig. 12 $\times$ 278.

PLATE 121

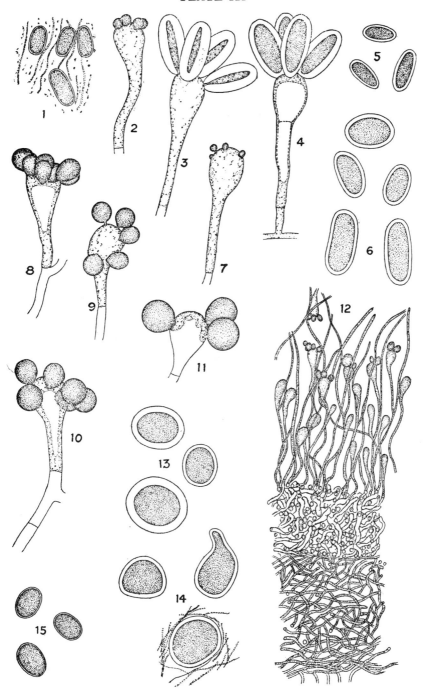

PLATE 122

Figs. 1–3. *Cyathus melanospermus*.   No. 23.
Fig.   4. *Cyathus melanospermus*.   Type.
Fig.   5. *Cyathus vernicosus*.   No. 1688.
Fig.   6. *Crucibulum vulgare*.   No. 7440.
Fig.   7. *Crucibulum vulgare*.   No. 647.
Figs.   8, 9. *Crucibulum vulgare*.   No. 5277.
Figs. 10, 11. *Nidularia pulvinata*.   Asheville, N. C.   Fig. 10 shows one of the sclerotic cells from the subhymenial layer.
Fig. 12. *Nidularia pulvinata*.   No. 7588.
Fig. 13. *Nidularia castanea*.   Newfield, N. J.

Figs. 1, 2, 8, 9 × 1013; figs. 3–7, 10 × 503; 11–13 × 1620.

PLATE 122

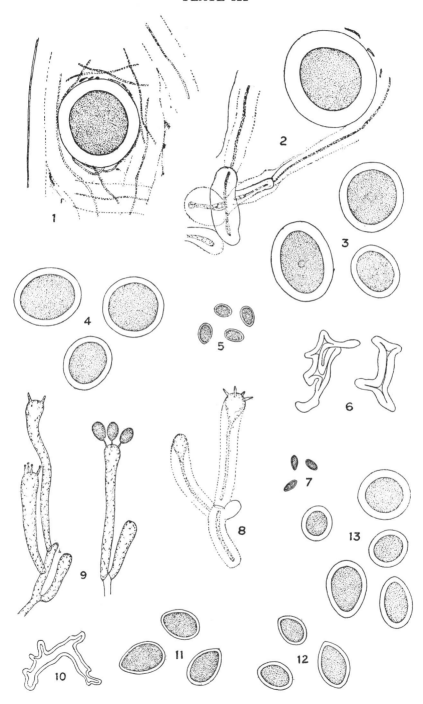

PLATE 123

Figs. 1–3. *Cyathus Lesueurii*. No. 7281 (showing spores embedded among gelatinizing threads).
Fig. 4. *Calostoma cinnabarina*. No. 5521.
Fig. 5. *Calostoma lutescens*. No. 1935.
Fig. 6. *Calostoma Ravenelii*. No. 1488.

Figs. 1–3 × 503; others × 1620.

PLATE 123

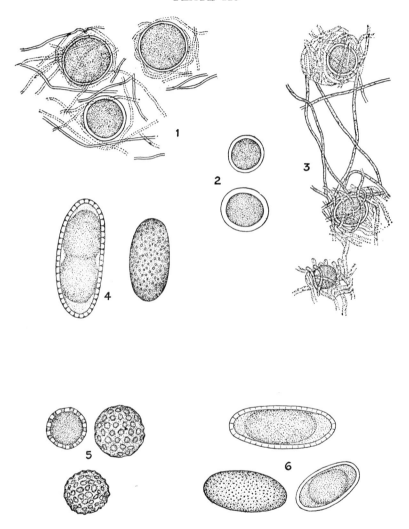

INDEX

Abstoma, 139
Agaricus tabularia, 63
Anthurus, 3, **8**
  aseroeformis, 8
  borealis, 4, **8**
  borealis var. Klitzingii, 9
  Mullerianus, 8
Arachniaceae, 1, **144**
Arachnion, 58, **144**
  album, 144, **145**
Arachniopsis, 144
Arcangeliella, 23
Astraeus, 105, 139, **185**
  hygrometricus, 124, **185**
  stellatus, 185

Battarea, 149
Boletus parasiticus, 165
Bovista, 58, 94, 96, **97,** 101, 139
  ammophila, 95
  brunnea, 100
  candida, 140
  circumscissa, 139
  gigantea, 62
  lilacina, 63
  minor, 95, 97, **99**
  montana, 97
  nigrescens, 98, 142
  ovalispora, 99
  pila, **97**
  plumbea, 90, 95, 97, 98, **99**
  radicata, 95
Bovistella, 58, 75, 86, **94,** 100
  ammophila, 95
  Davisii, 96
  dealbata, 100
  echinella, 95, **96**
  ohiensis, 95
  radicata, 75, **95,** 145
  tomentosa, 100
Broomeia, 143
  congregata, 143
  guadalupensis, 143

Calostoma, 139, 185, 187, **188**
  cinnabarina, **189,** 191
  lutescens, 189, **190**
  microsporum, 189, **192**
  Ravenelii, 189, **191**

Calostomataceae, 1, **185**
Calvatia, 1, 58, **59,** 60, 90, 94
  arctica, 66
  aurea, 60
  borealis, 66
  candida, 61
  caelata, 60, 61, 64, **68**
  craniformis, 60, **67,** 68
  cretacea, 60, **66**
  cyathiformis, 59, 60, 62, **63,** 64
  elata, 60, **65,** 81, 82, 83
  favosa, 68
  fragilis, 60, **64**
  lepidophorum, 60
  lilacina, 67
  lilacina var. occidentalis, 65
  maxima, 59, 60, 61, **62**
  novae-zelandiae, 63
  pachyderma, 60, 64, 65
  polygonia, 63
  rubro-flava, 1, 59, **60,** 93
  saccata, 65, 83
Carpobolus stellatus, 147
Catastoma circumscissum, 139
  pedicellatum, 142
Cauloglossum transversarium, 56
Chlamydopus, 149, 150
Claustula Fischeri, 3
Clathreae, 3
Clathrella, 6
Clathrus, **5,** 18
  albus, 6
  cancellatus, 4, 5, **6**
  columnatus, 4, **5,** 6
  flavescens, 6
  ruber, 6
  volvaceus, 6
Coilomyces Schweinitzii, 117
Colus, **6**
  Garciae, 7
  hirudinosus, 6
  javanicus, 7
  Mülleri, 6
  Schellenbergiae, 4, **7**
Crucibulum, 40, 173, 174, 175, **181**
  crucibuliforme, 181
  vulgare, 175, 181
Cyathia hirsuta, 175

Cyathus, 173, **174,** 175
  emodensis, 173
  fimentarius, 182
  hirsutus, 166
  intermedius, 175
  lentifera, 180
  Lesueurii, 175, 177, **179**
  Lesueurii var. minor, 178, 179
  melanospermus, 175, 178, **179**
  olla, 180
  Poeppigii, 175, **177**
  rufipes, 175
  rugispermus, 175, **178**
  stercoreus, 173, 175, **177,** 178, 179, 180, 181
  striatus, **175**
  vernicosus, 175, 178, **180**
Cycloderma ohiensis, 113

Dendrogaster connectens, 46
Dictyocephalos, 149
Dictyophora, 11, **13,** 16
  duplicata, 5, **13**
  phalloidea, 14
  Ravenelii, 11
Diplocystis, 58
  Wrightii, **143**
Disciseda, 1, 58, 59, 97, **139**
  candida, **139**
  circumscissa, 139, 141
  pedicellata, 139, 141, **142**
  subterranea, 139, **141**, 142
  verrucosa, **141**

Elasmomyces, 53, 55

Gallacea scleroderma, 51
  violacea, 51
Gautieria, 15, 20, **21,** 23
  graveolens, **22**
  morchelliformis, **22**
  Trabuti, 23
Geaster, 1, 59, 80, **102,** 185
  ambiguus, 132, 136, 138
  Archeri, 110, 135
  arenarius, 103, 105, **120**
  argentatus, 120, 138
  argenteus, 119
  asper, 105, 128, **135,** 137
  australis, 114
  avellaneus, 138
  badium, 137
  biplicatus, 132, 133
  Bryantii, 105, 129, 132, **133**
  caespitosus, 116
  calceus, 130

campestris, 135
Cesatii, 129
columnatus, 138
corallinus, 119
coronatus, 103, 105, 115, 121, 125, **129,** 132, 134, 136
Curtisii, 115
delicatus, 127
Drummondii, 103, 105, 120, **137**
elegans, 134, 137
fibrillosum, 185
fenestratus, 125
fimbriatus, 105, 106, 111, 113, 121, 123, 124, **125**
floriformis, 103, 105, 120, 121, **127**
fornicatus, 102, 103, 105, 106, 115, **124,** 129, 130
granulosus, 130
Hariotii, 103, 105, **135**
Hieronymi, 105, **123,** 124
hygrometricus, 166, 185
involutus, 137
juniperinus, 130
lageniformis, 106, 111, 112, 126, 128
leptospermus, 78, 105, **131,** 136
lignicola, 116
limbatus, 104, **107,** 122, 124, 127, 132
Lloydii, 105, **123**
lugubris, 119
mammosus, 103, 105, 111, **119,** 136, 137, 188
marchicus, 124
marginatus, 129
Michelianus, 106
minimus, 103, 127, 129
mirabilis, 105, 110, **116,** 118
Morganii, 103, 104, **109**
multifidum var. *a*, 132
papyraceus, 116, 117
pectinatus, 105, 108, **132,** 133, 134, 135
plicatus, 133
pseudo-limbatus, 109
pseudomammosus, 135
quadrifidum, 129
Rabenhorstii, 134
radicans, 103, 104, **115,** 124
Readeri, 113
rufescens, 103, 105, 106, 108, 109, **121,** 122, 123, 125, 126
saccatus, 104, 106, 109, **110,** 116, 126
saccatus, northern form, **111**
saccatus var. Walkeri, **113**
Schaefferi, 109
Schmidelii, 105, 132, **134,** 136, 137
Schweinfurthii, 137
Smithii, 132, 136
stellatus, 185

stipitatus, 102
striatulus, 136
striatus, 107, 134
striatus var. minimus, 137
subiculosus, 104, 114, 116, **118**
tenuipes, 133, 135
terreus, 130
trichifer, 105, 116, **118**
triplex, 104, **106,** 108, 109, 111, 112, 114, 115, 126
tunicatus, 125
umbilicatus, 105, **136**
velutinus, 104, 112, **113,** 115, 124
Welwitschii, 115
Geastrum fibrillosum, 185
minimum, 137
Granularia, 183
castanea, 184
pisiformis, 183
pulvinata, 183
Gymnomyces, 15, 21, **23**
vesiculosus, **23**
Gyrophragmium decipiens, 55
Delilei, 55
Gyropodium coccineum, 189

Holocotylon, 144
Hydnangium, 25, 47
carneum, 48
galathejum, 49
hysterangioides, 25
liospermum, 25
monosporum, 51
Ravenelii, 48
Stephensii, 49
Stephensii var. Ravenelii, 48
Hymenogaster, 24, **45,** 46
anomalus, 44, 45
decorus, 45, 46, 47
foetidus, **45**
Thwaitesii, 45, 46, **47**
utriculatus, 46
Hymenogastraceae, 1, **24,** 26, 173
Hypoblema, 60
Hysterangiaceae, 1, 3, **15,** 26
Hysterangium, 15, **17,** 21, 25, 36, 46, 51
calcareum, 18
clathroides, 15, **17,** 19, 20, 21, 26
coriaceum, 18
fragile, 18
membranaceum, 18
nephriticum, 18
pompholyx, 17, 18, **19**
rubricatum, 18
stoloniferum, 18, 21

stoloniferum var. americanum, 17, 19, **20**
stoloniferum var. mutabile, 21
Thwaitesii, 18

Ithyphallus, **11**
imperialis, 12
impudicus, 5, **12,** 13
Ravenelii, 5, **11,** 12
rubicundus, 5, **13**

Jaczewskia, 16

Key to the Families, 1
Key to the Phalloids of the United States, 4

Laternea columnata, 5
Leucogaster, 24, **42,** 45
anomalus, 42, **44**
araneosus, 42, **43,** 44
badius, 42, **44**
carolinianus, 42, **43**
fulvimaculosus, 42, **44**
luteomaculatus, **42**
Leucophleps, 51
magnata, 51
Lycoperdaceae, 1, **58**
Lycoperdon, 1, 58, 59, **69,** 84, 86, 93, 94, 139, 144, 145
abscissum, 89
acuminatum, 70, **78,** 132
atropurpureum, 70, **71**
atropurpureum var. stellare, 72, 74, 75
Berkeleyi, 67
bovista, 62
caelatum, 68, 166
calvescens, 87
candidum, 90
calyptriforme, 78
caudatum, 85
cepaeforme, 61, 75, 92
coloratum, 71, **93**
compactum, 74
constellatum, 73, 85
cretaceum, 66
cruciatum, 87
cupricum, 87
cupricum var., 76
Curtisii, 71, **89**
cyathiforme, 63
delicatum, 62, 67, 68
depressum, 69
dryinum, 87
echinatum, 70, 72, **73,** 85
elatum, 65
elegans, 77

excipuliforme, 82, 166
eximium, 71, 85, **86**
favosum, 68
Fontanesii, 68
Frostii, 72
furfuraceum, 93
fuscum, 71, 85, **87**
giganteum, 62
gemmatum, 65, 71, **82,** 85, 88, 89, 166
glabellum, 76
hirtum, 76
lepidophorum, 60
leprosum, 78, 113
macrogemmatum, 82
marginatum, 66, 71, 73, **87,** 90
Missouriense, 67
molle, 77, 78, 81, 82
muscorum, 65, 70, 71, **81,** 102
nigrescens, 83, 85
oblongisporum, 71, **91,** 92
papillatum, 87
Peckii, 71, **84**
pedicellatum, 71, **85,** 89
perlatum, 83, 84
polymorphum, 61, 69, 71, **92,** 94
polytrichum, 81
pratense, 88, 89
pseudoradicans, 70, 81
pulcherrimum, 70, **72,** 74, 85
pusillum, 69, 71, 90, **91,** 93, 94
pusio, 119
pyriforme, 70, 71, **79,** 83
recolligens, 188
rimulatum, 70, **75,** 76
saccatum, 65
sculptum, 70
separans, 87
Sinclairii, 68
subincarnatum, 71, **80**
subvelatum, 70, **76**
Turneri, 77
umbrinum, 70, 71, **76**
Warnei, 55
Wrightii, 89
Lysurus, 8
  australiensis, 9
  Clarazianus, 9
  Gardneri, 9
  Mokusin, 8
  Texensis, 8

Macowanites, 23, 53
Marasmius oreades, 63
Melanogaster, 24, 35, 36, **38,** 41
  ambiguus, 38, **41**
  mollis, 38

nauseosus, 38, **39**
odoratissimus, 40
rubescens, 38, **40**
variegatus, **38,** 40, 41
Mitremyces, 189
  lutescens, 191
  Tylerii, 192
Mutinus, **9**
  bovinus, 10
  caninus, 4, 10
  Curtisii, 4, **10**
  elegans, 10
  Ravenelii, 4, **9,** 10
Mycenastrum, 58, 97, **101**
  corium, **101**
  corium var. Kara-Kumianum, 101
  radicatum, 101
  spinulosum, 101
Myriostoma, 1, 58, 59, **138**
  coliformis, **138**

Nidula, 173, 174
Nidularia, 174, **183**
  alabamensis, 183
  castanea, 183, **184**
  fascicularia, 180
  globosa, 166, 183
  Juglandicola, 181
  pisiformis, 183
  pulvinata, **183**
  stercorea, 177
Nidulariaceae, 1, **173**
Nigropogon, 24, **37**
  asterosporus, **37**

Octaviania, 24, 25, **47,** 173
  asterosperma, 25, 48, **51**
  compacta, 25, 26
  purpurea, 38, 48, **50**
  Ravenelii, 48
  Stephensii var. Ravenelii, 48

Peziza striatus, 176
Phallaceae, 1, **3**
Phalleae, 3
Phallogaster, 3, 15, **16,** 20
  saccatus, **16**
  Whitei, 17
Phallus aurantiacus, 13
  imperialis, 13
  impudicus, 11
  indusiatus, 14
  Ravenelii, 11
  rubicundus, 11
  togatus, 14

Phellorina, 160
Phlyctospora fusca, 160
Pisolithus, 144, 160, **170**
    arenarius, 170
    tinctorius, 170
Podaxaceae, 160
Podaxon, 56, 160
Polysaccum, 170
    crassipes, 170
    pisocarpium, 170
Protophallus, 3, **15**
    jamaicensis, **16,** 21
Protubera, 3, 16
Pseudocolus, 6

Queletia, 149, **158**
    mirabilis, **158**

Rhacophyllus, 53
Rhizopogon, 24, **26,** 33, 37, 38, 41
    aestivus, 41
    albus, 29
    atlanticus, 27, 29, **35,** 36
    diplophloeus, 41
    graveolens, 27, 30
    luteolus, 27, 28, 29, **33,** 35
    maculatus, 27, **35**
    nigrescens, 27, 29, **30,** 35
    pachyphloeus, 41
    parasiticus, 26, **27**
    piceus, 27, 31, **34,** 35
    provincialis, 31
    roseolus, 26, 27, 29, 31, **32**
    rubescens, 27, **28,** 31, 32, 33, 34, 41, 48
    rubescens var. Vittadini, 29
    truncatus, 27, **36**
Rhopalogaster, 53, **56**
    transversarium, **56**

Sclerangium polyrhizon, 161
Scleroderma, 38, 101, **160,** 170
    aurantium, 66, 161, **165**
    bovista, 161, **163, 164,** 167
    cepa, 161, 163, 165, **167,** 169
    flavidum, 161, **162,** 165, 167
    fuscum, 160
    geaster, **161,** 163
    lycoperdoides, 160, 161, 165, **168**
    lycoperdoides var. reticulatum, 161, **170**
    pteridis, 160, 162
    tenerum, 168, 169
    Texense, 164
    verrucosum, 161, 168, 169
    vulgare, 165
Sclerodermataceae, 1, **160**
Sclerogaster, 24, **25**
    compactus, 26
    lanatus, 26
    minor, **25**

Secotiaceae, 1, **53**
Secotium, **53**
    acuminatum, 54, 55
    agaricoides, **54**
    arizonicum, 55
    australe, 55
    decipiens, 55
    krjukowense, 53
    rubigenum, 54, 55
    russuloides, 55
    tenuipes, 55
    Warnei, 54, 55
Simblum, 5, **7**
    rubescens, 7
    rubescens var. Kansensis, 7
    sphaerocephalum, 4, **7**
    texense, 4, 7
Sphaeria herculea, 56
Sphaericeps, 149
Sphaerobolaceae, 1, **146**
Sphaerobolus, **146**
    carpobolus, 147
    impaticus, 146
    iowensis, 146, **148**
    stellatus, 146, **147,** 148
    stellatus var. giganteus, 146, **148**
Stella americana, 161

Trichaster melanocephalus, 102
Tulasnodea, 150
    fimbriata, 158
Tulostoma, 150
Tylostoma, **149,** 158, 174, 185, 187
    albicans, 154
    americanum, 154
    Berkeleyii, 150, **157**
    brumale, 151
    campestre, 150, **156,** 157
    fimbriatum, 156
    Finkii, 150, **154**
    floridanum, 150, 151, **153**
    gracile, 154
    granulosum, 155, 156, 157
    kansense, 154
    Lloydii, 150, 154, **156**
    Longii, 154
    mammosum, 150, **151,** 152, 153, 158
    minutum, 154
    obesum, 155
    pedunculatum, 151, 152
    poculatum, 150, **155,** 156
    punctatum, 157
    pygmaeum, 153
    simulans, 150, **151,** 153
    squammosum, 154, 158
    verrucosum, 150, **153**
    volvulatum, 150, **155**
Tylostomataceae, 1, **149**

THE
GASTEROMYCETAE
OF OHIO
Puffballs, Birds'-Nest Fungi
and Stinkhorns

BY

MINNIE MAY JOHNSON

An unabridged reprint of an article that was originally
published in the *Ohio Biological Survey Bulletin 22,*
Vol. IV, No. 7, pp. 271-352.

TABLE OF CONTENTS

	Page
PREFACE	3
INTRODUCTION	4
DISTRIBUTION AND HABITAT	6
SYNOPSIS OF THE OHIO GASTEROMYCETAE	7
KEY TO THE GENERA OF THE GASTEROMYCETAE	7
ORDER I. HYMENOGASTRALES	9
Family Secotiaceae	10
Family Hymenogastraceae	10
ORDER II. SCLERODERMATALES	12
Family Sclerodermataceae	13
Family Arachniaceae	17
ORDER III. LYCOPERDALES	18
Family Lycoperdaceae	19
Family Calostomataceae	53
Family Tylostomataceae	55
ORDER IV. NIDULARIALES	62
Family Sphaerobolaceae	62
Family Nidulariaceae	64
ORDER V. PHALLALES	67
Family Clathraceae	67
Family Phallaceae	69
LITERATURE CITED	73
EXPLANATION OF PLATES	77

PREFACE

This study of the Gasteromycetae of Ohio was begun during the summer of 1923 at the suggestion of Dr. W. G. Stover and has been carried on under his direction. During this time the writer has examined the literature dealing with the group; has collected a large number of specimens in Ohio and in parts of Michigan; and has studied these specimens together with those in the Lloyd Museum and in the herbaria of Dr. W. G. Stover, and the Ohio State University. From these investigations a list of the genera and species found or likely to be found in Ohio has been prepared, descriptions for each of the genera and species have been written, and keys to aid in the identification of specimens have been worked out.

The principal writings consulted in the preparation of this paper have been those of Coker and Couch (7), Peck (54), Morgan (49), and Lloyd (21-44). These and others are listed under "Literature Cited" at the end of the paper. The most recent of these is "The Gasteromycetes of Eastern United States and Canada," by Coker and Couch. This is very complete work covering a much larger territory and a greater number of species than that undertaken by the writer in this paper. Coker and Couch also include many additional notes on the morphology of the Gasteromycetes and on individual species. Hard (13) and McIlvaine (46) also describe and illustrate many of the species and these works are available in most libraries.

In order to conserve space in this paper, the writer is not giving citations to the literature and illustrations under each species. If desired, this information may be found in Coker and Couch (7).

The writer here wishes to express her appreciation to Dr. W. G. Stover for his help and guidance; to Dr. J. H. Schaffner for his interest and helpful suggestions; to Miss MacKay of the Lloyd Library for the use of books and the privilege of studying the specimens in the Lloyd Museum; to C. G. Johnson, C. G. Brooks, R. B. Gordon, R. A. Dobbins, and F. H. Haskett for assistance in taking the photographs; and to others who have aided in the collection of specimens.

* Papers from the Department of Botany, Ohio State University, No. 250. Presented in partial fulfillment of the requirements for the degree of Doctor of Philosophy in the Graduate School of the Ohio State University.

INTRODUCTION

The Gasteromycetae are the highest of the fungi. They consist of a large assemblage of fungi quite unlike in external appearance, but all characterized by having their spores formed within the *peridium*. The sporebearing surface is composed of basidia which are usually arranged in a more or less definite layer, called the *hymenium*. Each basidium usually produces four spores which are either sessile or borne on a stem-like structure, called the *sterigma*, which is termed a pedicel when it remains attached to the mature spore.

There are five orders, twenty-eight genera, and ninety-two species of Gasteromycetae found in the north central section of the United States. All of these genera except three, Pseudocolus, Hymenogaster, and Queletia, are found in Ohio and it is quite probable that these may also occur here, since they are found in neighboring states. One genus, Rhizopogon, and four species are new records for this state.

On the basis of their different general characteristics the Gasteromycetae may be divided into three popular groups: the puffballs, the birds'-nest fungi, and the stinkhorns.

Many species of puffballs are edible if collected when young and with the interior still white. So far as known there are no poisonous species. In many cases the fruiting body is too small or too tough to be eaten with pleasure. Obviously the mature puffball, mainly consisting as it does of a mass of dry spores and fine threads, is not "edible," even though it is not poisonous. The species of Calvatia and a number of species of Lycoperdon are especially prized by mushroom lovers. The eggs of at least some of the stinkhorns are reported to be edible but they are certainly not appetizing. The fruiting-bodies of the birds'-nests are small and tough and are not used as food.

I. *The Puffballs.*

This is the largest and most commonly known group of the Gasteromycetae. The principal characteristic is that the sporebearing portion, or the gleba, which occupies the interior of the fruiting-body, becomes dry and powdery at maturity in all genera except Rhizopogon and Hymenogaster where it remains firm until its slowly decays. The gleba in some species fills the entire fruit-

4

ing-body, which is then said to be sessile. In other cases the lower portion does not develop spores and is called the sterile base.

In most species the whole interior of the very young puffball is an undifferentiated, soft mass of cells. Later, in most genera, countless numbers of irregular, minute cavities are developed in the cellular mass. Each cavity in the fertile portion is lined with basidia. As the spores mature the hymenial tissue deliquesces and disappears, leaving the fertile portion of the fruiting-body filled with a disarranged, powdery mass of spores and threads when dried. In one order of the puffballs there are no gleba cavities and the basidia are arranged irregularly throughout the fertile portion. At maturity the gleba then becomes either a powdery mass as in Scleroderma, or breaks up into small bodies called *peridioles* as in Arachnion.

No such change, however, takes place in the sterile base. It remains firm and is usually a long time persistent. In some species the sterile portion is more or less well developed, forming a long stem-like, or a cup-like base below the gleba. Sometimes the sterile base extends up into the gleba forming the *columella* as in Secotium and Geaster.

The mature gleba in most of the genera consists of spores and long intertwined threads called the *capillitium*. In some genera, as Scleroderma and Arachnion, the capillitium is very rudimentary or entirely wanting.

The interior of the fruiting-body is surrounded by a rind-like structure called the *peridium*. In a few genera, as Scleroderma and Arachnion, the peridium is a single layer. In other genera there are two rather distinct layers, termed the *inner peridium* and the *outer peridium*. Each of these may consist of a single layer or two or more structurally differentiated secondary layers. In most of the genera the inner peridium dehisces by means of a more or less definite opening, but in others it, together with the sporebearing mass, breaks into fragments which are blown away by the wind.

II. *Birds'-Nest Fungi.*

The fruiting-body of this group of the Gasteromycetes is cup- or bell-shaped, closed when young with a covering called the *epiphragm*, but open at maturity. The spores are borne in egg-like structures or *peridioles* which are within the fruiting-body. These fungi usually grow on decayed wood, leaves, sticks, or rubbish. Some species, however, grow directly on the ground. There are four genera commonly known as the "bird's-nest" fungi.

III. *The Stinkhorns.*

The Gasteromycetes having elongated fleshy or spongy fruiting-bodies with a slimy, ill-smelling spore mass are popularly known as "stinkhorns" or "carrion fungi." When young the whole fruiting-body is enclosed in a tough, white or pinkish-white peridium, ovoid to globose in shape and usually subterranean. In this stage it is referred to as a "phalloid egg."

In all genera except Phallogaster the fruiting-body at maturity elongates forming a hollow, cylindical, spongy stem or *stipe* with the sporebearing surface or *receptacle* at the apex. The tough outer covering of the "egg," remains as a cup-like structure, called a *volva*, at the base of the stipe. In Mutinus the receptacle is the apex of the stipe; in other genera it consists of a definite cap or *pileus*, or of a lattice work, or of finger-like projections, called arms, attached by their bases to the apex of the stipe.

Species of six genera have been reported in this region.

Distribution and Habitat

Ohio is situated in an interesting position in relation to the distribution of the Gasteromycetes. The northern part lies in the Great Lakes region and it is here that Tylostoma and Myriostoma are found. The prairie region extends into the western part of Ohio and the genus Mycenastrum, which is a common western species, occurs there. The genus Calostoma, which is generally reported in the Appalachian Mountain region, is found in the hills of southeastern Ohio. *Bovistella radicata* is found almost entirely in southern Ohio. Other genera of the Gasteromycetes are scattered more or less over the state with each species in its respective habitat.

There are both subterranean and aerial forms of the Gasteromycetes. The former are very rare in this section and the only species reported for Ohio, *Rhizopogon roseolus,* was collected by the writer at Old Man's Cave, Hocking County. Other hypogeal forms probably grow here, but they remain to be discovered. Some of the aerial forms are subterranean when young, but are exposed or extended above the soil surface at maturity.

Most of the Gasteromycetes grow in rich soil or on decaying logs and stumps in damp woods. Certain species are usually found growing among moss plants. Other Gasteromycetes are more xerophytic in habitat, some species inhabiting open woods, pastures, lawns, and even cultivated fields, while others are found in sandy soil in mixed and coniferous forests. The mycelium of some species is reported to form mycorrhizas with the roots of forest trees.

The Gasteromycetes are well distributed throughout the State. So far as the writer has found, the richest collecting field is in the Sugar Grove region. The fruiting period of these fungi occurs mainly during late summer and autumn. Calostoma, however, matures in April and May and some species of Rhizopogon are found during the winter months.

SYNOPSIS OF THE OHIO GASTEROMYCETAE

ORDER I.   HYMENOGASTRALES
        Family 1. *Secotiaceae*
            Genus: Secotium
        Family 2. *Hymenogastraceae*
            Genera: Rhizopogon, and Hymenogaster

ORDER II.   SCLERODERMATALES
        Family 1. *Sclerodermataceae*
            Genera: Scleroderma, and Pisolithus
        Family 2. *Arachniaceae*
            Genus: Arachnion

ORDER III.   LYCOPERDALES
        Family 1. *Lycoperdaceae*
            Genera: Mycenastrum, Bovista, Bovistella, Calvatia,
                 Lycoperdon, Disciseda, Astraeus, Geaster,
                 and Myriostoma
        Family 2. *Calostomataceae*
            Genus: Calostoma
        Family 3. *Tylostomataceae*
            Genera: Queletia and Tylostoma

ORDER IV.   NIDULARIALES
        Family 1. *Sphaerobolaceae*
            Genus: Sphaerobolus
        Family 2. *Nidulariaceae*
            Genera: Nidularia, Crucibulum, and Cyathus

ORDER V.   PHALLALES
        Family 1. *Clathraceae*
            Genera: Phallogaster, Anthurus, and Pseudocolus
        Family 2. *Phallaceae*
            Genera: Mutinus, Phallus, and Dictyophora.

KEY TO THE GENERA OF THE GASTEROMYCETAE

I. Fruiting-body usually without a marked odor; more or less persistent; gleba never apical or slimy...................................... II
I. Fruiting-body usually with a strong, disagreeable odor when fresh; soon decaying; globose or egg-shaped when young, inclosed in a thick peridium which at maturity persists as a cup at the base; usually stalked; spore mass slimy at maturity, borne at the apex of the stalk, or on a special cap-like, lattice-like or branched receptacle, or on the inner surface of the lobes of the split peridium. .23. Phallales (Stinkhorns)
   II. Fruiting-body usually fleshy or tough-fleshy when young; not cup-like; subglobose to top-shaped; gleba at maturity dry and dusty or powdery or more rarely firm with permanent cavities
      1. Hymenogastrales, Sclerodermatales, and Lycoperdales (Puffballs)
   II. Fruiting-body usually tough and leathery; persistent; cup- or in-verted bell-shaped; containing one or more egg-like peridioles which inclose the spores........20. Nidulariales (Birds'-nest fungi)

1.—PUFFBALLS

1. Fruiting-body usually subterranean; gleba firm, conspicuous with prominent subglobose to labyrinthiform cavities.................... 2
1. Fruiting-body aerial at maturity; gleba becoming dry and powdery, without permanent cavities.. 3
  2. Peridium with conspicuous external veins or fibrils, spores naked
                                                   3. *Rhizopogon*
  2. Peridium without superficial fibrils; spores surrounded by a sheath
                                             2. *Hymenogaster*
3. Outer peridium splitting radially and turning back into star-like segments 4
3. Outer peridium not splitting as above............................. 6
  4. Inner peridium with a single apical pore or opening............. 5
  4. Inner peridium with a number of openings...........15. *Myriostoma*
5. Capillitium much branched, columella absent, spores 8 microns or more in diameter; segments of outer peridium strongly incurved when dry
                                           13. *Astraeus*
5. Capillitium unbranched, columella present, spores less than 8 microns in diameter; segments of outer peridium incurved or not when dry
                                           14. *Geaster*
  6. Fruiting-body with a stem which is much smaller than the base of the spore-bearing portion.. 7
  6. Fruiting-body sessile or with a thick base of about the same diameter as the spore-bearing portion............................. 10
7. Fruiting-body with a central columella extending to the apex..1. *Secotium*
7. Fruiting-body without a columella................................. 8
  8. Stem inserted in a socket or depression in the base of the fruiting-body 9
  8. Stem or stipe-like sterile base a slender continuation of the spore-bearing portion, not inserted in a socket.................10. *Calvatia*
9. Fruiting-body opening by a definite apical mouth...........18. *Tylostoma*
9. Fruiting-body without a definite apical opening, the peridium breaking away irregularly.....................................17. *Queletia*
  10. Capillitium of cottony threads abundantly mingled with the mature spore mass... 11
  10. Capillitium wanting or scanty.................................... 16
11. Capillitium bearing scattered prickles or short spines; spores 9-12 microns in diameter; fruiting-body without prominent sterile base; inner peridium thick and rigid................................7. *Mycenastrum*
11. Capillitium without prickles; spores less than 8 microns, fruiting-body with or without thickened sterile base; inner peridium various........ 12
  12. Capillitium free, rather short, dichotomously branched several times, the branches short, tapering to a point................... 13
  12. Capillitium partly attached to the inner wall of the peridium, not dichotomously branched, branches long, not conspicuously tapering 14
13. Fruiting-body yellowish-brown with well-marked sterile base; outer peridium floccose, warty, or spiny........................9. *Bovistella*
13. Fruiting-body darker, reddish-brown, purplish-brown, or lead-colored; without sterile base; outer peridium thin, continuous, not spiny nor warty ....8. *Bovista*
  14. The upper portion of the inner peridium breaking away at maturity and containing the inner peridium which opens by a basal mouth ....12. *Disciseda*
  14. Not as above.. 15
15. Outer peridium very thin, membranous; inner peridium fragile, at maturity breaking up into fragments which fall away; fruiting-body large, usually more than 10 cm. in diameter....................10. *Calvatia*
15. Outer peridium composed of scales, spines, warts, or granules; inner peridium membranous to papery, persistent, usually opening by an apical mouth at maturity; fruiting-body less than 8 cm. in diameter
                                           11. *Lycoperdon*
  16. Columella extending to the apex of the fruiting-body and downward as a short stipe....................................1. *Secotium*

16. Columella absent..17
17. Fruiting-body with a thick rooting base made up of numerous anastomosing fibers; spore-bearing portion at the apex, subglobose; opening
by an apical stellate mouth............................16. *Calostoma*
17. Fruiting-body not as above......................................18
18. Peridium thick or thin, tough and leathery; at least persistent;
spores not in peridoles............................4. *Scleroderma*
18. Peridium very fragile, crumbling away at maturity or earlier;
spores borne in peridioles....................................19
19. Fruiting-body sessile or nearly so; spores 3-4 microns, smooth
6. *Arachnion*
19. Fruiting-body with stem-like base; spores 9-13 microns, warted
5. *Pisolithus*

20.—BIRDS'-NEST FUNGI

20. Fruiting-body 1-3 mm. in diameter, globose; dehiscing stellately;
peridiole single, shot away at maturity, leaving the peridium as a
cup...19. *Sphaerobolus*
20. Fruiting-body more than 4 mm. in diameter when mature, cup-, or
inverted bell-shaped; peridioles more than one..................21
21. Peridioles attached by a thread or cord (funiculus); covered when
young with a felt-like membrane (epiphragm)....................22
21. Peridioles adhering together; funiculus and epiphragh wanting
20. *Nidularia*
22. Peridioles white..................................21. *Crucibulum*
22. Peridioles dark gray, to brown or black.............22. *Cyathus*

23.—STINKHORNS

23. Gleba borne on a receptacle at the apex of a spongy stem............24
23. Gleba borne on the inner surface of the lobes of the split peridium
23. *Phallogaster*
24. Receptacle entire, tubular or conical, the gleba borne on the outer
surface 25
24. Receptacle divided into arms with the gleba borne on the inner surfaces 27
25. Receptacle a definite cap-like pileus 26
25. Receptacle not pileate, but consisting of the apical portion of the stem
26. *Mutinus*
26. Veil single, membranous, usually obvious; pileus smooth, granular
or reticulated..27. *Phallus*
26. Veils two, one net-like and well developed, the other membranous;
pileus prominently reticulated....................28. *Dictyophora*
27. Arms free...25. *Anthurus*
27. Arms united at their apices.....................24. *Pseudocolus*

GASTEROMYCETAE

The Gasteromycetae are those fungi in which the spores are
formed on basidia within the fruiting-body which is enclosed by a
peridium of one or more layers. The spores at maturity may be enclosed by the peridium or within peridioles, or they may be exposed
on a receptacle. They are disseminated in various ways.

ORDER I. HYMENOGASTRALES

Fruiting-body mostly subterranean; indehiscent; capillitium
wanting; spores borne in gleba chambers which are separated by

trama plates. Two families have been reported for Ohio and neighboring states.

Family 1. *Secotiaceae*. Columella axillary, extending from the sterile base to the apex and continuous with the peridium. Gleba composed of radiating tramal plates which are lamella-like. Secotium is the only genus found in Ohio.

1. Secotium Kunze. 1840

Fruiting-body obovate with a short stalk extending to the apex, forming a columella. Peridium varying in thickness, dehiscing irregularly at the base. Capillitium none. Cavities of the gleba separated by persistent, lamella-like folds radiating from the columella. Spores ovate, colored, smooth or rough.

Only one species is reported within our range.

Secotium agaricoides (Czern.) Hollos

Plate I. Figure 1.

Fruiting-body depressed globose to acute-ovate with a short stalk. Peridium persistent, usually continuous, sometimes scaly, white at first, then buff-colored; varying in thickness, dehiscing at the base in a circle about the stalk. Gleba olive-brown to brown, consisting of numerous chambers separated by lamella-like plates radiating from the columella and becoming powdery when mature; columella extending to the apex; capillitium none; spore mass yellowish-brown to brown. Spores smooth, ovate, 4-6.5 x 5.5-8 microns, often with a minute pedicel.

Habitat: Pastures and cultivated fields. May to October.

Distribution: In all parts of the United States except the extreme East.

S. agaricoides is very variable as to size and shape. The radiating tramal plates and the well-developed columella are the distinguishing characters. Immature fruiting-bodies are similar in appearance to unexpanded gill-fungi, such as species of Coprinus. The radiating tramal plates which resemble lamellae suggest relationship with the Agaricaceae. This species is occasionally found in all parts of the north central section. It has also been known in literature as *S. acuminatum* Mont.

Family 2. *Hymenogastraceae*. Fruiting-body indehiscent, sterile base present or wanting. Gleba conspicuous with permanent, irregular cavities which are separated by the sterile tissue or septa. Two genera, Rhizopogon and Hymenogaster, are found in this region.

2. Hymenogaster Vitt. 1831.

Fruiting-body entirely or partially embedded in the soil, irregularly globose to globose, sometimes with a well-developed sterile base. Peridium of one layer, thin or fishy. Gleba composed of irregular cavities, empty or stuffed, usually radiating from the base, but sometimes scattered throughout the fruiting-body. Spores colored, irregularly ovate to elliptical.

Only one species of this genus has been reported for this section.

Hymenogaster nanus Mass. & Rodw.

"Peridium globose, irregular, barely viscid, 1.5 cm. wide, grayish-brown, easily separated from the gleba; cavities radiating from the sterile base; septa thick, brown. Spores elliptical, subacute at both ends, minutely warted, bright yellow-brown, 14-15 x 8 microns."

Habitat: Subterranean.

Distribution: Tasmania and reported from Michigan.

This species, described by Massee and Rodway (2), was founded on a single specimen collected by Rodway in Tasmania. His notes state that this specimen resembled *Secotium gunnii* B. & C. The only other collection of this species which has come to the notice of the writer was made by Kauffman (16) at Ann Arbor, Michigan. He failed to publish a description of his collection and the writer has not seen it. The above description is a translation of the original description.

3. Rhizopogon Fr. 1817.

Fruiting-body 0.5-7.0 cm. in diameter, globose to elliptical, often very irregular, more or less covered with mycelial strands or fibrils, sometimes growing on the surface of the ground, but usually partially or entirely embedded. Peridium of one or two layers, composed of vesicular or floccose hyphae. Gleba gelatinous, with labyrinthiform or subglobose cavities which are separated by the tramal plates or septa and are more or less filled with spores at maturity. Spores smooth, elliptical, 1-2 guttulate, often with a short pedicel.

Although the genus Rhizopogon is widely distributed over the United States, it is mostly confined to the Atlantic, the Pacific, and the Gulf regions. Only two species have been reported in this section but other species may possibly occur here. Zeller and Dodge (68) have recently written a careful monograph of this genus.

KEY TO THE SPECIES

1. Peridium reddish- to dark-brown; septa 36-72 microns wide; spores 2-3.5 x 3.5-5 microns..................................1. *R. rubescens*
1. Peridium yellowish- to greenish-brown; septa 90-100 microns wide; spores 3-4 x 8-12 microns..................................2. *R. roseolus*

1.　Rhizopogon rubescens Tul.

Fruiting-body subterranean, subglobose, often irregular, 1-6 cm. in diameter, with a few scattered fibrils which are inconspicuous and flattened above, becoming more conspicuous and rhizomorph-like at the base. Peridium thin, simple, 160-220 microns wide, white at first, then reddish, and finally changing to dark brown or black when dry. Immature gleba white, becoming greenish-to tannish brown when mature; glebal cavities empty, irregularly subglobose to labyrinthiform with narrow septa, 36-72 microns wide. Spores elliptical, smooth, hyaline, 2-3.5 x 3.5-5.5 microns, usually with two oil drops.

Habitat: Sandy soil under pines and firs. Gregarious. Autumn and winter.

Distribution: In all parts of the United States except the North Central States.

Although this species is widely distributed over the United States, it is quite rare in this section, having been only reported from Pennsylvania. This species is somewhat similar to *R. roseolus* (Corda) Hollos, but it may be distinguished by the reddish-colored peridium, the narrow septa, and the smaller spores.

2.　Rhizopogon roseolus (Corda) Hollos

Fruiting-body 0.5-3 cm. in diameter, sub-globose, often irregular, whitish in color when fresh, but becoming yellowish to greenish-brown when mature, often with black spots; fibrils dark brown or black, usually wanting at the apex, but forming flattened ridges at the base. Peridium compact, single, 160-300 microns in thickness; gleba whitish or light yellow and gelatinous when fresh, becoming buff-colored to yellowish-brown and hard when dry; cavities labyrinthiform, empty; septa 99-100 microns thick, compact, composed of gelatinized hyphal threads; basidia elliptical, 1-2 spored. Spores smooth, elliptical, 3-4 x 8-12 microns, with two oil drops.

Habitat: Sandy soil in coniferous or mixed forests.

Distribution: Eastern and southern states; also Ohio.

In 1926 the writer collected this species at Old Man's Cave near Logan, Ohio. The fungus was growing in a pine-hemlock forest and the fruiting-body was partially embedded in the sandy-loam soil. The specimen was identified by Dr. C. W. Dodge of Harvard University. According to Zellar and Dodge (68) it had previously been reported only in the Atlantic and Gulf states.

ORDER II.　SCLERODERMATALES

Fruiting-body with or without sterile base. Gleba with or without cavities; in a few cases dividing up into minute peridioles;

finally becoming a dusty or powdery mass; basidia irregularly arranged throughout the fertile portion and not forming a distinct hymenium. Capillitium wanting or rudimentary, or well developed.

Family 1. *Sclerodermataceae*. Peridium thick, of one layer, usually warty or scaly; gleba breaking up into solid peridioles in one genus; capillitium rudimentary or wanting. Sterile base often present. Scleroderma is the most common genus. Pisolithus is also found in Ohio.

4. **Scleroderma** Pers. 1801.

Fruiting-body globose to depressed-globose, usually sessile, but occasionally tapering into a stem-like base. Peridium a single layer, usually very thick, tough, and hard, from which comes the term "scleroderm," but thin and leathery in some species; commonly covered with persistent irregular warts or granules, but comparatively smooth in a few species. Mouth irregular or with stellate segments. Gleba uniform, at first white, later becoming greenish to purplish-brown. Capillitium none or rudimentary, consisting of flocci. Spores large, globose, rough, 9-18 microns in diameter, mixed with remains of the tramal walls.

KEY TO THE SPECIES

1. Peridium rough with scales or warts.............................. 3
1. Peridium smooth or areolate (surface cracked or broken into small areas) 2
    2. Spores reticulated and spiny, 9-15 microns..............2. *S. bovista*
    2. Spores spiny but not reticulated 4.5-10 microns............1. *S. cepa*
3. Peridium thick and rigid with large warts or fleshy scales; spores reticulated 4
3. Peridium thin and flexible with smaller flat warts or scales; spores not reticulated 5
    4. Outer peridium with raised warts, opening irregularly, not with recurved stellate lobes, less than 1 mm. thick when dry; fruiting-body 2-5 cm.......................................4. *S. aurantium*
    4. Outer peridium with fleshy scales, at maturity opening by large stellate segments which turn backward, more than 1 mm. thick, fruiting-body 4-15 cm..............................6. *S. geaster*
5. Peridium opening at maturity by breaking into more or less stellate lobes...5. *S. flavidum*
5. Peridium opening irregularly, not stellately...........3. *S. lycoperdoides*

1. **Scleroderma cepa** (Vaill.) Pers.

Fruiting-body 1-5 cm. in diameter, globose to depressed-globose, usually sessile or with a short sterile base. Peridium reddish-yellow to reddish-brown, very thick at first, becoming thinner at maturity, smooth except for a few flat scales at the apex; dehiscing by an irregular breaking of the peridium. Gleba white at first, becoming purplish-black when mature, powdery, tramal tissue white. Spores globose, dark brown, acutely echinulated, 4.5-10 microns in diameter; 18.5 microns in diameter when still surrounded by nurse hyphae.

Habitat: Sandy soil in woods.

Distribution: Wisconsin, Ohio, North Carolina, Massachusetts, and Florida.

This is a rather rare species in this section, but has been collected in Ohio. The fruiting-body in general is quite similar to that of *S. bovista* Fr. and it is probable that the two species have been confused in American collections. The writer has studied several collections of each species. In *S. cepa* the spores are rather light-brown, spiny, not reticulated although an occasional spore appears reticulated, perhaps due to the position of the spines. According to Rea (59) the tramal plates are whitish, then grayish, tinged darker or lilac. As compared with *S. bovista* the spores are smaller, lighter colored, and the spines are shorter and less numerous.

2. Scleroderma bovista Fr.

Fruiting-body 2-5 cm. in diameter, subglobose, often irregular w,ith root-like mycelium at the base. Peridium thin, yellowish to tannish-brown, smooth, sometimes with a few flat scales, dehiscing by breaking irregularly. Gleba at first whitish, becoming olive to purple-brown and powdery at maturity; tramal plates yellow; capillitium rudimentary and floccose. Spores olive-brown, globose, 9-15 microns in diameter, spiny, reticulated.

Habitat: Damp sandy soil in woods and open places.

Distribution: North Carolina, Virginia, Ohio, Michigan and Wisconsin.

This is also an uncommon species in this section. Three collections have been made in Ohio, one by Isabelle Johnson at Sugar Grove, and two by W. G. Stover at Westerville and at Sugar Grove. These collections agree in every respect with authentic European specimens from Hollos which are in the Lloyd Museum. The spores are strongly reticulated and are larger and darker than those of *S. cepa* with relatively long crowded spines which sometimes almost form a mat, obscuring the reticulations. According to Rea (59) the tramal plates are yellow. Specimens in the Lloyd Museum collected by Morgan at Preston and labelled *S. bovista* were studied by the writer and were found to have spores which were not reticulated and which had other characters of *S. cepa*.

3. Scleroderma lycoperdoides Schw.
Plate I, Figure 4.

Fruiting-body small, globose, 1-2 cm. in diameter, usually sessile. Peridium yellowish to brownish, thin, papery, flexible, more or less smooth although covered with reddish-brown, flat warts or scales; more or less uniform in size; dehiscing by an irregular, apical opening. Gleba purplish-brown; capillitium rudimentary. Spores 8-11 microns in diameter, globose, olive-brown, spinulose, mixed with yellow flocci.

Habitat: Damp sandy soil of open woods.

Distribution: Widely throughout the United States.

This is a very common species in Ohio and Michigan. It is usually found in sandy woods mixed with deciduous and coniferous trees. The European species, *S. verrucosum* (Bull.) Pers., is similar to this species, but differs from it in the size and the nature of the peridium. Coker and Couch (7) have studied an authentic specimen of Schweinitz's *S. lycoperdoides* which is now in Michener's Herbarium and found that it is the same as *S. tenerum* B. and C.

4. Scleroderma aurantium (Vaill.) Pers.

Plate I, Figures 2 and 3.

Fruiting-body 2.5-8 cm. in diameter, depressed-globose, sessile, with a strong, fibrous mycelium. Peridium less than 1 mm. thick when dry, corky, pale yellow to brown or orange-brown; dehiscing by an irregular opening; outer surface breaking up into persistent raised warts, usually both large and small intermingled. Immature gleba grayish-white, becoming powdery, bluish to greenish-black with a purple tinge when mature. Spores 7-12 microns in diameter, globose, brown, reticulated, covered with spines, and mixed with yellow flocci.

Habitat: Sandy soil, either in deciduous or coniferous woods.

Distribution: Common everywhere in the United States.

This is perhaps the most common species of the genus in our territory. The outer surface of the peridium cracks into rather small areas which are often very symmetrical. In many cases the center of each area is occupied by a prominent wart with a circular base and this is currounded by a circle of smaller, oblong, radiating warts.

The fruiting-body is sometimes parasitized by *Boletus parasiticus* Bull. This condition is occasionally found in the Old Man's Cave area near Logan, Ohio, where W. G. Stover and the writer have collected several specimens. (See Plate I, Figure 3.) Sometimes as many as three fruiting-bodies of the parasites were found growing from the same host. This species is also commonly known as *S. vulgare* Horn.

5.   Scleroderma flavidum E. and E.

Fruiting-body entirely embedded in the soil when young, subglobose, 2-6 cm. in diameter, plicate at the base, with strongly developed rhizomorphs. Peridium yellowish-brown, thin, the top covered with flat, innate warts or scales which become fewer towards the base; mouth of irregular, stellate segments which often turn backward. Gleba dingy olive-brown to dark brown. Spores globose, dark brown, 5.5-12 microns in diameter, covered with dense, slightly curved spines.

Habitat: Sandy soil in open places.   June to November.

Distribution: Eastern United States and California.

This species has not yet been reported in Ohio, but it occurs in Michigan, Illinois, and Indiana.   Moffatt (48) states that it is quite common at Clarke and Millers, Indiana. *S. flavidum* is quite similar to *S. geaster* in its manner of dehiscing.   However, it is not so large, the peridium is not so thick or does not have reticulated spores. The most distinctive characters of *S. flavidum* are the comparatively flat scales of the peridium, the stellate dehiscence, and the non-reticulated spores.

6.   Scleroderma geaster Fr.

Unexpanded fruiting-body globose to subglobose, entirely or partially embedded in the soil, 4-15 cm. in diameter, usually irregular, sessile. Peridium 1-2 mm. thick, more or less covered with yellowish-brown warts, or rough with flaky scales; dehiscing at the apex in a stellate manner with irregular segments which extend half-way or more to the base and turn backward. Gleba dark greenish-brown to purplish-black with whitish tramal lines. Spores globose, 4.5-15 microns in diameter, brown, spiny, reticulated.

Habitat: Clay and sandy soil in woods and open places.

Distribution: Eastern United States.

This species of Scleroderma is rare in this section.   It was collected near Chillicothe by Hard (13) and at Preston by Morgan. *S. geaster* has reticulated spores like *S. bovista,* but it is easily distinguished by the large, rough fruiting-body and the stellate manner of dehiscence.   In external appearance *S. geaster* also resembles to some extent *Pisolithus tinctorius* (Pers.) Coker and Couch, but it lacks the peridioles.

5.   Pisolithus Alb. & Schw. 1805.

Fruiting-body partially embedded in the soil, irregularly subglobose, attenuated into a thick stalk-like base. Peridium simple, thick, corky, very fragile at maturity. Gleba composed of irregularly shaped sulfur to yellowish-brown peridioles which become free at maturity and crumble away. Capillitium rudimentary. Spores globose, rough.

The chief distinguishing characters of this genus are the large irregular, sulfur-colored peridioles and the crumbling nature of both the peridium and the gleba. Sometimes the walls of the peridioles disintegrate and the genus is confused with Scleroderma. The yellow coloring matter in the peridioles is used for dyeing purposes by the French peasants.

This genus was formerly known as Polysaccum D C. Only one species has been reported from this section and it is rarely found:

Pisolithus tinctorius (Pers.) Coker & Couch

Plate I, Figure 5.

Fruiting-body irregularly globose to depressed-globose, usually constricted into a thick stem-like sterile base. Peridium nearly smooth, becoming thin and fragile when mature, tannish- to greenish-brown, often mottled with dark brown to black areas. Gleba more or less gelatinous when young, greenish-brown to black with sulfur-yellow to brown, embedded peridoles which become dry and powdery and crumble away at maturity. Peridioles irregular, 1-3 x 1-5 mm., somewhat shaggy with hyphal threads, long persistent, but finally becoming a powdery mass. Capillitium rudimentary. Spores globose, brown, spiny, 3.5-6 microns in diameter.

Habitat: Sandy soil in open woods, old pastures and lawns.

Distribution: Ohio, Pennsylvania, South Carolina, Alabama and Florida.

This species which is usually named *Polysaccum pisocarpium* Fr., is rarely found in Ohio. Hard (13) collected it a few times near Chillicothe and Professor R. A. Dobbins found it near Lancaster. The writer has not studied young developing specimens. Coker and Couch (7) state that the peridioles in section are "whitish or yellow, then watery vinaceous, then through darker vinaceous to nearly black . . . peridioles separated by a nearly black jelly inclosing a densely woven mass of delicate threads."

Family 2. *Arachniaceae*. Peridium very thin, crumbling away at or even before maturity. Gleba granular, composed of small permanent cavities which form peridioles. Sterile base wanting. Arachnion is the only genus in this family.

6. Arachnion Schw. 1822.

Fruiting-body globose to subglobose, sessile, peridium simple, very thin, smooth, fragile, crumbling away at maturity. Gleba a powdery mass of minute granules, called peridioles, from whose outer walls extend hyphal threads. Spores smooth, usually globose, sometimes with a pedicel.

The genus Arachnion is very widely distributed throughout the world. Owing to the fact that it is extremely fragile, it is not commonly found. Superficially the fruiting-bodies are similar to the Lycoperdons, but they differ in that they have no capillitium, columella, sterile base, or mouth. Only one species is reported from this region.

Arachnion album Schw.

Plate I, Figure 6.

Fruiting-body globose to subglobose, sessile, 0.5-1.5 cm. in diameter with a root-like rhizomorph at the base. Peridium pure white when immature, smooth, thin, fragile, breaking into irregular fragments and crumbling away at maturity. Gleba white at first, then becoming grayish-colored, composed of irregularly subglobose peridioles, 96-180 x 180-250 microns, which are shaggy from the loosely woven hyphae of which the tramal wall is composed. Spores globose, smooth, 3-4.5 microns in diameter, often with a minute pedicel.

Habitat: On the ground in open fields, pastures and along paths. Summer and early fall.

Distribution: Eastern United States and Texas.

This species has been collected a few times in Ohio. No doubt it is more common than the number of collections would indicate. The fruiting-bodies are very fragile. On maturity they become ash-colored and crumble away until they are entirely inconspicuous in the soil. When immature they may be mistaken for small Lycoperdons, but on cutting the fruiting-body one can detect the granular mass of the peridioles. The writer has collected this species on the campus of the Ohio State University and also at McConnelsville, Ohio. Lloyd (34) and Morgan have also collected it in Ohio.

ORDER III. LYCOPERDALES

Peridium double, the outer peridium either consisting of spines, granules or warts, or of a continuous layer which splits stellately in some genera and scales off in others; interior of fruiting-body a powdery mass of capillitium and spores.

Three families, Lycoperdaceae, Tylostomataceae, and Calostomataceae are referred to this order in this paper. The various authors, however, are not in agreement as to the systematic position of the two latter. Pending further investigations the writer prefers to include them in this order.

Family 1. *Lycoperdaceae.* Fruiting-body sessile or with a more or less stem-like, sterile base which consists of the undifferentiated portion directly below the gleba. Capillitium well developed, consisting of long intertwined threads. The nine genera reported in this region are: Lycoperdon, Calvatia, Bovistella, Bovista, Mycenastrum, Disciseda, Geaster, Myriostoma and Astraeus.

7. Mycenastrum Desv. 1842.

Fruiting-body globose to subglobose, sessile. Outer peridium continuous, very thin, scaling or peeling off at maturity; inner peridium thick, hard, corky, dehiscing by means of irregular lobes or fragments. Capillitium threads thick, short, sparingly branched; branches pointed and with scattered prickles. Spores brown, globose, rough.

There is only one species in this genus.

Mycenastrum corium Desv.

Plate I, Figure 7.

Fruiting-body 5-13 cm. in diameter, globose to subglobose, sessile. Outer peridium thin, continuous, scaling off when mature; inner peridium thick, corky, dehiscing irregularly. Capillitium and spore mass dark purplish-brown when mature; capillitium threads thick, 8-9 microns in diameter, branched, with scattered, short, thick spines or prickles, most numerous near the tips of the branches. Spores brown, globose, rough, 8-12.3 microns in diameter.

Habitat: Rich sandy soil.

Distribution: North-central and western United States.

This species occurs abundantly in the western states, but is quite rare east of the Mississippi River. Several collections have been made in Michigan and Illinois. Only two have been reported from Ohio. These are in the Lloyd Museum. One of these was made at Troy by G. C. Fischer and was presented to Lloyd by Morgan. The other was collected at Toledo by W. R. Lowater. The thick, corky inner peridium and the spiny capillitium are the chief distinguishing features of this species. The name *M. spinulosum* Pk. has also been applied to this plant.

8. Bovista Pers. 1797

Fruiting-body globose to depressed-globose without a sterile base. Outer peridium usually smooth, very thin, deciduous; inner peridium smooth, thin, parchment-like, varying from lead color to reddish-brown, and dehiscing by means of a regular or an irregular mouth. Capillitium and spore mass very compact, firm, persistent; capillitium originating within the gleba, short, thick, distinct, dichotomously branched several times, with tapering branches. Spores smooth, globose or oval, sometimes with a pedicel.

The fruiting-body begins its growth partially embedded in the soil. At maturity it breaks away from the mycelium and is blown about the fields and pastures by the wind, whence the name "tumblers," which is so often applied to them. It is by this method that the spores are dispersed, since the fruiting-body may persist for several years.

KEY TO THE SPECIES

1. Fruiting-body 1-2.5 cm. in diameter; spores with long pedicels........ 2
1. Fruiting-body 2.5-6 cm. in diameter; spores sessile or with a minute pedicel...1. *B. pila*
   2. Spores oval, 5-6 microns in diameter; basal mycelial pad absent; common ....2. *B. plumbea*
   2. Spores globose, less than 5 microns in diameter; basal mycelial pad present; rare...................................3. *B. minor*

1. Bovista pila B. and C.

Plate I, Figure 8.

Fruiting-body 2.5-6 cm. in diameter, globose, with a cord-like mycelium. Immature outer peridium thin, smooth, and white, becoming a brownish-lead color at maturity and scaling off; inner peridium brown to purplish-brown, smooth, shining, parchment-like, dehiscing with an irregularly torn opening. Capillitium and spore mass firm, compact, purplish-brown; main capillitium threads 9-14.5 microns thick, much branched, with tapering branches. Spores smooth, globose, 3-5 microns, usually with a minute pedicel.

Habitat: In pasture fields and open woods. June to October.

Distribution: Eastern United States and Colorado.

The fruiting-body, when mature, breaks away from the mycelium and may be seen tumbling about over the ground for more than one season. This species can easily be distinguished by its irregular dehiscence, and globose spores with minute pedicels. Lloyd (27) states that it is similar to the European species, *B. nigrescens* Pers. which has wrongly been reported in this country.

2. Bovista plumbea Pers.

Plate II, Figure 9.

Fruiting-body globose to depressed globose, 1.5-3 cm. in diameter with fibrous mycelium. Outer peridium at first smooth and white, but scaling off at maturity; inner peridium lead-colored, parchment-like, smooth, dehiscing by means of a round or oblong mouth. Capillitium and spore mass greenish-brown to purplish-brown; main threads 9-14.5 microns thick, three to five times dichotomously branched, branches long, straight, tapering.   Spores oval, 3-5 x 7-9 microns, with a pedical 10-13 microns in length.

Habitat: On the ground in old pastures and meadows.   Late summer and fall.

Distribution: From the Atlantic coast west to Minnesota; also in California.

This species is either solitary or gregarious.   The characters by which it may be distinguished from the other species of Bovista are its color, absence of a basal mycelial pad, and the oval pedicellate spores.   *B. plumbea* is common in this section.

3. Bovista minor Morg.

Immature fruiting-body deeply embedded in the soil, anchored firmly by the universal mycelium.   Mature fruiting-body globose, 1-2 cm. in diameter. Outer peridium thick, rough, fragile, mostly adhering to the soil as it emerges except a small patch at the base; inner peridium reddish-brown, very thin, smooth, flaccid, dehiscing by a regular mouth.   Capillitium and spore mass greenish-brown to brown; main threads 5.5-7.5 microns thick, dichotomously branched two to four times, branches long, curled, flexuous, and tapering. Spores globose, smooth, 2.5-4.5 microns with long slender pedicels four or five times the diameter of the spores.

Habitat: On the ground in damp shaded places.

Distribution: Ohio, Nebraska and Massachusetts.

This rare fungus has only been collected twice in Ohio.   Morgan collected it at Cincinnati and gave some of his specimens to the Lloyd Museum.   In 1926, Dr. W. G. Stover collected it at Jackson. Stover's specimens agree in every respect with Morgan's collection.

9. Bovistella Morg. 1892.

Fruiting-body globose to depressed-globose; sterile base usually well developed; mycelium basal, thick, cord-like.   Outer peridium composed of small granules or spines which fall off at maturity; inner peridium thin, flaccid, dehiscing by means of a large irregular mouth.   Capillitium threads free, thick, dichotomously branched, with tapering branches.   Spores globose or oval, smooth or rough.

Bovistella is intermediate between Bovista and Lycoperdon. In general appearance it is similar to Lycoperdon, as the outer peridium consists of spines and granules in contrast with the continous layer in Bovista.   The capillitium, however, is like that of Bovista in that it is dichotomously branched.

There are only two species in our territory.

KEY TO THE SPECIES

1. Fruiting-body large, 3 cm. more in diameter; sterile base well developed...2. *B. radicata*
1. Fruiting-body small, less than 1 cm. in diameter; sterile base wanting or nearly so...1. *B. echinella*

1.   **Bovistella echinella** (Pat.) Lloyd

Fruiting-body globose to subglobose, very small, less than 1 cm. in diameter; sterile base wanting or nearly so. Outer peridium consisting of minute tufted spines which form patches over the inner peridium; inner peridium dark brown, thin, membranous, dehiscing by a definite, somewhat protruding mouth. Capillitium and spore mass olive-brown; main threads slender, about the diameter of the spores, dichotomously branched, branches long and tapering. Spores globose, smooth, 3.5-4.5 microns in diameter with pedicels up to 10 microns in length.

Habitat: On the ground usually among moss.

Distribution: Michigan, North Dakota, Washington, Ecuador, Jamaica, Mexico, Denmark and Lapland.

Although this little "puffball" is widely distributed over the world, it is quite rare in the United States, having only been reported twice. According to Lloyd (36), it is usually found growing among mats of the moss *Funaria hygrometrica*. The characteristic features of this species are the small size, the protruding mouth, and the long slender, dichotomously branched capillitium.

2.   **Bovistella radicata** (Mont.) Hollos

Plate II, Figure 10.

Fruiting-body globose to depressed globose, 3-7.5 cm. in diameter. Sterile base large, plicate beneath, persistent, occupying about one-half of the interior; mycelium thick, root-like. Outer peridium composed of a dense layer of soft, minute spines or warts, white at first, becoming brownish to buff-colored at maturity and gradually falling away; inner peridium yellowish-brown, smooth, shining, dehiscing by means of a large irregular mouth. Gleba greenish-brown to brown; capillitium fragile, free, 6-8 microns in diameter, branched dichotomously several times, branches tapering. Spores even, oval to globose, with persistent pedicels, 10-12 microns in length.

Habitat: On the ground in cultivated fields, old pastures, and open woods.

Distribution: From Missouri east to the Atlantic coast and south to the Gulf of Mexico.

This is the most common puffball of southern Ohio and it is

also frequently found in the neighboring states. It grows either singly or gregariously. This species resembles the Lycoperdons in external appearance, but can easily be distinguished from them by the nature of the capillitium, which in this case consists of thick main branches, dichotomously branched, with long slender branches. For a long time it was thought that the American species *Bovistella ohiensis* (Ell. and Morg.) Morg. and the European species *B. radicatum* (Mont.) Hollos were distinct. Hollos (15), however, has made a careful study of specimens of the American plant sent to him by Morgan, Burt, and Trelease, and the European sepcimens sent to him by Patouillard. He believes that they belong to the same species.

10.   Calvatia Fr. 1846-49.

Fruiting-body subglobose to turbinate, usually large, varying in size from 3-45 cm. in diameter, sessile or with a thick, long or short sterile base. Outer peridium very fragile, either thin, continuous, smooth and glossy, areolated, or consisting of minute deciduous spines or granules; inner peridium sometimes thick when fresh, but upon drying becoming thin and very fragile, breaking away at maturity from the top of the fruiting-body first, carrying fragments of the gleba with it. Gleba when mature a compact, powdery and cottony mass, yellowish-orange, to greenish-brown or purplish-brown, usually separated from the sterile base by a definite membrane. Capillitium threads partly attached to the inner wall of the peridium, long without spines or prickles, much branched but not dichotomous with conspicuously tapering branches. Spores globose, 3-7 microns in diameter, even or minutely warted, sometimes with a short pedicel.

KEY TO THE SPECIES

1. Spore mass violet to purple...................................... 2
1. Spore mass yellowish-, orange-, to greenish-brown.................. 3
   2. Fruiting-body 2-7 cm. in diameter; sterile base wanting or nearly so ....1. *C. fragilis*
   2. Fruiting-body 7-18 cm. in diameter; sterile base thick, appearing cup-shaped after spore mass breaks away..........2. *C. cyathiformis*
3. Sterile base scanty or entirely wanting............................ 4
3. Sterile base well developed.. 5
   4. Fruiting-body globose to subglobose, usually more than 15 cm. in diameter; gleba greenish-brown......................3. *C. maxima*
   4. Fruiting-body subglobose to turbinate; usually less than 10 cm. in diameter; gleba yellowish- to brownish-orange......4. *C. rubro-flava*
5. Sterile base long, rather slender, stem-like; outer peridium of minute spines or granules...7. *C. elata*
5. Sterile base short and thick...................................... 6
   6. Outer peridium of thick, floccose warts or spines; capillitium thick, 7-15 microns.......................................6. *C. caelata*
   6. Outer peridium thin, smooth, continuous; capillitium 2.5-4 microns wide ....5. *C. craniiformis*

1. Calvatia fragilis (Vitt.) Morg.

Fruiting-body subglobose to obovate, 2-7 cm. in diameter, with a very short, pointed base; sterile base compact, scanty or almost wanting. Outer peridium thin, smooth, very fragile, whitish at first, becoming brownish or purplish later, often areolate at the top; inner peridium thin, extremely fragile, purplish-brown. Capillitium and spore mass dark purple-brown, rather persistent; capillitium threads short, 2.5-6 microns in diameter, septa few, sparingly branched. Spores globose, 3.5-5 microns in diameter, minutely warted.

Habitat: On the ground in pastures and meadows.

Distribution: Northern United States and Canada.

This little purple-spored puffball is very common in this section. It is quite similar to *C. cyathiformis* except as to size. The distinguishing features of *C. fragilis* are the small size, the smaller minutely warted spores, and the scanty, compact, pointed, sterile base. In the Lloyd Museum there are several collections which have been labeled *C. occidentalis*, which no doubt is the name Lloyd (32) accepted for his so-called "western form" of *C. cyathiformis*. From a study of Lloyd's specimens, the writer is convinced that his *C. occidentalis* is the same as *C. fragilis* (Vitt.) Morg.

2. Calvatia cyathiformis (Bosc.) Morg.

Plate II, Figure 11.

Fruiting-body 5-15 cm. in diameter, depressed-globose to turbinate; sterile base short, thick, plicate, with a cord-like mycelium, appearing cup-shaped after the gleba breaks away, occupying one-third to one-half of the fruiting-body, long persistent. Outer peridium smooth, thin, fragile, soft, kid-leather-like, light pinkish to brown on top, often areolate; inner peridium velvety, thin, fragile, purplish in color, breaking away gradually after maturity with fragments of the gleba adhering to it until only the cup-shaped sterile base remains. Capillitium and spore mass at first violet, but becoming dark purple at maturity; threads sparingly branched, 1.5-2.5 microns in thickness; spores globose, sessile, 4.5-6.5 microns in diameter, distinctly warted.

Habitat: On the ground in pastures and meadows. July to November.

Distribution: Eastern and central United States.

This is the most common species of Calvatia found in this region. It is popularly known as the "cup-shaped puffball" from the large, long-persistent, cup-, or beaker-shaped sterile base which is often found during late autumn and winter, and even in the following spring. Smaller fruiting-bodies of this species are sometimes confused with *C. fragilis* (Vitt.) Morg. which also has purple spores. *C. cyathiformis* may readily be distinguished by the large and rougher spores and the larger, more porous, and cup-shaped sterile base. This species has also been known as *Calvatia lilacina* (Berk. and Mont.).

3. Calvatia maxima (Schaeff.) Morgan

Plate II, Figure 12.

Fruiting-body very large, 15-45 cm. in diameter, depressed-globose or ovoid, sessile, without a sterile base, with a thick cord-like mycelium. Outer peridium very thin, white to yellowish, glossy, or kid-leather-like, although sometimes slightly roughened with minute spines, yellowish to greenish-brown at maturity and quite fragile; inner peridium very thin, fragile, breaking away at maturity, with the gleba adhering to it. Capillitium and spore mass yellowish to brownish-green; capillitium very long, much branched, often septate. Spores globose, even, 3.5-5 microns in diameter, often with a minute pedicel.

Habitat: On the ground in rich pastures and open woods.

Distribution: Northeastern United States and Canada.

This species is the largest of the puffballs and is commonly known as the "giant puffball." In 1911 A. G. Pyle collected near Malta, Ohio, a specimen that weighed twenty-four pounds and had a circumference of 6 ft. and 4 inches. This specimen is illustrated in Plate II, Figure 12.

This species may easily be distinguished by its large size, absence of a sterile base, and the white to yellowish, glossy, kid-leather-like outer peridium. In literature it has been known by several names, the most common of which are *Lycoperdon bovista* L. and *Calvatia gigantea* (Batsch) Morg.

4. Calvatia rubro-flava (Cragin) Morg.

Fruiting-body subglobose to turbinate, 1.5-14 cm. in diameter, 1.5-6 cm. in height; sterile base compact, often scanty, plicate, usually tapering and occupying about one-third of the entire structure. Outer peridium reddish- to brownish-orange, consisting of floccose spines or dense granules; inner peridium reddish- to yellowish-orange, thick, becoming thin and fragile on drying. Capillitium and spore mass reddish- to yellowish-orange, persistent; capillitium long, branched, somewhat thicker than the spores. Spores globose, smooth, 3-4 microns in diameter, often with a short pedicel

Habitat: Cultivated ground, lawns, and gardens. Late summer and fall.

Distribution: Missouri east to the Atlantic Coast; Alabama.

This species is very distinct from the other species of Calvatia

and can easily be distinguished by the orange-colored fruiting-body.
According to Murrill (53), Cragin first described it in 1885 from
specimens collected in Kansas as *Lycoperdon rubro-flava*.   In 1899
Lloyd (22) described specimens collected in Ohio as a new species
under the name *Calvatia aurea*.   Later, however, he (23) decided
that these specimens might possibly belong to Cragin's species.
The writer has carefully examined specimens of both *C. aurea* and
C. rubro-flava in the Lloyd Museum and thinks that Lloyd is correct in considering them the same species.

5.   Calvatia craniiformis Schw.

Plate II, Figure 13.

Fruiting-body large, 7-18 cm. in diameter, 10-12 cm. high, depressed-globose, obovoid or turbinate, with a thick, often plicate, sterile base; mycelium
cord-like. Outer peridium very thin, fragile, smooth, whitish-gray to gray,
finally becoming areolated; inner peridium very thin, velvety, yellowish-brown,
fragile, breaking up into fragments when mature and falling away with portions of the gleba adhering. Sterile base cup-shaped, persistent, tapering to
a point, occupying from one-third to one-half of the fruiting-body. Capillitium
and spore mass yellowish to brownish-green; threads very long, branched, hyaline, 2.4-4 microns in diameter. Spores even, globose, 3-4 microns in diameter,
with a very short pedicel.

Habitat: On the ground in pasture fields and open woods.
August to October.

Distribution: East of the Mississippi River; also Texas.

This species is popularly known as the "Brain-shaped puffball."   It is commonly found throughout this region.   It is sometimes confused with *C. caelata* (Bull.) Morg. which also grows in
this section, but it can easily be distinguished by the smaller capillitium threads and the smoother outer peridium.

6.   Calvatia caelata (Bull.) Morg.

Fruiting-body 4.5-12 cm. in diameter, turbinate, with a thick sterile base
and cord-like root. Outer peridium a thick floccose layer of coalescent spines
or warts, at first white, later changing to a yellowish or brownish color, finally
breaking up into more or less persistent areola; inner peridium very thin and
fragile at the apex, causing a very irregular opening as it breaks away in
fragments; sterile base cup-shaped, persistent, occupying about one-half of the
entire fruiting-body, and separated from the fertile portion by a definite membrane. Capillitium and spore mass a yellowish-green color; threads branched,
7-15 microns thick; spores smooth, globose, 3.5-5 microns in diameter, often
with a short pedicel.

Habitat: On the ground in fields, lawns, and roadsides. Late summer and fall.

Distribution: From Kansas and Minnesota east to the Atlantic Coast.

This species has frequently been found in Michigan, but has not yet been reported in Ohio. It is often confused with *C. craniiformis* but may be distinguished from it by the flocculose outer peridium and the very thick capillitium threads.

7. Calvatia elata (Massee) Morg.

Fruiting-body turbinate, contracted abruptly into a long stalk-like sterile base up to 15 cm. in length. Outer peridium a thin layer of minute persistent spines or granules; inner peridium very thin, fragile, breaking into fragments. Spore mass greenish-brown to brown; capillitium slender, long, branched. Spores globose, even or minutely warted, 4-5 microns in diameter, often with a minute pedicel.

Habitat: Mossy and damp ground.

Distribution: New England, New York, and Ohio.

This species looks very much like the Lycoperdons in that the outer peridium is spinulose or granular. The fruiting-body, however, does not dehisce by means of a definite opening. The inner peridium together with the gleba breaks up into fragments and falls away. *C. elata* is said to be the American form of *C. sacata* (Vahl.) Morg. which it closely resembles. It differs from the latter mainly in that it has slightly smaller and smoother spores. The reported habitat of the two is the same. *C. elata* has been reported from Ohio by Hard (13) and from Michigan by Kauffman (16). Moffatt (48) and others report *C. saccata* to occur in this country. It has not been reported in Ohio. The difference between the two species is so slight that these reported collections may possibly be cases of mistaken identity. Since the writer has not examined any of the American collections, she is not including it in this paper.

11. Lycoperdon Tourn. 1719.

Fruiting-body subglobose to turbinate, with or without a thick sterile base, less than 8 cm. Mycelium usually fibrous, sometimes cord-like. Outer peridium deciduous or subpersistent, continuous or consisting of minute granules, warts, or long spines, at first white or cream-colored, becoming yellowish- to dark-brown with age; inner peridium thin, membranaceous, persistent, flaccid, dehiscing by means of an apical mouth which is usually irregular. Gleba cottony, yellowish-brown to olivaceous-brown, or purple; capillitium attached in part to inner peridium, threads without spines or prickles, simple or branched, but not dichotomous, branches often somewhat tapering but not conspicuously so. Spores usually globose, smooth or warted, pedicels deciduous except in a few species.

KEY TO THE SPECIES

1. Spore mass yellowish-brown to greenish-brown..................... 2
2. Spore mass purplish-brown....................................... 19
    2. Sterile base prominent, occupying one-third or more of the fruiting-body 3
    2. Sterile base small and inconspicuous or entirely wanting.......... 8
3. Sterile portion white, composed of minute cavities; mycelium white, cord-like; outer peridium consisting of reddish-brown persistent granules ....12. *L. pyriforme*
3. Sterile portion yellowish to purplish-brown, composed of large cavities 4
    4. Outer peridium deciduous, composed of crowded spines which peel off in flakes at maturity....................9. *L. marginatum*
    4. Outer peridium long persistent, composed of minute spines, warts, or granules... 5
5. Spines, warts, or granules uniform in size........................ 6
5. Spines, warts, or granules of different size....................... 7
    6. Spores with a short pedicel; growing on leaf mold...18. *L. umbrinum*
    6. Spores without a pedicel; growing on mats of moss, usually Polytrichum....................................14. *L. muscorum*
7. Cream-colored, flocculose spines scattered over the dense, persistent, tannish-brown granules...........................15. *L. floccosum*
7. Large, deciduous, "consolidated" warts intermingled with the smaller persistent ones; inner peridium reticulated.............16. *L. gemmatum*
    8. Outer peridium deciduous..................................... 9
    8. Outer peridium long persistent............................... 11
9. Warts or spines pinkish-brown; inner peridium conspicuously pitted 7. *L. subincarnatum*
9. Spines stout, convergent, white to buff-colored; inner peridium smooth 10
    10. Spores with long conspicuous pedicels...........10. *L. pedicellatum*
    10. Spores without pedicels..........................8. *L. curtisii*
11. Spines or granules yellowish-brown to reddish-brown................ 12
11. Spines or granules dark brown to black........................... 18
    12. Spores globose.. 13
    12. Spores oblong, 3-4 x 4.3-6 microns..............3. *L. oblongisporum*
13. Fruiting-body growing on wood.................................. 14
13. Fruiting-body growing on the ground............................ 16
    14. Fruiting-body less than 1 cm. in diameter, egg-shaped, pointed 6. *L. acuminatum*
    14. Fruiting-body more than 1 cm. in diameter, subglobose to pear-shaped 15
15. Peridium with conspicuous depressions or pits; spores 2.5-3 microns 13. *L. tessellatum*
15. Peridium without depressed areas; spores 3-5.5 microns..12. *L. pyriforma*
    16. Sterile base porous, spores 2-3.5 microns in diameter, minutely rough ....11. *L. turneri*

16. Sterile base compact or entirely wanting, smooth, 3.5-5 microns
in diameter.. 17
17. Outer peridium of minute bran-like scales; inner peridium flaccid
2. *L. pusillum*
17. Outer peridium thin, consisting of a coat of whitish- or buff-colored
minute spines which form patches over the parchment-like inner peridium ....1. *L. cepaeforme*
18. Fruiting-body 1-1.5 cm. in diameter, spores smooth.....4. *L. dryinum*
18. Fruiting-body 1.5-3.5 cm. in diameter; sterile base porous, spores
minutely warted.....................................5. *L. fuscum*
19. Outer peridium a smooth continuous layer becoming cracked and areolated at maturity...................................17. *L. rimulatum*
19. Outer peridium not continuous................................... 20
20. Outer peridium consisting of long prominent spines............. 21
20. Outer peridium consisting of warts, minute spines or granules.... 23
21. Spines dark brown or black, convergent, inner peridium reticulated
21. *L. echinatum*
21. Spines white or pale brown; inner peridium not reticulated 22
22. Spines 2-3 mm. long, dense, convergent at their apices; inner peridium shining.................................20. *L. pulcherrimum*
22. Spines about 1 mm. in length, usually free at their apices, intermingled with minute granules; inner peridium furfuraceous
19. *L. atropurpureum*
23. Inner peridium pitted, with one or more reddish-brown to dark brown
granules in each depression; sterile base scanty, whitish, compact
13. *L. tessellatum*
23. Inner peridium not pitted, sterile base well developed, porous........ 24
24. Outer peridium of dense, persistent, tannish-brown granules with
superficial flocculose spines........................15. *L. floccosum*
24. Outer peridium of warts, minute spines or granules; without
flocculose spines 25
25. Outer peridium of large deciduous warts intermingled with smaller
persistent ones; inner peridium reticulated.............16. *L. gemmatum*
25. Outer peridium of minute spines or granules; inner peridium not
reticulated ....18. *L. umbrinum*

1. Lycoperdon cepaeforme Bull.

Fruiting-body small, 1-3 cm. in diameter, globose or depressed-globose;
sometimes plicate below; sterile base scanty, composed of small cavities; mycelium root-like. Outer peridium consists of a whitish or pale brown coat of
very fine spines or granules which usually break up into patches and persist
for a long time. Inner peridium pale brown, parchment-like; mouth apical,
large. Gleba greenish-yellow to greenish-brown; columella present; capillitium
branched, colored. Spores 3.5-5 microns in diameter, globose, smooth, sometimes with a small pedicel.

Habitat: On ground in open woods and meadows. July to
August.

Distribution: New England to Wisconsin and south to Alabama.

L. cepaeforme has been frequently collected in Ohio. It is usually quite small in size and may be distinguished by the thick root-like mycelium, the papery inner peridium usually with the outer peridium adhering in patches, and the scanty sterile base. Coker and Couch (7) consider *L. cepaeforme* as synonym of *L. polymorphum* Vitt., but Lloyd treats it as a form of the latter. The writer, however, believes that it should be considered a distinct species. It differs from *L. polymorphum* Vitt. mainly in the absence of a well-developed stem-like sterile base. *L. pusillum* Batsch is also similar to this species, but it has no sterile base and has a very soft flaccid inner peridium.

2. Lycoperdon pusillum Batsch

Fruiting-body small, 1-2.5 cm. in diameter, globose, sessile; sterile base wanting; mycelium cord-like. Outer peridium thin, flaccid, consisting of minute, pale brown, bran-like scales which are quite persistent on the pale brown surface of the inner peridium. Gleba greenish-yellow to greenish-brown; capillitium much branched, about the same diameter as the spores. Spores globose, even, 3.5-4.5 microns in diameter.

Habitat: On the ground in pastures and open woods. June to late autumn.

Distribution: North Dakota east to the Atlantic coast and south to Florida.

This species is rare in Ohio. The writer has collected it at Old Man's Cave. *L. pusillum* is very similar to *L. cepaeforme* Bull. but may be distinguished from it by the fact that it has no sterile base and that the inner peridium is very flaccid. It is sometimes confused with small forms of *L. curtisii* Berk. but it may be distinguished by its smoother surface and bran-like scales.

3. Lycoperdon oblongisporum B. and C.

Fruiting-body globose to subglobose, 1-2.5 cm. in diameter; sterile base scanty and compact or entirely wanting; mycelium root-like. Outer peridium consisting of very minute, furfuraceous spines or granules which are long persistent on the light brown inner peridium. Gleba greenish-brown to brown. Capillitium colored, much branched. Spores even, oblong 3-4 x 4-6 microns, often with a minute pedicel.

Habitat: On the ground in dense woods.

Distribution: Ohio, Wisconsin, and North Carolina.

This is a rare species. The only known collection in Ohio was made by Lloyd near Cincinnati. This puffball is very similar to

L. cepaeforme Batsch but it may be easily distinguished by its oblong spores.

4. Lycoperdon dryinum Morg.

Fruiting-body 1-1.5 cm. in diameter, globose to subglobose; sterile base absent or nearly so; mycelium root-like. Outer peridium long persistent, composed of minute dark brown to black granules. Inner peridium smooth, grayish-brown and somewhat shining, dehiscing by an apical mouth. Gleba yellowish-brown to brown; capillitium pale greenish-brown, branched, about the same diameter as the spores. Spores globose, smooth, greenish-brown, 3-4 microns in diameter, often with a short pedicel.

Habitat: In the woods growing on leaf mold.

Distribution: Ohio and North Carolina.

L. dryinum is similar to *L. fuscum* Bonorden and is considered a form of the letter by most authors. However, after a study of the type collection in the Lloyd Museum, the writer believes that it should be treated as a distinct species. It differs from *L. fuscum* in that the fruiting-bodies are very small, that the sterile base is usually wanting, and that the spores are smooth.

5. Lycoperdon fuscum Bonorden

Fruiting-body subglobose to turbinate, 1.5-3.5 cm. in diameter; sterile base porous, occupying one-fourth or less of the interior. Outer peridium composed of very small persistent dark brown or black spines scattered all over the fruiting-body; inner peridium smooth, shining, dehiscing by means of an apical pore. Gleba olive-brown to brown, Capillitium colored, branched, about the same diameter as the spores. Spores globose, minutely warted, 2.5-5 microns in diameter, often with a short piece of the pedicel attached.

Habitat: In woods growing on leaf mold. August to October.

Distribution: North Carolina, Washington, D. C., Illinois, Pennsylvania, West Virginia, and Ohio.

This is a rare "puffball" in Ohio, having only been collected twice. The first collection reported for Ohio was made August 28, 1926, at Old Man's Cave, Hocking County, by the writer and party. On October 10, 1926 another collection was made at Sugar Grove by Dr. W. G. Stover and class. The small dark brown or black spines are the chief distinguishing characters of this species.

6. Lycoperdon acuminatum Bosc.

Fruiting-body 3-9 mm. in diameter, 6-13 mm. high, globose when immature, becoming egg-shaped and pointed at the apex at maturity; sterile base absent, mycelium white and fibrous. Outer peridium scurfy or granular, white, soft and delicate at first, but forming persistent grayish-brown, bran-like scales on the inner peridium when dried. Capillitium and spore mass yellowish-green to dirty gray; threads simple, hyaline, 6-9 microns in diameter. Spores globose, even, 3.3-4 microns in diameter.

Habitat: At the base of trees and on damp moss-covered logs.

Distribution: New York, New Jersey, North Carolina, South Carolina, Ohio, and Missouri.

This is a very small and comparatively rare species. It has been collected several times in Ohio. The distinguishing features by which it may be identified are its small size, its peculiar egg-shape, and its habitat. In literature it has been known as *L. calyptriforme* Berk. and Rav. and *L. leprosum* Berk.

7. Lycoperdon subincarnatum Pk.

Plate III, Figure 19.

Fruiting-body globose to depressed-globose, sessile or nearly so, 0.5-2.5 cm. in diameter; sterile base, scanty, composed of small cavities, sometimes entirely wanting; mycelium white, cord-like. Outer peridium consisting of dense, pale brown to dark brown, deciduous warts or spines which leave small deep depressions or pits on the surface of the grayish-brown inner peridium like the surface of a thimble. Inner peridium tough, leathery; mouth large, irregular. Gleba greenish-yellow to greenish-brown; capillitium long, hyaline, septate, sparingly branched, 4-8 microns in thickness. Spores brown, globose, minutely warted, 3.8-5 microns in diameter.

Habitat: In woods on decayed logs and stumps.

Distribution: Maine, New York, North Carolina, Pennsylvania, Ohio, and Wisconsin.

L. subincarnatum has been collected in Ohio at Akron, Preston, Malta, and Sugar Grove. It is a small "puffball" which may be easily identified by the dense uniform, brown warts or spines, and the leathery pitted inner peridium with a large mouth. It grows on wood and the white mycelial fibers penetrate the substratum as do those of *L. pyriforme* Schaeff.

8. Lycoperdon curtisii Berk.

Plate II, Figure 14.

Fruiting-body globose to depressed-globose, 0.6-3.5 cm. in diameter, usually sessile; sterile base scanty; mycelium fibrous. Outer peridium a dense layer of stout, convergent spines or pyramidal warts, white at first, later becoming buff-colored and falling away gradually toward maturity; inner peridium usually smooth, sometimes velvety, buff or clay-colored. Gleba yellowish to greenish-brown; capillitium hyaline, sparingly branched, thick, 6-12 microns in diameter, flaccid, septate. Spores globose, minutely rough, 2.5-4 microns in diameter.

Habitat: On the ground in lawns and pastures. July to late autumn.

Distribution: From Colorado east to the Atlantic Coast.

This puffball is very common in Ohio. It is usually found growing gregariously in short grass. *L. curtisii* is similar in appearance to *L. marginatum* Vitt., but may be distinguished by the smaller fruiting-bodies, the non-flaking outer peridium, and the minutely warted spores. According to Coker and Couch (7) *L. Wrightii* B. & C. is a synonym.

9. Lycoperdon marginatum Vitt.

Fruiting-body usually depressed-globose, 1.5-5 cm. in diameter; sterile base plicate, with large cavities, occupying about one-third of the interior but distinctly separated from the gleba by a membrane. Outer peridium white at first, becoming yellowish-brown with age, composed of crowded, adherent warts or spines with united apices, which at maturity peel off in large flakes. Inner peridium dull yellowish-brown or cinnamon color, slightly scaly or furfuraceous in appearance and often pitted; mouth irregular. Gleba greenish-brown to brown; capillitium hyaline 2.5-5 microns thick, sparingly branched. Spores globose, hyaline, smooth, 3-5 microns in diameter, often with long slender pedicels about the diameter of the spores.

Habitat: On the ground in lawns, pastures, and open woods. July to October.

Distribution: In all parts of the United States except the Pacific region. Very common in Ohio.

The distinguishing features of this species are the spiny outer peridium which flakes off in patches, and the furfuraceous, pitted inner peridium. Other names by which this species has been known in literature are *L. cruciatum* Rostk., *L. separans* Pk., *L. calvescens* B. & C. and *L. papillatum* Schaeff.

10. Lycoperdon pedicellatum Pk.

Plate II, Figure 15.

Fruiting-body globose to depressed-globose, 1.5-4 cm. in diameter, plicate at the base; sterile base small, with large cavities, forming a stem-like structure; mycelium of slender fibers. Outer peridium composed of long, stout, dense convergent spines which are usually deciduous, leaving the thin, shining, yellowish-brown inner peridium more or less reticulated. Gleba greenish-brown; capillitium 1.5-7 microns in thickness, hyaline, much branched. Spores usually globose, sometimes oval, 3-5 microns in diameter with long, persistent pedicels 12-18 microns in length.

Habitat: On the ground and on decayed wood.

Distribution: Ohio, New York, Alabama, North Carolina, and Wisconsin.

The long, persistent pedicels form a distinguishing character of this species. In this respect it resembles species of Bovistella and Bovista. On the basis of this character Lloyd (36) places it in Bovistella. The writer, however, believes it to be a true Lycoperdon since it does not have the dichotomously branched capillitium characteristic of Bovistella. *L. caudatum* Schroet. is a synonym.

11. Lycoperdon turneri E. and E.

Fruiting-body subglobose to obovate, 1.5-3.5 cm. in diameter; sterile base scanty, porous; mycelium fibrous. Outer peridium yellowish-brown, consisting of minute spines and warts which dry up and are long persistent; inner peridium smooth, shiny, yellowish- to greenish-brown, dehiscing by an apical mouth. Gleba at first greenish-yellow, becoming greenish-brown at maturity; capillitium branched. Spores globose, very minutely rough, greenish-yellow, 2-3.5 microns in diameter, usually with a minute pedicel.

Habitat: On the ground in woods.

Distribution: In the United States east of Missouri to the Atlantic coast and south to Florida.

L. turneri is quite commonly found in Ohio. It is similar in appearance to *L. umbrinum* Pers. After studying the type specimen which is in the Lloyd Museum the writer believes that it is a distinct species. In *L. turneri* the sterile base is scanty and the gleba is permanently greenish-yellow to greenish-brown, while in *L. umbrium* the sterile base is stem-like and the gleba becomes purplish-brown.

12. Lycoperdon pyriforme Schaeff.

Plate II, Figure 16.

Plate III, Figure 17.

Fruiting-body obovate to pear-shaped, 1-4.5 cm. in diameter and 2-4.5 cm. in height; sterile base well developed or scanty, with white, compact cavities. Mycelial strands long, white, cord-like, abundant, permeating the substratum. Outer peridium consists of reddish-brown granules or warts which are persistent on the inner peridium, often irregularly cracking; mouth apical, slow in formation. Gleba greenish-yellow, greenish-brown to brown, columella prominent; capillitium hyaline, long, branched, 3-5.5 microns thick. Spores brown, globose, smooth, hyaline, 3-4.5 microns in diameter.

Habitat: On decayed wood; seldom on the ground. Usually gregarious. July to November.

Distribution: New England to Wisconsin, and south to Florida and Kansas; also in California.

This is one of the most common species of puffballs in Ohio. It is easily distinguished by its small, reddish-brown, persistent granules; its white compact, sterile base; and long, white, mycelial strands which penetrate the substratum conspicuously. *L. pyriforme* is quite variable as to size and the nature of the outer peridium. Sometimes it is similar to *L gemmatum* Batsch in shape, but it differs in the nature of the outer peridium. *L. pyriforme* is also similar to *L. tessellatum* Pers. but it lacks the pitted inner peridium and the purplish-brown spores.

13. **Lycoperdon tessellatum** Pers.

Fruiting-body 2-3 cm. in diameter, subglobose to turbinate; sterile base scanty, compact, whitish or light brown in color; mycelium white, cord-like. Outer peridium consisting of grayish-brown to purplish-brown, persistent spines or warts which occur in groups in the irregular pitted depressions of the inner peridium; mouth apical, irregular. Gleba greenish-brown to purplish-brown; capillitium branched, about the same diameter as the spores. Spores smooth, globose, 1.5-2.5 microns in diameter.

Habitat: Growing on decayed wood, usually logs.

Distribution: Massachusetts and New York west to Nebraska.

L. tessellatum is considered as a form of *L. pyriforme* by Lloyd (33). After a careful study of specimens, the writer believes that it should be considered a distinct species for the following reasons: the peridium is conspicuously pitted, with a group of spines or warts in each depression; the mature gleba is brown to purplish-brown; and the spores are smaller than in *L. pyriforme* Schaeff. The first collection reported for Ohio was made June 14, 1925, by the writer at McConnelsville. On September 20, 1926, another collection was made by the writer in almost the same locality.

14. **Lycoperdon muscorum** Morg.

Fruiting-body depressed-globose to turbinate, 1.5-3 cm. in diameter, up to 4 cm. high; sterile base stem-like, porous, occupying about one-third of the interior. Outer peridium mostly persistent, composed of minute yellowish-brown to cinnamon-brown spines, granules, or scales. Inner peridium shiny when denuded, dehiscing by means of an apical mouth. Gleba yellowish-green to brown; capillitium yellowish-green. Spores globose, minutely warted, 4-5 microns in diameter.

Habitat: Growing in mats of moss, usually Polytrichum.

Distribution: Michigan, Ohio, Connecticut, Maine, New York, Massachusetts, Minnesota, and Mexico.

This species, although widely distributed, is relatively rare. It is peculiar in the fact that it grows among moss. It is similar in appearance to *Calvatia elata* (Massee) Morg., from which it may be easily distinguished by the methods of dehiscence. Other names by which it has been known are *L. pseudoradicans* Lloyd and *L. polytrichum* Lloyd.

15. Lycoperdon floccosum Lloyd

Fruiting-body turbinate, up to 4 cm. in diameter and 4-4.5 cm. high with a stem-like porous sterile base. Outer peridium felt-like, composed of dense, tannish-brown, persistent granules and scattered cream-colored, soft, flocculose spines; inner and outer peridium more or less rigid. Gleba greenish-brown to brown, sometimes purplish-brown; capillitium threads branched, greenish-brown, up to 3.6 microns in diameter. Spores globose, rough, 2-3.5 microns in diameter, with a short pedicel.

Habitat: On the ground in woods or rich meadows.

Distribution: Maine, Massachusetts, Pennsylvania, Ohio, Missouri, and Iowa.

This species may be easily identified by the cream-colored, flocculose spines which are scattered over the dense, persistent, tannish-colored granules. Lloyd (33) considered it a form of *L. umbrinum* Pers., but the writer thinks that it is a distinct species. *L. floccosum* is rare in Ohio. Morgan collected it at Preston, Smith at Akron, and the writer at McConnelsville. The *L. elongatum* Berk. of Morgan's paper (52) is probably to be referred to this species which was described at a later date. In fact there is a specimen in the Lloyd Museum collected by Morgan at Preston. A label inside the box bears the name *L. elongatum*. The outer label, however, bears the name *L. floccosum*.

16. Lycoperdon gemmatum Batsch
Plate III, Figure 18.

Fruiting-body depressed-turbinate, 2.5-6 cm. in diameter, 2-7 cm. in height; sterile base well developed with large cavities, elongated, tapering, occupying from one-third to one-half of the interior; mycelium fibrous. Outer peridium composed of whitish to gray, thick, consolidated warts, with smaller warts or spines intervening. The larger ones fall off at maturity, leaving scars which give a reticulated appearance to the yellowish-brown surface of the inner peridium. Inner peridium flaccid, tough, dehiscing by an apical mouth. Gleba yellowish-brown to greenish-brown when mature, often becoming purplish-colored when old; capillitium hyaline, sparingly branched, 2.5-5.5 microns in thickness. Spores pale brown, globose, minutely warted, 2.5-5 microns in diameter.

Habitat: On the ground in rich soil, on decayed leaves, and on decayed wood. Solitary or gregarious.

Distribution: Eastern United States, Kansas, and Washington.

L. gemmatum is very common in Ohio. It is considered one of the most beautiful puffballs and has been named "gemmatum" on account of the gem-like character of the warts. This species is quite variable as to size, shape, and the nature of the inner and outer peridia. Sometimes the inner peridium is so fragile that one could easily mistake it for a species of Calvatia. The gleba often turns a pale purplish-brown with age.

17. Lycoperdon rimulatum Pk.

Fruiting-body depressed-globose, 1.5-3 cm. in diameter, sterile base scanty, occupying one-third or less of the interior; mycelium root-like. Outer peridium grayish to yellow brown, a thin, smooth, continuous, adherent fibrillose layer which cracks on drying and scales off with age, becoming rimulose or areolate in appearance; inner peridium smooth, yellowish-brown to purplish-brown in color, more or less shiny; mouth apical. Gleba brownish to reddish-purple; capillitium sparingly branched, usually thinner than the spores. Spores dark brown, globose, rough, 5-7 microns in diameter, often with pedicels 2 microns in length.

Habitat: On sandy ground in fields and woods. Autumn.

Distribution: New York, New Jersey, North Carolina, South Carolina, Pennsylvania, Ohio, Michigan, and Wisconsin.

L. rimulatum may be easily distinguished from the other species of Lycoperdon with purplish brown spore-mass by its smooth, continuous outer peridium which becomes areolate with age. It is a rare "puffball" in Ohio and has only been collected at two different places. Morgan collected it several times at Preston and Stover collected it once near Columbus.

18. Lycoperdon umbrinum Pers.

Fruiting-body subglobose to pear-shaped, 1.5-3.5 cm. in diameter; sterile base stem-like, porous, occupying about one-third of the interior. Outer peridium yellowish-brown to tannish-brown composed of a coat of small, soft, persistent spines; inner peridium when exposed pale brown, glossy, dehiscing by a small apical mouth. Gleba at first yellowish-brown, slowly changing to purplish-brown; capillitium pale yellowish, flexuous, branched. Spores reddish-brown, globose, rough, 3.5-4.5 microns in diameter with a short pedicel.

Habitat: On leaf mold in woods and heaths. September to November.

Distribution: In the United States east of Colorado to the Atlantic Coast and south to North Carolina.

L. umbrinum has been collected in Ohio at Toledo, Oberlin, Westerville, and in the Sugar Grove region where it is quite common. It is often confused with old specimens of *L. atropurpureum* Vitt. which have lost their long spines, but have still retained their smaller ones. *L. umbrinum*, however, may be identified by the dense, small, yellowish-tan spines which are persistent on the shiny peridium. This plant has also been known in American literature as *L. glabellum* Pk.

19. Lycoperdon atropurpureum Vitt.

Fruiting-body 1-4 cm. in diameter, subglobose to turbinate; sterile base very porous, stem-like, sometimes plicate or lacunose, occupying one-third or more of the interior; mycelium fibrous. Outer peridium consisting of slender spines, 1 mm. or less in length, intermingled with minute spines or granules; the larger spines falling off at maturity and leaving the inner peridium more or less furfuraceous. Mouth small, irregular. Gleba at first greenish-yellow, slowly changing to dark purple-brown when mature; capillitium sparingly branched, 4.5-7 microns in diameter, pedicellate or mixed with detached pedicels.

Habitat: In woods on the ground or on decayed wood. August to October.

Distribution: Wisconsin east to New York and south to Alabama.

On account of the slow change in color of the spore mass, this species has often been misnamed by different authors. The gleba of the immature fruiting body is yellowish-brown to greenish-brown and if the specimens are collected at that time they remain the same color. *L. atropurpureum* is very variable as to size, shape, sterile base, and nature of the outer peridium, consequently it sometimes approaches the other purple-spored species in certain respects. The presence of slender spines intermingled with minute persistent spines, scales or granules is the chief distinguishing feature of this species.

20. Lycoperdon pulcherrimum B. & C.

Plate III, Figure 20.

Fruiting-body 2.5-7.5 cm. in diameter, subglocose to obovoid, smooth and plicate at the base; sterile base porous, occupying one-third of the interior, forming a thick, stout stem with cord-like mycelium. Outer peridium consisting of white to yellowish-tan, dense, slender, convergent spines, 2-3 mm. long, which fall off gradually at maturity. Inner peridium smooth, shining, brown or purplish brown. Gleba greenish-brown to brownish-purple; capillitium branched, branches long and slender. Spores globose, rough, 4-5.5 microns in diameter.

Habitat: Low ground in fields and woods. September to October.

Distribution: Kansas east to Vermont and south to North Carolina.

This is a most beautiful species as the name suggests. It may be easily identified by the long, dense, white or yellowish-tan, convergent spines, the shining, purplish-brown inner peridium, and the purple-brown gleba. *L. pulcherrimum* is comparatively rare in Ohio and has only been collected at Preston, Toledo, Columbus, and McConnelsville.

21. Lycoperdon echinatum Pers.

Fruiting-body 1.5-3.5 cm. in diameter, subglobose to ovate, sterile base a short compact stem-like structure occupying about one-third of the interior; mycelium fibrous, white. Outer peridium consisting of long (2-5 mm.), convergent, dark brown or black spines which at maturity fall off leaving the inner peridium somewhat reticulated and pale brown in color at first, due to the minute dark-brown granules, but becoming shining as the granules disappear. Gleba greenish-brown, becoming purplish-brown at maturity. Capillitium hyaline, 2.5-3 microns in width, branched. Spores globose, 3.5-6 microns in diameter, rough, sometimes with a long pedicel, but usually these have become detached and are mixed with the spores.

Habitat: On the ground among leaves in dense woods, groves, or sometimes in pastures. August to November.

Distribution: Eastern United States and Canada.

This is rather a rare species in this section. It has been reported from Michigan, Pennsylvania, and Ohio, where it is frequently found in the Sugar Grove region. The crowded, shaggy, dark brown, stout spines, the reticulated inner peridium, and the purplish-brown spore mass are the distinguishing characters of this species. *L. constellatum* Fr. is a synonym.

12. Disciseda Czern. 1845.

Fruiting-body globose to subglobose, entirely or partially embedded in the soil, without a sterile base; mycelium universal. Outer peridium of two layers, the outer thick, composed of a loosely interwoven mass of hyphae to which grass, soil, and other foreign material adhere, the inner, thick and fleshy when fresh, but becoming thin and papery at maturity; covering the inner peridium entirely when young, but slowly breaking away near the base thus freeing the inner peridium, and finally leaving only a pad at the apex in old specimens. Inner peridium subglobose to globose, tough, membranaceous, dehiscing by an irregular opening at the base; capillitium branched, fragile. Spores globose, minutely warted, sessile or pedicellate.

This genus was described by Morgan (52) in 1892 as Catastoma and was known in literature by this name until Hollos (15) discovered that it had been previously described as Disciseda by Czerniaiev in 1845. The inner peridium is entirely different from that of all other genera. The mouth develops not at the apex, but at the base of the inner peridium. This point can be determined only if the fruiting-bodies are collected while still attached to the soil. After being freed the fruiting-body at first appears a a "puffball" within a cup and with a mouth or opening at what appears to be the apex of the inner peridium. It should be remembered that in its development this is really at the base of the fruiting-body.

KEY TO THE SPECIES

1. Fruiting-body 0.5-2.5 cm. in diameter; spores less than 5 microns in diameter.. 1. *D. candida*
1. Fruiting-body 1.3-4 cm, in diameter; spores more than 5 microns in diameter.. 2. *D. subterranea*

1. Disciseda candida (Schw.) Lloyd

Plate III, Figures 21 and 22.

Fruiting-body depressed globose, 0.5-2.5 cm. in diameter, partially embedded in the soil. Outer peridium double, only partially enclosing the mature inner peridium; outer layer a thick, white, interwoven mycelial mass, usually dirty grayish or brown color from the adhering soil particles and grass; the inner layer spongy when fresh, becoming thin and papery on drying. Inner peridium thin, tough, light-brown to gray, covered with minute scales, dehiscing by means of a basal mouth. Gleba greenish-brown to purplish-brown; capillitium sparingly branched, 3-5 microns in diameter, hyaline, fragile; spores rough, globose, 3.5-4.5 microns in diameter, with a short pedicel.

Habitat: On clay soil and pastures, along roads, and paths.

Distribution: Cosmopolitan.

During the month of August, 1926, following a wet warm period, this species was very abundant on the campus of the Ohio

State University. The writer was able to collect many specimens in various stages of development. When young, the fruiting-body was completely surrounded by the outer peridium and was entirely embedded just beneath the surface of the soil. As the fruiting-body developed it extended above the surface, forming a little mound of mycelium more or less covered with adhering soil and grass, as is shown in Plate III, Figure 21. The rapid growth of the inner peridium causes the outer peridium to pull apart at the base, thus freeing the fruiting-body from the soil and giving it the appearance of a cup containing the inner peridium. After the fruiting-body is dislodged from the soil and blown about by the wind, fragments of the outer peridium break and fall away until in old specimens only a small pad is left adhering to the inner peridium. During these observations, the writer did not find any cup-like remains of the outer peridium in the soil as is reported in the literature. In no case was there any indication that the outer peridium splits into halves as previously reported. It seems merely to be a case in which the inner peridium outgrew its "jacket"—the outer peridium. The mycelium in young specimens was universal and there was no sign of a stalk as reported by Coker and Couch (7). The mouth is an irregular opening, formed even while the fruiting-body is firmly fastened to the soil.

From the time of Morgan's work this species was known as *Catastoma circumscissum* (B. & C.) Morg., then as *Disciseda circumscissa* (B. & C.) Hollos, until Lloyd (25) discovered that it had been previously described by Schweinitz as *Bovista candida*.

2. **Disciseda subterranea** (Pk.) Coker and Couch

Fruiting-body subglobose, 1.3-4 cm. in diameter. Outer peridium a thick mycelial mass, incrusted with soil and other foreign material, entirely covering the inner peridium when young; in older specimens mostly worn away leaving only a pad at the portion of the inner peridium opposite the mouth. Inner peridium brown, tough, membranaceous, covered with thin, light-colored scales, dehiscing by means of an irregular opening at the center of the part which was embedded in the soil. Gleba greenish-brown to purple-brown; capillitium fragile, 3-4 microns thick; spores rough, globose, 5.5-9.5 microns in diameter, with a short pedicel.

Habitat: Sandy soil.

Distribution: Michigan west to Washington; Colorado, South Carolina, Canada.

This species has not yet been reported in Ohio. It is quite similar to *D. candida* (Schw.) Lloyd, but differs from is in the large spores.

13. Astraeus Morg. 1889.

Immature fruiting-body subterranean, depressed-globose, to ovate; mycelium basal. Outer peridium thick, composed of four layers: a thin mycelial layer which soon wears off, next a thick fibrous layer; a thin horny layer; a thick, white, inner layer which becomes thin and cracked on drying. At maturity, the entire outer peridium splits radially into star-like segments which are expanded when moist and incurved when dry. Inner peridium sessile, tough or leathery, with a single, irregular mouth. Gleba dark brown; columella none; capillitium long, much branched and interwoven, originating from the inner peridium. Spores rough, globose.

There is a single species in this genus.

Astraeus hygrometricus (Pers.) Morg.

Plate III, Figures 23 and 24.

Unexpanded form embedded in the soil, depressed-globose to ovate, 1.5-2.5 cm. in diameter; mycelium basal, consisting of black, hairy, rhizomorphs. Outer peridium dark brown, rigid, strongly hygroscopic, split almost to the base into 7-20 acute segments which are strongly incurved and depressed over the inner peridium when dry; inner layer thick, grayish-white, becoming thin and cracked when mature. Inner peridium depressed-globose, 1.5-2.5 cm. in diameter, tough, gray or light-brown in color, scurfy or reticulated, sessile; mouth definite, irregular. Gleba reddish-brown to brown; columella none; capillitium threads branched, 3.5-6.5 microns in diameter, hyaline. Spores very large, 7-12 microns in diameter, globose, warted, brown.

Habitat: Sandy soil in coniferous or mixed woods. Late summer or fall.

Distribution: World wide.

This species was formerly included in the genus Geaster as *G. hygrometricus* Persoon. Morgan (51) was the first to realize that it differs too much from the other species of Geaster to be included in the same genus. He separated it and established a new genus, Astraeus, for it. Although Astraeus resembles the genus Geaster in external appearance, it differs in the following respects: (1) It has no columella; (2) the spores are much larger; (3) the threads of the capillitium are branched; and (4) the threads are continuous with the elemental hyphae of the peridium. Another name by which the plant has been known is *Astraeus stellatus* (Scop.) Fisch.

This species occurs frequently in Ohio, Michigan, and Pennsylvania, but only in sandy soil. It has been collected a number of times in the Sugar Grove region. In addition, there is in the Lloyd Museum a single collection from Lowater at Toledo.

In September, 1925, the writer and her brother collected it

near Lancaster, Ohio. The fruiting-bodies were all 2.5 to 5 cm. under the surface of the ground, and as many as a dozen were found attached to the base of the fruiting-body. Coker and Couch (7) observed the same condition in North Carolina. There were a few old fruiting-bodies of the previous season on the surface of the soil mixed with sand and leaves. Many of the old inner peridia had been long since lost, but the outer peridia were well-preserved and still possessed their hygroscopic character.

14. Geaster Mich. 1729.

Immature fruiting-body globose or acute, entirely or partially embedded in the soil; mycelium universal or basal. Outer peridium consisting of three layers; the outer or mycelial layer, the middle or fibrillose layer, and the fleshy inner layer, all of which split radially at maturity into star-like segments. The segments turn back, exposing the inner peridium, and raising the entire fruiting-body above the surface of the soil. In some cases the segments are hygroscopic, enclosing the entire inner peridium when dry, but exposing it when moist. Inner peridium thin, membranaceous, ovid to subglobose, with or without a pedicel, dehiscent by a plane, lacerate, or a raised, even sulcate mouth. Gleba yellowish-brown to dark-brown. Columella present, usually prominent. Capillitium long, slender, simple. Spores globose, 2.5-7.5 microns in diameter, hyaline to brown, rough.

The species of Geaster, Astraeus, and Myriostoma are extremely interesting on account of the peculiar behavior of the outer peridium. At maturity this layer splits radially into segments which turn backward from the inner peridium, forming a star-like body on the surface of the ground, whence the name "earth-star." In some species the outer peridium remains star-like only during wet weather, enclosing the inner peridium when dry. In such cases the segments are said to be hygroscopic.

In some species the inner peridium is borne on a stalk or pedicel. The columella or column-like sterile tissue, arising internally from the base of the inner peridium, and from which the capillitium arises, is conspicuous in many cases. The mouth in most species of "earth-stars" is quite prominent, often arising as a small cone at the apex of the inner peridium. It may be either even or sulcate (grooved).

There are fourteen species in this region. *Astraeus hygrometricus* (Pers.) Morg. is included in the key, because of its close resemblance to the Geasters among which it was long included, in order to facilitate the separation of the hygroscopic "earth-stars."

KEY TO THE SPECIES

1. Outer peridium markedly hygroscopic, segments strongly incurved when dry, expanded when wet.................................... 2
1. Outer peridium not hygroscopic.................................... 4
    2. Mouth definite, fibrillose, conical, surrounded by a silky zone .... 2. *G. mammosus*
    2. Mouth indefinite, irregular, plane, without a zone............... 3
3. Fleshy layer of outer peridium white when fresh; spores 8-12 microns in diameter.....................................*Astraeus hygrometricus*
3. Fleshy layer of outer peridium dark brown; spores 4.5-7 microns in diameter... 1. *G. floriformis*
    4. Inner peridium sessile; outer peridium saccate—the unsplit portion forming a cup and enclosing the lower part of the inner peridium 5
    4. Inner peridium with a short stalk or pedicel; outer peridium not saccate 9
5. Mouth surrounded by a definite circular area........................ 6
5. Mouth not surrounded by a definite circular area.................... 8
    6. Fleshy layer of outer peridium thick, breaking circumscissally near the middle and remaining as a free margined cup at the base of the inner peridium.................................. 6. *G. triplex*
    6. Fleshy layer of outer peridium thin, adnate, not breaking circumscissally and forming a free margined cup at the base of the inner peridium.. 7
7. Outer or mycelial layer of the outer peridium thin, adnate, glabrous, often with adhering soil................................ 4. *G. saccatus*
7. Outer or mycelial layer of the outer peridium thick and felt-like, partially separating from the middle layer.................. 5. *G. velutinus*
    8. Mouth sulcate....................................... 7. *G. archeri*
    8. Mouth not sulcate............................... 3. *G. fimbriatus*
9. Mouth sulcate or sulcate-plicate.................................. 10
9. Mouth not sulcate... 12
    10. Inner peridium with persistent granules or minute warts. 11. *G. asper*
    10. Innner peridium smooth or only furfuraceous................... 11
11. Inner peridium tapering downward from the middle, striate at the base; pedicel with a collar or ring at the base.......... 12. *G. pectinatus*
11. Inner peridium often constricted below the middle, then swollen at the base; striations and ring wanting..................... 10. *G. schmidelii*
    12. Mouth surrounded by a circular zone.......................... 13
    12. Mouth not surrounded by a circular zone at the base...8. *G. rufescens*
13. Circular zone surrounding the mouth bounded by a ridge; outer peridium at first covered with a shaggy mycelial layer.................. 14
13. Circular zone not bounded by a ridge; outer peridium glabrous .... 9. *G. limbatus*
    14. Segments of outer peridium 4-5, deeply cut......... 14. *G. coronatus*
    14. Segments of outer peridium 7-12, not deeply cut...... 13. *G. minimus*

1.   Geaster floriformis Vitt.

Unexpanded fruiting-body subterranean. Outer peridium hygroscopic, split into 6-10 unequal, acute segments, expanding 2-2.5 cm.; mycelial layer at first covered with adhering soil, later becoming a grayish tan-color; fleshy layer thin, dark brown. Inner peridium membranaceous, yellowish-brown to grayish-brown, subglobose, about 1 cm. in diameter, sessile; mouth indefinite, small, irregular. Gleba yellowish-brown to brown; capillitium threads about the same diameter as the spores. Spores globose, brown, 4.5-7 microns in diameter, distinctly warted.

Habitat: Sandy soil in woods.

Distribution: Western United States, Illinois, and Ohio.

G. *floriformis* is a western species. It is reported from Illinois by Moffatt (48) and there is a collection in the Lloyd Museum made by Morgan, at Preston, Ohio. Superficially, this little hygroscopic species resembles *Astraeus hygrometricus* (Pers.) Morg. It may be distinguished, however, by the less rigid outer peridium, the dark red or brown fleshy layer, the smaller spores, and the membranaceous inner peridium. G. *delicatus* Morg. is a synonym.

2. Geaster mammosus Chev.

Unexpanded fruiting-body subglobose to ovate, with a tapering apex; mycelium basal. Outer peridium very hygroscopic, split nearly to the base into 7-12 narrow, acute segments which expand 2.5-5.5 cm. when moist, inrolled when dry, usually umbilicate at the base; outer layer thin, soon flaking off; the middle layer fibrous, thin, whitish- to grayish-brown; the inner layer thick, porous, fleshy, and dark brown. Inner peridium sessile, depressed-globose or ovoid, pale yellow to brown, minutely pubescent, 1-3 cm. in diameter; mouth conical, ciliate, fimbriate, surrounded by a paler circular area. Gleba brown; columella short, cylindrical, with a broad base; capillitium 1.8-4.5 microns in diameter, light brown. Spores globose, brown, slightly rough, 2-5.5 microns in diameter.

Habitat: Sandy soil among leaves in woods and fields. July until late fall.

Distribution: Northern United States, California, and North Carolina.

G. *mammosus* is similar to *Astraeus hygrometricus* (Pers.) Morg. in the hygroscopic property of the outer peridium. Otherwise there are several features distinguishing the two. G. *mammosus* is much larger and has a pale brown outer peridium with a thick, fleshy, dark brown, inner layer. Its mouth is definite and conical in contrast to the irregularly torn mouth of *A. hygrometricus* (Pers.) Morg. G. *floriformis* Vitt. is also similar, but differs mainly from G. *mammosus* in the irregular mouth and the lack of a columella. This species has been collected at the following places in Ohio: at Preston by Morgan; at Linwood by Lloyd; and at Toledo by Lowater.

3.   Geaster fimbriatus Fr.

Unexpanded fruiting-body globose; mycelium universal, usually with adhering soil. Outer peridium flaccid, at maturity splitting about half way to the middle into 5-11 recurved segments, the undivided portion becoming deeply saccate; outer or mycelial layer very thin, membranaceous, usually deciduous; the inner fleshy layer thin, persistent, tannish-brown to reddish-brown. Inner peridium light to reddish-brown, subglobose, sessile, 0.9-1.5 cm. in diameter; mouth conical, indefinite, slightly raised. Gleba dark brown; columella very small; capillitium threads 1.8-7.5 microns thick. Spores globose, dark brown, 2.2-4 microns in diameter, minutely warted.

Habitat: On the ground in woods.

Distribution: Eastern United States, Wisconsin, Colorado, and Ontario.

This little "earth-star" belongs to the saccate group of the Geasters and is often confused with *G. saccatus* Fr. and *G. velutinus Jungh.* It differs from both of these species in that its mouth is not surrounded by a definite circular zone. The outer layer of the outer peridium of *G. saccatus* is adnate, while in *G. fimbriatus* and *G. velutinus* it separates either partially or entirely. In *G. velutinus* this layer is thick and felt-like, but in *G. fimbriatus* it is very thin and membranaceous. *G. tunicatus* Vitt. is a synonym.

Lloyd believes that *G. fimbriatus* occurs only in Europe, although it has been reported several times in this country. Coker and Couch (7), however, have carefully studied European specimens of *G. fimbriatus* and believe the American plants to be the same. There are three collections in the herbaria at the Ohio State University made at Oxford and Columbus by W. G. Stover and at Sugar Grove by the writer. These specimens as compared by the writer agree in every respect with European specimens in the Lloyd Museum identified by Hollos and by Bresadola as *G. fimbriatus.*

4.   Geaster saccatus Fr.

Plate IV, Figure 25.

Unexpanded fruiting-body entirely or partially embedded in leaf mold, acute, 0.6-1.2 cm. in diameter; mycelium basal. Outer peridium thin, membranaceous, cut to the middle into 6-12 acute segments with long tapering points expanding 1.5-4.5 cm.; the unsplit portion deeply saccate, forming a cup-like structure in which the inner peridium is seated; outer layer very thin, glabrous, often with some adhering soil; inner layer thin, yellowish-brown to reddish-brown, adnate, sometimes cracking slightly. Inner peridium sessile, globose, 0.5-1.5 cm. in diameter, lighter in color than the segments; mouth definite, conical, fibrillose, seated in a different circular area. Gleba dark brown; columella clavate, extending about half way to the mouth; capillitium light brown, 4-6 microns thick. Spores pale brown, globose, 3.6-5.5 microns in diameter, warted.

Habitat: On leaf mold in woods. Gregarious.

Distribution: Eastern United States, Minnesota, and Mexico.

G. saccatus is a common species of Geaster in Ohio. Hard (13) reports it to be very abundant about Chillicothe. Oftentimes its identity is confused with that of *G. velutinus* Morg. and *G. fimbriatus* Fr. which are also deeply saccate. It may be distinguished by the definite, conical, fibrillose mouth and the glabrous, adnate outer layer of the outer peridium.

5. Geaster velutinus Morg.

Unexpanded fruiting-body globose, sometimes with a pointed apex; mycelium basal, fibrous. Outer peridium flaccid, splitting about to the middle into 5-7 acute segments, spreading 3-4 cm.; outer layer thick, felt-like, buff to pale brown, often partially separating from the middle layer at maturity; inner layer thin, reddish-brown, sometimes cracking; unsplit portion saccate. Inner peridium sessile, globose to subglobose, 1-1.5 cm. in diameter, buff-colored to dark brown; mouth even, conical, surrounded by a distinct fibrillose zone. Gleba brown; columella prominent, subclavate; capillitium usually thicker than the spores. Spores distinctly warted, light brown, 2.5-3.5 microns in diameter.

Habitat: In the woods on leaf mold.

Distribution: Eastern United States and Canada.

This "earth-star" is quite similar in appearance to *G. saccatus* Fr. and *G. fimbriatus* Fr. The thick, felt-like outer peridial layer which often separates from the segments at maturity and the definite mouth are the characters by which it may be distinguished. *G. velutinus* has been found in Ohio and Pennsylvania. Lloyd collected it at Norwood, Ohio, and Morgan at Preston. In literature it has been known as *G. readeri* Cooke and Massee and *Cycloderma ohiensis* Cooke; the latter having been described from the unexpanded form.

6. Geaster triplex Jungh

Plate IV, Figure 27.

Unexpanded fruiting-body, 2.5-4 cm. in diameter, subglobose to ovate with a beak, partially embedded in the soil; mycelium basal, leaving a light colored scar when detached. Outer peridium when mature splitting to the middle or farther into 4-8, brown or reddish-brown segments, expanding 8-12 cm.; revolute and sometimes vaulted in the middle of the basal portion; fleshy layer usually breaking away from the segments at the middle, forming a cup-like structure around the inner peridium. Inner peridium 2-3.5 cm. in diameter, yellowish-brown, sessile, depressed-globose; mouth definite, conical, fibrillose, seated in a definite circular area. Gleba dark brown; columella clavate, elongated, distinct; capillitium threads light brown, 3-6 microns thick, Spores 3-4.5 microns in diameter, globose, warted, brown.

Habitat: Rich soil about decayed logs and stumps in the woods. Autumn.

Distribution: Northern United States.

This species is commonly found in Ohio and neighboring states. It can easily be distinguished by the acute unexpanded form, the cup-like structure at the base of the inner peridium, and the definite mouth. The entire fruiting-body is buff-colored or grayish-brown at first, but becomes reddish-brown with age. Plate IV, Figure 27, shows both the unexpanded and the expanded forms of fresh fruiting-bodies of *G. triplex* which were collected by W. G. Stover north of Columbus, Ohio.

7.   **Geaster archeri** Berk.

Plate IV, Figure 31.

Unexpanded fruiting-body acute, 1-2 cm. in diameter; mycelium basal. Outer peridium often cut beyond the middle into 6-10 segments with long tapering points, expanding 3.5-5 cm., usually somewhat saccate, though recurved when perfectly expanded; outer layer cracking and flaking off; fleshy layer reddish-brown to dark brown or black, often cracking as in *G. saccatus* Fr. Inner peridium sessile, subglobose, 1-2 cm. in diameter, yellowish-brown, spotted; mouth prominent, conical, sulcate-plicate. Gleba dark brown; columella globose to clavate; capillitium 2.5-7 microns thick. Spores slightly rough, brownish, globose, 2.5-4.5 microns in diameter.

Habitat: Old decayed stumps and logs.

Distribution: New York, North Carolina, Ohio, Illinois, and California.

G. archeri is the only one of the sulcate-mouthed species of Geaster which is saccate and has a sessile inner peridium. It has been collected frequently near Cincinnati, Columbus, and Chillicothe, Ohio. In 1902, Lloyd (26) described some specimens as *G. morganii*, a new species. Later, while studying European specimens, he discovered that his new species had been previously described by Berkeley as *G. archeri*. He (30) corrected this error in 1905. Coker and Couch (7) consider *G. morganii* and *G. archeri* as distinct species. The writer, however, believes that they are synonymous.

8. Geaster rufescens Pers.

Plate IV, Figure 28.

Unexpanded fruiting-body subterranean, globose to subglobose; mycelium universal. Outer peridium recurved, cut about to the middle into 6-12 segments, expanding 5-8 cm.; unsplit portion vaulted; fleshy layer thick, reddish-brown, porous, and cracked; mycelial layer usually adnate, covered with adhering dirt, but sometimes scaling off. Inner peridium depressed-globose to ovate, 1.5-3 cm. in diameter, usually with thick pedicel; mouth irregular, slightly raised, fibrillose. Gleba brown; columella large, distinct, globose; capillitium threads 3.5-5 microns in thickness. Spores 3-5 microns in diameter, globose, slightly warted.

Habitat: Very rich soil about old stumps in woods and pastures.

Distribution: Eastern and central United States.

This species is one of our most common Geasters. It is often confused with *G. limbatus* Fr., but it may be distinguished from it by the irregular and indefinite mouth, the large persistent columella, and the thick, porous, fleshy, inner layer of the outer peridium.

9. Geaster limbatus Fr.

Outer peridium glabrous, split stellately half-way or more back into 7-10 long, acute segments, recurved or expanded; mycelium basal; inner layer thin, dark brown or black, closely adnate, sometimes cracking. Inner peridium subglobose to ovate, 1-3 cm. in diameter, grayish-brown to dark brown, often constricted and then swollen with a tapering base; pedicel thick, short; mouth definite, conical, silky. Gleba brown to blackish-brown; columella subglobose, often indistinct; capillitium threads unbranched, about 7 microns thick. Spores brown, globose, warted, 3.5-5 microns in diameter.

Habitat: In woods about old stumps and trees.

Distribution: Northern United States and Canada.

G. limbatus is a rare "earth-star" of northern distribution. It has not yet been found in Ohio, but it has been reported from Michigan, Pennsylvania, and Illinois. This species is often confused with *G. rufescens* Pers. from which it differs mainly in the thin, dark brown, firm, adnate, inner layer of the outer peridium, the darker inner peridium often with constrictions, and the definite mouth.

10. Geaster schmidelii Vitt.

Outer peridium split about to the middle into 5-9 acute segments, revolute, expanding 1-2.5 cm.; mycelial layer adherent; inner layer yellowish to dirty brown, sometimes cracking. Inner peridium 1 cm. or less in diameter, plum-colored, sometimes covered with a whitish bloom, ovate to globose, often constricted near the base, seated on a short, slender pedicel; mouth beaked, prominent, sulcate-plicate, surrounded by a circular depression at the base. Gleba dark brown; columella large, ovate; capillitium light brown, long, 2-3.5 microns thick, often encrusted with a granular substance. Spores small, globose, 2-4.5 microns in diameter, minutely warted.

Habitat: On the ground in open woods.

Distribution: Eastern United States, Nebraska, and Texas.

This species is rarely found in the United States. It has been reported from Illinois and Michigan, but had not been found in Ohio until 1926, when W. G. Stover and the writer collected a single specimen at the Y. W. C. A. Camp near Westerville. This specimen agrees in every respect with the specimens of *G. schmidelii* in the Lloyd Museum which were identified by Hollos. The most characteristic features of *G. schmidelii* are the small size, the plum-colored inner peridium, and the prominent, sulcate-plicate mouth. This species is similar in appearance to *G. bryantii* Berk. and *G. pectinatus* Pers., but it differs in being smaller and in lacking the collar and striations at the base of the inner peridium.

11.   Geaster asper (Mich.) Lloyd

Unexpanded fruiting-body subterranean with universal mycelium. Outer peridium at maturity splitting about to the middle into 8-10 segments, expanding 2.5-3.5 cm.; unsplit portion vaulted. Inner peridium rough with warts or granules, gray or brownish, subglobose, 1-2 cm. in diameter, with a short, thick pedicel; mouth conical, sulcate-plicate, seated in a circular depressed zone. Columella prominent, persistent, globose, with a broad base; capillitium hyaline, simple, long, 2-10 microns thick. Spores globose, light brown, warted. 3.5-6.5 microns in diameter.

Habitat: Rich sandy soil in woods and grassy places.

Distribution: Northern United States and Texas.

G. asper has been found frequently in Ohio, but has not yet been reported in the surrounding states. The verrucose inner peridium and the sulcate mouth surrounded by a depressed zone are the chief distinguishing characters of this species. According to Lloyd (26) *G. asper* was first described in 1729 by Michelius, and since that time has been redescribed twice, once as *G. campestris* in 1887 by Morgan and again as *G. pseudomammosus* by Henning in 1900.

12.   Geaster pectinatus Pers.

Unexpanded fruiting-body subglobose, 3-6 cm. in diameter; mycelium universal. Outer peridium at maturity splitting stellately to the center into 5-10 acute, revolute segments; mycelial layer shaggy and mixed with fragments of leaves and sticks; inner layer fleshy at first, yellowish-brown to reddish-brown, later becoming thin, and cracking and scaling off. Inner peridium subglobose, 1-2.5 cm. in diameter, brown to purplish-brown, tapering and striate at the base; pedicel slender, 5-7 mm. high, often with a ring at or near the base; mouth beaked or conical, prominent, sulcate-plicate, with a depressed circular zone at the base. Gleba dark brown; capillitium light brown, threads 2-7.5 microns in thickness, encrusted. Spores globose, brown, 3.5-6 microns in diameter, rough with large, globose warts.

Habitat: On the ground in woods.

Distribution: Eastern United States.

G. *pectinatus* is rare in the north central section, having only been collected in Ohio and Pennsylvania. The only collection reported for Ohio was made at Cincinnati by the Reverend Marcus Kreke in 1911. This species of "earth-star" is similar to G. *schmidelii* Vitt. and G. *bryantii* Berk. However, it may easily be distinguished by the striations at the base of the inner peridium and the ring-like structure on the unsplit portion of the outer peridium at the base of the pedicel.

13. Geaster minimus Schw.

Plate IV, Figure 26.

Unexpanded fruiting-body subglobose, 1-1.7 in diameter, embedded in leaf mold; mycelial layer universal, mixed with adhering sticks and leaves. Outer peridium split stellately about to the middle into 7-12 segments, recurved, often until they are more or less vertical, expanding 1.5-2.5 cm.; mycelial layer mostly adnate, shaggy in appearance; fleshy layer yellowish-brown, thin, finally cracking and scaling off the segments, but remaining smooth on the unsplit portion. Inner peridium 0.5-1 cm. in diameter, ovate, yellowish to purple-brown, often with a whitish bloom; pedicel short; mouth even, slightly raised, surrounded by silky zone which is bounded by a ridge. Gleba brown; columella small, slender; capillitium 2-5 microns in thickness, hyaline. Spores brown, globose, minutely warted, 3.5-4.5 microns in diameter.

Habitat: Sandy soil mixed with leaf mold; often under cedars. April to autumn.

Distribution: Canada, eastern United States, and Iowa.

G. *minimus* is quite commonly found in this section. Evidently this species fruits much earlier than most of the Geasters as J. H. Schaffner made, in 1895, a collection of both unexpanded and expanded forms at Ann Arbor, Mich., as early as April 29th. Coker and Couch (7) consider G. *minimus* as a synonym of G. *coronatus* (Schaeff.) Schroet. However, after careful study of the specimens in the Lloyd Museum and in the herbaria at the Ohio State University, the writer believes that the two forms are distinct species. The outer peridium of *G. minimus* is more or less flaccid and is cut into more segments than in *G. coronatus*. The spores are also less rough.

14. Geaster coronatus (Schaeff.) Schroet.

Outer peridium split more than half way back into 4-5 segments, which recurve until almost vertical, expanding about 3 cm.; unsplit portion vaulted; mycelial layer universal, shaggy with adhering debris, separating completely from the middle layer and forming more or less of a cup at the tips of the arched segments; fleshy layer brown to buff-colored, usually adherent. Inner peridium 1-1.5 cm. in diameter, ovate to oblong, attenuated at the base; plum-colored, often powdery; pedicel short; mouth fibrillose, slightly raised, with a definite silky zone bounded by a ridge. Gleba dark brown; capillitium threads pale brown, 2-4.5 microns in thickness, rarely branched. Spores globose, brown to purplish-brown, 3.5-4.5 microns in diameter.

Habitat: On leaf mold in woods.

Distribution: Massachusetts, Kentucky, Michigan, Texas, and North and South Carolina.

This species is similar in general appearance to *G. minimus* Schw., but it differs in the fornicate outer peridium. Coker and Couch (7) consider them as synonyms. The writer, however, believes that they are distinct species. It is true that their inner peridia are the same, but the two species differ greatly in the character of their outer peridia. The outer peridium of G. *coronatus* splits into 4-5 deep arched or vaulted segments with their apices attached to the cup-like mycelial layer which has more or less completely separated from the middle layer. In *G. minimus* the segments of the outer peridium are more numerous, (7-12), and less deeply cut than in *G. coronatus,* and the mycelial layer is mostly adnate. The outer peridium of the former is less rigid than that of the latter. *G. coronatus* has not yet been found in Ohio, but it has been reported from Michigan by Povah (57) and has been collected in Kentucky by Fink.

15. Myriostoma Desv. 1809.

Unexpanded fruiting-body subglobose, mycelium basal. Outer peridium of three layers: an outer fibrous layer, a middle corky layer, and an inner fleshy layer. The entire outer peridium splits at maturity into several segments which turn back, leaving the thin, membranaceous inner peridium exposed. Inner peridium seated on several column-like pedicels; mouths numerous. Gleba reddish-brown to brown; columellae several; capillitium sparingly branched. Spores brown, globose, rough.

This genus closely resembles the genus Geaster in general appearance. It can be distinguished, however, by the numerous mouths and pedicels. There is only one species.

Myriostoma coliformis (Dick.) Corda

Plate IV, Figure 29.

Unexpanded fruiting-body subglobose. Outer peridium dark brown, split about to the middle into 4-14 acute segments, recurved, expanding to 4-11 cm., the inner layer often splitting and cracking. Inner peridium subglobose, grayish to reddish-brown, roughened, supported by several pedicels, dehiscing by means of numerous ciliated mouths. Gleba brown or reddish-brown, columellae several. Capillitium threads 1.8-4.5 microns in width, brown, unbranched, tapering. Spores brown, globose, spiny, 3-6 microns in diameter.

Habitat: Sandy soil rich in leaf mold under trees and shrubs. Summer and fall.

Distribution: Ontario, Colorado, South Dakota, Florida, and Ohio.

This species is of rather rare occurrence, but when found the individuals are often numerous. In 1902, it was collected at two different places in Ohio, at Cedar Point and at Green Island, by Prof. J. H. Schaffner (61). These specimens matured the latter part of July and August. The fruiting-bodies were very abundant and the mycelium was growing in sandy soil mixed with leaf mold in open woods.

Family 2. *Calostomataceae.* Sporebearing portion distinct from the stem which is made up of anastomosing, gelatinous, hyphal strands. Outer peridium more or less gelatinous, breaking up into scales at maturity. Inner peridium a definite membrane of two layers enclosing the gleba. Capillitium scanty, soon disappearing. In the writer's opinion Calostoma is the only genus properly to be included here, although others also include Astraeus (see Coker and Couch (7), p. 185).

16. Calostoma Desv. 1825.

Sporebearing portion of the fruiting-body globose to subglobose, borne on a thick-rooting base which is composed of branched and interlaced strands of cartilaginous mycelium. Outer peridium composed of two layers, the outer one which is thick and gelatinous and the inner one which is thin and cartilaginous. Both of the layers usually break up into flakes or scales at maturity. Inner peridium hard, and cartilaginous when dry, dehiscing by means of a raised, stellately rayed mouth which is either red or is lined with red. Gleba white to yellowish-white, enclosed by a cream-colored or yellow membrane which is a part of the inner peridium and is called the spore sac or gleba membrane. This membrane contracts at maturity, forcing the spores and capillitium out through the rays of the mouth. Capillitium scanty, fragile, originating from the inner peridium. Spores large, globose to elliptical, smooth, rough, or pitted.

This genus has also been known as Mitremyces Nees. It is found mostly east of the Mississippi River (Lloyd, 33), chiefly in the Appalachian Mountain region. There are only four species which occur in the United States. Three of these are found in this region, but they are quite rare. The genus Calostoma is highly specialized in several ways, the most striking being the methods of spore dispersal through the highly developed mouth by means of the spore sac.

KEY TO THE SPECIES

1. Outer peridium scaling off; spores elliptical........................ 2
1. Outer peridium forming persistent scales on the inner peridium; spores
   round... 1. *C. ravenelii*
   2. Spores smooth; collar present at the base of the inner peridium
   .... 3. *C. lutescens*
   2. Spores pitted or sculptured; collar wanting.......... 2. *C. cinnabarina*

1. Calostoma ravenelii (Berk.) Mass.

Sporebearing portion of the fruiting-body globose, about 1 cm. in diameter with a slender stem-like base, 1-5 cm. high. Outer peridium not gelatinous, buff-colored, thin, cracking into scales or warts of various sizes which are more or less persistent on the surface of the inner peridium. Inner peridium yellowish to buff-colored; mouth raised with rays, and bright red. Glebal membrane cream-colored; spore mass white. Spores elliptical, pitted, 4.5-5.5 x 6-12 microns.

Habitat: On clay soil in open woods.

Distribution: Appalachian Mountain region.

This fungus is rarely found in the north central section. It has not yet been reported in Ohio, but has been found in Pennsylvania and Kentucky. The fruiting-body is quite beautiful. This species may be readily distinguished by the red mouth and the non-gelatinous outer peridium which forms persistent scales on the inner peridium. The spores which the writer examined in the Lloyd Museum are smaller than the measurements given in Coker and Couch (7).

2. Calostoma cinnabarina Desv.

Plate IV, Figure 30.

Sporebearing portion of the fruiting-body globose, 1-2 cm. in diameter, with a short, brown, rooting base of anastomosing strands of mycelium, 1-2 cm.

high. Outer peridium double, with a thick, gelatinous outer layer and a thin, non-gelatinous, red inner one. Both layers usually break or scale off together in fragments when dry. Inner peridium at first red due to the powdery dust from the inner layer of the outer peridium, later becoming buff-colored or yellowish, fading with age, dehiscing by a red, rayed mouth. Spore sac cream-colored; spore mass whitish. Spores elliptical, 4.5-10 x 7.5-18 microns, sculptured or pitted.

Habitat: On the ground in woods.

Distribution: In the Appalachian Mountain region from Massachusetts south to Florida and west to Texas.

This is the most common and most widely distributed species of Calostoma. It has been reported from Pennsylvania and West Virginia and three collections have been made in Ohio. It was reported by Dr. W. G. Stover (63) in 1911 as having been collected twice near Gibsonville, Hocking County, on April 4, 1910 by Dr. R. F. Griggs and on April 12, 1911 by B. M. Wells. On May 1, 1926, W. H. Camp collected it in Jackson County. This species is quite striking and may be easily distinguished by the short, thick, cartilaginous base, pitted or sculptured spores, the reddish colored inner peridium which later becomes yellowish-brown, and the red mouth.

3. Calostoma lutescens (Schw.) Burnap.

Sporebearing portion of the fruiting-body subglobose with a long, thick, stem-like base 6 cm. or less in height. Outer peridium double: the outer layer gelatinous, the inner one thin, yellow, deciduous, breaking into irregular segments which curl backward and form a collar at the base of the inner peridium. Inner peridium smooth, yellowish, thin, hard; mouth raised, red, with 5-8 rays. Gleba membrane bright yellow; spores pale yellow, globose, 5.5-9.3 microns in diameter.

Habitat: On the ground in woods.

Distribution: Appalachian Mountain region.

C. lutescens (Schw.) Burnap. is another rare fungus for this region. Herbst (14) reported it from Allentown, Pa. It has been reported from West Virginia. The chief distinguishing features of this fungus are the yellow fruiting-body with a red mouth, the collar at the base of the peridium, and the round spores.

Family 3. Tylostomataceae. Fruiting-body with a specialized fibrous stem, the apex inserted in a pocket in the base of the globose sporebearing portion. Outer peridium thickish, deciduous or persistent. Inner peridium membranaceous, opening by an apical mouth, Capillitium well developed, threads septate. Two genera, Queletia and Tylostoma, are reported for this region.

17. Queletia Fr. 1871.

Sporebearing portion of fruiting-body subglobose with a sterile base in
the form of a distinct stem or stipe inserted in a "socket" at its base. Outer
peridium thin and deciduous; the inner hard, fragile, soon breaking away in
small pieces. Capillitium well developed, threads short, thick, with rounded
blunt ends, septa rare or wanting. Spores rough, globose with short pedicel.

This is a rare genus with only one species, *Q. mirabilis* Fr.
Ramsbottom (58) states that it has been collected only at five different places in the world.

Dr. Herbst collected it at Trexlertown, Pa., for several consecu-
tive years. This genus is somewhat similar in general appearance
to Tylostoma. Queletia, however, has a much larger fruiting-body
and dehisces irregularly.

Queletia mirabilis Fr.

Sporebearing portion of the fruiting-body globose to subglobose 2-4 cm. in
diameter. Stem 6.5-8 cm. in length, 1.5 cm. in diameter at the top and 2 cm.
at the base, solid, yellowish-brown with coarse scales. Outer peridium whitish,
thin, smooth, deciduous; inner peridium yellowish-brown, breaking away at
maturity with parts of the gleba attached. Gleba cinnamon to reddish-brown,
fragile. Capillitium threads branched, short, tubular, thick, sometimes collapsing; ends rounded, blunt; septa few or wanting. Spores globose, rough,
3.5-6 microns in diameter, often with a short pedicel.

Habitat: On tan-bark.   August.

Distribution: Pennsylvania, France and Great Britain.

The chief distinguishing features of this rare "puffball" are the
insertion of the stem in a collar or socket at the base of the spore-
bearing portion of the fruiting-body, the irregular method of dehiscing, and the solid stem.

18. Tylostoma Pers. 1801.

Sporebearing portion of fruiting-body globose to depressed-globose; sterile base in the form of a distinct stem or stipe inserted in a "socket" at the
base of the peridium; usually long, slender; smooth or scaly; striate or even;
with a bulb-like mass of mycelium at the base, hollow or stuffed with loose,
white, cottony fibers. Outer peridium usually deciduous, but sometimes persistent, consisting of scales, warts, or granules which are sometimes mixed with
sand; inner peridium membranaceous, dehiscing by one or more mouths, either
definite or indefinite. Capillitium hyaline or subhyaline, long, slender, branched,
tubular, hollow, usually septate, often irregular with swollen septa and constrictions. Spores globose, subglobose, or angular, smooth, or more or less
warted, or spiny.

This is an interesting genus in which little puffballs are seated
on long, slender, stem-like bases. These plants are mostly of western

distribution, but several species are found in the Great Lakes region. *T. campestre* Morg. is the species most frequent east of the Mississippi, according to Lloyd (35). Nine others have been reported here, but they are all very rare.

KEY TO THE SPECIES

1. Mouth definite, tubular, naked.................................... 7
1. Mouth indefinite, torn, fibrillose................................. 2
   2. Mouth raised, shield-shape.................................... 5
   2. Mouth not raised, lacerated................................... 3
3. Spores rough, fruiting-body 1-2 cm. in diameter, inner peridium grayish- to yellowish-brown................................. 4
3. Spores smooth, fruiting-body 1 cm. in diameter, inner peridium reddish-brown.................................... 3. *T. lloydii*
   4. Capillitium with transverse septa and numerous, narrow constrictions .... 2. *T. campestre*
   4. Capillitium with mostly oblique septa; constrictions inconspicuous .... 1. *T. berkeleyii*
5. Spores smooth, irregularly globose.............................. 6
5. Spores rough, globose; inner peridium whitish......... 5. *T. tuberculatum*
   6. Inner peridium dark reddish-brown; stem 5-8 cm. long, scaly, dark colored.................................... 3. *T. lloydii*
   6. Inner peridium grayish-white or fawn-colored; stem 1-3 cm. long, striate, yellowish-gray.................................... 4. *T. poculatum*
7. Outer peridium persistent, consisting of coarse warts or scales .... 9. *T. verrucosum*
7. Outer peridium deciduous, except a basal pad, granular............. 8
   8. Mouth dark-colored or surrounded by a dark-colored zone .... 6. *T. mammosum*
   8. Mouth of same color as inner peridium......................... 9
9. Spores rough, 3.5-7 microns in diameter........................ 10
9. Spores smooth, 2-3 microns in diameter..................... 10. *T. finkii*
   10. Capillitium threads regular, not swollen at the septa..... 8. *T. rufum*
   10. Capillitium threads irregular, swollen at the septa...... 7. *T. simulans*

1. Tylostoma berkeleyii Lloyd

Sporebearing portion of fruiting-body subglobose, 1-2 cm. in diameter, with a stem 1.5-3 cm. long and 2-3 mm. wide. Stem striate or sulcate, somewhat scaly, with a brown mycelial ball at the base. Outer peridium with adhering sand particles, yellowish- to reddish-brown, gradually peeling away, often leaving a pad at the base of the inner peridium. Inner peridium buff-colored to brown, tough, dehiscing by means of a lacerated, fibrillose mouth which is sometimes slightly elevated. Gleba yellowish- to reddish-brown; capillitium tubular, irregular, branched, septa few and usually oblique. Spores globose, 3.5-6 microns in diameter, rough, often irregular.

Habitat: Sandy soil.

Distribution: Southern United States and Indiana.

This "puffball" is southern in its range. Its most northern point of distribution is Indiana where it is reported by Lloyd (35). According to Lloyd it has been wrongly called *T. fimbriatum* Fr. in American literature. The oblique septa of the capillitium are characteristic of this species.

2.   Tylostoma campestre Morg.

Sporebearing portion of fruiting-body subglobose, 1-2 cm. in diameter; stem, 2-10 cm. in length, 3-6 mm. in diameter, yellowish- to reddish-brown, scaly, with a mycelial ball at the base. Outer peridium yellowish-brown, granular, deciduous except for a persistent patch at the base of the inner peridium which forms a collar about the top of the stem. Inner peridium dirty gray to pale yellowish-brown; mouth usually irregular, somewhat fibrillose. Gleba yellowish-brown to brown; capillitium sparingly branched, very irregular with numerous twistings and constrictions, swollen at the septa. Spores globose often irregular, 3-4.5 microns in diameter, rough.

Habitat: Sandy soil.   Late summer and autumn.

Distribution: Northern United States.

This is the most common species of Tylostoma east of the Mississippi River where it is frequently found in the Great Lakes region. Two collections have been made in Ohio. Morgan collected it at Preston and Kellerman at Cedar Point. Lloyd (35) states that this species is a form of the European species, *T. granulosum* Lev. However, from a study of specimens of *T. granulosum* identified by Torrend, Bresadola, and Hollos, the writer considers *T. campestre* to be a distinct species. She found, as did Coker and Couch (7), that the spores of *T. granulosum* were much smaller and smoother than those of *T. campestre*. The capillitium also differed in that there were fewer constrictions, fewer septa, and less swelling at the septa in the European species.

3.   Tylostoma lloydii Bres.

Sporebearing portion of fruiting-body subglobose, about 1 cm. in diameter. Stem long, slender, stuffed, dark colored, scaly, 5.5-8 cm. long and 2.5 mm. thick, tapering towards the apex. Outer peridium thin, deciduous from all parts of the inner peridium except at the base. Inner peridium dark reddish-brown, papery, smooth; mouth fibrillose, shield-shaped, elevated at first, but later becoming a round, plane, naked opening. Capillitium threads irregular, 3-7.5 microns thick, subhyaline, septate, slightly and unequally swollen at the septa. Spores 3.5-4 microns in diameter, smooth, often irregular.

Distribution: Ohio.

Tylostoma lloydii is a rare species of Tylostoma which so far has only been collected near Cincinnati, Ohio, by Professor W. H. Aiken in March, 1897. Lloyd (35) sent some of the specimens to Bresadola who described it as a new species in his honor. The chief distinguishing features of this species are the small fruiting-body and the long, dark-colored, scaly stem.

4. Tylostoma poculatum White

Sporebearing portion of fruiting-body subglobose, 1-2 cm. in diameter; stem slender, 1-3 cm. long, and 2-6 mm. thick, thicker towards the base, yellowish-gray, striate, usually stuffed with white, cottony fibers. Outer peridium grayish-brown, granular, separating from the entire surface of the inner peridium except at the base where it forms a thick pad. Inner peridium membranaceous, pale grayish-white to fawn-colored, smooth, dehiscing by means of a raised, shield-shaped, fibrillose mouth. Gleba reddish-brown; capillitium threads sparingly branched, 3.5-7 microns wide, septa few and slightly swollen. Spores 3.5-5.5 microns in diameter, irregularly globose to angular, smooth.

Habitat: Sandy soil. Single or gregarious. October.

Distribution: Indiana, Nebraska, Colorado, and Alabama.

This rare puffball is widely scattered over the United States. Moffatt (48) reports it from Indiana, but it has not yet been found in Ohio. It is quite distinctive and may be easily identified by the raised shield-shaped mouth, the smooth inner peridium, the smooth spores, and the striate stem.

5. Tylostoma tuberculatum White

Sporebearing portion of friuting-body depressed-globose, 1-1.8 cm. in diameter; stem slender, 2-3 cm. in length and 3 mm. in diameter, hollow or stuffed. Outer peridium scaly, deciduous except at the base of the inner peridium. Inner peridium whitish, smooth, dehiscing by means of a round, raised, fimbriated mouth. Capillitium threads hyaline, branched, 4-8 microns thick, septate, swollen at the joints. Spores globose, 3-5 microns in diameter, with tuber-like warts.

Habitat: Sandy soil.

Distribution: Washington, Texas, Illinois, and Ohio.

This species is a close relative of *T. poculatum* White, from which it differs mainly in the more regular, globose and warted spores. Lloyd (35) considers it to be a form of *T. poculatum*, but the writer believes that it should be considered a distinct species. Lloyd (44) reports that it has been collected in Ohio by Professor F. O. Grover.

6.   Tylostoma mammosum (Mich.) Fr.

Plate V, Figure 32.

Sporebearing portion of fruiting-body globose to subglobose, 0.5-1.5 cm. in diameter, pale chestnut-colored to yellowish-brown; stem darker colored, 1-3 cm. long and 1-3 mm. thick, slightly striate and often slightly scaly. Outer peridium thin, scaling off except a sheath-like pad at the base of the inner peridium. Inner peridium smooth, membranaceous, yellowish-white, dehiscing by a small, tubular mouth of a darker color or surrounded by a darker colored zone. Capillitium threads branched, irregular, 2-7.5 microns thick, rarely septate; septa swollen. Spores globose to angular, 3-4.5 microns in diameter, slightly rough.

Habitat: Sandy soil, on old walls and dry banks.

Distribution: Texas, North Dakota, and Indiana.

Lloyd (35) stated in 1906 that *T. mammosum* (Mich.) Fr. is a European species which does not occur in this country. He believed that the American plants which have been identified as this species should be referred either to *T. simulans* Lloyd or *T. rufum* Lloyd, both of which he regarded as forms of *T. mammosum*. He evidently changed his mind about this later, for there are several American collections in his museum which are labeled *"T. mammosum."* The writer has made a careful study of these specimens together with European specimens identified as *T. mammosum* by Bresadola and by Hollos, and has found that they agree in every respect. Coker and Couch (7) found the same thing to be true. This species, however, is rare in the United States. Moffat (48) reports it from Indiana. It remains to be found in Ohio. The chief distinguishing feature is the pale inner peridium with a darker colored, protruding round mouth. Other names by which this species has been known are *T. pedunculatum* (L) Schroeter and *T. brumale* Pers.

7.   Tylostoma simulans Lloyd

Sporebearing portion of fruiting-body subglobose, 0.7-1.8 cm. in diameter; stem slender, 1.5-3 cm. in length and 1.5-2.5 mm. thick, slightly striate and scaly, stuffed, with mycelial ball at the base. Outer peridium granular, long persistent. Inner peridium chestnut-colored to pale brown, dehiscing by means of a tubular mouth which is usually of the same color. Capillitium threads 4.5-6.5 microns thick, branched, septate, swollen at the septa. Spores globose to subglobose or oval, 4-6 x 4.5-7 microns in diameter, distinctly warted.

Habitat: Sandy soil.

Distribution: Ohio, Texas, and North Carolina.

Lloyd (35) considers this species of Tylostoma to be a form

of *T. mammosum* (Mich.) Fr. The writer believes that it is a distinct species, since it differs from *T. mammosum* in the long persistent outer peridium and the larger and more distinctly warted spores. *T. simulans* is also similar to *T. rufum*, Lloyd, but it may easily be distinguished by the swollen septa. This "puffball" is rare in our section.

8. **Tylostoma rufum** Lloyd

Sporebearing portion of fruiting-body 1-1.5 cm. in diameter, depressed-globose; stem slender, dark reddish-brown, up to 3 cm. in length, 1-2 mm. thick, tapering and scaly towards the apex, striate, stuffed with white cottony fibers, mycelial ball present at the base. Outer peridium thin, brown, granular, long persistent. Inner peridium brown to reddish-brown, dehiscing by means of a long, tubular mouth of the same color. Gleba cinnamon-colored; capillitium threads 3.5-5.5 microns, regular, branched, septate, not swollen at the septa. Spores regular, globose, spiny, 3.5-5.5 microns in diameter.

Habitat: Sandy soil.

Distribution: Florida, Alabama, Texas, Iowa, and Illinois.

Although this species is widely scattered over the United States, it is quite rare. It was collected at Urbana, Illnois, by W. B. McDougal. Lloyd (35) states that it is an American form of *T. mammosum* (Mich.) Fr. However, after a careful study of the specimens in the Lloyd Museum, the writer believes that *T. rufum* is a good species. It differs from *T. mammosum* in that it has capillitium without swollen septa, larger and more spiny spores, and a more persistent outer peridium.

9. **Tylostoma verrucosum** Morg.

Sporebearing portion of fruiting-body globose to depressed-globose, 1-1.5 cm. in diameter; stem 5-10 cm. in length and 2-3 mm. thick, very firm and rigid, covered with large, brown, spreading scales which are deciduous, leaving only the smaller ones, stuffed with a large mycelial bulb present. Outer peridium thin, consisting of dense minute scales or warts which are persistent on the inner peridium. Mouth prominent, entire, tubular, small. Gleba brown; capillitium branched, long, hyaline, 3.5-6 microns thick, often septate, not swollen at the septa. Spores 4-6 microns in diameter, minutely warted or spiny, irregularly globose, pale brown.

Habitat: Rich sandy soil in woods.

Distribution: Ohio, Illinois, and Texas.

The persistent warts or scales, the larger mycelial bulb, and the tubular mouth are the chief distinguishing features of this species. According to Morgan (51), the mycelial ball at the base of the stem is often larger than the sporebearing portion. *T. verrucosum* has been collected by Morgan and Lloyd at Preston, and by Dr. Bruce Fink at Oxford.

10. Tylostoma finkii Lloyd

Sporebearing portion of fruiting-body reddish-brown, subglobose, 0.9-1.4 cm. in diameter, with a darker colored stem, 1.8-2.7 cm. long and 1.5-3.2 mm. wide, covered with scales which finally fall away. Outer peridium separating from the inner peridium and leaving a collar at the base. Inner peridium reddish-brown; mouth small, tubular, concolorous. Capillitium irregular, with constrictions and swollen septa, 3.5-8 microns in diameter, pale, septa few. Spores globose, often irregular, about 3 microns in diameter, smooth.

Habitat: Woods in autumn.

Distribution: Ohio and North Carolina.

This is a new species described by Lloyd (43) from specimens collected by Dr. Bruce Fink on the campus of Miami University, Oxford, Ohio, in 1923. Lloyd states that this species, in general, is similar to *T. squamosum* Pers., except for the smooth spores. Coker and Couch (7) collected a Tylostoma in North Carolina which they determined to be *T. finkii* Lloyd. Some of their specimens had as many as four mouths, while in the original collection by Fink each individual had a single mouth. The writer has not compared the two collections. Further study is necessary to determine the position of the North Carolina specimens. There are several American species with more than one mouth, though none of them occur within our range.

ORDER IV. NIDULARIALES

Fruiting-body globose to cup-shaped or vase-shaped, open at maturity; spores borne within the fruiting-body in egg-like structures called peridioles; capillitium wanting. There are two families in this order.

Family 1. *Sphaerobolaceae.* Fruiting-body very small, peridium of four layers, dehiscing stellately. Gleba fleshy, forming a single peridiole-like structure which is forcefully ejected at maturity. Sphaerobolus is the only genus.

19. Sphaerobolus Tode. 1790.

Fruiting-body minute, tough-fleshy, usually growing on decayed wood or leaves, partially or entirely embedded either in the substratum or in the dense white, fibrous mat of mycelium which often covers the substratum. Peridium whitish or cream-colored, dehiscing stellately, composed of four layers; a mycelial layer; a pseudoparenchymatous layer; a thin fibrous layer;

and a thick collenchyma layer of specialized cells. Gleba very minute, peridiole-like, ejected at maturity to a great distance; glebal cavities indistinct, with or without a definite hymenium. Spores subglobose to elliptical. Dense, irregular cells, called gemmae, which are capable of forming new hyphae are present in the gleba.

Only one species is found in Ohio and the neighboring states. The genus Sphaerobolus is very interesting in the fact that the peridium dehisces stellately and the single peridiole or glebal mass is shot out with great force.

Sphaerobolus stellatus Tode

Fruiting-body sessile, subglobose to globose, more or less fleshy, 1.5-3 mm. in diameter, entirely or partially embedded either in the substratum or in the dense white mycelial mat which often covers the substratum. Peridium cream-colored or yellowish at first, darker and brownish with age, dehiscing stellately at maturity and ejecting the gleba or the spore mass to a great distance. Gleba globose, viscid, about 1 mm. in diameter, cream-colored or buff-colored at first, becoming reddish-brown with age. Spores ovate to elliptical, 3.5-5 x 6-10 microns, mixed with gemmae.

Habitat: Decayed wood, twigs, and leaves. May to September.

Distribution: Louisiana, North Carolina, Pennsylvania, Michigan, and Ohio.

Although *S. stellatus* has a world-wide distribution, it is a comparatively rare fungus in the United States, having been reported from only a few states. On August 15, 1926, Margaret Shaw Humphrey and the writer collected some specimens on old leaves at Glenmary Park, near Worthington, Ohio. Dehiscence had not yet occurred, but the peridioles were ejected soon after the fruiting-bodies were placed in a Petri dish. About two weeks later the writer collected at the same place some specimens in which the peridioles all had been shot. The fungus in the second collection was growing on decayed wood. At the time this was believed to be the first collection of this species to be made in Ohio. However, when studying in the Lloyd Museum in 1927, the writer found two collections which Lloyd had made at Cincinnati in 1910. This species has also been known as *S. carpobolus* (L.) Schroeter and *Carpobolus stellatus* (Mich.) Desv.

According to Walker and Andersen (65) the distance to which the glebal mass is shot is often as great as fourteen feet or more. This interesting phenomenon has been studied both morphologically and microchemically by Walker and Andersen, who found that the forceful ejection of the glebal mass is due to the changing of glycogen in the cells of the inner peridial layer to sugar which greatly increases the osmotic pressure.

Family 2. *Nidulariaceae.* Fruiting-body cup-shaped or vase-shaped; tough and leathery; persistent; peridium consisting of one to three layers; peridioles numerous, with a hard, flinty layer. Three genera, Nidularia, Crucibulum, and Cyathus, are found in this region.

20. Nidularia Fr. & Nordh. 1818.

Fruiting-body globose to subglobose, sessile. Peridium cinnamon-brown, of a single layer, tomentose, fragile, breaking away at maturity either irregularly or circumscissally, leaving the peridioles exposed; epiphragm wanting. Peridioles dark brown to reddish-brown, not attached to the base of the peridium by a cord-like funiculus, but adhering together due to a mucilaginous substance, left exposed after the rupture of the peridium.

The name Granularia Roth has been used sometimes for this genus. Only one species is found within our range.

Nidularia pulvinata (Schw.) Fr.

Fruiting-body globose to subglobose, sessile, 6 mm. or less in diameter, whitish at first, becoming cinnamon-colored or brownish at maturity. Peridium of one layer, tomentose, covering the entire structure, fragile, dehiscing irregularly at maturity. Peridioles dark brown, numerous, entirely filling the fruiting-body, disc-shaped, small 0.8-1.5 mm. in diameter, without a cord-like funiculus, but glued together more or less by adhering mucus. Spores smooth, ovoid to elliptical, 4-6 x 6-8 microns, hyaline.

Habitat: On decayed wood.

Distribution: Maine, Connecticut, New York, North Carolina, Alabama, Louisiana, and Minnesota.

N. *pulvinata* is a very rare species in this section. It has not yet been found in Ohio, but Dr. Herbst (14) has reported it from Pennsylvania. The distinguishing features are the fragile peridium and the numerous, small, brown peridioles. N. *pisiformus* (Roth.) Zell., N. *alabamensis* Atk., and N. *globosa* (Ehr.) Fr. are other names by which it is known.

21. Crucibulum Tul. 1844.

Immature fruiting-body sessile, subglobose to ovate, often with a knob at the apex, tawny-yellow, tomentose or felted, becoming vase-shaped or cup-shaped and more glabrous at maturity. Peridium of two layers; the outer felt-like, extending over the apex and forming an epiphragm which becomes thinner and finally ruptures upon the expansion of the fruiting-body; inner layer thin, membranaceous, grayish. Interior of young fruiting-body filled with a white cottony substance which gelatinizes at maturity. Peridioles numerous, white on account of the thick, white layer (tunica) which covers up the dark brown or black layer beneath, attached by a cord or funiculus.

According to Lloyd (37) and Coker and Couch (7), there is only one layer in the peridium. The writer, however, agrees with Smith (62) and Ramsbottom (58) that there are two distinct layers. There is only one species in the genus Crucibulum.

Crucibulum vulgare Tul.

Mature fruiting-body sessile cup-shaped or vase-shaped, 5-8 mm. high and about 5 mm. wide. Outer layer of peridium at first thick, felted, tawny becoming smoother and grayish brown with age; inner layer membranaceous, thin, grayish-white; epiphragm yellow to tannish-brown present in young specimens but lacking in older ones. Peridioles white, numerous, disc-like, 1-1.3 mm. in diameter, attached to base of fruiting-body by an elastic cord or funiculus. Spores elliptical, hyaline, 3.5-6 x 4-10 microns.

Habitat: On wood and various kinds of debris. Rarely on soil. July to late autumn.

Distribution: Cosmopolitan.

This is a very common species of the "birds'-nest" fungi in this section. It may be easily distinguished by the tawny-colored, cup-shaped fruiting-body and the white peridioles. It is almost universally found growing on dead wood. Other names by which it has been known are *C. crucibuliforme* (Scop.) White and *Nidularia juglandicola* Schw.

22. Cyathus Hall. 1768.

Fruiting-body cylindrical or obconical, becoming cup-shaped or bell-shaped at maturity, with or without a mycelial pad at the base. Peridium of three layers: the outer shaggy to strongly tomentose or glabrous; the fibrous middle layer; and the inner membranaceous layer, smooth or striate. Epiphragm present in young specimens, but absent in the matured ones. Peridioles few, disc-shaped, dark brown or black, attached by an elastic cord or funiculus; tunica usually very thin and white, sometimes wanting. Spores elliptical, hyaline, varying greatly in size.

KEY TO THE SPECIES

1. Inner layer of peridium striate............................ 3. *C. striatus*
1. Inner layer of peridium not striate................................ 2
    2. Outer surface of peridium with fine hairs, not shaggy; peridioles large, 2-3.5 mm. in diameter; spores small, 5-8 x 8.5-11 microns
    .... 1. *C. vernicosus*

2. Outer surface of peridium shaggy with a mat of coarse hairs; peri-
    dioles 2 mm. or less in diameter; spores large, 18-30 x 22-35 microns
    .... 2. *C. stercoreus*

1.   Cyathus vernicosus DC.

Fruiting-body cup-shaped to vase-shaped, 8-12 mm. high, 5-15 mm. broad,
usually flaring, but sometimes incurved at the mouth. Outer layer of peridium
ochraceous to grayish-brown, covered with fine hairs at first which may wear
off with age; inner layer even, shining, grayish-brown to lead-color; epiphragm
present in young specimens. Peridioles disc-shaped, large, 2-3.5 mm. in diameter, attached by whitish funiculi; black, although covered with a thin,
white tunica. Spores hyaline, small, oval, 5-8 x 8.5-14 microns.

Habitat: On the ground usually on partially buried wood or
other vegetable matter.

Distribution: Northern United States, North Carolina, and
California.

This species is quite similar in general appearance to *C. stercoreus* (Schw.) De Toni. It may be distinguished, however, by
the wide flaring mouth, the large peridioles, and the small spores.
The habitat of *C. vernicosus* is also different from that of *C. stercoreus* as it grows in unmanured soil, while *C. stercoreus* is found
on highly manured soil or even pure manure. This species has been
frequently found in Ohio and neighboring states, but it is not as
common as *C. stercoreus*.

2.   Cyathus stercoreus (Schw.) De Toni

Fruiting-body cylindrical, obconical to vase-shaped, 5-15 mm. high and
4-8 mm. wide, with or without a stalk-like base. Outer peridial layer pale to
grayish brown, at first more or less shaggy with coarse hairs, becoming
smoother with age; inner layer even, without striations, grayish to dark brown
or black. Epiphragm present in young specimens. Peridioles disc-shaped,
dark brown or black, about 2 mm. in diameter, attached by funiculi, tunica
wanting. Spores hyaline, oval, 18-30 x 22-35 microns.

Habitat: On manure or richly manured ground. Gregarious.

Distribution: Widely distributed throughout the United
States.

C. stercoreus is the most common species of the "birds'-nest"
fungi in this section. It is usually found growing in lawns and
gardens and frequently the fruiting-bodies cover the soil for several
square feet. The distinguishing features of this species are the
coarse matted hairs of the peridium, the small peridioles and the
large spores.

3. Cyathus striatus Willd.

Plate V, Figure 33.

Immature fruiting-body cylindrical or obconical, becoming vase-shaped or bell-shaped at maturity, 5-9 mm. wide at the apex and 8-13 mm. high; base stem-like, arising from a reddish-brown mycelial mat. Peridium of three layers; the outer layer tawny, becoming yellowish-brown or grayish-brown, very shaggy with coarse, matted hairs which may become worn off with age; the middle layer fibrous; and the inner layer gray to grayish-brown, membranaceous, striate. Epiphragm tawny to grayish-brown, shaggy with coarse hairs in young specimens, becoming thinner and smoother as the fruiting-body matures until it finally breaks away. Peridioles disc-shaped, about 2 mm. in diameter, grayish-brown to dark brown or black, attached by a funiculus; tunica thin, often flaking off. Spores ovoid to elliptical, smooth, hyaline, 6-12 x 12-22 microns.

Habitat: On dead wood, bark, or twigs and leaves. Rarely if ever on the soil. Usually gregarious.

Distribution: Eastern and northern United States.

This "birds'-nest" fungus is quite striking and may be easily distinguished by the yellowish-brown, shaggy outer peridial layer and the striations within. It is commonly found in Ohio. This species also has been known as *Cyathia hirsuta* (Schaeff.) White.

ORDER V. PHALLALES

Immature fruiting-body egg-like with cord-like mycelium, surrounded by a tough peridium which ruptures irregularly at maturity, and remains as a cup or volva at the base of the stem in most genera. Sporophore of various forms as indicated in the descriptions below. Gleba greenish-brown to brownish-black, slimy, ill-smelling, usually borne on a definite receptacle. Spores smooth, elliptical to cylindrical, embedded in the gleba.

Family 1. *Clathraceae.* Fruiting-body subglobose to pear-shaped or elongated. Stem present or absent. Receptacle irregularly lobed, latticed, or consisting of separate arms. Gleba and spores borne on the inner surface of the lobes or of the bars of the lattice work, or on either surface of the arms of the receptacle. Phallogaster, Anthurus, and Pseudocolus are genera of this family occurring in our region.

23. Phallogaster Morg. 1892.

Fruiting-body ovate to pear-shaped, often with a short, stem-like base; mycelium fibrous, branched. Peridium single, smooth, glabrous, dehiscing with irregular lobes, exposing the green, slimy, ill-smelling, adhering gleba. Immature gleba composed of irregular masses, deliquescing at maturity. Spores smooth, cylindrical.

There is only one species in this region.

Phallogaster saccatus Morg.

Plate V, Figure 34.

Fruiting-body ovate to pear-shaped, 2.5-5 cm. high and 1.5-2.5 cm. in diameter, often with stem-like base; mycelium fibrous. Peridium flesh-colored to pale brown, composed of one layer, dehiscing irregularly at the apex into 3-5 lobes, forming an open cup or volva. Gleba at first in lobed masses, later deliquescing and often coating the inner surface of the peridium with a green, slimy, ill-smelling substance. Spores greenish, smooth, elliptical to cylindrical, 1.5-2 x 3.5-5.5 microns.

Habitat: Well-decayed wood, single or gregarious. May to September.

Distribution: Connecticut and New York west to Iowa.

Although *P. saccatus* is a native of the northern part of the United States it is found but rarely. It has been collected at four different places in Ohio; viz., Cincinnati by C. G. Lloyd, Granville by Professor C. J. Herrick, McConnelsville by the writer, and Trumbull County by H. A. Runnels. This species may easily be distinguished from the other "stinkhorns" by the pear-shaped fruiting-body which dehisces irregularly at the apex.

24. Pseudocolus Lloyd. 1907.

Immature fruiting-body globose; at maturity elongating into a hollow stem with a volva at the base and a receptacle at the apex. Receptacle of elongated arms or columns which are united at their tips. Gleba slimy, dark greenish-brown, borne on the inner surface of the arms.

Lloyd (39a, 40) in 1907 proposed the genus Pseudocolus to include those species formerly referred to the genus Colus Cav. & Sech. in which the arms or columns of the receptacle arise from a stem and are united at their apices.

In the original description of the genus Colus, as given by Fischer (9) in Saccardo's Sylloge Fungorum (Vol. 7, p. 21), the receptacle is described as "clathrate," that is, in the form of a net or lattice.

Only one species is reported in the northern hemisphere.

Pseudocolus schellenbergiae (Sumstine) nov. comb.

Immature fruiting-body globose; volva dark brown, smooth, 2-3 cm. in diameter, breaking at maturity into several irregular segments. Stem in the mature form short, cylindrical, hollow, white below to orange above, reticulate-pitted, with the volva at the base, dividing at the apex into an orange-colored receptacle, consisting of three arms, transversely wrinkled, cylindrical or compressed, 3-6 cm. long, arched outward and united at the tips. Gleba ill-smelling, dark greenish-brown, borne on the inner surface of the arms. Spores hyaline, ellipsoid-ovoid, 4.5-5.5 x 2-2.5 microns.

Habitat: On the ground.

Distribution: Pennsylvania.

This is a rare species of the "stinkhorns" which has only been reported once. Sumstine (64) described this fungus as a species of Colus in 1915 from specimens growing in the yard of Mrs. F. F. Schellenberg, Pittsburgh, Pa. The writer has not seen the specimen, but has adapted the above description from that of Sumstine.

Family 2. *Phallaceae.* Fruit-body consisting of a hollow, spongy stem with a basal volva and an apical receptacle. Receptacle the upper part of the stem or a distinct cap or pileus. Gleba external. Three genera, Mutinus, Phallus, and Dictyopora, are found in Ohio.

25. **Anthurus** Kalch. & MOw. 1880

Immature fruiting-body or "egg" subglobose to ovate; mycelium cord-like, basal. Mature form consisting of volva, stem, and receptacle. Stem hollow, cylindrical, usually enlarged upward. Receptacle apical, divided into 5-8 segments or arms which bear the slimy, ill-smelling gleba on the inner surface and on the sides. The volva is the peridium which remains as a cup-like sheath at the base of the stem.

There is only one American species. *Anthurus borealis* Burt, and it is found in this region. This species was described by Burt (6) in 1894 and placed in Anthurus after a careful taxonomic and morphological study. A number of other authors, however, have placed it in the genus Lysurus. The writer believes this to be due to a misconception of the characters of this genus. In the original description of Lysurus by Fries (10), published in 1823, the gleba is said to be borne on the outer surface of the free arms of the receptacle. The genus Anthurus was established in 1880 by Kalchbrenner (17) and MacOwan, who state that the stem is cylindrical, dilated from below upward, and divided into 7-8 simple, lanceolate arms with the gleba borne on their inner surfaces. The position of the gleba seems to the writer to be of generic importance.

Anthurus borealis Burt

Plate V, Figure 35.

Immature fruiting-body or "egg" entirely or partially embedded in the soil, subglobose to ovate, 1.5-3 cm. in diameter; mycelium white, cord-like. Stem hollow, white, 10-12 cm. high, somewhat enlarged upward and constricted where it joins the receptacle. Arms of receptacle 5-6, lance-shaped, rounded on the inner surface, with a pale pinkish, smooth, outer surface, continuous with the stem. Gleba borne on the inner surface and the sides of the arms; greenish-brown to brownish-black, shiny at maturity. Spores elliptical, hyaline, smooth, 1.5-2 x 3-4 microns. Volva cup-like, sheathing the stem.

Habitat: Usually in cultivated soil of flower beds and gardens.

Distribution: Connecticut, Massachusetts, New York, New Jersey, Pennsylvania, and Ohio.

A. borealis is frequently found in Ohio. During August and September, 1926, a large number of both "eggs" and mature fruiting-bodies of this "stinkhorn" were collected independently on different dates in the botanical garden of the Ohio State University by Professors Schaffner and Stover, and the writer.

26. Mutinus Fr. 1849.

Immature fruiting-body or "egg" subglobose to ovate, white, with a pinkish tinge, 1-2 cm. in diameter, at first subterranean; peridium tough, ruptured by the elongating stipe or stem, and forming a sheath or volva at the base. Stipe cylindrical, perforate at the apex, porous, fleshy, hollow, some shade of red. Receptacle or sporebearing portion apical. Gleba slimy, greenish-brown, ill-smelling, borne on the outer surface. Spores elliptical.

KEY TO THE SPECIES

1. Stem or stipe 10-17 cm. long, receptable undifferentiated; spores 2-3 x 4-7 microns... 1. *M. elegans*
1. Stem or stipe 6-8 cm. long; receptacle differentiated; spores 1.5-2.5 x 3.5-5 microns.. 2. *M. caninus*

1. **Mutinus elegans** (Mont.) Ed. Fischer

Immature fruiting-body at first globose to ovate, white with a pinkish tinge, later elongating to a height of 10-17 cm. with the peridium forming a sheath or volva at the base; mycelium basal, root-like. Stipe fleshy, spongy, hollow, cylindrical, tapering and perforated at the apex, white or pinkish white at the base, to deep red above. Sporebearing portion or receptacle indistinct from the stem. Gleba slimy, ill-smelling, greenish-brown, occupying from 2.5-5 cm. at the apex. Spores elliptical, 2-3 x 4-7 microns, smooth.

Habitat: Rich soil in woods and cultivated fields. Summer and autumn.

Distribution: Eastern United States.

M. elegans may be easily identified by the long, spongy, hornlike fruiting-body which tapers at the apex and bears the slimy, foul-smelling spore mass on the undifferentiated apical portion.

This species is frequently found in Ohio. The names *M. bovinus* Morg. and *M. curtisii* (Berk.) Ed. Fischer are both regarded as referring to this plant. The name *M. elegans* apparently antedates the other two and is, therefore, to be preferred.

2. Mutinus caninus (Huds.) Fr.

Mature fruiting-body 6-8 cm. high; stipe clavate, hollow, red and somewhat thickened above, tapering and paler below, with a conspicuous volva at the base. Sporebearing portion occupying about 2.5 cm. of the apex, marked off definitely from the sterile region. Gleba greenish-brown, slimy, somewhat ill-smelling. Spores cylindrical to elliptical, 1.5-2.5 x 3.5-5 microns, smooth.

Habitat: In rich soil usually about decayed logs or stumps. August to October.

Distribution: Eastern United States.

This species is similar to *M. elegans* (Mont.) Ed. Fischer. It may be distinguished by the shorter clavate receptacle, and the smaller more cylindrical spores. *M. caninus* has been reported from Ohio, Pennsylvania, and Illinois. Lloyd (38, 39) considers *M. ravenelli* (B. & C.) Ed. Fischer to be distinct from the species, but Burt (6a) considers them the same. Coker and Couch (7) state that they find no structural difference between the two. Since *M. ravenelli* is the later name it must be regarded as a synonym.

27. Phallus (L) Pers. 1801.

Immature fruiting-body or "egg" subglobose to ovate with root-like basal mycelium. Mature with stem, volva, and pileus. Stem hollow with sheathing volva at the base. Receptacle apical, in the form of a pileus attached at the apex of the stem, smooth, granular, or reticulated. Veil rudimentary or well developed, thin, membranous, usually inconspicuous, situated between the pileus and the stem. Mature gleba slimy, ill-smelling, greenish-brown, borne on the outer surface of the pileus. Spores smooth, elliptical.

This genus is also known as Ithyphallus (Fr.) Ed. Fischer in recent literature. According to the rules of the Botanical Congress at Brussels in 1910, the starting date for the nomenclature of the Gasteromycetes is 1801, the date of the publication of Persoon's (56) Synopsis Methodica Fungorum. Persoon recognized the genus Phallus. Since *P. impudicus* is the first species listed, it becomes the type species of the genus Phallus.

Desveaux, in 1809, described the genus Dictyophora with *D. phalloidea* as the type species. In 1823, Fries (10) divided the genus Phallus into several subgenera which Fischer (9) later raised to generic rank. It is the writer's understanding that the name Phallus must be retained as a genus of the phalloids.

Two species occur in our range.

KEY TO THE SPECIES

1. Pileus strongly reticulated; apex without a broad ring-like structure
....1. *P. impudicus*
1. Pileus not reticulated, but minutely granular; apex with a broad, ring-like structure...2. *P. ravenelii*

1.   Phallus impudicus (L.) Pers.

Immature fruiting-body subglobose to ovate, 3-5 cm. in diameter, white or pinkish colored; mycelium cord-like, basal. Stem of a mature form 7.5-25 cm. high, tapering at each end, white, hollow, cylindrical, about 3 cm. in diameter; volva basal. Pileus strongly reticulated, 4.5 cm. or less in length, attached to the apex of the stem; veil rudimentary. Gleba greenish-brown, slimy, fetid, covering the outer surface of the pileus and at first filling the reticulations. Spores oblong to elliptical, smooth, 1.5-2 x 2-5 microns.

Habitat: On the ground in woods, lawns, or gardens. Usually under trees and shrubs.

Distribution: Western United States east to Washington, D. C.

Lloyd (40) states that this is the most common "stinkhorn" found in the west and that it is rarely found east of the Mississippi River. Only one collection has been reported for Ohio. It was made at Cincinnati by B. H. Faris.

2.   Phallus ravenelii B. & C.

Plate V, Figure 36.

Unexpanded fruiting-body or "egg" white or pinkish white, subglobose to ovate, about 3.5 cm. in diameter; mycelium basal, cord-like. Mature form cylindrical, hollow, 10-17.5 cm. high and about 2.5 cm. thick, with a receptacle at the apex of the stem and a volva at the base. Receptacle in the form of a cap or pileus attached to a smooth, broad, raised ring at the apex of the stipe, minutely granular, veil present, membranous, lying between the pileus and the stipe. Gleba greenish-brown, slimy, ill-smelling, covering the surface of the pileus. Spores elliptical, smooth, 1.2-2 x 3-5 microns.

Habitat: In woods in the soil, or on decayed wood. Autumn.

Distribution: Eastern United States.

This species of "stinkhorn" has been frequently found in Ohio. It is usually gregarious and a number of fruiting-bodies may be attached to the same white, cord-like, mycelial mat. *P. ravenelii* may be identified by the granular, smooth, pileus and the hidden veil.

28. Dictyophora Desv. 1809.

Immature fruiting-body or "egg" subglobose to ovate; mycelium basal, cord-like. Mature form consisting of a hollow, cylindrical stem, with a strongly reticulated, campanulate pileus and a basal volva. Veils two: one a very thin and inconspicuous membrane; the other prominent, net-like and projecting below the pileus for some distance. Gleba fetid, slimy, dark green, to greenish-brown. Spores smooth, elliptical.

Dictyophora duplicata (Bosc.) Ed. Fisch.

Immature fruiting-body or "egg" subglobose to ovate, 4-5 cm. in diameter, plicate at the base, with a thick cord-like mycelium. Stem of the expanded form cylindrical, hollow, 15-20 cm. high, 2.5-3 cm. in diameter with a whitish or pale brown volva at the base and tapering towards the apex. Pileus strongly reticulated, about 5 cm. long, attached to the ring-like apex of the stem. Membranous veil white, usually in fragments; net-like veil prominent, extending below the pileus half-way or more to the volva. Gleba greenish-brown, slimy, offensive, borne on the outer surface of the pileus. Spores slender, elliptical, 1.5-2 x 3.5-4.5 microns.

Habitat: On the ground in woods about decayed stumps and logs. Autumn.

Distribution: Eastern United States.

This is a very beautiful species of the "stinkhorn," although it has a most offensive odor. It may be easily distinguished from the other species by the robust receptacle and by the long, white, lacy veil. *D. duplicata* is frequently found in Ohio.

LITERATURE CITED

1. **Albertini, J. B. de** and **Schweinitz, L. B. de.** Conspectus fungorum in Lusatiae, etc. 1-376. pl. 1-12. 1805. The Gasteromycetes are treated on pages 78-83.
2. **Anonymous** (Massee, George?). Fungi Exotici, II. Bull. Miscell. Inform. Roy. Gard. Kew 1899: 164-185. (See p. 180). 1901.
3. **Atkinson, George Francis.** Mushrooms, edible, poisonous, etc. 1-275. f. 1-223. 1900. The Gasteromycetes are treated on pages 209-216.
4. ——————— Origin and taxonomic value of the "veil" in Dictyophora and Ithyphallus. Bot. Gaz. *51*: 1-20. pl. 1-7. 1911.
5. **Berkeley, Rev. M. J.** Notices of North American fungi. Grev. *2*; no. 16: 49-53. 1873.
6. **Burt, E. A.** A North American Anthurus, its structure and development. Mem. Bost. Soc. Nat. Hist. *3*: 487-505. pl. 49-50. 1894.
6a. ——————— The development of *Mutinus caninus* (Huds.) Fr. Ann. Bot. *10*: 343-372. pl. 17-18. 1896.

7. **Coker, William Chambers** and **Couch, John Nathaniel.** The Gasteromycetes of Eastern United States and Canada. 1-201. pl. 1-123. 1928.

8. **Ellis, J. B.** and **Everhart, Benjamin M.** Canadian fungi. Lycoperdineae. New species of fungi. Journal of Mycology *1:* 89-93. 1885.

9. **Fischer, Ed.** Phalloideae in Saccardo's Sylloge fungorum. *7:* 1-27. 1888.

10. **Fries, Elias Magnus.** Systema mycologicum, etc. *2:* 1-620. 1823.

11. **Gäumann, Ernest Albert.** Comparative Morphology of the fungi. Translated and revised by Dodge, Carroll William. 1-701. 1928. The Gasteromycetes are treated on pages 467-519.

12. **Gwynne-Vaughan, H. C. I.** and **Barnes, B.** The structure and development of the fungi. 1-384. 1927. The Gasteromycetes are treated on pages 303-316.

13. **Hard, M. E.** The mushrooms, edible and otherwise. 1-609. f. 1-504. 1908. The Gasteromycetes are treated on pages 517-573.

14. **Herbst, Dr. William.** Fungal flora of the Lehigh Valley, Pa. 1-229. The Gasteromycetes are treated on pages 158-171. 1899.

15. **Hollos, Dr. Ladislaus.** Die Gasteromyceten Ungarns. 1-278. Tab. 1-29. 1904.

16. **Kauffman, C. H.** Outlines of the Gasteromycetes. Mich. Acad. Science. *10:* 70-84. 1908.

17. **Kalchbrenner, C.** and **Cooke, M. C.** Australian Fungi. Grevella *9:* 1-4. 1880.

18. **Linnaei, Caroli.** Flora Svecica exhibens plantes per regnum Sveciae crescentes, Systematica. 1-419. 1745. The Gasteromycetes are treated on pages 384-387.

19. ——————— Species Plantarum. *2:* 784-1684. 1763. The Gasteromycetes are treated on pages 1653-1655.

20. ———————Systema Naturae *2:* pt. 2: 885-1661. Gasteromycetes are treated on pages 1448-1466. 13 ed. (J. F. Gmelin). 1796.

21. **Lloyd, C. G.** Mycological writings. v. 1-7. 1898-1924.

22. ——————— *Calvatia aurea.* Myc. Notes *1:* 9-16. (See note 22.) 1899.

23. ——————— 84 Notes. Myc. Notes *1;* no. 4: 25-32. 1899.

24. ——————— The genera of the Gasteromycetes. 1-24. pl. 1-11. 1902.

25. ——————— Bovista and Bovistella. *Bovistella dealbata.* Myc. Notes *1;* no. 9: 81-96. f. 47-56. 1902.

26. ——————— The Geastrae. 1-43. f. 1-80. 1902.

27. ——————— The Bovistae. Mycenastrum. Myc. Notes *1;* no. 12: 113-120. 1902.

28. ——————— Catastoma. Mitremyces. Myc. Notes *1;* no. 13; 121-132. 1903.

29. ——————— Tylostomeae. The Podaxineae. Secotium. Arachnion. Myc. Notes *1;* no. 14: 133-148. f. 66-70. 1903.

30. ——————— The Lycoperdaceae of Australia, New Zealand, and neighboring islands. 1-42. pl. 25-34. f. 1-49. 1905.

31. ——————— The genus Lycoperdon in Europe. Myc. Notes *2;* no. 19: 205-220. pl. 41-54. 1905.

32. ——————— Myc. Notes *2;* letter 4: 1-7. (See note 11.) 1905.

33. ——————— The Lycoperdons of the United States. The genus Mitremyces. Myc. Notes *2;* no. 20: 221-244. pl. 9, 41-69. 1905.

34. ——————— The genus Arachnion. Myc. Notes *2;* no. 21: 245-260. 1906.

35. ——————— The Tylostomeae 1-28. pl. 10-22; 74-85. 1906.

36. ——————— The genus Bovistella. Myc. Notes 2; no. 23: 277-292. f. 124-128. 1906.

37. ——————— The Nidulariaceae or "birds'-nest fungi." 1-32. pl. 102-107. f. 1-20. 1906.

38. ——————— Concerning the phalloids. The common birds' nests. Myc. notes 2; no. 24: 293-308. f. 131-143. 1906.

39. ——————— Concerning the phalloids. Myc. Notes 2; no. 26: 325-340. pl. 92-121. 1906.

39a. ——————— The phalloids of Australia. 1-22. f. 1-25. 1907.

40. ——————— Synopsis of the known phalloids. 1-96. f. 1-104. 1909.

41. ——————— The genus Arachnion. Myc. Notes 5; no. 46: 643-645. 1917.

42. ——————— Report on specimens received from correspondents. Myc. Notes 7; no. 1, whole no. 66: 1122-1128. 1922.

43. ——————— Tylostoma finkii from Professor Bruce Fink, Ohio. Myc. Notes 7; no. 68: 1169. 1923.

44. ——————— Specimens received from correspondents. Myc. Notes 7; no. 6, whole no. 71: 1263-1267. (See p. 1264.) 1924.

45. **Massee, George.** British fungi. 1-551. pl. 1-40. 1911. The Gasteromycetes are treated on pages 452-483.

46. **McIlvaine, Charles** and **Macadam, Robert K.** One thousand American fungi, 1-729. pl. 1-181. 1902. The Gasteromycetes are treated on pages 577-618. (Dover Reprint).

47. **Michelio, Petro Antonio.** Nova plantarum genera, etc. 1-234. tab. 1-108. 1729.

48. **Moffatt, Dr. Will Sayer.** The higher fungi of the Chicago region. Nat. Hist. Survey 7; pt. 2: 1-24. pl. 1-26. 1923.

49. **Norgan, A. P.** The North American Geasters. Amer. Nat. 18: 963-970. f. 1-12. 1884.

50. ——————— The North American fungi. The Gasteromycetes. Jour. Cin. Soc. Nat. Hist. 11: 141-149. pl. 3. 1889.

51. ——————— Do. Lycoperdaceae. (Myriostoma. Geaster. Astraeus. Mitremyces. Tylostoma. Calvatia.) Ibid. 12: 8-22, 163-172. pl. 1, 2, 16. 1890.

52. ——————— Do. (Lycoperdon. Bovistella. Catastoma. Bovista. Mycenastrum.) Ibid. 14: 5-21; pl. 1-2; 141-148. pl. 5. 1892.

53. **Murrill, William A.** An orange-colored puffball. Mycologia 11: 319-320. 1919.

54. **Peck, C. H.** United States species of Lycoperdon. Trans. of Albany Inst. 9: 285-318. 1879.

55. **Persoon, D. C. G.** Commentarius D. Iac. Christ. Schaefferi . . . . fungorum Bavariae indigenorum icones pictas. 1-130. 1800.

56. ——————— Synopsis methodica fungorum. 1-706. f. 1-5. 1801. The Gasteromycetes are treated on pages 129-157.

57. **Povah, Alfred H.** Some non-vascular cryptogams from Vermilion, Chippewa County, Michigan. Mich. Acad. Science, Arts and Letters. 9: 253-272. 1929.

58. **Ramsbottom, John.** A handbook of the larger British Fungi. 1-222. 1923. The Gasteromycetes are treated on pages 161-177.

59. **Rea, Carleton.** British Basidiomycetae. 1-799. 1922. The Gasteromycetes are treated on pages 29 to 53.

60. **Saccardo, P. A.** Sylloge fungorum. *7:* 1-882. 1888. The Gasteromycetes are treated on pages 1-151 and in the addenda, pages 469-492.
61. **Schaffner, John H.** Ohio stations for Myriostoma. Jour. of Myc. *8:* 173. 1902.
62. **Smith, Worthington George.** Synopsis of the British Basidiomycetes. 1-531. 1908. The Gasteromycetes are treated on pages 459-494.
63. **Stover, Wilmer G.** An Ohio Station for *Mitremyces cinnabarinus*. Ohio Nat. *11:* 350-351. 1911.
64. **Sumstine. David R.** A new species of Colus from Pennsylvania. Mycologia *8:* 183-184. 1916.
65. **Walker, Leva B.** and **Andersen, Emma N.** Relation of glycogen to spore ejection. Mycologia *17:* 154-159. pl. 18. 1925.
66. **White, V. S.** The Tylostomaceae of North America. Bull. Torr. Cl. *28:* 421-444. pl. 31-40. 1901.
67. **White, V. S.** The Nidulariaceae of North America. Bull. Torr. Cl. *29:* 251-280. pl. 14-18. f. 1-20. 1902.
68. **Zeller, Sanford M.** and **Dodge, Carroll W.** Rhizopogon in North America. Ann. Mo. Bot. Gard. *5:* 1-36. pl. 1-3. 1918.

INDEX TO GENERA

Anthurus 69
Arachnion 17
Astraeus 42
Bovista 19
Bovistella 21
Calostoma 53
Calvatia 23
Crucibulum 64
Cyathus 65
Dictyophora 73
Disciseda 40
Geaster 43
Hymenogaster 11
Lycoperdon 27
Mycenastrum 19
Myriostoma 52
Mutinus 70
Nidularia 64
Phallogaster 67
Phallus 71
Pisolithus 16
Pseudocolus 68
Queletia 56
Rhizopogon 11
Scleroderma 13
Secotium 10
Sphaerobolus 62
Tylostoma 56

EXPLANATION OF PLATES
Plate I

1. Secotium agaricoides (Czern.) Hollos. Photo C. G. Johnson.
2. Scleroderma aurantium (Vaill.) Pers. Photo C. G. Johnson.
3. Scleroderma aurantium (Vaill.) Pers. Parasitized by *Boletus parasiticus* Bull. Photo R. B. Gordon.
4. Scleroderma lycoperdoides Schw. Photo F. H. Haskett.
5. Pisolithus tinctorius (Pers.) Coker and Couch. Photo F. H. Haskett.
6. Arachnion album Schw. Photo R. A. Dobbins.
7. Mycenastrum corium Desv. Photo C. G. Johnson.
8. Bovista pila B. & C. Photo C. G. Johnson.

Plate II

9. Bovista plumbea Pers. Photo C. G. Johnson.
10. Bovistella radicata (Mont.) Hollos. Photo C. G. Johnson.
11. Calvatia cyathiformis (Bosc.) Morg. Photo C. G. Johnson.
12. Calvatia maxima (Schaeff.) Morg. Photo C. G. Brooks.
13. Calvatia craniiformis Schw. Photo C. G. Johnson.
14. Lycoperdon curtisii Berk. Photo C. G. Johnson.
15. Lycoperdon pedicellatum Pk. Photo C. G. Johnson.
16. Lycoperdon pyriforme Schaeff. growing on a stump. Photo R. B. Gordon.

Plate III

17. Lycoperdon pyriforme Schaeff. Photo C. G. Johnson.
18. Lycoperdon gemmatum Batsch. Photo F. H. Haskett.
19. Lycoperdon subincarnatum Pk. Photo F. H. Haskett.
20. Lycoperdon pulcherrimum B. & C. Photo F. H. Haskett.
21. Disciseda candida (Schw.) Lloyd growing in the ground. Photo R. A. Dobbins.
22. Disciseda candida (Schw.) Lloyd showing the basal mouth. Photo F. H. Haskett.
23. Astraeus hygrometricus (Pers.) Morg. segments closed. Photo C. G. Johnson.
24. Astraeus hygrometricus (Pers) Morg. segments expanded. Photo C. G. Johnson.

Plate IV

25. Geaster saccatus Fr. Photo C. G. Johnson.
26. Geaster minimus Schw. Photo C. G. Johnson.
27. Geaster triplex Jungh. Photo F. H. Haskett.
28. Geaster rufescens Pers. Photo C. G. Johnson.
29. Myriostoma coliformis (Dick.) Corda. Photo F. H. Haskett.
30. Calostoma cinnabarinum Desv. Photo F. H. Haskett.
31. Geaster archeri Berk. Photo F. H. Haskett.

Plate V

32. Tylostoma mammosum (Mich.) Fr. Photo F. H. Haskett.
33. Cyathus striatus Wild. Photo F. H. Haskett.
34. Phallogaster saccatus Morg. Photo F. H. Haskett.
35. Anthurus borealis Burt. Photo F. H. Haskett.
36. Phallus ravenelii B. & C. Photo F. H. Haskett.

PLATE I

PLATE II

PLATE III

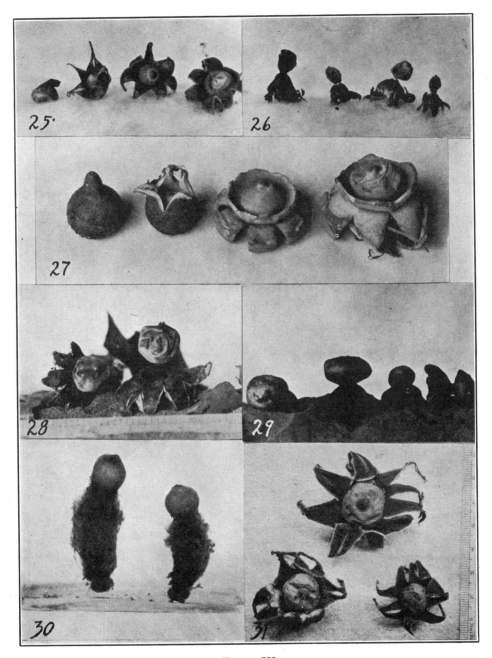

PLATE IV

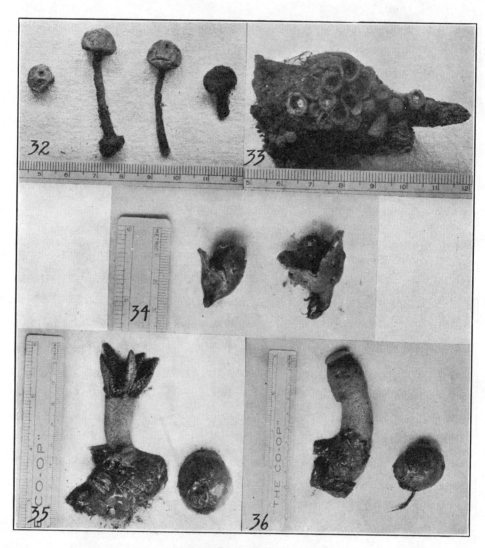

PLATE V

N5